A Glimpse Inside the Third Edition:

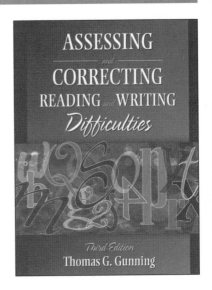

- **Discussion of No Child Left Behind (NCLB) and the concept of adequate yearly progress,** and their implications for instruction of struggling readers, demonstrate how NCLB might be used to help them assist struggling readers.

- Includes **assessment measures and techniques for assisting English language learners** to acquaint users with practical knowledge needed to help English language learners.

- **Emphasis on building higher level thinking skills** will enable teachers to understand that struggling readers need to learn higher level thinking skills along with basic strategies and be taught challenging content.

- **Focus on accelerating the progress of students who are behind** in the context of the three tier model, in which Tier 1 represents prevention of difficulties, Tier 2 provides added instructional time for children who have falling behind, and Tier 3 provides an in-depth diagnosis and specialized instruction for students who do not benefit from Tier 2 instruction.

- **Added coverage of fluency** provides teachers with more techniques for fostering fluency.

- **Emphasis on continuous progress monitoring** show teachers how they might use continuous progress monitoring to ensure that students are making adequate progress.

- **Critical discussion of widely used assessment devices**, such as the DIBELS and the Developmental Reading Assessment. Students will be better able to select appropriate assessment instruments.

THIRD EDITION

ASSESSING AND CORRECTING READING AND WRITING DIFFICULTIES

THOMAS G. GUNNING

Professor Emeritus, Southern Connecticut State University

Adjunct Professor, Central Connecticut State University

PEARSON

Boston ■ New York ■ San Francisco
Mexico City ■ Montreal ■ Toronto ■ London ■ Madrid ■ Paris
Hong Kong ■ Singapore ■ Tokyo ■ Cape Town ■ Sydney

Senior Series Editor: *Aurora Martínez Ramos*
Editorial Assistant: *Kevin Shannon*
Senior Marketing Manager: *Krista Groshong*
Editorial Production Service: *Tom Conville Publishing Services, LLC*
Manufacturing Buyer: *Andrew Turso*
Electronic Composition: *Omegatype Typography, Inc.*
Cover Administrator: *Kristina Mose-Libon*

For related titles and support materials, visit our online catalog at www.ablongman.com.

Between the time Website information is gathered and then published, it is not unusual for some sites to have closed. Also, the transcription of URLs can result in typographical errors. The publisher would appreciate notification where these errors occur so that they may be corrected in subsequent editions.

Library of Congress Cataloging-in-Publication Data

Gunning, Thomas G.
  Assessing and correcting reading and writing difficulties / Thomas G. Gunning.—3rd ed.
    p. cm.
  Includes bibliographical references and index.
  ISBN 0-205-44326-5
  1. Reading disability—Evaluation. 2. Reading—Ability testing. 3. Reading—Remedial teaching. 4. English language—Composition and exercises—Ability testing. 5. English language—Composition and exercises—Study and teaching. I. Title.

LB1050.5.G846 2006
428.4'076—dc22

                                                                    2005063784

Printed in the United States of America

10   9   8   7   6   5   4   3   09   08   07

CONTENTS

CHAPTER THREE

Overview of Assessment   61

CHAPTER FOUR

Placing Students and Monitoring Progress   82

CHAPTER FIVE

Assessment of Reading and Writing Processes   **119**

CHAPTER SIX

Assessment of Cognitive, School, and Home Factors   **152**

CHAPTER SEVEN

Emergent Literacy and Early Intervention Programs   180

CHAPTER EIGHT

Teaching Phonics, High-Frequency Words, and Fluency   223

CHAPTER NINE

Syllabic, Morphemic, and Contextual Analysis and Dictionary Strategies   304

CHAPTER TEN

Building Vocabulary   335

CHAPTER ELEVEN

Building Comprehension   359

CHAPTER FOURTEEN

Severe Problem Cases, Students Acquiring English, and Older Students   500

PREFACE

Although it is grounded in theory and research, *Assessing and Correcting Reading and Writing Difficulties,* Third Edition, is, above all else, a practical text. It specifies in careful detail how to assess students and how to use assessment results to provide effective instruction. Some forty-six sample lessons, covering virtually every major skill or strategy, are presented. The lessons are described in easy-to-follow, step-by-step fashion. The emphasis in the text is on teaching students strategies that they can use independently for improving word recognition, vocabulary knowledge, comprehension, reading in the content areas, writing, spelling, and study skills.

Realizing that one reason low-achieving readers have fallen behind is because they typically read less than their higher-achieving peers, the text provides numerous suggestions for books that can be used to provide additional reinforcement or that students might want to read for enjoyment. Because low-achieving readers read below grade level, books that are easy to read but are appealing to older students have been emphasized. Appendix B contains an extensive listing of high-interest, low-readability texts. Realizing, too, that low-achieving readers and writers need lots of practice, the text contains numerous suggestions for reinforcement activities.

In order to make the text as concrete as possible, numerous examples of low-achieving readers being assessed and instructed are presented. Most chapters also present Exemplary Teaching, a vignette of especially effective instruction, and a Minicase Study that exemplifies the major principles explored in that chapter. (Note that when a student in general is discussed, the text alternates between use of the pronouns *he* and *she* to avoid repetition of the awkward *he or she*.)

Because there are many approaches to teaching low-achieving readers and writers and varying philosophies behind these approaches, this text presents those techniques and practices that seem most promising. Low-achieving readers and writers need explicit instruction. They also need the opportunity to derive satisfaction and enjoyment from reading and writing for real purposes. This text recommends planned, systematic instruction within the context of lots of reading and writing.

Because there are many valid ways of teaching reading and writing, the text frequently provides a choice of methods. The chapter on phonics, for instance, explores both holistic and direct, systematic instructional techniques. Regardless of which technique is selected, emphasis is on providing contextual, functional instruction with many opportunities for real reading and writing.

Today there is an emphasis on collaboration between the classroom teacher and the specialist. At times, specialists use techniques that are different from those used by the classroom teacher, and specialists from different fields might choose different methods. For instance, when working with students who have severe reading problems, the reading specialist might show a preference for a teaching method known as the Fernald tracing technique, whereas a specialist with a learning disabilities orientation might use a multisensory technique known as the Orton–Gillingham method. It is important that you be acquainted with both these techniques so that you have a basis for choosing the approach that seems best suited to your situation and also so that you are able to work knowledgeably and effectively with other professionals.

The first portion (Chapters 1 and 2) of the text provides an overview of reading and writing difficulties and a summary of factors that contribute to reading and writing problems. The second section (Chapters 3–6) presents ways of assessing the strengths and weaknesses of low-achieving readers and writers. Because assessment and instruction are often intertwined, additional information on assessment is presented in the chapters on instruction. Emphasis is on obtaining information that will help you plan an effective program.

The bulk of the text explores techniques for teaching low-achieving readers and writers. The third section of the text (Chapters 7–10) explores methods for improving word recognition and includes a chapter on phonics, high-frequency words, and fluency, and a chapter that includes syllabic analysis, morphemic analysis (meaningful word parts), contextual analysis, and dictionary skills and strategies. The section ends with a chapter on developing vocabulary.

The fourth portion of the text (Chapters 11 and 12) is devoted to understanding the written word and includes chapters on general comprehension and reading in content areas, together with study skills. The last section of the text (Chapters 13–15) explores writing; techniques for helping students who have severe word-learning problems; programs for teenage and adult problem readers; and programs for students who are still acquiring English. The text concludes with a chapter on organizing a program for low-achieving readers and writers, including providing for materials, voluntary reading, and technology.

With its broad coverage, detailed lessons, and numerous suggestions for reinforcement, it is my hope that this text will be a practical guide and ready reference as you work with low-achieving readers and writers.

CHANGES IN THE THIRD EDITION

The No Child Left Behind Act (NCLB) has changed the face of intervention instruction. Because of the provisions of NCLB, a greater number of struggling readers and writers will be getting the help they so desperately need. The third edition explains the major provisions of NCLB and some of the ways in which these provisions might be met. As a result, closing the gap between achieving and struggling readers is a major theme of the third edition. The text emphasizes those approaches and techniques that help underachieving readers narrow the gap. Because the key to bringing all students to proficiency is to build language, background, and thinking skills, increased attention has been given to each of these areas. Both vocabulary (Chapter 10) and fluency (Chapter 8) have been given increased coverage as has monitoring progress (Chapter 4). Increased coverage has also been provided for the concept of response to intervention (Chapters 1 and 15.) The response approach to intervention is succeeding in obtaining help for struggling readers sooner and is demonstrating the power of sustained instruction. It has also demonstrated that there is a small percentage of struggling readers who will need sustained assistance for two years or more.

For a number of topics, there is a greater depth of coverage. The discussion of phonological awareness, for instance, (Chapter 7) looks into language factors that might have an impact on this essential skill. The process of deriving meanings of words from context (Chapter 9) also goes into greater depth. Considering key areas in greater depth has led to suggestions for more effective instruction. Because of the importance of vocabulary, descriptions of highly effective programs, such as Text Talk and FAME, have been added (Chapter 9).

Given the growing number of English language learners, increased emphasis throughout the text has been placed on ways in which English language learners' language and literacy development might be fostered. The role of technology has been more fully addressed. In addition to discussions in the main body of the text, notes in the margin make suggestions for making effective use of technology.

Overall, the text has taken a proactive position. Intervention rather than remediation is stressed throughout. Also emphasized is the power of instruction. The text takes the stance that students can be taught to be smarter through wide reading and programs such as Accountable Talk that foster thinking skills (Chapter 11). The Strategic Instructional Model (SIM) program (Chapter 12) demonstrates the power of strategy instruction to raise the performance of struggling learners' literacy. The success of high poverty schools that beat the odds has demonstrated the power of extended writing (Chapter 13). Realizing that, although programs are important, it is the teacher who is the key to intervention, Chapter 15 of the text recommends enhanced professional development, including grade-level meetings and study groups, especially those in which teachers discuss the progress of their students.

ACKNOWLEDGMENTS

I owe a debt of gratitude to Virginia Lanigan of Allyn and Bacon, who saw value in the original, unwieldy manuscript and offered the kinds of suggestions and support that enabled me to pare it down but enrich it. I am also grateful to Aurora Martínez, senior editor at Allyn and Bacon, who oversaw the revision of this text, and to her capable assistants, Erin Beatty and Kevin Shannon, who shepherded the manuscript through the many phases that led to publication. Many thanks, too, to the following reviewers, who offered numerous suggestions that were both thoughtful and valuable: Sherryl Macaul, University of Wisconsin–Eau Claire; Patricia Richardson, Salisbury University; Jeanne Shay Schumm, University of Miami; and Darren J. Smith, Arkansas State University.

CHAPTER ONE

INTRODUCTION TO LITERACY DIFFICULTIES

USING WHAT YOU KNOW

This first chapter of this text serves as an overview and introduction to a complex topic: reading and writing difficulties. Before reading the chapter, think about the knowledge that you bring to the topic, so that you will be better prepared to interact with the information presented. Have you read books or articles on reading and writing difficulties? Do you remember from your school days what steps were taken to help those classmates who struggled with reading or writing? If you are teaching now, think about students of yours who may have difficulty with reading or writing. What problems are they manifesting? How are these students being helped?

After reflecting on your knowledge of the topic, complete the Anticipation Guide that follows. The Anticipation Guide is a device that will help you interact with the chapter's main concepts. Most of the statements in the Anticipation Guide are open-ended and often do not have a right or wrong answer. These statements are designed to help you explore your beliefs and attitudes. They can also help indicate topics about which you might need additional information. The Anticipation Guide is a device that you can use with your students. Suggestions for teaching the Anticipation Guide are presented in Chapter 12.

ANTICIPATION GUIDE

Read each of the following statements. Put a check under "Agree" or "Disagree" to show how you feel about each one. If possible, discuss your responses with classmates.

	AGREE	DISAGREE
1. A problem reader is one who is reading below his or her grade level.	————	————
2. In most instances, reading problems can be prevented.	————	————
3. Most cases of reading difficulty should be handled by the classroom teacher.	————	————

	AGREE	DISAGREE
4. Low-achieving readers need to have tasks broken down into their component parts.	_____	_____
5. There is no one best approach for working with low-achieving readers.	_____	_____

READING DIFFICULTY DEFINED

There are many ways of defining reading difficulty, but the most telling definition was uttered by Awilda, a fourth-grader in a large urban school. When asked how school was going, she replied, "I got trouble with my reading."

Counting the extra year spent in second grade, Awilda had received more than four years of formal instruction in reading. However, despite having average intelligence, she was reading only on an early first-grade level. Although she had a stable personality, a caring family, and dedicated, highly competent teachers, she was reading at a level far below what might reasonably be expected. Intervention attempts including one-to-one instruction, had failed to help her. Further, Awilda's difficulty was interfering with her functioning both in school and the larger society. She lacked the skills necessary to read the literature, social studies, and science selections typically required of a fourth-grader. Outside school, she was unable to read the letters her grandmother sent from Houston, use the newspaper's TV guide to find out the evening's schedule, read the ads on cereal boxes, or engage in any of the literacy tasks that fourth-graders might encounter. Worst of all, Awilda's self-esteem was being eroded.

Awilda was manifesting a reading difficulty in three related but different ways. There was a discrepancy between overall cognitive ability and her reading achievement. Although she had average ability, she was reading well below grade level. And her lack of reading ability was interfering with the demands made by her life circumstances. Awilda was evidencing a functional difficulty. In addition, when provided with extra help, first by the classroom teacher, and then by the reading specialist, who implemented an intervention approach that worked with most students, she failed to make progress.

Discrepancy Definition

When considering whether a person has a reading difficulty, the reader's intellectual capacity and/or language development are frequently taken into consideration. Theoretically, students should be able to read at a level equal to their intellectual capacity or level of oral language development. Gifted students would be expected to read above grade level because their capacity is above average (Rosenberger, 1992). On the other hand, a student with mental retardation would not be expected to read on grade level because her or his capacity is well below average. Students with below-average intelligence are often denied corrective services because it is believed that diminished intellectual functioning is the cause of their reading problem. However, if a student with mental retardation is reading below the level indicated by his or her listening and/or cognitive ability test, that student is demonstrating a reading problem. A problem reader, then, is one who is reading below intellectual capacity or oral language development.

> **Discrepancy** definition of reading disability: a difference exists between the student's ability and achievement. A fifth-grader with the ability of a seventh-grader would be expected to read on a seventh-grade level.

Defining problem readers as those reading below capacity is known as the **discrepancy** definition of reading disorders. Traditionally, discrepancies have been described in terms of students reading one or more years below their capacity—for instance, an average fifth grader reading on a third-grade level. In many programs, discrepancies are expressed in **standard deviations.** A standard deviation is a measure of the degree to which scores are above or below average. For placement in programs for students with serious reading disabilities, many states set the discrepancy at 1½ standard deviations between performance on a test of academic ability and a reading achievement test (Snow, Burns & Griffin, 1998).

> Standard deviations are explained in more detail in Chapter 3.

Although it is the most widely accepted concept of reading difficulty, the discrepancy definition does have some major problems. First of all, there is no agreement on a definition of intellectual ability or on how to measure it. Gardner (1999), for instance, speaks of many kinds of intelligences—linguistic, musical, logical-mathematical, spatial, bodily-kinesthetic, intrapersonal, and interpersonal—but concedes that there may be more. Recently he added naturalist intelligence, spiritual intelligence, and an existential intelligence. The fairness of intelligence tests has also been called into question. If students have not had an equal opportunity to learn material, such as vocabulary or assembling puzzles, then intelligence tests may underestimate their abilities. The tests may also fail to include items from the students' culture (Salvia & Ysseldyke, 1998). IQ tests tend to discriminate against students from lower socioeconomic groups. Since IQ scores, at least in part, reflect the environment in which students grow up, students from disadvantaged environments tend to score lower on IQ tests (Siegel, 1998). Having lower IQ scores, students from lower socioeconomic groups who are struggling readers are less likely to meet the discrepancy cutoff scores and may be deprived of special services even though they have severe reading problems. Because students in the early grades would not have had much opportunity to achieve, it is difficult to find a large discrepancy, so many school districts adopt a "wait and fail" tactic: they wait until the student has encountered serious difficulty.

> If a discrepancy definition were not used, many of the brighter students would not be selected as having a reading difficulty, but more of the slower students would be.

One solution to the IQ controversy has been to use listening tests as measures of students' potential (Spring & French, 1990; Badian, 1999). Listening comprehension is the level of material that students can understand when the material is read to them. If a student's listening comprehension is at a fifth-grade level and the student is reading on a first-grade level, then there is a four-year discrepancy between capacity and achievement.

> To see how the discrepancy concept works, try Test Score Discrepancy Analyzer 2.0 at http://www.intervention central.org/tools.shtml.

However, in both listening and intelligence tests, there is the issue of the confusion of cause and effect. Because they are unable to fully utilize reading, which is a major source of intellectual or language development, poor readers may do less well on verbal intelligence and listening tests (Stanovich, 1991). Through wide reading, verbal abilities such as word knowledge and the ability to use and comprehend language are fostered, so that the reading process actually makes students "smarter" (Stanovich, 1992). As Siegel (1998) notes, "It is a logical paradox to use IQ scores with learning disabled children because most of these children are deficient in one or more of the component skills that are part of these IQ tests and, therefore, their scores on IQ tests will be an underestimate of their competence" (p. 128). In addition, because they are poor readers, they read less. Reading less, they pick up less knowledge and learn fewer vocabulary words, areas that are tapped by many IQ tests, so that as students get older their scores on IQ tests are likely to become more depressed. In fact, Siegel found that the IQs of older disabled readers were lower. She also found that the proportion of severely disabled readers decreased with age. Why might this be? If the IQ scores of older struggling readers decrease with age, then it is more difficult to establish a large discrepancy between ability and achievement.

A sizable discrepancy can be a sign of a severe difficulty. Badian (1997) found that students with large gaps between ability and achievement had a greater number of deficits.

Some students may have a discrepancy because of some internal characteristic that makes it difficult for them to learn. Others may have a discrepancy because of illness, absenteeism, a mismatched reading program, or high mobility. Recently I worked with a fourth-grader reading on a first-grade level, who had slightly above average intelligence. She easily met the discrepancy definition. However, when instructed, she learned word analysis skills easily and made rapid progress. The family had moved often, so she had missed large chunks of school. When the family finally settled down and she attended the same school for a sustained period of time and was given an appropriate program, she made rapid progress.

In addition to having a discrepancy, students should evidence difficulty in learning to read despite adequate instruction in order to be classified as disabled readers. In the latest version of the Individuals with Disabilities Education Act (IDEA, 2004), it is not necessary to show a discrepancy between a student's aptitude and achievement in order to establish a reading disability that is so severe that it qualifies as a learning disability. **Response to intervention** may be used to identify students with a learning disability. A response to intervention means that the student has been provided with high quality instruction but has failed to make adequate progress. This is typically a three-tier process. In the first tier, the student is provided with high quality instruction in the regular general education program. If the student falls behind, he or she is given supplementary instruction—either in a small group or one-to-one. If the student still fails to make adequate progress, he or she is assessed for possible placement in special education and/or provided with an intensive intervention program.

Response to intervention is an approach to the identification of reading/learning disabilities in which struggling students are provided with reading instruction that increases in intensity from high quality classroom instruction to specialized one-on-one intervention in order to assess the students' ability to learn. Instruction is typically combined with diagnosis.

The advantage of the response to intervention approach is that the focus is on prevention and remediation rather than on waiting for the student to fail. Because students are provided with high quality classroom instruction and then supplementary instruction and finally, intensive instruction, most children will make progress.

Functional Definition

Functional definition of reading disability: achievement fails to meet a certain standard or interferes with the reader's functioning in or out of school.

Many programs now use a **functional** definition in identifying problem readers. They simply provide instruction for the lowest achievers in reading. All states now administer proficiency tests in grades 3 through 8 and in high school. In many areas, students who fail to reach the proficiency cutoff scores are provided with intervention, regardless of ability. Reading Recovery, a highly successful program designed to boost the reading performance of low-achieving first-graders, provides intensive one-on-one instruction for those students identified as being in the bottom 20 percent of reading achievement. Again, academic aptitude is not a factor. All students within the lowest 20 percent are provided with assistance. Although it may overlook some bright underachievers, the functional approach provides added help for the poorest readers, regardless of any labels that may have been attached to them.

Another way of looking at reading difficulty from a functional approach is to judge whether or not it interferes with the reader's life circumstances. Does it hinder her or him from engaging in reading and writing activities that others in similar circumstances encounter? Awilda was unable to write to her grandparents or complete her school work. For high school students, it might take the form of reading so slowly that they cannot keep up with outside reading assignments. For a police trainee it might be the inability to read the department's manuals or write coherent reports. Barr, Blachowicz, and Wogman-Sadow (1995) define a reading problem on the elementary school level as one in which "a student cannot adequately understand the materials used for regular classroom instruction" (p. 9). As Klenk and Kibby (2000) comment, the goal of remedial instruction is for every child to be able to read the "texts generally considered appropriate for children's age or grade" (p. 684).

In this text the emphasis will be on a combined discrepancy and functional definition of literacy disorders and response to intervention. Keeping in mind the limitations of intelligence and listening tests, it is recommended that one adopt a broad view of ability. Students can manifest ability in a variety of ways: by the thinking and language abilities they display in classroom discussions and discussions with peers, by their ability to solve everyday problems, or by their knowledge of the world around them. One way of estimating students' learning abilities is by teaching them and seeing how much they learn. Many students who have been written off bloom when provided with the right kind of instruction (Hiebert & Taylor, 2000).

INCIDENCE OF READING PROBLEMS

What proportion of the population has a reading difficulty? How many Awildas are there? The National Assessment of Educational Progress found that the following percentages of students were unable to function on a basic level, which means that they could not comprehend text at a literal level, relate it to their lives, and make simple inferences, or draw conclusions based on the text (Donahue, Daane, & Grigg, 2003).

For the latest information on NAEP performance, consult http://nces.ed.gov/nations reportcard/site/home.asp.

Grade 4: 37 percent
Grade 8: 26 percent
Grade 12: 26 percent

Based on National Assessment and other data, it is estimated that up to 25 percent of the population has some difficulty with reading. Not all of these students have serious problems. Most have mild to moderate difficulty. They may be functioning a year or two below what might be expected. Only a small percentage have severe problems (Awilda would be classified as having a severe reading problem). Approximately 10 percent of the school

Students who have severe reading difficulties can be difficult to remediate. In one program, despite 2½ years of intensive instruction, 2.4 percent were still operating substantially below grade level (Torgesen, Wagner, & Rashotte, 1997).

population have a mild problem, 12 percent have moderate difficulties, and up to 3 to 6 percent have a more serious difficulty (Badian, 1999; McCormick, 1999; Torgesen, 2004; Vellutino et al., 1996). The percentage of poor readers will vary with locality. For instance, British researchers Rutter and Yule (1975) found a reading disability rate of 3.6 percent among the Isle of Wight's ten-year-olds but 9.3 percent among ten-year-olds in London's inner-city schools.

However, based on a functional concept of literacy, there is a "quiet crisis" in the secondary school (Schoenbach, Greenleaf, Cziko, & Hurwitz, 1999). Thousands of middle and high school students are struggling with their academic texts. The National Research Council (Snow, Burns, & Griffin, 1998) concluded that "The educational careers of 25 to 40 percent of American children are imperiled because they do not read well enough, quickly enough, or easily enough to ensure comprehension in their content courses in middle and secondary school" (p. 98). The good news is that most of these students have mild or moderate problems and can succeed if given some additional assistance by the classroom teacher or literacy specialist. A variety of programs have been shown to be highly successful (Curtis & Longo, 1999; Schoenbach, Greenleaf, Cziko, & Hurwitz, 1999).

PERSISTENCE OF SEVERE PROBLEMS

Reading problems may be growing worse. Scores of fourth graders whose achievement was within the lowest 10 percent dropped significantly between 1992 and 2000 (Donahue, Finnegan, Lutkus, Allen, & Campbell, 2001).

Unlike mild or moderate difficulties, severe reading problems can be chronic and require intensive intervention. These are students "who have unusual difficulty learning to read and whose reading problems cannot be accounted for by other disabilities, broad intellectual limitations, impoverished home environment, or generally inadequate instruction. Although the number of these children is likely much smaller than the number currently identified in schools as having RD (reading disability), many of these children do require ongoing, intensive educational support in order to learn to read" (Spear-Swerling, 2004, p. 517). Students who are poor readers in the early grades tend to be the lowest-achieving readers in the upper grades. Poor readers improve, but the gap between their achievement and that of average and superior readers remains (Shaywitz, 2003). Severe reading disability can be persistent. When a group of adults, who had been given intensive instructional assistance as children, were retested at age thirty-three, about half were found to be proficient readers. The other half were found to be deficient in reading. Half of these were only slightly below the proficient readers, but the remaining half (one-quarter of the total) still had serious reading problems (Myers, 2000).

Despite underlying deficits, students with severe reading problems do learn to read if given appropriate instruction, but their reading may continue to be slow and laborious. Because their reading skills are weak, they often rely on their background knowledge and language skills and use context fairly heavily. However, if they specialize in an area such as astronomy, physics, medicine, or business, they frequently learn the printed forms of the vocabulary in their particular area of interest, and this fosters improved reading. Having mastered a particular discipline, they can go on to have highly successful professional careers (Shaywitz, 2003).

ENGLISH LANGUAGE LEARNERS AS STRUGGLING READERS

> **Using Technology**
> The National Clearinghouse for English Language Acquisition and Language Instruction Educational Programs can be accessed at http://www.ncela.gwu.edu/. This web site provides information about programs for ELL students.

Disproportionate numbers of English language learners (ELL) are classified as struggling readers (Valencia & Buly, 2004). However, poor performance on an English reading test does not mean that an ELL student is a struggling reader. Newly arrived students who are still learning the rudiments of the language would not be expected to be reading on grade level in English. It would be helpful to know how well the student is reading in his native language. If an ELL student is having difficulty with both reading in English and his native language then this is an indicator of a reading difficulty. On the other side of the coin, if an ELL child is struggling to learn to read, you can not dismiss this as being due to the fact that he speaks another language. You need to have some measure of the student's knowledge of English and opportunity to learn to read before that judgment can be made.

For most ELL students, their progress in literacy is limited by their command of English. As they learn English, they will be better able to improve their English reading skills. However, because they are still learning the language, ELL students will need extra assistance learning to read. Most will improve in reading as they acquire English and are given appropriate instruction. Another important piece of information would be whether the ELL student can read in his or her native tongue. Students who can read in their native tongue can transfer many of their skills to reading in English.

THE PROBLEM WITH USING LABELS

> **Dyslexia** originally referred to the loss of the ability to read because of damage to the central nervous system but now is used to refer to a serious reading disorder.

A few years ago, I got an urgent phone call from a distraught parent. "I just found out my son has dyslexia," she announced. "What should I do?" It was not my first **dyslexia** call; nor was it my last: I receive several a year. The problem with the term is twofold. First, the term *dyslexia* itself has very little meaning. The term is used by some to mean a serious reading problem, others use it for a spelling problem, and some use it to describe mild or moderate reading problems. The second problem with the usage of that term is that it suggests a neurological condition (Shaywitz & Shaywitz, 2000). The term *dyslexia* may be taken to mean that there is something neurologically wrong with the student, which accounts for his or her problems learning to read. However, the problem may well be in the program. When proper adaptations are made, nearly all children learn, including those whose difficulty may be rooted in a neurological condition. Referring to students who are slow to learn to read as "slow learners," Marie Clay (1993b), the major force behind Reading Recovery, explained:

What is possible for slow learners is different from what we used to think was possible . . . slow learners are slow learners only because of the ways in which we have tried to teach them. In society and in education we categorize them, and they grow to fit our categories. All we had to do was rearrange the teacher's talents, change the delivery conditions, and provide opportunities to succeed; then, slow learners caught up with their average classmates. (pp. xiii–xiv)

What is true for the term *dyslexia* also applies to other terms used to label underachieving students: *learning disability, at-risk, corrective, reading disabled,* and *remedial.* As C. Weaver (1994a) explains:

Nowadays, students diagnosed as dyslexic or learning disabled are often referred to as students with special needs. I like to think of them simply as "special learners"—and I hope that someday the educational bureaucracy will recognize that *all* learners are unique, *all* are special, and *all* need to be treated and taught accordingly. (p. 501)

> The **variability** concept is replacing the deficit model of remedial reading. When working with struggling readers and writers, teachers think in terms of matching instruction to varying needs rather than overcoming deficits.

Being unique, individual students have and always will vary in their reading and writing abilities, just as they vary in running, playing basketball, singing, or solving math problems. Some students seem to learn words after seeing them once or twice; others struggle with words they have seen a hundred times or more. Instead of considering struggling readers as being disabled, Roller (1996) believes that we should learn to accept the variability that students display as being normal, and adjust instruction to meet the needs of each student.

Unfortunately, labels seem to be here to stay. Often, in order to receive special services, students must first be labeled as *learning disabled, at risk, special needs, remedial, reading disabled,* or *corrective.* A label may be a device for getting a child the specialized services that he needs. What we need to do is to look beyond the label and see the individual.

THE NATURE OF CORRECTIVE INSTRUCTION

Corrective instruction comes in many forms. Although specialized techniques are sometimes used, corrective instruction is often simply more individualized application of methods employed in the regular classroom. Corrective techniques can be classified as being part-to-whole, whole-to-part, or interactive.

Part-to-Whole Approach

> In a **bottom-up** approach (part to whole), students are taught letters and sounds before being taught to read words. Emphasis is on processing the text rather than making use of the reader's background.

In a **bottom-up** or part-to-whole approach, students learn the nuts and bolts of reading and assemble them into a whole. Proceeding from the bottom of the process, they learn letter sounds and then blend them into whole words, which are then read in brief stories. Incorporating the belief that reading is easier if it is broken down into its parts and then reconstructed, many corrective programs have taken a part-whole, or bottom-up, approach.

Whole-Part Approach

> A **top-down** approach (whole to part) emphasizes constructing meaning through the readers' use of background knowledge and language ability.

In a **top-down** or whole-part approach, students start at the top of the reading process and proceed downward to letters and sounds. Instruction is initiated by reading whole stories with teacher assistance. Through reading whole stories and by using their knowledge of language patterns, students learn individual printed words and letter–sound relationships. Holistic approaches are based on a top-down view of reading. Children learn to read and write by being immersed in meaningful literacy activities. Whereas in a bottom-up approach, meaning is constructed by decoding words and assembling sentences and paragraphs, in a top-down approach, meaning is predicted. K. Goodman (1974) refers to reading as being a psycholinguistic guessing game in which the readers use their background knowledge and language ability to predict the meaning of a sentence or passage. Instead of processing the sentence letter by letter, word by word, readers use as few cues as possible. For instance, according to this view, seeing the sentence, "The sun is shining," readers need not decode *shining* letter by letter. Using their knowledge of what the sun does and the context of the sentence, readers predict that the word will be *shining*.

> Theorists with a bottom-up approach would posit that readers would process all or most of the letters of *shining* and get little help from context. An interactive approach emphasizes that reading is a parallel, simultaneous process.

An Interactive View

> An **interactive** approach stresses parallel use of processing of text and use of background knowledge.

In this text, reading is viewed as an interaction between part-whole and whole-part or top-down and bottom-up processes. As Rumelhart (1985) hypothesized in his classic **interactive** model, reading is not linear. We don't proceed from letters to words to meaning in step-by-step fashion. Nor do we proceed from the whole to the part. Rather, we engage in parallel processing so that we simultaneously use knowledge of language as well as contextual and letter–sound cues. Reading is both simultaneously top-down and bottom-up.

The truth is that readers, especially ones who have serious problems, need to use all the reading processes. Because low-achieving readers often have difficulty decoding words (Bader & Wiesendanger, 1986), there is a temptation to focus on lower-level processes, such as sounding out words. However, reading is very much a total language process. The most effective programs for struggling readers seem to be those that include a strong decoding component along with plenty of opportunity to apply skills by reading (Santa & Høien, 1999). The efficient reader simultaneously uses background knowledge, facility with language, ongoing comprehension of a selection, and decoding skills. For instance, when reading the following sentence, Jason, a fourth-grade low-achieving reader who has been receiving intensive instruction in decoding strategies, used a variety of sources to help him decipher the word *cocoa,* which for him was an unfamiliar print form:

After shoveling the snow, grandpa had a cup of hot cocoa.

Because Jason has had experience with hot cocoa, his ability to use the context of the sentence enhances his use of decoding skills so that he is able to process the word faster and more readily that he would have if the word *cocoa* had not been in his listening vocabulary. Top-down processes, including language ability and background knowledge, have made it easier for him to apply lower-level decoding processes. Had the context been weak or had the word *cocoa* simply been in a list, Jason would have had to rely more heavily on decoding.

One indication that students use parallel processing is that context aids their decoding. When students encounter words in context that they missed when presented in list form, they are able to read about 25 percent of the missed words correctly (Alexander, 1998).

Using a computer analogy, Adams (1990) theorizes that orthographic (letter), phonological (sound), meaning, and context processors all work simultaneously to decode words. However, the way that processors are brought into play is partly dependent on the nature of the task. As adept readers, our decoding skills become so well learned and rapid that they function automatically. There are occasions, however, when bottom-up processes are brought to the fore. Notice how consciously you use decoding skills as you read the following sentence:

Thēz wrdz ar speld fənetiklé.

Did you notice that you had to deliberately sound out each word? With your processes being slowed down, were you also able to notice how you used your knowledge of language and background of experience along with decoding skills to reconstruct the sentence?

Approaches to intervention can also be categorized as being cognitive-process or sociocultural or a combination of the two. A combination approach is probably more effective. As Stone (2004) noted, "Both perspectives have added to our understanding of language and literacy" (p. 4). A cognitive-process perspective focuses on the individual and emphasizes perceptual abilities, the limitations of memory, and the use of strategies to foster more efficient processing. Background knowledge is also stressed, and the learner is seen as an active participant who constructs meaning in terms of his or her background of experience. Socioculturalists see students as learning from more knowledgeable others. Reading and writing are seen as social processes in which participants learn from each other. What students learn is heavily determined by the social and cultural context in which it is learned. When assessing a struggling reader, from a cognitive-process perspective, focus would be on the mental process and strategies that the student uses. From a sociocultural point of view, emphasis would be placed on the student's culture and the environment in which he or she is being taught. Cognitive scientists emphasize neurocognitive functioning of individuals. Socioculturalists emphasize the influence of the environment and cultural ties. Both, of course, are important. Problems are likely to rise when one approach is overemphasized to the detriment of the other. One of the most successful intervention approaches, reciprocal teaching, combines strategy instruction with collaboration.

STAGES OF READING DEVELOPMENT

Although reading is a continuously developing ability that emerges from a child's experience with oral language and print and that grows and expands as the child progresses through the grades, reading can be divided into phases or stages (Chall, 1996). The reading tasks that a beginner faces are not the same as those encountered by an advanced reader. Programs provided for struggling readers should take into account the stage they are in. Although she may be older, a middle school student who has a serious reading problem may be in an early stage of reading development and will make the most progress if her program matches her level of functioning. Stages of reading development are described below.

Stage 1. Emergent Literacy

During the emergent literacy stage, students generally learn the function of print and may develop phonological awareness: the ability to detect rhymes and the sounds in words. Toward the end of this stage, children may be able to read signs and labels and may explore writing in the form of scribbles, letterlike forms, or invented spelling. Although it is usually associated with younger children, some older disabled readers may be in this stage.

Stage 2. Early Reading (Grades K–1)

Older students may have lingering weakness in phonological awareness, which hinders their progress in acquiring decoding skills.

A key characteristic of the early reading stage is an evolving grasp of the alphabetic principle. Students begin using their knowledge of letter–sound relationships and context to decode printed words. Many struggling readers are at this stage. Older students at this level need direct instruction in necessary decoding skills. They also need materials that are age appropriate but that reinforce the phonics elements they are learning (Curtis & Longo, 1999).

Stage 3. Growing Independence (Grades 2–3)

The main characteristic of the stage of growing independence is children's evolving fluency. As the process of decoding becomes automatic, students are able to concentrate on meaning. By the end of this stage, students are able to read about 3,000 words (Curtis & Longo, 1999).

Not having had enough practice with reading materials on their level, older disabled readers may spend an inordinate amount of time sounding out words. Their rate of reading is very slow and may be painfully dysfluent. These students need many opportunities to read materials that are relatively easy for them.

Stage 4. Reading to Learn (Grades 4–6)

The stage of reading to learn is marked by the wide application of word-attack and comprehension skills. Greater emphasis is placed on comprehending informational text. Although struggling readers may have acquired the necessary decoding skills, they may have difficulty with the vocabulary and conceptual load of the materials. They need systematic instruction in vocabulary, morphemic analysis, contextual clues, and dictionary skills. They may also need help with comprehension and study strategies.

Stage 5. Abstract Reading

At the abstract reading stage, students can construct multiple hypotheses, consider several viewpoints, mull over logical alternatives, and evaluate what they read. Their school texts are longer, more complex, and more abstract. Struggling readers at this stage need advanced study and comprehension skills as well as further vocabulary and concept development.

Using a stage development theory of reading, Curtis and Longo (1999) have created a highly successful reading program for older struggling readers. It has helped them to note "what has failed to develop, what has developed differently, and most importantly, what still needs to be developed . . ." (p. 10). To demonstrate their point they cite the example of Chrissy, a fifteen-year-old ninth-grader. Chrissy was having difficulty understanding what she read, but teaching her comprehension strategies wasn't helping. A beginning stage 3 reader (growing independence), Chrissy was reading very slowly. To quicken the pace of her reading, she guessed at words based on the first few letters rather than taking the time to analyze the whole word. The result was that she read *calendar* for *cylinder* and *efficiently* for *effectively,* and thus her comprehension suffered. What she needed was instruction that would foster automatic word recognition so that she could then focus on what she was reading rather than how she was reading.

Using a stage model along with careful assessment has another benefit. By understanding the stages of reading development, the teachers in the Boys Town program have been able to focus instruction so that they can concentrate on the knowledge and skills that are most critical for helping students progress to the next stage of development.

A SYSTEMS APPROACH

Reading and writing problems, especially when they are severe, affect all aspects of a student's life. Although he was easily the brightest student in first-grade, Robert was facing possible retention. Robert had serious difficulty learning to associate spoken words with their printed symbols. Despite special assistance, he had learned only a half-dozen words by the end of the year. Unfortunately, he learned to fear reading in the process. By the time he was referred to a university reading clinic, he was refusing to attempt to read. Why try, when failure was virtually guaranteed? The wall he had built around himself to prevent further failure was so impenetrable that counseling was required.

Robert's reading problem also manifested itself physically. Complaining of stomach pains, Robert was given a thorough examination. Unable to find a medical cause for the pains, the doctor believed they were caused by stress at school. Even Robert's social relationships were harmed by his reading difficulty. Classmates teased him for his slowness in catching on to reading. Baffled by Robert's difficulty, his family was torn between sympathy for his plight and a suspicion that maybe the source of Robert's problem was lack of effort. Meanwhile, at school, Robert mentally withdrew from all tasks involving reading and writing. He noted that his favorite part of school was "the bus ride home."

Understanding a student's reading difficulty, especially when it is a severe one, means finding out how it affects and is affected by the significant aspects of his life: family, school, and friends. For older low-achieving readers, society at large and the world of work must also be figured into the equation. The understanding must be ecological. For instance, it is important to see how the low-achieving reader functions in her or his classroom. Questions that need to be answered include: How does the student interact in the classroom? How do other students respond to her or him? What changes might be made to improve the student's progress? If the student is in a corrective program, the key question becomes: How might the corrective and regular classroom program be coordinated so as to achieve maximum benefit for the student? How can the classroom teacher and the reading specialist support one another's efforts? How might the home be involved? A comprehensive plan of assistance must take into account how the school, the home, and other institutions might play a role in remediation.

As Bartoli and Botel (1988) note, we need to see the interrelationship of the student with peers, with teachers, with any specialists who might be involved, and with parents. The idea is not to place blame but to see how all systems of learning or nonlearning are working and to integrate the cognitive with the emotional and the social. Under a **systems** approach, the role of corrective specialist becomes that of a collaborator who works closely with the classroom teacher. Rather than focusing on the causes of the child's failure, the corrective specialist and the classroom teacher work together to adjust the total environment so the student achieves success. The home is also involved in the process, and measures are taken to meet the student's out-of-school literacy needs. In a systems approach, instead of worrying about who did what wrong, emphasis is on getting the child on the right track.

> **Systems** approach: looks at all aspects of the student's life and the effect each has on the student.

INTERLOCKING ASPECTS OF READING

In addition to considering the student's literacy activities at home, in school, and in the wider world, a program of correction needs to take into account the five major interlocking aspects of reading: reader, task, text, instructional approach, and situational context (Walker, 1992). At the center of reading is the reader. Reading is a highly personal activity. Each of us brings to reading a unique blend of background, ability, perspective, interests, and proficiency. We interpret a text in the light of who we are and what we know.

Rosenblatt (1978, 1994) describes the interaction between reader and text as a **transaction.** The text is transformed by the reader and the reader, in turn, is transformed by the text. The ease of reading, the degree of interest, the organization of the text, and the use of illustrations affect the quality of the transaction. The degree of involvement will be minimal if the text is boring, too difficult, or both.

> **Transactional theory:** the reader transforms text through personal perspective, yet is also changed by the text. Meaning is created by the transaction between reader and text.

The task is also a key factor. Will the reader be skimming the material, reading it casually, or studying it in preparation for a test? Will the material be read silently or orally? Interacting with the task is the instructional approach used. Some students may respond well to highly structured direct instruction. Others thrive with approaches that focus on student involvement and stress discovery learning. Teachers of low-achieving readers need to ask: What instructional approach works best with this student or group?

■ ■ ■ ■ ■ ▬▬▬▬▬▬▬▬▬▬▬▬▬▬▬▬▬▬▬▬▬▬▬▬▬▬▬▬▬▬▬▬▬▬

EXEMPLARY TEACHING
BECOMING EMPOWERED

Although she was a year older than the other fifth-graders in her class, eleven-year-old Angela seemed shy and immature (Five, l992). Classified as learning disabled, she spent most of her mornings working on academics in a pullout program. In the afternoons, she returned to her classroom. Believing that Angela could benefit from process writing, Cora Lee Five, her teacher, included her in the afternoon writing program. At first, Angela's writing, which she restricted to brief journal entries, was very limited. Angela also refused to take part in writing conferences but did sit near the conference table, where she could overhear what was being said. Through

listening in, Angela was slowly drawn into the process. In time, Angela started conferring about her writing with a friend. This was a turning point. Little by little, she began to become involved in the class's activities. Throughout the year Angela's writing skills improved, as did her social skills. Angela began taking control of her learning and her life.

As Five noted, by being included in the class's activities, "Angela changed dramatically. The shy, dependent child who had no confidence and no real connection to her classmates and to learning turned into an animated involved girl who thought of herself as a learner" (Five, l992, p. 25).

All the other factors—reader, text, task, and technique—are affected by the context. Discussions, for instance, are altered dramatically by context. Students who are stone silent in a large group may become very expressive in a small cooperative learning group. (The Exemplary Teaching lesson demonstrates how Angela changed when her setting, teacher, and instructional approach were altered.)

PRINCIPLES OF CORRECTIVE INSTRUCTION

Problem readers are a diverse group. The majority have difficulty decoding; however, there are a number of excellent decoders who have difficulty understanding what they read. Degree of difficulty ranges from mild to severe. Possible causes run the gamut from inappropriate materials to poor nutrition. Depending on the nature, severity, and source of the problem, programs for low-achieving readers will vary. However, a number of basic principles should be incorporated in any program created to help students who are struggling with reading and writing.

Prevention versus Correction

Prevention, of course, is vastly superior to remediation. Prevention safeguards self-esteem, eliminates ineffective strategies before they are hardened into habits, and saves limited corrective resources for those who most desperately need it. The best prevention is a high-quality literacy program. A national committee charged with making recommendations to help prevent reading difficulties concluded, "Excellent instruction is the best intervention for children who demonstrate problems learning to read" (Snow, Burns, & Griffin, 1998, p. 33).

Importance of Success

In reading as in life, nothing succeeds like success. With success, there is increased effort, and more success. Marjorie Johnson (1966) describes the dawning of hope in a student with a severe reading problem who had spent several weeks laboriously, but successfully, learning a basic reading vocabulary.

> When Francis first learned that he could read a particular preprimer [beginning reading book] which happened to contain no words which he did not know at this point, he was amazed. It had been a long, hard struggle for him to acquire any immediate recognition vocabulary. His reaction showed both his recognition of his difficulty and his hope for the future—an awareness that he could and would progress. (p. 156)

Building On the Known

A close corollary of teaching for success is building on what is known. All too often, corrective instruction focuses on what the student doesn't know or can't do. In this text, both assessment and instruction will be presented as positive forces. The emphasis will be on building on what the student already knows.

Building on the known also means taking into consideration the student's background. In today's highly diverse classrooms, students come from a variety of cultures. It is important to use examples with which the student will be familiar. It is important to use materials that incorporate the student's culture and to use discussion and responding styles that the student finds comfortable and familiar. If the student is learning English as a second language, it is important to be aware of the student's language proficiency and to build on that proficiency.

Fostering Independence

The phrase "learned helplessness" is often used to describe low-achieving readers. Having a history of failure, they see themselves as unable to cope successfully with reading and writing tasks. In a study of poor readers, Butkowsky and Willows (1980) found that these students lacked confidence in their reading, had lower expectations of success, and gave up more easily. Poor readers are also more likely to attribute their success to luck (Wigfield & Asher, 1984) and failure to a lack of ability. Since luck and ability are beyond their control, they are inclined to give up too quickly or seek help, rather than rely on their own resources. Relying too heavily on others, their reading development is further stunted and they conclude that they are "helpless."

Often, well-meaning teachers fall into the trap of unwittingly reinforcing learned helplessness. Realizing that a student has limited skills and is struggling, the teacher supplies answers or figures out hard words for him because she feels sorry for him. Over time, some students develop a negative reflex reaction to academic challenges. Upon encountering a difficult word, they immediately lift their heads from the page and look to the teacher for help. Upon answering a discussion question, they study the teacher's face for a sign indicating whether the answer was correct. They seldom venture opinions. Browbeaten by a cycle of failure and self-defeating behaviors, they feel like outcasts in the community of readers and writers. In addition to teaching these students strategies, the teacher must also build confidence, instill an openness to taking risks, and a willingness to take responsibility for one's learning.

To foster independence, never do for students what they can do for themselves. A corollary is never to accept anything but the student's best. If they are accustomed to having substandard work accepted by overly sympathetic teachers, students internalize their lowered expectations. The greatest compliment a teacher can pay a student is to reject inferior efforts. By accepting only the student's best, the teacher is saying, "I have faith in you." Expectations, of course, need to be realistic.

Active Involvement

Being an independent learner requires active involvement in the task at hand. Unless the student is actively involved, the most carefully planned program will fail by default. In explaining the success of VAKT, an instructional program that makes use of *v*isual, *a*uditory, *k*inesthetic (sense of movement), and *t*actile modalities, and which was designed for students with the most serious reading problems, M. S. Johnson (1966) notes:

> Learning takes place through purposeful activity. It is an active process. It grows out of reacting to stimuli in a purposeful way. A child using VAKT is participantly involved to a maximum degree. He formulates the ideas to be worked with. They are expressed in his own words. He listens, speaks, writes, and reads to reach his goals. If he failed to involve himself, he suffers the immediate consequence of his lack of involvement in that things do not go well for him—he does not learn what he sets out to learn. (p. 155)

Personalized Instruction

In addition to providing direct instruction to low-achieving readers, it is important to adapt instruction to meet individual variations in interest and background and in preference for strategies. Some low-achieving learners do best with holistic instruction, others learn best when instruction is parceled out in manageable bits. No one corrective package fits all needs. The structured phonics system that works so well with some low-achieving readers is frustrating to students who prefer a more holistic approach.

Continuous Assessment

Teaching and assessment should merge. Initial instruction should be based on an assessment that highlights the students' strengths and weaknesses and establishes an appropriate level of instruction. As the instruction proceeds, the teacher is guided by the students' responses. If the materials are too hard or lacking in interest, the teacher obtains more appropriate materials. If students have difficulty applying a strategy, the teacher provides on-the-spot support and guidance.

A Full Range of Literacy Experiences

Because low-achieving readers and writers often manifest difficulty with subskills such as decoding, poor oral reading, spelling, or handwriting, there is a natural temptation to remedy the deficiency by providing lots of extra practice in the poorly developed skill. As a result, corrective students may end up working on fragmented skills. Instead of reading intriguing trade books or composing imaginative stories, they spend their time filling in blanks on worksheets or reading brief, unrelated selections and answering low-level multiple-choice questions.

Graves (1991) describes Billy, a third-grader with a learning disability who put so much effort into his spelling and handwriting that the final product was a badly smudged series of disconnected sentences. While Billy had serious handwriting and spelling problems, what he needed most was a program that encouraged him to express himself. Because he was focusing on the things that he did poorly, Billy failed to see himself as a writer. As far as he was concerned, he had nothing of value to say. An appropriate program for Billy would begin with Billy's concept of himself as a writer. Once he is convinced that he has something to say and begins to express himself on paper, Billy will see the need for conventional spelling and readable handwriting. At that point, Billy will be ready for helpful instruction related to his handwriting and spelling.

Direct, Systematic Instruction

Although it is an essential ingredient, surrounding students with interesting, readable books and intriguing writing and reading tasks is not enough. The skills and strategies that achieving readers soak up through immersion all too frequently escape low-achieving readers unless they are provided with explicit explanations and demonstrations. Low-achieving readers and writers need a program of direct, intensive, systematic instruction presented in the context of lots of real reading and writing. In one instance, below-level readers were carefully taught strategies for making inferences; they were soon operating on the same level as the average readers (Hansen & Pearson, 1982).

Intervention programs should maximize success by developing needed background, vocabulary, concepts, and skills before students read a selection. As Curtis and Longo (1999) warn, "When you work with students who have a history of academic failure, you set them up to fail again unless you start with the first step: direct instruction" (p. 23). For instance, in some intervention programs, students are given books to read that contain unknown words or that contain phonic elements they have not been taught. Although the teacher prepares the students by conducting a book introduction, all of the difficult words or new phonic elements are not introduced directly. If the student has difficulty, the teacher provides prompts. However, students would undoubtedly be more successful if new words were more thoroughly introduced or if necessary phonic elements were taught beforehand.

Direct instruction should not be misinterpreted to mean the fragmented teaching of isolated skills and the use of workbooks and worksheets (Roller, 1996). Direct instruction should be conducted within the context of real reading and writing and should focus on guidance in the purposeful use of strategies.

An Integrated Approach

> A **unit** is a plan of study that includes objectives, teaching techniques, learning activities, materials, and assessment.

Poor readers and writers often have difficulty organizing and relating new knowledge to what they already know. Using a **unit** or theme approach is one way of helping low-achieving readers form the kind of cognitive connections that adept readers make on their own. By providing varied and sustained experience with key concepts or themes, students develop a depth of understanding. In addition, studying commonalities improves students' cognitive performance. In a study in which low-achieving readers read and discussed a series of passages, those who read passages that developed a common theme showed a greater increase in overall comprehension. They also demonstrated significant improvements in their ability to construct generalizations and to infer the theme when reading about new topics (Palincsar & Klenk, 1992).

> Unfortunately, not only do poor readers read less on their own; they also have fewer opportunities to read independently in school (Applebee, Langer, & Mullis, 1988): "poor readers presumably have more difficulty reading on their own and, therefore, are less likely to be encouraged to do so" (pp. 38–39).

Wide Reading

We literally learn to read by reading. In order to develop their capacities fully, poor readers need to make up for lost time. They need to read more, not less, than their higher-achieving peers. In a carefully controlled study of a program designed for struggling readers, Leslie and Allen (1999) found that the students who read the most in their free time made the most progress. Guthrie (2004) estimates growth based on the amount of time students spend reading, both in school and out. Based on observations, questionnaires, and studies, Guthrie speculates that the average student in grade 4 reads about two hours a day. This includes thirty minutes in language arts, thirty minutes in the content areas, thirty minutes during self-selected reading, and thirty minutes at night doing homework or voluntary reading. With reading a total of two

> Wide reading builds fluency, vocabulary, syntactical knowledge, and background knowledge. It also contributes to the development of thinking and memory skills (Stanovich & Cunningham, 1992).

hours a day, the student achieves an average score on the typical standardized test. Students who read more achieve higher scores; those who read less have below-average scores. A fourth-grade student who has been reading just thirty minutes a day will be at the second-grade level. A student who reads three hours a day will be at the sixth-grade level. Each thirty minutes of additional reading is associated with about a year's growth in reading. However, assuming that students have been reading at an average rate since second grade, a fourth-grader would have to read an additional 270 hours (thirty minutes times three years times the 180 days of an average school year) to gain an added year's growth. Of course, this is very approximate, but it can function as a rule of thumb.

Providing Materials at the Appropriate Challenge Level

If students are to engage in wide reading, reading should be relatively easy. In instructional settings, students apparently do best when they know 95 to 98 percent of the words in the selection (Berliner, 1981; Gambrell, Wilson, & Gantt, 1981; Nation, 2001). When given

Time on task increased from 20 percent to 50 percent when low-achieving readers were given a text that was one year below their grade level (Anderson, 1990).

texts on or close to the appropriate level, poor readers spend more time on task. Achievement also improves. When poor readers know most of the words, they are better able to use context clues and so do not have to overrely on sounding out the words. They read with more fluency and understanding. Struggling readers who used texts on their instructional level did better in word recognition, fluency, and comprehension than students who used grade-level texts (O'Connor et al., 2002). When students are reading at their instructional level, there is a greater overlap of known words than when they are reading text at their frustration level. This means that they are more likely to see the same words over and over again. This fosters fluency. One characteristic of all successful intervention programs is making sure that students are reading books that are on their level. Unfortunately, a number of intervention programs have set the criterion for instructional level at 90 to 95 percent word recognition. This means that students will have difficulty with as many as one word in ten. If students have difficulty with every tenth word, their reading is more likely to become halting and dysfluent. It will be more of a struggle than it need be. Students will make more rapid progress and will be more confident if they are given materials in which they can read at least 95 percent of the words.

All too often students reading below grade level are given books that are too difficult for them. To help students with the many hard words they encounter in their basal readers or chapter books, the teacher proceeds slowly through the book. Perhaps the group spends an entire week on a single story. As a result, they end up spending a minimum amount of time reading. However, actual reading is what these students need most. Instead of inching their way through a book that is too hard, they should be given lots of books that have the appropriate level of challenge. Examples of easy reading materials are provided throughout the body of this text and also in Appendix B.

A Sense of Community

Low-achieving readers also need a sense of community. By being accepted and valued in the classroom and in reading and writing groups, low-achieving readers are motivated to try harder. And, of course, they then are better able to learn from their peers. Describing the struggling readers and writers that they had been observing, Allen, Michalove, and Shockley (1993) explain that "Reggie learned how to choose classmates who could really help him read. Lee learned to write initially by copying what his friends wrote; eventually, he became a genuine collaborator, first in the oral composing of the story, and then in the physical writing" (p. 249).

SOURCES OF HELP FOR LOW-ACHIEVING READERS

An essential source of help for low-achieving readers is the classroom teacher. Often, a well-implemented program will prevent problems. Foorman, Fletcher, Francis, Schatschneider, and Mehta (1998) found that effective classroom instruction can reduce the number of underachieving readers in the lower grades to just 6%. Low average is defined as a score at the 30th percentile or better. In addition, some struggling readers may not qualify

Allington (1995) comments, "The longer we allow children's development to lag behind that of their peers the more difficult it becomes to accelerate their learning" (p. 8).

for special services, and even if they do, they will benefit from the additional reinforcement provided by the classroom program. And when they are discontinued from the corrective program, a well-planned classroom program will build on what they have learned and prevent future problems (Duffy-Hester, 1999).

Complementing the classroom teacher, a number of specialists work with low-achieving readers and writers: the reading/language arts specialist, the Title I teacher, learning disabilities specialist, and speech-language therapist. Professionals in migrant and bilingual or ESL (English as a second language) education might also be involved (Johnston & Allington, 1991). Why are so many different professionals involved in assisting low-achieving readers? Federal regulations are one probable cause. Two of the major pieces of legislation that provide for corrective services are Title I and the Individuals with Disabilities in Education Act (IDEA).

Title I Legislation

Title I is designed to foster improvement in math and literacy skills of students living in poverty areas.

Using Technology
No Child Left Behind can be accessed at http://www.ed .gov/nclb/landing.jhtml?src=fb. This web site provides information on NCLB and the progress currently being made by schools.

A key segment of Title 1 is the No Child Left Behind Act (NCLB). NCLB is changing the face of remedial and corrective reading. The purpose of NCLB is "to ensure that all children have a fair, equal and significant opportunity to obtain a high quality education and reach, at a minimum, proficiency on challenging state academic achievement standards and state academic assessments." More specifically, the goal requires that 100 percent of all students reach the proficient level in math and reading/language arts by school year 2013–2014. As of the 2005–2006 academic year, all public school students in grades 3 through 8 must be assessed in reading and math on a yearly basis and at least once during grades 10 through 12. Effective 2007–2008, an assessment in science is also required in one of the grades in each of the following ranges 3–5, 6–9, and 10–12.

Schools are required to make acceptable yearly progress (AYP) toward meeting the goal. The key indicator of progress is performance on state achievement tests. If underperforming schools fail to meet AYP for two years in a row, they are subject to corrective action. Not only must the student body as a whole meet the AYP, but each subgroup must also meet AYP. Subgroups include: economically disadvantaged, major ethnic and racial groups, students with disabilities, and limited English–proficient students. Some schools with overall high achievement might be cited because their ELL or economically disadvantaged students are not making adequate progress. There is a safe harbor provision. Schools will not be cited if the percentage of nonproficient students in the group (subgroup or entire school) that did not meet the goal has been reduced by 10 percent from the previous year, and the group has also met the requirement for the additional indicator.

As schools implement the provisions of NCLB, the number of reading difficulties should decrease. In fact, this is already happening. However, because NCLB specifies that all students pass state proficiency tests in reading, the number of students identified as needing assistance is sure to increase. In the past many special education students were not provided extra help with reading because they were judged to have emotional, physical, or cognitive problems of such a nature that they couldn't be brought up to proficiency. Since the aim of NCLB is to bring all students to proficiency, these students will be provided with needed assistance. Struggling readers in regular education who are not making adequate progress will also be provided with more assistance.

Individuals with Disabilities Education Act

Learning disabilities: "a disorder in one or more of the basic psychological processes involved in understanding or in using language, spoken or written, which may manifest itself in an imperfect ability to listen, think, speak, read, write, spell, or to do mathematical calculations" (PL 94-142).

In the 2004 reauthorization of IDEA, there is a call for more widespread use of scientifically based literacy programs and early intervention in regular education so that there will be fewer unnecessary referrals to learning disabilities programs because of reading difficulty.

Inclusion: policy of educating all students, including those with special needs, within the regular classroom. With partial inclusion, students may be included for some classes but not others.

Another major source of funding for students with reading and writing difficulties is IDEA (Individuals with Disabilities Education Act of 2004). About 8.8 percent of students ages six through twenty-one are served by IDEA (U.S. Department of Education, 2002). Slightly more than half of students served by IDEA are categorized as being learning disabled. In the decade of the 1990s, the number of students identified as being learning disabled increased by nearly 40 percent. Although **learning disabilities** is defined as "a disorder in one or more of the basic psychological processes involved in understanding or in using language, spoken or written" (PL 94-142), the disorder most frequently manifests itself as a reading difficulty. Snow, Burns, and Griffin (1998) estimate that approximately 80 percent of students diagnosed as having learning disabilities evidence a reading problem. As a result, often the students who have the severest reading problems are taught by the learning disabilities specialist.

Because of a past lack of coordination between corrective and classroom programs and a concern that pullout programs fragment instruction, current trends are toward collaboration and **inclusion.** Increasingly, Title I teachers are working within the classroom, as are special education teachers. Under revised regulations, special education teachers may now work with regular education students and up to 15 percent of special education funds may be used to assist struggling learners not identified as being eligible for special education services. In addition, under the Regular Education Initiative, children with learning difficulties, especially those who have moderate problems, are being returned to the regular classroom. As of the 1999–2000 school year, the latest year for which figures were available, 53 percent of special education students received instruction within the regular classroom from 79 to 100 percent of the time (U.S. Department of Education, 2002). Collaborating with the classroom teacher, the learning disabilities specialist, Title I instructor, and reading specialist function as resource persons or team members.

THE ROLE OF STANDARDS

Standards are instructional objectives that state what students should know and be able to do. The idea behind the standards is to improve the quality of instruction. Clearly stated

EXEMPLARY TEACHING
COLLABORATING TO HELP STRUGGLING READERS

Realizing that many students were coming to school with limited literacy experiences and were struggling with reading in the early grades, the principal of the Roosevelt School sought help in setting up a program that would provide the extra help these students needed. Believing that the program should be school-based, Karen Broadus (Broadus & Bloodgood, 1999), a literacy consultant, involved the teachers during the planning and the instructional stages as the group set up a one-to-one tutoring program. In fact, all three first-grade teachers and the two Title I teachers, along with community volunteers, became tutors. Arrangements were made for the first-grade teachers' aides to take over the class while they tutored. As a result, the professional staff got to know the program from the inside out. As they tutored the children, they got a close-up look at the kinds of techniques and materials that worked best with struggling readers. Many of these,

they adapted for use with their classes. As one teacher explained:

> I'm really glad I was able to be part of this program. I can't say that enough because not only have I done it, but I understand it now and I understand a lot more about what I can do as a teacher. . . . That's such a strength for all the children I'll ever work with. (Broadus & Bloodgood, 1999, p. 437)

With typical pullout programs, teachers are bypassed and may feel that they lack the necessary expertise to help struggling readers or that it is not their responsibility. However, the reality is that students spend only a small proportion of their time in intervention or remedial programs. Most of their instruction is provided in their regular classrooms. Without an effective classroom program, the best intervention programs will fall short.

objectives should lead to improved instruction, especially if assessment is closely tied to the standards and if there are adequate instructional resources for helping students meet standards.

Because of the adoption of a standards-based approach to literacy instruction, students are now expected to perform at a certain level. Although standards have been set by states and local districts and so vary, standards require that students be reading on or close to grade level. In the past, the expectation was that struggling readers would make reasonable progress. However, now the goal is for them to achieve the same level of performance as other students. This has raised the bar (Quenemoen, Thurlow, Moen, Thompson, & Morse, 2003). In the past, fewer than 10 percent of special education students were assessed. Now there is a regulation that requires all students, except for 1 percent who have severe cognitive deficits, to be tested. The decision to hold all students to grade-level standards is a controversial one. As Quenemoen et al., 2003 note:

> There is considerable rhetoric in some quarters that asserts all children can learn to grade-level content and achievement standards. There is considerable rhetoric in other quarters that asserts that *not* all children can learn to grade-level content and achievement standards and that it is unfair to schools, educators, and even the children to expect them to achieve to this level. There is general agreement that children in the earliest grades of school should be held to high expectations so that they do not fall behind from the beginning.

THE WHYS OF READING PROBLEMS

Although it is possible to remediate literacy difficulties without knowing their causes, it can help us plan a better program if we know why a student is struggling. For instance, there is a condition known as a word-finding difficulty, in which a student has a problem remembering common words. If, through a careful assessment, we become aware that a student has that difficulty, modifications can be made in the program that can help the student build word retrieval skills; there are also strategies that we can teach the student that will help him or her cope with this difficulty. The next chapter will take a look at the major factors involved in reading and writing difficulties, to shed light on a vital area in hopes that we might better help the many students who suffer some form of reading or writing disorder.

SUMMARY

According to a discrepancy definition, a problem reader may be defined as one who is reading below intellectual capacity. According to a functional definition, a problem reader may be defined as one whose reading ability is significantly below-grade level or whose functioning in his or her life situation is hindered by a deficiency in reading ability. According to a response-to-intervention concept, a problem reader is one who fails to benefit from instruction that is effective with other students. Approximately 25 percent of students have a reading problem. However, most of these have a mild or moderate problem. Only about 3 percent have a severe difficulty. In general, disproportionate numbers of ELL students are classified as struggling readers.

Corrective instruction may be part-whole, whole-part, or interactive. Reading is a parallel rather than a sequential process, with four processes working simultaneously: orthographic, phonological, meaning, and context. Approaches to intervention can also be categorized as being cognitive-process or sociocultural or a combination of the two.

The No Child Left Behind Act (NCLB) is changing the face of remedial and corrective reading. Under the provisions of NCLB, struggling readers will be getting more assistance.

Reading develops in overlapping stages or phases. Instruction should be linked to students' stage of development. Since reading affects all aspects of one's life, it is advisable to take a systems approach, which considers the reader's functioning in school, in the family, with friends, and—for older low-achieving readers—in the workplace. Reading instruction also has five interlocking aspects: reader, text, task, instructional approach, and context.

Although the nature and severity of reading difficulty may vary, a number of principles undergird the teaching of problem readers. These include emphasizing prevention, fostering success, offering a full range of literacy experiences, and providing direct instruction with integrated and personalized approaches. Also helpful is gearing instruction to ongoing assessment, building on the known, fostering independence, demanding active involvement, providing wide reading of material on an appropriate level of challenge, and building a sense of community.

In corrective programs, students are helped by a variety of professionals: classroom teachers, Title I personnel, reading/language arts specialists and consultants, learning disabilities specialists, and migrant and bilingual educators. Although taught by professionals from diverse fields, corrective reading programs tend to be similar. Current trends are toward collaboration between the specialist and the classroom teacher and the provision of corrective instruction within the classroom. The standards movement has resulted in improved performance by some struggling students. The most economically disadvantaged students have improved when states have adopted a standards system that features assessment and adequate resources, including preschools and smaller classes in the lower grades.

APPLICATION ACTIVITIES

1. Go back to the Anticipation Guide that you completed at the beginning of the chapter. Respond to the items once more. Have you changed your mind about any of the items? If so, what caused you to change your response? Even if your responses stayed the same, your reasons for agreeing or disagreeing may be different.

2. Interview the literacy specialist at a local school. Find out what kinds of help are given to students who are experiencing difficulty with reading.

3. Read "A Case Study of Middle School Reading Disability," (*The Reading Teacher, 49,* February 1996, pp. 368–377), which describes how a sixth-grader was provided corrective assistance. What roles did the home, school, and reading clinic play in this successful intervention?

4. Think about the way you process information. Which do you favor, a holistic, part-to-whole, or an interactive approach?

■ ■ ■ ■ ■

CHAPTER TWO

FACTORS INVOLVED IN READING AND WRITING DIFFICULTIES

USING WHAT YOU KNOW

This chapter explores factors involved in the attainment of proficiency in reading and writing. One factor is the ability to pay attention. All other things being equal, students who are better at paying attention become better readers. This does not mean that a student who has difficulty paying attention cannot or will not become a proficient reader or writer, but it does mean that adjustments might need to be made in the student's program. For instance, allowing students to choose their own books and establishing eye contact when you give directions might help the student better pay attention (Weaver, 1994b).

From your experience, what do you think might be essential factors in the attainment of reading and writing proficiency? What might be some factors that hinder progress? As you mull over these questions, think about possible intellectual, physical, environmental, psychological, and educational causes. Also, think in terms of the stages of reading and writing. What might make it difficult for a beginning reader to make adequate progress? What factors might be associated with a reading problem in the middle grades? In the upper grades?

ANTICIPATION GUIDE

Read each of the following statements. Put a check under "Agree" or "Disagree" to show how you feel about each one. If you can, discuss your responses with classmates.

	AGREE	DISAGREE
1. The major cause of reading problems in young children is failure to teach phonics.	————	————
2. Reversals can be a sign of a serious reading problem.	————	————
3. Deficiencies in auditory processes are more likely to cause reading problems than are difficulties in visual processes.	————	————

	AGREE	DISAGREE
4. Fortunately, most low-achieving readers do not suffer from emotional difficulties.	_____	_____
5. The ultimate origin of severe reading difficulty is probably neurological.	_____	_____
6. Low-achieving readers need to have tasks broken down into their component parts.	_____	_____

INTERACTING FACTORS IN READING AND WRITING DIFFICULTY

Although Josh and Chip were eight years old, both were virtual nonreaders when their parents enrolled them in a special after-school program for struggling readers. Chip was able to read a few words such as *I* and *me* at sight and could write his full name and a few other words. Josh was only able to read the word *I* on the word recognition test that was administered to him and was able to write his first but not his last name. Although the manifestations of their difficulties were similar, the boys had very different backgrounds. Josh was language delayed and neurologically impaired. He had extreme difficulty learning new words.

It was easy to see why Josh had failed to learn to read. Chip, however, was something of a puzzle. Although Chip experienced some difficulty learning new words, he had average intelligence, adequate language development, and no obvious physical, psychological, social, or emotional problems. During instructional sessions, however, Chip gave up easily. If he did not get a difficult word on the second or third try, he threw up his hands. Because there were so many words he did not know, he found reading very frustrating. Because he was also easily distracted, much of the instructor's time was spent getting and maintaining his attention. Although his parents expressed a sincere desire for him to succeed, they did not back up their words with supportive action. Chip was frequently absent or tardy and often failed to complete assignments, which his parents had been asked to supervise. Although he was showing some limited progress, Chip dropped out of the program.

Realizing that Josh would have difficulty attaining proficiency in reading and writing, his parents had vowed to support him in any way they could. They read to him regularly, conversed with him continuously, took him on frequent trips, and vigorously supported his academic efforts. Friendly and outgoing, Josh set about the task of learning to read with dogged determination. He was never late for his sessions and rarely absent. All assignments were completed. Noting Josh's interest in dogs and cats, the teacher built many of the activities around the topic of pets. Whenever possible, she gave Josh a choice of activities and materials. Working closely together, Josh's special program instructor and classroom teacher supported each other. Josh's progress surpassed the most optimistic predictions.

> Chip might have been more successful if text, approach, and context had been adjusted until a mix was found that better met his needs.

The same factors that contributed to Josh's success—effort, drive, healthy self-esteem, parental support—were lacking in Chip's situation and so contributed to his lack of success. In addition, the suitability of the instructional programs differed. Josh's teacher built on his interests and gave him choices. Chip's teacher, however, had apparently given him material that was too difficult, which intensified his feelings of frustration and failure. Moreover, his teacher did not seem to have effective techniques for handling his distractibility.

As suggested by these two cases, reading difficulty is often the result of a host of interacting factors or contributing causes. These factors may be classified as cognitive, linguistic, psychological, social-emotional, physical, and educational. Although placed last, educational factors are often key. For instance, had Chip had a more satisfying, more appropriate program, he might have persevered. Perhaps, too, greater efforts could have been made to enlist parental support.

Although each of the major factors will be discussed in isolation, it should be emphasized that often no one factor causes reading problems. In general, the cause is an interaction of several factors (Kibby, 1995).

COGNITIVE FACTORS

A number of cognitive factors are possible causes of reading problems. These include overall cognitive ability or ability to learn, memory, associative learning, and the ability to pay attention.

Overall Cognitive Ability

Recognizing that some students have serious cognitive limitations, NCLB allows schools to assess up to 1 percent of their students through checklists rather than through state proficiency tests.

Generally speaking, the brighter the students, the better they read. Cognitive ability affects language development. Students with mental retardation, for instance, are slower to develop language, show a depressed rate of vocabulary development, and have a lower final level of language development (Ratner, 1993). Language development, in turn, places limitations on reading development (Carroll, 1977). Reading requires bringing to a conscious level one's implicit knowledge of language (Menyuk, 1991). Delayed language development may hinder reading development.

Students with very limited language or cognitive ability—for instance, those who have profound retardation—may never learn to read. Students with mental retardation who are classified as being educable, on the other hand, should meet with some success in learning to read but may not progress beyond a second- or third-grade level. Often these students do well with decoding but have difficulty with comprehension. As noted in Chapter 1, student's reading levels should match their level of cognitive or oral language development. An average fifth-grader who can understand fifth-grade selections that are read to her or him should be able to read on a fifth-grade level. A teen with mental retardation who can understand language typical of third-graders should be able to read on a third-grade level. Of course, the relationship between cognitive ability or language development and reading achievement is not one to one. Other factors, such as the quality of the program, the amount of voluntary reading, and the motivation of the students, enter into the equation (Singer, 1977).

It should also be noted that the relationship between reading and language and cognitive growth is reciprocal. As Ratner (1993) notes, it seems likely that linguistic and cognitive ability develop in parallel. Moreover, reading leads to fuller development in vocabulary and syntax and may also promote greater cognitive efficiency. Our ability to process information is based, in part, on how much we know. Through reading, we acquire a broader base of knowledge, which should foster cognitive growth (West, Stanovich, & Mitchell, 1993). As Resnick (1999) has pointed out, if given a well-planned challenging program, students can be taught to be smarter.

In addition to general cognitive capacity, a number of specific cognitive and linguistic abilities are involved in learning to read. These are discussed in the following sections.

Memory

> Memory is developmental. As children grow, their capacity to **encode, store,** and **retrieve** material increases.

To investigate the role that memory plays in reading difficulty, it is important to understand the current concept of working memory. Memory is composed of three essential processes: **encoding, storage,** and **retrieval.** Simply put, outside data are translated into a code (encoded) that is placed into working memory and then long-term memory, from which they can later be retrieved through recall or recognition. The memory process begins when raw data enter the sensory register. The data are held there for only about a second. During that time, attentional processes select from the masses of data entering the sensory register those stimuli that we wish to process further. Stimuli not chosen fade away. Sensory data that have been chosen enter a short-term storage facility known as working memory.

> **Working memory:** temporarily holds all the information of which we are conscious, including what has just been perceived and what is being thought.

Working memory "holds all the information that we are currently thinking about or are conscious of at any given time" (Gordon, 1989, p. 199). As such, it has a limited capacity that depends on the type of data being held there. Working memory is the system that temporarily stores information during the performance of such cognitive tasks as reading a sentence or working out a math problem in one's head (Hulme & MacKenzie, 1992). Working memory simultaneously stores and processes information and is composed of three subsystems: the central executive; phonological memory, which temporarily stores verbal information; and a visuospatial sketch pad, which temporarily stores visual images (Baddeley, 1992) (see Figure 2.1).

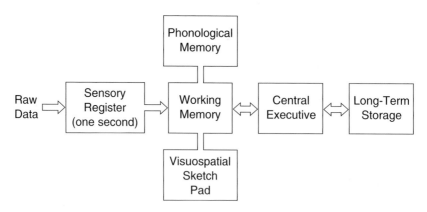

FIGURE 2.1   Model of Working Memory

> **Phonological coding:** ability to use the sounds in a word to store that word in working and long-term memory and, later, to retrieve that word.

Most information is encoded **phonologically.** Even if we saw three geometric figures and wanted to remember them, we would more than likely encode them verbally by saying their names: "circle, square, triangle." New data entering working memory will replace old information. Therefore, we must rehearse the representations that we wish to retain, or it, too, will fade away. Unless rehearsed, representations will fade away within about two seconds. To see how working memory operates, try the following experiment (Carlson, 1993). Read the letters below and try to remember them. Look away from the book for a few seconds and then see if you can recite them.

E Q M T B X A

How did you keep the letters in working memory? First of all, you probably verbally encoded the letters by retrieving their names from long-term memory. That is, you said the names of the letters. Then you probably rehearsed them. You said them to yourself or said them out loud over and over so you would not forget them.

> Although we also have memories for smells, tastes, motor movements, and nonverbal sounds, only visual and verbal working memory are included in the model.

Working memory, then, makes use of information stored in long-term memory as well as information that enters from sensory store. In similar fashion, when you read words at the end of a sentence you relate them to words at the beginning of the sentence (which are stored in working memory). However, you also relate the unfolding meaning of the gist of sentences and paragraphs read previously and now stored in long-term memory and relate it to experiences you have had, which is also information stored in long-term memory. As information is being placed into phonological memory, the executive system can retrieve information from other parts of the memory system and form associations so that data from working and long-term memory can be integrated.

How much information can be held in working memory? As a rule of thumb, as much verbal information as phonological memory will hold, which is approximately as much as you can say in two seconds (Baddeley, 1992). In a classic experiment, this averaged out to about seven bits of information for most people (Miller, 1956).

Verbal encoding of the type noted by Baddeley is an essential process in reading. Inefficient verbal encoding may be at the heart of word recognition, comprehension, and vocabulary difficulties. As Brady (1991) notes, "The most striking characteristic of poor readers is the common occurrence of verbal memory problems" (p. 130). When compared with higher-achieving readers, low-achieving readers have more difficulty remembering a series of letters, words, numbers, and similar verbal tasks. However, according to Brady (1991), low-achieving readers have no difficulty with tasks that require visual rather than verbal encoding. They do just as well as good readers when asked to remember a series of nonsense doodles or photos of unfamiliar people. The difficulty that low-achieving readers have remembering words or a series of verbal items such as digits apparently reflects a deficiency in verbal encoding (Brady, 1986). Poor readers can code incoming stimuli phonologically, but they apparently form less accurate and less stable representations. As a result, it is more difficult for them to hold onto information in working memory. Because of processing limitations, bits of data are lost. Both decoding and sentence comprehension suffer.

Torgesen and Hecht (1996) found a subgroup of children who have difficulty using a phonological code to store letter sounds or words. Because some children have difficulty encoding words and letter sounds into working and long-term memory, they have difficulty retrieving them and experience problems learning phonics and sight words.

Based on their extensive study of memory, Gathercole and Baddley (1990) concluded that phonological memory appears to make a critical contribution to reading development at the point at which relationships between letter groups and sounds are being acquired. Learning letter sounds and words requires acquiring a stable phonological representation of the sounds, which is what phonological memory helps achieve. For instance, a student with weak phonological memory may only partially code the word *bug* when he learns it initially. Later, when he encounters the word in print, he may have difficulty retrieving its spoken form because it was stored without adequate phonological cues.

Inefficient use of working memory may also hinder comprehension. Good readers process information more efficiently and also store more information than do poor readers (Daneman & Carpenter, 1980). In addition, better readers pass information into working memory faster (Jackson, 1980). Because the words in the beginning of a sentence are stored in working memory while the rest of the sentence is being processed, an efficient working memory is crucial to comprehension. Otherwise, by the time the reader reaches the end of the sentence, she may have forgotten the content of the beginning of the sentence (McCormick, 1987).

Associative Learning

Randall is a nine-year-old third-grader. According to informal reading inventory results, Randall has a listening capacity of grade three. However, Randall is operating on a beginning reading level. He is able to read just a few words at sight and knows initial but not final consonants. When presented with a word-learning test in which he was taught a series of seven words, with each word being presented a minimum of ten times, Randall learned only one word (see the Word Learning Test in Appendix A). Randall does no better in actual classroom teaching–learning situations. Even when new words are carefully presented in context, he fails to learn them.

When given this same word-learning test, Maria, a ten-year-old fourth-grader who was also reading on a beginning level, learned all seven of the words. However, when retested just thirty minutes later, Maria was able to read only two of the words. Both Randall and Maria have associative word-learning problems. They have extreme difficulty learning to associate printed words with their spoken equivalents. In kindergarten and first grade, both students, according to their teachers' reports, had difficulty learning to associate letters and their names, and later, letters and sounds. Despite having had excellent teaching, they have made very little progress in reading. The two students have a condition known as specific or primary reading disability. As described by Rosner, Abrams, Daniels, and Schiffman (1981):

More recently, McGregor (2004) defined dyslexia as a "specific reading impairment in which the most prominent weakness is the inability to decode words" (p. 310).

> The dyslexic's major problem is symbolization or association. He experiences basic difficulty in the association of common experiences and the symbols (words) representing them. Since reading is a process of association, difficulty in this area means that the child will frequently encounter many problems in acquiring a sight vocabulary . . . the major presenting symptom is the tremendous difficulty in decoding. (p. 442)

This description echoes the first account of a student identified as having a severe reading disorder. The account was written more than a 100 years ago by Pringle Morgan, a physician, who was describing a fourteen-year-old who was struggling with beginning reading skills despite seven years of intensive tutoring. Morgan believed that the boy was showing the same signs as adults who had lost the ability to read because of brain damage. He believed that the boy's difficulty, which he termed "word blindness," was due to a congenital condition that involved defective development in the left angular gyrus.

> Percy F has always been a bright and intelligent boy, quick at games, and in no way inferior to others of his age. His great difficulty has been—and is now—his inability to learn to read. This inability is so remarkable, and so pronounced, that I have no doubt it is due to some congenital defect. . . . In spite of . . . laborious and persistent training, he can only with difficulty spell out words of one syllable. (Morgan, 1896, p. 1378)

> **Associative word-learning difficulty:** serious difficulty learning to associate symbols and their spoken equivalents: letters and sounds; written words and their oral equivalents.

Although we do not know the cause of Percy's difficulty, he obviously had an **associative word-learning** problem. Associative word-learning problems are most likely rooted in phonological coding difficulties and inefficient memory and represent the most severe reading difficulty. However, there are several techniques for remediating this deficiency; these are discussed in detail in Chapter 14.

Attention

> **Attention:** act or state of directing one's consciousness to stimuli.

Another important condition for learning to read is **attention.** There can be no learning without attention (Simon, 1986). Attention fulfills three functions: screening out irrelevant stimuli, selecting relevant elements, and shifting from one stimulus to another (Robeck & Wallace, 1990). Recently I assessed and instructed a high school student who had a very low measured IQ and difficulty paying attention. Her progress was very limited, but it was not her low cognitive ability that was impeding progress; it was difficulty paying attention. When she was on-task, she made quite encouraging gains. When she was off-task, she made no progress. The most essential part of her program was planning ways to maximize her attention.

> **Attention-deficit/ hyperactivity disorder (ADHD):** "persistent pattern of inattention and/or hyperactivity-impulsivity that is more frequent and severer than is typically observed in individuals at a comparable level of development" (American Psychiatric Association, 2000, p. 78).

A condition that interferes with attention is the somewhat controversial **attention-deficit/hyperactivity disorder (ADHD).** ADHD sometimes occurs with anxiety, depression, conduct difficulties, and learning disorders. According to the American Academy of Pediatrics (2000), estimates of students with ADHD vary from 3 to 5 percent of students aged six to twelve. The number of boys diagnosed outnumber the number of girls diagnosed by three to one. A large proportion of the girls referred have been diagnosed as having ADHD of the inattentive type.

According to the *DSM-IV-R* (American Psychiatric Association, 2000), the essential feature of ADHD is a "persistent pattern of inattention and/or hyperactivity-impulsivity that is more frequent and severer than is typically observed in individuals at a comparable level of

Using Technology
CHADD (Children and Adults with Attention Deficit/Hyperactivity Disorder) can be accessed at http://www.chadd.org/. This web site provides a wealth of information on ADHD.

development" (p. 78). Indications of inattention include difficulty sustaining attention to tasks in school and at play, not listening or following instructions, not completing tasks that require sustained effort, being easily distracted and forgetful, doing work in a careless fashion, shifting from one unfinished task to another, and losing items. Signs of hyperactivity include not being able to sit still, excessive motion, inability to play quietly, talking excessively, and impulsivity. Impulsivity includes interrupting others, blurting out responses, and difficulty waiting in line or waiting for one's turn. Symptoms usually occur by the age of seven and should be evident in a variety of situations: at home, at school, and at play. The symptoms should not be the result of anxiety, personality, or other mental disorder, and should not be occasioned by a temporary period of stress. One reason that ADHD is difficult to diagnose and controversial is that the symptoms are subjective and occur to some degree in many students.

Some professionals wonder whether ADHD could be controlled by altering the instructional environment and teaching better self-management skills, using medication only as a last resort.

Although most children with ADHD will manifest signs of both inattention and hyperactivity-impulsivity, there are three subtypes of ADHD: a combined type that includes both inattention and hyperactivity-impulsivity, a predominantly inattentive type (ADD), and a predominantly hyperactive-impulsive type.

Students who have ADHD also seem to be at greater risk for a reading disorder. In a recent study, about 30 percent of boys and 17 percent of girls who had serious reading problems were also judged to have ADHD (Willcutt & Pennington, 2000). In contrast, only about 5 percent of boys and 3 percent of girls without severe reading problems were assessed as having ADHD. However, the two disorders, ADHD and reading disability, do not seem to be neurologically related. Students who have severe reading problems are characterized by increased brain activity, especially in areas in the left hemisphere, which are critical for reading, whereas those suffering from attention deficit disorder have a lowered pattern of brain activity (Wood, 1994). ADHD is additive: it adds to the disabled reader's woes.

Zentall (1993) sees ADHD as a bias rather than a deficit: ADHD students are biased toward strong stimuli, so a very strong stimulus may hold their attention more fully than it should and neutral or less attractive stimuli are ignored. The student may home in on an interesting fact and miss the main idea.

Even if ADHD is overdiagnosed, as some critics contend, there are students who do have difficulty paying attention and who are overly active and impulsive. Some suggestions for working with these students include the following.

- If students have difficulty with tasks requiring sustained attention, have them read brief rather than lengthy selections, or break lengthy selections into segments.
- Use color or boxes or other means to highlight important details. This will call their attention to essential items.
- Plan assignments that involve the students in activities. This will help focus their attention. For instance, creating a web or semantic map or composing a timeline will sustain attention better than simply answering questions.
- Provide a variety of interesting practice activities to attract and hold students' interests.

- Provide students with strategies that will help them compensate for their difficulties. For instance, impulsive students do poorly on multiple-choice items because they have difficulty delaying a response until they have read all the items (Zentall, 1993). Teach them a test-taking strategy that helps them read and consider all options before responding. Also teach strategies for planning and organizing work to impulsive students, who tend to jump in without thinking ahead.
- Provide structure and remove distractions or competing stimuli so that there is a better chance that students will focus in on relevant stimuli.
- Keep oral directions brief and to the point.
- Provide students with stretch breaks and opportunities to move around.
- Use positive reinforcement. Praise the students for rules followed and activities completed.
- Because ADHD students often respond better to visual stimuli, add visual elements to oral directions. A middle school teacher in Pennsylvania placed a model on the board to illustrate the steps in organizing assignments. Students were encouraged to

---

■ ■ ■ ■ ■ ■

EXEMPLARY TEACHING
FOSTERING ATTENTION

Although ADHD can conjure up associations of a student who calls out answers, cannot sit still, bounces around the classroom, acts impulsively, and has difficulty getting along with the other children, Randy Lee Comfort (1994), an assessment and remediation specialist, has worked successfully with these students because she builds on their positive characteristics: their energy, creativity, spontaneity, and humor. Building on the students' creativity and energy, Comfort involves them in planning goals and the activities needed to achieve those goals. As she explains, "Too often we forget to talk to children about what they want and need; we forget to include them in their own growing up and learning process. Asking a child what kind of help is needed or listening to a student talk about when he or she wants to work on something independently might give teachers and parents clues as to the child's particular learning style" (Comfort, 1994, p. 67). Being involved in the planning also gives the child a sense of being in control. ADHD children need structure and routine, but they also need choice and independence. As Comfort explains, they become anxious when they

don't know the routine, and this increases their activity level. However, they also react to a structure that is too rigid, so they need to be able to make choices. ADHD children also do better when the work is intrinsically interesting and involves higher thinking processes. If the work consists of completing low-level worksheets, they tend to rush through it. If the task requires thoughtful responses and is also interesting, then they become more deeply engaged and they are less likely to speed through the activity. Working with Brad, a bright seven-year-old who could not seem to stay in his seat or concentrate on his work, Comfort and Brad set a goal of having Brad work for ten continuous minutes. After that, Brad would be allowed to play for five minutes to get rid of tension that might build up as he worked for ten minutes. In order to provide challenge and to make the task interesting, Comfort gave Brad a series of answers to word problems. Brad had to create the problems. Brad became so involved in the task, which used his creativity and analytic skills, that he skipped his five-minute break. Given the right kind of situation, Brad's ADHD is minimized.

compare their work with the model before turning it in. As a result, students' organizational skills improved (Burcham, Carlson, & Milich, 1993).

VISUAL PROCESSING DEFICITS

Although auditory and linguistic abilities are more important to reading than visual skills, visual processing does play a varied, sometimes surprising, role in reading. While linguistic coding and other deficits seem to be a major cause of reading disability, visual perceptual deficits may be complicating factors. In a series of studies, neuroscientists (Chase, 1996; Chase & Stein, 2003) found that some poor readers were slower at processing visual information. Older struggling readers were found to be still processing individual letters, whereas achieving readers of the same age were processing words in chunks (Chase, 1996).

Reversals

As commonly used, **reversals** is a generic term that encompasses a number of confusions. These include:

> Orientation or rotation errors—*b* for *d* or *p* for *q*
> Mirror images— Ǝ for *E*
> Letter sequence or transposition errors—*was* for *saw*

As students first encounter print, it is natural for them to transpose, rotate, and reverse letters. Beginning at birth, perception develops and matures as the child grows older. Perception is selective. As visual perception develops, a student becomes more adept at searching out critical information in a display. Perception also becomes more differentiated. Thus, the child becomes better able to detect slight differences between *m/n, b/d,* and other easily confused letter pairs (Gibson & Levin, 1974).

At four years of age, children make a high proportion of mirror-image and rotation errors (Gibson, Gibson, Pick, & Osser, 1962). In a sense, however, these are not errors at all for a young child. Real objects do not change their identity when their position in space is altered. A chair is a chair whether it is upright, upside down, or lying on its side. However, depending on its orientation, a letter formed with a vertical line and a circle can be *b, d, p,* or *q*. Rotation errors, then, are natural. More than half of all kindergartners make these errors, with right–left rotation errors (*b/p*) posing special problems (Gibson & Levin, 1974).

The discrimination of graphic features is an ability that continues to develop through the age of eight. By age eight, most students make few mirror-image or rotation errors. However, low-progress readers may continue to make transposition and rotation errors beyond the age of eight if they are still learning beginning reading skills. They may simply be going through the stages of letter and word discrimination that younger readers have already completed. In addition, according to Vellutino and Scanlon (1988), low-achieving readers make more reversal errors because their decoding skills are weak, and they are therefore less analytical in their processing of printed words. In their research, students taught through an approach that stressed phonological awareness and phonics made far fewer reversals than a control group.

Some classic confusions also seem to be memory rather than perceptual problems. Younger and low-achieving readers often confuse letter pairs such as *b* and *d* that have very similar appearance. However, this confusion, when it persists, is not because they cannot see the difference between a *b* and a *d:* they cannot remember whether the symbol they see is a *b* or a *d.* So what seems to a perceptual confusion may be a further indication of the difficulty that disabled readers have making associations between letters and their names and letters and their sounds.

As far as sequencing errors are concerned, Gibson and Levin (1974) believe these may be caused by the manner in which novice readers process words. Inexperienced readers proceed letter by letter (*h-o-p*), whereas more mature readers use patterns of letters to read words (*h + op*). Because they process words letter by letter, rather than in chunks, poor readers are more likely to mix up the order of the letters.

Delayed or Faulty Directionality

> **Directionality:** ability to detect left, right, up, and down consistently and automatically.

Although most children learn to process print naturally and with little difficulty, Marie Clay (1991) discovered students who continued to have problems processing print in proper order for a period of at least three years. Persistent errors in processing print may be caused by a faulty or slow developing sense of **directionality.** Clay speaks of the child developing "sensory postural awareness of one side as being different from the other" as being necessary to develop directionality (1991, p. 116). Our sense of left and right and up and down grow out of motor explorations (Kephart, 1966). As children reach to the left and to the right, and up and down, they develop an internal sense of directionality. If the development of that sense is delayed or disturbed, students may have difficulty perceiving letters in a consistent left-to-right order and so transpose letters.

In summary, rotating or transposing letters is a natural part of learning how to process print. In most instances, it is not a factor in reading disability. Although often equated in the popular press with letter transpositions and visual deficits, most cases of reading disability seem to spring from auditory language deficits. "Far from being a visual problem, dyslexia appears to be a limited facility in using language to code other types of information" (Vellutino, 1987, p. 34). However, if reversals persist beyond the age of seven or eight, despite careful instruction, they may be a sign of an underlying disorder in directionality (Harris & Sipay, 1990).

If students do manifest directional difficulties, observe and decide which of the following is the most probable description of the situation:

- The student is a novice reader and writer and is still learning to process print in a consistent manner. There is evidence that reversals or other signs of directional confusion are decreasing.
- Despite extended instruction and practice, there is continued evidence of directional errors. However, most of the errors have to do with substitution of *d* for *b* or *p* for *q* or

other easily confused items. These suggests a memory or associative learning rather than a perceptual problem.

- Despite extended instruction and practice, there is continued evidence of directional errors. These errors involve confusing the order of letters in words, syllables in words, or words in sentences. Older low-achieving readers may make subtle transposition errors, such as mixing up the order of syllables in multisyllabic words, thus reading "enmentjoy" for enjoyment (Robeck & Wallace, 1990). If they persist, errors such as these may indicate an underlying processing problem.

Although in most instances poor readers simply outgrow orientation and sequencing errors, their progress is aided by good teaching practices, which stress consistent movement from left to right. These include the following.

- When reading from the board, chart paper, or a big book, emphasize that you read the words from left to right. Also note the return sweep. Demonstrate that after coming to the end of a line, you return to the beginning of the next line.
- When drawing objects on the board or decorating a wall, proceed from left to right.
- Insofar as possible, arrange and present displays from left to right.
- Using a chart with arrows or other devices, stress the need to form letters in a consistent fashion. For instance, when presenting the letter *t,* emphasize drawing the initial stroke from top to bottom and the second stroke from left to right. If students sometimes cross the *t* from left to right and at other times from right to left, they are opening themselves up to directional confusion.
- Directionality grows out of our physical sense of left and right. Plan a wide variety of games and activities, such as the Hokey Pokey, that foster development of that internal sense.

For those few children who continue to have difficulty with letter orientation and sequencing, try the following.

Tracing. Tracing, especially if supervised, helps children with both orientation and directionality.

Keyboarding. Encourage the use of word processing programs or even ordinary typewriters. The slower, more deliberate selection of letters aids proper sequencing.

Context. Always have students check their reading to make sure it makes sense. Children should be alerted to make adjustments when they read sentences like "I have on pets" for "I have no pets," or "I saw sad" for "I was sad."

Sounding out. Encourage the use of sounding out along with context. Students are less likely to read "I saw sad" if they are using initial consonants or, preferably, all the letters in a word along with context to help them decode words. When such an error does occur, ask if the sentence makes sense and also ask them to tell what letter *saw* begins with so that they can see that, both semantically and phonologically, their response is wrong.

Mechanical aids. Encourage the use of finger pointing and markers if they help. Although discouraged when used by more capable readers because it is believed to foster word-by-word reading, finger pointing can be a helpful aid for novice readers.

LANGUAGE FACTORS

Deficits in oral language are a major characteristic of low-achieving readers. According to Wiig (1994), approximately 70 to 80 percent of learning-disabled students—most of whom have reading problems—have language disorders. They may have difficulty following a story, show little interest in verbal activities, and have difficulty with word retrieval (e.g., remembering the names of objects). Syntax may be similar to that of a younger child. Verbal concept development may also be deficient. Upon entering school, they may not be able to name colors, letters, or days of the week. These children may have limited vocabularies and difficulty with listening comprehension. Students who evidence language disabilities for which there are no obvious causes, such as hearing impairment or neurological damage, are referred to as having a language learning disability or specific **language impairment** (Catts & Kamhi, 1999).

> A **language impairment** is a condition in which children have difficulty learning or using language but there is no obvious cause.

Some students are **language delayed.** Their language development follows the same sequence as that of other children, but it is slower. For the most part, these children catch up to their peers. In contrast, the language of language-impaired children develops differently. They do not grow out of their impairment. Even when language-delayed children grow out of their difficulties, they may still have problems learning to read and write. Because of language delay, they may not have in place the necessary development for learning phonemic awareness when it is presented in kindergarten and first grade. Without adequate phonemic awareness, they are unable to learn phonics skills.

> A **language delay** is a condition in which language development follows a normal but slower path of development.

Children's expressive language milestones have been found to be particularly effective predictors of later reading achievement. Milestones include the age at which children say their first word, speak in sentences, and so forth. For more information on developmental milestones, see Chapter 6.

Students with language difficulties are almost sure to have problems with reading. However, in addition to instruction in reading, they will also need help developing needed language skills. Ideally, the language specialist and the reading teacher should map out a joint program. Here is how the reading specialist and the language specialist worked together to help Burt.

Burt, a third-grader, baffled his teachers. Burt had excellent decoding skills, but his comprehension was almost nonexistent. He had extreme difficulty answering questions about stories that he had read, and his score on the district's standardized test of comprehension was extremely low. While working with Burt, the reading specialist noted that Burt had difficulty understanding questions. When the specialist asked where the story had taken place, Burt gave the names of the main characters. When the specialist asked Burt when the story had taken place, he told where it was taking place. Burt also had difficulty answering questions in ordinary conversation. Referred to the language specialist, it was found that Burt had difficulty understanding and formulating questions. As the language specialist worked with Burt and the reading specialist implemented suggestions provided by the language specialist, Burt's reading comprehension improved. Burt and other students with serious language problems need help from both the language and the reading specialists. Because their reading problems are rooted in language, the key to helping them is to build needed language skills.

Articulation Difficulties

Speech articulation problems may also contribute to reading difficulties. Students may experience increased difficulty learning letter–sound relationships for sounds they are having difficulty forming, for instance. However, reading and speech should not be confused. Just because the child is not able to articulate a sound, this does not mean that the child cannot perceive that sound or cannot make sense of words in which the sound appears. When working with students who have articulatory or other language problems, it is best to consult with the school's speech and hearing specialist. Many children with articulation problems also have concurrent language disorders (Ratner, 1993).

Additional language difficulties that might contribute to a reading difficulty include poor phonological awareness, inadequate automatized rapid naming, and deficient word finding.

Phonological Factors

> **Phoneme:** smallest unit of sound that distinguishes one word from another. **Phonemic awareness:** the ability to detect the separate phonemes in a word: /b/ /a/ /t/.

A widely accepted theory of reading disability holds that a major cause is a deficiency in phonological processing. Phonological processing includes phonological awareness, phonics, working memory, and lexical retrieval. (Phonological awareness includes detecting groups of sounds as in rhyming and individual sounds as in phonemic awareness.) As novice readers process a printed word, they use phonological awareness to detect its separate sounds; retrieve orthographic and phonological information from the lexicon, which is a mental dictionary; and hold this in working memory as they connect sounds to the letters in the word they are reading (Troia, 2004). Phonological awareness, retrieval of information phonologically encoded, and phonological coding in working memory are key processes in decoding (Troia, 2004). A phonological-processing difficulty most often manifests itself in deficient **phonemic awareness,** which involves detecting sounds in words, and a phonological coding deficit, which is a slowness or difficulty in using the sounds of a word to help remember that word (discussed earlier). Students who are deficient in phonological awareness have difficulty dealing with language in an abstract way. For instance, although they can understand the word *hat* and use it in normal conversation, they are unaware that *hat* is composed of three sounds: /h/, /a/, /t/. These students might also have difficulty identifying initial consonants in words or even detecting rhyme. Not being able to perceive individual sounds in words, these students are unable to match up letters with sounds and are also unable to learn phonics. As might be expected, disabled readers have more difficulty learning phonological awareness (National Reading Panel, 2000) and so need more intensive instruction for longer periods of time.

Although it is often associated with young children, phonological awareness can be a problem for older disabled readers, too. Weaknesses in phonological awareness have been found in disabled readers of all ages (Bruck, 1992). This does not mean that older disabled readers will not be able to learn to decode words. It does mean that their program should include a very explicit phonological awareness element. In fact, without a strong foundation of phonological awareness, students may not acquire decoding skills, or they may learn phonics patterns but be unable to transfer that knowledge to new words (Lovett et al., 1994). (See Chapter 7 for a fuller discussion of phonological factors.)

Rapid Automatized Naming

Even when students do have adequate phonological awareness, they may have difficulty naming or processing language rapidly and automatically. Famed neurologist Norman Geschwind (1972) conjectured that young children's ability to name colors would be an indicator of how well they would learn to read. Naming a series of colored blocks, explained Geschwind, would be a simulation of the cognitive processes activated in decoding, because the child would be required to attach a word to an abstract symbol, a block of color. Three decades of ensuing research have confirmed Geschwind's thesis (Wolf, 1991). In a test known as **Rapid Automatized Naming (RAN),** low-achieving readers, in numerous studies and at various ages, have been slower to name a series of colored squares, pictures of common objects, digits, and letters. In a RAN task, the student is asked to name a series of five different colors, objects, digits, or letters. These same five digits arranged in random order are repeated ten times so that, for each subtest, the child is asked to name fifty items as quickly as possible. Figure 2.2 shows what a RAN digit-naming task would look like. Manis, Seidenberg, and Doi (1999) theorize that RAN taps processes used in skilled reading: visual motor coordination, serial scanning of text, accessing word names and meanings rapidly from memory, and articulation. Believed to be an index of the automatization of word recognition skill, naming speed is slower among struggling readers. However, struggling readers, when provided with adequate reading practice, do increase their speed in reading words (Levy, Abello, & Lysynchuk, 1997).

> **Rapid automatized naming (RAN):** ability to name letters, numbers, colors, or objects quickly with a minimum of cognitive effort. Slowness in naming numbers and letters is a sign of a slowness in underlying processes and could hinder decoding.

FIGURE 2.2   Sample Rapid Automatized Naming Tasks

5	2	9	2	7	5	9	4	7	4
4	9	2	7	2	5	9	7	4	5
7	5	9	5	2	4	9	7	4	2
9	2	4	7	5	2	5	4	9	7
2	5	9	7	4	9	2	4	7	5

For most people, the order of naming speed from slowest to fastest is objects, colors, letters, and digits. The average adult can name digits or letters approximately twice as quickly as colors or objects. Naming letters and numbers is a more highly automated process than naming colors or pictures of objects. (Slowness in naming letters and numbers suggests a deficiency in automating the processing of the basic symbols of reading.) Naming pictures of objects and color squares requires semantic processing—you must attach meaning to the pictures and the squares—and so takes longer.

At the kindergarten and first-grade level, students who later become poor readers are slow at all four naming tasks. In grade two and beyond, they are generally slower at naming letters and digits than are achieving readers. However, only rate of naming letters and numbers correlates with achievement in reading. Poor readers are slower in reading letters, words in lists, and text. Biemiller (1977–1978) concludes that this may be due to slower visual processes. Poor readers may need to examine more features to identify letters. Slowness in recognizing letters may lead to slowness in word recognition or a disruption of the process. As Manis, Seidenberg, and Doi (1999) explain:

> Children who are slow to name printed symbols may not activate visual and phonological codes for printed letters in memory close enough in time to encode the letter combinations that occur most frequently in print. Hence, they do not acquire knowledge of orthographic patterns or form orthographic representations of words as quickly or easily as a child with faster letter identification. (pp. 131–132)

A child who is slow to recognize letters is slow to retrieve the letter's sound and slow to build up awareness of the common letter patterns found in words. Without quick recognition of letters, they might process words letter by letter rather than in patterns (Bowers, Sunseth, & Golden, 1999). Struggling readers need more practice than achieving readers to learn to read words immediately and, even with added practice, still take longer to read high-frequency words (Reitsma, 1989; Ehri & Saltmarsh, 1995).

Some poor readers have slower lexical (word) access speed. This means that once they have processed the spelling of a word that they are reading, it takes them longer than the average reader to locate that word in their lexicon, which is a mental dictionary. RAN is an indicator of speed of lexical access. Theoretically, the slower the student is at rapid automatized naming, the slower she or he is at lexical access. Slowness in naming is persistent. Long after low-achieving readers are 100 percent accurate in naming letters and numbers, their speed at doing so remains less than that of achieving readers (Samuels, 1994).

Word-Finding Problems

> **Word-finding** deficit: persistent slowness or inability to generate a word to name a specific object, event, and idea, even though the word is in the speaker's vocabulary.

A process related to but on a higher level than speed of naming of familiar objects and symbols is word retrieval or **word finding.** Deficiencies in word finding affect comprehension and higher-level word recognition skills, such as using context.

Burly, good-humored, and talkative, ten-year-old Mel was reading on a first-grade level, despite having average ability. In addition to his obvious reading disability, Mel's speech was marred by "you knows," hesitations, and roundabout expressions for common words. He referred to the carpet on the classroom floor as "the thing you walk on." It was not that the word *rug* or *carpet* wasn't in his vocabulary. Mel simply could not retrieve *rug* or *carpet* from his store of words. When the teacher said, "Do you mean *rug?*" Mel quickly responded, "Yes. The rug."

All of us have difficulty finding the right word on occasion—whether it be the name of a co-worker's spouse, a technical term, or a distinctive word that would be especially appropriate for a special situation. However, Mel's difficulty was ongoing and frequent. His word finding difficulty interfered with reading and writing as well as speech. Although Mel's difficulty was so severe that it was noticeable to even the casual observer, many students suffer from less obvious forms of word finding.

Symptoms of word-finding difficulty include frequent pauses, circumlocutions or roundabout language, repetitions, misuse of nonspecific words such as "things" or "stuff," frequent use of expressions such as "you know" or "I can't think of the word," and the frequent use of *ums* and *ahs* and similar meaningless sounds (Snyder & Godley, 1992). Frequent "I don't knows" when called upon to answer in class can also be a sign of word-finding difficulty. The "I don't know" may mean that the student cannot think of the words to express the answer.

Seen in children with brain damage and students who have learning and communication disorders, word-finding deficits have until recently been the responsibility of the communication disorders and/or learning disabilities specialists. However, a growing body of research indicates that there is a strong relationship between deficits in word finding and reading disability. Just as some problem readers have difficulty with the automatic naming of numbers and letters, some also have difficulty retrieving words (Wolf & Goodglass, 1986).

Students with word-finding difficulties may have difficulty using picture and text clues. Stumped by the word *penguin,* Sandy was encouraged by her teacher to use the story's illustration, which showed a penguin, to help her decode the word. Unable to retrieve the name of the pictured animal, Sandy finally responded with the word *bird.* Deficient word-finding ability had hampered her use of a picture clue. Her use of other contextual clues will also be hampered by word-finding difficulties. Encountering a difficult word, she will be less able to predict what word might logically fit the sense of the sentence, because retrieving words from her mental storehouse is both slower and less accurate. However, this does not mean that students with word-finding difficulties should not use context. Ironically, although hampered in the use of context, they rely on context more heavily than students who have no difficulty retrieving words. Since context provides added clues, it aids in the retrieval of words.

> Had Sandy used phonics along with picture clues, she would have had a better chance of retrieving the word.

Compensatory Programming. Traditionally, the speech therapist or communication disorders specialist works with students who have word-finding difficulty. However, there are a number of steps that you can take to help these students compensate for their difficulties.

- In discussions, provide more clues and additional wait time. Keep in mind that these students may know more than they can say. (Remember how you felt taking a test and

Remembering what they have read may also be a problem for students with word-finding difficulty, since there is a greater chance they will be unable to retrieve the words encapsulating key concepts or events in the text.

Having difficulty retrieving the necessary words, students with word-finding deficits will be less likely to join in class discussions of the selections they have read; if they do join in, they may not always be able to express the information they have garnered from their reading.

getting items wrong when you knew the date or name or word but could not remember it until after your test paper was turned in. Students with retrieval problems may experience these feelings on an almost ongoing basis.)

- Before reading, provide an overview of the selection or give a preview of the story. Place key words from the story on the board. Prominently displaying semantic maps and webs helps prepare students for the story. They also help cue retrieval during the reading of the selection and during the subsequent discussion.
- Stress the use of phonics in decoding unfamiliar words. Hampered in their use of context clues, these students should be taught to use phonics as a compensatory device. However, use of phonics should be integrated with context.
- Adjust evaluation procedures. Students with retrieval problems may have special difficulty with tests of expressive vocabulary that involve having the students retrieve words. They may also have difficulty with tests that require them to supply dates, names, and terms. Consider using a multiple-choice format with these students, because this lessens retrieval requirements.

ORTHOGRAPHIC PROCESSING

Orthographic processing is the visualization or visual awareness of letter patterns.

Being able to process spoken rhyming words faster because they have similar spelling is known as the **orthographic** effect and provides evidence that the student is able to access, use, and integrate orthographic and phonological information automatically (Zecker, 1991). At age seven, normally achieving readers show the orthographic effect. However, reading-disabled students do not begin to show the effect until age ten, and the effect is smaller than that of normally achieving readers.

Why might students be faster at saying that the spoken words *coat* and *boat* rhyme than they would be at saying that *boat* and *vote* rhyme, keeping in mind that the words were spoken and that they were not shown the printed versions of the words? This phenomenon, which has been found in several experiments (Zecker, 1991), highlights the importance of orthographic processing and also suggests that we process information in parallel fashion. **Orthographic processing** is the visualization or memory of letter patterns so that students can distinguish between or spell words such as *pear, pair,* and *pare.* Since the systems work in parallel, while the phonological processing system is detecting whether the two words end with the same sound, the orthographic system is being accessed. Words that are spelled the same often have the same sounds, so the orthographic system helps speed the detection process. There is a visual effect on what seems to be an auditory task. On the other hand, phonological similarities facilitate the recognition of visual similarities. Students were faster at recognizing that word pairs such as *pouch* and *couch* were spelled the same than they were at recognizing that word pairs such as *touch* and *couch* had the same spellings. Seeing the words activated both the orthographic and phonological codes.

When students learn to read, an orthographic identity is added to the phonological, semantic, and syntactic identity of words in their mental storehouse. Disabled readers who have phonological deficits may have difficulty creating adequate orthographic images because the links between sound and letters or letter patterns are more difficult for them to grasp (Berninger, 1990). Although it is partially a visual skill, orthographic awareness is not the same as visual perception. As Berninger (1990) notes, "Children who mix up letter order in words may have inefficiencies in processing orthographic information, but that cannot be equated to an organically based deficit in visual perception" (p. 519).

Students may have strong phonological processing skills but weak orthographic processing ability. This can be seen in students who are good phonetic spellers but who have difficulty with words that are not phonetic. Orthographic processing takes on more importance after grade three (Badian, 2000). Experience with print builds orthographic awareness. Students who lack orthographic awareness overrely on phonics

> Although weakness in orthographic processing may affect both reading and spelling, in some students it only affects spelling. These students may have sufficient orthographic memory for reading but not spelling (Orton, 1966).

and are slower in their reading. In extreme cases, they may continue to sound out words that they have encountered many times—words that normal readers would recognize immediately. They are better at reading and spelling regular words (Stanovich, 1992). They tend to confuse words such as *what* and *want* that are orthographically similar and may continue to reverse and transpose letters longer than students who have a stronger orthographic ability (Badian, 2000).

Orthographic processing may be related to naming speed. Students who are slow at naming letters and numbers are less sensitive to orthographic information or letter patterns and may have difficulty with tasks

> Phonological and visual processing difficulties may be due to a cognitive deficit in timing that affects all brain modalities.

such as recognizing the word spelled correctly when presented with *tite, tight,* and *tait.* Since both *tight* and *tite* have the same pronunciation, students have to rely on orthographic information to determine which spelling is correct. Difficulty in using orthographic information slows the reader down because the reader has to rely more heavily on phonological information and does not get the extra boost that orthographic

information provides. Notice how the following sentence is difficult to read because the orthographic information is misleading, and so you must rely strictly on a phonological coding:

Due ewe no hymn?

> Speed in letter naming was found to be related to choosing the correct spelling, an orthographic task (Hultquist, 1997). Letter-naming speed was measuring the speed with which students accessed orthographic representations.

Orthographic ability is related to decoding ability. In the early stages of reading, students rely heavily on phonics to decode words. As decoding skills are developed, orthographic processing becomes an important factor. Students who have difficulty with orthographic processing may have difficulty storing irregular words. Because they have difficulty with orthographic processing, they overrely on phonics, which means that their reading may be slow and laborious. They confuse letters and words that are similar in appearance, especially if the words are irregular. They frequently confuse word pairs such as *were*

and *where.* Their spelling is phonetic. They spell what they hear and so have difficulty with irregular words such as *because* and *often.* They continue to misspell high-frequency words that they have encountered many times.

Unfortunately, many struggling readers are weak in both the phonological and orthographic areas (Roberts & Mather, 1997). In her study of disabled readers, Badian (1997) found that 90 percent of the students had a double deficit. They had difficulty with both phonological awareness and orthographic processing or rapid automatized naming. And 40 percent had a triple deficit: the most severely disabled readers evidenced weaknesses in phonological processing, orthographic processing, and naming speed.

SOCIAL AND EMOTIONAL FACTORS

Although she was gifted, Florence had difficulty learning to read in first grade. Seeing her friends learn with relative ease, she wondered why she could not make sense of the words on the page. The words that she had worked so hard to learn on Monday were forgotten by Tuesday. A naturally outgoing, confident child, she became withdrawn as her concept of herself as a competent learner plummeted. Within a few months, she gave up trying. She had acquired a condition known as learned helplessness.

> **Learned helplessness:** children believe, based on repeated failures, that their efforts to learn will be ineffective and they must rely on others to help them.

According to Seligman (1975), **learned helplessness** is the response manifested by people who believe they are unable to exert any influence over a situation. Feeling that her efforts to learn to read were futile, Florence gave up trying. Instead of attempting to read the easy story books that her teacher gave her, she persuaded a friend or her mother to read them to her. When she came across a word she could not read, instead of trying to work it out, she immediately asked another student or the teacher for help. Believing that she could not learn to read became a self-fulfilling prophecy for Florence. Because she had judged her efforts to be futile, Florence no longer worked on reading, learned less, and fell further behind, thus confirming her feelings of defeatism.

Fight or Flight

> Although the main reactions to danger or stress have been described as fight or flight, scientist have recently discovered a third alternative: tend and befriend. Seen mostly in females, tend and befriend is a reaction in which people turn to friends or family members in times of stress (Taylor, Klein, Lewis, Gruenewald, Gurung, & Updegraff, 2000).

Social and emotional maladjustment can be the cause of a reading problem, an effect, or a mixture of both. In Florence's case, learned helplessness was an effect of a reading difficulty, but in time it became a cause of her continued lack of progress. Being asked to read caused obvious stress in Florence. Students who have serious reading difficulties often display a fight-or-flight reaction to escape the stress caused by having to engage in a behavior that they find virtually impossible. Students who adopt a fight reaction are soon noticed because they engage in confrontational or disruptive behavior, or they may simply refuse to read. They may criticize the reading material, complaining that it's a stupid book. They may say that reading is boring or deny having a reading problem. The student may refuse to begin an assignment, yell, or even have a tantrum (Gentile & McMillan, 1987). The purpose behind the behavior is to avoid reading at all costs. For the aggressive problem reader, being chastised, kept after school, or sent to the principal's office is preferable to reading.

The behaviors of students who exhibit a flight reaction are generally more subtle and more socially acceptable than those engaged in by the fight group. Instead of criticizing reading and displaying outward signs of anxiety, the students turn inward. They engage in self-criticism, blame themselves for their failure to read, become withdrawn and silent, and may escape into daydreams. When they do engage in reading activities, they adopt a learned helplessness approach and frequently seek help from peers and teachers.

Developing a Sense of Self-Efficacy

> **Self-efficacy:** belief in one-self as a learner.

> Students' **self-efficacy** is enhanced when the learning task is perceived as being doable, the text is on the appropriate level, instruction is clear and well organized, and students feel comfortable.

> Struggling readers who were persuaded to put forth more effort made substantial gains (Marzano, Gaddy, & Dean, 2000). One way to help students understand the connection between effort and success is to give them real-life examples of people who have met the challenge, including yourself (Marzano et al., 2000).

Whether through fight or flight, students with negative associations with reading avoid it—or if they do read, they engage in the task with less intensity. Students are more likely to undertake an activity such as reading or writing if they have a sense of self-efficacy. Bandura (1977) describes **self-efficacy** as students' belief in their ability to complete a task successfully.

Success breeds success. What students need above all else to build a sense of efficacy is a history of success. The tasks that students complete successfully must be at the proper level of challenge. Tasks that require too much effort or are judged to be very easy do not build a sense of self-efficacy. As Bandura (1977) comments, "To succeed at easy tasks provides no new information for altering one's sense of self-efficacy, whereas mastery of challenging tasks conveys salient evidence of enhanced competence" (p. 201). In reading, this means providing students with materials that they can handle. It also means carefully teaching strategies and making sure that students have ample opportunity to apply those strategies independently. Students who lack an adequate sense of self-efficacy need to see that they can use strategies successfully on their own. "Independent performance, if well executed, produces success experiences, which further reinforce expectations of self-competency" (Bandura, 1977, p. 202).

Strategy instruction is especially effective when students see the value of the strategy and understand when and where to apply it (Schunk & Rice, 1987). Praise and feedback also help. However, feedback should be specific. "I like the way you used context to figure out those hard words" is a more effective form of feedback than the general comment, "You're doing great." Both effort and ability should be praised. "You're really working hard," should be complemented by, "You really know what you're doing," or "You caught on fast." After an erroneous response, help the student see what she might do to achieve a successful experience: "You weren't able to sound that word out or find a part that you know, but try saying *blank* for the word and reading to the end of the sentence. Read the whole sentence again and then see if you can tell what word might be placed in the blank."

In summary, self-efficacy can be enhanced by group and individual goal setting, careful teaching with emphasis on building independence in use of strategies, positive expectations, using peers as models, and providing positive feedback. It also helps if you have high expectations and convey these to the class. Having materials and instruction on the proper level of challenge is also important.

Exemplary Teaching: Building Self-Efficacy.   Struggling readers often lack a sense of self-efficacy. As Torgesen (2004d) noted, "They frequently have given up on the idea of ever becoming a good reader." Concept Oriented Reading Instruction (CORI) is a highly effective approach that builds background knowledge, strategies, and intrinsic motivation so that students read because they enjoy it or they have questions they want answered. Students become engaged readers with a strong sense of self-efficacy (Guthrie, 2003b). If students lack essential decoding or comprehension skills, CORI teachers provide these students with extra instruction. They work with them in groups of four to six. They teach simplified versions of the strategies and gradually move up to the more complex versions. For questioning, for instance, students might be limited to just one page or one question, and they will be asked initially to compose just one question, not multiple ones. The teacher provides more modeling and more guidance. Teachers supply a bridge from the text to the response. They might use semantic maps or frames that guide students as they summarize. These scaffolds are gradually faded out.

Parental Pressure

Undue parental pressure to perform may also affect the disabled reader adversely. On the one hand, parental support is important as the child learns to read and write. The child sees that his parents value achievement and, in response, works hard, takes necessary risks, gives up play for work, and generally takes responsibility for learning. If undue pressure is added, however, the child may judge that "if I don't do well, Mom and Dad will be angry with me." If the pressure is increased even more, the child may see failure as catastrophic, thus creating in the child a genuine fear of failure (Bricklin, 1991). Under intense fear of failure, the child may engage in avoidance behavior or even give up trying, reasoning that if you don't try, you don't really fail.

Helping Students Overcome Negative Behaviors

Using Technology
For practical tips on handling behavior problems, visit Intervention Central at http://www.interventioncentral.org/.

Children with serious emotional and adjustment problems should be helped by the school social worker, psychologist, and other appropriate professionals. In addition to implementing the suggestions of mental health workers, try the following measures when working with students whose academic self-esteem is deficient.

■ Provide a stable, caring learning environment. Be positive. Build on the students' strengths, rather than focusing on their weaknesses. Supply clear instructions and establish orderly, consistent routines and high, but realistic, expectations. Be accepting of individual differences. Through example and instruction, teach mutual respect. Value each individual because of who he or she is, not because of what he or she does.

■ Reprimand students in private rather than in public. Avoid sarcasm and condescending or demeaning remarks.

■ Greet students when they enter the class; say good-bye when they leave (Curtis & Longo, 1999).

■ Handle oral reading with care. Oral reading practices that discourage low-achieving readers include: asking them to read difficult passages or read parts in difficult plays orally; having them read books that are beneath their maturity level; frequently correcting them or allowing other students to correct them; and stopping them from reading but assigning a better reader to continue with their part or to help them (Gentile & McMillan, 1987). On the other hand, don't exclude low-achieving readers from oral reading activities, but see to it that they are adequately prepared. Working with a disabled reader whose oral reading was dysfluent, Bradley and Thalgoot (1987) found that when the student read a selection silently before reading it orally, his rate of reading doubled and the number of misread words was significantly reduced. The student also seemed more relaxed and involved. In contrast, when reading orally at sight in the classroom, he mumbled the words, made frequent errors, and appeared both anxious and embarrassed.

■ Acknowledge difficulties. When students evidence obvious fight-or-flight reactions, judiciously acknowledge the difficulty and the emotion behind it. "You don't seem to like reading group," or "You seem to have a difficult time choosing a book to read," or "Tests seem to make you nervous." These acknowledgements need to be expressed "in an emotionally accepting way" (Bricklin, 1991, p. 212). The acknowledgment shows that you care and gives the child the opportunity to talk about the difficulty. Once the difficulty is acknowledged, steps can be taken to remedy it through encouragement, use of strategies, or, for more serious problems, sessions with a mental health professional.

■ Promote independence. Don't fall into the trap of providing unneeded assistance for students who have learned helplessness. As noted in Chapter 1, a general principle of remedial education is never to do for the students anything that they can do for themselves. Don't sound out a word that a student can sound out for herself. And if she cannot sound out the whole word, encourage her to sound out as much as she can and then build on that. If she cannot recall an important fact from a selection she read, encourage her to go back and find it. Teach students strategies that they will be able to apply independently. Although they may need guidance in the beginning, gradually lead them to a stage of independence. Also, redirect questions that indicate a lack of independence, especially if asked by students who are overly dependent (Glazer, 1991). For instance, if a student asks, "Should I read this again?" redirect the question so that the student must exercise her own judgment. Ask: "Would you like to read it again?" or "Do you think you need to read it again?" If the student asks, "Which book should I read?" redirect that to "Which book would you like to read?"

■ Give students choices whenever possible. Allow them to select books and stories to read and to choose activities. Involve them in setting up classroom rules and procedures. If they are involved, they will put more of themselves into their work. And you are also telling them that their thoughts and judgments are important. This will boost their self-esteem and give them a sense of control over their lives.

In many instances, students' mental health takes a turn for the better once they begin to make progress in reading. Because they feel good about themselves, they try harder and

> Ironically, undue fear of failure leads to behaviors that cause failure (Bricklin, 1991).

do better, which leads to even more success. It is the beginning of a very positive cycle. However, some students have such severe emotional problems that professional intervention is needed before they can make progress. For instance, a student who is deeply depressed may need mental health assistance before she or he is able to invest energy in improving reading skills or even take an interest in schooling. Although it is always a good idea to work collaboratively with other professionals, it is essential when teaching deeply disturbed students.

PHYSICAL CAUSES

In a holistic assessment, it is important to look at the student's mental and physical condition. Neurological and health factors, as well as vision and hearing, need to be considered.

Neurological Factors

> Mysterious as well as complex, the brain is organized in ways that may seem strange to us. For instance, the part of the brain responsible for sequencing letters also controls rhythmic activities (Luria, 1970). An awkward gait may be accompanied by letter reversals.

The most severe instances of reading difficulty—and, perhaps, some less severe cases—are caused or complicated by variation in neurological development, including subtle damage or changes in neurological organization that may not be readily apparent. In several studies, patterns of underactivation of posterior regions of the brain and overactivation of frontal regions when participants were asked to perform phonological analysis tasks suggest a disruption in the systems of the brain responsible for phonological functioning (Shaywitz & Shaywitz, 2000; Shaywitz, 2003). Differences in lateralization were also noted. Lateralization means that one side of the brain, usually the left, is dominant for language activities. Participants whose brains were more lateralized were faster at processing words. Functional disruptions in the areas around the angular gyrus were also found. For participants with dyslexia there was a weakened connectivity in the left hemisphere between the angular gyrus and the temporal (responsible for hearing) and occipital (responsible for vision) lobes. This portion of the brain is thought to be the area in which associations between letters and sounds or printed words and their spoken equivalents are made (Shaywitz et al., 2000). However, research indicates that many parts of the brain are dynamically involved in reading. As Riccio and Hynd (1996) comment, "It is clear that there is no unitary neurological factor that results in dyslexia. Rather, the research to date suggests a combination of structural or functional differences" (p. 11).

Hearing Impairments

In the past, most children with serious hearing problems were taught in residential schools or day schools that had special full-time programs. Today, more and more students are being taught within the regular classroom. This is due to a change in philosophy and advances in technology and techniques. With inclusion, it is important that the classroom teacher and reading specialist have a basic understanding of hearing difficulties.

The Individuals with Disabilities Education Act (IDEA) defines hearing impairment as "an impairment in hearing, whether permanent or fluctuating, that adversely affects a child's educational performance." Deafness is defined as "a hearing impairment that is so severe that the child is impaired in processing linguistic information through hearing, with or without amplification."

Frequency: number of sound waves emitted per second.

Hertz (Hz): unit of measurement for sound waves. One hertz equals one cycle or sound wave per second.

Decibel: unit for measuring loudness of a sound.

Otitis media: inflammation of the middle ear—a fairly common and sometimes persistent and recurring condition in young children.

Degree of Physical Loss. Hearing loss is measured in terms of pitch and intensity (National Dissemination Center for Children with Disabilities, 2004). Sound waves vibrate. The number of vibrations or cycles per second is the sound wave's pitch or **frequency,** which is measured in a unit known as **hertz.** The higher the frequency, the higher the hertz. Humans are sensitive to sounds in the 20–20,000 hertz range, but testing is generally done in the 125–8,000 range, which encompasses speech frequencies. There may be loss across all frequencies or a loss in specific frequencies.

In addition to measuring pitch, the intensity or loudness of sounds is also assessed. The higher the **decibel** level, the louder the sound. A whisper is 20 decibels, conversation about 55–60, heavy traffic 90, and thunder 120. Losses from 20 to 60 decibels are classified as mild or moderate, from 60 to 80 are severe, and 90 or above are profound.

Extent of Impairment. While hearing loss can be measured in terms of frequencies and decibels, the extent of impairment is dependent on a number of factors. These include age of loss, age of intervention, and type of communication input (Meyen & Skrtic, 1988). Generally speaking, the earlier the loss, the more profound its impact. Children who lose their hearing before acquiring speech are much more seriously impaired than those whose loss occurred after the acquisition of language. However, early intervention, which could include use of an assistive device such as a hearing aid or a special microphone used by the teacher, special teaching, and training of parents can significantly lessen negative effects. The use of sign language and other means of communication can also have a positive impact. Even so, children who are hearing impaired have a more difficult time learning vocabulary, grammar, word order, and idiomatic expressions.

The Reading Teacher's Role. While severe and profound cases of hearing impairment are generally handled by speech and hearing specialists, you can help by noting children who seem to have undetected hearing difficulties and referring them for testing, by making appropriate program adjustments, and by collaborating with the speech therapist. Having deficits in vocabulary, syntax, and figurative language, hearing-impaired students generally lag significantly behind in reading comprehension. They may also be deficient in their knowledge of story structures and so experience difficulty comprehending narratives. Corrective students who are hearing impaired or who lost but regained hearing because of **otitis media,** which is an inflammation of the middle ear and is a fairly common and sometimes persistent and recurring condition in young children, may evidence language deficits and so need additional assistance.

Signs of a possible hearing problem include talking too loudly or too softly, poor articulation, asking to have directions repeated, difficulty listening, and frequent ear

FIGURE 2.3   Observation Checklist: Signs of Possible Hearing Problem

Faulty pronunciation or other speech difficulties   _____

Poor spelling   _____

Frequent requests to repeat directions and questions   _____

Lack of attention   _____

Inappropriate responses   _____

Focusing on speaker's lips   _____

Earaches   _____

Frequent rubbing of the ear   _____

Unnatural pitch of the voice   _____

Cupping ear or turning ear toward speaker   _____

Complaints of ringing or buzzing in ear, dizziness,
or closed feeling in the ear   _____

Sores in ear or discharge   _____

Frequent sore throats, colds, or tonsillitis   _____

infections. An observational checklist of possible symptoms is presented in Figure 2.3. It is especially important for teachers of young children to be on the lookout for signs of otitis media.

> **High-frequency hearing loss:** one in which students can hear low frequency sounds but not high-frequency sounds such as /f/, /s/, /th/.

High-Frequency Loss.   One type of impairment that sometimes evades detection is a **high-frequency hearing loss.** Students can hear sounds in the lower range, which includes most consonants and the vowel sounds. However, they are unable to hear certain consonants, such as /f/, /s/, and /th/, that are at the higher end of the range (Harris & Sipay, 1985). Since these children can hear most speech sounds and can understand some words, their impairment may escape detection, especially if only a few consonants are involved. However, because they miss some words, these students find school confusing and, of course, have special difficulty learning letter–sound relationships.

Because her hearing impairment was subtle, Mandy's high-frequency loss was not detected until she entered school. As a result, her vocabulary was limited, as were her general background of knowledge and concepts. Once Mandy's impairment was discovered, she was fitted with a hearing aid and given special help by the speech therapist.

Mandy acquired a fairly substantial sight vocabulary, but she experienced difficulty learning decoding skills, and her comprehension was poor. Decoding skills showed an improvement when her reading teacher began using a modified version of a pattern approach. Through careful testing, the speech therapist had been able to determine what sounds Mandy could hear and which she still had difficulty with. The reading specialist taught those patterns that were composed of sounds that Mandy could hear. Working with the speech therapist, she also devised techniques in which she was able to show Mandy how high-frequency sounds, the ones she could not hear, were formed. In a sense, she added a step to her phonics lesson. In order to compensate for Mandy's hearing impairment, she helped Mandy form difficult-to-hear sounds with her mouth. Mandy's teacher also helped Mandy with her writing. Because Mandy was overly concerned with spelling, she did virtually no writing. Mandy's writing consisted of a sentence or two of the plainest of prose, devoid of all embellishment and elaboration. Encouraged by her teacher to spell as best she could, Mandy was finally convinced to try invented spelling. Little by little, her writing grew in content and quality of expression. Wide reading and lots of discussion helped expand Mandy's meager background.

Vision Impairments

> **Myopia:** condition in which the light rays fall in front of the retina so that distant objects are not seen clearly; also know as nearsightedness.

About 20 percent of students have visual problems by the time they reach their late teen-age years (American Academy of Pediatrics, 1996). The most common problem is nearsightedness. Although poor vision is rarely a cause of poor reading, blurred, fuzzy, or strained vision can certainly add to the problem.

Vision is initiated when light rays from an object enter the cornea and pass through the lens. The lens bends the rays so that they are focused on the retina. An optic nerve connects the retina with the visual cortex, which interprets the signal. In order for the light rays to be focused on the retina, the eye must be properly shaped. If the eyeball is too long, light rays fall in front of the retina, resulting in nearsightedness or **myopia.** If the eyeball is too short, light rays fall behind the retina, resulting in farsightedness or **hyperopia. Astigmatism,** a third major structural defect, results from an irregular curvature of the cornea and causes a blurred or misshapen image. All three of these conditions can be corrected with lenses.

> **Hyperopia:** condition in which the light falls behind the retina so that close objects are not seen clearly; also know as farsightedness.

> **Astigmatism:** irregularity in the cornea that causes blurred vision.

Accommodation and Convergence.   Acuity of vision is not sufficient, however. Vision is both structural and functional. In order to have correct vision, our eyes need to be properly shaped. However, having properly shaped eyes is not enough. It is possible to have a vision system that is physically perfect but still have vision problems. Vision is functional, a learned act. Through experience, humans literally learn to see. Because of the physiology of the eyes, we should see two objects. However, we learn to fuse dual images into one. The student's eyes must also function in such a way that she or he can see a single object at all working distances. Accommodation and convergence mechanisms must work in tandem. In **accommodation,** the shape of the lens is adjusted according to the distance of the target object. In **convergence,** a group of six pairs of muscles move the eyes so that they focus on the object. As an object gets closer, for instance, the lenses contract and the eyes turn inward.

> **Accommodation:** automatic focusing of the lens.

> **Convergence:** automatic adjustment of the pointing of the eyes in order to maintain clear vision.

> **Strabismus:** muscular imbalance of the eyes so that the eyes point in different directions.

Two visual conditions that contribute to reading difficulties include **strabismus,** which is a condition in which the eyes are misaligned and point in different directions (American Academy of Ophthalmology, 1984, 1990), and insufficient convergence, which means that the eyes are not fixating on the same spot at near point. Because these conditions strain the visual system, eyes may become tired, with resulting redness, itching, and burning. A headache may ensue. For some students, reading also may be disturbed. They may experience

> letters and words that appear to overlap, letters and lines that appear to be crooked, parts of words that disappear, letters that become unclear, and problems with finding the next line of print. (Aasved, 1989, p. 192)

Struggling readers sometimes complain that the letters seem to be moving or that the words won't stand still. Reading requires, among other skills, binocular stability, which means that both eyes work together in such a fashion that they are able to fixate on small targets and maintain a single, clear fixation as the reader moves his eyes across and down a page. Binocular stability is developmental. Based on assessments of nearly 1,000 children, Stein (1996) found that only 54 percent of six-year-olds had achieved binocular stability, but 70 percent of seven-year-olds, and 85 percent of nine-year-olds had. However, a much higher proportion of binocular instability was found in disabled readers. When binocular instability was corrected through the use of special glasses, the disabled reader made nearly twice as much progress as did a group of controls. Fortunately, binocular instability can be partly alleviated by using large print.

Amblyopia: suppression of vision in one eye. Because that eye is not used, it becomes weakened. Lost vision can be restored by stimulating the affected eye if the problem is detected early enough.

The Special Case of Amblyopia. Although eight-year-old Amy passed her vision screening test, frequent complaints of headaches and squinting alerted her teacher to a possible vision problem. An examination by a vision specialist revealed a serious problem. Amy had **amblyopia,** which can be caused by strabismus. Vision in her right eye was 20/20, but vision in her left eye was 20/100. Amy saw at 20 feet what people with average vision could see at 100 feet. Suppressing vision because of a lack of coordination with the right eye, the left eye had lost much of its power through disuse. Glasses and patching of the strong eye were prescribed. Patching the stronger eye forced the weaker eye to go back to work.

Amy was fortunate. According to Jobe (1976), amblyopia is best treated when the child is young. If untreated until the age of eight or nine, there is danger of a complete loss of vision in the weaker eye. However, after months of patching, Amy's vision improved. Vision in her left eye improved to 20/50.

Color Vision.   When the class was reading *Little Blue and Little Yellow* (Lionni, 1959), which explains how colors can be mixed to form new ones, Raphael seemed confused. Later, a visual exam revealed that Raphael is unable to distinguish the colors yellow and blue. The ability to see color ranges from those who can distinguish all hues to those who see only one color. In between are those who have difficulty detecting one or more of the primary colors: red, green, and blue. Most people who are color blind confuse red and green and are said to have red-green color blindness. However, some color-blind persons may also confuse blue and yellow. To them, blue is green, and yellow appears to be pink. A few color-blind persons are achromatic, and see only white and shades of gray including black. An inherited, X-linked trait, color blindness is far more prevalent among boys. About one boy in twenty has some degree of color blindness, but only about one girl in every 200 is color blind (Carlson, 1993).

It is important to be aware of children's ability to see color. Color blindness cannot be corrected and does not affect reading directly. However, it can be a source of confusion when teaching students how to read color names or when reading stories such as *Little Blue and Little Yellow,* in which color figures prominently, or when materials are color coded. Children who are color blind should be aware of their condition and should be taught strategies for adapting to it.

Screening Vision. Although poor vision is usually not a cause of reading problems, it can make reading and related learning activities, such as copying from the board, more difficult. Therefore, it is important for the school to screen students for possible vision problems. Sometimes, signs of difficulty are obvious. The student holds the book too close or too far, or squints when copying from the board. Other signs are more subtle: tilting the head or covering one eye when reading, headaches or nausea after reading, or frequent tearing or redness in the eye. A list of symptoms is presented in Figure 2.4.

> While working with students, you might inquire as to whether they have had a vision exam and whether glasses were prescribed. Often, students do not wear their glasses.

FIGURE 2.4   Vision Checklist

Reddened eyes or lids	_____
Frequent sties	_____
Frequent tearing	_____
Squinting	_____
Headaches	_____
Eyes turn in or out	_____
Burning or itching sensation in eyes after reading or writing	_____
Rubbing eyes while reading or writing	_____
Excessive blinking while reading or writing	_____
Double vision	_____
Closing or covering one eye while reading or writing	_____
Tilting head while reading or writing	_____
Holding printed material too close	_____
Frequently changing distance between eyes and printed material	_____
Difficulty copying from board	_____
Skipping or rereading lines	_____
Omitting words	_____
Using finger to keep his or her place	_____
Difficulty writing on lines when writing or staying in lines when coloring	_____
Writing with ragged left margin	_____
Writing or doing math problems crookedly on page	_____

Adapted from C. Beverstock, *Your Child's Vision Is Important,* Newark, DE: International Reading Association, 1991, pp. 10–11.

The Role of the Reading Specialist.   Through your observations, note any students who may have visual problems and refer them for testing. Also encourage teachers to adopt practices that foster good vision. Lighting should be adequate, work on boards should be large enough so that it is easy to see, reading materials should be legible, students who need glasses should obtain and wear them.

Vision Training.   As noted earlier, there is more to vision than just acuity. Vision is a learned act. Although children may start kindergarten as early as age four, vision does not mature until about the age of seven and one-half. Young children tend to be farsighted. However, school demands a wide range of visual activities. Years ago, noted child developmental researchers Ilg and Ames (1964) claimed that the following visual skills should be required for reading: ability to focus and point eyes together as a team, speed of perception, accuracy in looking from one object to another, ability to sustain focus at the reading distance, and eye–hand coordination. The authors recommended training for those found to be deficient in visual skills. They felt that for many children, visual therapy—that is, being taught how to move, focus, and fixate the two eyes so that they coordinate properly—is essential for efficient visual development.

Now, years later, visual training is controversial (American Academy of Pediatrics, 1998; Casbergue & Greene, 1988), but its effectiveness has not been disproved. One conclusion that is clear is that visual training in isolation is ineffective. Visual training must be combined with instruction in reading and writing in order to have an impact. By and large, low-achieving readers and writers will improve in reading and writing when given careful instruction in these areas and lots of opportunities for practice and application. If students do evidence problems maintaining their place or sweeping their eyes across a line of print, steps can be taken to ease visual tasks. For one, the student can be shown how to use a marker. Clearly designed books with large print might be used. Periods of reading and writing might be interspersed with activities that involve far-point vision so as to give the child's near-point visual mechanism a rest. Copying from the board might be kept to a minimum, as the shifting from far to near point and back again makes maximum demands on the accommodation/convergence systems. Use of big books and chart stories, on the other hand, should be stressed, because these make use of the child's far-point vision.

> At one time, using a marker was discouraged, but one should be recommended for students who would benefit from its use. Older students might use a 6-inch ruler or similar device.

Physical Health

> Kevin's case demonstrates the importance of an interactive approach. The first step in helping Kevin would be encouraging his family to make sure he was well rested.

Seven-year-old Kevin was having difficulty learning to read. Although he was in second grade, he still was operating at a beginning reading level. Observation indicated that Kevin was inattentive and seemed to lack energy. Kevin was also frequently absent due to colds and other minor illnesses. When questioned by his teacher, Kevin revealed that he stayed up late at night watching TV. Sleepy and irritable the next day, he had little energy to devote to the strenuous task of learning to read. His progress was further hampered by his frequent absences, which caused him to miss crucial instruction. Tragically, Kevin's reading difficulty was caused by inadequate care.

Unfortunately, more and more children are receiving substandard care. In a three-year-study by a blue-ribbon panel of experts and leading citizens, it was determined that the quality of child care in the United States has deteriorated dramatically. Almost one child in every five lives in poverty (Carnegie Corporation, 1994). The number of children raised in foster care has increased by more than half, from 200,000 to nearly half a million. More than half of the mothers of children under one year of age are working outside the home, as compared to fewer than one in five in 1960. The number of children born to unmarried mothers and being raised in single-family homes has also risen dramatically. There is also an increase in child abuse, homelessness, and violence in the lives of children. These factors are having a negative impact on the emotional and cognitive development of children and, of course, on their reading and writing development.

Also on the increase is asthma. Nine million children have been diagnosed with asthma (Centers for Disease Control and Prevention, 2004). There is some evidence that low-achieving readers have a greater incidence of asthma and other allergic conditions (Hugdahl, 1993). Asthma and other chronic illnesses can impede progress in reading in one of five ways: increased absenteeism, side effects of medication, lessened ability to engage in learning activities because of the effects of the illness, interference from anxiety and other emotional facts caused by the illness, and teachers' or parents' perceptions that the student is too fragile to engage in learning activities (Celano & Geller, 1993).

Research suggests that students who have asthma do not necessarily experience greater difficulty with reading. However, asthma may combine with other factors, such as low socioeconomic status and behavior problems, and then impede progress in reading (Celano & Geller, 1993).

Educational programs designed to help children better understand and manage asthma can help improve school performance. When planning programs for these children, it will be helpful to involve health care professionals and parents. Providing instruction in management of the illness and consulting with parents and health care professionals are effective procedures for working with any youngster who has a chronic health problem. The child's reading and writing difficulties should be considered in the total context of all of the child's needs.

EDUCATIONAL FACTORS

On the basis of a longitudinal study, Vellutino et al. (1996) concluded that experiential and instructional deficits were at the heart of the reading difficulties of the middle-class students studied. All but 15 percent of students classified as being disabled readers made substantial progress in a carefully planned instructional program. In follow-up studies, Vellutino found that most children at risk for having difficulty with reading overcame these risk factors when instructed in a well-planned literacy program in kindergarten. A small number needed additional help in first grade in order to overcome risk factors. As Vellutino (2003, summary) concluded, "Early and long-term difficulties in the majority of impaired readers are caused primarily by experiential and instructional deficits rather than biologically based cognitive deficits." Factors that contribute to poor performance include failure to gear instruction to the needs of the student. Unfortunately, as a group, poor readers spend less time reading silently, do more oral reading, are asked a greater proportion of lower-level questions, are given fewer prompts, and have less time to answer (Barr & Dreeben, 1991; Allington, 1983).

Using inappropriate materials, especially materials that are too difficult, is also a major educational factor in reading difficulty. In her longitudinal study of poor readers, Juel (1994b) found that, on average, these students could only read about 50 percent of the words in their beginning readers. From first through fourth grade, they were able to read only between 70 and 80 percent of the words in their basal readers. In fourth grade, the average poor reader was able to read just 74 words in 100. In other words, for four years these youngsters were forced to read materials that were far too difficult for them. It is small wonder that they disliked reading. When interviewed in fourth grade, 26 of 29 expressed a distaste for reading. When asked whether they would rather read or clean their rooms, 40 percent opted for cleaning. Poor pacing, inadequate classroom management, and failure to develop independence are other factors that contribute to reading problems (Harris & Sipay, 1990).

> Goodman (1982) comments, "Coping with school texts, especially in upper elementary and secondary grades, is a problem that most troubled readers face even as they are improving in their ability and self-confidence" (p. 89).

Lack of effective instruction is also a major factor in reading difficulty. Although benefitting from immersion in print, many emergent readers require systematic instruction in phonological awareness and letter knowledge (Pinnell & McCarrier, 1994). Later, they need direct instruction in decoding, comprehension, vocabulary, and study skills. As Richek, Caldwell, Jennings, and Lerner (1996) comment, "Although the typical student often learns word recognition and comprehension strategies from extensive reading, low-achieving students may need direct, sequenced lessons" (p. 7). However, the program should be balanced. An overemphasis on phonics or oral reading can be detrimental (Allington, 1984). Students need ample opportunity to apply skills, so there should be an emphasis on reading a variety of materials. As Goodman (1982) notes, "Readers in trouble are more likely to be the victims of too much skill use than not enough" (p. 89). What they need, Goodman explains, are "opportunities to read and write, and most of all, the experience of success." They need to realize that "the easiest things for them to read are going to be the very ones they have the most interest in, the most background for, and that they get the most pleasure from" (p. 90).

> Students' behavior is a key factor in the amount of progress students make. In a study of early-intervention programs, Torgesen (2000) found that students who benefitted the least were those who had low scores on phonological awareness and were rated by their classroom teachers as having the broadest range and highest frequency of behavior problems.

Poor instructional planning can also be a factor in reading problems. As noted earlier, a small percentage of students who participate in Reading Recovery prove to be difficult to accelerate. Observations undertaken to note instructional factors that foster or hinder progress found that the major factor associated with a lack of success was failure to plan daily lessons. Other negative factors included not using consistent, specific language; not demonstrating enough; and not noting whether a student had gained control of a skill in a variety of contexts (Lyons, 1995).

The Role of Basal/Anthology Series

Most students in grades K through 5 are taught through basal reading/ literature anthology series. Unfortunately, in a way, these series shortchange struggling readers. Basals recommend whole-class teaching of the anthology's main selections, which are written on grade level, so that everybody reads the same selection. The best readers read the target independently, average readers get help, and struggling readers have the selection read to them or they read along with a recorded version. As a result, struggling readers do less reading than average or above-average readers. Struggling readers need to do more reading, not less. Use materials that are on the students' level rather than the selection in the basal if it is too difficult for them.

On the plus side, basals provide suitable materials for struggling readers and may even provide a parallel program written on a lower level or easy-to-read alternates for the anthology selections. The parallel selection is on the same topic as the main text selection but is easier to read and has activities designed to foster prerequisite skills. Because the program for struggling readers parallels the main program, some of the preparation and extension activities can be conducted with the whole class. Today's basals also provide bibliographies and libraries of below-level books.

Scientifically Based Instruction

Using Technology
For more information on NCLB, go to the NCLB web site at http://www.ed.gov/nclb/landing.jhtml.

Concerned that schools adopted methods that had no validation and which often proved to be ineffective, No Child Left Behind legislation has demanded instruction that has been scientifically validated; that is, the technique or approach has been compared to another technique or approach and found to provide superior results. Key elements found to be a part of effective programs for the early grades are phonological awareness, phonics, fluency, vocabulary, and comprehension (National Reading Panel, 2000). The International Reading Association advocates evidence-based rather than scientifically based instruction. Evidence-based validation is a broader term and would include qualitative studies as well as those that had an experimental and control group.

SOCIAL AND CULTURAL FACTORS

In many ways, reading and writing are social activities. When we talk about a book we have read or ask a friend to explain a passage or, as members of a club, draft a letter to the editor, we are working with others to construct and create meaning. In schools, students read to each other, discuss books in small and large groups, work with a partner in reading, and share their writing in small and large groups. Students' learning is dependent, in part, on their role in the group, how the group perceives them, and how effectively they operate in the group. Unfortunately, students who are poor readers are frequently rejected by their classmates (Richek, Caldwell, Jennings, & Lerner, 1996). Feeling rejected, they become passive, stop participating, and fail to get help from their peers. Motivation and sense of self-efficacy also suffer. As noted in Chapter 1, building a sense of community in which everyone is valued is essential for all students, especially those who are struggling.

Students also do better when materials reflect their cultural heritage and when the reading and writing activities in which they engage are ones that are important in their cultures. It is all too easy to underestimate the rich heritages that students from diverse cultures bring to the school (Taylor & Dorsey-Gaines, 1988).

FAMILY FACTORS

Children of parents who had reading difficulties are three to six times more likely to experience reading difficulties themselves (Smith, Brower, Cardon, & Defries, 1998). Genetic studies suggest a complex interaction between several genes and environmental factors (Gilger & Wise, 2004).

The home literacy environment is, of course, a critical factor in children's literacy development. Key factors include:

- *Parental reading habits.* Children are more likely to value reading if they see their parents reading.
- *Reading to children by adults.* Reading to children is one of the most valuable things that parents can do. Reading to children develops language and literacy skills and builds a closer relationship between parent and child.
- *Availability of reading and writing materials.* Just having literacy materials available fosters their use.
- *Parental expectations.* By expressing high expectations and providing help, parents foster enhanced achievement.
- *Stimulating verbal interactions.* Discussions, explanations, dinner-time conversations, and reading to children and discussing what has been read all contribute to children's language and conceptual development. Research indicates that both middle-class and poor, uneducated parents engage in many of the same type of verbal interactions, but middle-class children are exposed to a greater quantity of interactions (Hart & Risley, 1995).

ECONOMIC FACTORS

About 17.6 percent (12.9 million) of the nation's children under eighteen still live in poverty (DeNavas-Walt, Proctor, & Mills, 2004). Poverty makes its mark early. At eighteen months, all children have an equal vocabulary, regardless of the educational or economic status of their families (Hart & Risley, 1995). However, after that, vocabulary growth starts to diverge. Children raised in poverty may come to school knowing 3,000 or fewer words, whereas children from affluent families may have vocabularies of 8,000 or more words. By the time students enter kindergarten, 66 percent of students can recognize the letters of the alphabet. However, only 41 percent of children whose caregivers are receiving welfare can recognize the letters of the alphabet (West, Denton, & Germino-Hausken, 2000). According to National Assessment of Educational Progress (NAEP) data, children raised in poverty lag behind in reading. More than twice as many students eligible for free or reduced-price lunch programs read below the basic level (Grigg, Daane, Jin, & Campbell, 2003).

Although teachers want the best for their students, they may structure instruction for the poorest readers in such a way that their growth is unintentionally limited. In her study of fifth-graders, Anyon (1980) found that schools in poverty areas emphasized more rote learning, less student involvement, and lowered expectations when compared with schools in more affluent areas. Students in poverty areas are also less likely to be taught comprehension strategies and may not be asked to do out-of-class reading, because the teachers judge they would not do them (García, Pearson, & Jiménez, 1994). When poor students are given similar reading instruction to that given to middle-class students, their achievement is similar.

One reason why poor children are at greater risk for having reading difficulties is that they may be attending substandard schools. As the Committee on the Prevention of Reading Difficulties in Young Children (Snow, Burns, & Griffin, 1998) note, "A low-status child in a general moderate or upper-status school or community is far less at risk than that same child in a whole school or community of low-status children" (p. 127).

Poverty can interact with other factors. Childsight, a division of Helen Keller International, estimates that approximately 25 percent of secondary school students who live in poverty cannot see what is written on the board. They need glasses but their families can't afford them. Targeting the eleven- to fourteen-year-olds, because that is the age group most likely to be hit with visual problems, Childsight has screened more than 200,000 students and distributed 30,000 pairs of eyeglasses (Helen Keller International, 2004).

SUMMARY

Reading problems are often the result of a host of interacting factors or contributing causes. Possible factors include cognitive, visual perceptual, linguistic, emotional, physical, educational, social, cultural, and economic factors. Having adequate intelligence is not a guarantee that one will not have a reading problem. Specific cognitive factors, such as memory, associative learning, and attention, apparently play roles in reading disorders. Although deficits in memory can affect reading in a variety of ways, inefficient verbal coding may be at the heart of word recognition, comprehension, and vocabulary deficiencies. Related to and possibly caused by inefficient verbal encoding is a deficit in associative learning. A deficiency in associative learning is characteristic of students who have the most serious reading difficulties.

Students who have difficulty paying attention have difficulty learning. As many as 30 percent of boys and 17 percent of girls who have reading problems have been diagnosed as having the somewhat controversial condition, attention deficit disorder. Although auditory processing deficits seem to lie at the heart of many reading disorders, visual processing difficulties, including difficulty with orthographic processing, can contribute to the problem.

Deficits in oral language are a major characteristic of low-achieving readers. These deficits may take the form of articulation problems; auditory discrimination and phonological difficulties; deficiencies in vocabulary, syntax, and knowledge of story grammar; slowness in rapid automatized naming; and slowness in word retrieval.

Failure to learn to read can be both a cause and an effect of social and emotional problems. A multidisciplinary approach should be used when working with students who have social/emotional problems.

Reading difficulties can be rooted in physical factors or intensified by them. Both vision and hearing should be screened. Poor health does not necessarily affect reading development adversely. However, chronic conditions such as asthma, when combined with factors such as poverty, may hinder progress in reading.

Educational factors are at the heart of many instances of low achievement in reading. Inappropriate materials, poor pacing, lack of effective instruction, and overuse of skill and drill may lead to reading problems.

Failure to provide for the social nature of learning and the diversity that exists in today's classrooms can impede growth in reading. Poverty can also be a barrier to progress in reading and writing development.

APPLICATION ACTIVITIES

1. To get a concrete sense of a severe reading difficulty and what its effect might be, read the case study cited below. As you read, ask: What are the possible causes of Peter's difficulty? How was his difficulty treated? McCormick, S. (1994). A nonreader becomes a reader. *Reading Research Quarterly, 29,* 157–176.

2. Read the Executive summary of Snow, C. E., Burns, S. M., & Griffin, P. (1998). *Preventing reading difficulties in young children.* Washington, DC: National Academy Press. What are the committee's major recommendations?

3. Choose one of the possible causes of reading difficulty and investigate it in more detail.

CHAPTER THREE

OVERVIEW OF ASSESSMENT

USING WHAT YOU KNOW

Have you ever had the feeling, after taking a test, that the test was not a valid indicator of your knowledge, that you really knew more but the test did not allow you to show it, or that the test seemed unfair because it asked questions about topics not covered in the class? This chapter looks at some basic principles of assessment. It also looks at a number of different kinds of tests and the ways in which tests and other assessment devices can be chosen and used so as to provide the most accurate and useful information.

ANTICIPATION GUIDE

Read each of the following statements. Put a check under "Agree" or "Disagree" to show how you feel about each one. If you can, discuss your responses with classmates.

	AGREE	DISAGREE
1. In assessment, how a student gets an answer is more important than whether the answer is right or wrong.	_____	_____
2. Most tests do not yield useful information because they distort the reading/writing process.	_____	_____
3. In general, informal tests are better than formal ones.	_____	_____
4. One of the best ways to assess a student is to teach him or her in a weak area and see how much and how well she or he learns.	_____	_____
5. Time spent assessing low-achieving readers would be better spent instructing them.	_____	_____

PRINCIPLES OF EFFECTIVE ASSESSMENT

Tracy, a fourth-grader, was a puzzle. She had above-average academic ability, and her word-recognition skills were superior. She could read multisyllabic words with ease. Her oral reading was smooth and expressive. However, her comprehension was surprisingly

Although assessment and instruction are placed in separate sections in this text, in practice, the two are blended. Assessment should be an integral part of all instruction.

poor. On both informal and formal tests, she missed all but the easiest questions. The test results revealed that Tracy had a comprehension problem, but they did not suggest any reasons for Tracy's problem, nor were there any suggestions in the results as to the best way to teach Tracy. The testing had been static. It provided the end product of Tracy's reading achievement and academic ability, but it provided no information about the processes Tracy used. It did not indicate what Tracy needed in order to perform adequately. Nor did it suggest how much help Tracy might need. Also missing was information about other important aspects of Tracy's performance: How did she respond to classroom instruction? Were there some kinds of tasks that she enjoyed or found easier than others? How did she feel about herself as a learner? What was her relationship with her classmates? What was her family life like? Was her family supportive of her efforts in school?

What Tracy required was an assessment that was both interactive and dynamic. An interactive assessment considers both top-down and bottom-up factors. It also postulates that the reader changes as the task changes. For instance, the student who daydreams her way through a science article may read a biography of her favorite sports star with intense interest. An interactive approach to assessment recognizes that five major factors have to be considered: the reader, the text, the techniques being used, the reading or writing task involved, and the situational context in which the reading or writing is performed (Walker, 1992). The student who is lost in a large-group situation may do quite well when taught in a small group. A student who responds negatively to a technique that is teacher directed might react more positively when taught by a method that relies more heavily on student input.

Standards for assessment endorsed by the International Reading Association and National Council of Teachers of English (Joint Task Force on Assessment, 1994) stress that the primary purpose of assessment is to improve teaching and learning.

Because reading and writing are such complex activities, the assessment must also be multidimensional. Depending on the age and level of literacy development of the student and the nature of the difficulty, it should include the following areas: general cognitive ability; other cognitive processes, such as memory and associative learning; phonological and orthographic processing, the ability to use independent learning strategies in decoding, comprehension, and study skills; vocabulary knowledge; writing; spelling; and handwriting. Language development and physical factors, such as overall health, vision, and hearing, as well as home and school factors should be considered. Being holistic and interactive, the assessment needs to consider the interplay among the factors and how they affect each other. For instance, chronic ear infections might impair hearing, which might make learning phonics more difficult. This, in turn, will lower the student's self-esteem as a learner, which will reduce effort and achievement.

Assessment also needs to be realistic. The best assessment is that which is closest to the skill or strategy in its actual use in the classroom (Meltzer, 1993). The Informal Reading Inventory, which is presented in Chapter 4, is one of the most effective assessment devices because it involves actual oral and silent reading and oral retellings or the oral answering of questions, which is similar to the way reading is conducted in the classroom. This assessment is even more realistic if the reading series, trade books, or content area texts used in the students' program are a part of the assessment.

DYNAMIC ASSESSMENT

Assessment must reflect changing academic demands as students move up through the grades and encounter higher-level comprehension and study tasks. Dynamic assessment fits in with the concept of response to intervention discussed in Chapter 1.

Under No Child Left Behind (NCLB), all students except for 1 percent who have been excluded because of serious cognitive deficits, must be assessed in terms of grade-level standards.

Assessment must also be dynamic. It should not just measure what the student can do now, it should also predict the student's potential for change. For instance, two students may both do poorly on a test of word-reading ability. Although their scores may be identical, their potential for learning the words might be very different. But how does the teacher know this? The solution is to teach the students a sampling of the unknown words and to note carefully what each student required in order to learn them. You might do this in a number of ways. First, select the words to be taught. You might choose, from those missed on the test, seven words of medium difficulty. Teach the words by using an approach that you feel should be effective for this particular student. Place the words on cards. Display a word and ask the student to read it. If the student is not able to read it, say the word and have the student repeat it. Point out distinctive features of the word or call attention to familiar phonic elements, and use it in a sentence. Each time you say the word, point to it. Then present the next word in the same way. After all the words have been presented, shuffle them, and present them again in the same way they were presented the first time. Keep a record of the number of words that the student is able to read correctly. See how many trials it takes the student to learn all seven words, but set a limit of approximately ten trials so that the student does not become frustrated. If the student learns all the words in a few trials, then you can infer that the student has good word-learning ability and should make rapid progress.

If the student has difficulty with the task, try other teaching approaches. You might use a word-building approach as explained in Chapter 8. In a dynamic assessment you do not just find out what the student doesn't know, you explore the student's level of knowledge, the amount of instruction needed to teach the element, and, in some instances, the way in which the student learns best. Dynamic assessment answers the all-important questions: How does the student learn? What must be done in order for the student to learn? As such, instruction is linked to assessment.

Dynamic assessment is based on Vygotsky's view of learning (Haywood, Brown, & Wingenfeld, 1990), which holds that children learn higher-level concepts through their interactions with peers and adults (Vygotsky, 1978). Vygotsky suggested that in addition to measuring student's current functioning level, we should also assess how well the child might do if helped by an adult. The difference between what a child can do on his own and what the child can do with the assistance of an adult or more knowledgeable peer is known as the **zone of proximal development.** This is what is measured in dynamic assessment.

Zone of proximal development: difference between what students can do on their own and what they can do under the guidance of an adult or more knowledgeable peer.

In a sense, dynamic assessment provides a more realistic estimate of students' potential because it yields information about their learning ability. As Feurstein, Rand, and Hoffman (1979) have shown in their research, lack of knowledge may be mistaken for lack of ability to acquire that knowledge. Dynamic assessment has the potential for providing a more accurate, fairer estimate of learning ability in children who may not have had adequate opportunity to learn because of an impoverished home life or substandard schooling.

ADMINISTERING A DYNAMIC ASSESSMENT

In general, administering a dynamic assessment involves the following steps:

Step 1: Gather baseline data. Administer the test the way it is normally given. This will provide baseline data.

Step 2: Teach and record. Provide assistance or instruction so that the student can reach an acceptable level of performance on the task or a sample of the task. Record the amount and type of help required to reach an acceptable level.

Step 3: Retest. Give the original test once again and chart improvement from first to final testing. Degree of change suggests the extent to which students will benefit from instruction.

Step 4: Evaluate intervention. Note the student's response to your assistance. What helped? What didn't? Is the student able to apply or use in new context what she or he learned? Also note any difficulties the student had during the learning trials. Then describe the conditions and procedures most likely to improve the skill or strategy tested (Haywood, Brown, & Wingenfeld, 1990; Haywood, 1993).

Dynamic assessment is time consuming, but for students with severe reading problems, dynamic assessment could mean finding techniques that work. "In such cases, the cost of dynamic assessment may be much less than the cost of not finding the answers to important educational questions" (Haywood, Brown, & Wingenfeld, 1990, p. 417). Dynamic assessment also helps identify the number of students who have severe problems. Vellutino, Scanlon, and Tanzman (1998) found that when students initially identified as having serious reading problems were provided with well-planned instruction, most responded positively and made enough progress so that they were reclassified as achieving readers or as students with mild reading problems.

Assisted Testing

Assisted testing is an easy-to-apply form of dynamic assessment in which students are given cues or prompts to see how much help they need in order to respond correctly (Johnson, 1993). At first, provide an easy cue. Then gradually provide more substantial cues until the student is able to respond correctly, or you run out of prompts. Based on the cues you have given, determine what the student already knows or can do and what she or he would need to know in order to be able to perform successfully. For instance, on a test of word recognition, the student responded "I don't know," to many of the words. Going back over

In **assisted testing** you ask: "How much help and what kind of help do I have to provide in order for a student to perform successfully?" You start off by giving a little assistance and then increasing it until the student can respond correctly.

a sampling of the missed words, the teacher first asked the student if there was any part of a missed word that she knew. If that didn't work, the teacher covered up the first portion of the word and had the student read the second portion. Then uncovering the second portion, the teacher had the student read that, combine the two parts, and read the whole word. For instance, for the word *morning,* the student said she could not read any parts. But when the teacher covered up all but the *or,* the student had no difficulty reading it. When *m* was uncovered, the student was able to add *m* to *or* to form *mor* and then, reading the *ing,* add it to *n* and combine all the elements into the word *morning.* With similar help, the student was able to decode a number of the multisyllabic words that she had gotten wrong on the first pass through. The teacher concluded that the student knew the elements of which the words were composed, but needed help locating known elements in multisyllabic words and then reconstructing the words.

On the basis of the initial testing the teacher would have concluded that the student simply could not handle polysyllabic words. Using assisted testing, she could see that the student had some knowledge of multisyllabic words. The teacher also had discovered a way of helping the student learn what she needed to know in order to be more successful in decoding polysyllabic words. Figure 3.1 shows an analysis of the dynamic testing of the student, including recommendations for future instruction.

Levels of Knowledge

When assessing students, also try to determine their level of knowledge. If they cannot respond on a higher level, move to a lower level. In the *Durrell Analysis of Reading Difficulty* (Durrell & Catterson, 1980), alphabet knowledge is tested on five levels. The highest

Finding a student's knowledge level provides a realistic starting point. Often we assume that problem learners have no knowledge in a particular area and we waste time reteaching what they already know.

level requires students to write the letters of the alphabet. If the students cannot do that, they are asked to identify a series of letters. Failing to do that, students recognize letters by choosing from four letters the one that the teacher says. Students who cannot do that are asked to match letters from memory. For example, shown the letter *m,* which is then removed from sight, the student picks the *m* from a series of four letters. The lowest level is a straight match. The students, while looking at the letter *m,* select its match from a series of four letters. The point of having these levels is to find out where the students are in terms of alphabet knowledge so that instruction can proceed from there.

All too often, when students miss an item or a series of items, we assume they have no knowledge in that area. However, using a level-of-knowledge approach, we retest until we determine on what level the students are operating. For instance, if a student cannot read the word *where* on a test of word reading, the task could be made into one of recognition rather than recall by saying the word *where,* and then having the student pick it out from among two or three other words.

Also vary the mode of response. If students are unable to write a summary, perhaps they can give one orally. If students have difficulty with certain questions, you might reword them. Perhaps they were too vague or too complex (Johnson, 1993).

FIGURE 3.1   Dynamic Assessment Analysis

Title of Assessment: *Basic Reading Inventory, Graded Word Lists B*

Original Results

Level	Number Correct
pp	*20/20*
p	*19/20*
1	*17/20*
2	*17/20*
3	*10/20*

Did well with single-syllable words but had difficulty with multisyllabic words.

Retest Results

Level	Number Correct
pp	*20/20*
p	*20/20*
1	*19/20*
2	*19/20*
3	*16/20*

Was able to read 11/17 multisyllabic words previously missed.

Assistance Provided
Showed student how to look for familiar word parts in words she had difficulty with and use those familiar parts to reconstruct whole word. Needed four prompts.

Recommendations
Needs to be taught multisyllabic patterns, especially the less common ones. Needs more instruction in use of decoding strategies. Stress application of strategies.

Trial Teaching

Also known as diagnostic teaching (Walker, 1992), trial teaching is based on the information yielded by an assessment. It works best if the assessment has been dynamic, because a dynamic assessment provides insight into the student's learning processes. Constructing hypotheses based on an analysis of assessment data, you, in cooperation with the student, construct a tentative approach that you feel will work best. You also carefully monitor the instruction to make necessary changes in approach, materials, setting, pacing, or any other aspect of the situation. As Lipson and Wixson (1991) note, diagnostic teaching is "thoughtfully planned" and contains "our best guesses" about what may work for a particular student (p. 74).

> See Chapter 6 for more information on trial teaching.

> Assessment should emphasize the students' strengths so that these provide a foundation for instruction.

Fittingly, the first step in trial teaching is to consult with the student. Discuss with the student the results of the assessment and explain that there are several ways of helping her or him and that you—teacher and student—will be trying out different ways of teaching and different materials to find out which works best (Roswell & Natchez, 1989). Depending on the skill or strategy being taught, the student is invited to choose materials and, in some instances, activities. Using your strongest hypothesis, try out one or more instructional procedures. If one doesn't work out, try another.

Diagnosis does not stop with dynamic or assisted testing or even trial teaching. It is an ongoing process. As Doris Johnson (1993) notes, "It goes on forever." In assessment, you create a hypothesis and evaluate it through testing, including dynamic testing, observation, trial teaching, and carefully monitoring the student's performance. In a sense, every lesson that you teach should be a trial or diagnostic one.

ASSESSMENT CATEGORIES

Assessment measures fall into four main categories: screening, diagnostic, monitoring, and outcome. Screening devices are assessments used to identify students who need additional assessment because they appear to be at risk. For emergent readers, tests of alphabet

---

ESSENTIAL STEPS IN THE ASSESSMENT PROCESS

As adapted from Kibby (1995), the assessment process consists of six essential steps.

Step 1: Establish an estimate of the levels on which the students are operating.

Step 2: Gather and evaluate information about students' reading/writing strengths and weaknesses.

Step 3: Assess and evaluate students' teaching–learning situation. Through dynamic testing and trial teaching, determine under what circumstances students learn best. Also assess the home situation.

Step 4: Evaluate materials used in the students' program.

Step 5: Integrate information and design a long-term program.

Step 6: Continually assess and evaluate the program and make modifications as necessary. In general you will be asking the following questions:

- On what levels are students functioning?
- What are the students' potential for growth?
- What are the students' strengths and weaknesses in reading and writing?
- What are the students' most immediate or most essential needs in reading and writing?
- What would be the most effective materials for these students?
- Under what circumstances and in what setting would these students learn best?
- What are the most effective techniques or approaches for teaching these students?
- Are there any physical, psychological, social, or other factors that need to be considered?
- How might the home, larger community, and school work together to help students?

To answer these questions you will need assessment instruments, which are devices for gathering information about students' performance.

knowledge or phonological awareness might function as screening tests. Word-list tests composed of words that gradually increase in difficulty or oral or silent reading selections might also be used as screening tests. Students are usually screened at the beginning of the school year, or, if they are transfer students, when they enter the school. Students who score very low on screening measures should be provided with additional assessment and/or an intervention program. If students fail to make progress despite careful teaching and placement in intervention programs, an in-depth diagnosis might be required. Diagnosis is typically conducted by a team of professionals and might include assessment by the school psychologist, learning disabilities specialist, reading specialist, and other professionals.

Once they are in a program, students' progress is monitored to make sure they are making adequate progress. Outcome measures are designed to indicate whether the goals of a program have been met. Outcomes measures are generally given at the end of the semester or year. Assessment is sometimes described as being formative or summative. *Formative assessment* is ongoing assessment designed to provide teachers with data they can use to plan and revise instruction. Monitoring is an example of formative assessment. *Summative assessment* is given at the end of a program to evaluate its effectiveness. Outcome assessment is summative.

AUTHENTIC ASSESSMENT

> Every child can learn, given the right kind of instruction, materials, tasks, and situation. The purpose of assessment is to determine the optimal learning circumstances for a particular student.

Given an interactive transactional theory of reading, which is based on the premise that students use both top-down and bottom-up processes to construct meaning, it follows that assessment should involve the kinds of reading and writing tasks that students are called on to perform in and out of school—reading whole books, studying texts, and writing stories or letters. Although the term *assessment* might conjure up visions of tests, testing is just one way of getting information about students' reading and writing performance. You will also use observations, interviews, questionnaires, and samples of students' work. In addition, student records and portfolios can provide insight into students' reading and writing experiences and capabilities. Portfolios, which are collections of samples of students' writing and reading, are especially useful sources of information.

This chapter will provide an overview of the kinds of tests that are frequently used in literacy assessment and some basic measurement concepts. Chapter 4 will explore the informal reading inventory and related tests. Chapter 5 will focus on gaining insight into students' reading and writing processes using observations, interviews, questionnaires, work samples, and formal and informal tests. Appendix C contains a listing of key devices frequently used to assess reading and writing and related areas.

TESTS

Although widely used, standardized tests have a number of shortcomings. Most do not require students to create meaning. Rather, they provide students with a series of multiple-choice items, so that they select rather than create responses. In addition, higher-level skills are neglected. Furthermore, group tests generally assess the product rather than the process of reading. Tests results may indicate the percentage of answers correct, or compare students with others who have taken the test, but they do not generally provide insight into the strategies that students use to respond to test items.

Despite their shortcomings, results of group tests can provide useful information. They can function as screening devices. Low scores on group tests can indicate possible problems. Individuals with low scores might be given individual assessments. Low scores by groups of students in key areas such as comprehension or vocabulary development might suggest the need for changes in the instructional program or materials.

Norm-Referenced versus Criterion-Referenced Tests

> **Norm-referenced test:** the performance of students is compared to that of a norming or sample group.

Norm-Referenced Tests.   Group tests of reading and writing generally fall into one of two categories: norm-referenced or criterion-referenced. In **norm-referenced tests,** which are often referred to as standardized tests, students are compared with a norm group, which is a sample of others who are in the same grade or are the same age. The score indicates whether students' performance is average, above average, or below average compared to the norm group. Scores are commonly reported in one or more of the following ways:

- Raw score is the total number correct. It has no meaning until transferred into a percentile rank, grade equivalent, or other score.
- **Percentile rank** indicates where a student's score falls on a ranking of percentages from 1 to 99. A percentile rank of 10 indicates that the students did better than 10 percent of the norm group. A rank of 50 is average and indicates that the student did better than 50 percent of the norm group. Percentile rank is the most frequently used norm score. However, percentile ranks are not equal units. A percentile rank of 80 does not mean that the student did twice as well as a student with a percentile rank of 40. Therefore, percentile ranks should not be added, subtracted, divided, or multiplied, or used for subtest comparison.

> **Percentile rank:** the most-used score for norm-referenced tests of reading and writing.

- Grade-equivalent scores characterize performance as being equivalent to that of other students in a particular grade. A grade equivalent score of 6.2 indicates that the student answered the same number of items as the average sixth-grader in the second month of that grade. The grade-equivalent score does not indicate at what level the student can read. A score of 6.2 does not mean that a student is reading on a sixth-grade level.

> Percentile rank is a measure of comparative standing. If students progress at the same rate, their percentile ranks stay the same. To move up to a higher percentile, they must make a better-than-average gain.

The International Reading Association opposes the use of grade-equivalent scores because they are open to misinterpretation. For instance, a grade-equivalent of 6.2 earned by a third-grader does not mean that the third-grader can handle sixth-grade material. Chances are the third-grade test does not even contain selections on a sixth-grade level. On the other hand, a grade-equivalent of 3.2 obtained by a sixth-grader does not mean that the sixth-grader is reading on a third-grade level. It does indicate that the student is reading significantly below grade level. Grade-equivalent scores are most meaningful when the test students have taken is at the right level and the score is not more than a year above or a year below average. Grade-equivalent scores are misleading and easily misunderstood and so should be used with care.

- Normal-curve equivalents (NCEs) place students on a scale of 1 through 99. The main difference between NCEs and percentile ranks is that NCEs represent equal units and so can be added and subtracted and used for comparing performance on subtests.

- Stanine is a combination of the words *standard* and *nine* and describes a nine-point scale. The stanines 4, 5, and 6 are average points, with 1, 2, and 3 being below average and 7, 8, and 9 above average. Stanines are useful when making comparisons among subtests.

- Scaled scores are a continuous ranking of scores from the lowest levels of a series of norm-referenced tests through the highest levels—from kindergarten or first grade through high school. Scaled scores, which generally range from 000 to 999, are useful for tracking long-term growth. Two specialized forms of scaled scores are the DRP and Lexile units. DRP units are used to report performance on the Degrees of Reading Power Tests. DRP units range from 15 for the easiest materials to 85 for the most difficult reading material. The advantage of DRP units is that the same type of measurement is used to indicate students' reading levels and also the difficulty level of reading material. A student with a DRP score of 50 is able to read materials that have a readability of 50 or below or slightly above. Lexile scores are also used for reporting test scores and the difficulty level of texts. The Lexile framework is a scale from 200 to 1700 with 200 being very easy reading material—about mid-first-grade level—and 1700 being very difficult reading material of the type found in scientific journals. A student with a lexile score of 600, which is about a sixth-grade level, is able to read materials with a readability of 600 or below or slightly above. Lexile units are also used to indicate both the students' level of reading proficiency and the difficulty level of reading material. The Stanford 9 and Stanford Diagnostic, although traditional standardized tests, provide lexile units along with percentiles and other scores.

Many of the scores provided for norm-referenced tests are based on the concept of the normal curve. According to this concept, if a large number of people took a test and the scores were depicted graphically, most of the scores would fall in the middle. As scores fell more and more above or below average, there would be fewer cases, so that a bell-shaped curve would be formed as in Figure 3.2. A line drawn through the middle would depict the average or mean score. In addition to having a mean, scores have a standard deviation. The standard deviation indicates the degree to which scores are above or below the mean. The more the scores vary, the higher is the standard deviation. Because of the shape of the curve, about 68 percent of the cases fall within one standard deviation above or below the mean, close to 96 percent fall within plus or minus two standard deviations, and nearly 100 percent fall within three standard deviations. Figure 3.2 shows standard deviations and how norm-referenced test scores relate to the normal curve and to each other. Also shown are scores from two intelligence tests: the Wechsler scales and the Stanford-Binet. Both have a mean of 100, but the

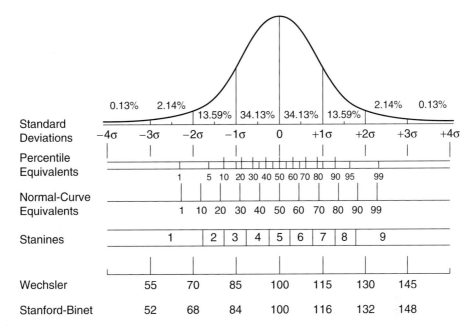

FIGURE 3.2 Comparison of Norm-Referenced Scores

Wechsler scales have a standard deviation of 15 and the Stanford-Binet has a standard deviation of 16. This means that a score of 130 on the Wechsler is equivalent to a score of 132 on the Stanford-Binet, since both are exactly the same distance from the mean.

Standard deviations are sometimes used to classify students as being severely disabled readers. Typically there must be a difference of 1.5 standard deviations between ability and reading achievement in order for a student to be classified as having a serious reading disability. A number of major ability and achievement tests have been constructed so that the tests have an average or mean score of 100 and a standard deviation of 15. To meet the 1.5 standard deviation discrepancy, a student with an average IQ score of 100 would have to obtain a reading achievement score of 77.5 or lower and would place at about the 7th percentile on a test of reading. In other words, although the student did better than 50 percent of those who took the intelligence test, the student outperformed only 7 percent of the sample of students who took the reading achievement test. There is a wide discrepancy between ability and reading achievement.

The Meaning of Norm Scores. Newspapers often report the number of students reading below grade level. There seems to be an expectation that every student should be reading at grade level. However, norm-referenced tests are set up in such a way that 50 percent of those who take the test will score below the norm. The norm is where the average student scores. It is not a standard that all students should meet. The norm is the grade level of the test or the 50th percentile, the 5th stanine, or the 50th NCS. Here is how the publisher of a norm-referenced test explains the situation:

If the norm group was tested in the sixth month of grade 4, the average score for the group would convert to the grade equivalent of 4.6. But note that even in that norm group, fully half of all pupils actually in the sixth month of fourth grade scored at or below that norm or "grade level." If the same test is then given to another group, it would not be surprising to find many pupils scoring "below the norm." Remember, half of the norm group itself scored at or below the norm; that's the meaning of the word (Harcourt Educational Measurement, 2000).

If reading instruction improves and students start doing better on standardized tests, then the norms will be changed:

Suppose that to score at the norm on a fourth-grade test, a pupil must answer 25 questions out of 40 correctly. Then, suppose we improve the teaching of reading so that all fourth-grade children in the nation score at least 25 and many score much higher than 25. Now all children are reading "at or above the norm," right? Wrong! As the scores have changed, so has their average—the norm. If you were to standardize the test again, you might find that the middle or average score for the national norm group is now 31 out of 40. So, the norm now is 31, not 25, and half the pupils are still reading at or below the norm and half are reading above the norm. In other words, if everybody is above average, it's not the average anymore! This is the reason that the norm is not an absolute goal for everyone to attain. It is simply a statement of fact about the average of a group. If they all read better, then the norm moves higher. You've done something worthwhile, indeed, but it didn't bring everyone "up to the norm"! (The norm for a test which was standardized in the 1950's is no longer the norm, since more than half the pupils now read better than that. This is one of the reasons new tests must be standardized by the publishers every few years.) (Harcourt Educational Measurement, 2000).

Purpose of Norm-Referenced Tests.   Norm-referenced tests serve a sorting function. They indicate how students scored in comparison to the reference group. Were they average, above average, or below average? Teachers and school systems might want to know how their students did in comparison with other students. However, if used to judge the effectiveness of a program—whether for an individual, a class, or a school district—norm-referenced tests have serious limitations. First, and foremost, the test might not measure what has been taught. Second, norm-referenced tests are designed to sort students, so most of the items are designed so that only 40 to 60 percent of the test takers will get them right. The tests are deliberately designed so that there are low, average, and high scores. Items that most students get right are likely to be removed from the test because they do not discriminate. As a result, norm-referenced tests tend to eliminate items on which most students do well. But the items on which most students do well are drawn from the areas that the teacher emphasized because they were the ones that encompassed the most important content or skills. In addition, norm-referenced tests often include items that students can answer because of knowledge they picked up outside school. In their attempt to include items that discriminate, test creators include items that require reasoning skills not typically taught as part of the content domain being assessed, so the items are assessing intellectual *aptitude* rather than content or skill achievement. As assessment expert W. James Popham (2000) comments, "Standardized achievement tests should be used to make the comparative interpretations that they were intended to provide. They should not be used to judge educational quality" (p. 401).

Criterion-referenced test: student performance is measured against a standard. A typical standard of performance on a criterion-referenced comprehension test is 75 percent.

Benchmark: standard of performance against which students' achievement might be assessed. An end-of-first-grade benchmark might be the ability to read an excerpt from a Frog and Toad book with 95 percent word recognition and 75 percent comprehension.

Criterion-Referenced Tests. Instead of comparing students with each other, a practice that fosters sorting and competition, **criterion-referenced tests** compare students' performance with a criterion or standard. On measures of comprehension, a typical criterion is 75 percent. On measures such as knowledge of the letters of the alphabet or initial consonants, the criterion might be set at 100 percent. One problem with criterion-referenced tests is that the standard is set arbitrarily. For instance, no one actually tries out the test with a representative group of students to set what a reasonable criterion or standard might be. If they are constructed carefully, criterion tests, because they indicate how well students did on specific reading and writing tasks, provide information that can be used to plan instruction.

One form of criterion-referenced assessment is the **benchmark,** a description of a key task that students are expected to perform. For instance, in one intervention program for struggling readers, the benchmark is that they be able to read a children's book entitled *A Kiss for Little Bear* (Minarik, 1959) (Hiebert, 1994). Benchmarks need not be tied to a specific book but might be stated in more general terms:

- Uses context and phonics cues to decode difficult words.
- Can read fourth-grade material and retell the main events or details in the selection.

Survey versus Diagnostic Tools

Reading tests can also be categorized as being survey or diagnostic tools. Survey tests typically provide an overview of general comprehension and word knowledge. Diagnostic tests assess a number of areas or assess key areas in greater depth. The Stanford Diagnostic Reading Test, one of the best known of the group diagnostic tests, assesses comprehension, reading or listening vocabulary, word analysis skills, and, at higher levels, the ability to scan. A list of survey and diagnostic tests is presented in Tables 3.1 and 3.2.

Formal versus Informal Tests

Standardized test: assessment tasks and administration are carefully specified so that anyone taking the test does so under similar conditions. The term *standardized test* is also used to mean a norm-referenced test.

Tests can also be categorized as being formal or informal. Formal tests may be **standardized.** They are designed to be given according to a standard set of circumstances. These tests have sets of directions, which are to be followed exactly. They may also have time limits. All norm-referenced tests are standardized. The advantage of formal standardized tests is that typically they have been constructed with care and tried out on hundreds or thousands of students.

Informal tests generally do not have a set of standard directions, so there is a degree of flexibility in how they are given. In fact, the main

TABLE 3.1 **Survey Reading Tests: Norm Referenced**

NAME	PUBLISHER	GRADES	SKILL AREAS
Group Tests			
Degrees of Reading Power	Touchstone	1–college	Comprehension
Gates-MacGinitie Reading Test	Riverside	K–12	Comprehension, vocabulary; early levels measure emergent literacy and decoding skills
GRADE	AGS (American Guidance Services)	K–12+	Listening, vocabulary, comprehension; early levels measure emergent literacy and decoding skills
Iowa Tests of Basic Skills (ITBS)	Riverside	K–12	Comprehension, vocabulary, word analysis, listening, optional performance items, writing prompts
Iowa Tests of Achievement and Proficiency	Riverside	9–12	Comprehension, vocabulary
Metropolitan Achievement Tests	CTB/McGraw-Hill	K–12	Comprehension, vocabulary
Nelson-Denny	Riverside	9–16	Comprehension, vocabulary reading rate
Stanford Achievement Tests	CTB/McGraw-Hill	K–12	Comprehension, vocabulary
TABE (Tests of Adult Basic Education)	CTB/McGraw-Hill	Adult (ranges from limited literacy to advanced literacy)	Comprehension, vocabulary
Terra Nova CAT (California Achievement Test)	CTB/McGraw-Hill	K–12	Comprehension, vocabulary
Terra Nova CTBS (California Test of Basic Skills)	CTB/McGraw-Hill	K–12	Comprehension, vocabulary
Individual Tests			
Kaufman Test of Educational Achievement (K-TEA)	AGS	1–12	Comprehension, decoding
Peabody Individual Achievement Test Revised (PIAT-R)	AGS	K–12	Comprehension, letter and word recognition
Wechsler Individual Achievement Test	Psychological Corporation	K–12	Word reading, comprehension

TABLE 3.2 Diagnostic Reading Tests

NAME	PUBLISHER	GRADES	SKILL AREAS
Group Tests			
California Diagnostic Reading Test (CDRT)	CTB/McGraw-Hill	1–12	Comprehension, vocabulary, decoding, reading speed, study skills
Stanford Diagnostic Reading Tests (SDRT)	Harcourt	1–13	Comprehension, vocabulary, decoding, scanning; optional assessment for strategy use, interest and attitude questionnaire, and story retelling
Individual Tests			
Diagnostic Assessment of Reading with Trial Teaching Strategies	Riverside	1–6	Comprehension, decoding, oral reading, reading levels, listening capacity
Diagnostic Reading Scales— Revised	CTB/McGraw-Hill	1–7+	Comprehension, oral reading, word reading, reading levels, decoding
Durrell Analysis of Reading Difficulty	Harcourt	1–6	Comprehension, oral reading, word reading, decoding, reading levels, letter knowledge, spelling, visual memory
Gates-McKillop-Horowitz Reading Diagnostic Tests	Teacher's College	1–6	Comprehension, oral reading, word reading, decoding, auditory discrimination, blending, spelling, letter knowledge
Woodcock Reading Mastery Tests—Revised	AGS	K–13	Comprehension, vocabulary, decoding, letter knowledge, visual-auditory (associative) learning
Woodcock Diagnostic Reading Battery	AGS	K–13	Letter–word identification, word attack, reading vocabulary, comprehension, incomplete words, sound blending, oral vocabulary, listening comprehension, memory for sentences, and visual matching

advantage of informal tests is their flexibility. They may be designed to assess almost any skill or area, and may be tailored for any population. Informal tests are typically constructed by teachers. Their disadvantage is that they may not be constructed with sufficient care, and their reliability and validity may be unknown. One of the most widely used assessment devices in the field of literacy is the informal reading inventory, which is explored in the next chapter.

EVALUATING ASSESSMENT DEVICES

Reliability

> **Reliability:** the consistency of an assessment device. It is the degree to which the device would yield similar results if given to the same person or group again.

In order to be useful, assessment devices must be both reliable and valid. A reliable device is one that yields consistent results. For a test, **reliability** means that if students retook the test they would get approximately the same score. For an observation guide, it means that if two or three observers rated the same student at the same time, their ratings would be similar. In the rating of essays, it means that a single rater would give the same essays similar ratings if she or he rated them on different occasions, or that the scores given by different raters to the same piece of writing would be similar.

Validity

> **Validity:** degree to which an assessment device measures what it intends to measure; also, the degree to which the results can be used to make an educational decision.

Validity means that a device measures what it says it measures, such as vocabulary, comprehension, rate of reading, attitude toward reading, and so forth. It also means that the device will provide information that will be useful in making an instructional decision, deciding, for instance, whether students' comprehension or word recognition is adequate or if a program or approach is working (Farr & Carey, 1986). Moreover, the way a skill or strategy is assessed should be dictated by the way it was taught and the materials used. If students were taught to write brief summaries of informational text using their science books, then a multiple-choice test that only requires them to select from four options the best summary of a brief, narrative piece would not be valid. Validity is also concerned with the interpretation of test results. When test results are used for purposes for which they are not suited or intended, then the interpretation is invalid, even if the test itself is valid.

> **Correlation coefficient:** statistical measure that expresses in mathematical terms the degree to which two variables are related.

For commercially produced tests, information about a test's reliability and validity are generally contained in the test administration or technical manual. Reliability is expressed as a **correlation coefficient.** A correlation coefficient can range from 0, which means no relationship, to 1, which means a perfect relationship, and can be positive or negative. For making decisions about a group, a correlation of .8 is adequate. However, when making individual decisions, a correlation of .9 is desired.

Validity may also be expressed as a coefficient of correlation. One way of indicating the validity of a new reading test, for instance, is to compare students' performance on the new test with their performance on an established test or some other criterion. The correlation should be high but not too high. A correlation of .9, for instance, would indicate that the tests are so closely related that they seem to be measuring the same thing, so what's the purpose of the new test? This type of validity is known as *statistical* or *concurrent validity.* Some tests also have *predictive validity.* That is, they predict how well a student will do on a related task at some later date. For instance, tests of alphabet knowledge and phonemic awareness given in kindergarten can be used to predict how students will do in reading in first grade.

NCLB programs such as Reading First require the use of tests that have proven scientific technical validity and reliability. While tests might possess technical validity and reliability, they might be lacking in content validity. They might not measure skills that are essential in reading or might measure them in such a way that they do not provide helpful information to teachers.

They typically yield correlations as high as .5 or .6, indicating a strong relationship between these factors and later success in reading.

Test makers also frequently include descriptions of construct and content validity. **Construct validity** is the degree to which a test measures a theoretical trait or construct such as critical reading, learning ability, or phonological awareness. The construct on which a test of phonological awareness is based is the theory that phonological processes are essential for the acquisition of reading skill. This theory is supported when students who have high scores in phonological awareness do well in beginning reading. **Content** or **curricular validity** is the degree to which the content of a test reflects reading or tasks as they are taught in the schools. Many of the national standardized tests are based on the content standards adopted by major professional organizations, such as the International Reading Association, state standards, and the content of basal readers and other materials used to teach literacy. The best way to judge content or curricular validity is to see how close a match there is between what you teach and what the test assesses. If possible, go beyond the general description of content validity in the technical manual and examine the test items themselves. Note whether the items are measuring behaviors or knowledge that is important. Also note what proportion of the content that you think is important is being assessed. Content validity is especially important in criterion-referenced tests

Standard Error of Measurement

Standard error of measurement (SEM): estimate of the difference between the obtained score and what the score would be if the test were perfect.

In judging the quality of a test, it is also important to know the **standard error of measurement (SEM).** The SEM is a statistical estimate of the amount that a test score might vary if the test were given again and again. Although tests yield a particular score, that score should be thought of as a range of likely scores. For instance, if a norm-referenced test has a SEM of 5 percentile points and you got a score of 50, that means that if you retook that test there is a two-thirds (one standard deviation) chance that your score would fall between 45 and 55, which is plus or minus one SEM. Because standard error of measurement is an index of the consistency of test taker's scores, it is also a measure of reliability.

Fairness

Tests, of course, should also be fair. As the Joint Task Force on Assessment (1994) notes, "Because traditional test makers have all too frequently designed assessment tools reflecting narrow cultural values, students and schools with different backgrounds and concern often have not been fairly assessed" (p. 41). Test bias can take many forms. A test can be biased on the basis of geography, gender, socioeconomic status, ethnicity, or race. For instance, a reading selection on ice hockey would seem to favor middle class males living in the northeast. Today's tests are typically examined by teams of experts for bias. However, other forms of bias include opportunity to learn and familiarity with test situations.

Students who have not been taught critical content will, of course, be at a disadvantage. So, too, will students from other countries who may not be familiar with U.S. testing situations. These youngsters should be provided with practice and instruction that will acquaint them with the form of the testing and the testing procedures (Popham, 2000).

For additional information about tests, see the *Fifteenth Mental Measurements Yearbook* (Impara, Plake, & Spies, 2003), or *Tests in Print VI* (Murphy, Plake, Impara, & Spies, 2002), which lists more than 4,000 tests. You might also consult the Buros Institute, which specializes in test information: http://www.unl.edu/buros/.

FUNCTIONAL-LEVEL ASSESSMENT

When group tests are used, struggling readers are often assessed unfairly. It is a widespread practice to administer the same norm-referenced or criterion-referenced test to an entire class, even though there may be a wide range of reading ability in that class. For instance, a seventh-grade student reading on a second-grade level would find a typical seventh-grade test to be extremely frustrating. Moreover, the test would yield misleading results. Norm-referenced tests have a bottom. As soon as the student answers a question or two on a seventh-grade-level test, he might earn a grade-equivalent score of 3.5 or so. With a little bit of lucky guessing, the student might achieve a grade-equivalent score of fourth grade or higher. Thus, the teacher might assume that the student can read on a fourth- or fifth-grade level, so the student is given materials that are too difficult. In addition, the experience of taking a test that is far too difficult can be very demeaning and discouraging. How can you tell if a test is too easy or too hard? A test is probably too hard if a student fails to obtain a score that is better than he would have gotten if he had merely guessed. If on a multiple-choice test there are four answer options, a student has one chance in four of getting an answer correct. If a student does not get more than 25 percent of the attempted items correct, his score is at a chance level. A test is too easy if a student gets all or most of the items correct.

The solution is to assess students on the level at which they are functioning (Gunning, 1982). This might mean giving a student an out-of-level test. For a seventh-grader reading on a second-grade level, this means giving the student a test that actually has second-grade material on it. If the material is too juvenile for the student, then you might use a test designed for older students or adults who are reading on a second-grade level. Grade-equivalent and scaled scores can be used with out-of-level testing. However, out-of-level norms should be used to report percentile and stanine scores, because these scores involve comparing students who are in the same grade. Another possible solution is to select a test that assesses a wide range of reading levels. Administering the right-level test means that you need to know students' approximate reading levels. Approximate reading levels may be obtained from teacher judgment, informal reading inventories, running records, or observing which level of materials the students can handle. You may also use a locator test. A *locator test* is generally a brief test of reading vocabulary or reading comprehension that covers a broad range of levels. The GRADE Locator Test (American Guidance Service) covers levels from grade 2 through secondary school) and can be given to a group in about ten minutes.

As noted in Chapter 1, federal and state regulations are calling for a wider inclusion of students in high-stakes tests, including some students who were previously excused. Unfortunately, except for the 1 percent excused because of severe cognitive deficits, all students are now required to take the state's grade-level proficiency test. This creates a potential problem for struggling readers because they will be reading below grade level. The solution is to create tests that have enough "bottom" for virtually all students. Knowing that a large percentage of students will be reading below grade level, the tests should be so constructed that there are some passages that would be on the appropriate level for struggling readers. A fourth-grade test, for instance, might have a passage or two on the second-grade and third-grade levels. Taking a test with sufficient bottom would allow below-grade-level readers to demonstrate what they know and can do. Struggling readers would feel less humiliated; educators would be provided with useful assessment information. Teachers of struggling readers would feel better about having their students assessed.

HIGH-STAKES TESTS

High-stakes tests, such as college entrance exams, have long been part of education. However, the number and uses of high-stakes tests has increased dramatically. High-stakes tests are now used in many school districts to determine whether young children pass or fail. Although assessment is an essential part of education, there are some problems with high-stakes tests. For one, tests provide only a limited sample of reading behavior and can yield misleading results. When important decisions are being made, it is important that several sources of information, such as actual samples of the students' work or teacher observations, be consulted. Second, when single tests are used to make important decisions, the tests take on inflated importance and may become the curriculum. This is especially true in high-poverty schools where test scores tend to be low (International Reading Association, 1999). If too much time is spent on test preparation, there is a loss of instructional time. If the tests have a cutoff score, sometimes there is an overemphasis on those who just missed the cutoff and a consequent neglect of the lowest scorers. Lastly, high-stakes tests reduce decision making at the local level. Teachers are forced to gear their curriculum to what is being tested. This thwarts the basic intent of assessment, which is to measure what has been taught so that adjustments can be made. To counter some of the possible problems arising from high-stakes tests, The International Reading Association (1999) recommends the following:

- Construct more systematic and rigorous assessments for classrooms, so that external audiences will gain confidence in the measures that are being used and their inherent value to inform decisions.
- Take responsibility to educate parents, community members, and policy makers about the forms of classroom-based assessment, used in addition to standardized tests, that can improve instruction and benefit students learning to read.
- Understand the difference between ethical and unethical practices when teaching to the test. It is ethical to familiarize students with the format of the test so they are familiar with the types of questions and responses required. Spending time on this type of instruction is helpful to all and can be supportive of the regular curriculum. It is not ethical to devote substantial instructional time teaching to the test, and it is not

ethical to focus instructional time on particular students who are most likely to raise test scores while ignoring groups who are unlikely to improve.

- Inform parents and the public about tests and their results.
- Resist the temptation to take actions to improve test scores that are not based on the idea of teaching students to read better (p. 262).

REPORTING TO PARENTS

Parents are understandably concerned about their children's performance. When discussing assessment results, focus on the child's strengths. Also avoid comparisons with other children, if possible. Discuss the student's performance in the light of what he might reasonably be expected to do. If the student has below-average scores, stress signs of progress: Jan could read only one-syllable words when the school year began, but now she is able to read many words that have two or three syllables. If parents want to know how their child is doing in comparison with other children, use general categories rather than precise numbers. Instead of saying that Juan is reading at the 20th percentile, explain that he is reading below average. However, do explain that the child does have a reading problem. Parents have a right to that information. When explaining assessment results, suggest ways in which the parents might build on strengths and try to shore up weaknesses. Show samples of the student's work. Highlight evidence of effort and improvement. End the conference on an encouraging, hopeful note.

SUMMARY

Assessment is an interactive process and should consider the reader, the text, the techniques being used, the reading or writing task involved, and the context in which the reading or writing is performed. Assessment should also be dynamic. Through instruction provided after initial testing, or through trial or assisted teaching, it should attempt to discover what the student's true learning potential is and how the student learns best.

Assessment devices should be authentic. They should reflect the kinds of reading and writing tasks that students undertake in and out of school. Because they consist mainly of brief passages and multiple-choice items, traditional group tests have limited authenticity. Assessment measures fall into four main categories: screening, diagnostic, monitoring, and outcome. Assessment measures can also be classified as being formative or summative.

There are many different kinds of reading and writing tests. Tests can be norm referenced or criterion referenced. Norm-referenced tests compare a student's performance with that of a sample or norm group. Although they are most often reported in percentile ranks, test performance can also be expressed in stanines, normal-curve equivalents, scaled scores (including DRP and Lexile units), or grade equivalents. Criterion-referenced tests compare students' performance with a criterion or standard, which may be a percentage of answers correct, or a benchmark such as being able to read a book on a certain level. Tests can also be classified as being group or individual, survey or diagnostic, formal or informal. Some categories overlap. For instance, a test can be both criterion and norm referenced.

Tests are expected to meet standards of reliability and validity. A reliable test is one that yields the same approximate score if taken over and over again. A valid test is one that measures what it says it measures. In order to be valid, a test should also provide useful information for an educational decision. Kinds of validity include concurrent or statistical, predictive, curricular or content, and construct. Tests are not precise measures but have a standard error of measurement, which can be used to estimate the scores that students would achieve if they took the same test over and over.

High-stakes tests are those that are used as the basis for making important decisions. Although high-stakes tests can provide valid information about students' performance, several sources of assessment should be used when making important decisions. In addition, tests should not be used to dictate curriculum. Assessment data should be shared with parents. Students' strengths and signs of progress should be emphasized.

APPLICATION ACTIVITIES

1. Start a collection of sample informal and formal tests and other assessment devices that you might use. Also, collect ideas for assessing students in reading and writing.

2. Examine a norm-referenced or criterion-referenced test. Note the skills being tested and the way they are being assessed. What does this suggest about the content validity of the test? What information does the test maker provide about reliability, validity, and fairness? What suggestions, if any, does the test publisher give for using test results?

3. Become acquainted with the literacy standards in your state and with tests or other systems used to assess students' performance on standards. Although the tests themselves are usually secure so that you cannot examine them, a list of standards or skills assessed and sample items are usually provided. Note the consequences of not meeting the standards and whether assistance is provided for students identified as not meeting standards. Most state departments of education provide this information on their web sites.

CHAPTER FOUR

PLACING STUDENTS AND MONITORING PROGRESS

USING WHAT YOU KNOW

Have you ever had to read a book that was simply too difficult for you? How did you feel? How would you feel if, day after day, you were asked to read books that were too hard for you? What do you think might be the overall effect on your attitude and your progress? One of the most important decisions that you will make as a literacy teacher is matching students with materials that have an appropriate level of challenge. One of the best devices for placing students is the informal reading inventory or devices modeled on the inventory. A simple but powerful device, the inventory consists primarily of a series of selections that gradually grow more difficult.

ANTICIPATION GUIDE

Read each of the following statements. Put a check under "Agree" or "Disagree" to show how you feel about each one. If possible, discuss your responses with classmates.

	AGREE	DISAGREE
1. Although they are subjective, informal tests are more useful than formal tests.	————	————
2. When estimating a student's reading level, the most important factor is the ability to read words.	————	————
3. When estimating a student's reading ability, silent reading performance is more important than oral reading.	————	————
4. For most students, group tests provide adequate data about reading performance.	————	————
5. Analyzing a student's errors is one of the best ways of diagnosing a reading difficulty.	————	————

THE INFORMAL READING INVENTORY

Informal reading inventory (IRI): a series of passages that gradually increase in difficulty, used to assess oral reading and comprehension.

When properly administered and interpreted, the **informal reading inventory (IRI)** yields much of the information about a student that the reading teacher needs. Although it only takes about thirty minutes to administer, the informal reading inventory indicates the student's reading level and approximate level of language development. It provides insight into word analysis and comprehension strategies, background knowledge, work habits, and interests. Once you are familiar with the IRI, it can be used as a framework with which to observe and interpret students' reading behavior.

One of the most valid and reliable measures of reading, the IRI is the basis for a number of commercially produced diagnostic assessments as well as the running record, which is an essential ingredient in Reading Recovery, and the technique of miscue analysis, an important element in whole-language assessment. Like many important developments in other fields, the IRI is simple and sensible. In its original form, administering an IRI was like having a customer try on shoes. The teacher had a series of graded readers and tried them on for size until finding the one that fit just right—neither too easy nor too difficult.

As originally conceived, inventories were constructed by teachers. Typically, IRIs were created using passages from basal readers. In keeping with the spirit of using children's books to teach reading, it is also possible to construct an inventory based on a series of children's books that increase in difficulty. (Instructions for creating an inventory can be found in Johnson, Kress, & Pikulski's [1987] *Informal Reading Inventories,* 2nd ed.) Teacher-constructed inventories are more valid because they reflect the types of materials you actually use in your class. This fits in with the concept of curriculum-based assessment. *Curriculum-based assessment* (CBA) is designed to assess students' academic skills from instructional materials actually used by students (Shapiro, 1996). A CBA IRA would use the texts that students are reading in their language arts or content-area classes.

Because of the time involved in creating a curriculum-based informal inventory, many teachers use commercially produced IRIs. Most commercial inventories range from a preprimer level through grade 8. However, the Bader Reading and Language Inventory (Bader, 1998), Informal Reading Inventory: Preprimer to Twelfth Grade (Burns & Roe, 2002), Ekwall/Shanker Reading Inventory (Ekwall & Shanker, 2000), the Flynt–Cooter Reading Inventory for the Classroom (Flynt & Cooter, 1995), the Informal Reading-Thinking Inventory (Manzo, Manzo, & McKenna, 1995), and the Qualitative Reading Inventory (Leslie & Caldwell, 2001) extend up through grade 11 or 12, which makes them especially useful with older students. There are also specialized inventories such as Read: Reading Evaluation Adult Diagnosis: An Informal Inventory for Assessing Adult Student Reading Needs and Progress (Colvin & Root, 2000), which is distributed by Literacy Volunteers and contains an inventory designed for adults.

Although most inventories start at a preprimer level, which is early first grade, some inventories assess below the preprimer level. The Basic Reading Inventory (Johns, 2001) includes a selection on the picture and easy sight words level and also a number of early literacy assessments. The Stieglitz Informal Reading Inventory (Stieglitz, 1997) uses a procedure known as dictated story assessment to test students who are reading below a first-grade level. Students discuss a photograph and dictate a story about it, which they then read. Both

The Flynt–Cooter Reading Inventory uses brief sentences that gradually increase in difficulty rather than lists of words to establish a starting point. The Stieglitz Informal Reading Inventory provides both words in isolation and words in sentences.

the Basic Reading Inventory and the Bader Reading and Language Inventory (Bader, 1998) contain a series of preliteracy assessments for students who are unable to read preprimer passages. A listing of commercial inventories is presented in Table 4.1.

One problem with testing older low-achieving readers is that the easiest passages in most inventories are written for young children and would be both demeaning and boring for older students. However, the Classroom Reading Inventory (Silvaroli & Wheelock, 2001) has three forms, two of which contain passages, even at the easiest levels, that are appropriate for older students. Forms A and B are designed for elementary school students. Form C is meant for students in junior high, and Form D is designed for assessing high school students and adults. Even at their easiest levels, Forms C and D present selections that deal with cars, sports, and other mature topics. The Bader Reading and Language Inventory (Bader, 1998) also has a form designed for older students and one created for adults.

The typical IRI, whether teacher created or commercially produced, consists of two major components: graded word lists and graded passages. The graded word lists consist of separate lists of ten to twenty words on a preprimer through an eighth- or twelfth-grade level. The passages consist of a series of graded selections beginning at preprimer level and extending to eighth, ninth, or twelfth grade. Generally, there are two passages at each level, one to be read orally and one to be read silently. Some inventories provide only an oral passage and, to save time, some teachers omit the administration of the silent reading passages in inventories that assess both oral and silent reading. However, omitting silent reading passages lessens both the validity and reliability of the IRI. Moreover, in some students there is a marked difference between performance on oral and on silent reading passages.

Besides the comparison of oral and silent reading performance, other important information is lost when the administration of silent reading passages is omitted. The teacher is unable to observe the strategies that a student uses when reading silently and is unable to gauge silent reading speed. The teacher also misses the opportunity to note whether the students finger-point, subvocalize, or engage in other similar behaviors that may be symptomatic that the material is too difficult and/or that the readers are inefficient.

Administering the inventory is fairly straightforward. The inventory is administered individually and begins with the student being asked to read the words on the word lists, starting with the easiest list. Using the results of the word-list administration, the teacher locates a probable starting point for the reading of the graded passages. Beginning with passages where comprehension and word recognition are virtually flawless, the student continues to read until the material is obviously too difficult. As the student reads, the teacher carefully observes the student's comprehension, word recognition, use of strategies, oral language development, and how he or she handles the testing situation. The more careful the observation, the greater will be the insight obtained.

The IRI as a Placement Device

A primary purpose of the IRI is to obtain placement information. The teacher needs to know what level of material is most likely to produce optimum results. This is especially crucial

TABLE 4.1 Commercial Inventories

NAME	AUTHORS	GRADES	ADDED SKILL AREAS
Analytic Reading Inventory	Woods & Moe	1–9	Contains science and social studies passages.
Bader Reading and Language Inventory	Bader	1–12 and adult	Also assesses phonics, language, spelling, and emergent literacy.
Basic Reading Inventory	Johns	1–8	Includes assessment of emergent literacy.
Classroom Reading Inventory	Silvaroli & Wheelock	1–8	Forms C and D can be used with older readers.
Critical Reading Inventory: Assessing Students Reading and Thinking	Applegate	1–12	Drawing conclusions and critical thinking.
Ekwall/Shanker Reading Inventory	Shanker & Ekwall	1–12	Includes assessment of emergent literacy, word analysis, and reading interests.
Informal Reading Inventory	Roe & Burns	1–12	
Informal Reading-Thinking Inventory	Manzo, Mano, & McKenna	1–11	Includes assessment of prior knowledge and higher-level thinking skills.
English-Espanol Reading Inventory for the Classroom	Flynt & Cooter	K–12	Emergent literacy. Has an English only version.
Flynt–Cooter Reading Inventory for the Classroom	Flynt & Cooter	1–12	Features longer pieces, retellings, picture reading, and an observation guide to assess emergent literacy.
Informal Reading Inventory	Burns & Roe	1–12	
English-Espanol Reading Inventory for the Classroom	Prentice Hall	K–12	Emergent literacy. Has an English-only version.
Qualitative Reading Inventory III	Leslie & Caldwell	1–12	Features longer pieces, assessment of prior knowledge, retelling procedures, and think-alouds.
PALS	Invernizzi & Meir	K–3	Emergent literacy, IRI, word reading, spelling.
Stieglitz Informal Reading Inventory	Stieglitz	1–8	Assesses emergent literacy and prior knowledge.
Texas Primary Reading Inventory	Texas Education Agency	K–3	Emergent literacy, phonics. Has a Spanish version.

Independent level: level of material that a student can read with at least 99 percent word recognition and 90 percent comprehension.

Instructional level: level of material that a student can read with at least 95 percent word recognition and 75 percent comprehension. The 95 percent word-recognition figure has recently been validated by ESL researchers (Nation, 2001). At the 90 percent level, a few students had limited comprehension. At 95 percent, most students were able to construct a reasonable understanding of the selection.

Frustration level: level of material where a student's word recognition is 90 percent or less or comprehension is 50 percent or less.

Listening capacity: level of material that a student can understand with 75 percent comprehension when it is read to him or her.

for low-achieving readers, who tend to be given materials that are too difficult for them, a condition that leads to frustration and makes it impossible for them to apply a balanced set of reading strategies (Clay, 1985).

The IRI yields four levels: independent, instructional, frustration, and listening capacity. As its name suggests, the **independent level** is the point at which students can read on their own, without any help from teachers, parents, or peers. They recognize at least 99 percent of the words, and comprehension is nearly perfect. At the **instructional level,** students can read at least 95 out of 100 words, and they recall at least 75 percent of what they read. If given instructional assistance, they can read with confidence and competence. At the **frustration level,** the material is simply too difficult for the student to read, even with assistance. Students miss ten or more words out of a hundred and/or remember only half of what they read. Students may exhibit lip movement during silent reading, may be easily distracted, or may engage in hair twisting, grimacing, or other stress-signaling behaviors (Johnson, Kress, & Pikulski, 1987).

Once a student has reached the frustration level, the teacher reads the inventory selections to her or him in order to assess the student's ability to understand written language when decoding is not a factor. The highest level at which the student can understand 75 percent of the material that is read to her or him is the **listening capacity.**

Although guidelines vary somewhat, the most accepted standards for the four levels are presented in Table 4.2. Powell (1971) and others have argued for lower standards and/or standards that vary according to grade levels. However, a study by Fuchs, Fuchs, and Deno (1982) found that levels obtained using the 95 percent word-recognition criterion agreed fairly substantially with levels obtained by teacher estimates and standardized tests. Using a lower word-recognition percentage resulted in placing a greater proportion of students above the level estimated by the classroom teacher. As noted in Chapter 1, research indicates that students do best when they can cope with at least 95 to 98 percent of the

TABLE 4.2   Informal Reading Inventory Standards

LEVEL	WORD RECOGNITION IN CONTEXT		COMPREHENSION
Independent	99%	(and)	95%
Instructional	95%	(and)	75%
Frustration	90%	(or)	50%
Listening capacity			75%

There is some disagreement about the percentage of word recognition required for adequate comprehension. See Baumann (1989) and Powell (1971) for a discussion.

words (Berliner, 1981; Biemiller, 1994; Gambrell, Wilson, & Gantt, 1981). Indeed, Enz (1989) found that relaxing IRI standards resulted in a deterioration of both achievement and attitude. Students placed according to higher standards spent a greater proportion of time on task, had a higher success rate, and had a more positive attitude toward reading.

Administering the Word-List Tests

The graded word lists provide a starting point for administration of the graded passages. They also yield valuable information about a student's ability to recognize words immediately and to use word-level processing strategies to decode words that are not immediately recognized. In a sense, the task is artificial because in actual reading words are generally encountered in running text, thus providing the opportunity to use context. Because the words in the word-list tests are presented in isolation, students have no recourse but to use word-analysis strategies; so this brief, but important, test provides excellent insight into a student's ability to use phonics, syllabic analysis, and other word-level decoding skills.

In order to get the most information from word-list tests, they should be given in a timed (flash) and an untimed (analysis) administration. In a timed administration, each word is flashed for a second, so that the student is assessed on her or his ability to pronounce words immediately, without recourse to decoding. The student should be seated to the side of you and should be reading from her or his copy. Use a second copy for marking, but keep that on your desk or a clipboard.

Using two three-by-five cards, flash each word for a second as shown in Figure 4.1. A word is flashed by pulling down the card in the left hand while keeping the card in the right hand in place for one second. As the word is being exposed, it is important that the card in the right hand be held steadily and not dragged down, preventing the student from getting a clear, unobscured look at the word. To make sure that the word is exposed for a second, but no longer, say, "One thousand," to yourself and then snap the opening closed by pushing down the card in

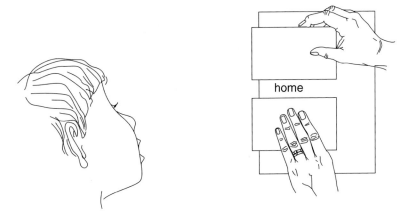

FIGURE 4.1   Administering Word-List Test

the right hand. Continue to flash the words in this fashion until the student misreads a word or is unable to read a word within one second. At that point, record the student's response in the flash column and open up the cards so the student can then analyze the word she or he missed. The student is then encouraged to use word-analysis skills to try to figure out the word. The student's response is recorded in the untimed column, and testing is resumed. Continue testing until the student misses half the words under the flash condition on two consecutive levels. Extending the testing to a level where the student is meeting difficult words provides you with the opportunity to observe the student's word-analysis skills in isolation in full operation.

When the student makes an error, record her or his performance. If the student mispronounces or substitutes a word, write the mispronunciation or substitution. If the student says, "I don't know," write *dk* in the blank. Write *o* if the student makes no response. A check indicates a correct response. (However, to keep the test moving, you need not record checks in the flash column until later. Because you don't need to write anything in the flash blank unless the student fails to respond or makes an error, you can assume that the blanks that have not been written in are correct items.)

If a student reads correctly a word that she missed on flash, then place a check in the untimed column. If a student makes the same mistake, record it with a check with a tail. If the student gives a second mispronunciation or substitution, one that is different from the first, record that. It is important to record a student's errors, because they provide information about the kinds of elements he has mastered and those with which he is having difficulty. A list of symbols used to mark the word-list test is presented in Figure 4.2. A marked word-list test is presented in Figure 4.3.

Before giving the word-list test, explain its nature and purpose. Say, "I am going to ask you to read some words for me. At first, I will only show you the word for a second, because I want to see how well you can read words without needing time to figure them out. If you are unable to read a word in one second, then I will give you time to figure it out. That will help me to see how you figure out words. As you go through the lists of words, they will become harder, but do the best you can."

Interpreting the Results of the Word-List Tests

After the entire inventory has been administered, analyze the results, beginning with the words in isolation, the word-list tests. First, make a gross comparison between performance on the flash list and performance on the untimed list.

FIGURE 4.2   Word-List Test Marking Symbols

	Flash	Untimed		
saw	✓	____	✓	(Correct response.)
then	*they*	____	*they*	(Substitution. The substitution is written on the line.)
wet	*we*	✓	✓	(Made same error on untimed as on flash.)
was	*dk*	*dk*	*dk*	(Said, "Don't know.")
boy	*0*	*0*	*0*	(No response.)

FIGURE 4.3   Performance on Word-List Test

	Flash	Untimed
1. me	✓	
2. get	✓	
3. home	✓	
4. not	*no*	✓
5. he	✓	
6. tree	*tee*	✓
7. girl	✓	
8. take	*tack*	✓
9. book	✓	
10. milk	*more*	*my*
11. dog	✓	
12. all	✓	
13. apple	✓	
14. like	✓	
15. go	✓	
16. farm	✓	
17. went	*when*	✓
18. friend	*dk*	*dk*
19. about	*above*	✓
20. door	*do*	*dot*
Percent correct:	*60%*	*75%*

The flash score represents the student's ability to recognize words automatically, without resorting to decoding them. The untimed score indicates the student's ability to use phonics, syllabication, and morphemic analysis to decode words that are not recognized immediately. A high flash score indicates a high sight or immediate-recognition vocabulary.

> Because they test only students' ability to pronounce printed words, word lists should not be used to obtain students' reading levels. However, they are useful for estimating immediate-recognition vocabulary.

An improved analysis score is a gauge of decoding ability. The larger the difference between the two scores, the greater is the decoding ability. However, a very large difference may indicate that the student has few words that she or he can recognize at sight and so must sound out nearly all words. This can be a problem. If too much of a student's working memory is taken up by word analysis, too little will be left for comprehension (Samuels, 1994). What does the performance shown in Figure 4.3 suggest about the student's ability to recognize words immediately and her decoding skills?

After making a global analysis of a student's ability to recognize words at sight versus his ability to decode words, examine the kinds of words that were read correctly and those that were read incorrectly. Choose from the following questions those that apply to the student you have tested. The questions address gradually increasing levels of difficulty. The first questions are most appropriate for novice readers. The later questions are more suitable for advanced readers. If word-list tests are analyzed carefully, they should yield as much or more information about decoding skills as a word-analysis or phonics test.

- What parts of the word can the student read? Beginning? Middle? End?
- Can the student read beginning consonants? Can the student read ending consonants?
- Can the student pronounce short-vowel patterns *(cat, pet)?*
- Can the student read double-letter long-vowel patterns *(goat, rain)?*
- Can the student read final-*e* long-vowel patterns *(wave, home)?*
- Can the student read *r*-vowel patterns *(car, chair, here, store, sir)?*
- Can the student read other-vowel patterns *(choice, how, crawl, brook, spoon)?*
- Can the student read multisyllabic words?
- Does the student's difficulty pronouncing words seem to be caused by a lack of familiarity with the words in oral language? Is this essentially a vocabulary problem? To check to see whether a word the student has missed is in her listening vocabulary, say the word and ask the student to tell what the word means. For instance, if the student misread the word *solar,* say the word after the word-list test has been completed and ask the student to tell what the word means. If the student does not know what the word means, then the miscue is signalling a vocabulary need. If the student knows the meaning of *solar,* then a decoding need is being indicated (Jesse Turner, personal communication, October 10, 2000).

Assisted Testing.   As a further analysis, try assisted testing, which was explained in the previous chapter. Students might miss words on the word-list test because they were rushing, were nervous, or felt the pressure of being assessed. After administering the word-list tests, reassess the students on some of the missed items. First, give them another chance to say the word. If they are unable to respond, provide them with a prompt. A good prompt to use is "Are there any parts of that word that you can say?" This will tell you whether they know the element but need the assistance of prompting. If the student is unable to respond to the prompt, cover up all but a part of the word that you think the student might know and invite the student to read that. Then uncover the rest of the word and see if the student can read it. Make a note of the prompts you supplied and the student's response. One student misread *ran/run, us/use,* and *got/goat.* Her results suggested difficulty with short vowels and long vowels. However, when asked to read the words again she read all of them correctly. The student also had misread *struggle, sunup, several,* and *survive.* When given another chance to read them, she still had difficulty, nor was she able to respond to the prompt: "Is there any part of this word that you can say?" However, when provided with a prompt that included covering up a portion of the word so that she could focus on a part of the word that was probably familiar she was able to read all four words. (For instance, all of the word *struggle* was covered except for *rug.*) The results indicated that she was a better decoder than the original test results suggested. The improved performance also indicated that teaching her the pronounceable word part and other strategies would most likely be fruitful. As a side benefit, the student felt better about her performance because she could see that she had improved when given a second chance to read the words.

Administering the IRI Passages

> Some informal reading inventories use longer passages to reflect the kinds of sustained reading that students actually do. The disadvantage is that these inventories take longer to administer.

Procedures for administering and interpreting inventories vary. The procedures presented in this text are drawn from those described in *Informal Reading Inventories* (Johnson, Kress, & Pikulski, 1987), which is a widely used, highly respected source.

To determine the students' starting point for reading the oral and silent passages, locate the student's last perfect performance on the flash list. The starting point for the passages is the level below the last perfect performance. If the student's last perfect performance on flash was fourth grade, begin testing at the third-grade level. If you suspect a comprehension problem, you might start at an even lower level (Johnson, Kress, & Pikulski, 1987). Looking at Sheila's scores (Figure 4.4), you can see that her starting point would be grade 2.

As conceived by Betts (1946), the IRI is modeled on the directed reading activity (guided reading lesson), except that the emphasis is on evaluation rather than instruction. A second major difference is that one passage at each level will be read orally without any

> **Retelling:** process of recounting orally or in writing a story or an information piece. The purpose of a retelling is to assess comprehension.

preparation. Normally, passages are read silently before being read orally. The steps in administering the inventory, which, except for assessing listening comprehension, are similar to those in a traditional reading lesson, include: preparing for reading a passage, assessing background knowledge, setting a purpose for reading, reading of passage, **retelling** of passage or answering questions about the passage, oral rereading of a selected segment of the silent passage (optional), and assessing listening comprehension.

The inventory begins with the reading of the oral passage at the level below the student's last perfect performance on the flash portion of the word-list tests. The oral passage

FIGURE 4.4   Sheila's Test Results

	WORD-LIST SCORES	
Level	*Flash*	*Untimed*
PP	100	100
P	100	100
1	100	100
2	100	100
3	100	100
4	75	90
5	50	60
6	40	50

is read at sight. The student does not read it silently first. Before a student reads the oral passage, explain the test and its purpose. Explain that he or she will be reading a series of stories (articles). State that you will be taking notes on the reading so that you can get some information on how they read. Tell the student that after he has read the passage, you will ask him to answer some questions (or retell the story or article in his own words).

Preparation for Reading a Passage.   Ask a question or two about the title, topic, or illustration to explore briefly the student's knowledge of the topic. Before reading a selection about possums, you might direct the student's attention to the illustration of a possum and ask him what the picture shows. If there is no response, this might indicate a lack of background information about possums. To verify this, you might ask the student what she or he knows about possums. As the student responds, evaluate the depth and accuracy of her or his background knowledge. Since reading is very much a matter of bringing meaning to a page or activating schema, it is important to have an estimate of the quality of the student's store of information. However, make sure that you don't give away major ideas or key vocabulary in the preliminary discussion. As part of a discussion, set a purpose for reading. This might be a general purpose, such as to find out more about the topic, or it may be more specific. Most commercial inventories contain a preliminary discussion and/or purpose-setting question. In the Basic Reading Inventory (Johns, 2001), for instance, the student is asked to read the title and tell the examiner what she or he thinks the passage will be about.

> As the student reads orally, note his or her fluency. Fluency is the smoothness with which students read. A fluent reader groups words into meaningful phrases and reads with appropriate expression.

Once the purpose has been set, have the student read the selection aloud to answer the purpose question. As the student reads aloud, use a series of symbols to describe her or his reading behavior. Note mispronounced words, omitted and inserted words, asking for help, correction of errors, hesitations, repetitions, misread punctuation, word-by-word reading, inaccurate intonation, head movement, finger-pointing, and other behaviors that might yield insight into the manner in which the reader processes print. Symbols for each of these behaviors are presented in Figure 4.5.

Mispronunciations that are occasioned by the student's dialect or because the student's native language is not English are not counted as errors. For instance, if students habitually omit endings in their speech, this is not counted as an error if they drop endings when they are reading. If a student who is not a native speaker of English pronounces *shoes* as *choose*, this is not counted as an error if this is the way the student pronounces the word in conversation and if the student understands that the word refers to footwear. In fact, translation of printed symbols into one's dialect is a positive sign (Goodman & Goodman, 1978). It indicates that the student is reading for meaning and not just making sounds.

As a practical matter, only uncorrected mispronunciations, omissions, insertions, and words supplied by the teacher count as errors. Repetitions and hesitations and other behaviors provide qualitative information about the student's reading. If a student reads so rapidly that it is difficult to record all his errors, then focus on noting those misreadings that count as errors. You may also record any other behavior that would shed light on the student's reading. In the sample marked-up inventory selection in Figure 4.6, the examiner included a comment in which the student stated that he likes animals. This information about the student's interests will come in handy when selecting materials.

FIGURE 4.5   IRI Oral Reading Symbols

QUANTITATIVE ERRORS

the angry *orange* cat   Mispronunciation (Substitution)

the angry cat   Omission

the (angry) cat   Asked for word

the *big* angry cat   Insertion

the angry *angle* ✓ cat   Self-correction (not counted as an error)

QUALITATIVE ERRORS

the|angry cat   Hesitation

<u>the</u> angry cat   Repetition

the angry cat *w × w*   Word-by-word reading

The angry cat hissed⊗
And away ran the dog.   Omitted punctuation

This is your cat. ↑   Rising inflection

Is this your cat? ↓   Falling inflection

HM   Head movement

FP   Finger pointing

As students are decoding difficult words, be sure to record all their attempts. This can yield valuable insight into their decoding processes. You might see, for instance, that a student is decoding a word sound by sound or using familiar word parts.

Comprehension Check.   After the student has read the passage, comprehension is checked. The traditional procedure for assessing comprehension of an IRI selection is to ask comprehension questions. Students' responses to questions should be recorded so you can take time later to examine any responses about which you are unsure. If the student has not supplied enough information for you to make a determination as to whether the answer is right or wrong, you can ask the student to tell you more. However, do not supply any clues or hints. After scoring the comprehension responses, analyze them in terms of their quality.

**FIGURE 4.6   Sample Informal Reading
Inventory Performance**

The Pet Shop

*Commented,
"I
like
all
kinds
of
animals."*

Maria really wanted a little dog. One

day she went with her parents to the pet

shop. They looked at the fish, turtles,

par-rots
parrots, and many kinds of dogs. Maria

and her parents saw one nice puppy that
likely ✓
acted very lively. It looked like a small
little
bouncing black ball of fur. The puppy was
fat
a fluffy black poodle. It jumped around in

its cage. When Maria petted the puppy, it
barked
sat up and begged. Maria and her parents

laughed because the poodle looked so cute.

They decided to buy the poodle. After all,
rest
who could resist such a nice dog.

From J. L. Johns, *Basic Reading Inventory: Pre-Primer Through Grade
Twelve & Early Literacy Assessments,* 8th ed., 2001, p. 259. Copyright ©
2001 by Kendall/Hunt Publishing Company. Reprinted with permission.

Were they complete? Was additional information volunteered? What level of language did
the student demonstrate as she or he answered questions.

As an alternative to asking questions, you might check comprehension by requesting
a retelling. In a retelling, a student is asked to recall a selection in her or his own words.
Generally, the teacher uses a guide that indicates the main points that should be covered in
a retelling. Figure 4.7 presents a sample retelling guide from the Qualitative Reading Inventory (Leslie & Caldwell, 2001).

The major advantage of the retelling procedure is that students reconstruct the piece
according to their personal interpretations. The teacher is provided with the opportunity to
observe how the student organizes her retellings and what kind of information she recalls or

FIGURE 4.7   Retelling Scoring Sheet Sample

SETTING/BACKGROUND

_____ John Chapman was born
_____ in 1774
_____ He became a farmer
_____ and grew crops.
_____ John liked
_____ to grow
_____ and eat apples.
_____ People were moving west.
_____ Apples were a good food
_____ for settlers to have.

GOAL

_____ John decided
__5__ to go west.
_____ He wanted
__3__ to plant apple trees.

EVENTS

_____ John got many seeds
_____ from farmers
_____ who squeezed apples
_____ to make a drink
_____ called cider.
_____ He left
_____ for the frontier.
_____ He planted seeds
_____ as he went along.
_____ He gave them away.
_____ John walked miles.
__6__ He crossed rivers

__7__ and went through forests.
_____ He was hungry
_____ and wet.
_____ He had to hide
__8__ from Indians
_____ unfriendly Indians.
__9__ His clothes were torn.
_____ He used a sack
_____ for a shirt
_____ and he cut out holes
_____ for the arms.
__11__ He wore no shoes.

RESOLUTION

_____ John's fame spread.
__1__ He was nicknamed
__2__ Johnny Appleseed.
_____ Settlers accepted seeds
_____ gratefully.
_____ Thanks to Johnny Appleseed
__12__ trees grow
__13__ in many parts
_____ of America.

Other ideas recalled including inferences

4   lived in Massachusetts
10   didn't give up

chooses to include. A retelling also shows what the reader inferred or added to the selection (Irwin & Mitchell, 1983). For more information on retellings, including sample questions, refer to pp. 123 to 124.

Because asking questions and requesting a retelling both have distinct advantages, you might assess comprehension by doing both. First, have the student provide a retelling. Then ask questions about any essential information not included in the retelling or follow-up probes.

Administering Silent Reading Passages.   Immediately after discussing the oral passage, administer the silent reading passage on that same level. After administering the third-grade oral passage, for instance, have the student read the third-grade silent passage. Do not administer all the oral passages at once and then the silent passages.

> Because students are not allowed to look back at the passage when answering comprehension questions, recall, as well as understanding, are being tapped.

Just as was done when administering the oral passage, background should be explored in preparation for reading the passage and a purpose should be set. The student should be directed to read the passage silently. As the student reads silently, make notes on his behavior. Using the symbols presented in Figure 4.8, indicate lip movement, head movement, finger-pointing, and vocalization. Also note any words for which the student asks for assistance. (You may supply a word if the student asks for it, but if that word is part of the answer to a comprehension question, the student is not given credit for the answer even if she gets it correct. The rationale is that the student would not have gotten the answer without the help you supplied.) At the conclusion of the silent reading, request a retelling or seek answers to traditional questions as you did for the oral passage.

Except as an optional procedure on the Qualitative Reading Inventory-III (Leslie & Caldwell, 2001), students are not allowed to go back over the selection to locate information that would help them answer questions. This means that retention as well as comprehension is being assessed. Allowing students to look back would provide information about students' comprehension when memory is not a factor and also about their ability to locate appropriate information. However, the inventory should be scored according to students' ability to answer questions without using look-backs.

Oral Rereading.   Although it is not included in most commercial inventories, a valuable activity is to plan an oral rereading of a portion of the passage that was read silently. This rereading accomplishes three aims. It provides: "(1) a gauge of the student's ability to skim for the relocation of specific information; (2) a measure of ability to read for a specific purpose and to stop when that purpose has been satisfied; and (3) an index of the ability to profit from previous silent reading of the material, and thus improve the fluency of oral performance over oral reading at sight at the same level of difficulty" (Johnson, Kress, & Pikulski, 1987, p. 35).

> Because the student has already read the passage silently, the oral rereading should be more fluent than the reading of the oral passage at that level.

The oral rereading should be marked in the same manner as the oral selection was. A comment should also be placed on the teacher's copy to indicate how successfully the student reread the passage in question.

FIGURE 4.8   Symbols for Silent Reading

HM	Head movement
LM	Lip movement
FP	Finger pointing
SV	Subvocalization
PC	Use of picture clue

Rate of Reading.   Another valuable piece of information that the inventory can yield is the rate of reading. The rate at which a student reads can provide insight into her or his fluency. Slow reading can be a sign that decoding is taking an excessive amount of time, or the student may be reading word by word. Or it may be an indication that the student processes information slowly. Another possibility is that the student may be very anxious about remembering all the details in a selection and may believe that the best way to foster comprehension and retention is to read very slowly. Slow reading, especially among older students who have adequate decoding skills, is often a sign of an underlying problem.

> Rate of reading and *fluency* are not identical. Rate of reading is speed of reading and does not consider whether words are grouped into phrases and read with expression. A slow rate of reading on independent and instructional-level material suggests that the student's reading is not fluent (Rasinski & Padak, 1996).

Once students have mastered basic decoding skills, oral reading should match the student's rate of speaking (the average rate of speaking is 100 to 140 words per minute) and, beyond grade 2, silent reading speed should surpass rate of oral reading. To assess rate of reading, use a stopwatch but be unobtrusive. Students might feel pressured if they see that they are being timed.

Approximate average rates of reading for both oral and silent selections in grades 1 through 7 are presented in Table 4.3 (from Powell, cited in Lipson & Wixson, 1991). In seventh grade and beyond, students' rate of silent reading is approximately 200 to 250 words per minute (Harris & Sipay, 1990).

Reaching the Frustration Level.   Students continue reading oral and silent passages until they reach their frustration level. The frustration level is the point at which students have a score of 90 percent or less on the word recognition of the oral passages or when average comprehension of oral and silent passages is 50 percent or less. If students have acceptable word recognition but comprehension is 50 percent or less, test at the next highest level to make sure that the students have truly reached their frustration levels. Because of a lack of interest or inadequate background in a specific topic, students' comprehension may dip temporarily but rebound on a higher-level selection.

Establishing Listening Capacity.   Once students have reached the frustration level, you should have them stop reading. At that point, you begin reading the passages to them. The

TABLE 4.3   Median Rates of Reading

INSTRUCTIONAL READING LEVEL	ORAL READING	SILENT READING
Grade 1	55	55
Grade 2	85	85
Grade 3	115	130
Grade 4	135	155
Grade 5	145	185
Grade 6	150	205

object is to locate the highest level at which students can understand printed materials, once the barriers posed by translating print have been removed. Two selections at each level are read to students in order to find the highest point at which students can understand 75 percent of the material. Again, be prepared for dips in performance. Do not stop as soon as the student reaches the 75 percent mark. Even if the performance slips below 75 percent, test at the next level. Listening comprehension may rebound.

Obtaining a listening-capacity level yields important information. The expectation is that students will be able to read up to their listening capacity level. The listening-capacity task is an approximate measure of overall receptive language development. Students whose instructional level is below their listening comprehension level are judged to be reading below their potential. Average students can typically grasp listening materials at their grade level. Below-average students generally have a listening level that is below grade level, and above-average students generally are able to comprehend material that is above their grade level. Note the scores presented in Table 4.4. Although all three students whose scores are reported in the table are in the same grade and have different instructional levels, none is classified as a problem reader because all are reading up to their listening capacities. Jonathan, the first youngster, has a listening level of grade 2 but also is reading at a grade-2 level. Jonathan's language development seems to be below average. Maxine's instructional level of grade 4, which is at grade level, matches her listening level. Maxine's language development is apparently average. Benjamin, on the other hand, has an instructional and listening level of grade 8. His scores suggest superior language development.

> Because listening develops faster in the primary grades than reading does and some students have difficulty processing oral language, listening levels must be interpreted with care (Sticht & James, 1984).

As with the oral and silent passages, background should be explored and purposes set before the listening passages are read to students. For testing purposes, use the passages that the student has not yet read. However, if these are too hard, read easier passages from alternative forms. In the majority of cases a student's listening capacity will match or exceed the instructional level. However, some students have listening difficulties and will do even worse on a listening-comprehension test than they do on a reading test. They may have depressed listening scores because of emotional or attentional problems. A small percentage have difficulty processing information presented orally. For these students, it may be necessary to read passages to them that are below their instructional level. To get a measure of receptive language development in instances where the listening-capacity test does not seem to be working out, administer the Peabody Picture Vocabulary Test or a similar instrument.

TABLE 4.4   Performance of Three Fourth-Graders on an IRI

	JOHNATHAN	MAXINE	BENJAMIN
Independent	1	3	4
Instructional	2	4	8
Frustration	3	5	6
Listening capacity	2	4	8

Interpreting Inventory Results

Informal reading inventories do much more than just give reading levels. Because IRIs include a variety of lengthy selections and duplicate, in a controlled setting, the act of reading, they provide an excellent opportunity for insightful, in-depth observation. To interpret an inventory, begin with the most general information, the levels. The listening-comprehension level provides information about the student's cognitive ability and language development. The higher the student's listening comprehension, the more fully developed are his language and cognitive abilities. Listening comprehension that is significantly above grade level indicates better-than-average potential. Now take a look at the instructional level. Some students may have a range of instructional levels. Remember that a student is instructional if her word-recognition-in-context scores fall between 95 and 98 percent and comprehension is between 75 and 89 percent. Note Angela's levels in Figure 4.9. Her instructional levels are grades 2 and 3. Angela's basic instructional level, which is the highest level at which she

FIGURE 4.9 Sample IRI Levels

Name _Angela_   Age _____

Date _____

Grade _____   School _____   Examiner _____

Informal Reading Inventory Summary Sheet

| | WORD-LIST SCORES | | PASSAGE SCORES | | | | |
| | | | Word Recog. | Comprehension | | | Listening |
Level	Flash	Untimed	in Context	Oral	Silent	Avg.	Capacity
PP	100	—					
P	100	—					
1	90	100	99	100	90	95	
2	85	90	98	80	90	85	
3	75	85	95	80	70	75	
4	60	70	89	60	50	55	
5	50	60					80
6	40	50					80
7							50
8							
9							

LEVELS

Independent	1
Instructional	2–3
Frustration	4
Listening Capacity	6

SUMMARY OF NEEDS

Difficulty with main idea questions and multisyllabic words.

meets the criteria, is grade 3. Her immediate instructional level is grade 2. That is the level at which the student begins to show needs. In deciding at which level to place Angela, a number of factors need to be considered. If Angela is older, it might be better to place her in the higher level, since that will make it easier to obtain materials that are age appropriate. If Angela seems insecure and gives up easily, it is advisable to place her in lower-level materials, so she does not feel overwhelmed.

An examination of the levels yields other valuable information, too. They provide an estimate of the degree of discrepancy between ability and achievement in reading. For instance, the greater the difference between listening capacity and instructional level, the more serious is the problem. Note that Angela is reading three years below her listening capacity. Although both Orlando and Maria, whose levels are presented in Figure 4.10, have the same instructional level and are in the same grade, Orlando apparently has the more serious problem. With a listening capacity of 7, Orlando is five years below capacity whereas, Maria with a listening capacity of 5, is only three years below capacity.

Another comparison that should be noted is the magnitude of the difference between the instructional and the frustration levels. There is a buffer between the instructional and frustration level that is at least 5 percent in word recognition and 25 percent in comprehension, because the criteria for the instructional level are at least 95 percent word recognition and 75 percent comprehension but 90 percent word recognition or 50 percent comprehension for the frustration level. The greater the distance between the instructional and frustration levels, the more likely it is that the student will make rapid progress because this indicates a gradual, rather than a steep, drop-off in skills.

FIGURE 4.10   Comparison of IRI Levels

	ORLANDO	MARIA
Independent	1	1
Instructional	2	2
Frustration	3	4
Listening	7	5

LEVEL	WORD RECOGNITION IN CONTEXT	AVERAGE COMPREHENSION	WORD RECOGNITION IN CONTEXT	AVERAGE COMPREHENSION
PP	—		—	
P	100	100	100	90
1	99	90	100	90
2	95	80	96	80
3	86	60	93	70
4	—	—	91	60
5	—	—	90	60
6				
7				
8				

Take a look at Orlando's and Maria's instructional and frustration levels. Orlando's word-recognition score takes a nose dive after he reaches the instructional level at grade 2. His 86 percent word recognition score at grade 3 indicates that he will need lots of work in that area to bring word recognition up to an acceptable level. Maria's scores, on the other hand, taper off. With a little work, she should be able to bring up those 91 and 93 percentages to the 95 percent level.

After comparing levels, take a look at the student's scores in the two major areas assessed: word recognition and comprehension. Is there a discrepancy between the two? Is word recognition high but comprehension low, or vice versa? Or do both dip as the selections get harder, which is the typical pattern? Once you have a global sense of the student's reading performance, make an in-depth analysis of major areas, noting, of course, that reading is a holistic act so that ultimately information from all areas will need to be integrated.

Word Recognition.   Keeping in mind the information gathered from an analysis of the word-list tests, analyze the student's performance on word recognition in context. Is the student's percentage of word recognition in context higher at each level than her or his percentage of words recognized in isolation in the untimed condition? Was the student able to read some words in context that she or he had missed in isolation? Because of the availability of clues, most students are better able to recognize words in context than in isolation.

On the other hand, there are a few students whose word recognition skills are actually worse in context. These students have poor decoding skills. Deciphering words is a struggle for them. Given words in isolation, they are forced to apply their weak phonics skills. However, given words in running text, they overuse context, which is easier for them to apply than their weak phonics skills. If a picture is available, they may use that, too. Because they overrely on pictorial and verbal context and do not use the decoding skills they possess, they actually miss some words that they could read in isolation if they tried. They need to learn to use context along with phonics, not instead of phonics. They also need to have their phonics skills strengthened, with ample opportunity to apply them so they become automatic.

> If the student's performance on the word lists and oral passages portions of the IRI has been carefully analyzed, this should provide a wealth of information on word-analysis abilities, so it may not be necessary to give a separate phonics test.

Also observe the processes the student uses to decode words that posed problems. Did the student process the word sound by sound, saying /k/, /r/, /u/, /n/, /ch/ for *crunch*? Did the student use chunks of the word saying "un-run-crunch" or "run-crunch"? And what about the integration of strategies? Ideally, students should be making balanced use of the three language systems to decode words. These include the graphophonic, syntactic, and semantic. As you examine a student's errors, ask yourself the following questions:

- When the student encounters a difficult word, what does she or he do?
- Does the student try to sound it out?
- Does the student use verbal context?
- Does the student use picture cues?
- Does the student ask for help or give up without trying to work out the difficult word?
- Are student's miscues (misread words) meaningful?

- Does the student monitor her or his reading? Does the student self-correct when the text is not making sense or the word decoded does not fit? Self-corrections indicate that the student is reading for meaning and is monitoring her or his reading, and so are a positive sign. Self-correction of minor miscues, however, could indicate an over-concern with pronunciation. Good readers tend not to correct minor miscues that do not have an effect on the meaning of the passage (Y. Goodman, 1992).
- What strategies does the student use to correct an error?

At this point, take a look at the qualitative markings on the inventory. Slow or word-by-word reading, frequent hesitations, and repetitions are signs that the student is having difficulty with decoding. Take a little time, too, to examine the student's mastery of the "content" of phonics. What word-analysis elements was the student able to use? With what word-analysis elements did the student have difficulty? Using the list of word-recognition skills presented earlier in the chapter, examine the student's word-recognition-in-context performance. What phonic (consonants, consonant clusters, single vowels, vowel combinations, short vowels, long vowels, other vowels), syllabic, or morphemic elements (prefixes, suffixes, roots) was the student able to use? With which did she or he have difficulty?

Word recognition in isolation lends itself to dynamic testing. After students have completed the first run-through, go back and see if they can read some of the words they missed. For instance, pointing to a missed word, ask the student if there is any part of the word that she can read. If the student can read a part of the word, see if she can read the whole word. If the student says that she can't read any part of the word, cover up all but a part that seems relatively easy and see if the student can read that. (You might cover up all but the *par* in *particular*.) If the student can read that part, see if she can use that part to help her reconstruct the whole word. You may discover hidden strengths on which you can capitalize when you work with the student.

Comprehension.   Comprehension is affected by a number of factors, including language development, cognitive ability, background of experience, word recognition, and appropriate use of strategies. A good starting point for assessing comprehension processes is to look at the preparatory portion of each of the oral and silent selections. What background of information did the student bring to the selection?

If the student has answered traditional questions, analyze responses. What kinds of questions did the student answer best? What kinds of questions posed problems? Note in particular what the student's performance was on key questions and hypothesize what this implies about underlying cognitive processes. Literal questions, those whose answers are stated explicitly in the story, require selection and retention of details. Inferential questions and questions that require drawing a conclusion may require that a student integrate comprehension of details and background knowledge. Vocabulary questions hinge on word knowledge and, depending on the nature of the item, the ability to use context. Main-idea questions involve the ability to organize or categorize details and draw a conclusion as to what the main idea is. Instead of simply noting how many details, main idea, or inferential questions the students answered, take note of the basic comprehension processes that these responses suggest. Ask: How is the student processing printed information? What are the student's strengths? What are the student's weaknesses?

Listening.   Along with establishing the student's listening level, note his performance. Was he attentive during the reading of the selections? What kinds of questions was he able to answer with ease? What kinds of questions posed problems? How do listening and reading comprehension compare?

Supplementary Questions.   To get a more complete look at the student's use of comprehension strategies, supplement the administration of the IRI with key questions about the use of strategies. After administering the comprehension portion of the IRI, ask such questions as: What do you do before you read an article or story? (Students should be surveying the text, predicting, setting purposes.) What do you do as you read? What do you think about? (Students should be selecting important details, organizing and evaluating information, relating new information to old, creating mental images.) What do you do if there is a part that you don't understand? (Students should be rereading, or perhaps using graphic cues.) What do you do after you read? (Students should integrate new and old information, evaluate information, and think about how the new information might be applied or used.) To get a fuller look at a student's use of strategies, you may wish to supplement the administration of the IRI with an administration of a think-aloud, which is discussed in Chapter 5.

Shortcomings of IRIs

Commercial IRIs may overestimate the difficulty level of material that students can read. A possible consequence is that students may be placed in materials that are too difficult for them.

Despite the obvious utility, IRIs have their shortcomings. If they are not administered by trained professionals, or if the professional does not heed the standards, they may yield inflated levels (Enz, 1989). If selections are unappealing, require backgrounds that students do not possess, or contain questions that are ambiguous or which can be answered without reading the selection, then they may yield erroneous results (Lipson & Wixon, 1997). In many inventories the selections are very brief and so are easier to read than typical selections. Inventory selections for a particular grade may also be written at an easier level than the selections contained in basal readers and other materials designed for that grade. This is especially true of first- and second-grade selections (Gunning, 2000d). Many of these shortcomings can be overcome by trying out several inventories and selecting the one that you feel gives the best results. Also, as you become familiar with an inventory, you will learn its strengths and weaknesses, and can take steps to compensate. You may find that the sports selection on level four penalizes students who know little about sports but motivates reluctant readers who like sports to do their best and often reveals hidden strengths. In addition, levels yielded by an inventory should be thought of as estimates. Observe students' actual performance reading their texts and make adjustments as necessary.

MISCUE ANALYSIS

Miscue analysis, which is a way of examining and interpreting students' oral reading errors, is based on the premise that not all oral reading mistakes are equal or even negative. For instance, if a student substitutes the word *car* for *automobile* in the sentence, "The automobile

Miscues: oral reading responses that differ from the expected responses.

in the showroom window caught my eye," he is demonstrating that he is reading for meaning, because *car* is a synonym for *automobile*. The word **miscues** rather than *errors* is used "to avoid the negative connotation of errors (all miscues are not bad) and to avoid the implication that good reading does not contain miscues" (K. Goodman, 1969, p. 12).

As noted earlier, according to K. Goodman, the reader draws on three basic sources of information: graphophonic or phonics, syntactic, and semantic, which includes the sum total of the reader's background of knowledge. By comparing miscues to the original text, we can gain insight into the reader's processes. For instance, we can surmise whether the reader is using a balanced strategy or is overusing graphophonic strategies or fails to use semantic cues. The promise of miscue analysis is that it provides insight into the reading process (K. Goodman, 1974).

Adapted Miscue Analysis

Reading miscue analysis, originally designed for research purposes, can be time consuming. Therefore, you may want to use the simplified miscue analysis procedures described below. To save more time, it is recommended that the procedures be used in conjunction with the oral reading passages of an IRI. If miscues from an IRI are used, select only those miscues that occur at the independent and instructional levels and on any passages that occur between the instructional and frustration levels. Do not choose miscues from the frustration level. As material becomes too difficult, both good and poor readers tend to overuse graphophonics cues because they are not able to read enough words to use context.

On a sheet similar to the one in Figure 4.11, make a list of the student's miscues. List twenty-five, if you can. If there are fewer than twenty-five, list as many as are available. But remember that the fewer the miscues, the less dependable will be the conclusions that you can draw from the data. Next to each miscue, write the word that was misread—the actual text. Then compare the miscue with the text. Assess whether the miscue fits the sense of the selection. Ask: "Is the miscue meaningful? Does it fit the sense of the selection?" If so, put a check (✓) in the first column. If not, put a minus (–).

Next, determine whether the miscue is graphically similar. A miscue is graphically similar if at least half the graphic elements in the miscue are the same as those in the text. Note in the next two columns whether the beginning, middle, and end of the miscue are similar to the beginning, middle, and end of the text word. If the word has only two graphemes (*he, bee*), assess only the beginning and the end. A two-grapheme word is similar if one of the graphemes is the same. A three-grapheme (*goat, red*) word is similar if two of the three graphemes are the same.

After assessing a miscue for graphic similarity, note whether it was self-corrected. Self-corrected miscues do not count as errors on an IRI but provide valuable information about a student's reading processes, and so are included in the analysis. In the next column, note whether the miscue is a nonword. Production of nonwords is significant because it indicates a failure to read for meaning and suggests the overuse of decoding.

After filling in each column, tally the check marks and convert the total in each column to a percentage. Note which strategies the student is using. A high percentage of meaningful miscues and self-corrections indicate the use of context. A high percentage of

FIGURE 4.11   Miscue Analysis of a Fourth-Grader's Reading

Miscue	Text	Semantic Similarity	Graphic Similarity	DEGREE OF GRAPHIC SIMILARITY			Self-Corrections	Non-Words
				Beg.	Mid.	End		
1. be	beyond	—	—	✓	—	—	✓	
2. wild	wide	—	✓	✓	—	✓		
3. milk	Mike's	—	✓	✓	—	✓		
4. letter	leather	—	✓	✓	—	✓		
5. his	him	—	✓	✓	✓	—		
6. out	up	✓	—	—	—	—		
7. was	were	✓	—	✓	—	—		
8. title	titles	✓	✓	✓	✓	✓		
9. books	book	✓	✓	✓	✓	✓		
10. covers	covered	✓	✓	✓	✓	—		
11. full	fell	—	✓	✓	—	✓		
12. men	mean	—	✓	✓	—	✓		
13. talking	taking	—	✓	✓	—	✓	✓	
14. out	ought	—	✓	✓	—	✓		
15. de-shed	demolished	—	✓	✓	—	✓		✓
16. schap	scrap	—	✓	✓	—	✓		✓
17. wreaked	wrecked	—	✓	✓	—	✓		✓
18. being	be	✓	✓	✓		—		
19. collection	collectors	—	✓	✓	✓	—		
20. budding	building	—	✓	✓	—	✓		
21. a	one	✓	—	—	—	—		
22. Claude	Claudia	✓	✓	✓	✓	—		
23. five	fife	—	✓	✓	✓	—		
24. tree	three	—	✓	—	✓	✓	✓	
25. dis-tor	destroy	—	✓	✓	✓	—		✓
Totals		32%	84%				12%	16%

graphically similar words indicates the use of graphophonics strategies. Compare percentages to determine whether strategies are being used in balanced fashion. Is there an overreliance on meaning or sounding out? Does one strategy area seem to be weak?

If phonics is a problem area, examine the columns to see which elements are being used. Most poor readers fail to use the middles of words because they have difficulty with vowel correspondences. Some rely too much on initial consonants. Reexamine the miscues and see if you note any particular needs in phonics or structural elements.

Most important of all, as you analyze the data, set up tentative hypotheses to describe the current state of the student's reading development and some steps that might be taken to foster the student's growth in literacy. As you administer additional assessment measures or work with the student, be prepared to amplify and revise your hypotheses.

Examine the sample miscue analysis in Figure 4.11. This is an analysis of the reading performance of Madeline, a fourth-grader who was receiving special help because of comprehension problems. The percentages tell the story. Madeline's miscues were graphically similar 84 percent of the time but fit the context only 32 percent of the time. In addition, she self-corrected only 12 percent of her miscues. It is clear from even a quick survey of the results that Madeline is neglecting context clues. Note that she produced four nonwords, a further sign that she does not always read for meaning.

A program for Madeline would emphasize reading for meaning and monitoring one's reading so the student is constantly asking: "Does this sound right? Does this make sense? What word would fit here?" Madeline also needs to integrate the use of context with her deciphering skills. With help from context, she should have been able to figure out words such as *leather* and *wrecked*. Although she overrelies on sounding out, Madeline needs some instruction in the use of word-analysis skills. She does well with single-syllable words but has difficulty with multisyllabic words. Vocabulary knowledge may also be a factor. She may have missed *demolished* because it is not in her listening vocabulary.

Retrospective Miscue Analysis

In retrospective miscue analysis (RMA), the reader and teacher listen to a tape of the student's reading and discuss whether the miscue made sense, if it was corrected, and if it needed to be corrected. In their work with struggling readers in a detention facility, Moore and Aspegren (2001) found that students who used RMA improved their use of contextual clues and also improved their comprehension as indicated by richer and fuller retellings. The students also came to a better understanding of themselves as readers.

RUNNING RECORDS

A useful adaptation of the informal reading inventory and miscue analysis, **running records,** are a quick, easy assessment of a student's oral reading behavior. Like miscue analysis, running records are designed to reveal the processes the student is using to read text.

Running record: an oral reading assessment with a dual purpose: determine (1) whether the material being read is on the appropriate level, and (2) which strategies the reader uses to decode hard words.

When the performance is less than perfect, there are opportunities to record the work done by the child to get it right, to puzzle it out. This reveals something of the process by which the child monitors and corrects his own performance. When he encounters something new we can observe how he approaches the novel thing, and what he learns from the encounter (Clay, 1993a, pp. 21–22).

Unlike miscue analysis, running records are quick and easy to administer, and no special material is needed. Generally, the student is given material felt to be on her instructional level and asked to read orally. As with other assessment procedures, the purpose of the running record is explained to the student. As the student reads, the teacher records the student's performance, using the symbols presented in Figure 4.12.

FIGURE 4.12 Running Record Symbols

1. Words read correctly are marked with a ✓.
   John ran home.

   ✓　✓　✓ _____

2. Substitutions are written above the line.
   Pam was hungry.

   ✓　✓　*angry* _____
   　　　hungry

3. Self-corrections are marked "SC."
   Pam was hungry.

   ✓　✓　*angry* | *SC* _____
   　　　hungry

4. A dash is used to indicate no response.
   I will see her tomorrow.

   ✓　✓　✓　✓　— _____
   　　　　　　　tomorrow

5. A dash is used to indicate an insertion
   of a word. The dash is placed
   beneath the inserted word.
   A dog.

   ✓　*big*　✓ _____
   　—

6. A "T" is used to indicate that a child
   has been told a word.
   I will see her tomorrow.

   ✓　✓　✓　✓　*T* _____
   　　　　　　　tomorrow

7. The letter "A" indicates that the child
   has asked for help.
   A small mouse

   ✓　✓　*A* _____
   　　　mouse

8. At times, the student becomes so tangled by
   a misreading that it is suggested that she or
   he "Try That Again," which is coded with
   "TTA" and is counted as an error.
   The horse ran into the barn.

   　　　　　　　　　　　　TTA
   [✓ *house*　✓　✓　✓　*bus*]
   　horse　　　　　　　*barn*

9. A repetition is indicated with an "R." Although
   not counted as errors, repetitions are often part
   of an attempt to puzzle out a difficult item.
   The point to which the student returns in the
   repetition is indicated with an arrow.
   The horse ran into the barn.

   ✓　*house* | *SC*　✓　✓　✓ *bus* | *R*
   　horse　　　　　　　　*barn*

A blank sheet of paper may be used to record a student's performance on a running record. Two lines of words and symbols are used to indicate each line of text. For most reading behaviors, the student's performance is written on the top line. The bottom line is left blank; later, after the running record has been administered, it is filled in with the words from the text. A check mark is written on the top line to indicate words read correctly.

Although running records are typically recorded on a blank sheet of paper, they may be recorded on a photocopy of the text that the student is reading (Learning Media, 1991).

Substitutions are also written on the top line. If a student sounds out a word, that is indicated by using lowercase letters: *p-e-t*. Uppercase letters are used to indicate words that the student has spelled out (*L-I-O-N*). Insertions are indicated by writing the insertion above the line and a dash below it. Omissions are recorded by writing a dash above the line. The letters "SC" indicate a self-correction, "T," being told the word, and "A," an appeal for help. The letter "R" symbolizes a repetition with a line and arrow used to indicate the extent of the repetition.

In general, you should take a neutral stance when assessing oral reading. Be supportive and encouraging but do not give assistance, as it will invalidate your results. Although as a teacher your natural inclination is to provide instruction, when you are assessing you need to see what students can do on their own. Occasionally, however, students may make so many errors in a passage that they need to be redirected. This can be accomplished by asking them to "Try that again." If you resort to this intervention, which should be used sparingly, bracket the text in question and label it "TTA" for "try that again."

On some occasions, a student may be blocked by a key word that she or he is unable to decode but that is important to the sense and the flow of the passage. For instance, it might be the word *cheetah* in an informational piece about cheetahs. If he is unable to decode the word, the student will be blocked from using background knowledge to process the text. For this type of situation, you may tell the student the word, but code your assistance with a "T" to indicate "told word," and count it as an error.

As in the IRI, substitutions, omissions, insertions, appeals for help and being told a word are counted as errors. Self-corrections are not counted as mistakes. A repeated error, saying *there* for *this,* counts each time it occurs, but a proper noun, no matter how many times it is mispronounced, counts as only one error.

After scoring the running record, calculate the percentage of errors. Divide the number of errors by the number of words in the selection and subtract from 100 percent. Using a more lenient standard than the IRI, guidelines for running records are presented in Table 4.5. The instructional level for word recognition, for instance, is 90 to 94 percent, rather than the 95 to 98 percent required by IRI standards. Note that only word recognition is included in the standards. As an option, you might also calculate the self-correction rate and assess comprehension. The self-correction rate is the percentage of errors that the student self-corrects. To determine the self-correction rate, divide the number of self-corrections by the number of errors. An acceptable rate would be approximately 25 percent or 1/4. To check comprehension, have the student retell the story, or you might ask a series of questions as is done with the IRI.

TABLE 4.5   Running Record Standards

TEXT	WORD RECOGNITION
Easy	95–100%
Instructional	90–94%
Hard	80–89%

Analyzing Miscues in a Running Record

Just as with the informal reading inventory, it is important to code students' miscues and self-corrections when analyzing a running record. Note for each miscue and self-correction the cue or cues being used. To interpret the student's oral reading, Clay (1985) suggests that the teacher examine every error and ask, "Now what made him say that?" (p. 21). As you analyze miscues, ask yourself: "Is the student using meaning? Does the miscue make sense? Is the student using syntax? Does the miscue fit grammatically? Is the student using visual cues? Does the miscue fit the graphic construction of the word? Does it begin and/or end with the same sound? Does it have the same vowel sound?" Code the miscues, "M" to indicate use of meaning, "S" for syntax, and "V" for visual (phonics). Or students might be using two or even three strategies so you would code the miscue "MV, SV, SM," or "SVM." Also note whether the student engages in cross-checking, that is, using one type of cue to support another. For instance, a student reads "The dog were barking" for "The dogs were barking." Noting that *dog* does not fit with *were,* the student went back to the beginning of the sentence and saw that *dog* ends in an *s* and self-corrected by adding *s* to the noun. A syntactic cue alerted the student that she had misread, but a visual cue, the *s* at the end of *dogs,* was used to verify her correction so the item should be coded "SV."

Look for a pattern. One or two miscues in the meaning category would be inconclusive. In order to obtain a sufficient number of miscues on which to base a valid conclusion, students should read a passage of about 100 words or more. The passage should be challenging but not overwhelming. As the text becomes too difficult, students' skills disintegrate, so the examiner will get a false impression of their reading. At the maximum, students should be making no more than one error for every ten words read. For a thorough analysis of student's use of strategies, you might try a running record on easy, medium, and difficult selections, but not one in which the student's error rate exceeds 90 percent. You might also compare a student's performance on a new story with one that has been read previously. Note the running record displayed in Figure 4.13. What strategies does the student seem to be using?

> Using running record procedures, you focus on what the students can do because you make a check mark for each word read correctly.

As you become familiar with the running record technique, you can make more detailed analyses of strategies used. This is especially true in the visual category. Note, for instance, whether a student seems to sound out words letter by letter or is chunking sounds. Is the student breaking down a word such as *rat* into *r + a + t,* or is the student chunking sounds so that he analyzes it as *r + at.* Is he using the first letter and combining that with context, or is he attempting to use larger sections of the word?

> For more information on running records, see M. M. Clay, (1993a). Still another source of information about running records is Johnston (2000).

Note how effectively and efficiently strategies are being used. Ask: Are any strategies being overused or used inappropriately? Are meaning strategies used when visual strategies are called for or vice versa? To what extent are strategies being used in a balanced, integrated fashion?

As you assess, consider the student's stage of development. Over-attention to one or another cue source is very common for brief periods of time in students' development. It is quite common for students just getting the hang of letter–sound relationships to devote an overabundance of effort to them, even to the extent that meaning is lost as attention is exhausted by the process of decoding words.

FIGURE 4.13   Sample Running Record

The Elves and the Shoemaker

				CUES USED			
				E	S	E	SC
The shoemaker was very poor.	✓ T ✓ ✓ ✓ shoemaker			1		M S V	M S V
He had just enough leather	✓ ✓ ✓ every letter enough leather			2		M S Ⓥ M Ⓢ Ⓥ	M S V M S V
to make one more pair	✓ ✓ ✓ ✓ |poor pair			1		M S Ⓥ	M S V
of shoes.	✓ ✓					M S V	M S V
He cut out the leather	✓ ✓ ✓ ✓ letter leather			1		M Ⓢ Ⓥ	M S V
for a new pair of shoes,	✓ ✓ ✓ poor SC ✓ ✓ pair			1		M S Ⓥ	Ⓜ Ⓢ V
and then he went to bed.	✓ ✓ ✓ ✓ ✓ ✓					M S V	M S V
He was soon fast asleep.	✓ ✓ ✓ first SC ✓ ᴿ fast			1		M Ⓢ Ⓥ	Ⓜ S Ⓥ

Commercial Running Records

Based on the Reading Recovery model, the *Developmental Reading Assessment (DRA)* (Beaver, 1997) functions as a informal reading inventory/running record for students in grades 1 through 3. The DRA consists of twenty Benchmark Books ranging in difficulty level from beginning reading through grade 5. In addition to providing levels, the assessment is designed to provide information about students' use of strategies so that instructional goals can be established. From the second-grade level on, students are invited to select one that is on the appropriate level from among three or four booklets that range in difficulty. The student reads the first page orally and, if the book is on the appropriate level of challenge, reads the rest of the book silently and, later, retells the story.

A Spanish equivalent *(Evalucaion Del Desarrollo De LA Lectura)* is also available. A unique feature of the DRA is the "What's Next? Focus for Instruction," which is a checklist containing possible steps that the teacher might take to help the student improve in the areas assessed. Suggestions include fostering extended reading, modeling predicting and previewing, and building decoding skills.

The Developmental Reading Assessment (DRA) (Celebration Press) functions as an informal reading inventory/running record in grades 1 through 3. The Developmental Reading Assessment 4–8 (Celebration Press) combines oral responding with writing. The DRA 4–8 is an individually administered instrument, which consists of having students read passages orally and answering questions in writing. Teachers can administer the oral passages in as little as 5 to 10 minutes, but administration can take longer if students have difficulty with the passage or the passage is too easy. Students' written responses can take almost an hour. Students who have good comprehension but poor writing skills would be penalized by this assessment.

PLANNING INSTRUCTION BASED ON IRI, MISCUE ANALYSIS, OR RUNNING RECORDS RESULTS

In addition to indicating instructional levels, IRIs, running records, and miscue analysis provide a wealth of data that can be used to plan a reading program for students, especially if the results have been carefully analyzed and you have carefully observed the student during the administration of one of these instruments and, if possible, during class time. After assessing a student, note strengths and weaknesses to help you determine what kind of instruction might be most effective. Consider strategies that might be used before, during, or after reading. Both decoding and comprehension strategies should be planned, along with ideas for book selection and fostering reading. Take your cues from the students' performance. For instance, if the student failed to preview before reading, stress previewing activities. If the student overused context, focus on decoding strategies. Suggestions for developing the strategies and skills listed are developed in Chapters 7 through 14.

COMPARING IRI, MISCUE ANALYSIS, AND RUNNING RECORDS

All three devices, the IRI, miscue analysis, and running record, play a role in assessment. The IRI is the most versatile of the three, and the easiest to administer and interpret. The IRI is also the best of the three instruments for placing pupils and, when interpreted with care, can provide a wealth of information about the student's reading process.

The more specialized miscue analysis provides extensive information about the way in which the student processes printed language, information that can be used to plan a program of instruction. However, in an interview with Mellor and Simons (1991), K. Goodman warns that miscue analysis is of no value unless it is rooted in an understanding of its underpinnings.

The running record, a direct descendant of miscue analysis, is most valuable as an ongoing indicator of strategies that students are using and as a check on the suitability of materials they are reading. Easy to administer, the running record is a useful, practical instrument; but because of its focus on decoding, it works best with students who are operating on the earlier levels of reading.

The major benefit of the IRI, miscue analysis, and running record is that they provide a peek into students' reading processes. Using an IRI perspective whenever you examine students' reading performance, you are mentally estimating whether the material they are reading is on their independent, instructional, or frustration level. From a miscue analysis or running record perspective, you would be asking: What cues is the student using to process print? As Y. Goodman notes:

> Once you are aware of what is involved in miscue analysis, you are always listening with what I call a "miscue head"; you have the scheme of miscue analysis in your head. Sometimes, working with students whose strategies are not very efficient, you may need to do a very full, complete miscue analysis, but if kids are developing appropriately, it's not necessary to use a miscue inventory because you know that they're using the strategies in an appropriate way, and you just keep monitoring it yourself. (quoted in Mellor & Simons, 1991, p. 100)

IRI-BASED TESTS

A number of reading assessment instruments are based on the concept or embody some of the major features of an IRI. These include oral reading tests, group reading inventories, cloze and modified cloze tests, and word-opposites and word-list tests.

Oral Reading Tests

As their title suggests, oral reading tests do not include the assessment of silent reading. As such, they are quicker to administer, but they are less valid because they neglect silent reading, and less reliable because they assess the student on just one passage for each level instead of two. One advantage of oral reading tests such as the Gray Oral Reading Test (GORT) is that many of them are norm referenced and standardized so they may be used in situations that demand validated instruments, such as in pre- and posttesting for an experimental or government-funded program.

Word-List Tests

To save time, teachers and diagnosticians sometimes administer word-list tests instead of IRIs. As discussed earlier, a word-list test consists of a series of words in isolation that gradually increase in difficulty. There is a close correlation between the ability to pronounce words in isolation and overall reading (Manzo & Manzo, 1993). However, because they require only the ability to pronounce words, these tests neglect comprehension and may report misleading levels for students who are superior decoders but poor comprehenders or vice versa. In a comparison of commercial and teacher-made IRIs with the reading subtest of the WRAT (Wide Range Achievement Test), which requires only the pronouncing of isolated words, the WRAT yielded estimates that were one to two grade levels above the estimates yielded by IRIs (Bristow, Pikulski, & Pelosi, 1983). The two most popular word-list tests are as follows:

The Slosson Oral Reading Test (SORT) presents twenty words at each grade level from preprimer through grade 12. The student is required only to pronounce the words and does not have to know their meanings. Standardized and norm referenced, the Slosson yields grade equivalents, percentile ranks, and stanines.

Similar in format to the SORT, the Oral Reading Subtest of the WRAT also assesses reading through the pronunciation of isolated printed words. The WRAT is frequently administered by school psychologists.

Group Inventories

Because of the time involved, it may be impractical to administer individual IRIs. However, you may choose to administer a group reading inventory. Information about constructing and administering group reading inventories can be found in *Informal Reading Inventories* by Johnson, Kress, and Pikulski, (1987). Some reading series contain group reading inventories. There are also three standardized tests that function as group inventories: the Degrees of Reading Power, the Scholastic Reading Inventory, and STAR.

The major shortcoming of group inventories is that they assess only comprehension. They don't assess students' ability to read words. To obtain this information, you might use oral-words reading tests such as the Slosson Oral Reading Test (norm referenced) or the Word Reading Survey (informal) (see Figure 4.14). Taking only about 5 minutes to administer, these tests give a quick estimate of the students' reading abilities. Because comprehension is not assessed, results have to be interpreted with care. Administer the Word Reading Survey just as you would an IRI word lists test. The students's estimated instructional reading level is the highest level at which the student can read seven or eight words out of ten.

Degrees of Reading Power (DRP).   The Degrees of Reading Power is designed primarily to provide an instructional level. A modified cloze test, the DRP has no questions. Composed of a series of passages that gradually increase in difficulty, the DRP assesses overall reading ability by having students choose from among five options the one that best completes a portion of the passage from which words have been omitted. Each passage has nine deletions. As in a classical IRI, the passages gradually increase in difficulty

FIGURE 4.14   Word Reading Survey

1	2	3	4	5	6	7	8	9–12
I	please	branch	reason	escaped	absence	continuously	calculator	administrative
the	never	middle	distant	business	instinct	application	agriculture	spontaneous
we	hour	stronger	lonesome	continue	responsible	incredible	prohibited	molecule
go	climb	picture	silent	obedient	evaporate	maximum	legislation	ritual
hat	field	hunger	wrecked	entrance	convenience	environmental	translucent	recipient
help	spend	several	decided	applause	commercial	accumulate	astronomical	conscientious
coat	side	empty	certainly	government	necessary	geographical	optimistic	infectious
are	believe	since	favorite	celebration	recognition	triangular	narrate	beneficiary
how	happen	impossible	realized	microscope	vertical	pollutant	persuasive	attribution
work	suddenly	straight	solution	navigate	starvation	currency	obnoxious	paralysis

From Gunning, T. (2003). *Building literacy in the content areas.* Boston: Allyn & Bacon.

and encompass a wide range of difficulty so that slow, average, and superior readers' ability may be assessed adequately. Instead of yielding a grade-level score, the instrument provides a DRP score. The DRP score indicates what level of material the student should be able to read. A complementary readability formula is used to indicate the difficulty level of books in DRP units. The basic intent of the DRP is to match students with books that are on their levels (see pp. 538 and 540 for information on using DRP scores to match students with books on the appropriate level).

The Scholastic Reading Inventory.   The Scholastic Reading Inventory, which also uses a modified cloze procedure, yields lexile scores. Lexile units progress from 200 to 1700. Table 15.1 in Chapter 15 provides an estimated grade equivalent for both lexile and DRP scores. Scholastic's Inventories come in six levels, one for each grade. Very poor readers may need to be reassessed on a lower-level test than the one indicated for their grade level.

Computed Administered Placement Test

STAR.   A third instrument that functions as a placement device is STAR (Advantage Learning Systems), which is administered and scored by a computer and so does not require valuable teacher time. The STAR has a branching component; that is, the program is set so that if students do well they are given higher-level passages, but they are given lower-level passages if they do poorly. The STAR uses vocabulary and modified cloze.

MONITORING PROGRESS

Progress monitoring is a key element in every intervention. You need to collect data that indicates whether or not students are making reasonable progress. Progress monitoring measures can be informal. You might administer an IRI periodically, use running records, or end-of-unit assessments. When monitoring students' progress, don't rely on just one source of information. Work samples, checklists, and observations should be used to shed light on students' performance and track students' progress. Charts of books read also enable you to monitor student progress. If students are lagging behind in their book reading, you can intervene.

An economical but effective way to track students is to assess key skills. For emergent and very early readers, these might be alphabet knowledge or phonological awareness. Students are assessed on their ability to name the letters of the alphabet, provide initial sounds when shown illustrations, or segment spoken words into their separate sounds. For developing readers, it might be phonics or the ability to read words that become increasingly difficult. For more advanced readers, it might be comprehension of increasingly difficult passages. Because tests of word analysis are not readily available, these are included in the text and can be found in Appendix A.

Continuous Progress Monitoring

Continuous Progress Monitoring (CPM) is a systematized way of tracking students' progress. You create a chart for each child. You mark the end point and the beginning point

CPM can be used to mark a starting point, set a reasonable progress goal, and then track progress toward meeting that goal. If the student fails to make adequate progress, adjustments are made in the program.

Using Technology
DIBELS homepage can be accessed at http://dibels .uoregon.edu/. This web site provides extensive information about DIBELS along with downloads of the subtests.

and then decide about how much progress students have to make in order to reach the end point or the objective. Periodically—this could be quarterly, monthly, or even weekly—you note where students are so that you can judge whether they are on a trajectory for success. If not, you can then decide how you might revise their program so that they are on the road to success. If students aren't making progress, they can be provided with intervention programs or additional help. CPM can also be used to track the effectiveness of interventions so that more effective ones can be designed (National Center on Student Progress Monitoring, 2004).

Curriculum-based measurements are sometimes used to monitor progress. Curriculum-based measurements are quick probes that measure the same skill over and over again. DIBELS (Dynamic Indicators of Basic Early Literacy Skills), the most popular CBM, assesses alphabet knowledge, phonological awareness, vocabulary, and fluency. The tests are timed. Students read as many letters, nonsense syllables, or words in a passage as they can within one minute. DIBELS is designed to be given three times a year. However, it has many forms and could be given monthly or even weekly. If students are having serious difficulty with their reading, you might want to administer the CPM more frequently, perhaps even once a week. That way you can make necessary adjustments more quickly.

The emphasis in the DIBELs is on lower-level processes such as speed of pronouncing printed words. Higher-level comprehension and vocabulary skills are neglected. However, in the oral reading fluency assessment the system does offer a number of passages at each level that might be used to track growth. These might be given as directed or modified and administered in the same fashion as an IRI or running record. If given in both standard and modified fashion, the passages would yield reading rate scores, reading levels, and retelling scores. If a miscue analysis is administered, it would also yield qualitative data about students' use of word-analysis skills and strategies. If adapted, the DIBELS would be more time-consuming to administer but would yield more valuable data.

Using Technology
For additional information on CBM along with a web-based template for creating a progress monitoring graph, visit Intervention Central at http://www.interventioncentral.org/.

Constructing a CPM Assessment. To construct a CPM assessment, first determine the area to be assessed (Wright, 2004). Then obtain baseline data on the students' performance. To set performance goals, determine, as best you can, what the norms for the grade are or what a reasonable expectation for desirable progress might be. For many literacy skills, it will be the ability to read grade-level material with 70 percent comprehension. For fluency, it will be the ability to read at the speed at which the typical student reads. Median rates for oral and silent reading are listed in Table 4.3. Norms will help you determine whether the students you are assessing are reading at an average, above-average, or below-average rate. Your next step is to obtain or construct assessments. You can use selections from basals or trade books or you might use already prepared selections, such as DIBELS or you might use a series of high-frequency or orthographically "regular" words. For passages, record errors and percentage of accuracy along with rate (Wright, 2004).

After obtaining baseline data on your students, set a target. The target will depend on the amount of time available for the intervention and the rate of progress that you believe the student can make. For instance, if the student is a fourth-grader reading at 40 words a minute who was assessed at the beginning of the year, you might estimate that this student can improve his reading rate by 2 words a week. Over a period of thirty weeks, you estimate that the student can gain 60 words a minute in reading rate and so reach a target rate of 100 words a minute. Since the student is reading on a mid-third-grade level, you might also estimate that the student will gain a year and a half's growth. The probes that you use will begin at the mid-third-grade level but will continue up through the fourth-grade level.

Create a graph to show progress. Place reading rate on the vertical axis and time of year on the horizontal axis. Plot the student's beginning level and the ending level. Draw a line to show the student's expected progress. Then weekly or monthly plot the student's scores. If the student has a serious problem, monitor more frequently. With frequent monitoring, you are quicker to note when students are lagging behind and so need additional instruction, more review, or better materials. The progress monitoring chart in Figure 4.15 shows a second-grader's scores on the Word Pattern Survey. The student's beginning score was 20. A target score of 70 was set because that represents second-grade performance and seemed achievable if the student was given extra tutoring. If the student fails to make adequate progress, strengthen the intervention. You might provide more intensive instruction or additional practice, or you might try an approach that seems more in keeping with the student's learning style.

FIGURE 4.15   Continuous Progress on Word Pattern Survey

Name _____   Grade _____   School Year _____

	Sept	Oct	Nov	Dec	Jan	Feb	Mar	April	May	June
80										
70										
60										
50									✓	✓
40					✓	✓	✓			
30				✓						
20		✓	✓	✓						
10	✓									

MINICASE STUDY

Mike, the new boy in third grade, was something of a puzzle. Although he had been in the class for three weeks, he hadn't made any friends. The other children didn't pick on him, but they didn't seek him out for inclusion in their games.

Quiet and undemanding, Mike was easily overlooked in the hustle and bustle of the classroom. Although Mike did well with math calculations, he had difficulty with any activity that required reading or writing. Because he was struggling with his third-grade basal reader, the school's reading specialist gave Mike an IRI.

The source of Mike's reading difficulties soon became obvious. According to the word-list tests, Mike's ability to recognize words at sight or immediately was adequate up through the preprimer grade level. Although he did better with word recognition in context, Mike's instructional level turned out to be first grade. Actually, Mike was able to read second-grade material with 80 percent comprehension, but his word recognition was only 85 percent. Having a rich background of information, Mike was able to make maximum use of context to reconstruct the story.

Mike also had excellent listening comprehension. When selections were read to him, Mike was able to answer at least 75 percent of the comprehension questions up through the seventh-grade level. This suggested that Mike had highly developed oral language and cognitive abilities.

Based on the IRI results and the classroom teacher's observations, Mike was provided additional assistance with word-recognition skills. The program included systematic instruction in phonics and in the use of context clues, with heavy emphasis on applying those skills by reading lots of books and other materials on the appropriate level. Writing also became a prominent part of the program.

In order to build on Mike's excellent cognitive and oral language skills, he was encouraged to listen to books on tape and to view informational CD-ROM programs. Mike was also placed in a cooperative learning group composed of students who were especially friendly and outgoing. After a slow start, Mike made rapid progress.

SUMMARY

The widely used informal reading inventory consists of graded word lists and oral and silent passages that extend from the preprimer through the eighth- or twelfth-grade level. The IRI yields four levels: independent, instructional, frustration, and listening capacity. The independent level is the point at which the student's word recognition is 99 percent and comprehension is 90 percent. Figures for the instructional level are 95 percent word recognition and 75 percent comprehension. The frustration level is reached when word recognition slips to 90 percent or below, or comprehension is 50 percent or less. After a student has reached the frustration level, selections are read to her or him. The listening capacity, which provides an estimate of the level of material that a student could handle if she or he had the necessary processing skills, is the highest point at which the student can understand 75 percent of the material that is read to her or him.

When analyzed carefully, inventories are a rich source of information about a student's reading behavior. Miscue analysis, which can also be used with an IRI or a running record, builds on the concept of the IRI and yields information that opens a window to the strategies that the student is using and the reading process itself. In miscue analysis, an attempt is made to determine to what extent contextual and graphophonic cues are used.

Built on the concept of miscue analysis, the running record is an efficient way to assess students' oral reading. Used extensively in Reading Recovery, the main objectives of running records are to make sure students are reading on the appropriate level and to provide insights into the strategies they are using as they decode words.

A number of other tests are modeled on the format or purpose of the IRI. These include oral inventories, word-list tests, group inventories, and cloze tests.

Progress monitoring is a key element in every intervention. Progress monitoring may be formal or informal. One device used to monitor progress is curriculum-based measurement, which measures the same continuously developing skill, rather than a series of subskills, over and over again, often with brief probes.

APPLICATION ACTIVITIES

1. Compare two of the inventories mentioned in this chapter. Pay particular attention to the quality of the selections and questions. Which inventory seems to be better? Why?

2. Administer an informal reading inventory. Using the modified miscue analysis recommended in the chapter, analyze the inventory results. Based on this analysis, what strategies are used by the student you tested? What might be done to improve this student's reading?

3. Administer a running record to a student in a primary grade. Analyze the results and answer these questions: Was the text that you used on the appropriate level of difficulty? What strategies did the student seem to be using? What seemed to be the student's greatest strengths and weaknesses?

CHAPTER FIVE

ASSESSMENT OF READING AND WRITING PROCESSES

USING WHAT YOU KNOW

This chapter complements the previous one on informal reading inventories, miscue analyses, and running records. It continues to look into ways in which reading and writing problems are assessed and analyzed and to provide techniques for assessing critical areas, such as decoding and comprehension, in more depth. It also discusses ways of assessing such related areas as spelling and writing. In addition, it goes beyond formal and informal tests and looks at other ways of gathering information.

What do you know about assessing reading, writing, and spelling difficulties? In addition to knowing at what level the student is reading, what else would you wish to know if you were teaching a student with a reading difficulty? How would you go about gathering that data in order to get the most useful information in the shortest amount of time?

ANTICIPATION GUIDE

Read each of the following statements. Put a check under "Agree" or "Disagree" to show how you feel about each one. If you can, discuss your responses with classmates.

	AGREE	DISAGREE
1. The most useful way to gather information about reading and writing processes is through observation.	_____	_____
2. Decoding is the most important reading area to assess.	_____	_____
3. When testing decoding skills, it is better to use nonsense words than real words.	_____	_____
4. Having students retell a story is a better way to assess comprehension than asking them questions about the selection.	_____	_____
5. If a student has good comprehension, you do not need to test decoding or vocabulary skills.	_____	_____

READING PROCESSES: DECODING

Having insight into a student's decoding processes will help you decide on the most promising approaches to use when instructing the student and determine what kinds of instruction he or she might need. In the previous chapter, you learned how to interpret the results of word-list tests and word recognition in context on informal reading inventories and also how to interpret running records. Through interviews, observation, and occasional informal questions, you can verify findings and gain additional information about the student's decoding processes.

> By asking students to tell you how they figured out a hard word, you are helping them become more aware of their thought processes.

As students read aloud, note the processes that they are apparently using. Note, first of all, whether they seem to have strategies that are effective. Do they use context? When they decode a word, do they sound it out letter by letter *(B + e + n)*, or do they attempt to put large elements together *(B + en)*. Do they integrate context and sounding out? Do they try another pronunciation when the word they have reconstructed is not a real word or does not make sense?

For novice readers, note whether their errors or miscues are phonological. Reading *big* for *bag* or *run* for *ran* shows that students are beginning to use phonological skills. Reading *man* for *dad* would be a nonphonological representation. The point at which phonological errors outnumber nonphonological ones indicates that the student has attained functional phonological ability (Stuart & Colthheart, 1990).

After students have successfully decoded a difficult word, ask them how they figured out the word; or, as they are unsuccessfully attempting to decode a word, ask what you might do to help them. For students who have serious decoding and word-learning problems, you might use the interview presented in Figure 5.1. It is not necessary to ask all the questions listed. Simply ask those that seem most pertinent.

If you want to find out what phonic elements a student knows, administer the Word Patterns Survey in Appendix A. The Survey consists of eighty words that include most of

FIGURE 5.1   Word Identification Interview

Name of Student _____

Date _____

Age _____   Grade _____   Reading Level _____

1. How do you feel about reading?
2. Is reading hard?
3. What do you think makes reading hard?
4. What is the hardest thing for you to do in reading?
5. Why do you think that it's hard for you to learn words?
6. What is the hardest thing about learning words?
7. What would make it easier?
8. What do you do when you come across a hard word?
9. What makes it hard to figure out words?
10. What kinds of words are the hardest to learn?

the major word patterns found in single-syllable words. If students do poorly on the Word Patterns Survey, administer the Beginning Consonant Correspondences test, which can be found on the author's web site: http://thomasgunning.org/. The Consonant Correspondences test consists of presenting students with a letter and asking them to tell what sound that letter makes. If students do well on the Word Patterns Survey, administer the Syllable Survey in Appendix A to see how well they can decode multisyllabic words.

A number of tests use nonsense words to assess decoding. The rationale is that students will not have seen these items before and therefore will not be responding to them as words that they had memorized. However, as noted earlier, decoding involves using four processors: orthographic (letter), phonological (sound), meaning, and context. When students decode a word, there is a feedback step in which they note whether the item they have decoded is a real word. If the item being decoded is a nonword, then the semantic process cannot be brought into play. Because of this missing feedback step, decoding nonsense words is apparently more difficult than decoding real words (Cunningham et al., 1999). Walmsley (1978–1979) also found that pseudo-words and rare words were more difficult to read than real words and words in common use. Moustafa (1995) noted a tendency for students to misread pseudo-words as real words. In all three studies, nonsense words were harder to read than real words. Using nonsense words provides some information about a student's ability to decode words. However, because the test task is more difficult than the task the student will actually face when reading, tests using nonsense words underestimate students' ability to decode words and may indicate a problem where there is none.

Sometimes spelling is used to assess students' knowledge of phonics. To assess knowledge of beginning consonant correspondences, students may be asked to spell such words as *ball, cat,* and *dog.* They are given credit if they are able to spell the first letter of each of the words, because that is what is being assessed. The problem with using spelling is that it is not the same process as that used in reading. In reading, the student must retrieve sounds for letters. In spelling, the student retrieves letters for sounds. Spelling is generally more demanding than reading. However, in some rare cases a student can spell a word that he cannot read. Given the sounds of the words, he may be able to retrieve the letters that represent the sounds. Seeing the letters, however, he may not be able to retrieve the sounds.

Published Phonics Tests

Many of the diagnostic tests listed in Chapter 3 assess decoding skills. There are also a wide variety of informal phonics tests. However, many of these either use nonsense words or spelling and so are of doubtful validity. Two published tests that use real words to assess phonics are the Beginning Phonics Skills Test (Shefelbine & Newman, 2000a) and the Phonics subtest of the Diagnostic Assessments of Reading (Riverside).

READING PROCESSES: COMPREHENSION

Dependent on but more complex than decoding, comprehension is more difficult to assess. Poor comprehension can be caused by a number of factors, including inadequate background, lack of necessary concepts or vocabulary, poor use of strategies, lack of basic decoding skills or fluency, lack of attention or concentration, poorly developed thinking skills, or inadequate language development. In addition to these internal factors, comprehension difficulties can be caused or made worse if the materials students are reading are too difficult or poorly written, or if comprehension instruction is inadequate.

Comprehension can be assessed in a variety of ways. In addition to administering and analyzing an informal inventory, observing students in a discussion in class, noting students' performance on teacher-made comprehension tests or on end-of-book unit tests provides an overall sense of a student's ability to comprehend what has been read. Group standardized norm-referenced tests, such as the Metropolitan, Iowa, Gates-MacGinitie, California, GRADE, Stanford, or other similar tests, provide overall measures of comprehension. As noted in Chapter 3, guessing is a factor in most norm-referenced tests, because they generally have a multiple-choice format; in light of this, the tests are measures of recognition of information rather than recall or construction of meaning. A better test of comprehension is the informal reading inventory or a similar measure, because guessing does not play a role, and the students must construct their responses.

When assessing comprehension, make sure that students are reading material on their instructional level. If they are not able to read at least 95 percent of the words, comprehension will be hampered. Similarly, check reading rate. If their reading rate is very slow, if they are reading grade 3 material or above and are reading at less than eighty words a minute, their reading rate is too slow. If they are reading first- or second-grade material and their reading rate is less than fifty words a minute, their reading rate is too slow. In fact, their reading rate is so slow that it is probably interfering with comprehension (Monti & Cicchetti, 1996). To assess comprehension adequately, select a passage in which at least 95 percent of the words are known and the student can read the passage with a fair amount of fluency. Otherwise, a low comprehension score may be due to lack of fluency or inadequate word recognition.

Comprehension assessments have been criticized because they oversimplify the complexity of understanding texts. They focus on a few skills, and don't provide teachers with very much information that they might use to help struggling readers (RAND Reading Study Group, 2004). Along with other recommendations, the RAND Reading Study Group called for comprehension assessments that contain

> *Capacity to identify individual children as poor comprehenders.* An effective assessment system should be able to identify individual children as poor comprehenders, not only in terms of prerequisite skills such as fluency in word identification and decoding, but also in terms of cognitive deficits and gaps in relevant knowledge (background, domain specific, etc.) that might adversely affect reading and comprehension, even in children who have adequate word-level skills. It is also critically important that such a system be able to identify early any child who is apt to encounter difficulties in reading comprehension because of limited resources to carry out one or another operation involved in comprehension. (p. 746)

In addition to determining the status of struggling comprehenders, it is essential to find out what is causing their comprehension problems. Is it lack of background or vocabulary? Is it an attention problem? Are they failing to use strategies? Or are there some other factors at work?

RETELLING OF INFORMATIONAL PIECE

As noted when discussing informal reading inventories, an excellent way to assess comprehension is to arrange for a student to read a selection of the type typically read in class and then request a retelling. To use a retelling to probe comprehension of an expository piece, try the following procedures:

Step 1: Provide material. Provide a student with expository material on his level. The material should not be so hard that it is frustrating, but it should be challenging so that you can observe what strategies the student uses to read difficult materials.

Step 2: Observe student reading. Observe the student to see if he does anything before reading. Watch to see if he gets an overview of the selection, uses the title, headings, or illustrations, or simply dives right in. As the student reads, note whether he looks at illustrations, uses the glossary, or rereads.

Step 3: Have student retell. Have the student retell the selection. To elicit a retelling, start off with open-ended questions, so the student has complete freedom to formulate her responses. For an informational selection, ask such questions as: "Tell me in your own words as much information as you can from the selection that you just read." Or, "Tell me what you learned from the selection." If the student does not provide sufficient information, ask, "Can you tell me more about what you just read?" Note the quality and organization of the retelling. Is the student able to restate the main idea of the selection or provide a summary? Are most of the major points included in the retelling? Does the student seem to have an adequate understanding of the information? Does the student relate the information to her personal life or other information that she possesses?

Step 4: Ask follow-up questions. If the student was not able to retell the selection adequately, then ask follow-up or probing questions designed to assess how well the main idea and supporting details were comprehended. Ask: "What was this selection mostly about? What important details did the author include in the selection?" If the student has difficulty, provide assistance, but note what kinds of help are needed and how much help is required. Also try to gain insight into the student's reasoning processes so that you have a sense of what kind of help will be effective. If you are working with a group, you might have them write a summary of a brief expository piece.

Retelling

Questions mold responses into a certain form. Retellings provide insight into the processes students use to construct meaning and organize information.

A retelling of a piece of fiction would take a somewhat different format and be structured around the main elements of a story: setting, characters, plot, goal, story problem, and theme. After the student has read the selection, ask her to retell it. For a younger student you might say something like, "Pretend I have never heard this story. Tell it to me." If necessary, use prompting questions, such as the following:

Setting: Where did the story take place? When did it take place?
Characters: Who are the main characters in the story? What can you tell me about them?
Problem(s): What problem(s) did the main character have to solve?
Goal: What is the main character's goal? What is she trying to do?

After analyzing retellings, reflect on what this information tells you about students' reading–thinking–speaking processes and their ability to organize, integrate, and evaluate.

Plot: What are the main things that happened in the story?
Outcome: How was the story problem resolved?

When eliciting a retelling, tell students that they should pretend that they are telling the story to someone who has never heard it. Otherwise, they may assume that you know the story and omit important details because they believe you are familiar with the story events and characters (Benson & Cummins, 2000). In assessing a retelling, ask such questions as:

- Are major events or ideas highlighted?
- Are appropriate inferences made about characters and events?
- Is the retelling accurate?
- Is information from the selection integrated with the student's background of information?
- Does the student evaluate information?
- Does the student use the author's organizational pattern?
- What does the retelling reveal about the student's oral language development and presentation style?

You might try using five-finger retelling. As students retell, they make a fist and then release one finger for each story element in a piece of fiction or important idea in an information piece.

To make the assessment of a retelling more efficient and more accurate, list the main elements from an informational piece or story to check off as students mention them. You might use numbers to indicate the sequence of items included in the retelling. Put a "1" next to the plot element that the student mentioned first, a "2" next to the second element mentioned, and so forth. Code items with a *p* that were mentioned as a result of probing. (A sample retelling scoring sheet was presented in Figure 4.7.) Also note the overall completeness and quality of the retelling.

Because of difficulties with expressive language or other problems, some students may have difficulty retelling a story even though they fully comprehend it. Careful use of

A written retelling assesses students' ability to construct meaning from what they have read and organize that in written form. Poor readers are typically penalized when written responses are required (Simmons, 1990).

probes should help you discover to what extent students understood a piece. Using the levels-of-difficulty concept of assessment, start with a request for a retelling. If the student is unable to retell the selection, use probes. If the student has difficulty with probes, ask recognition-type questions in which the student only has to recognize or select the right answer: "At the end of the story, did the dog return to its first owner, find a new home, or join a pack of wild dogs?" The idea is to find out at what level the student understands the selection and in what format she or he is best able to respond. Students who have adequate comprehension but encounter difficulty in retelling should be taught how to retell a story. If it is not possible to obtain individual retellings, you might arrange for students to create written retellings.

Think-Alouds

A key component in comprehension is the appropriate use of background knowledge when reading text. Poor comprehenders may read in bottom-up fashion, focusing on decoding

> **Think-alouds:** readers or writers describe their thought processes as they read a selection or compose a piece.

rather than understanding the passage, or they may overrely on background knowledge and insert their own information for what the text actually conveys. One way to determine how students are processing text is to use a think-aloud. As its name suggests, a **think-aloud** involves having readers discuss what is going on in their minds as they read. This reveals the processes the reader uses. Think-alouds can be brief and informal. For instance, during a discussion of a selection, you might ask questions similar to the following:

- What was the selection mainly about?
- How did you get the main idea of the selection?
- What were you thinking about as you read the selection?
- What do you think will happen next in the selection? What makes you think so? (Gunning, 2000a)

To conduct a more formal think-aloud, use a selection that is 100 to 200 words in length. Mark off sections of the text where you want the students to stop and discuss their thought processes. This might be after each sentence or after brief segments of text. Ask questions designed to reveal students' thought processes. These might include the following:

Before reading: What do you think this selection might be about? What makes you think so?

During reading (after reading each marked-off segment): What was going on in your mind as you read the selection? What were you thinking about? Were there any parts that were hard to understand? What did you do when you came across parts that were hard to understand? Were there any hard words? What did you do when you came across hard words?

After reading (after reading entire selection): Tell me in your own words what this selection was about.

If students have not previously engaged in thinking aloud, they may be reluctant to do so or may tell you what they think you want to know. To get students used to the idea, model the process. Tell them to take time every once in a while to think about what they are doing. This will get them used to noticing their thinking and, if done before you conduct a think-aloud, it should enhance the richness of the think-aloud. Think-alouds are also more productive if the student feels secure and accepted (Johnston, 1992).

> Think-alouds can focus on aspects of reading. Wade (1990) created think-alouds to assess students' ability to predict, read flexibly, and integrate text information with background knowledge.

As students think aloud, record their responses word for word. Then analyze their responses. Note use of strategies listed below (these strategies are discussed in Chapter 11). Then come to conclusions about the effectiveness of the strategies that the student is using and the extent to which the student is monitoring for meaning.

- Made predictions
- Revised prediction or conclusion based on new information

- Considered information previously read
- Made inferences
- Drew conclusions
- Made judgments
- Visualized or created images
- Paraphrased
- Summarized
- Constructed questions
- Reasoned about reading
- Monitored for meaning
- Noted difficult words
- Noted confusing passages
- Reread difficult sections
- Used illustrations as an aid
- Used context or other decoding skills

If possible, think-alouds should be used with actual school texts. One advantage of using think-alouds with actual school texts is that this increases the validity of the procedure and also increases the possibility that the results can be used to plan a program of intervention (Myers & Lytle, 1986). Myers and Lytle have constructed think-alouds specifically for use with low-achieving readers. They use passages that are fifteen to twenty sentences in length and retype the passage so that each sentence is on a separate line. Sentences are uncovered one by one. After reading a sentence, students are asked to tell what they were thinking about or what event went through their minds as they were reading. Particular emphasis is placed on having the students tell what is going through their minds when they encounter difficult sentences, because it is at this point that insights into their way of processing difficult text are garnered.

Caroline, a fourth-grader, was referred to a university reading clinic because she was having difficulty comprehending what she read. Through administering a Think-Aloud Protocol Analysis, Myers and Lytle (1986) found that she used a number of strategies including paraphrasing, inferring, and elaborating on the text by adding information and visualizing. However, Caroline failed to monitor for meaning, with the result that she sometimes failed to comprehend difficult passages and was not aware of her lack of comprehension.

Building on Caroline's strengths, the teacher affirmed her use of strategies and overall comprehension, with the result that Caroline increased the use of her strategies and seemed more confident about her reading. She was also shown how to monitor her comprehension so she could take corrective action when she did not understand a passage. Strategies such as predicting and creating hypotheses about the reading were also demonstrated.

Based on their work with struggling readers, Monti and Cichetti (1996) found that they tend to have the following profile:

- Focus on decoding and pronunciation rather than meaning
- Rarely activate background knowledge before reading a text
- Fail to monitor or take stock of their comprehension
- Rarely raise questions about meaning during reading (p. 16)

Questionnaires and Interviews

Another way of getting information about reading processes is through questionnaires or interviews. Some questions that might be asked include the ones listed in the comprehension interview presented below. Of course, all these questions would not be asked in one sitting. First, you would determine which area or areas of comprehension you want to explore and then choose or compose questions designed to tap into these areas. The five italicized questions are the most open-ended. Encourage students to respond to these. If more information is desired, ask the probing questions listed under each italicized query.

> A good example of a well-designed questionnaire is The Elementary Reading Attitude Survey in the May 1990 issue of *The Reading Teacher.*

BEFORE READING

What do you do before you read?

Do you read the title and headings?

Do you look at the pictures?

Do you predict what the selection might be about?

Do you ask yourself what you know about the topic?

Do you plan how you are going to read the selection—fast, medium, or slow?

DURING READING

What do you do while you're reading?

Do you think about what you're reading?

Do you stop every once in a while and ask yourself what you've read so far?

Do you picture in your mind the people, events, and places that you are reading about?

Do you make up questions in your mind as you read?

Do you imagine that you are talking to the author as you read?

What do you do if the passage is confusing?

Do you read it again?

Do you just keep on reading?

Do you try to get help from photos or drawings?

What do you do if you run into a hard word?

Do you use context to try to figure it out?

Do you try to sound it out?

Do you use a dictionary or a glossary?

AFTER READING

After reading the selection, what do you do?

Do you think about what you've read?

Do you do something with the information that you've learned?

Do you compare what you've just learned from your reading with what you already know?

A less formal way to assess students' use of strategies is to include some of these questions in pre- and postreading discussions. An easy way to assess the difficulty students might be having with text—especially text that they're reading on their own—is to have students jot down the locations of words or passages that are posing problems or simply to place a sticky note under a difficult word or confusing passage (Gunning, 2000a).

Observations

To enhance the validity and reliability of observations, determine which behaviors you wish to observe, for how long, and under what conditions. Construct an observation checklist so you can focus on target behaviors. Schedule several observations.

Direct observation is also a valuable source of information about comprehension and other processes. Although observations may be made at any time, some situations provide especially rich sources of information. In a reading conference or a group discussion of a selection, note the level of comprehension, the degree of interest and involvement, the grasp of strategies, and the immediate needs of students. During a period of voluntary reading, observe the kinds of books students select to read and the interest with which they read. In cooperative groups, note how students interact. During writing workshop, note how students approach their writing and how they use their time. It is especially helpful to observe students as they encounter a difficult word or confusing passage: What strategies do they use? How successful are they at applying these strategies?

Since memory is fleeting and deceptive, it is helpful to keep a record of observations. A checklist is useful for recording observations because it helps us to focus on key areas. You might also compose anecdotal records.

Anecdotal Records

Anecdotal record: recording of an incident or behavior that provides information about a student.

An **anecdotal record** is the recording of an event that sheds some light on the student's reading/writing behavior. An anecdotal record may be very brief but should contain a summary portrayal of the event, the time, date, names of persons involved, and a description of the setting. In addition to providing information about comprehension and other reading processes, anecdotal records may be used to obtain data about interests, attitudes, strategy use, work habits, interaction with others, or other elements of the program. Records might be kept daily, weekly, or monthly. It is helpful to make records of the same type of behavior in a variety of situations. For instance, a student might achieve excellent comprehension under some circumstances but evidence poor comprehension under others. When making anecdotal records, include a number of observations so that you do not form a conclusion based on limited data. Also take note of successful efforts as well as unsuccessful ones. There is a tendency to stress the

Using Technology
Programs such as Learner Profile (Houghton Mifflin) can be used to record observations and other assessment data. Data can be loaded back and forth between a desktop or laptop computer and a handheld device.

failures and omit the successes, but this results in an inaccurate portrayal (Bush & Huebner, 1979).

In addition to being an accurate description of behavior, an anecdotal record should also describe the setting in sufficient detail "to give meaning to the event" (Thorndike & Hagen, 1977, p. 525). If the record includes an interpretation or evaluation of the event, that should be kept separate from the description of the event. The interpretation might be placed in parentheses. Presented in Figure 5.2 are a series of anecdotal records. What do they reveal about the student? How might this information be used in planning instruction for the student?

> A convenient way to take anecdotal records is to summarize the behavior on a sticky note and, later post it in a notebook set aside for keeping anecdotal records.

In order for anecdotal records to be used effectively, they should be reviewed periodically and summarized. Teachers should look for developmental trends or patterns. Strengths and weaknesses should be noted and used as a basis for gaining insight into the student's learning and planning instruction (Rhodes & Nathenson-Mejia, 1992).

FIGURE 5.2   Anecdotal Record

Student: _Marcia_   Date: _10-11_

During reading workshop, Marcia listened to Three Billy Goats Gruff on tape. I asked her if there were any books that she wanted to take home but she said no and said that all the books in the room had too many hard words. I told her that I had some new books that she might like because they didn't have so many hard words. I showed her Have You Seen My Cat?, The Good Bad Cat, Cat on the Mat, and Let's Get a Pet. After looking over the books, she chose Have You Seen My Cat?, which I share-read with her.

Student: _Marcia_   Date: _10-12_

Marcia rushed in this morning and claimed she could read Have You Seen My Cat? Relying heavily on pictures, she was able to retell the story. Marcia asked if she could take another book home and chose Cat on the Mat. I share-read it with her. I asked her to point to words as I read them, which she did.

Student: _Marcia_   Date: _10-14_

When Marcia returned Cat on the Mat, she said she would like to read it to me. She was able to read it, but continued to use pictures to help her. However, she was obviously using the print. She only used the pictures when she had difficulty with a word. She asked if she could take Let's Get a Pet home. She said that she was getting a pet and wanted to see if the book had any good ideas.

Background Knowledge

Because comprehension is a constructive process in which we build meaning based on what we know about a topic, background knowledge is a key component of comprehension. Background knowledge can be assessed informally through classroom discussions. A simple word-association task can also be used to assess background knowledge. Students are given a key word or phrase and told to write down as many words as they can think of that the key word brings to mind (Zakaluk, Samuels, & Taylor, 1986). If students are about to read about oil, gas, and coal, the keywords might be *fossil fuels.* For longer selections, those that are three to five pages in length, provide two or three key words. Students are given three minutes for each key word or phrase to write down as many words as they can think of. Responses are then tallied. Students are given one point for each reasonable association. For fossil fuels, students might be given one point for coal but no credit for wood.

The greater the number of reasonable associations, the greater is the likelihood that the student has a rich store of background knowledge. As a result of tryouts, students were given the following scores:

0–2 points: low prior knowledge
3–6 points: average prior knowledge
7+ points: high prior knowledge

A number of teaching techniques include brainstorming. The quality and quantity of students' responses can be used to assess students' prior knowledge. A technique known as PReP was designed specifically to assess background knowledge. Brainstorming techniques are discussed in Chapter 12.

ASSESSING STUDY SKILLS

Students are frequently required to go beyond comprehension. They are called upon to remember and/or apply what they have read. This entails studying. Lack of adequate study skills is a major reason for referring older students for corrective help. Study skills may be diagnosed through observation, interviews, questionnaires, and by subtests of standardized tests. One way to assess the effectiveness of study skills is to see how well students do on quizzes, tests, and assignments that require home preparation. If students are doing poorly, you might conduct an interview to determine the source(s) of the difficulty. Since effective studying involves habits, attitudes, and motivation as well as study strategies, your interview should cover all these areas. Because students may tend to tell you what they think you want to hear, ask questions in an open-ended fashion. Sample interview questions are presented in Figure 5.3.

To save time, pick from the group of questions in Figure 5.3 the ones that are most pertinent. Also feel free to add questions, and to reword questions to fit the needs of your students. If you are working with groups of students and do not have time for individual interviews,

> In preparation for assessing students' study skills, determine what skills and work habits students will need in order to complete assignments and prepare for tests.

> Study skills consist of strategies students might use to help them learn and retain information: outlining, note-taking, reading to retain information.

FIGURE 5.3   Study Strategies and Habits Interview

I'm going to ask you some questions about the way you study. Your answers will help me understand how you study, so that I should then be able to give you suggestions for improving the way you study.

1. Which subject is your hardest to study for?
2. What makes that subject hard for you to study?
3. Which subject is easiest to study for?
4. What makes that subject easy for you to study?
5. What do you do when you are studying and there is something that you don't understand?
6. What do you do to try to help you remember the material you have studied?
7. How do you know when you have studied enough?
8. What do you think could be done to improve your studying?
9. What kinds of tests do your teachers give?
10. What's the best way to study for a test in which you have to fill in blanks?
11. What's the best way to study for a multiple choice test?
12. What's the best way to study for an essay test?
13. Where do you study?
14. What supplies do you have in the place where you study?
15. When do you study?
16. Do you study at the same time each day?
17. How long do you study?
18. Do you listen to the radio or a CD or tape player or watch TV while you are studying?
19. Do you take breaks during your study periods? If so, when and for how long?
20. Do you ever study with other students? If so, do you find that helpful?
21. Which of your school books do you have to study the most? Pretend that you are studying for a quiz on a short section of this book. Show me how you would study for the quiz.

hold a group discussion on the topic. Often, students will be more open with their peers than they will be with their teachers. A checklist of study strategies is presented in Figure 5.4.

In order to see whether students possess study strategies, observe them as they use study strategies in the class. You might stage a study session in which they prepare for a test on a brief informational passage, study vocabulary words, memorize dates or facts, or study a list of spelling words. For more information on assessing and teaching study skills, see Chapter 12.

ASSESSING VOCABULARY KNOWLEDGE

Assessment of vocabulary may not require additional testing. You can get some sense of students' listening and speaking vocabularies by noting the kinds of words that they use in their conversations with you and the quality of their responses to questions. How does their use of words compare with the demands of the situation? Is it adequate? Is it more than adequate? Is it less than satisfactory? If the vocabulary portion of an individual intelligence test has been given, check to see how the student performed. If there still seems to be a need for vocabulary testing, you might administer the Peabody Picture Vocabulary Test or another

FIGURE 5.4   Checklist of Study Strategies

1. Does the student use SQ3R (see Chapter 12 for explanation of SQ3R) or some other study approach?	usually	sometimes	never
2. Does the student clarify difficult concepts or passages?	usually	sometimes	never
3. Does the student take notes on her or his reading?	usually	sometimes	never
4. Does the student outline important information?	usually	sometimes	never
5. Does the student organize the information into a semantic map or another type of graphic organizer?	usually	sometimes	never
6. Does the student rehearse the information by saying it over and over again, visualize the information, or use some other strategy for remembering it?	usually	sometimes	never
7. Does the student integrate material from notes and text?	usually	sometimes	never
8. Does the student self-test herself or himself on the material?	usually	sometimes	never
9. Does the student take adequate notes in class?	usually	sometimes	never
10. Do study efforts manifest themselves in the student's earning higher grades?	usually	sometimes	never

receptive test of vocabulary. Some diagnostic tests also assess oral vocabulary. The DARTTS (Riverside), Gates–McKillop–Horowitz (Harcourt), and the first two levels of the Stanford Diagnostic Reading Test (Harcourt) and all levels of the new Grade (AGS) standardized tests assess listening vocabulary. Also look at the informal reading inventory results. How did the students do with items that involved difficult vocabulary? How did they do on the word-list tests? Were they able to pronounce the difficult words? Did they mispronounce some of the multisyllabic words in such a way that suggests that these words are not part of their listening vocabulary?

Note students' reading vocabulary as well as their listening and speaking vocabularies. If students have difficulty with decoding, there may be a number of words in their listening or speaking vocabularies that they do not recognize in print. Most norm-referenced tests contain a reading vocabulary subtest. Generally, vocabulary and comprehension scores are comparable. When vocabulary is high, comprehension is high. When vocabulary is low, comprehension is low. A high-vocabulary, low-comprehension score suggests that the student has the potential to read better but is not using it. The cause could be an attention problem, weakness in strategy use, or difficulty seeing relationships among words or ideas. A low-vocabulary, high-comprehension score suggests that the student has a language difficulty or might still be learning English. Students who are still acquiring English may have a wealth of background to bring to a selection and so are able to answer a number of comprehension questions, but their English vocabulary is limited because they lack extended experience with the language.

ASSESSING WRITING

More than any other subject, writing lends itself to assessment. The product is there for all to see and can be analyzed in many different ways. However, although an analysis of the final product will yield important information, it is also important to examine the process of writing. Combining product and process information provides a fuller understanding of your students as writers, and so helps you to plan the best possible program for them. In your evaluation, include an assessment of the teaching techniques that you have used.

Role of Students

Include students as an integral part of the evaluation process. Evaluation starts with the assessment of needs and the setting of goals. Discuss with students their goals for the writing program and discover what their needs are. These goals and needs do not have to be expressed all at one time, and will change as the students' writing ability changes. An opportune time to discuss goals and needs is when examining the student's writing **portfolio,** a collection of pieces of the student's writing or other work samples, lists of books read, test results, and other data. While going over the portfolio with the student, you might ask such questions as:

> **Portfolio:** collection of pieces of writing or other work samples, lists of books read, test results, and other data.

- What kinds of writing do you do in school?
- What kinds of writing do you do outside of school?
- How do you feel about writing?
- What do you like about writing?
- What do you like best about writing?
- What is hard for you in writing?
- What kinds of writing would you like to learn to do better?

Assessment Techniques

Observations. Observe students as they write. How do they go about choosing topics? About what kinds of topics do they like to write? What kind of preplanning do they do? How much effort do they put into composing? What are their work habits like? How do they go about revising and editing?

As you hold conferences with students, note strengths and needs. Also note strengths and needs during discussions and sharing. Keep a chart similar to the one shown in Figure 5.5. Also keep anecdotal records on actions and events that offer special insight into the student as writer.

Journals. Students' journals provide insight into their writing. Journal entries may include a description of the topics they have explored, some of the struggles they have had

FIGURE 5.5   Writing Conference Notes

STUDENT	DATE	SUBJECT	STATUS	STRENGTHS	NEEDS	PLANS
Alberto	1/9	Letter to friend	2nd draft	Lots of information	Show interest in other person	Ask person questions
Georgia	1/9	New sister	1st draft	Warm tone	Weak beginning	Work on beginning
Latisha	1/9	Grandmother	planning	Interesting personality	Examples of courage & kindness	
Raphael		Editorial: rats				
Stephanie		Dancing Contest				

with their writing, and some of their achievements as writers. Of course, the journal itself might show how the students' writing has changed. Are the selections longer? Are they more specific and purposeful? Are they more alive?

Evaluating Pieces of Writing

How should a piece of writing be assessed? Should it be evaluated holistically, according to the general impression that it makes? Or, should it be analyzed element by element, including content, style, originality, and mechanics? As you will see in the next two sections, both holistic and analytic approaches have merit.

Holistic Scoring.   In **holistic scoring,** the teacher reacts to the piece as a whole, rather than being unduly influenced by any one of the major elements of writing. The piece is assessed in terms of its overall effectiveness: Does it work? Is it convincing or moving? To score a piece holistically, you might compare it to three anchor pieces that have already been rated as being good, fair, or poor. Determine which of the three pieces the composition being assessed is most like. You should also use a written **rubric** as a guide. A rubric is a descriptive set of guidelines used to assess the comparative quality of a piece of work.

Rubrics are more than just scoring guides. Rubrics have the power to improve instruction. They serve as "instructional illuminators." As Popham (2000) notes, "Appropriately designed rubrics can make an enormous contribution to instructional quality" (p. 292). Well-

> **Holistic scoring:** process of assessing compositions on the basis of an overall impression of the piece.

> **Rubric:** overall description of standards, often accompanied by example pieces, for assessing a composition or other assignments.

constructed rubrics specify the essential tasks that the students must complete or the key elements that must be included in order to produce an excellent piece of work. This helps both the teacher and student focus on key skills. In order to be effective, rubrics should be concise. They should contain only three to five evaluative criteria; otherwise, both student and teacher get lost in details. Second, each evaluative criterion must encompass a teachable skill. For instance, evaluative criteria for a persuasive piece might include use of examples and/or reasons to advance a position, effective organization, use of persuasive language, and correct use of mechanics. All of these criteria are teachable.

The first step in developing a rubric is to identify the key characteristics or traits of the performance or piece of work to be assessed. For a rubric on a written piece, the key traits might include content, style, organization, and mechanics. If possible, examine finished products to see what their major traits are. Write a definition of each trait. What exactly is covered by content, style, organization, and mechanics? Develop a scale for the characteristics. It is usually easiest to start with the top performance. If you have examples of students' work, sort them into piles—best, worst, and middle. Look over the best pieces and decide what makes them the best. Look at the poorest and decide where they are deficient. Write a description of the best and poorest performances. Then fill in the middle levels. For the middle levels, divide the pile into two, three, or four piles from best to worst, depending on how many levels you wish to have. However, the more levels you create, the more difficult it becomes to discriminate between adjacent levels. You may find that four levels suffice. Evaluate your rubric. Use the following checklist to assess your rubric:

- Does the rubric measure the key traits in the students' performance? Of the analytic scales, 6-trait writing is the most popular and is used in virtually every state and a number of countries around the world. The six traits include
  - *Ideas*—the author's message and the details that support it.
  - *Organization*—the way the ideas are arranged.
  - *Voice*—the unique expression of the author's ideas.
  - *Word choice*—aptness and originality of the words the author uses.
  - *Sentence fluency*—the way the sentences enable ideas to flow.
  - *Conventions*—correctness of mechanics (could include layout) (Spandel, 2005).
- Are differences in the levels clearly specified?
- Does the rubric clearly specify what students are required to do? The criteria need to be constructed in such a way that they are geared to the skill being taught and to the specific task used to assess mastery of the skill. For instance, a task to measure students' ability to write a story might have students describe a day in the life of a talking pencil. If evaluative criteria assess the students' ability to make an inanimate object seem like a person, then the criteria are too task specific. A more universal and more valuable criterion might be "creating believable characters." This criterion applies to all fictional writing and leads to teaching a skill that can be applied in many situations rather than teaching to a specific task. On the other side of the coin, evaluative criteria can be too general, so that it is difficult to use them to discriminate between an average and above-average performance (Popham, 2000).

> The foundation of a rubric is the set of evaluative criteria that will be used to assess students' work. The criteria should function as an instructional guide so that the teacher can use them to plan lessons and activities that will help the students master the skills being taught.

- Can the rubric be used as a learning guide by students?
- Can the rubric be used as an instructional guide by the teacher? (Chicago Public Schools, 2000)

Show the rubric to colleagues and discuss it with students and ask for feedback. Try out the rubric, revise it, and then use it. As you use the rubric with actual pieces of students' work, continue to revise it.

Rubrics are more effective if students participate in their construction. Through helping in the creation of the rubrics, students form a clearer idea of what is expected in the task being assessed. In one study with fourth-graders, students used cooperatively created rubrics to assess their writing (Boyle, 1996) and also took part in peer evaluation sessions in which the rubric was used. As a result of creating and using the rubric, students' writing of persuasive pieces showed significant improvement.

> **Analytic scoring:** process of scoring compositions through a consideration of major features of the pieces.

Analytic Scoring. While holistic scoring is an excellent device for gaining an overall impression of a piece of writing, **analytic scoring** helps the teacher note specific strengths and weaknesses in students' writing. When using analytic scoring with writers who have difficulties, it is best to focus on a few essential features that you have been emphasizing, rather than noting all the errors in a piece. This provides a framework for both you and the student and helps keep the struggling writer from becoming disheartened. Although important for assessment, the traits help students read their writing with a writer's eye so that they can develop an inner ear for what sounds right and what doesn't. Through a study of the traits they learn to hear their voices. Since it makes known the qualities of effective writing, the 6-trait rubric provides a guide for writing and revision. For the most valid results, multiple samples of students' writing should be assessed. A sample analytic scoring guide is presented in Table 5.1.

Using Portfolios to Assess Writing

Although portfolios are intended primarily as a way to assess writing, they can also be used to assess progress in reading and in content areas. Modeled on the artist's portfolio, a student's portfolio includes samples of the student's work. As such, it displays the breadth of her or his work and shows development over time. Portfolios serve the following purposes:

1. By assembling a portfolio and examining it periodically, students see how they have grown and developed as learners, what their strengths are, and in what areas they need to work. Portfolios help students to gain insight into themselves as learners and to be self-evaluative.

> To assess the processes a subject uses, include samples from various stages of a project. For writing, include prewriting sheets, first draft, revisions, and final copy.

2. Portfolios provide teachers with a means of assessing the growth of their students so they can plan activities to foster further growth. They also give teachers a deeper understanding of the way students develop as learners.

3. Portfolios can help parents better understand the development of their children's abilities. They can see areas in which their children

TABLE 5.1 Analytic Scoring Rubric for Expository Prose

	LEVEL 4	LEVEL 3	LEVEL 2	LEVEL 1
Ideas	Develops topic clearly and fully. Develops main point with interesting examples or ample detail.	Develops topic clearly. Uses several examples or details. Examples or details are adequate to develop topic but lack originality or interest.	Develops topic with examples or details. Does not use enough examples or details to be convincing. Some details may not pertain.	Topic is not clearly developed. Does not use details or examples to develop topic, or uses details or examples that are not related to the topic. Statement of topic may not be clear.
Organization	Shows a definite pattern of organization. All elements clearly relate to main topic and are in proper sequence. Uses signal words or other devices to show how ideas are related. Piece has a natural flow.	Shows a definite organizational pattern. Details are in proper sequence. Uses some signal words to indicate organization. Piece lacks a natural flow.	Shows some sense of organization. Details generally relate to main idea. However, may not show how details relate to each other and main idea. May include extraneous details. Fails to use signal words or other organizational devices.	Fails to develop a main idea. Details do not relate to main idea.
Voice	The writing is distinctive and bears the author's stamp. The reader is pulled into the piece.	The writing includes some attempts to make the piece come alive, but does not do so consistently.	The writing is serviceable but plain.	The writing is noticeably flat as though it were written in a monotone.
Word Choice	Word choice is appropriate and varied. Uses vivid words. Use of advanced vocabulary.	Word choice is appropriate and varied. Uses words typical of average student.	Word choice is generally appropriate but lacks variety and vividness.	Uses limited stock of words. Some words may be inappropriate.
Sentence Fluency	Uses varied sentence structure. Includes complex and compound as well as simple sentences. Sentences are grammatically correct.	Uses some complex sentences but primarily uses simple or compound sentences. Makes few sentence errors.	Uses simple sentences primarily. Sentences are brief and lack development or expansion. Includes run-ons and sentence fragments.	Sentences are brief and inadequately developed or may contain one or two very long sentences connected with a series of *ands*. Many sentence fragments and run-ons. Inadequate use of adjectives and adverbs.
Conventions	No or very few errors in use of basic mechanics.	Few errors in spelling, punctuation, or capitalization.	Shows a grasp of rudimentary mechanics: capitalization of first word in sentence and correct use of end punctuation but has several spelling, punctuation, or capitalization errors.	Numerous errors in rudimentary mechanics.

have grown and areas in which they need additional work. Seeing how their children have developed is more meaningful to them than numerical or letter grades.

Physically, portfolios can be folders, oversized manila envelopes, small boxes, or accordion folders. Contents can range from rough drafts through finished copies, to videotapes of an enactment of an original drama. In order to fulfill their promise, portfolios have to be carefully planned. There are five steps to using portfolios: establishing goals, deciding on indicator tasks, establishing standards, managing portfolios, and evaluating (Paris, 1993).

Steps to Using Portfolios

Step 1: Establishing Goals.   As with any evaluation, you must first establish goals. These will be overall goals for your program and individual goals or objectives for each student. If you have constructed an Individual Education Plan (IEP, required for students who are assigned special education services) or if students in your class have such plans, that could be one source from which objectives can be drawn.

> Poor writers do better on portfolio assessment than on test compositions. Portfolios provide them with the time they need to do their best work (Simmons, 1990).

Step 2: Deciding on Indicator Tasks.   Once you have decided on your goals, you must select indicator tasks that you will be able to use to tell whether the goal has been reached. For instance, if one goal is to increase students' ability to write expository prose, then samples of expository writing could be used as a basis for assessing that goal.

Step 3: Establishing Standards.   You need to decide what counts as adequate performance. For example, what qualities must an expository essay meet before you can say that a student's performance is adequate? As noted earlier, a type of standard frequently used in the assessment of writing and other literacy tasks is the rubric. Rubrics can be composed for individual literacy tasks and also for the portfolio as a whole.

Step 4: Managing Portfolios.   Portfolios can get out of hand. They can become a warehouse for a student's work, including virtually every piece of writing he or she has done. So that you and the student can focus on what is important, portfolios should include only key samples of work. These samples are chosen because they can be used as indicators of progress toward one or more of the goals that have been specified. Samples from the beginning, middle, and end of the instructional period should be included so that progress can be assessed. Encourage students to include samples of work done outside school in addition to work done in school. If students are composing poems, taking part in a play put on by a community group, reading books on their own, or engaging in other

> To examine a portfolio, have the student explain it to you. Ask: "What is your favorite piece of work?" Or "What does the portfolio show about your progress as a reader and writer?"

significant literacy activities outside school, this should be noted in their portfolios. Both teacher and student should agree on a system for deciding which pieces of writing or other work samples are to be included in the portfolio. The student may want to include only her or his best pieces. However, you may want to select a variety of pieces so that the portfolio reflects multiple aspects of the students' literacy development. You might adopt a system in which the student chooses a third of the pieces to be included, you choose a third, and you agree mutually on a third. Whichever system you choose, the student should be involved in the process.

> To build students' sense of self-efficacy, demonstrate how much they have improved. Examine pieces written at different times of the year that show a progression.

A checklist or summary sheet placed on the inside cover or other suitable spot should provide an overview of the contents of the portfolio. Students should also provide statements in which they list their goals, the activities undertaken to reach their goals, and a reflection on their progress in meeting their goals. Students might also note continuing needs and future goals and plans for meeting those needs and reaching those goals. Some teachers use the three-column chart presented in Figure 5.6 to help students reflect on their progress (Hansen, 1987). These charts were designed for writing folders but can be used in portfolios as well.

Step 5: Evaluating Portfolios. Both teacher and students evaluate the contents of the portfolio. Portfolio conferences should be held at least four times a year (Farr & Farr, 1990), but may be held more frequently, especially if you are working one-on-one or with small groups of low-achieving readers and writers. Portfolios should also be assessed with a rubric, so that teachers and students can use the assessment of the portfolio to plan instructional activities (Popham, 2000).

Assessing Writing Samples

If a portfolio is not available, the next best source of information is to obtain writing samples. Samples can be obtained in a number of ways. You might give students a drawing or photo and ask them to write a story about it. For young students, you might ask them to draw a picture of something they like to do, and then have them write a story about the picture. This prompt could also be adapted for use with older students. Omitting the drawing portion, you might ask them to tell about things they like to do, including hobbies and sports and other interests.

Another prompt that might be used with students of varying ages is to have them write a letter telling about themselves. Picture prompts might be used to elicit narrative

FIGURE 5.6   Portfolio Reflection

THINGS I CAN DO WELL	THINGS I'M WORKING ON	THINGS I PLAN TO LEARN
Write a letter	*Writing pieces that explain or tell how to do something*	*How to write interesting beginnings*
Capitalize, use periods and question marks		
	Spelling	*How to write better endings*
	Better sentences	

tales. Prompts from topics such as those listed below might elicit a variety of narratives, informational, or persuasive pieces:

> My Favorite Book
> The Most Important Person in My Life
> How to Make My Favorite Sandwich
> The Importance of Taking Care of Our Home, the Earth
> Why We Should or Should Not Build a Station in Space
> Why Cats Make Better Pets than Dogs (or vice versa)
> What I Would Do if I Had a Million Dollars
> If I Had Three Wishes

If possible, obtain two or three samples of students' writing. Also try to obtain pieces written for varied purposes. Students might be more proficient in narrative than in expository writing, for instance. When obtaining the samples, emphasize that students should do their best but should not worry about handwriting or spelling. Because you want to obtain an estimate of what the student can do independently, do not provide help with spelling or mechanics.

Analyze the writing samples along a variety of dimensions ranging from content (ideas) to handwriting. Start with the highest-level aspect—content—and work down to the lowest-level aspect—handwriting. Areas that might be assessed are listed as follows:

> *Ideas:* Does the piece have a main idea or theme? How well developed is the main idea or theme?
>
> *Organization:* How well organized is the piece? Do all the details support the main idea? Are the details in their proper order?
>
> *Voice:* How distinctive is the writing?
>
> *Fluency:* How well structured are the sentences? Are there a variety of sentences? Are the sentences well developed?
>
> *Word choice:* What is the quality of the word choice? Are a variety of words used? Are words used correctly? Is there an attempt to use language in an imaginative way?
>
> *Conventions:* Has correct style been used? Is the capitalization, punctuation, spelling, and usage correct?
>
> *Handwriting:* How legible is the handwriting? Is the handwriting readable? Are all the letters formed correctly? Is spacing between words and letters accurate?

As students write their sample pieces, observe their performance. Note whether they spend time planning or revising. Note, too, how much effort they put into their writing.

Commercial Tests of Writing

Commercial tests might also be used to assess writing achievement. One of the best-known writing tests is the Test of Written Language-3 (TOWL-3). The TOWL-3, which is designed for students from age seven through seventeen, assesses the mechanics of writing, sentence combining, spelling, and the ability to write a story. The Wechsler Individual Achievement Test, the Diagnostic Achievement Battery, the PIAT-R, and the KETA, which are discussed in Chapter 3, contain writing assessments. (For additional information on the assessment of writing, see Chapter 13.)

Exemplary Teaching: Using Portfolio Assessment

An especially rich source of information is the portfolio. At the Simpson-Waverly School portfolios are used to make sure that every child is making adequate progress. Although 95 percent of its students live in poverty, Simpson-Waverly's (Hartford) scores on the demanding Connecticut Mastery Test are equal to those of suburban schools. Strong leadership, a dedicated staff, a push for excellence, and help from community institutions, such as lectures provided by Trinity College professors to students in grades 4 through 6 help account for the school's success. However, a key factor is the school's monthly portfolio review process. Once a month the school's review team meets with each teacher. The review team consists of the principal, reading specialist, curriculum specialists, and other staff members. Team members examine test scores, quizzes, writing samples, logs of books read, and any other artifacts that might shed light on students' progress. The team plans the program and makes suggestions for teachers, with special attention being paid to students who are not making progress. Although individual folders are analyzed, sometimes common needs are noted, so suggestions are made for techniques or materials that might be used with a group or the whole class. Cumulatively, the review process reveals schoolwide needs and so the review sessions are used to plan professional development (Gottlieb, 2004, March 9, B1 & B70).

SPELLING

> Although poor spellers can be good readers, the reverse is almost never true. Poor readers are virtually always poor spellers.

Although sometimes thought of as a visual memory process, spelling is that and more. Spelling is deeply rooted in linguistic knowledge. "These linguistic foundations include knowledge and awareness of phonology, orthography, semantics, and morphology, as well as clear and concise mental orthographic images" (Apel, Masterson, & Niessen, 2004, p. 645). Research conducted by Henderson (1990) and his colleagues indicates that spelling develops in stages. By knowing what stage a student is in, the teacher can build on that knowledge and teach spelling and decoding more effectively. However, in order to understand the developmental stages of spelling, it is important to understand the basic principles of spelling development.

Spelling is based on three principles: alphabetic, pattern, and meaning (Henderson & Templeton, 1986; Templeton & Morris, 1999). On its most primitive level, English spelling is alphabetical. Letters represent sounds. In the word *hat,* for instance, the letters *h-a-t* represent the sounds /h/, /a/, /t/. However, there are a large number of words in which there is not a one-to-one relationship between a word's letters and sounds. The pattern principle means that spelling is frequently determined by the patterning of letters within a word. For instance, the *e* marker at the end of a word indicates that a vowel is long rather than short, as in *hat/hate.*

When students spell correctly words they have misread, they may not be analyzing the words in their reading. They may be creating a pronunciation on the basis of a quick look.

According to meaning, the third principle, words that have similar meanings have similar spellings, even if their pronunciations differ. For instance, the italicized letters in the following word pairs have different pronunciations even though the letter in each pair is the same: com*pe*te/com*pe*tition, ser*e*ne/ser*e*nity. Spellings have been kept the same to show the similarity in meanings. As students' knowledge of spelling develops, they learn first the alphabetic principle, then the pattern principle, and finally, the meaning principle. As their understanding of the spelling system changes, it becomes more conceptual and more abstract.

Stages of Spelling

Based on the alphabetic, pattern, and meaning principles, spelling development is divided into five broad stages: prephonemic, alphabetic (letter-name), word pattern (orthographic, within-word pattern), syllabic (syllable juncture), and morphemic (derivational constancy).

In the prephonemic stage, children have not grasped the alphabetic principle. They do not realize that letters represent sounds.

Prephonemic.   The student in this stage does not use the alphabetic principle. The student may create letter-like forms, use a mixture of letters and numbers, or just use letters. However, the letters do not represent speech sounds.

Spanish-speaking English learners apply their knowledge of Spanish pronunciations to their invented spellings (Nathenson-Mejia, 1989). For instance, /t/ and /th/ sounds in English are often pronounced /d/ by Spanish speakers, so a word like *the* would be spelled *de* or *di*. The word *little* might be spelled *ldl.*

Alphabetic.   The student's writing incorporates the alphabetic principle. In the earliest stages, a single letter may represent a whole word: *K* for *car.* Later, the student represents the first and last consonant sounds: *KR* for *car.* As the student progresses, she or he begins using vowels. Long vowels are spelled with letter names: *FET* for *feet, BOT* for *boat.* Fortunately for the inventive speller, the names of the long vowels incorporate their sounds. Because short-vowel sounds are not incorporated by a distinctive set of letters, many inventive spellers use the letter name for the long vowel that is formed in approximately the same place in the mouth as the short vowel they are attempting to spell. Say "ay," the long-vowel sound for *A,* and "eh," the short-vowel sound for *E,* and you will notice that both are very close in their place of articulation. Since short *e* is articulated in approximately the same place as long *a, bed* is often spelled as *bad* in the alphabetic stage. This is known as the "close to" tactic. Other "close to" spellings include spelling short *i* with an *E* (*BET* for *bit*), short *o* with an *I* (*TIP* for *top*), and short *u* with an *O* (*COT* for *cut*) (Read, 1971).

Students in the early alphabetic stage rely not only on how words sound but also on how the sounds feel as they are articulated. /v/ feels like /f/, so *love* is spelled *LF* (Bear, Invernizzi, Johnston, & Templeton, 1996).

For some consonant spellings, the spelling–sound connection is not apparent at first glance. For instance, *tr* is frequently spelled *ch,* as in *CHAN* for *train* and *dr* may be spelled *JR* as in *JROM* for *drum.* To see why these spellings are logical from the student's point of view, listen carefully as you say *chain* and *train.* Did you notice that the beginning sound of *train* is very similar to the beginning sound of *chain?* And if you say *chree,* it sounds like *tree* (Temple, Nathan, Temple, & Burris, 1993).

In similar fashion, the *d* in *dr* has a /j/ sound, so *drop* may be spelled *JRUP* or simply *JUP*. During this stage, spellings with nasal sounds such as *m* and *n* are omitted when they occur before a consonant, so that *bump* is spelled *BUP*. At the end of this stage, students begin to spell regular short-vowel words (*hat, pet*) correctly.

Word Pattern.   Through encountering standard spelling in books and other printed matter in their environment, children begin to notice certain spelling conventions: the consonant cluster at the beginning of *train* is spelled with *tr; e* at the end of a word is a marker for a long vowel (*rake*), and so forth. They begin to use visual features in addition to sound features to spell words and enter the orthographic word pattern stage. Their spelling is no longer based solely on sound. Although their spelling is not always correct (they may spell *rain* as *RANE*), it is becoming more standard and incorporates such features as final-*e* markers and double vowel letters to spell long-vowel sounds. A sign that students have entered this stage is the use of silent letters (Templeton & Morris, 1999). As students progress in this stage, they learn to spell most single-syllable words accurately. This is when students with poor orthographic processing ability begin to experience difficulty.

> The key understanding in the word pattern stage is that words are not spelled by sound alone. Orthographic patterns such as final *e* (*brave*) and digraphs (*plain*) must be incorporated.

Syllabic.   With additional experience with print, students begin encountering multisyllabic words. They have a firm grasp of single-syllable patterns, but now they must be able to apply their knowledge to multisyllabic words. Students learn when to double the final consonant or drop the final *e* when an ending such as *ing* is added (*dropping* or *taking*). They also learn about the double consonants in closed syllables, as in words like *battle,* which have syllables that end with a consonant (*bat-tle*), with the vowel usually being short. The word *battle* has a double consonant just as the word *batting* does. Students also learn about open syllables, which are syllables that end with a vowel: *ba-by,* with the vowel usually being long.

> The key characteristic of the syllabic (syllable juncture) stage is applying knowledge about spelling single-syllable words to spelling multisyllabic ones—for instance, knowing when to double the final consonant when adding inflectional endings (*hop + ing = hopping*).

Morphemic.   In this stage, students apply the principle of meaning. Words that have similar meanings have similar spellings even though pronunciations may be different. From a phonemic point of view, a better way to spell *sign* would be *SIN*. However, the *g* is retained to maintain the semantic connection among *sign, signal,* and *signature* (Venezky, 1965). Other examples include *compose/composition,* where the long *o* in the second syllable of *compose* becomes the short *o* in the second syllable of *composition,* and *contribute/contribution,* where the short *i* in the second syllable of *contribute* becomes a *schwa* in the second syllable of *contribution* (Ganske, 1993). A chart of the major stages of spelling can be found in Figure 5.7.

> In the (morphemic) derivational-constancy stage, focus is on meaningful elements rather than sound elements. Students break up words into prefixes, suffixes, and roots rather than syllables.

As the description of the phases of spelling suggests, learning to spell is a constructive, conceptual process. Through the experience of reading and writing words, students create hypotheses about the way words are spelled and then test them. In the alphabetic phase, for instance, students conceive of spelling as being a

FIGURE 5.7   Spelling Stages

Prephonemic *zq*	Use of random letters to spell words. Letters have no relation to sound.
Alphabetic *td, tod*	Letters represent sounds. In early stage, an initial or an initial and a final consonant may be used to represent the whole word. Later, long-vowel sounds are spelled with their letter names, and short-vowel sounds are spelled with the long-vowel letter formed closest to the place where the short vowel is articulated. At end of stage, regular short-vowel words are spelled correctly.
Word Pattern *tode, toad*	Realizes that there is a visual component to spelling. Thus, a final *e* or another vowel letter would be added to *tod* (toad) to signify the long *o* sound. At the end of this stage, most single-syllable words would be spelled correctly.
Syllabic *planning*	Students begin to form hypotheses about how to spell multisyllabic words. They become aware of dropping final *e* or doubling the final consonant when adding certain endings.
Morphemic *sign, signal*	Students realize that words with a common derivation and meaning have similar spellings even if the pronunciations vary.

> For a more thorough analysis of children's spelling, use the *Developmental Spelling Analysis* (Ganske, 2000) or the *Spelling Performance Evaluation for Language and Literacy (SPELL)*, a computer software assessment tool.

process of writing one letter for each sound. In the orthographic pattern phase, they realize that the pattern of a word, and not just its individual sounds, must be considered when the word is being spelled.

Because spelling is constructive, conceptual, and progresses through various phases, it is important that spelling instruction match students' level of word knowledge (Henderson & Templeton, 1986). Vowel markers or the doubling rule for consonant–vowel–consonant words (*hopped, planning*), for instance, is too difficult conceptually for students who are still grappling with alphabetic phonics. They might be able to memorize words like *hate* or *planned,* but they will not grasp the underlying principles that determine their spellings. Words should be presented that fit students' developmental levels so they can discover and make use of the underlying regularity of the language.

Determining the Stage of Spelling

Spelling stages can be assessed by observing the kinds of spellings students create. You can also give a screening test to assess students' spelling development. One such test is presented in Table 5.2. The Elementary Spelling Inventory (Bear & Barone, 1989) presents twenty-five words that gradually grow more difficult. Start with the easiest item for each student and continue testing until the words are obviously too difficult. Encourage students to spell the words as best they can. Before giving the test, explain its purpose. Tell students that you want to find out how they spell words. Explain that some of the words may be hard

TABLE 5.2 The Elementary Spelling Inventory (with Error Guide)

STAGE	EARLY ALPHABETIC	ALPHABETIC	WORD PATTERN	SYLLABIC	MORPHEMIC
1. bed	b bd	bad	bed		
2. ship	s sp shp	sep shep	sip ship		
3. drive	jrv drv	griv driv	drieve draive drive		
4. bump	b bp bmp	bop bomp bup	bump		
5. when	w yn wn	wan whan	wen when		
6. train	j t trn	jran chran tan tran	teran traen trane train		
7. closet	k cs kt clst	clast clost clozt	clozit closit		
8. chase	j jass cs	tas cas chas chass	case chais chase		
9. float	f vt ft flt	fot flot flott	flowt floaut flote float		
10. beaches	b bs bcs	bechs becis behis	bechise beches beeches beaches		

STAGE			WORD PATTERN	SYLLABIC	MORPHEMIC
11. preparing			preparng preypering	preparing preparing	
12. popping			popin poping	popping	
13. cattle			catl cadol	catel cattle cattel cattle	
14. caught			cot cote cout cought caught		
15. inspection			inspshn inspechin	inspecshum inspechion inspection	
16. puncture			pucshr pungchr puncker	punksher punture puncture	
17. cellar			salr selr celr seler	seller sellar celler cellar	
18. pleasure			plasr plager plejer pleser plesher	plesour plesure	pleasure
19. squirrel			scrl skwel skwerl	scqoril sqrarel squirle squirrel	
20. fortunate			forhnat frehnit foohinit	forchenut fochininte fortunet	fortunate

STAGE			WORD PATTERN	SYLLABIC	MORPHEMIC
21. confident				confedent confedint confedent conphident confiadent confedent confedent confedent confident	
22. civilize				sivils sevelies sivilice cifillazas sivelize sivalize civalise civilise civilize	
23. flexible				flecksibl flexobil fleckuble flecible flexeble flexibel flaxable flexabal flexable	flexible
24. opposition			opasion opasishan opozcison opishien opasitian	opasition oppasishion oppisition opposision opposition opposition	opposition
25. emphasize				infaside infacize emfesize emfisize imfasize ephacise empasize emphasise emphisize	emphasize

Note: The preliterate stage is not presented here.
Copyright 1989 from Donald Bear and Diane Barone, *Reading Psychology 10*(3), 1989, pp. 275–292. Reproduced by permission of Taylor & Francis, Inc., http://www.routledge-ny.com

Although it was designed for elementary school students, the *Elementary Spelling Inventory* can be used with older poor spellers who are operating on an elementary school level. See Bear, Invernizzi, Templeton, and Johnston (2004) for a variety of spelling inventories.

Graded lists of spelling words can be found in the *Classroom Reading Inventory* (Silvaroli & Wheelock, 2001) and *My Kid Can't Spell* (Gentry, 1997).

The Reading and Language Inventory (Bader, 1998) also contains a series of diagnostic spelling tests designed to show whether students can spell phonetically regular words, words with silent letters, words that follow key spelling patterns, and high-frequency words.

but they should do their best to spell as much of each word as they can. Say each word, use it in a sentence, and then say the word once more.

To estimate students' stage of development, carefully analyze their spelling in terms of the major characteristics of each stage. For instance, students are in the early alphabetic stage if they are representing whole words by one or two consonant letters, as long as those letters are intended to represent sounds. They are in the late alphabetic stage if they are beginning to represent long vowels with single letters containing the vowels' names. They are in the word pattern stage if they use two vowel letters or a final *e* to represent long-vowel sounds. Students might also show signs of being in two stages at the same time or moving back and forth between stages. An error guide designed to help you determine students' spelling stages is also presented in Table 5.2. Verify the results of the Elementary Spelling Inventory by analyzing spellings that appear in students' writing. Misspellings are better indicators of stages, because words spelled correctly might be ones that the student has memorized without understanding the basic principles behind the spellings. For instance, a student might memorize the spelling of *like* without realizing that the final *e* marks the *i* as being long (Schlagal, 1992).

Based on the student's spelling stage, you can estimate the student's spelling level. The alphabetic stage is kindergarten and first grade. Word pattern encompasses grades 1 and 2. The syllabic stage is equivalent to grade 3. Figure 5.8 shows the performance of a student on the Elementary Spelling Inventory. What stage is he in?

You can also give a placement test to assess students' spelling development. A Spelling Placement Assessment is presented in Table 5.3. The Spelling Placement Assessment has five levels. Level 1 consists of easy sight words and short-vowel patterns and is equivalent to grade 1 spelling. Level 2 consists of long-vowel patterns and is equivalent to grade 1 and 2 spelling. Level 3 is comprised of *r*-vowels and other vowels and is equivalent to grade 2 and 3 spelling. Level 4 consists of multisyllabic words and is equivalent to grade 3 and 4 spelling. Level 5 is equivalent to grade 5 spelling.

To administer the Spelling Placement Assessment, explain to students that you will be dictating some words. Tell them that some words may be hard to spell, but urge them to do their best. Tell them that even if they can't spell the whole word, they should spell as much as they can, even if it's just the first letter. Say each word in isolation, in a sentence, and then in isolation. Start with the first list, unless you know that the students are advanced spellers. Stop when students are missing most of the words in a list.

The criterion for an instructional level for spelling is lower than it is for reading. Students are instructional at the level at which they are able to spell between 50 and 75 percent of the words correctly (Temple, Nathan, Temple, & Burris, 1993). After you have obtained a student's level, analyze the results to determine which stage he is in and also his major needs. Students who are unable to spell any of the words are at the emergent stage. Those who are able at least to represent initial consonants are at the beginning

FIGURE 5.8   Student's Performance on Elementary Spelling Inventory

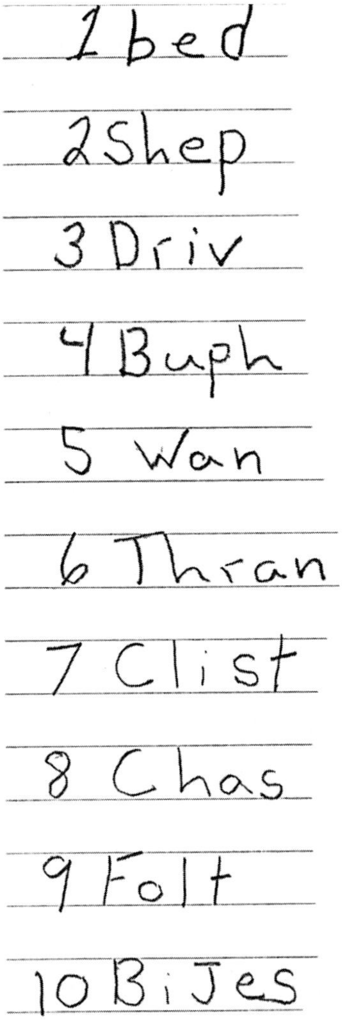

```
1 bed
2 Shep
3 Driv
4 Buph
5 Wan
6 Thran
7 Clist
8 Chas
9 Folt
10 BiJes
```

alphabetic stage. Those who are able to spell the short-vowel patterns are at the end of the alphabetic stage. Those who show some knowledge of long-vowel patterns, even if their spelling of long vowels is not always correct (they may spell *train* as *TRANE*) are in the word pattern stage. Those who are able to spell most single-syllable words correctly are at the end of the word pattern stage. Students who are able to spell multisyllabic words and who know when to drop final *e (hoping)* and when to double final consonants *(planning)* are in the multisyllabic stage. Spelling can lag behind reading. A student in the multisyllabic stage in reading may be in the word pattern stage in spelling.

TABLE 5.3   Spelling Placement Assessment

LEVEL 1	LEVEL 2	LEVEL 3	LEVEL 4	LEVEL 5
cat	name	star	happen	damage
the	what	guess	everyone	happiness
sad	like	care	metal	opposite
is	any	laugh	welcome	laughter
ten	read	school	between	adventure
one	want	build	holiday	passenger
not	show	farm	carried	caution
was	been	young	against	ninety
hop	train	turn	middle	voyage
you	from	touch	famous	president
get	sleep	should	question	magazine
were	put	learn	absent	government
sun	use	south	weather	probably
on	once	sure	yesterday	mention
sit	place	cloud	thousand	separate
do	are	month	success	continue
bug	night	join	student	description
give	your	knee	mountain	future
fish	smile	caught	neighbor	information
come	milk	warm	problem	electric

As noted earlier, it is important to know what stage students are in so instruction can be geared to their conceptual understanding of the spelling system. For instance, students in the early alphabetical stage do not have sufficient grasp of the spelling system to grapple with final-*e* words such as *hope* and *plane.* They still conceptualize spelling as being one letter for each sound. They might spell *eighty* as *A-T-E* (Gentry, 1997). They are not quite ready to spell by eye but will be ready to do so once they have encountered more final-*e*, long-vowel words in print.

> A spelling placement inventory, the McGuffey Qualitative Inventory of Word Knowledge, is available in Bear, Invernizzi, Templeton, and Johnston (2004).

Also note the kinds of words that students had difficulty with. Many words can be spelled auditorially. Words such as *hat, went,* and *stop* are spelled just the way they sound, so they can be spelled correctly if students sound them out. Some words, such as *mention* and *future,* require advanced knowledge of phonics before they can be spelled correctly. And some words, such as *money, do, where,* and *police,* are only partially spelled the way they sound and so require students to memorize them visually as well as auditorially. Still other words, such as *hopped* and *liked,* can be spelled correctly if students apply the correct rules for adding the past-tense marker. Knowledge of roots, suffixes, and prefixes helps students spell words like *finally* and *actually.* Realizing that *final* and *actual* are the base words, the student adds *ly* to create adverbs and so spells the words correctly as *finally* and *actually.* In the first two levels of the Spelling Placement Assessment, the odd-numbered words are highly predictable and lend themselves to auditory spelling. However, the even-numbered words have less predictable spellings and so require the use of visual memory or orthographic processes.

To further assess students' spelling, examine their written pieces and observe them during the writing process to see whether they are able to detect spelling errors. Note how they go about correcting their errors. Does the student try several spellings? Does the student use a reference, such as a word wall or dictionary? Also assess the student's ability to learn to spell. Choose five words from the ones that the student has misspelled and ask the student to study them because she or he will be tested on them. Note how the student goes about studying the words. Retest the student on the words and note how effective her or his study techniques were. Also use the Student Spelling Interview in Figure 5.9.

Although the two processes of spelling and reading differ somewhat—spelling requires producing letter sounds, reading requires only the recognition of letter sounds—students' spellings can offer insights into their knowledge of the phonics system, especially in the early stages. If a student is only using initial consonants to spell words, for instance, that suggests that he has not grasped vowels yet. This could be a good time to introduce short-vowel patterns, but teaching long-vowel patterns is probably beyond the student's level of development. In general, spelling lags a bit behind reading. For example, students can usually read long vowels before they can spell them (Stahl, Stahl, & McKenna, 1998).

In addition to determining what stage students are in and what level they are operating on, it is important to know what strategies they are using. Are they using sound, visual, structural (roots, prefixes, suffixes), rules, and meaning strategies in balanced fashion, or are they neglecting a particular area? Chapter 13 provides additional suggestions for assessing students' use of strategies to spell words and also students' strategies for studying spelling words.

Commercial Spelling Tests

In addition to the many informal tests of spelling, there are several commercially produced tests of spelling. The Test of Written Spelling-3 (Pro-Ed), which can be administered to students ages six to eighteen, uses fifty predictable words and fifty unpredictable words to assess

FIGURE 5.9 Student Spelling Interview

Name _____   Date _____

Grade _____   Age _____

1. What kinds of words are easy for you to spell?
2. What words are hard for you to spell?
3. What makes a word hard to spell?
4. How do you go about spelling a hard word?
5. How do you go about studying spelling words? Show me how you might study a list of words for a test.
6. How do you check to see if the words are spelled correctly in a story that you have written?
7. What might you do to become a better speller?

spelling. Norms are provided. A thorough assessment of spelling is presented in The Spelling Performance Evaluation for Language and Literacy (SPELL) (Laureate), a software program that analyzes students' misspellings and makes instructional recommendations. The Reading and Language Inventory (Bader, 1998) also contains a series of diagnostic spelling tests designed to show whether students can spell phonetically regular words, words with silent letters, words that follow key spelling rules, and high-frequency words. Ganske (2000) also has a very thorough spelling assessment in her book, *Word Journeys: Assessment-Guided Phonics, Spelling and Vocabulary Instruction.*

HANDWRITING

Although it is often associated with severe reading difficulty, poor handwriting tends to be neglected in remediation programs. Perhaps because there are higher-level skills that need remediating, handwriting is given a low priority. However, even though it is a low-level skill, deficient handwriting can lead to lowered grades and lowered self-concept. Written work that is not neat or legible is frequently downgraded and is also a constant reminder to the student and his teachers of his other learning difficulties.

Dysgraphia: a neurological condition in which the person loses the ability to write. A dysgraphic student can read but has difficulty writing.

Although it is a low-level skill, handwriting is a complex task (Bain, 1991). Poor handwriting may reflect poorly developed motor skills, deficient visual or kinesthetic memory, or **dysgraphia,** which is a disorder that occurs between the visual memory system and the motor system (Bain, 1991; Johnson & Myklebust, 1967).

Because handwriting disorders may be manifested in many ways, observation is an important element in their assessment. Different tasks make different demands, so the student should be observed in a variety of situations: copying from material on her desk, copying from material on the board, composing a piece, and—if older—taking notes. Posture, grip, handedness, quality of writing, and speed of writing should be noted; and the product of the student's writing should be compared with a standard piece of writing (Bain, 1991; Rowell, 1992). When appropriate, both manuscript and cursive writing should be compared.

Observation of handwriting is important because this can lead to a better understanding of a handwriting deficiency. Slowness in copying from the board, for instance, may be caused by inattention, by forming letters one at a time rather than as part of a group, or by poor visual memory that requires the student to check the board for each new letter that is being copied (Bain, 1991). It can even be caused by a lack of automatized skill in letter formation, so that the student has to look several times at a single letter that is being copied to see how it is formed.

Scales for assessing quality of handwriting are available from publishers who distribute handwriting material, such as Zaner Bloser (traditional) and Scott-Foresman (D'Nealian). Cursive writing may be assessed on the Handwriting Scale of the Test of Written Language (TOWL) (PRO-ED) or the Test of Legible Handwriting (TOLH) (PRO-ED). The TOLH assesses the readability of handwriting, manuscript or cursive, in grades 2 through 12.

SUMMARY

Both decoding and comprehension processes can be assessed in greater detail through the administration of formal and informal tests, observations, questionnaires, and think-alouds. The emphasis should be on gaining insights into the processes that the student is using. For comprehension, retellings generally yield more information than asking questions. However, if students have difficulty with retellings because of language processing or other problems, then answering questions is a more appropriate means of assessment. Study skills, a leading area for referrals for corrective help for older students, should also be assessed. Questionnaires, interviews, observations, and an analysis of content-area test results are among the methods that can be used to assess study skills.

Vocabulary knowledge can be assessed through observation and informal or formal tests. Writing can be assessed through examination of portfolios and obtaining and analyzing writing samples. A developmental spelling inventory can be administered and analyzed to estimate what stage students are in, and to see how this data might be used to plan spelling and word-analysis instruction. The effectiveness of the methods students use to study spelling words can be assessed by providing them the opportunity to study five words that they misspelled and then giving a retest. Diagnostic and placement spelling tests are also available. Handwriting can be assessed informally or with the aid of commercial scales.

APPLICATION ACTIVITIES

1. Focusing on one aspect of behavior, observe a student and compose an anecdotal record. If possible, observe the student on three different occasions. Then compare the records. What conclusions can you draw?

2. Examine one or more of the tests presented in this chapter. Note what the test is measuring and its format. Note, too, its strengths and weaknesses.

3. Read Marie Clay's *An Observation Survey of Early Literacy Achievement* (Portsmouth, NH: Heinemann, 1993a) and "Evaluating Beginning Readers" in Francine Johnston et al.'s *Book Buddies* (New York: Guilford, 1998). Which of the assessment measures described in these books do you feel are most useful? Why?

4. Pick a level and view the videos demonstrating PALS at http://pals.virginia.edu/PALS-Instruments/. What kinds of information are the assessment measures providing? How might you make use of this information?

CHAPTER SIX

ASSESSMENT OF COGNITIVE, SCHOOL, AND HOME FACTORS

USING WHAT YOU KNOW

This chapter looks at the ways of assessing students' cognitive and related capabilities: academic aptitude, memory, attention, and associative learning, which includes the crucial ability to learn printed words. Because of the interactive nature of assessment, personal, home, and school factors are also explored. What has been your experience with intelligence and other tests of cognitive abilities? What might be some effective ways to gather information about personal, home, and school factors as they affect reading and writing development?

ANTICIPATION GUIDE

Read each of the following statements. Put a check under "Agree" or "Disagree" to show how you feel about each one. If you can, discuss your responses with classmates.

	AGREE	DISAGREE
1. The main problem with intelligence tests is that no one knows exactly what intelligence is, so it cannot be measured accurately.	_____	_____
2. Tests of listening capacity are more equitable measures of ability to learn to read than are tests of intelligence.	_____	_____
3. Questionnaires and interviews lack validity because people are inclined to tell the questioners what they want to hear.	_____	_____
4. Parents are reliable sources of information about their children.	_____	_____
5. The best way to gain insight into students' reading problems is to talk to them.	_____	_____

ASSESSMENT OF CAPACITY

One of the most basic questions asked in an assessment is what is the student's aptitude for reading? Or, to ask the question in another way, given optimum development—one in which any reading deficiencies might be remedied—on what level should the student be reading? There are three main ways to assess a student's capacity: administer a test of academic aptitude, obtain the student's listening capacity, or provide the student with the opportunity to learn and see how she or he does.

> What we call intelligence is the result of interaction between heredity and environment. The richer the environment, the more fully our mental capabilities are developed (Carnegie Corporation, 1994).

Because of past misuse and misinterpretation, the testing of intelligence is highly controversial. Intelligence tests have been criticized for favoring some cultures over others, with the result that members of some groups were believed to obtain artificially low scores. Today's tests are constructed with greater sensitivity and are carefully screened for items that are culturally biased. However, as Carlson (1993) notes, "Unfortunately, the problem of cultural bias has not been solved. Even though questions with obvious cultural bias are no longer incorporated into intelligence tests, different experiences can lead to different test-taking strategies" (p. 448). In addition, intelligence tests reflect not only innate ability but also the opportunity to develop that ability. Students who come from environments where there is limited interaction with adults may have depressed scores. And, of course, motivation is a factor. Students who try harder often achieve more.

Intelligence tests sample those behaviors that the author of the test believes manifest cognitive ability. Different authors use different items, so the same student taking three different tests might get three different scores. In some instances, there might be significant differences among the scores. Most intelligence tests are really measures of academic aptitude. They measure such behaviors as vocabulary development, background information, ability to see likenesses and differences, ability to complete verbal and figural analogies, ability to complete patterns, and other similar abilities that are good predictors of school performance (Salvia & Ysseldyke, 1998). However, intelligence tests fail to include items that assess practical problem-solving abilities, which may be a good predictor of how one does in life.

Sternberg (1985) concludes that there are three main areas of intelligence: componential, experiential, and contextual. Componential intelligence includes verbal ability and deductive reasoning. Experiential intelligence refers to the ability to handle novel situations or problems and to learn from experience. Contextual intelligence refers to the ability to adapt to the environment, to find one's place in the environment, and to shape the environment to fit one's needs. Emphasizing practical intelligence, Sternberg (1996) believes that intelligence involves the ability to plan and organize one's life. Gardner (1999) theorizes that the mind reflects the structure of the brain and is composed of a number of separate structures or modules. Gardner (1983) also theorizes that intelligence encompasses seven areas: linguistic, musical, logical-mathematical, spatial, bodily-kinesthetic, intrapersonal, and interpersonal. To these Gardner (1999) recently added three new candidates: naturalist, spiritual, and existential.

Wechsler (1989) warns against equating intelligence with the score on tests he has devised or those others have created.

Professionals who use the WPPSI-R and other intelligence tests should avoid the temptation to equate test performance with general intelligence. Because scores on intelligence scales summarize performance on a particular sample of discrete tasks, the scores and their meanings are tied to specific test content. . . . (p. 10)

More importantly, the role of *nonintellective* factors, such as motivation and temperament, precludes the equating of test scores and intelligence. It is widely recognized that children with similar test scores may not cope equally well with similar environmental challenges for reasons unrelated to their cognitive abilities. Traits such as anxiety, persistence, enthusiasm, and impulse control are not directly assessed by current measures of intelligence, but strongly influence the child's overall effectiveness at meeting the world and its challenges. Thus the task of assessing a child's intelligence necessarily involves more than simply obtaining the child's intelligence test scores. (p. 2)

Resnick (1999) has challenged what she sees as an overemphasis on aptitude. As she explains,

What we learn is a function of both our aptitudes for particular kinds of learning and the effort we put forth. However, there is a widespread belief that ability determines, in large measure, what we learn in school. Therefore, students who score low on aptitude tests or seem to be lacking in ability are not provided with challenging learning. Basic skills are emphasized. As a result, not having been presented with tasks and materials that demand higher level thinking these students score low on tests of reasoning ability. However, research over the past quarter-century has demonstrated that, when taught, students can and do learn higher level thinking skills. In experimental programs and in practical school reforms, we are seeing that students who, over an extended period of time are treated *as if* they are intelligent, actually become so. If they are taught demanding content, and are expected to explain and find connections as well as memorize and repeat, they learn more and learn more quickly. They think of themselves as learners. (p. 1)

Because of these changes in students, Resnick defines intelligence as

. . . the habit of persistently trying to understand things and make them function better. Intelligence is working to figure things out, varying strategies until a workable solution is found. Intelligence is knowing what one does (and doesn't) know, seeking information and organizing that information so that it makes sense and can be remembered. In short, one's intelligence is the sum of one's *habits of mind.* (p. 4)

According to Resnick, students can literally be taught to be smarter. Teaching students to be smarter starts with the belief that well planned instruction combined with effort will improve students' ability to reason. The curriculum must be stated in clearly understood terms, must focus on covering key concepts in depth, and provide opportunities for reasoning with those concepts.

Bias against Poor Readers

Unfortunately, intelligence tests are biased against poor readers. Even on individual intelligence tests, which require no reading, low-achieving readers may be penalized. For instance, poor readers typically read less, which restricts their ability to learn new vocabulary and build a background of information—two areas that are frequently assessed by intelligence tests (Stanovich, 1991). As Siegel (1998) notes, "It is a logical paradox to use IQ scores with learning disabled children because most of these children are deficient in one or more of the component skills that are part of these IQ tests and, therefore, their scores on IQ tests will be an underestimate of their competence" (p. 128). In addition, because they are poor readers, they read less. Reading less, they pick up less knowledge and learn fewer vocabulary words, areas that are tapped by many IQ tests, so that as students get older their scores on IQ tests are likely to become even more depressed. In fact, Siegel found that the IQs of older disabled readers were lower. She also found that the ratio of poor readers to dyslexic students increased with age. Why might this be? If the IQ scores of older struggling readers decrease with age, then it is more difficult to detect a large discrepancy between ability and achievement.

IQ tests also discriminate against students from lower socioeconomic groups. IQ scores, at least in part, reflect the environment in which students grow up, so students from disadvantaged environments tend to score lower on IQ tests. Having lower IQ scores, students from lower socioeconomic groups who are struggling readers are less likely to meet the discrepancy cutoff scores and may be deprived of special services even though they may have severe reading problems.

Lowered Expectations

The most significant criticism of intelligence tests is that they may lead to an underestimation of what students can do. Carlson (1993) points out:

> Another problem with intelligence tests is that they may lead low-scoring students to underestimate themselves. Children who discover that they have scored poorly on an intelligence test are likely to suffer feelings of inferiority and may become disinclined to try to learn, believing that they cannot. (p. 448)

Low scores may also lead teachers to believe that students cannot achieve. Believing this to be so, they may not challenge them sufficiently or give them as rich a program as they should. Carlson (1993) comments, "Clearly, schools should use intelligence tests with great caution. If the results are not themselves used intelligently, such tests are actually harmful" (p. 418).

ROLE OF INTELLIGENCE TESTS

Despite their obvious limitations, intelligence tests can play an important role in the assessment of reading problems, if results are interpreted with awareness of the above limitations. For one thing, intelligence tests provide an indication of the extent of a student's reading difficulty. They may also indicate potential. Problem readers, especially if they have retreated into themselves, may be judged to have lesser cognitive ability. For instance, Frank, an eight-year-old reading on a first-grade level, spent much of his time daydreaming

Frank meets the functional and discrepancy definitions. He was reading below grade level and was unable to handle his school texts. Achievement was also below ability.

Interpreted with caution, individual intelligence tests can provide insights into students' cognitive functioning and so can be used to plan a more effective intervention.

Wechsler scales have a standard deviation of 15. Since 68 percent of the population have a score of 100 ± one standard deviation, this means that 68 percent have an IQ score of between 85 and 115. Some 14 percent have an IQ of between 115 and 130. Another 14 percent have scores that fall between 70 and 85. Only 2 percent have scores above 130 and 2 percent have scores below 70.

and seldom spoke in class. That, together with his unkempt appearance, created the impression of a student who had average or low-average ability. When he was tested, however, Frank achieved a score of 141, which put him in the top 1 percent of the population. Realizing that Frank was intellectually gifted and that his reading problem was even more severe than it had seemed, because Frank should have been reading far above grade level, Frank's teacher obtained additional services for him.

As a practical matter, most intelligence testing is conducted by a school psychologist. However, knowing the contents of the major intelligence tests and what scores on subtests signify will put you in a position to make use of that information. If it is analyzed carefully, information about a student's performance on specific elements of an intelligence test can shed light on the student's reading difficulty and can be used to plan a program of remediation.

Wechsler Scales

The most popular of the intelligence tests are the Wechsler scales, which define intelligence as the "overall capacity of an individual to understand and cope with the world around him" (Wechsler, 1974, p. 5). Although Wechsler conceived of intelligence as being global and multifaceted, he created scales that included a number of subtests. The WISC-III (Wechsler Intelligence Scale for Children III), which can only be administered by a qualified examiner, is designed for students between the ages of six and sixteen. In addition to obtaining an estimate of a student's overall functioning intelligence level, the teacher can, by examining performance on subtests, determine a student's relative strengths and weaknesses in several crucial areas. A description of each subtest and its relevance is presented as follows:

Verbal Scale

Information.   The subject is asked questions about general knowledge. This subtest measures how well the subject has interacted with the environment and recalls information. Because poor readers are cut off from one source of information, their scores may be somewhat depressed. A low score suggests a need to build a background of information.

Comprehension.   Students tell what they would do in a variety of social situations. The subtest measures common sense and social judgment. Since school-type learning is not being assessed, poor readers are not penalized.

Arithmetic.   This subtest requires students to solve arithmetic problems mentally. It measures ability to pay attention and concentrate and to remember the elements that need to be manipulated. Poor readers frequently do badly in those areas, and so they tend to do badly on this test.

Similarities. The subject tells how two items are alike. This subtest measures the ability to form concepts. Poor readers can do well on this subtest. A low score suggests the need to teach thinking skills such as noting similarities and differences and categorizing.

Vocabulary. Subjects are asked to define words. This subtest measures students' store of concepts and is generally considered to be the best assessment of academic aptitude. Older low-achieving readers may have somewhat depressed scores because they are cut off from one avenue of learning new words: reading. Scores should not be too depressed, however, because there are many ways, besides reading, of learning new words. A low score suggests a need to develop vocabulary.

Digit Span. Subjects say a series of numbers forwards and backwards. This subtest measures attention, concentration, and working memory. Because poor readers may have problems in one or all three of these areas, they tend to do poorly on this subtest.

Performance Scale

Picture Completion. The subject is asked to identify the missing part in a picture. The subtest measures attention to detail and the ability to differentiate between essential and nonessential elements. Poor readers are not penalized on this subtest.

Picture Arrangement. The youngest subjects assemble three-piece puzzles. Older subjects arrange cut-up pictures in order so that they tell a story. This subtest measures the ability to see sequential, cause–effect, and other relationships and the ability to plan. Poor readers can do well on this subtest.

Block Design. Students use blocks to reproduce a design. The subtest measures nonverbal concept formation and the ability to detect and construct relationships. Poor readers are not penalized on this subtest, but students with neurological impairments may do poorly.

Object Assembly. Subjects assemble puzzles. This subtest measures the ability to see visuo-spatial relationships. Poor readers can do well on this subtest.

Coding. The subject associates the code that goes with a symbol and writes it in a blank. The subtest measures the ability to make, remember, and record associations. Because some low-achieving readers have difficulty making associations, they may do poorly on this task.

Mazes (optional). Using a pencil, subjects make their way through a maze. This measures the ability to plan ahead. Poor readers are not penalized on this subtest.

Symbol Search (optional). Measures visual-motor speed and concentration.

With the addition of several new subtests, the WISC IV, which is designed to be more diagnostic, assesses cognitive processes in four areas: Verbal (Similarities, Vocabulary, Comprehension, Information, Word Reasoning), Perceptual (Block Design, Picture Concepts, Matrix Reasoning, Picture Completion, Word Reasoning), Working Memory (Digit Span, Letter-Number Sequence, Arithmetic), Processing Speed (Coding, Symbol Search, Cancellation). A number of the tests are optional.

> Students with learning problems may evidence "scatter." Often, they have some surprisingly low scores on some subtests but surprisingly high scores on others and miss easy items but get difficult items correct.

The WPPSI-III (Wechsler Preschool and Primary Scale of Intelligence—Third Edition) is designed for children between the ages of two years, six months and seven years, three months. Many of the tests are similar to those on the WISC IV.

As a group, poor readers tend to do poorly on the Arithmetic, Digit Span, Information, and Coding portions of the Wechsler scales. As Galvin (1981) notes, except for Information, the subtests have in common paying attention to, and keeping in memory, abstract symbols, an area in which poor readers often have difficulty.

Stanford-Binet

The *Stanford-Binet,* which is based on the earliest intelligence test, one devised for French children in 1905 by Albert Binet, was most recently revised in 1985 and assesses the following areas: verbal reasoning, comprehension, quantitative reasoning, abstract/visual reasoning, and short-term memory. The Stanford-Binet can only be given by a qualified examiner.

Peabody Picture Vocabulary Test

A test that can be administered by teachers and reading specialists is the Peabody Picture Vocabulary Test. Sometimes used as a test of verbal ability, the Peabody measures only one aspect of intelligence, receptive vocabulary (Salvia & Ysseldyke,

> The Peabody Picture Vocabulary Test is frequently used as a measure of receptive vocabulary rather than of academic ability.

1998). The Peabody measures vocabulary by having the student point to the picture that best represents the meaning of the word that the examiner says. Because it only requires the student to point to a picture, the Peabody works especially well with students who are shy or are withdrawn or who have difficulty expressing themselves. However, guessing is a factor. The authors of the Peabody warn, however, that the Peabody can only be used as a measure of verbal ability if the student is a native speaker of English (Dunn & Dunn, 1997). It may yield erroneous results if it is administered to those with hearing difficulties, non-native speakers of English, or to those who have in some other way not had a full opportunity to learn standard English vocabulary. Additional tests of cognitive ability are listed below.

Other Individual Tests of Cognitive Ability

Tests that are frequently used in the assessment of students with reading disabilities include the following.

> *Woodcock–Johnson Psychoeducational Battery—Revised.* Ages: 3–70+. Contains twenty-one cognitive and fourteen achievement subtests. Features several memory tests, language tests, and a reasoning subtest. Two cognitive subtests provide potentially useful information about associative word learning: Memory for Names, in which the student learns the names of nine space creatures, and Visual-Auditory Learning, in which the student learns to associate words with made-up symbols.

Detroit Tests of Learning Aptitude, Fourth Edition. Ages: 6–17. Includes ten subtests: Word Opposites (vocabulary), Design Sequences (visual sequential memory), Sentence Imitation (auditory memory), Reversed Letters (auditory memory), Story Construction (using a picture to tell a story), Design Reproduction (visual memory and motor skill, visual-motor integration), Basic Information, Symbolic Relations (nonverbal reasoning), Word Sequences (auditory memory), and Story Sequences.

Detroit Tests of Learning Aptitude—Primary, Second Edition (DTLA-P-2). Ages: 3–9. Subtests include: Articulation, Conceptual Matching, Design Reproduction, Digit Sequences, Draw-A-Person, Letter Sequences, Motor Directions, Object Sequences (memory), Oral Directions, Picture Fragments, Picture Identification, Sentence Imitation (auditory memory), and Symbolic Relations.

Kaufman Assessment Battery for Children. Ages: 2.6–12.6. Includes two scales. Sequential Processing Scale: Hand Movements (recall and reproduce hand movements), Number Recall, and Word Order (remember names of objects in order). Simultaneous Processing Scale: Magic Window (identify a picture on the basis of seeing parts of it), Face Recognition (recognize faces previously shown), Gestalt Closure (complete a drawing and name it), Triangles (copy designs), Matrix Analogies (complete visual analogies), Spatial Memory, and Photo Series (arrange photos to tell a story).

Group Intelligence Tests

Although they were once used widely, use of group intelligence tests has decreased. Group tests of intelligence are even more problematical than individual tests of intelligence. Guessing is a factor, and the tests are timed. In addition, because the tests are administered in group fashion, there is no one-on-one administration designed to elicit the student's best performance. Beyond the primary level, group intelligence tests may involve reading. Unless students can read the test items with relative ease, they may be unfairly penalized: scores will reflect both reading and intelligence. Neville (1965) states that valid performance on a group intelligence test requires at least a fourth-grade reading level.

The two most widely used group tests of academic aptitude are the Cognitive Abilities Test (Riverside) and the Otis–Lennon School Ability Test, Eighth Edition (Harcourt). The Cognitive Abilities Test measures abilities in three areas: Verbal, Quantitative, and Nonverbal. The Otis–Lennon School Ability Test measures verbal and nonverbal reasoning. Despite their shortcomings, the tests do provide an indication of the reasoning abilities of students and can be used as screening devices. In addition, the tests can indicate whether students are reading up to their ability. The Cognitive Abilities Test has been co-normed with the Iowa tests. The Otis–Lennon has been co-normed with the Stanford and the Metropolitan. If students take both an aptitude test and an achievement test, it is possible to note whether reading and other scores are commensurate with measured academic ability.

TESTS OF LISTENING

As noted in Chapter 3, tests of listening can also be used to estimate students' potential. Tests of listening from an informal reading inventory (IRI) can be used, or you might also use a test of listening vocabulary in which words and possible definitions are read to a student, and the student marks the correct definition. Tests of this type can be found on the GRADE, some levels of the Stanford Achievement Tests, the first two levels of the Stanford Diagnostic Reading Tests, and the WIAT-II. The DARTTS and other individual diagnostic reading tests feature listening vocabulary tests in which the student supplies definitions for target words that are read by the examiner. One advantage of a listening test is that it does not pigeonhole students into a particular cognitive category as an intelligence test does. Another measure of ability is to provide students with opportunities to learn under optimum conditions and see how they do.

TESTS OF LANGUAGE

Through tests such as the Peabody and the informal reading inventory, you can assess students' vocabulary and listening ability. Through analyzing students' responses, you can also informally assess the quality of their language. Students who seem to have speech or language problems should be referred for additional assessment. One assessment device that is widely used by speech and language professionals is the Clinical Evaluation of Language Fundamentals-3 (CELF-3). The CELF-3 is designed to assess students in grades K–12 in the areas of word meaning, sentence and word structure, and memory. Both expressive and receptive language are assessed (Semel, Wiig, & Secord, 1995). The Woodcock–Johnson–III Tests of Achievement (Woodcock & Mather, 2001) contain a number of tests of language. Test of Word Knowledge Test (TOWK) (Harcourt) evaluates receptive and expressive language. This is a lengthy but thorough test that would best be administered and interpreted by the speech-language specialist.

ASSESSMENT OF MEMORY

Working memory may be assessed through both verbal and nonverbal tests. Auditory working memory can also be assessed by having students repeat a series of words, sentences, or nonsense syllables or recall orally a series of pictured objects. A popular test for working memory is digit span, which involves having the student repeat a series of digits forward or in reverse. Digit Span is one subtest given on the Wechsler scales. The arithmetic subtest may also be used to assess working memory. To see if there is a possible memory problem, you should compare the student's scaled score on Digit Span with scores on the other subtests to see if there is a significant difference. Each of the subtests on the Wechsler yields a score between 1 and 20, with 10 being an average score. Because the scores are all on the same scale, they can be compared. However, only a difference of 3 points or more is considered to be significant. (Working memory is assessed on the WISC-IV with the subtests: Digit Span, Letter–Number Sequence, and Arithmetic.

If Wechsler scores are not available, you can administer digit-span items from the Slosson Intelligence Test. To use these items to assess auditory memory, simply regroup them and ask them, one series at a time, starting with the shortest span of numbers and working up to the highest number. Administer digits forward and then digits reversed. To analyze performance, note the highest age level at which the student is able to repeat all the digits. Memory for sentence items, which involves having the student repeat sentences, can also be regrouped, administered, and analyzed in the same way that digit-span items are. Other sources of auditory memory items include the following two subtests of the Detroit Tests of Learning Aptitude (American Guidance Service).

Sentence Imitation.   The student repeats sentences that gradually increase in length.

Word Sequences.   Students repeat a series of unrelated words. A useful comparison is to see whether students do better with Word Sequences or Sentence Imitation. Are they able to use the sense and structure of the sentences in Sentence Imitation to remember more words?

The Detroit Tests of Learning Aptitude also have a test of visual memory, which is described as follows:

Design Sequences.   In Design Sequences, students choose from a set of six cubes, each of which contains five shapes, the ones that are the same as those presented by the examiner before being hidden from view. Because the figures are nonsense shapes, the student will have difficulty using a name to help him remember the shapes, and so visual memory is tapped. A useful comparison is to contrast visual and verbal memory. Many low-achieving readers apparently have difficulty using a verbal code to help them store and/or retrieve items but do fine with visual memory.

Attention and concentration are also involved in memory tasks. Students may have difficulty with a memory task because they are tired, are feeling anxious, are distracted by a problem that is bothering them, or are having difficulty paying attention or concentrating for some other reason.

ASSOCIATIVE WORD LEARNING

> Difficulty learning the printed forms of words is the major hurdle faced by students who have the severest reading problems.

> To assess word-learning ability, also note the student's performance when new words are presented. How many words does he learn? How many does he retain?

Of all the diagnostic areas mentioned so far, associative word learning is probably the most crucial. Associative word-learning difficulty is the defining characteristic of a severe reading difficulty. All the students with the most serious reading problems that I have encountered have had a serious, dramatic unmistakable problem in this area.

Associative word learning can be diagnosed in many ways. One indication of a problem in this area is a noticeable difficulty learning letter names, letter sounds, and high-frequency words. Poor performance on the word-list tests of an IRI despite ample opportunity to learn is a possible sign of an associative word-learning problem. To assess a student's word-learning ability, use a procedure similar to that employed for dynamic testing. Gather seven words that are in the student's listening vocabulary but that she does not recognize in print (these might be seven words that she missed on the word-list test). After pretesting to make sure that the student cannot read the words, see how many presentations it takes before the student learns all seven words. In the first presentation, help the student to analyze each word. Go over any elements, such as initial consonant, vowels, or vowel patterns, that the student might use to help her to learn and remember the word. For instance, when presenting a word such as *hat,* help the student sound out the word, /h/-/a/-/t/, if the student knows these elements. If the student knows vowel patterns, point out the *h* and the *-at* pattern. If the student knows only consonants, point out the *h* and the *t.* For the remainder of the presentations, simply tell the student what the word is if she gets it wrong. If the student gets the word right, simply say, "Yes, the word is _____." Stop after ten presentations so that the student does not become too frustrated. Note the number of words known at the last presentation. Then retest thirty minutes later and then the next day to assess delayed recall. (A Word-Learning Test is presented in Appendix A.)

The average student will learn all seven words within ten trials and will be able to recognize most, if not all, the words thirty minutes later and the next day. Students with associative word-learning difficulties may learn only one or two words in ten trials; but even if they do learn them all in the ten trials, they will be able to recognize only one or two thirty minutes or a day later. These same students will also do poorly on other tests of associative learning that use visual symbols. Additional tests of associative learning can be found in the Woodcock–Johnson Cognitive Abilities Battery (Riverside) and are listed below.

> *Visual-Auditory Learning.* The student learns to associate familiar spoken words with symbols in the context of a story.
>
> *Memory for Names.* The student learns to associate nonsense names with drawings of space creatures.

WORD FINDING

Word-finding difficulties can be diagnosed by comparing performance on a test of receptive vocabulary, such as the Peabody or Receptive One-Word Picture Vocabulary Test (ROW-PVT) with a test such as the Boston Naming Test or The Expressive One-Word Picture Vocabulary Test (EOWPVT), both of which require the students to supply a word when shown an illustration, so that comparisons can be easily made between an individual's expressive and receptive language. Students with word-finding difficulty generally do better on receptive vocabulary tests because they do not have to retrieve words from memory. An instrument designed specially to diagnose word-retrieval difficulties is the Test of Word Finding (Riverside). Word finding can also be assessed through observation. A word-finding observation checklist is presented in Figure 6.1.

If you do suspect that a student has a word-finding difficulty, involve the speech therapist. The speech therapist will be in a better position to evaluate the student's overall language ability and might work with the student if the student turns out to have a word-finding difficulty. The speech therapist might also give you assistance as you plan a program for the student.

FIGURE 6.1   Observation Guide for Word-Finding Difficulties

1. Does the student use roundabout phrases (the thing that you cut with)?	rarely	sometimes	often
2. Does the student frequently answer "I don't know" when you believe that she or he does know the answer?	rarely	sometimes	often
3. Does the student frequently pause or use "ums" and "ahs" when speaking?	rarely	sometimes	often
4. Does the student frequently say "I forgot," "I can't remember" or "I can't think of the name of that"?	rarely	sometimes	often
5. Does the student frequently use vague or general words such as "that boy," "that place," or "something" rather than the specific name of the person, place, or object?	rarely	sometimes	often

ASSESSING THE INSTRUCTIONAL SITUATION

In an interactive assessment, the student's instructional situation should be observed and analyzed. At the Reading Clinic at Southern Connecticut State University, students who have severe reading problems may receive services for two or even three years. Having a different student teacher for each semester, they may have as many as six instructors over a period of three years. The amount of progress that students make varies from instructor to instructor, sometimes to a considerable degree. Although all the instructors are well trained and carefully supervised, each has a different personality and a unique style of interacting. Each has different preferences in materials and teaching approaches. When students have exceptional teachers, they generally make exceptional progress.

Although the teacher is the most important factor in determining the amount of progress, other essential elements include amount of instructional time, how the time is used, the degree to which the student is actively involved, the types of materials used, and the kinds of activities pursued. In general, time spent on actual reading—including voluntary reading—and writing has a greater payoff than time spent on worksheets. Students also benefit more when instruction is pegged to their interests and abilities. Overall, the instructional situation has an enormous impact on students' learning and is particularly crucial for low-achieving readers.

If you are assisting a student but are not his or her classroom teacher, explore the student's school situation as part of your assessment. Talk to the student's teachers. Get an overview of the major tasks that the student is expected to complete and an assessment of the student's performance. Ask about the student's strengths and weaknesses in key subject areas. Ask, too, about the student's work habits and overall adjustment. Invite the student's teacher(s) to provide any insight they might have about the student's difficulty with reading and writing. Find out what kinds of approaches have been used with the student. Balanced programs seem to work best. The student may have been in a program that did not provide systematic instruction in crucial skills or in a program where there were insufficient opportunities for application. In particular, try to find out what kinds of activities and materials work particularly well and which don't. Assessing the instructional setting is important. Knowledge of instructional presentation, feedback, class structure, and nature of materials used can provide insight into the kinds of interventions that might be planned (Shapiro, 1996). The assessment should consider classroom requirements. Students' ability to handle their texts and complete typical assignments should also be assessed. Analyzing the student's portfolio and completed class and homework assignments will shed light on the student's ability to function in the classroom and also the kinds of tasks he is required to complete and his proficiency in completing these tasks (Shapiro, 1996).

It is also helpful to get the student's perspective on the instructional setting. Does the student feel competent in the target area? Does the student understand typical directions? Does the student know what to do when he runs into difficulty? Are there areas or tasks, such as spelling, that pose particular problems?

Also observe the student on two or more occasions during reading and writing sessions. If the student attends subject-matter classes, observe those. If the student is receiving special help, arrange for a conference with the specialist and observe the student working with the specialist. In addition to conducting observations and interviews, evaluate the student's ability to cope with her or his school books (Broaddus & Bloodgood, 1994). Ask the student how textbooks are used. Does the student read them in class, or is he expected to read them independently at home? If they are read at home, is the student provided with some sort of study guide? If they are read in class, are they read silently or are they read aloud?

Have the student indicate what chapter the class is on in each text and then read a portion of the next chapter. In IRI test style, assess whether or not the texts are on the student's instructional level. Also note the strategies the student uses to comprehend the text.

> According to the Family Educational Rights and Privacy Act (20 U.S.C. & 1232g; 34 CFR Part 99), schools may not release information from school records without parental permission. When requesting information, it is advisable to obtain a written release from parents.

Assess the student's home assignments and how they are handled. Find out if the student makes a note of homework assignments so he knows what to do. If the student does, ask to see a record of the assignments. Note whether the record of the assignments is clear. If the student does not keep a record, ask the student how she or he remembers what the homework assignments are. Also find out whether the student completes assignments on a regular basis (Meltzer, 1993).

School records can be a valuable source of information, especially if the student has been tested extensively, or if the school keeps a portfolio. If you are not working in the student's school, you need to get written parental permission to examine records. All information should be kept confidential. Pertinent information includes the following.

Attendance.   Spotty attendance can interfere with learning.

Retentions.   Students who spent a year in a transition class or who were retained in first-grade or another grade may have a more serious problem than those who were not, because they have had an additional year of schooling.

Grades.   Look at overall performance and areas of strength and weakness.

Performance on achievement and aptitude tests.   Look at all areas, not just reading and writing. Sometimes a student will show strengths in areas such as math or art, where reading and writing are not as important.

Special help given.   If the student has been given help and is still having difficulty, it may indicate a more serious problem exists.

Transfers.   Moving from school to school can cause gaps in students' learning.

CASE HISTORY

> When obtaining a case history, interview both parents together, if possible. Maintain a nonjudgmental, professional attitude.

In order to get a fuller understanding of the student's background, it is important to obtain a case history from the parents or other primary caregivers. A case history will provide a backdrop for interpreting test results and other data. The focus of the history is on obtaining data about the biological and environmental factors that affect the student's physical, emotional, social, and cognitive development (Abrams, 1988). To obtain needed information, the following six areas should be explored:

1. Family constellation and student's role within the family.
2. History of the mother's pregnancy, and her child's birth and infancy.
3. Developmental milestones, such as the age at which the student sat up, crawled, and walked, with special emphasis on language development. Major developmental milestones are listed in Table 6.1. The sequence of these milestones is the same for all children. Children coo and babble and then say single words before they speak in sentences. However, there is enormous variation within each stage. For instance, although most children speak in two-word phrases or sentences by about the age of two, some normal children may not do so until they are three or four (Lenneberg,

TABLE 6.1   Developmental Milestones

Lifts head	2 months
Coos	4 months
Babbles	6–9 months
Sits without support	6 months
Stands alone	11 months
Walks	12 months
Says one or more words	12 months
Scribbles randomly	18 months
Speaks in two-word sentences	24 months
Speaks in three-word sentences	36 months
Makes word-like scribbles	36 months
Writes letters but letters do not represent sounds	48–60 months
May attempt invented spelling in which letters represent sounds	48–72 months

cited in Stewig & Nordberg, 1995). A delay in reaching developmental milestones may not be significant in and of itself. However, a pattern of late development takes on more significance, especially when accompanied by other indicators of slow development and learning problems.

4. Medical and psychological history, with emphasis on factors that might influence reading and writing development.
5. School history with emphasis on elements that might have an impact on reading and writing development (Abrams, 1988).
6. Personal adjustment.

> If parents express feelings of guilt about their children's learning problems, explain that they should not blame themselves but should focus on working to improve their children's reading and writing.

A case history should be obtained from both parents or the student's primary caregivers. The interview should be held in a relaxed, private setting. Take a few minutes to put the parents at ease and also explain the purpose of the interview: that you wish to obtain information that will give you a total picture of their child so that you can reach a fuller understanding of their child's reading and/or writing difficulty. Explain that it is important for you to gain an understanding of the problem from their perspective. In order to obtain a maximum amount of information, questions should be asked in open-ended fashion. Sample questions are listed in the following. Some questions touch on sensitive areas. Be sensitive to parents' reaction. Adapt questions to fit your particular situation.

FAMILY FACTORS
Can you tell me about your family? Who lives in your home? What are the names and ages of the other children? Have any of your other children had problems in school? Did you or your spouse have any difficulty in school?

PREGNANCY
How would you describe your pregnancy? Did you experience any illnesses during your pregnancy? Did you take any medications? How would you describe the birth? Did you have any difficulties or complications? Was the baby full term or did the baby come early? (37 weeks is considered full term.) How much did your child weigh? (5.5 pounds is considered full-term weight.)

EARLY YEARS AND OVERALL HEALTH
What was _____ like as an infant? Was _____ easy or difficult to care for? What kinds of childhood illnesses did _____ have? Has _____ ever had her/his eyesight or hearing checked? Did she/he have any high fevers? Did _____ ever have any convulsions? Were there any head injuries? Did _____ ever lose consciousness? How would you describe _____ health now? Is _____ on any medication now? How much sleep does _____ get each night? Does she/he have any difficulty sleeping? How would you describe her/his appetite? Does she/he eat most foods? Does she/he eat breakfast? Has _____ ever been diagnosed as being hyperactive or having an attention deficit disorder?

> Parents can provide valuable insights into their child's attitude toward school, response to different kinds of instruction, and self-feelings as a learner.

DEVELOPMENTAL MILESTONES

Did you keep any records telling when _____ talked or walked? At what age did _____ sit up? At what age did _____ crawl? Stand? Walk? Say first word? Say first sentence? How would you describe _____ speech as she/he was growing up?

EARLY LANGUAGE AND LITERACY DEVELOPMENT

What language or languages are spoken in the home? What language does _____ use at home? Did _____ play with pencils and crayons? Did _____ try to write? Did _____ have favorite storybooks? Did anyone read to her/him? Did _____ ever pretend to read to you, to teddy bears or dolls, or to younger children? Did _____ watch TV? How often did she/he watch? What kinds of shows did she/he like best? As a young child did _____ ever ask questions about signs? Did _____ ever ask you how to write her/his name or other words? Did _____ try to write before going to school?

SCHOOL HISTORY

What can you tell me about _____ reading/writing difficulty? How do you see the problem? What do you think is the cause of the problem? When did you first notice that _____ had a difficulty? What has been done to help _____ solve the problem? What else, if anything, do you think should be done? Does _____ like school? What are _____ favorite subjects? Which subjects does she/he like least? Did _____ attend preschool? Kindergarten? In what ways have you or other members of the family tried to help _____? How is _____ school attendance? About how many days a year does _____ miss? Has _____ ever missed a long period of schooling because of illness or other reasons?

HOME FACTORS

Do you or anyone else in the family try to help _____ with homework? About how much homework does _____ have each evening? Where does _____ do homework? Do you take _____ to the library? If so, how often? Do you buy books or magazines for _____? Do you read to _____? Did you read to _____ when she/he was younger? Do you like to read? About how much reading do you do each day? Do you subscribe to any newspapers or magazines? What plans do you have for _____? What plans does _____ have for herself/himself? What does _____ plan to be when she/he grows up?

> Questioning parents about the student's homework can yield valuable information about the student's study strategies and habits.

INTERESTS/PERSONAL ADJUSTMENT

How does _____ get along with the other children at school? Does _____ belong to any clubs or teams? How does _____ spend her/his free time? Does _____ like to read? How much time does _____ spend reading each week? About how many books would you say _____ read last month? Does _____ have any hobbies or other interests? How does _____ get along with the children in the neighborhood? How does _____ get along with the other members of the family? Is there anything else you would like to tell me about _____?

The questions do not have to be asked in order. Rather, you should follow the natural flow of the interview. When asked a health question, parents may get into the area of school history because the child got sick in school. To get the most information, follow the parent's lead. Rearrange questions as the situation dictates. Also spend added time in those areas that seem to have the most bearing on the particular student you are examining. If chronic illness is a major factor, for instance, spend additional time discussing the student's medical background. Also, keep in mind that parents are not always objective. Some information may be omitted or distorted. And some information, such as the age of some of the developmental milestones, may not be remembered accurately. If parents have medical or developmental records, these should be consulted. All information should, of course, be kept confidential.

If you are unable to interview parents or school personnel, you might use a written questionnaire to obtain information. Although interviews are more effective in eliciting information, using a questionnaire is better than obtaining no information at all. Since school personnel are busy, questionnaires should be succinct. Because some parents of poor readers and writers may also have experienced difficulty with reading and writing, parent questionnaires should be easy to read and easy to answer. Sample questionnaires are presented in Figures 6.2 and 6.3.

STUDENTS' VIEWS

> Students' responses can help you determine assessment/instructional priorities. If students say the words make reading hard, look into their decoding skills or the difficulty level of the reading material.

An essential element in the assessment is to obtain the students' views of their reading and writing. How do they think they are doing? What kinds of skills would they like to learn? What kinds of help, if any, would they like to have? Some possible questions that might be asked are listed below. Choose the questions that seem most appropriate. Also feel free to add questions. Instead of using a formal interview approach, ask the questions in an informal, conversational style.

> By asking children what they would like to learn to do in reading and what would help them to become a better reader, you involve them in setting goals.

- What are your favorite school subjects? Why?
- Are there any subjects that are hard for you? What makes them hard? What might make them easier?
- What things are easy for you in reading?
- What things are hard for you in reading?
- What kinds of things would you like to learn to do in reading?
- What would help you to become a better reader?
- Do you read on your own at home?
- What kinds of things do you like to read?
- What are your favorite books?
- Who are your favorite authors?

All of the above questions can also be asked about writing. Responses can be supplemented by observational data and other information that you obtain about the students and their perception of reading and writing.

FIGURE 6.2 Parent Questionnaire

Name of child_____   Date of birth_____
Name of school_____   Grade in school_____
Mother's name_____   Occupation_____
Father's name_____   Occupation_____

Names and ages of brothers and sisters

_____
Main language spoken in home _____ Other languages spoken in home _____
How would you describe your child's overall health?

_____
Does your child now have any major illnesses?

_____
Has your child had any major illness or had any accidents that caused an injury?

_____
Does your child wear glasses? _____ When was the last time your child's eyes were checked?

_____
Has your child ever had any difficulty with hearing? _____
When was the last time your child's hearing was checked? _____
Has your child ever repeated a grade or been placed in a transitional class? _____
What difficulty does your child have in reading or writing?

_____
When was this difficulty first noticed?

_____
Has the school tried to help your child? If so, how?

_____
Have you tried to help your child? If so, how?

_____
Except for help that you have given, has your child been helped outside of school? _____ If so, how?

_____
Has your child been tested for a learning problem? If so, what kind of testing was done?

_____
Is your child in any special programs for children with learning problems?

_____
Has your child missed a lot of time from school? _____ If so, please describe.

_____
What does your child like to do when not in school?

_____
What special interests or hobbies does your child have?

_____
Is there anything else that you can tell us that would help us to understand your child's reading or writing difficulty?

_____

FIGURE 6.3 School Questionnaire

Name of student _____ Grade _____ Date _____

Name of school _____ Teacher _____

School address _____ Phone _____

1. Student's reading level _____
2. Name and level of materials now being used _____
3. Results of standardized tests _____
4. Results of IEP or other special assessments _____
5. Grades for last marking period _____
6. Results of vision test _____ Hearing test_____
7. Description of speech or behavior problems, if any_____
8. Any extended or frequent absences _____
9. Grades repeated or placement in a transition class _____
10. Description of any extra help given _____

Classroom teacher's or specialist's description of the child's problem in reading or writing and suggestions for helping the child.

_____

_____

Is the child now being considered for special placement or retention? If so, please describe.

_____

_____

_____

READING EXPECTANCY

An assessment should include some indication of the level at which the student should be reading. This is the student's **reading expectancy.** As a general principle, students should be able to read up to their cognitive or linguistic capacity. Tests of cognitive ability such as the WISC-III, WISC IV, or the Stanford-Binet can be used to estimate a student's reading capacity. The higher the score on these tests, the higher is the student's reading expectancy. As a rough rule of thumb, to get a measure of expectancy, subtract 5.6 from the student's mental age (5.6 is the average age at which students start kindergarten). If the test does not give a mental age, you can calculate that by multiplying the student's chronological age by the test's standard or IQ score. Thus a nine-year-old with an IQ of 133 has a mental age of 12 (1.33 times 9) and a reading expectancy of 6.6. (11 years, 12 months minus 5 years, 6 months). The student can be expected to be able to read on a sixth-grade level. Still another way to calculate reading expectancy is to use the following formula: ([IQ/100 times years of reading instruction] + 1 = Reading Expectancy) (Bond, Tinker, Wasson, & Wasson, 1994). Using this formula, the student's reading expectancy is grade 5 ([133/100 times 3] + 1 = 5), so this formula gives a more conservative estimate. In calculating years in school, begin with first grade, not kindergarten, even though there may have been some formal reading instruction in kindergarten. If a student repeated a grade or spent an extra year in a transition class, that should be included when calculating years in school.

> **Reading expectancy:** estimate of the level at which a student should be reading, based on tests of academic aptitude, listening capacity, or estimated ability to learn.

When calculating reading expectancy, also consider opportunity to learn. A very bright first-grader, for instance, who has a reading expectancy of 4.0, might not have had sufficient exposure to reading for this to be a realistic expectation.

Using Technology
The web site at http://www
.interventioncentral.org/index
.shtml provides information
and a device for calculating
discrepancies between ability
and achievement.

When determining a reading
expectancy, consider several
sources of information. Use
an IQ score if available and
also the listening level
yielded by the informal reading inventory.

Technical procedures are sometimes used to determine reading expectancy, reading achievement, and whether there is a significant gap between the two. Typically a substantial discrepancy is one in which there is a difference of 1.5 standard deviations between achievement and ability (Spear-Swerling & Sternberg, 1996). This means that if a student achieved an average score of 100 on the Wechsler scales, which have a standard deviation of 15 points, then his achievement on a standard measure of reading, also having a standard deviation of 15, would have to be 77.5 or lower.

As noted earlier, it is not necessary to administer a test of cognitive capacity to obtain a measure of a student's reading expectancy. There are also a number of measures of language development that may be used to gauge a student's reading expectancy. The simplest of these is a test of listening capacity. The informal reading inventory, which was covered in detail in Chapter 4, yields a listening level. This is obtained by reading stories to students and finding the highest level at which the students can understand 75 percent of the questions asked about a selection that has been read to them. If a third-grader reading on a first-grade level obtains a listening level of grade 5, that is the student's reading expectancy. Other sources of language capacity are listening vocabulary subtests found in some norm-referenced group tests and some individual diagnostic tests as noted in Chapter 5. The grade equivalent yielded by these subtests is an estimate of the student's reading expectancy.

SUMMARIZING THE DATA

Once you have assembled all the data from your assessment, it is important to organize the information so that trends can be noted and comparisons made. Use a form similar to the one in Figure 6.4 to help you group data about reading in one block, data about spelling and writing in another, data about emergent literacy in a third, and so on. Suggestions for placing data are presented in Figure 6.5.

After placing the data in blocks, examine each of the blocks in terms of the first one, which summarizes the student's estimated cognitive ability, listening capacity, and reading expectancy. Looking at the reading block, for instance, note how the student is doing in terms of reading expectancy or listening capacity. Is the student reading above or below reading expectancy or listening capacity? Looking at the writing and/or spelling block, note whether performance is above or below the student's estimated capacity or expectancy. After examining each block in this way, make comparisons among the blocks. How do writing and spelling compare with reading or word analysis? Also look for strengths and needs. Examining the categories at the bottom of the page, note major findings from the case study. These might include long-term illnesses, grades repeated, or indications of extra help given at school. Including only the most essential information, such as reading level, reading expectancy or listening capacity, major strengths and needs, summarize the data. Hold off on making recommendations until you have conducted a **trial teaching** lesson (see pp. 174–175).

Trial teaching: use of sample lessons to determine which instructional approaches are most effective, based on assessment data.

FIGURE 6.4 Case Summary

Name ___Robert Lawlor___   Date of Birth ___4-19-91___   Grade ___3___   Date ___3-10-02___

COGNITIVE	IRI & OTHER RDG. TESTS	WORD RECOG.	EMERGENT	SPELLING/ WRITING	ORAL LANGUAGE	ASSOC. LRNG.	MEMORY	ACH. TESTS
WISC 110	Ind. pp	F U		1–50	Seems	Word Lrng.	Digits 8	Stanf.
High	Inst. p	pp 75 85		2–20	adequate	Imm.–7/7	Arith. 9	Rdg. 10 P.R.
Comp-13	Frus. 1	p 65 75		Letter		Delayed-6/7		Math 40 P.R.
Vocab.-12	List. 5	1 50 55		name				Lang. 11 P.R.
Low		2 40 40		stage				
Block-7	Stan.	Word		writing				
Obj.-7	Tot-10 P.R.	patterns—		sample—				
Listening	Comp-11 P.R.	diff		very				
Capacity	Wd.St. 9 P.R.	with		rudimen-				
5	Vocab. 9 P.R.	long		tary				
		vowels						
Reading								
Expect.								
5.4								

CASE HISTORY HIGHLIGHTS

Repeated 1st grade
Lagged in overall motor & lang. dev.
Emotional outbursts
Likes sports

SCREENINGS

Vision—squints & holds book close

TRIAL TEACHING

Responded best to whole-part teaching of word analysis skills

SUMMARY

High/avg. ability
Possible diff with memory & attention
Signif. behind in reading, writing, & spelling

RECOMMENDATIONS

Use easy-to-read sports books
Use whole-part approach to word analysis
One-on-one instr.

Note: P.R. stands for percentile rank.

FIGURE 6.5 Suggestions for Filling Out the Case Summary

Cognitive Ability	Give results of IQ test. Note high and low scores on subtests or areas in which student did well and areas in which student did poorly.
Listening Capacity	Note listening capacity from IRI.
Reading Expectancy	Use IQ or listening test or both to estimate reading expectancy.
Reading Achievement	List IRI levels. Give results of other reading tests, think-alouds, or observations of reading.
Word Recognition	Give results of word-lists tests. Provide information from the Word-Patterns Survey, Syllable Survey, the Word-Identification Interview, think-alouds, and observations.
Writing/Spelling	Give results of the Elementary Spelling Inventory, a test on graded lists of spelling words, and examination of writing samples and portfolio.
Oral Language	Provide test results of vocabulary assessment or other language measures and note observational data. Include word finding data, if this area was assessed.
Assoc. Learning	Provide results of Word-Learning Test. Note results of symbol learning tests and observations.
Memory/Attent.	Note results of tests of memory and attention.
Emergent	If pertinent, note knowledge of concepts of print, letter knowledge, phonemic awareness, and beginning sounds. Note interest in reading and writing and awareness of the purposes of reading and writing.
Case History	Note both major positive and negative factors. Note school situation.
Screenings	Note hearing, vision, health or other screenings.
Trial Teaching, Response to Intervention	Briefly describe trial teaching or response to intervention and note results.
Summary	Indicate reading expectancy; reading, writing and spelling levels; major strengths, weaknesses, and needs.
Recommendations	Suggest type of assistance (small group, one-on-one), major areas of needed instruction, and possible techniques or approaches and possible materials. Also recommend needed screenings.

MAKING RECOMMENDATIONS

Make recommendations on the basis of the assessment data and trial teaching. Recommendations might include suggestions for level of help—one on one, small group, regular classroom—and for the approach that might be taken—language experience, reading workshop, and so forth. Recommendations might also be provided for major needs—comprehension of main ideas, application of study strategies, ability to read short-vowel patterns, or ability to decode multisyllabic words, for instance. Possible teaching techniques,

Upcoming chapters explore materials, methods, and settings for corrective instruction. You will be better able to plan an intervention program after reading the rest of the text.

especially if these have been tried and shown to be successful, should be listed. The recommendations should answer the key questions established in Chapter 3.

- On what level is the student functioning?
- What is the student's potential for growth?
- What are the student's strengths and weaknesses in reading and writing?
- What would be the most effective materials for this student?
- Under what circumstances and in what setting would this student learn best?
- What are the most effective techniques or approaches for teaching this student?
- Are there any physical, psychological, social, or other factors that need to be addressed in order for the student to do his best?
- How might the home, larger community, and school work together to help the student?

PROFESSIONAL REPORTS

Reading specialists, along with psychiatrists, psychologists, communication disorders specialists, and other professionals are called upon to summarize the results of their assessments and make appropriate recommendations. Although they differ from profession to profession, these reports or case studies have a number of commonalties. In terms of style, they are typ-

■ ■ ■ ■ ■

APPLYING TRIAL TEACHING

Once you have assembled all your assessment data, except for trial teaching, reflect upon the data and construct hypotheses as to what the student's major strengths and weaknesses are and what might be the best way to instruct the student. To test out your hypotheses, arrange for a trial teaching lesson, as explained in Chapter 3. A trial teaching lesson consists of the following steps:

Step 1: Plan. Based on an analysis of assessment data, construct hypotheses and plan tentative techniques for teaching one or two key strategies. Assemble materials on the appropriate level of difficulty that you think would be appealing to the student.

Step 2: Explain to student. Inform the student of the results of the assessment in a concrete but positive way. Emphasize strengths

and note that many bright students have difficulty with reading. Explain to the student the techniques that you will be using and how they will help her or him.

Step 3: Present choice. Give the student a choice of materials and activities.

Step 4: Implement, assess, adjust. Implement the technique and assess its effectiveness and also the student's reaction to it. Make adjustments as necessary.

Step 5: Discuss with the student. Discuss the effectiveness of the technique, activities, and materials with the student. Explain to the student that this session shows that she or he is a capable learner and should make progress using this and similar techniques. Invite the student's suggestions and implement them as fully as possible.

ically written in formal English and attempt to be both objective and conservative. Care is taken to base conclusions and recommendations on test data and observations. Since these reports may be used to place students, obtain additional services, or plan a program of remediation, they should be complete, clear, and precise. Although the reports should embody a professional tone, they should be free of jargon and written in clear, simple language so they may be understood by parents and others outside the profession, as well as school principals, school counselors, and other professionals. Technical terms should be used with care, and, if

■ ■ ■ ■ ■ ▬▬▬▬▬▬▬▬▬▬▬▬▬▬▬▬▬▬▬▬▬▬▬▬

EXEMPLARY TEACHING
TRIAL TEACHING

Maria, a fifteen-year-old ninth-grader, was reading on a fourth-grade level despite having average ability as indicated by a WISC administered by the school psychologist. Her listening level indicated adequate language development. Based on the results of the listening comprehension score, Maria was reading five years below her capacity.

During interviews with teachers, Maria's parents, and Maria, it was revealed that Maria disliked school in general, and reading in particular. During her interview Maria stated that she hated reading because it was boring and she couldn't see any sense in reading all that dumb stuff. When the examiner looked over the texts from content-area subjects, she could see that they were all written at or above grade level, which was well above Maria's fourth-grade reading ability.

During the trial teaching session, the examiner explained to Maria that she could understand ninth-grade stories and articles that were read to her. This meant that she was a bright person and had a good vocabulary and knew lots of things. The examiner also explained to Maria that she was good at reading one-syllable words, but because she had difficulty reading words that had two or more syllables, she would have a hard time reading ninth-grade books.

Looking frustrated, Maria said she had been taught all the syllable rules but they didn't help much. The examiner explained that she had a special way of teaching multisyllabic words, one she had used to help other bright students who had trouble with long words. She showed Maria how she could use her knowledge of single-syllable words

to read multisyllabic words. Writing the words *side, beside, divide, decide,* and *provide* on the chalkboard, she helped Maria use her knowledge of *side* to read *beside, divide, decide,* and *provide.* Maria had missed both *provide* and *decide* during her testing.

Sensing that Maria had a negative attitude toward traditional classroom material, probably because she had been given texts that were too hard for her, the examiner displayed an array of easy-to-read novels, the local newspaper, and *Action* (Scholastic), a magazine written on a third- through fifth-grade level. Maria found *Action* to be appealing, especially after reading the cover selection and seeing that it wasn't too long or too hard to read.

Based on Maria's reactions, a program was planned in which she was taught high-frequency syllable patterns and shown how to use her knowledge of single-syllable words to decode multisyllabic words. Patterns introduced were drawn from materials that she was reading, so that she would see the value of learning the skill and apply it in the context of real reading. She was also provided with high-interest materials on a fourth-grade level of difficulty. Because her content-area texts were too difficult for her, tapes were made so she could read along with the tapes. A variable-speed tape recorder was obtained so she could set the reading speed at a comfortable pace. Because she was so far behind, she was given help in the classroom and also after school by the reading specialist. By year's end, Maria was able to handle sixth-grade material. Her attitude toward school also showed a marked improvement, as did her grades.

When sharing results, emphasize the student's strengths and the practical steps that the parents or teacher might take to help the child.

When constructing reports, avoid judgmental language. Instead of "Frank was lazy during the testing sessions," say, "Frank needed encouragement to continue working."

The focus of an assessment will vary, depending on the stage the student is in. For beginning readers, decoding might be the emphasis. For more advanced readers, focus might be on comprehension and study skills.

Some assessment reports also include a listing of tests administered along with test scores on the first page. This provides the person reading the report with an overview of the test results.

The assessment outline is a sample and should be adapted to fit your situation. Include categories that may have been left out; delete areas that you do not assess.

used, should be explained. For instance, instead of saying, "Mario had difficulty with vowel digraphs," state that "Mario had difficulty with words like *rain* and *bean,* in which two letters are used to spell the vowel sound." Instead of talking about a student's independent level, translate this into a phrase that a nonspecialist would understand: the level at which Mario can read on his own, without any help from the teacher."

The content of the assessment report will vary, depending on the complexity of the case and the extent of the assessment procedures. A diagnostic report may range from two or three pages to twenty or more. However, the reports written by reading specialists for schools are generally brief.

Although the assessment report may include information about the student's health, interests, social and psychological adjustment, school record, cognitive abilities, vision, and hearing, the emphasis should be on reading and writing and the kinds of programs that seem to work best with the student. Presented below is an outline for a full report. Reports vary somewhat in both format and content, so the outline should be adapted.

I. Identifying Information (on cover sheet)
  A. Student's name
  B. Date of birth and chronological age at start of assessment
  C. Sex
  D. Grade in school
  E. Name of school
  F. Examiner and place of assessment
  G. Dates of assessment

II. Reason for Referral and Summary of Observations (on inside pages)
  A. Name, age, grade, school, reason for referral
  B. Test-taking behavior, best-liked and least-liked tasks
  C. Results of interview about reading/writing problems, interests, and vocational plans

III. School History
  A. Summary of progress in school
  B. Achievement in specific subjects
  C. Results of achievement and other tests
  D. Attendance, repeated grades
  E. Description of classroom program
  F. Notes on special placement or special help given
  G. Classroom and special placement observations

IV. Results of Assessment
  A. Physical
    1. Vision
    2. Hearing

        3. Other
    B. Cognitive
        1. Academic aptitude
        2. Memory
        3. Associative learning
        4. Auditory and visual discrimination
    C. Reading achievement
        1. Word recognition
        2. Informal reading inventory levels
        3. Fluency, reading rate
    D. Phonological awareness, letter knowledge, if applicable
    E. Concepts of print—if applicable
    F. Special phonics testing
    G. Writing
    H. Spelling
    I. Handwriting
    J. Results of dynamic testing, response to intervention, and/or trial teaching

V. Summary of Assessment
    A. Highlights of cognitive testing
    B. Highlights of reading achievement and other testing
    C. Conclusions

VI. Recommendations
    A. Setting and approach
    B. Major needs to be addressed
    C. Ways in which school can be supportive
    D. Ways in which parents can be supportive

VII. Description of Intervention (if applicable)
    A. Setting, approach
    B. Major needs that were addressed
    C. Skills/strategies taught
    D. Techniques used
    E. Materials employed
    F. Evaluation of progress

ASSESSMENT: AN ONGOING PROCESS

Assessment should be ongoing and continuous. Whenever a student is engaged in a learning activity, assess the activity. How does the student cope with the activity? Which activities cause difficulty? Which are done with ease? What factors are hindering the student's progress? What factors are accelerating progress? What changes might be made to improve the student's chances for success? For instance, one student was struggling with a word-pattern approach, but began making progress when taught by a sound-by-sound approach. Apparently, his phonemic awareness was weak, and he needed added instruction in letter–sound relationships. Later, building on his improved phonemic awareness and solid knowledge of letter–sound relationships, he did quite well with a pattern approach. Another student made very little progress learning new words until a tracing technique was used. Chances are that even the most comprehensive assessment would not yield this information. This is the kind of information that continuous assessment, and trying out different approaches and materials, is most likely to reveal. The important thing is to ask two questions as you work with the corrective reader: How is this approach/material/setting working? If it isn't working out, what might work better?

A MULTIDISCIPLINARY APPROACH

A reading problem, especially one that is severe, can have many causes, and can affect many aspects of a student's life. It is important to involve other professionals, parents, and the individual student in the process of assessment and remediation. The school psychologist can shed light on cognitive and affective factors and, perhaps, provide help with the emotional aspects of the problem. The language therapist can test language abilities and provide help with articulation, word finding, and other difficulties. The learning disabilities specialist can test in math and cognitive processing areas. The nurse can provide insight into health issues and screen for auditory, visual, or health problems. Working collaboratively with other professionals is not just an excellent way to obtain a full array of information on a student, it is also an excellent way to enlist needed support.

MINICASE STUDY

Josephine is an eight-year-old second-grader, who, when tested, was able to read only two words: *I* and *am*. Referred for testing by the school psychologist, Josephine was given the WISC-III. What do the results of the test suggest about Josephine's cognitive functioning? How might the following information from the WISC-III be used to plan a program of intervention for her?

WISC-III FULL SCALE IQ, 97 VERBAL SCORES
Information, 8
Similarities, 12
Arithmetic, 9
Vocabulary, 12
Comprehension, 10
Digit Span (not counted), 4

PERFORMANCE SCORES
Picture Completion, 11
Coding, 9
Picture Arrangement, 9
Block Design, 5
Object Assembly, 10

Note that, overall, Josephine has average ability. However, there is weakness in information, which suggests that building background would be an important part of her program. Her high score in vocabulary and similarities suggests good ability to form concepts. Her low score in digit span suggests a possible attention/concentration problem or difficulty with short term/working memory for verbal, sequential material. Low score on the block assembly suggests difficulty in the visual perceptual motor area. A program for Josephine would build on her strong language skills, but include elements such as manipulatives and tracing that would help her pay attention and concentrate.

SUMMARY

A student's literacy capacity can be assessed through administering an intelligence or a listening test. Focusing as they do on academic aptitude, and encompassing tasks that all students may not have had an equal opportunity to learn, intelligence tests need to be interpreted with care and should be supplemented by observation of what the student can actually do. The most popular intelligence tests are the Wechsler scales, whose subtest scores can be analyzed to yield diagnostic information. Only qualified personnel can administer the Wechsler scales; however, reading professionals may administer the Slosson Intelligence Test and the Peabody Picture Vocabulary Test, a measure of receptive vocabulary.

Specific areas of cognitive functioning that should be assessed in a thorough assessment include memory and associative word learning. If a student is showing symptoms of word-finding difficulty, this area should also be assessed.

As part of an interactive assessment, the student's school situation should be observed. If possible, observe the student in reading and writing and content-area classes. Also interview the student's teachers and analyze school records. If it is not possible to interview teachers, ask the school to complete a concise questionnaire. A case history obtained by interviewing the student's parents provides a backdrop for interpreting other assessment data. To determine whether a student has a reading disorder and the degree of severity, if there is a disorder, it is essential to establish where the student should be in terms of reading achievement. In general, students are expected to read up to their capacity as indicated by an IQ test, a listening test, or an oral vocabulary test. If possible, complement test and observational data by conducting condensed trial teaching lessons in a key area.

Reading professionals may be expected to summarize assessment data in a professional report. Such a report follows the same general style and format of that in a psychological report.

APPLICATION ACTIVITIES

1. Talk to a school psychologist or a reading specialist about the kinds of measures that she or he administers. Discuss the value and limitations of the measures.

2. Complete an assessment and write a professional report based on your findings. If time and circumstances permit, write a full report. If not, write a minireport based on a reading assessment that focuses on informal reading inventory results.

CHAPTER SEVEN

EMERGENT LITERACY AND EARLY INTERVENTION PROGRAMS

USING WHAT YOU KNOW

Emergent literacy, which encompasses both reading and writing, acknowledges that all students come to school with some experience with reading and writing. Emergent literacy refers to those early reading and writing behaviors that ultimately emerge into conventional literacy. What might be involved in making the transition from the informal literacy activities engaged in at home to a formal introduction to reading and writing? How might the literacy backgrounds of students differ? What difficulties might students encounter, especially those who are at risk because of poverty or other factors, as they enter into reading and writing programs? What might be done to alleviate these difficulties? What kinds of early intervention programs might be effective in helping students who otherwise might experience failure in their attempts to learn to read and write?

ANTICIPATION GUIDE

Read each of the following statements. Put a check under "Agree" or "Disagree" to show how you feel about each one. If you can, discuss your responses with classmates.

	AGREE	DISAGREE
1. Children learn to read and write in much the same way as they learn to speak.	_____	_____
2. Early interventions should not be started too soon, because some students may simply need more time to mature.	_____	_____
3. For at-risk students, a structured emergent literacy program works best.	_____	_____

AGREE   DISAGREE

4. Older students just learning to read and write may need to go through the same stages of learning to read and write as average kindergartners and first-graders do.

5. Direct instruction in phonics should be an essential element in early intervention programs.

_____ _____

_____ _____

EMERGENT LITERACY AND INTERVENTION

> **Emergent literacy:** reading and writing concepts and behaviors of young children that develop into conventional reading and writing (Sulzby & Teale, 1991).

According to Sulzby (1989), **emergent literacy** can be described as "the reading and writing behaviors of young children that precede and develop into conventional literacy" (p. 84). In reading, these behaviors might range from leafing through a picture book to reading a repeated phrase or, in writing, from drawing or scribbling to composing a message in invented or even conventional spelling.

Although emergent literacy recognizes that all students who come to school have some knowledge of and experience with reading and writing, that knowledge and experience can vary enormously. Some students will be able to write their names, recognize most of the letters of the alphabet, and, perhaps, read a few words. A few, about one in a hundred, will be able to read on a level comparable to that of the average second- or third-grader. On the other end of the continuum, some will not be able to write their names or recognize any letters. A few will never have held a book or a pencil. In one study, five-year-olds who came from impoverished backgrounds had approximately the same level of literacy development as four-year-olds who came from enriched backgrounds. As Gillet and Temple (1994) comment:

> Four out of five children make a host of useful discoveries about print before and during kindergarten. From being read to, from reading back favorite storybooks, and from attempting to make messages with pencils, these children pick up a range of concepts about print that enable them to grow as readers and writers with the help of normal tutelage. One out of five children are not so fortunate, however. These children do not have their early print concepts in place when they begin first grade, and things do not go well for them. (p. 58)

> **High Scope,** one of the best-known of the preschool preventive programs, can be accessed at http://www .highscope.org/Educational Programs/EarlyChildhood/ preschoolkeyexp.htm. This web site provides information about setting up a program using High Scope principles.

Preventive Programs

Children who end up in the one-out-of-five group would benefit from a program of prevention. One way of preventing reading problems is to develop children's language and preliteracy skills in the preschool. This does not mean that there should be formal instruction in reading. Reading aloud regularly, shared reading, setting up areas for dramatic play and for reading and writing, creating a classroom library, developing oral language skills, modeling reading and writing, and providing opportunities for children to write, draw, and explore language will naturally develop emergent literacy (Campbell, 1998). Low-income four-year-olds showed encouraging gains when stories were read to them on a regular basis and the teacher engaged them in discussions in which they made predictions, reflected on the story, and talked about words (Dickinson & Smith, 1994). It is also helpful to develop rhyming and other phonological awareness skills, letter knowledge, and concepts of print. Since this instruction is designed for preschool students, the goal is exposure and awareness rather than mastery. Three excellent preschool programs are described below.

Para Los Niños. Designed for four-year-old Spanish-speaking preschool children, the program included Big Books shared reading, writing and reading centers, and a take-home library and workshops for parents. The students outscored native speakers of English who had participated in other preschool programs despite the fact that the emergent literacy tests were administered in English (Yaden et al., 2001).

Language Enrichment Activities Program (LEAP). This program boosted poor four-year-olds' performance from the 30th to the 50th percentile (Community Update, 1996). To build language and vocabulary, teachers read at least five theme-related books a day, used posters and activities to stimulate oral language, built phonological awareness and concepts of print, and introduced the alphabet. Children also learned color and shape names and other basic concepts.

■ ■ ■ ■ ■ ▬▬▬▬▬▬▬▬▬▬▬▬▬▬▬▬▬▬▬▬▬▬▬▬▬▬▬▬▬▬▬▬▬▬▬▬

EXEMPLARY TEACHING
BOOKS FOR PRESCHOOL CHILDREN

In a project known as Books Aloud, 330 child-care centers in poverty-stricken areas in and around Philadelphia were provided with libraries of five books per child (Neuman, 1999). The books became a focal point and impetus for a host of activities. With attractive, high-quality books available, teachers began reading aloud to children and talking about books. They talked about how books are read and how to care for them. The children began examining books and "reading" them. Discussions of authors and stories ensued. Word games were introduced. Children began using story-type language, such as "Once upon a time." Library corners and writing centers were set up. The curriculum of the day-care centers was expanded to include reading and writing and talking about books. Children in the Books Aloud program, who were three or four years of age at the time, showed encouraging gains in a number of literacy measures. They also did better in kindergarten than children who attended control day-care centers. Although some training was involved, the key change agent in the project was the presence of and access to books.

Webbing into Literacy   http://curry.edschool.virginia.edu/go/wil/home.html. Webbing into Literacy is a downloadable program designed to provide Head Start teachers with materials and instruction that will foster language development, phonological awareness, alphabet knowledge, and concepts of print.

Kindergarten Preventive Program

The foundation of a preventive program is to build an atmosphere that fosters emergent literacy. Being developmental, emergent literacy is a natural outgrowth of learning oral language and is fostered in much the same way as oral language is fostered, through interaction with adults and peers. In the classroom this means providing a literacy-rich environment in addition to instruction. On the surface, a **literacy-rich environment** is one in which the student is surrounded by the tools of literacy: books, signs, posters, labels, paper, envelopes, and writing instruments of every kind, including word processors, and rubber stamps. On a deeper level, a literacy-rich environment is more than an impressive display of the artifacts of literacy; it is one in which "a thoughtful teacher capitalizes on opportunities to focus on . . . print and make children aware of its various functions in real contexts" (Learning Media, 1991, p. 55).

> **Literacy-rich classroom:** one in which children have many opportunities to read to themselves and each other and to write using invented and/or conventional spelling.

> To foster literacy, Morrow (1994) suggests setting up centers of learning. These may incorporate content areas or may be devoted to particular activities such as reading, writing, and viewing.

Because literacy is an outgrowth of oral language, language development should be the foundation for the program. Literacy activities should be accompanied by opportunities to discuss what, how, and why we read and write. Students should also share orally what they have read and written. Talking about an experience before writing about it, for instance, both develops oral language and fosters better writing.

Benefits of Reading Aloud

A key element in a literacy-rich environment is reading to students. Some children enter kindergarten having been read to for 1,000 to 1,700 hours (Adams, 1990). Others have never been read to by anyone. According to the Commission on Reading, "The single most important activity for building the knowledge required for eventual success in reading is reading aloud to children" (Anderson, Hiebert, Scott, & Wilkinson, 1985, p. 23). Reading aloud to a child builds background of experience, vocabulary, syntax, and comprehension (Dickinson & Smith, 1994). It also builds an acquaintance with literary language and a sense of story so that students have a framework for understanding narratives. Discussing books that have been read aloud is also very valuable. Adults tend to use enriched language when discussing books with children, and children pick up this enriched language (Kaderavek & Sulzby, 1999).

Literally thousands of books are available for reading to students. The important thing is to read books that both you and the students enjoy. It is also a good idea to include informational books so that you build background as you build language. However, also select books that will be understandable to the students. For fiction, you might start with simple narratives and work up to more complex selections. Let the students' responses be

Reading aloud to students is a vital element in a literacy program for low-achieving readers. Because they are hampered in their ability to read, they are cut off from one source of developing language and background.

your guide. If they are interested in the text and can answer most of the questions that you ask, then you are probably on the right level. If they are restless and seem confused, try a simpler book. When reading informational text, read about topics that students can comprehend and to which they can relate. Select books that introduce and explain new ideas or topics, but without overwhelming students. As students' language and background develop, introduce more complex selections. Being introduced to more complex language patterns helps students to internalize these patterns (Kaderavak & Sulzby, 1999).

How a book is read has a bearing on how much students benefit. Students seem to benefit most when the book is given an introduction, read through without much interruption, and then discussed fairly thoroughly (Dickinson & Smith, 1994). An important component of the discussion is "child-involved analytical talk" (p. 117). Child-involved analytical talk includes analyzing characters or events, predicting events, making connections between events or characters in the story and events and people in the listeners' lives, talking about words and their meanings, summarizing portions of the story, evaluating the story, and clarifying comments students make about the story (Dickinson & Smith, 1994).

The following read-aloud lesson incorporates the principles just discussed, which lead to increased development of vocabulary, overall language, and comprehension.

READ-ALOUD LESSON

BEFORE READING
Read the title and display the cover, and encourage students to predict what the story might be about. Have them justify their predictions. Introduce any concepts that might hinder students' comprehension of the story. Have students listen to the story to compare their predictions with what actually happens.

DURING READING
Clarify any elements that might be confusing. Also check students' predictions, and when appropriate, encourage them to make new predictions. However, emphasize the story itself. Do not allow long discussions to interrupt the flow of the story.

AFTER READING
Discuss students' predictions. Have them compare their predictions to what actually happened in the

story. Discuss events in the story and characters. Have students justify and explain their responses so that they are analyzing the text and the language of the story. For instance, after reading *Anansi Goes Fishing* (Kimmel, 1992) and after discussing the main events of the story, ask why Anansi went to the justice tree. Also ask why the tree is called a "justice tree" and why the judge didn't believe Anansi. Discuss why Anansi didn't speak to Turtle for a long time. Talk over, too, the good that came out of the story and the meanings of some of the difficult words: *disgrace, justice, judge, warthog.* Also have students relate characters and events to their own lives.

Fostering Emergent Literacy

Within the context of holistic reading and writing activities and being read to, students grow in literacy. Although many children may develop literacy naturally, with a minimum of instruction, low-achieving readers and at-risk students need direct instruction in addition to

Kindergarten programs can help prevent reading difficulties. Children at risk for reading difficulties perform better in reading if their kindergarten programs spend more time on activities such as phonemic awareness, spelling, and writing (Vellutino et al., 1996).

numerous opportunities to engage in reading and writing. Areas in which direct instruction are especially important are concepts about print, phonological awareness, letter knowledge, and knowledge of beginning consonant correspondences.

Concepts about Print

Even though they may have been in school for a while and have had experience with reading and writing in their homes, low-achieving readers may not have acquired essential **concepts about print.** These include the following.

Concepts about print: basic understanding about written language—printed words represent spoken words, are composed of letters that represent sounds, are read from left to right, and so on.

BOOK-ORIENTATION CONCEPTS
- Locating the front and back of a book
- Recognizing the function of the cover and title page
- Recognizing the function of print and pictures

PRINT-DIRECTION CONCEPTS
- Reading from left to right
- Reading from top to bottom

PRINT CONCEPTS
- Understanding that words can be written down and read
- Recognizing a letter, a word, and a sentence
- Understanding that printed words are composed of letters
- Understanding that words are composed of sounds
- Understanding that letters represent sounds
- Being able to point to separate words in print and match these with words that are being read by oneself or another
- Understanding the difference between uppercase and lowercase letters
- Understanding the function of punctuation marks

Above all, students should understand that reading is a meaningful act. Reading is not primarily a task involving translating letters into sounds but is mainly a matter of constructing understanding.

Some of the print concepts are interdependent. For instance, students' concept of words and their ability to form letter–sound relationships are apparently related. One device students use to follow a line of print is the use of initial consonants. In fact, being able to segment and pronounce or spell initial consonants seems to be a prerequisite for following a line of print by pointing to each word with one's finger (Morris, 1992). Knowing initial consonants apparently helps students locate the beginnings of words. Being able to fingerpoint, in turn, seems to contribute to further development of letter–sound relationships. Once students are able to detect individual words, they are then able to note the functions of final, and later, medial letters.

Informal Assessment of Concepts of Print. To assess students' concepts about print informally, give the child a copy of *Brown Bear, Brown Bear, What Do You See?* by Bill

The Bader Reading and Language Inventory (Bader, 1998) contains several tests for assessing emergent literacy, including one for noting separate words in a sentence.

Martin (1983), or a similar book. Ask questions to probe the student's knowledge of print conventions: "Have you ever seen this book? What do you think this book might be about? How can you tell what a book is about? What do you do with a book?" Opening to a page that has an illustration and text, say, "I'm going to read this page to you. Where should I start reading? (Lipson & Wixson, 1997). Point to the first thing I should read. (Note whether the child points to print or an illustration and whether the child points to the first word.) Now I'm going to start reading. Point to each word as I read it." (Read two facing pages of text slowly. Note whether the child can point to each word as you read it. Note, too, whether the child goes from left to right, makes a return sweep, and goes from top to bottom and from the left page to the right page.) Pointing to a line of print, ask, "How many words are in this line?" Pointing to a word, ask, "How many letters are in this word? Can you read any of the words?" After assessing the child's knowledge of print, note the child's overall level of development, and fill in the Concepts about Reading section of the Observation Guide presented in Figure 7.1.

Writing Sample.   As part of your assessment of the child's emergent literacy, ask the child to write her name. If the child seems hesitant, encourage her to write it as best she can. If she can write her name, then ask her to write any additional words that she knows. Also ask the child to write a story. Ask her to write a story telling about games that she likes to play or other things that she likes to do. Encourage her to write as best she can or to write the way she usually does. (Accept drawing, scribbling, letterlike symbols, and other forms of written expression.) Note the child's overall level of development. With this information, complete the Writing section of the Observation Guide.

In addition to observing the child's performance on the structured reading and writing observations, note whether she understands the functions of reading and writing. As you observe, ask: "Does the child enjoy listening to stories? Is she able to retell a story? Does she enjoy browsing through books? Does she attempt to read or retell a story from a book? Does she attempt to write? Does she write for a variety of purposes: to tell a story, to send a message, to make a list?" For additional suggestions for assessing young students, see Marie Clay's *An Observation Survey of Early Literacy Achievement* (1993a).

When assessing young children, it is essential that you consider their opportunity to learn. As Meisel (1998) cautions, "Not only do children—especially young children—acquire skills at different rates and in different ways, children are also exquisitely sensitive to opportunity to learn. If a child has . . . not been exposed to opportunities to acquire these skills, then that information will not be available to the child" pp. (16–17). With these children, try dynamic assessment. If students are unable to name letters of the alphabet or identify rhyming words, for instance, teach them these skills and note how readily and under what circumstance they learn these skills or, if they do not learn them, what seems to be causing them problems.

DEVELOPING LITERACY CONCEPTS

Literacy concepts are best developed through an immersion in reading and writing activities. As you read books to children, point out the cover, the front of the book, the title, and

FIGURE 7.1 Emergent Literacy Observation Guide

Student's Name _____   Age _____

Date _____   Native Language _____

Put a check (✓) in the blank if satisfactory, minus (–) if has a need in that area, and plus (+) if advanced. Comments may also be written on the blanks.

Oral Language

Can express self clearly _____

Asks questions when necessary _____

Uses a vocabulary appropriate for age _____

Uses sentence structure appropriate for age _____

Listens to and understands stories _____

Can retell a story _____

Can follow oral directions _____

Can converse effectively with peers _____

Can converse effectively with teacher _____

Concepts about Reading

Understands the main purpose of print _____

Recognizes environmental print _____

Can name the letters of the alphabet _____

Can point to each word as a line of print is read _____

Can detect individual sounds in words _____

Can detect rhyme _____

Can detect beginning sounds _____

Can read own name _____

Recognizes some words in print _____

Interest in Reading

Responds to being read to _____

Shows an interest in books _____

Pretends to read books _____

Attempts to read books _____

Asks questions about words, letters, or pictures in books _____

Writing

Understands the functions of writing _____

Writes or draws stories, letters, or lists _____

Uses invented spelling _____

Uses writing to communicate _____

Can write name _____

Attitude and Work Habits

Wants to learn to read and write _____

Can work independently _____

Is able to sustain attention _____

Can work with others _____

Is willing to experiment and risk making mistakes _____

Has confidence in own ability _____

the author's name. Discuss illustrations as you read. As you write messages or lists of names or schedules on the chalkboard, reinforce appropriate literacy concepts. Display and discuss signs, labels, notes, letters, announcements, and students' writing. Also use techniques such as shared reading.

Shared Reading

In a **shared reading,** you read an enlarged text as students follow along. In subsequent rereadings of the text, students join in the reading. Enlarged text may take the form of commercially produced big books, big books that you create yourself, poems or songs written on the chalkboard, or experience stories written on large sheets of paper or on the chalkboard. Because the text is enlarged, the class can follow along as you read a selection. This procedure can be used to introduce or reinforce nearly any skill or understanding in early reading, from the concept of going from left to right to the reading of words, phrases, and sentences. Just as with oral reading, it is essential that you select Big Books that are on students' conceptual level and that engage them. Start off with Big Books that contain familiar rhymes or stories and that have just one line of print per page. Listed below are procedures for conducting a shared reading activity (Gunning, 1994a).

> **Shared reading:** technique in which the teacher reads aloud from a big book or other enlarged text and students follow along. It is used to introduce concepts of print and high-frequency words.

■ ■ ■ ■ ■ ▬▬▬▬▬▬▬▬▬▬▬▬▬▬▬▬▬

SHARED READING LESSON

Step 1: Preparing to read the selection. Prepare students for a shared reading by discussing the cover illustration and the title and, if you wish, some illustrations from the text. Based on a discussion of the cover (and text illustrations) and the title, have them predict what the selection might be about. Set a purpose for reading. If the students have made a prediction, the purpose might be to compare their predictions to what actually happened in the text.

Step 2: Reading the selection. As you read the selection, run your hand under it, pointing to each word as you say it so students get the idea of going from left to right and that there is a one-to-one match between the spoken and the printed word. Stop and clarify difficult words and concepts. Discuss interesting parts and have students evaluate their predictions, revising them if they see fit.

Step 3: Discussing the selection. After students have followed along as you read the selection, discuss it with them. Begin by talking about their pre-

dictions. Also try to relate the selection to experiences that students may have had. Try to elicit responses to the characters and situations portrayed, asking such questions as, "Do you know anyone like the main character? Has anything like this ever happened to you?"

Step 4: Rereading the selection. During a second reading of the text, point out and discuss words, letters, punctuation marks, and other elements of print. During this second reading, encourage students to join in and read parts that they can handle. This may be a repeated word or phrase or a whole sentence. If the book is a popular one, schedule several rereadings. Each time, the students should take more responsibility for the reading.

Step 5: Extending the lesson. As a follow-up, students may want to listen to taped versions of the big book, or read regular-size versions to a partner. Depending on the student's development, this may be a pretend reading, a retelling based on pictures, or a genuine reading.

Concept of Separate Words

One of the most essential print concepts for students to learn is that each printed word represents one separate spoken word. One way of developing a concept of separate words is through voice pointing. Beginning readers often memorize stories that have been read to them over and over again or use the illustrations in highly predictable books to "read" a text. Although they seem to be reading the words on the page, actually they are reciting a memorized story or constructing a story based on the picture. This is especially true of students who are experiencing difficulty learning to read. To convey the concept of separate words and to teach children to begin to take note of the details of individual words, point to each word as the class share-reads a story and encourage the children to look at each word as you point to it. When you come to a repeated line of text such as, "Are you my mother?" slow down the pace, very deliberately point to each word, and make sure that the students say the word as you point to it. Have a volunteer read the repeated sentences, pointing to each word as he does so.

The concept of word is facilitated by awareness of beginning sounds. Using beginning sounds, students can mark the beginning of a word and use that as an anchor point. Once students have a concept of word and can follow along as a book is being read, they are better able to pick up additional letter–sound knowledge. Because they are able to follow along in shared reading, they begin to match sound with letter and they learn whole words and additional letter–sound relationships. The process is aided if the teacher points to words in the Big Book and if the teacher reads Big Books that contain just one line of print so that students are better able to match spoken and printed words (Morris, Bloodgood, Lomax, & Perney, 2003).

As individual students are reading a predictable book with you, occasionally have them point to each word as they read it. Also request finger pointing whenever you feel that a student is reciting a memorized sentence rather than really reading it. Besides helping to build a concept of separate words in a sentence, it helps students notice the details of printed words and to learn some printed words incidentally. After all, if students are not looking at words as they read on their own or through shared reading, or are not looking at the right words, then they will not learn anything about the makeup of the words.

Although typical shared reading lessons benefit everyone, the benefit can be intensified for struggling readers if the students are grouped by their level of proficiency so that the shared readings can be geared to their needs (Koskinen, Blum, Bisson, Phillips, Creamer, & Baker, 1999). In focused shared reading, the teacher selects a book for struggling readers that would best fit in with the needs she has observed. For students who are still learning initial consonants, the teacher might pick a very simple book, one that contains a number of repetitions of the target consonant. The teacher provides an overview of the text and asks students to predict what the selection will tell if it is nonfiction or what will happen if it is fiction. The teacher then does a text or picture walk, in which she gives the gist of the story and reviews difficult words or expressions that might occur or any other elements that might pose problems. The teacher then reads the book aloud, pointing to the words she is reading. The book is then share-read. The book is made available for students to reread during the day and/or take home and read.

STUDENTS' WRITING

To further foster the development of literacy concepts, encourage students to write. In the past, children were discouraged from writing, except for copying, until they had been taught

Invented spelling: intuitive spellings that students create before being introduced to conventional spelling, or as they are learning to spell. Invented spelling is sometimes referred to as "developmental" or "transitional" spelling.

how to form letters of the alphabet and were taught how to spell some words. As a result, their writing was limited to words that they could spell and whose letters they could form. The current conception is that writing is a developmental ability that has its roots in language, starts with scribbling, and evolves into drawing and ever more complex representations, including the use of random letters, **invented spelling,** and, eventually, conventional spelling (Calkins, 1994; Temple, Nathan, Temple, & Burris, 1993).

As they progress, children create or invent a system of representing sounds that, in the early stages, might use a letter or two to represent a whole word such as *lion* (which might be spelled *LN*) but that becomes increasingly accurate. Through invented spelling, children explore the nature of the spelling system and advance in their ability to spell and to decode printed words. (See pp. 141–150 for additional information about the stages of spelling.)

Daily writing activities in which invented spelling is encouraged foster development in both reading and writing. Initially, the writing activities might start with drawing a picture and then writing a story about the picture. Other writing activities include describing trips and memorable events, writing pieces telling about themselves and others, composing lists, writing notes and letters, creating fictional pieces, and keeping a journal.

Unfortunately, many low-achieving readers have had negative experiences with writing and may be extremely reluctant to write. Having had their erroneous spelling corrected on many occasions, they may also be unwilling to try invented spelling. Part of fostering a willingness to write is the approach that one takes. Sulzby and Barnhart (1992) suggest incorporating three elements in your approach. First, accept whatever form of writing children choose to use, whether this be drawing or scribbling or using random letters. Second, make your request simple. Say, "Write a story" or "Write a letter to your mother." Third, be reassuring. Say, "It doesn't have to be like grown-up writing. Just do it your own way" (p. 126). You might even model some of the forms of writing that novice writers choose.

After a student has written his piece, have him read it back. If the writing is not decipherable, some teachers choose to write a translation beneath the child's writing so they have it for later reference. As the student reads her piece, note how she reads it. If the student is reading a story, does it sound like storybook reading? Does a friendly letter sound and look different from a story? As the student reads, does she attend to the symbols that she wrote? How close is the match between the symbols that the student wrote and the reading? Whether children use drawings, squiggles, or letters to write, emphasis should be on using these representations to create meaning (Calkins, 2003).

In general, students should be encouraged to write every day. One good way to start is to have them draw a picture and then write a story about it. The picture actually helps them to encapsulate their thoughts so they can better structure what they want to write.

Foster a variety of writing activities: stories, letters, lists, signs, advertisements, and announcements. Strike a balance between providing topics or story starters and having children choose what they want to write about. Also strike a balance between the writing children generate on their own and dictated pieces that are created through a language–experience approach.

Language–Experience Approach

> **Language–experience** approach: a single student or group dictates a story, which is scribed by the teacher and then used to teach reading and writing.

In a **language–experience approach,** students discuss an experience that they have had, such as a trip to a farm, getting a new classroom pet, the arrival of a baby brother, and so forth, and then dictate a story about the experience. Through careful questioning, the teacher may structure the story, but the language of the piece should be the students' own. The story can be one that is created by the group or one that a student dictates to the teacher or an aide. After it has been written, the teacher reads the story back as the student follows along. The student is invited to make any changes that he wishes. After changes have been made, the teacher reads the story and the student joins in, just as in a shared-reading lesson.

Because they incorporate their own experiences and their own language, many low-achieving readers and students learning to speak English find language–experience stories easier to read than texts composed by others. Another advantage of the language–experience approach is that it can be used with students of all ages and is an excellent method of instructing older novice readers. A sample language–experience story is presented in Figure 7.2.

Use conventional spelling when scribing a student piece. To avoid confusion between your mature writing and students' emerging form, you might explain that you use grown-up writing when you write down their stories and that someday they will use grown-up writing too. But it's okay for them to write the way other students do.

Shared Writing

> **Shared writing:** differs from language experience because both the teacher and the student share in composing the piece. In interactive shared writing, students do some of the physical writing of the story.

Modeled on shared reading, **shared writing** is a collaborative process in which both teacher and students take part in composing, scribing, and reading a piece of writing (Pinnell & McCarrier, 1994). Just as in traditional language experience, the class writes about experiences they have had or books that have been read to them. Often a shared reading of a favorite book forms the basis for the class's writing. If their writing is to be based on a story, the story is read several times so that they have a firm grasp of the plot and are familiar with the language of the story.

A story-based piece of writing can take a number of forms. After hearing "Goldilocks and the Three Bears," one class created a labeled

FIGURE 7.2   Language-Experience Story

Hermit Crabs
Hermit crabs are sneaky.
They do not have homes of their own.
They steal shells from snails.
Then they make their homes in the shells.

drawing of the interior of the three bears' home. Another class, after hearing a version of Tolstoy's *The Enormous Turnip,* summarized it by creating a mural in which each character had a completed speech bubble.

Whatever form the written piece takes, students play an active role in deciding the content. For instance in creating the mural for *The Turnip* (Domanska, 1969), each student drew one of the characters in the tale and, in a conversation bubble drawn by the teacher, decided what the character would say. One student decided that his character would say, "One, two, three, pull" (Pinnell & McCarrier, 1994).

In addition to suggesting content, students also participate in the writing. In a form of shared writing known as interactive writing, the teacher encourages students to scribe initial consonants, parts of words, or even whole words. One strategy that these novice writers are encouraged to use is knowledge of the spellings of their names. For instance, Tiffany was able to supply the first letter of *turnip* because *turnip* begins like *Tiffany,* and Paul was able to supply the first letter of *pull.* The students' names are also placed on the wall in alphabetical order so these can be used to help with the spelling of words. The teacher also uses prompts to call students' attention to the number of words in the sentence and to reinforce the concept of separate words and other print concepts. Some prompts that might be used include the following (Pinnell & Fountas, 1998):

- How many words are there in our sentence?
- Can you clap as I say each word?
- What is the first word that we want to write?
- Say the word slowly. What sounds do you hear?
- What sound do you hear at the beginning of the word?
- Whose name begins like that word?
- What letter stands for that sound?
- Can you write the letter that stands for that sound?

Here is sample dialog to show how shared writing might be implemented. It is based on work by Martin (1995). After reading *All I Am* (Roe, 1990), students discuss things they can do. The class decides to compose a shared story telling what they can do.

Robert: I can sing.

Teacher: How shall we write that in our story?

Tanya: Robert can sing.

Teacher: (pointing to spot on chalkboard) Robert, will you write your name here?

Teacher: (pointing to and reading "Robert") What goes next?

James: *can.*

Teacher: How does can begin? Who has a name that begins like *can?*

Carmelita: I do.

Teacher: How does your name begin?

Carmelita: With a *c.* My name begins with a *c.*

Teacher: Can you write a *c* here? (Judging that the class does not know the sound of the short *a,* she adds an *a* and reads /ca/.) What do we need to add to /ca/ to make *can?*

Class: *n.*

Teacher: Who can add an *n?*

Nina: I can.

Teacher: (after *n* has been added, reads while pointing to each word as she says it), Robert can. What can Robert do?

Class: Sing.

Teacher: How does *sing* begin? Whose name begins like *sing?* (Getting no response) How about *Sandra?* Does *sing* begin like *Sandra?*

Teacher: Sandra, can you make an *s* here?

Teacher: (Adds *ing* to *s* and reads), *sing.* Robert can sing. Is this right? Is this what we wanted to write?

The scaffolding and explanations that the teacher offers are geared to the students' level of understanding. Skills and understandings that students are currently working on are the concepts of word and beginning sounds. Later, the teacher might focus on ending and then medial sounds or high-frequency words. Stories are posted and students are encouraged to read them from time to time. As a reference, all of the students' first names are listed in alphabetical order on a chart that is displayed prominently. Also listed are color words and other words that the class has studied. An alphabet strip is also available in case students forget how to form a letter. As students learn high-frequency words such as *the,* these are listed on the class's word wall.

Handwriting

Even though they may have been in school for several years, low-achieving readers may not have learned how to form correctly all of the letters of the alphabet. As they explore writing, students will naturally learn some aspects of letter formation. Displaying a large model alphabet and individual alphabet cards will help. However, they should also be provided with direct instruction. (See Chapter 13 for suggestions for teaching handwriting to older students whose handwriting skills are deficient.)

PHONOLOGICAL PROCESSES AND READING

Upon entering school, the average child has a command of some 6,000 words and has mastered the basics of a breathtakingly complex language system. They would have no difficulty distinguishing between the statements "I stepped on my cat" and "I stepped on my hat," even though the two statements differ by only a single speech sound. When they are communicating, children are operating on automatic pilot and are attending to the meaning of what they hear and say, rather than the structure of their utterances. However, reading demands that students be able to deal with the structure of language in an abstract way. For instance, students must be able to abstract the beginning sounds of words before they can learn that *b* represents the sound /b/, as in the beginning of *ball.*

In conversation, students are not aware that words have separate sounds. They may not even have a concept of what a word is or may not be able to tell how many words are in a sentence. "What did you say?" may seem like a single speech event to them: "Whatyasay?"

Speech sounds, or phonemes, vary according to the environment. The sound of /p/ in *pat* is not the same as the sound of /p/ in *tap*.

Without being able to detect the separate words in a sentence, students will not be able to match printed words with their spoken equivalents.

Although most students learn the necessary phonological skills with little difficulty, a significant number do have problems in this area. Clay (1991a) found that a large percentage of six-year-olds who were having difficulty learning to read could not detect the separate sounds in words. Juel, Griffith, and Gough (1986) found that most of the children who had difficulty learning to decode in first grade had been deficient in phonemic awareness when they entered first grade. The prestigious Committee on the Prevention of Reading Difficulties in Young Children declared that phonemic awareness is the "key to understanding the logic of the alphabetic principle and thus to the learnability of phonics and spelling" (Snow, Burns, & Griffin, 1998, p. 15). Phonological awareness is not the only skill that readers need, but it might just be the most essential.

What makes detecting the sounds of a word like *sun* or *cat* so difficult? First of all, speech sounds are not articulated separately. "Spoken language is seamless. There are no breaks in speech signaling where one phoneme ends and the next begins" (National Reading Panel, 2000, Sec. 2, p. 11). For instance, the word *hat* is not articulated *h-a-t*. Nor is it perceived as three sounds. The word *hat* is spoken as one continuous flow of sound. Its sounds are formed and perceived more or less simultaneously. Because of a speech phenomenon known as coarticulation, the lips form /h/ and at the same time the tongue articulates an /a/ and glides into a /t/. The /h/, /a/, and /t/ overlap and form a single pulse of sound (Liberman & Mattingly, 1989). This is an advantage for the listener. It speeds the perception of speech. However, coarticulation makes detecting individual sounds difficult.

Metalinguistic ability: the ability to think of language as an object itself: to think of words as words and speech sounds as speech sounds.

In addition, phonological awareness requires dealing with language on an abstract or metalinguistic level. **Metalinguistic ability** requires that the child deal with the form as well as the content of language. Metalinguistic skills go beyond using language and involve playing with language, thinking and talking about language, and making judgments about the correctness of language. Children begin to show some evidence of metalinguistic awareness at the age of three (Snow, Burns, & Griffin, 1998). However, this ability develops slowly and continues into the school years. For a time children have difficulty considering words apart from their meanings. For instance, when asked to tell which word is longer, *snake* or *caterpillar,* many children will respond that *snake* is longer because they are thinking of the creature named by *snake* and not the word. When they are asked to segment sentences into words, young children tend to supply meaningful phrases rather than individual words: The little boy / has a red wagon.

Metalinguistic awareness requires a certain degree of cognitive development. Speaking of tasks that require the manipulation of beginning sounds, Harris and Sipay (1990) comment, "The ability to abstract a beginning sound from a spoken word and compare it with the beginning sound of another word is a cognitive ability that many five- and six-year-olds have not yet developed. In Piaget's terms, it requires 'decentration' " (p. 42).

Decentration, a hallmark of the stage of concrete operations, means that a child must be able to consider two aspects of a situation at that same time. In language, the child must realize that *cat* represents an animal and is a word composed of sounds. Watson (1984) posits a decentration lag for those who have difficulty noting sounds in words.

> **Decentration:** cognitive operation in which a child has the ability to consider two or more aspects of an object or event at the same time.

Some students who perform normally on general language measures are slow to develop decentration ability, which in turn slows down development of phonemic awareness, which in turn blocks progress in reading. These students would need additional experience with phonemic awareness activities.

Phonological awareness is deeply rooted in language. At the earliest stages, words may be represented in memory holistically. Over time, the holistic representations become more and more segmented, so that words may be represented as syllables and, later, by individual sounds. Children's earliest words may be stored holistically. As children mature, this holistic storage may become more segmented, until eventually it reaches the phoneme level (Fowler, 1991). This development from holistic to segmented continues until about age eight. Segmentation ability apparently develops as children's vocabularies grow and as they acquire larger numbers of words that have similar pronunciations, such as *hat, hot, hop, hope.* Distinguishing these words means that they must be able to segment words into increasingly smaller units of pronunciation until they are segmenting words sound by sound. If students' vocabularies are limited, they may have difficulty with phonological awareness. Students may also have difficulty with phonemic awareness if their pronunciation of sounds lacks accuracy and distinctiveness (Elbro, Borstrøm, & Petersen, 1998).

Phonological awareness develops from larger to smaller units. For most students, the easiest phonological awareness task is detecting rhyme. Rhyming does not require the student to manipulate sounds (Yopp, 1988). However, rhyming does require a level of abstraction. In order to be able to tell whether the words *cat* and *hat* rhyme, the child must be able to abstract *at* from each word, compare them, and note that they are the same. Rhyming poses problems for some kindergarten students and even a few students in grade 1. The next easiest task is blending, in which students are required to synthesize a series of speech sounds into words. Hearing /h/, /a/, /t/, the student blends it into the word *hat.* Blending words in this way can be good preparation for noting initial sounds. Blending onsets and rimes (*m + an = man*) is easier than blending all the sounds in a word but still provides preparation for detecting initial consonant sounds. Segmenting sounds is a more advanced task. When segmenting sounds, students break down a word into its component sounds. Given the word *house,* they say, /h/, /ow/, /s/. Segmenting words into syllables, into onset and rime, or simply isolating the first consonant is easier than segmenting words into individual sounds. Segmenting a word into individual sounds is a struggle for many kindergarten children (Liberman, Shankweiler, Fischer, & Carter, 1974; Yopp, 1995). At age six, one child in six still had difficulty segmenting a word into its individual phonemes (Sawyer, 1987). The ability to segment words into individual phonemes develops last.

> Phonemic awareness goes beyond merely noting separate sounds in words. It requires mentally holding onto and manipulating sounds in words (Gentry & Gillet, 1993).

> The **onset** is a word's initial consonant or consonant combination.

> The **rime** is the rhyming part of a word, the part that begins with a vowel (*-et, -oat*).

> Perhaps because they are dealing with the beginning of words, ELL students may find detecting beginning sounds easier than detecting rhyme.

Phonological Awareness and ELL Students

Native speakers of another language do best if they learn phonemic awareness in their own language. These skills transfer. However, difficulties arise when English language learners are taught phonemic awareness in English. There will be a number of sounds in English that are not present in the students' native language. They may be asked to detect sounds that are foreign to them. When teaching phonemic awareness to English learners, focus on sounds that are the same in both languages. For instance, there is no long *e* in Spanish but there is a long *o,* so start with the long-*o* sound. Table 7.1 compares sounds in English and Spanish.

Assessing Phonological Awareness

Phonological awareness can be assessed in a variety of ways: by telling which words rhyme or which begin with the same sound, by having the student tell how many sounds are in words, by having students blend individual sounds to compose a word (/r/ + /a/ + /t/ = rat), or by deleting a sound from a word: taking /k/ from *cat,* for instance, or deleting and sub-

TABLE 7.1   Comparison of Speech Sounds in Spanish and English

English Vowel Sounds Not Present in Spanish

Short *a*: cat
Short *i*: wish
Short *u*: cup
Short double *o*: book
Schwa: sofa

English Consonant Sounds Not Present in Spanish

/j/: jump
/v/: vase
/z/: zipper
/sh/: shoe
/ŋ/: sing

Possible Confusions

/b/ pronounced /p/: *cab* becomes *cap*
/j/ pronounced /y/: *jet* becomes *yet*
/ŋ/ pronounced /n/: *sing* becomes *sin*
/ch/ pronounced /sh/: *choose* becomes *shoes*
/v/ pronounced /b/: *vote* becomes *boat*
/y/ pronounced /j/: *yet* becomes *jet*
/sk/, /sp/, /st/ pronounced as /esk/, /esp/, /est/
/i/ pronounced /ē/: *sit* becomes *seat*
/ē/ pronounced /i/: *seal* becomes *sill*
/u/ pronounced /o/: *cut* becomes *cot*
/oo/ pronounced /oo/: *look* becomes *Luke*

Adapted from C. A. O'Brien (1973). *Teaching the Language Different Child to Read,* Columbus, OH, Merrill.

stituting /p/ for /w/ to make *pet* from *wet*. Key skills to be assessed for initial reading are beginning sounds and segmentation.

Rhyming.   Rhyming can be assessed informally by having students match picture cards that rhyme. For instance, give student three cards, two of which rhyme: *cake, snake, dog*. Have students tell which two pictures have names that rhyme: *cake, dog, snake*. Do several examples so that students understand the directions. Also be sure to name the pictures so that students do not misinterpret a picture of a snake for a worm, for instance. A Rhyming Survey can be found on the author's web site at http://thomasgunning.org/. The criterion for the survey is 8 out of 10. If students do poorly, it may be due to limited experience with rhyme, or they may find the terminology confusing. You might try working on rhyme with the lowest-scoring youngsters to determine how readily they learn this concept.

Beginning Sounds.   Awareness of beginning sounds can be assessed informally by having students sort picture cards according to beginning sound (Johnston, Invernizzi, & Juel, 1998). Provide the students with fifteen picture cards that depict three different beginning sounds. Choose sounds that are relatively easy to discriminate and that are very different from each other, such as /s/, /m/, and /h/. Introduce the task by presenting a model picture for each beginning consonant sound: *sun, moon,* and *hat*. Put *sun* at the top of the table or desk and explain: "This is a picture of the sun. *Sun* begins with a sss sound." Pointing to the other cards, say, "Put all the cards whose names begin with sss as in *sun* under the picture of the sun." Putting the picture of the moon next to the picture of the sun, say, "This is a picture of the moon. *Moon* begins with mmm. Put all the pictures whose names begin with mmm as in *moon* under the picture of the moon." Holding up a picture of a hat, explain, "This last picture shows a hat. *Hat* begins with a hhh sound." Place the picture next to that of the moon and explain, "Put all the pictures whose names begin with hhh as in *hat* under the picture of the hat."

To make sure the student understands what to do, sort three sample cards. Holding up the picture of the numeral 6, say, "This is a picture of a sssix. Where does sssix go?" Also place the pictures of the mop and hand. Give help as needed with the samples, but then direct students to place the rest of the cards on their own. First, however, make sure that the students can name all the cards. Beginning sounds can also be assessed by having students match pictures whose names begin with the same sound.

If students are unable to perceive most of the beginning sounds, it may be because they have little experience with beginning sounds or find the terminology unfamiliar. You might further probe low scores in this area by teaching beginning sounds to low-scoring youngsters and noting how they respond to instruction. Also check the performance of low-scoring students in the rhyming subtest. Low scores in both Rhyming and Beginning Sounds indicate a need for intensive work in phonemic awareness.

> Instruction in phonological awareness that is focused on one or two skills is more effective than instruction that includes a variety of phonological awareness skills. Segmenting is an especially essential skill (National Reading Panel, 2000).

Segmentation Ability.   **Segmentation** may be partial—noting the beginning sound in a word—or it may be complete—noting all the sounds in a word. Identifying a phoneme requires at least partial segmentation of a word. A student must first segment beginning sounds before being able to tell whether the words begin with the same sound.

However, segmentation does not necessarily involve identifying the sound, which is critical in word analysis (Byrne & Fielding-Barnsley, 1995). Segmentation ability can be assessed on three levels: by having a student say a word in syllable parts: *cow–boy,* by having the student say a word in onset-rime parts *b–ook,* and by having a student say the separate sounds in a word: *b–oo–k.*

A Segmentation Survey can be found at http://thomasgunning.org/. Students do not have to be able to segment words completely in order to start work on initial consonants, but they should be able to segment the first sound and they should be able to detect beginning sounds. If students are unable to segment words sound by sound, they need continued work with phonemic awareness as they learn initial consonants. Work on phonemic awareness can be integrated with phonics instruction.

Commercial Tests.   A number of commercial tests assess phonological awareness. TALS (Test of Awareness of Language Segments) (Sawyer, 1987) assesses a student's ability to segment sentences into individual words, long-spoken words into syllables, and short-spoken words into individual phonemes. To make the task of segmenting concrete, the student uses blocks or chips to indicate segments. Although it was designed primarily for children between the ages of 4½ and 7, TALS has been used with older disabled readers and with adults. The Phonological Awareness Test (Lingui Systems) assesses all aspects of phonological awareness and also basic phonics. The Comprehensive Test of Phonological Processing (CTOPP) (Pro-Ed) assesses phonological awareness, phonological memory, and rapid naming. There are two versions: one for kindergarteners and first-graders and a second for students in grades 2 through college. All subtests of commercial tests of phonological awareness need not be given. Time can be saved by giving just those that are critical for reading. For instance, since the ability to delete or substitute phonemes is not required for beginning reading instruction, you may omit subtests that assess these skills. The Phonological Awareness Literacy Screening (PALS) (University of Virginia) uses picture sorts to assess rhyming and phonological awareness.

Techniques for Building Phonological Skills

Developing phonological awareness should be seen as being part of a program of overall language development. Since phonological awareness apparently grows out of vocabulary knowledge, the more words children know, the easier it will be for them to develop phonological awareness. As children's vocabularies develop, they acquire an increasing number of words that have similar sounds, so that they have to distinguish between words like *bat, bet, bit, but, beet,* and so on (Metsala, 1999). As their vocabularies grow, children develop the ability to make finer discriminations and begin processing words on a phonemic rather than a holistic level. Because they have more experience with everyday words, students are better able to discriminate between familiar, everyday words with similar sounds than they are between unfamiliar or infrequently heard words that have similar sounds. Beginning elements are easier to segment or isolate than ending ones. Middle elements are the

Given intensive instruction, children who lack phonemic awareness can catch up to students whose phonological awareness is more advanced (O'Connor, 2000). However, the gap widens if students who are poor in phonological awareness are not provided with instruction (McBride-Chang, Wagner, & Chang, 1997).

most difficult. Words with fewer sounds are easier to work with than words with more sounds (Troia, 2004).

One way to foster overall phonological awareness is through natural activities such as word play and listening to rhymes, riddles, puns, jokes, songs, and stories that call attention to words as words and sounds as sounds. When students play with language, instead of just listening to the meaning, they are drawn to words and sounds as abstract units of language.

Rhyme.   A good place to begin the development of phonological skill is with rhyme. An enjoyable way to develop the concept of rhyme is to read nursery rhymes and other rhyming tales to students. At first, just read and discuss the rhymes, so that students build a kind of subconscious storehouse of rhyming knowledge. Maclean, Bryant, and Bradley (1987) found that children who knew nursery rhymes were better at detecting rhyme and learned to read faster than children who lacked that knowledge. For older students, who might perceive nursery rhymes as being too babyish, substitute humorous verses or jump-rope rhymes similar to the following:

> *When you're old and think you're sweet*
> *Pull off your shoes*
> *And smell your feet.*

As students become familiar with rhyming pieces, stress the rhyming elements. As you develop a concept of rhyme, also build the language used to talk about rhyme: *same, sounds, rhyme, words,* and so forth.

Building Rhymes.   To extend the concept of rhyme, build rhymes with students. Using the element *at,* here is how a rhyme might be built. Say "at." Have students say "at." Tell students that you are going to make words that have *at* in them. Say "c-at," emphasizing the *at* portion of the word. Ask students if they can hear the *at* in *c-at.* Holding up a picture of a cat, have them say *cat* and listen to the *at* in *c-at.* (By using pictures, you are reducing the burden on students' memories). Hold up a picture of a hat. Have students tell what it is. Tell students that *h-at* has an *at* in it. Ask them if they can hear the *at* in *h-at.* Introduce *rat, bat,* and *sat* in the same way. Ask students if they can tell what sound is the same in *cat, hat, rat, bat,* and *sat.* Stress the *at* in each of these words. Explain that *cat, hat, rat, bat,* and *sat* rhyme because they all have *at* at the end. Invite students to suggest other words that rhyme with *cat: mat, pat, fat, that.*

Ask students if *hen* rhymes with *cat.* Discuss the fact that *cat* ends with *at* and *hen* ends with *en,* so they don't rhyme. Ask if *sat* rhymes with *cat.* Discuss why these two words rhyme. Emphasize that they both end with *at,* so they rhyme. Other groups of words that might be used to build rhymes are listed below.

bag, rag, tag, flag	*cape, tape, grape*
hay, clay, tray	*cake, rake, snake*
mail, nail, pail, sail, snail, tail	*car, jar, star*

bed, red, sled, bread, thread   *sock, block, clock, lock, rock*
king, ring, wing, string, swing   *boat, coat, goat*

Identifying Rhymes.   Have students tell whether word pairs such as the following rhyme: cat—hat, hat—pan, mat—rat, can—man. If the students give correct responses, affirm their answers and explain why the answers are correct. "Yes, *cat* and *hat* do rhyme. They both end with an *at* sound. If students provide a wrong response, gently supply the correct response and an explanation, or rephrase the question so the students have a better chance of getting it correct: "Do you hear the same sound at the end of *hat* that you hear at the end of *pan*? No, *hat* and *pan* do not rhyme. *Hat* ends with an *at* sound and *pan* has an *an* sound. *An* and *at* are different sounds." To make the task more concrete and to aid students' memories, show pictures of word pairs as you say them. From time to time, reexplain what a rhyme is. Some possible pairs of words that might be used in this activity are listed below:

bag—rag	*bee—tree*
cat—hat	*king—ring*
cake—man	*ball—net*
car—star	*fish—dish*
bee—car	*boat—goat*

Sorting Rhymes.   Sorting is also an excellent way to reinforce the concept of rhyme. In sorting, students group objects or pictures whose names rhyme. If possible, begin with objects. Objects are more concrete than pictures and less likely to be misinterpreted. Using toys and dollhouse furniture, assemble sets of objects similar to the following: boat, coat, goat; bug, mug, rug, plug. Display two boxes, one with a toy bug in front of it and one with a goat in front of it. Tell students that they will be putting the objects that rhyme with *bug* in the "bug" box and those that rhyme with *goat* in the "goat" box. Sort one or two objects as examples. Holding up a rug from a doll house or a small piece of rug, say its name, emphasizing the *ug* portion, then say "*Rug* rhymes with *bug*. Both have an *ug* sound, so I'll put it in the 'bug' box."

Once students understand what they are to do, have them sort the objects. Have them name the object, tell which of the two boxes it should be placed in, and why. After all the objects have been sorted, have students name the objects in each box and note that all the objects rhyme.

Another way of sorting rhymes is to give each child a picture card. In a pocket chart, place the example cards (cat, goat) and have students come up and place their picture cards under the example cards with which they rhyme (Gentry & Gillet, 1993).

Also have students sort pictures. Some pictures that might be used in sorting rhymes include: bat, cat, hat, rat; nail, pail, sail, snail; cake, rake, snake; bed, bread, sled; car, jar, star; king, ring, string. Pictures are sorted in much the same way as are objects. Select a picture to serve as a model for each rhyming pattern and have students place rhyming pictures underneath.

Students can work individually, in pairs, or in small groups. After a sort has been completed, have students say the name of each picture in a category. If students are slow or hesitant, discuss any questions they might have and ask them to sort again. If students have completed a sort under your guidance, have them sort the items a second time for additional practice. Also use the following activities to teach or reinforce the concept of rhyme.

- Call attention to rhyming sounds in nursery rhymes and rhyming tales.
- When reading rhyming lines, read all but the last word and have students suggest a word to complete the couplet.

> *Twinkle, twinkle, little star, How I wonder what you* _____.
> *Up above the world so high, Like a diamond in the* _____.

- Hold up an object (or picture of an object) and have students choose from a display another object whose name rhymes with the name of the object you are holding. Holding up a stuffed cat, for instance, have students say "cat." Then have them choose from a display of a ball, a hat, and a box, the one that rhymes with *cat.*
- Give students a single word and have them supply words that rhyme with it. Have them supply rhyming words for *cat, hill, cake,* for instance.
- Have students sort objects whose names rhyme: can, toy van, toy man; bat, toy cat, toy rat; toy house, toy mouse; toy rake, rubber snake, toy cake; toy goat, toy boat, coat.
- Give each student three pictures, of a star, a nail, and a boat, for instance. Discuss the names of the three objects. Hold up pictures that rhyme with one of the students' three pictures. Say the picture's name and have students say it. Have them hold up the picture that rhymes with the one you are holding up. Ask, which one of your pictures, the star, the nail, or the boat, rhymes with *goat*? The students should hold up a picture showing a boat. After students have held up their pictures, confirm their responses. Say, "Yes, you are right, *boat* and *goat* do rhyme. They both have an *oat* sound.
- Have students tell which word in a group does not rhyme: *hat, soap, cat; goat, bell, coat.*
- Using one of Bruce McMillan's terse verse books as a model, help the class create a book of terse verses: fat cat, goat boat, school pool, rag bag, nail pail.
- Have students create rhyming books. Each page contains drawings of items that rhyme: man, pan, van, Dan, for example.
- Read rhyming riddles to students. The answer to the riddle is two rhyming words. Some riddles that you might read to the class include the following. Provide hints as needed.
    What do you call a small rug that a cat sleeps on?   *(cat mat)*
    What do you call a star that is many, many, many miles away?   *(far star)*
    What do you call a dog or cat that has been out in the rain?   *(wet pet)*
    What do you call a seal's lunch or dinner?   *(seal meal)*
    What do you call a skunk's suitcase?   *(skunk trunk)*

- Have students draw rhyming pictures. Provide students with a paper that has a drawing of a cat at the top. Have students draw objects whose names rhyme with *cat.*
- Have students add rhyming verses to open-end songs, as in *Down by the Bay* (Gunning, 2000b).

DOWN BY THE BAY
Down by the bay, where the watermelons grow
Back to my home I dare not go.
For if I do my mother will say,
Did you ever see a bear combing his hair
Down by the bay?

Did you ever see a bee with a sunburned knee
Down by the bay?

Did you ever see a moose kissing a goose
Down by the bay?

Did you ever see a whale with a polka dot tail
Down by the bay?

Did you ever see a fish sailing in a dish
Down by the bay?

Blending Onsets and Rimes.   Blending onsets and rimes is an intermediate step between rhyming and detecting beginning sounds. The **onset** is the consonant or consonant cluster preceding the rime: *s-, sl-, tr-*. The **rime** is the pattern's vowel and any consonants that follow it: *-oap, -eep, -ee*. Rhyming focuses on the rime, the ending sounds of words. Blending onsets and rimes builds on the students' growing awareness of rhyme and introduces the onset. Using a puppet, tell students that the puppet says its words in parts. Instead of saying *fish* the way we do, it says *f-ish*, so we have to help him by putting the parts of the word together. Have students help put the following words together: *b-ee, h-at, b-ook, d-eer, s-un*. Present the words in groups of five. As a way of involving all students, supply each student with a set of five pictures showing the five words. Be sure to discuss the names of the pictures. When you say the word to be blended, students choose the picture that shows the word and hold it up. By observing the students, you can tell who is catching on and who is having difficulty. After students have held up the picture for the word being blended, have them say the word. Confirm students' efforts but correct wrong responses. For a correct response, you might say, "*Hat*. That is correct. When you put /h/ and /at/ together, you get *hat*." For an incorrect attempt, you might say, "That was a good try. But when I put /s/ and /un/ together, the word is *sun*. You say it, 's-un—sun.'" After students have completed a set, go through it again. Challenge them to put the words together faster.

Create riddles that incorporate both rhyming and blending. "I'm thinking of a word that

begins with /b/ and rhymes with *toy*.
begins with /m/ and rhymes with *pan*.
begins with /r/ and rhymes with *cat*.
begins with /f/ and rhymes with *sun*.
begins with /k/ and rhymes with *make*.

Blending might be difficult for students who have problems with articulation and short-term memory for sounds (Swanson & Alexander, 2001). Steps should be taken to reduce the memory load. Stretching the sounds (hhhaattt) and then asking students to repeat the stretched form and then asking them to identify the word help make the task easier (O'Connor & Bell, 2004). Sounds that cannot be stretched can be iterated or repeated: b-b-b-all.

Beginning Sounds.   Once students have demonstrated some ability to deal with language on an abstract level, as evidenced by their ability to detect rhyme and play with and manipulate sounds, introduce the concept of beginning sounds. A delightful way to do this is through reading Dr. Seuss's *There's a Wocket in My Pocket* (Geisel, 1974), which combines rhymes and perception of beginning sounds.

Another book to introduce beginning sounds is *The Story of Z* (Modesitt, 1990), in which the letter *Z* leaves the alphabet. As you read this book aloud, highlight the missing sound and discuss beginning sounds in words.

After reading the text, discuss the rhymes and the words that Dr. Seuss made up. Lead students to see that Dr. Seuss made up his silly words by changing the first sound of a real word: *pocket—wocket*. Supply real words and help students create silly words by changing the first sound. In the exercise below, students change the first sound in the last word in each sentence.

There's a _____ in my book.
There's a _____ in my lunch box.
There's a _____ in the room.
There's a _____ on my desk.
There's a _____ on the bus.

Also use names to convey the concept of beginning sounds. Ask students if you are Ms. ___eynolds. When they say no, and say you are Ms. Reynolds, ask them what was missing from ___ eynolds. Lead them to see that the beginning sound was missing, that you are Ms. RRReynolds, drawing out the initial /r/. Go around the room and ask: Is this ___ am? Is this ___ eth? Is this ___ uis? Have students add the beginning sound to each name. Repeat the child's name, stretching the initial sound as you do so, "SSSam."

Follow the same procedure with objects or pictures of objects: Is this an ___ ail (nail)? Is this an ___ en (pen)? Is this an ___ ook (book)? Is this an ___ orse (horse)? If students have difficulty with this task, drop down to a lower level, one that requires only sound discrimination. For instance, holding up a real object or a picture, ask the following questions.

(Holding up a pen) Is this a pen or a ten?
(Holding up a pan) Is this a pan or a tan?
(Holding up a hat) Is this a hat or a bat?
(Holding up a ball) Is this a ball or a tall?

When introducing initial sounds, there is a tendency to supply the letter that represents the sound. However, doing so may distract the child from the task, which is perceiving sounds.

To further reinforce the concept of beginning sounds, choose a book that lends itself to this activity, such as *Morris and Boris* (Wiseman, 1959). Discuss how *Morris* and *moose* begin in the same way. Also read alliterative tales or alphabet books to students. If reading the *s* page of an alphabet book that contains a number of items that begin with /s/, discuss how all the items begin with the same sound.

Emphasize the /s/ in each word so that students can clearly hear it. Say the sound in isolation and in the context of a whole word. Talk about the sound of /s/ as in *sun*. Discuss students' names that begin with /s/: *Sam, Sarah, Sandy.*

Also read alliterative verses and sing alliterative songs. Discuss the names of common objects that begin with /s/ and create a bulletin board of objects whose names begin like *sun.*

During the normal course of the day's activities, take advantage of naturally occurring opportunities to reinforce awareness of beginning sounds: if it is a *Monday* in *May,* discuss how *Monday* and *May* begin with the same sound. If you are discussing animal sounds, note that cows make a *moo* sound.

Correspondences for sounds that are incorporated in the names of letters are easier to learn than those that aren't. Thus, it is easier to learn *b* = /b/ (bee) or t = /t/ (tee) than it is *h* = /h/ (aich). Long vowels and the following consonants incorporate their sounds in their names: *b, e, d, f, j, k, l, m, n, p, r, s, t, v, z* and the soft sounds of *c* and *g* (Durrell, 1980; Ehri & Snowling, 2004). Students typically have a more difficult time learning correspondences for *h, w, y,* hard *g,* and hard *c.* The letter name *y* is especially difficult because it begins with a /w/ sound.

Other Activities

■ Have students identify which of two pictures begin with a target sound. Because the student only has to choose between two items, this is an easy task. Holding up a picture of a hat and a man, the teacher asks, "Which picture, the hat or the man, begins with /m/ as in *moon*? Other possible practice items include:

/s/	sun	dog
/m/	man	boy
/h/	hat	pig
/k/	bird	car
/r/	ring	goat

■ Have students sort objects or pictures whose names have the same beginning sound. Follow the same procedures that you followed for sorting rhymes.
■ Have students create sound booklets. A sound booklet contains drawings or pictures of items that begin with the same sound. An /s/ booklet might contain drawings of the sun, a sock, a sandwich, a saw, and a six and a seven.
■ Say a rime (part of a word that follows the initial consonant or cluster) and have students make as many words as they can by adding initial consonants. For instance, say "-eep." Students might say, *beep, deep, jeep,* and so forth. As an alternative, say a word and have students make new words by changing the first sound of the word so that *cat* becomes *bat, hat, pat, sat,* and so forth.
■ Give the rime of a word and a clue. Have students guess what the word might be. Say, "ay." Monday is a _ay. Give me some money. _ay me. Feed this to a horse. _ay.

Sounds in Words: Segmentation.   To introduce the concept of sounds in words—which is phonemic awareness because a phoneme is an individual speech sound—play this game with students. Pointing to a picture of a goat, ask, "Is this a /g/?" When the class says, "no," agree

> If students have difficulty segmenting single sounds, have them note the syllables in words, which is an easier task. Show students how to clap for each syllable in a series of multisyllabic words that you say.

and explain, "That's right. I didn't say all of the word's sounds. I said, 'Is this a /g/?' " Then say, "Is this a /g/, /ō/?" (emphasize each sound). Explain that no, this is not a /go/. It doesn't have enough sounds. Next, ask, "Is this a goat?" Once again, carefully enunciate all three sounds, /g/, /ō/, /t/. When the class says, "yes," explain that they are right. *Goat* has three sounds and you said all three of them. Present *sun* and *cat* and other three-sound words in this same way.

If students have difficulty segmenting words into sounds, practice with words that have just two sounds: *go, no, me, he.* Also present two-sound words in which the vowel comes first*: ape, ate, at, eat, it.* Words that begin with a vowel are a little easier to segment than those that begin with a consonant (Uhry & Ehri, 1999). Avoid words like *on,* in which it is hard to separate the vowel from the consonant. A list of easy-to-segment words is given in Figure 7.3.

Detecting sounds in words is not only difficult because the sounds overlap, but also because the sounds are fleeting; they quickly fade (Castiglioni-Spalten & Ehri, 2003). Calling attention to the way sounds are formed can also help students learn to detect sounds, especially when the means of articulation is readily detectable. For instance, have students say "mmm" and discuss how the lips are used to make this sound. Noting the separate movements can help students become more fully aware of the speech sounds they are making. This is a concrete way of experiencing phonemes. Realizing how phonemes are articulated helps lay a conceptual foundation for phonemic awareness (Lindamood & Lindamood, 1975, 1998). For instance, the three phonemes in *meat* can be seen in the three successive mouth movements needed to articulate *meat.* Lips are pressed together to form /m/, teeth are shown to form /e/, and the tongue is used to articulate the final /t/ sound. Using articulatory movements to explore sounds may help students who have difficulty perceiving them auditorially (Torgesen, 1994). It might also be that producing the articulatory gestures needed to make speech sounds requires more focus and more concentration (Castiglioni-Spalten & Ehri, 2003). Articulating the speech sounds also seems to be more motivational. In one study students in an articulatory group required fewer corrections for inappropriate behavior than the comparison group. For students who are having a serious struggle developing phonemic awareness, including articulatory movements as part of instruction might mean the difference between learning and not learning. Skjelfjord (1976) reported on two students who made no progress learning to segment sounds until an articulatory component was added

FIGURE 7.3   Easy-to-Segment Words

at	moo	pie
ape	too	tie
age	zoo	toe
ate	bee	Joe
Ed	see	Sue
eat	we	new
it	he	who
us	she	my

(Skjelfjord, 1977). At that point their progress was rapid. Because it creates strong bonds, requires more concentration, and seems to be motivational, an articulatory component should probably be added to phonemic awareness training.

> **Elkonin technique:** method that teaches phonemic awareness by having students put tokens in boxes to show how many sounds a word has.

Elkonin Technique. Using markers can also help students segment sounds. To reinforce and also to extend the concept of sounds in words, use the **Elkonin technique** (Elkonin, 1973). Through the use of sound boxes, Elkonin sought to "materialize" the analysis of a word into its component sounds (phonemes). Children are given a picture of an object whose name contains two or three sounds. Underneath the picture appear boxes that match the number of sounds the picture's name contains. One block is drawn for each sound. For the word *cat,* three blocks are drawn, one each for /k/, /a/, /t/. Three boxes are also drawn for the word *goat*. Although *goat* has four letters, it has only three sounds: /g/, /ō/, /t/. Students indicate the number of sounds in a word by placing a marker in the box for each sound they hear. Figure 7.4 shows Elkonin boxes.

Playing with Sounds. To further develop students' implicit knowledge of the sounds of language, sing songs and read books to them that play with language. For instance, read *Jamberry* (Degen, 1983), a humorous picture book in which the word *berry* is used to form dozens of words:

> One berry   Two berry   Pick me a blueberry.
>
> Hatberry   Shoeberry   In my canoe berry.

As you read the book, have the students clap out the rhythm of the piece—one clap for each syllable. After discussing the tale, ask students to form *berry* words, the sillier the better. Other children's books that play with language include:

> Geisel, T. (1991). *Mr. Brown Can Moo! Can You?* New York: Random House.
> Geisel, T. (1979). *Oh Say Can You Say?* New York: Random House.
> Hutchins, P. (1976). *Don't Forget the Bacon.* New York: Morrow.
> Hutchins, P. (1976). *Follow That Bus.* New York: Knopf.
> Lunn, C. (1990). *A Buzz Is Part of a Bee.* Chicago: Children's Press.

Riddles. Read riddles and jokes to students, especially those that involve a play on word sounds. Discuss riddles that call attention to sounds in words. For instance,

> What kind of key can climb a tree?   (A mon-*key*.)
> What kind of pet can play in a band?   (A trum-*pet*.)
> What kind of vegetable can take you for a ride?   (A *cab*-bage.)

Adding Sounds. Say *and* and tell children that you will be making a new word. Say *sssand*. Discuss what sound you added to *and* to make *sand.* Create other words in this same

Sounds in Words

Say the word that names the picture. Put a marker in the first box as you say the first sound of the word. Put a marker in the second box as you say the second sound of the word. Put a marker in the third box as you say the third sound of the word.

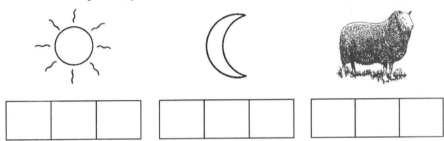

FIGURE 7.4   Elkonin Boxes

From T. Gunning (1994a). *Word Building: Beginnings*, New York: Phoenix Learning Resources. Reprinted by permission of Galvin Publications.

way. Some possibilities include: *eat—seat, ate—gate, air—hair, an—can, am—ham, at— rat, in—pin, it—sit, and—band.*

A Reciprocal Relationship

Phonemic awareness apparently enjoys a reciprocal relationship with reading (Perfetti, 1992; Perfetti, Beck, Bell, & Hughes, 1988). Thus, adults who have never learned to read are lacking in phonological awareness (Alegria & Morais, 1991). Although some awareness of sounds in words is necessary for the acquisition of initial reading skills, experience with initial reading tasks further develops phonemic awareness. You do not have to wait to introduce letter–sound relationships, sight vocabulary, and other beginning reading skills until children have mastered phonemic awareness. Based on their studies, Vandervelden and Siegel (1995) believe that initial phoneme recognition and some segmentation ability are all that is required for instruction in beginning phonics. Segmentation ability might be partial. Being able to isolate the first sound in a word should be sufficient for instruction in initial consonant correspondences.

Phonological Awareness and Word Analysis

Phonemic awareness is most effective when students learn to segment and identify phonemes as part of learning to read and write rather than as an isolated skill (Vandervelden & Siegel, 1997; Bus & van Ijzendoorn, 1999). Because the letters in a word represent the word's sounds, working with letters is a way of marking sounds. "Learning to attend to

> "It is during writing that the relationship between individual letters and phonemes might be the most vivid. That is, a child with pencil in hand as she sounds the phonemes in her mouth and attempts to represent these." (Juel & Minden-Cupp, 1999, p. 30)

letters in words and relating these to how words sound appeared to make explicit the underlying phonemic structure" (Vandervelden & Siegel, 1997). Students taught by an integrated approach outperform those who are taught either phonological awareness or phonics in isolation. Neither a literature immersion nor a skills-first program of phonological awareness is most effective. What works best is to combine both reading of nursery rhymes and other pieces of good literature and systematic instruction in phonemic awareness. "Letters may draw the child's attention to the sounds in spoken words, and a distinct visual symbol for each phoneme may anchor the phonemes perceptually" (Bus & van Ijzendoorn, 1999, p. 412).

Another effective technique is to gear the program to the students' level of understanding. One highly successful program used speech-to-print recognition. Students were required only to recognize the printed form of a word spoken by the teacher. This is a relatively easy task and might be used with students who are struggling with typical approaches. The teacher presented a correspondence and then asked students to point to the word that contained that correspondence. After two correspondences were presented, the students were shown two words, one of which started with the correspondence just taught. For instance, having taught the correspondences *s* = /s/ and *m* = /m/, the teacher presented the words *man* and *sun* and asked students to point to the word that says *man*. After a third correspondence has been taught, have them choose from all three. However, as additional correspondences are introduced, drop one so that students are not required to choose from more than three correspondences. This activity works best with continuants, since they are articulated with a continuous stream of breath and so may be emphasized without being distorted. Continuants include /f/, /m/, /n/, /r/, /s/, and /w/. Also choose correspondences whose letter names are known by students. At-risk students who took part in speech-to-print recognition activities of this type improved in phonemic awareness, letter–sound recognition, and the ability to learn new words (Vandervelden & Siegel, 1997). An adapted lesson is presented below.

■ ■ ■ ■ ■ ▰▰▰▰▰▰▰▰▰▰▰▰▰▰▰▰▰▰▰▰▰▰▰▰▰▰▰▰▰▰▰▰▰▰▰▰▰▰▰

SPEECH-TO-PRINT LESSON

Step 1: Introducing the correspondence. Present the correspondence *m* = /m/. Emphasize the way that the lips are pressed together to form the sound /m/. Explain that the letter *m* stands for the sound /m/ heard at the beginning of *mmman* and *mmmoon.*

Step 2: Guided practice. Assuming that the correspondences *s* = /s/ and *f* = /f/ have been introduced, present groups of word cards similar to those on the right. To make the activity more concrete, you might have the students place a plastic letter on the word they have identified, placing an *m* on *man,* for example.

Which word says *man*?	man	sun	fish
Which word says *sun*?			
Which word says *fish*?			
Which word says *me*?	me	see	five
Which word says *five*?			
Which word says *see*?			
Which word says *mat*?	mat	sat	fat
Which word says *fat*?			
Which word says *sat*?			

Affirm students' responses: Yes, that word says *man.* You can tell it says *man* because it begins with the letter *m.* The letter *m* makes the sound *mmm* that you hear at the beginning of *man.*

After students have learned initial consonants, they are introduced to final consonants and make matches based on both the initial and final consonants. For instance, giving the students the word cards, *cat, can, cap,* the teacher would say, "Which word spells *can*? Which word spells *cat*? Which word spells *cap*?" After vowels were introduced, choices are made on the basis of vowels. Given the word cards, *bit, bet, but,* the students are asked, "Which word spells *but*? Which word spells *bet*? Which word spells *bit*?"

Step 3: Guided spelling. In guided spelling, the teacher carefully articulates the words and the student spells it with a set of plastic letters. Initially, the student might simply select from three plastic letters the one that spells the beginning sound. Later, as the student learns to spell whole words, he might be asked to spell two- or three-letter words and might be given the letters in mixed-up order.

Step 4: Real-world words. Also use real-world materials. Holding up a milk carton, have students point to the word *milk.* Holding up a tub of margarine, have students point to the word *margarine.*

Road to the Code

Road to the Code is a research-based eleven-week program designed to teach phonemic awareness and two short vowel and six consonant correspondences. Vowels are included so that a series of words can be created by combining consonants and vowels. The program consists of forty-four lessons, each fifteen- to twenty-minutes long, that feature three activities: Say-It-and-Move-It, Letter Name and Sound Instruction, and Phonological Awareness Practice. Say-It-and-Move-It is similar to using Elkonin boxes. First the target word is spoken; then each sound is spoken in an elongated fashion as a disk is moved for each sound.

LETTER KNOWLEDGE

Although there is an association between students' ability to write their names and their knowledge of letter names and letter sounds, some students can write their names but do not know the names or sounds of the letters that make up their names. They have learned their names logographically. Some know the names of the letters in their names and even the sounds represented by the letters but cannot produce their names (Bloodgood, 1999).

A key prerequisite to learning to read is knowing the letters of the alphabet. If students do not know the identity of *s*, then they will not be able to associate it with the sound it represents. If they confuse *m* and *n*, they may assign the sound of /n/ to /m/ and vice versa. The learning of letter–sound relationships will be greatly hindered. Knowing the name of a letter aids memory. Students who know the names of the letters are better able to learn letter–sound relationships (Ehri, 1983). According to Murray, Stahl, and Inez (1993), "Identifying letter names is a suboperation in the task of learning letters sounds" (p. 5). Instruction in letter knowledge and phonological awareness helps students learn from other activities. For instance, students will not pay attention to or learn from environmental print in the classroom if they do not know any letters of the alphabet. And students have difficulty following along as the teacher reads a big book if they do not know beginning sounds. Knowing beginning sounds helps children determine where words begin (Morris, 1992).

Assessing Letter Name Knowledge

To test students' knowledge of letter names, give the Letters Name Test presented on the author's web site: http://thomasgunning.org/. If students are unable to name the letters when they are shown them, drop down to a lower level of knowledge. Say the name of a letter and have students pick it out from a series of four letters in a row.

Teaching Letter Names

Children learn the letters of the alphabet by contrasting distinctive features rather than by memorizing shapes (Gibson, Gibson, Pick, & Osser, 1962). Distinctive features include curves, slants, and whether lines are open or closed. To foster the learning of distinctive features, it is important that letters be presented in such a way that one can be compared with another so that students can note how *t* differs from *d* or *l* differs from *t*. It is best, however, not to present easily confused letters such as *b* and *d* or *p* and *q* at the same time.

A logical starting point for teaching letter names is with students' own names. There is a close relationship between children's ability to write their names and their knowledge of letter names and letter sounds (Bloodgood, 1999). If students know any letters at all, chances are these are the letters used to spell their names. Write the names of students on the board and discuss the letters that make up their names. Note names that begin with the same letter. List and discuss, for example, names that begin with *B* or *T*. If students cannot write both their first and last names, this is a good time to teach that skill. At this point, you might also want to review correct letter formation, if necessary. Often low-achieving readers form some letters incorrectly or inconsistently. Forming letters consistently builds perceptual and organizational skills. Because poor readers often have difficulty remembering visual-verbal material, it may be helpful if you supply them with copies of the alphabet that they can paste in their notebooks and refer to as needed. (See Chapter 13 for additional suggestions on handwriting instruction.)

> Just because students represent a whole word with a single letter, this does not necessarily mean that they are not aware of all the sounds in a word. At first the task of thinking what letter represents each sound may simply be too overwhelming to students (Hughes & Searle, 1997).

One of the best ways to reinforce knowledge of letter names is to surround students with examples of letters and reasons to use them. Display a model alphabet and have available old typewriters, computers, stamp sets, letter stencils, magnetic and felt letters, and a wide assortment of writing instruments and paper. Encourage students to experiment with the alphabet and to play alphabet games. Also encourage wide writing with invented spelling. Most important of all, read and discuss alphabet books, and encourage students to read these texts. Simply reading alphabet books to students seems to increase their letter knowledge and their sensitivity to sounds in words (Murray, Stahl, & Inez, 1993). Other activities that might be used to reinforce letter knowledge include the following.

- Using a magnetic letter board, mix several examples of the letter being taught with letters that have already been learned. Don't mix letters that are similar in form—*m* and *w*, for example. Have students assemble all the examples of the target letter—all the *s*'s, for example (Clay, 1993b).
- Help students create an alphabet book. Set aside twenty-six pages in a composition book. As students learn a letter, write that on the appropriate page in upper- and

lowercase forms. Write a model word that begins with the letter, so that students can see the letter in the context of a word and also begin to get a sense of the sound that the letter represents. Have students paste in or draw an illustration of the model word.

■ Use environmental print. This is an especially useful approach if you work with older students, who will see environmental print as being mature. Bring in cereal boxes, milk cartons, and other items that have labels. Have students "read" the labels and identify the letters that make up the labels.

■ Develop letter knowledge as a natural part of your routines. As you list names or write messages on the board, spell out the words and names. Also surround students with the tools of writing, so that they are encouraged to experiment with writing and make discoveries about the alphabet as they do so. One especially useful device is to load talking software, such as *Dr. Peet's Talk/Writer* (Hartley) or *Write Out Loud* (Don Johnston) into your computer so that when a key is pressed it says the name of the key's letter. Later, as students move into letter sounds, the software's operation can be changed so that when a key is pressed, the sound of the letter, rather than its name, is spoken.

> Children can make essential discoveries about letter–sound relationships through their attempts to write. Children "reinvent writing and thereby make it their own" (Ferreiro, 1986, p. 37).

> Watching and listening as children spell words is a good way to gain insights into the processes they are using. Writing slows down the student's processing, so it lends itself to observation (DeFord, 1997).

Invented Spelling

Encourage experimentation with writing and spelling. Through their attempts at spelling, students provide themselves with a valuable analysis of letter–sound correspondences. Invented spelling also opens a window onto the child's processing of letter–sound relationships. By examining samples of a student's invented spelling, it is possible to estimate where a student is on the path to understanding the alphabetic system. Does the student understand that words are composed of letters? Does the student realize that letters can be used to represent sounds? Does the student know some basic letter–sound correspondences? If so, which ones? (See Chapter 5 for additional information about spelling development. See Figure 5.7 for a chart of stages of spelling development.)

EARLY INTERVENTION PROGRAMS

Children who experience difficulty in the early stages of reading do learn. Unfortunately, what they most often acquire from the experience are ineffective strategies and a concept of themselves as nonlearners. Speaking of delaying instruction until the child has experienced failure, Marie Clay (1985) notes, "The difficulties of the young child might be more easily overcome if he had practiced error behavior less often, had less to unlearn and relearn, and still had reasonable confidence in his own ability" (p. 10).

Reading Recovery

Programs of early intervention are both more effective and less expensive in terms of time, money, and emotional damage than are traditional corrective programs. The best known of the early intervention programs is Reading Recovery.

Growing out of her observations initiated in 1962 of how children in New Zealand learn to read, Marie Clay and several colleagues made an intensive two-year study of procedures used by teachers working one-on-one with low-achieving readers. After a year of observing, discussing, and piloting promising techniques, a set of procedures was established and refined.

The plan of the program is to accelerate children's progress by providing intensive one-on-one instruction, thirty minutes a day, five days a week, for a period of twelve to twenty weeks. The intent is to develop students' skills and abilities so that they can function as well as the average child in their class. In New Zealand, this was accomplished for 95 percent of the students who took part in the program (Clay, 1991). In the United States, the recovery rate is approximately 81 percent, not including students who dropped out or, because of absenteeism, did not complete at least 60 lessons (Lyons, 2000). There is also a Spanish version of Reading Recovery, Descubriendo La Lectura. This has a success rate of 84 percent. In one study of Reading Recovery, it was concluded that students who failed to make adequate progress had lower pretest scores on tests of phonemic awareness, word analysis, and oral cloze, a test that requires students to use their knowledge of language to fill in the blanks of a story that has had words deleted from it (Center, Wheldall, Freeman, Outhred, & McNaught, 1995). In view of this and an earlier study in which Reading Recovery students did better when systematic phonics were added to the program (Iverson & Tunmer, 1993), the authors concluded that the addition of systematic instruction in phonological awareness and phonics might strengthen the program.

Reading Recovery does not have a systematic approach to teaching phonological awareness and phonics. These are taught through spelling, through the make-and-break technique, through discussions with the student when the student has difficulty reading a word, and through an activity known as "fluent write."

A Reading Recovery Lesson.   A typical thirty-minute reading recovery lesson includes the following components.

> **Using Technology**
> Extensive information about Reading Recovery can be found at http://www.readingrecovery.org/.

Fluent Write.   At the start of the lesson, Reading Recovery teachers dictate one or two words for the students to practice writing. The purpose of this very brief exercise is to foster fluency. The words chosen might be high-frequency words, or they may be words such as *cat* or *we* that the student can use to build additional words. If the student seems unable to write a word but knows an analog, the teacher might prompt the student to use the analog to write the unknown word. For instance, when one student balked at writing the work *rake*, the teacher reminded him that he knew the word *make* and asked him to write it. After writing the word *make*, the student was then able to use his knowledge of *make* to write *rake*.

> A key feature of *Reading Recovery* is the lists of hundreds of children's books grouped by level of difficulty.

Reading of Familiar Books.   The child rereads orally two or more familiar books. The purpose of this rereading is to build fluency and confidence. It also gives the child the chance to apply previously taught strategies, such as using context or letter–sound relationships. Because the books have been read previously, the child should find that it is easier to apply the strategies.

Rereading of Previous Day's Book and Taking a Running Record. As the child reads the book orally and, generally, without any help from the teacher, a running record is taken. In a running record, which is somewhat similar to the administration of the oral selection of an informal reading, both of which were explained in Chapter 4, the teacher makes note of words read successfully and also errors or miscues. An analysis of the running record provides an assessment of the child's progress but, more important, yields information about the kinds of strategies the student is using. Is the student using verbal or pictorial context? Is the student using phonics? Is the student monitoring the reading so that miscues are corrected? At the end of this segment, the teacher praises the student for the quality of the reading, notes an instance or two when she applied strategies effectively, and points out one or more instances in which a strategy that was not used could have been applied or an instance where she might have applied a strategy more effectively.

Working with Letters. While reviewing the child's rereading or whenever appropriate, the teacher and student can build words together, using magnetic letters and a metal board. The magnetic letters might be used to help the child see the similarities in pattern words (*cat, hat, sat*), note *-s* or *-ed* endings, or focus on the sequence of letters in a sight word. Magnetic letters are also used to present the make-and-break technique, in which students construct, break apart, and reconstruct common word patterns (Clay, 1993b). (See Chapter 8 for a fuller explanation.)

Writing a Story. One of the basic assumptions of Reading Recovery (Clay, 1991) is the concept that reading and writing are closely related and that writing can be used as a means for understanding reading. Depending on her or his competence, the child is asked to dictate or write a one- or two-sentence story or message, with the teacher's help if necessary. The piece might be related to a previously read book, some event in the child's life, or another topic of interest. A notebook or looseleaf binder containing unlined paper turned sideways is used. The student tells the story to the teacher, who jots it down on a separate piece of paper so the story is not forgotten or distorted. The teacher repeats the story exactly as the student dictated it, and the student writes as much of the story as she can on the bottom page. The top page functions as an instructional or practice page. Here the student attempts to write words she is unsure of. The teacher may provide assistance by drawing Elkonin boxes and coaching the student as she fills in the letters of the target word. If the student knows just one or two letters in the word, the initial and final consonants, for instance, the student might write those in the appropriate boxes. The teacher then helps the student fill in the rest of the boxes. The teacher might also write words here, if the student has little or no chance of writing them successfully. A sample story is presented in Figure 7.5.

After the story has been written by the child on the bottom or story page and it has been read and reread, the teacher rewrites it on a strip of tagboard. The sentence is then cut up and the student reassembles it and reads it. Reassembling the sentence fosters comprehension and knowledge of syntactic structures. The cut-up sentence is placed in an envelope so the student can practice reading it at home.

Reading a New Book. The culmination of a Reading Recovery lesson is the reading of a new book. Reading a new book is last on the schedule, so that the child can apply and

FIGURE 7.5   Sample Story

In a storybook introduction or text walk, the teacher provides a scaffold so that students can get more out of the story and are better able to use strategies.

For additional examples of a text walk, see M. M. Clay (1991), "Introducing a new storybook to young readers," in *The Reading Teacher, 45,* 264–272.

integrate strategies introduced in the earlier part of the lesson. New books are carefully chosen and introduced. If a variety of books is available, the child takes part in the selection process. Books provided by the teacher present some challenge, but not too much. Students should know at least 90 percent of the words in the text (this text advocates a 95 percent standard). Having previewed the book in terms of the child's capabilities, the teacher "walks" through the book with the child, pointing out the title and author, and using illustrations to provide an overview of the text. The child is invited to relate the text to other books he has read or relevant experiences that he has had. The teacher may recite from the text unfamiliar terms, expressions, or syntactic structures. These may be pointed out in the text and the student may be asked to repeat them (Clay, 1991). The basic purpose of this orientation is to prepare the child for a successful reading of the text. The new book may be reread if there is time. It is always read the next day, during which time the teacher prepares a running record of the child's reading. Because introducing a book is a highly effective technique and can be used in any program, an adapted version of this procedure is presented in the box that follows.

INTRODUCING A BOOK

Step 1: Analyzing the text. Analyze the text. Note concepts, background information, words, or language structures that might be barriers for the prospective reader. In the book, *The Hungry Giant* (Cowley, 1980, 1990), for instance, the word *bommy-knocker* would be unfamiliar. To under-

stand the story, the reader would need to have a concept of a giant and background information about bees, beehives, and honey.

Step 2: Introducing the title and topic. Introduce the title and the topic of the text to the student. Help the student relate the topic to her own background of experience. Do not dwell on the title, as this will detract from the main purpose, which is a successful reading of the text. When introducing *The Hungry Giant,* read the title to the student and ask her to point to the giant on the cover. You might note that the giant is angry because he is hungry.

Step 3: Highlighting the story. Walk the student through the story page by page so that she has an overview of the tale. Knowing the gist of the story and who the main characters are, the student will be better able to use contextual and other clues to achieve a successful reading. As you walk the student through the story, preview words, concepts, and language structures that you think she might have difficulty understanding. Paraphrase key portions of the text that contain difficult items. Then help the student point out these items. For instance, after paraphrasing the first page, in which the unfamiliar word *bommy-knocker* is used, ask the student to point to the bommy-knocker in the illustration and tell how a bommy-knocker might be used. Then ask the student to point to the word *bommy-knocker* on the page. Also have the student point to *bread, roared,* and *giant,* which are words that would be in her listening-speaking vocabulary, but which she might have difficulty reading. As you walk through the text, paraphrasing the story, have the student point out other words that might be hard for her to read: *people, butter, honey, everywhere,* and *bee-hive.* To build necessary background, briefly discuss with the student what a beehive is and the fact that bees make honey and store it in a beehive. Do not display the last page. Instead, ask the student to tell what she thinks will happen when the giant smashes the beehive with his bommy-knocker. Although the student will know most of the story before she reads the book, she will still have the enjoyment of finding out how the story ends.

Step 4: Reading the story. As the student reads the story, note whether the selection seems to be on the appropriate level and also analyze the student's performance to see what strategies she is using and which strategies she might need to improve. Encourage the student to read the story on her own, but provide guidance and support as needed. If the student has difficulty with the word *with* in the sentence, "Get me some honey, or I'll hit you with my bommy-knocker," prompt the use of context. Have the student read "blank" for the unknown word *with* and then reread the sentence and use context to see what word would make sense there (these strategies are described in detail in Chapters 8 and 9).

Step 5: Discussing the story. Discuss the story. Start with the student's purpose for reading, which was to find out what happened when the giant hit the beehive with his bommy-knocker. Discuss, too, what the people did when ordered to bring the giant food and why they brought him a beehive.

Step 6: Skill/strategy instruction. Praise the student for her use of strategies: "I like the way you used the meaning of the story to help you read *with.*" Call attention to strategies that might need introducing or refining. "You read this word (pointing to *zoomed*) as *ran.* The word *ran* makes sense in the story. But what letter does *ran* begin with? What letter does this word begin with? What word that begins with *z* might make sense here?"

Step 7: Rereading. Encourage the student to dramatize the story. You might take the part of the people while the student takes the role of the giant.

Other Intervention Programs

Early Intervention in Reading. Although Reading Recovery is the best known and most carefully documented of the early intervention programs, a number of other programs also attempt to prevent, rather than remediate, reading problems. One inexpensive but highly effective preventive program is Early Intervention in Reading (EIR) (Hiebert & Taylor,

2000). Although it uses many of the techniques that makes Reading Recovery so successful, EIR students are taught holistically, with phonemic awareness and word identification and other skills and strategies being presented in the context of reading children's books.

Boulder Project. Hiebert (1994) also created a successful intervention program. Her program emphasizes building phonemic awareness, using word patterns (-*at, -en*), repeated readings of predictable books, especially those that reinforce patterns, writing sentences in journals, and taking books home. Teachers work daily with groups of three to six children for twenty to twenty-five minutes. A key component is reading books that reinforce the pattern being taught. For instance, after learning the -*ake* pattern, students might read *The Cake That Mack Ate* (Robart, 1986). Journal writing and taking books home to read are also integral parts of the program (Hiebert & Taylor, 2000).

> Intervention programs need not be expensive. Effective programs have been conducted by classroom teachers who provided additional assistance to those who needed it.

Ready Readers. Designed for K through grade 3, Ready Readers (Pearson/Modern Curriculum Press) combines systematic instruction in phonemic awareness and phonics with the reading of a series of readers that reinforce the patterns taught. Although the readers are decodable, they have a natural flow that is missing in most other decodable texts. For maximum effectiveness the 50 books at each level should be resequenced. Some of the earlier books are easier than the books designated to be used later.

> In addition to one-on-one tutoring for those who need it, Success for All also attempts to eliminate obstacles to learning, such as poor attendance.

Success for All. Another promising program that stresses prevention rather than remediation is Success for All (Slavin, Madden, Karweit, Dolan, & Wasik, 1994). More extensive than Reading Recovery, Early Intervention in Reading, or the Boulder Project, Success for All encompasses grades 1 through 6. The basic principle on which Success for All is based is that the school must do whatever it takes in order for children to be successful. As the creators of the program explain:

> **Using Technology**
> Success for All Foundation can be accessed at http://www.successforall.net/. This web site provides information about SFA programs.

The most important idea in Success for All is that the school must relentlessly stick with every child until that child is succeeding. If prevention is not enough, the child may need tutoring. If this is not enough, he or she may need help with behavior or attendance or eyeglasses. If this is not enough, he or she may need a modified approach to reading. The school does not merely provide services to children, it constantly assesses the results of the services it provides and keeps varying or adding services until every child is successful (Slavin, Madden, Dolan, & Wasik, 1996, p. 3).

Focusing on prevention and intensive intervention, Success for All provides students with ninety-minute periods of sustained, direct instruction. During these sessions, tutors and reading specialists along with classroom teachers instruct whole groups. With the use of these additional instructors, class size is reduced from an average of twenty-five students to fifteen. During the ninety-minute sessions, students are regrouped according to reading level, so that first-, second-, and third-graders with similar needs find themselves in the same group. This makes it possible to offer whole-group instruction, thus eliminating the

need for the teacher to assign seatwork to two groups while she works with a third group, as would be the case in a traditional three-group arrangement.

Although the program is carefully planned, Success for All tends to be rigid. Teachers are expected to follow highly structured guides and move at a predetermined pace. There is little allowance for exploring a topic in more depth, providing added review, or pursuing an alternative approach if the scripted approach does not work.

Volunteer Tutoring Programs

Carefully planned, professionally supervised tutoring programs do work. Twice-weekly tutoring sessions for a period of at least twenty weeks result in encouraging gains. Training and supervision of volunteers are key factors (Invernizzi, Rosemary, Juel, & Richards, 1997). Other essential factors in successful tutoring programs include the presence of a coordinator, structured lessons that include opportunities to read on-level materials and instruction in strategies (Wasik, 1998). Gains can be substantial. Morris, Shaw, and Perney (1990) reported gains of from 0.5 to 1.5 years for students who were tutored, as compared to a control group. In the Read to Succeed program (Bader, 1998), students typically gain two years in one, but some gain two years in a single semester. However, a small percentage of students in tutoring programs make little or no progress (Juel, 1996). These students may have severe problems and may require the services of a seasoned professional.

One of the most effective of the tutoring programs is the Howard Street Tutoring Program. Initiated in 1980 by Darrell Morris (1999) in order to provide help for struggling readers on the North Side of Chicago, the program, which is sometimes known as Early Steps, has the following components.

- *Rereading books (fourteen minutes).* Student rereads a familiar book. A beginning reader will echo-read pattern books, a mid-first-grade reader will partner-read or read every other page, and an end-of-first-grade reader will read with limited support from the tutor.
- *Word study (eight minutes).* Depending on their knowledge of phonics, students will sort beginning consonants, short-vowel patterns, long-vowel patterns, or whatever element they are working on. Sorting is the way that phonics is presented in this program. This text recommends direct instruction in phonics but using sorting to reinforce phonics. During word study the student might also play any one of a number of word games.
- *Sentence writing (eight minutes).* The student composes a sentence about a topic of interest. Although the teacher provides some support, the students write much of the sentence on their own. The purpose of having the student write the sentence is to encourage the student to make discoveries about the spelling system, so some of the words will not be spelled conventionally. This is a departure from the procedure used in Reading Recovery, in which all words are written correctly. After the student has written the sentences, the teacher writes it correctly on a strip of tagboard, cuts it up, mixes up the words, and has the student reassemble the sentence. This activity is dropped once students are able to read long-vowel patterns.
- *Introducing a new book (ten minutes).* Teacher previews the new book. After discussing the title and predicting what the book might be about, the teacher walks

through the book, discusses illustrations, and has the student point to words that have been discussed but that may pose problems.

■ *Reading to the child (seven minutes, if time allows).* The tutor reads and discusses a high-quality selection to the student.

Using Technology
For information about Book Buddies, a highly successful volunteer reading program, access their web site at http://curry.edschool .virginia.edu/reading/projects/ bookbuddies/what.html.

Early Steps has been adapted and used successfully in the Book Buddies program (Johnston, Invernizzi, & Juel, 1998) and has resulted in substantial gains (Invernizzi, Rosemary, Juel, & Richards, 1997). In the Early Steps and Book Buddies tutoring programs, lessons are planned by professionals and then given to tutors. However, Early Steps is also used by professionals who do their own tutoring. When used by professionals, Early Steps worked particularly well with the lowest achievers. Reading Recovery is successful with about 81 percent of the low achievers. In Reading Recovery, phonological awareness and phonics is taught primarily through writing and helping children when they encounter difficult words. Through using activities such as sorting phonics elements and encouraging invented spelling, Early Steps may reach some of the students who need a more intensive, more explicit approach to phonics than that offered by Reading Recovery (Santa & Høien, 1999).

Key factors in the early intervention programs are number of rimes introduced, amount of reading the students do at home, and parental involvement in the children's at-home reading (Leslie & Allen, 1999).

Although many students benefit from a twenty-week or full-year programs, Morris (1999) cautions that some students may need a second year of instruction before they catch up. Hiebert and Taylor (2000) concur.

Although studies of early intervention programs are encouraging, approximately from 10 to 30 percent of the students selected for these programs fail to make adequate progress (Spear-Swerling, 2004). These students, who make up approximately 2 to 6 percent of the total school population, may need more extensive assistance and one-on-one help with a highly trained professional (Scanlon & Vellutino, 1997; Torgesen, 2000, 2004). Chapter 14 contains suggestions for working with students who have the most serious reading problems.

Model Program for Early Intervention

Based on a review of the research, a careful look at successful group intervention programs, and practical experience, a program for group intervention should include the following.

■ Beginning assessment to find out where students are. This should include alphabet knowledge, ability to segment words into sounds and/or identify beginning sounds, knowledge of letter–sound relationships, and knowledge of high-frequency words. Your own judgment should also be a factor.
■ Instruction in small groups of three to five.
■ Instruction should cover phonological awareness (rhyming, segmentation, identification of beginning sounds), decoding (initial consonants and patterns), high-frequency words, and essential conventions of print. Each session should include a five- to ten-minute lesson on a consonant, pattern, or other element that appears in the text to be read. An approach known as Word Building, which is explained in the next chapter, is highly recommended. Because students do not always apply skills, have them exam-

ine in the selection to be read sentences containing words that incorporate the element that has been taught. This should be done in preparation for a reading of the selection.

- Reading and rereading of books that reinforce the pattern or other element that has been taught. These books should be on the appropriate level of difficulty. Students should be able to read them with 95 percent accuracy. In order to achieve this high level of performance, books should be carefully selected (see listing of books on pp. 258–261) and thoroughly introduced using the Reading Recovery procedure for introducing a book, which was described earlier. This introduction (text walk) includes introducing difficult words and concepts before students read the book. This should be done in addition to the word-analysis lesson.

- As the opportunity arises, students should be guided in the use of word-analysis and comprehension strategies. Word-analysis strategies should include using pronounceable word parts, analogy, context, and—in some cases—letter-by-letter sounding out (see Chapters 8 and 9 for a full discussion of these strategies). Students should also be monitoring for meaning.

- Students should be provided with as many opportunities as possible to read one-on-one with the teacher, an aide, a volunteer, or even an older student. Helpers should receive training so they are able to guide the student in the use of strategies.

- Students should read independently as much as possible. This could include rereading familiar books or reading easy books for the first time. Students should take books home to read or reread on a daily basis.

- The program should have a writing component. Students might write, with your guidance, a single sentence about a book that they read, as in Reading Recovery. The sentence may be cut up and taken home to be put together and read to parents.

- Parents should be involved. Parents need to understand the program so that they can support their children's efforts by listening to them as they read books and their segmented sentences.

- The program needs ongoing assessment. Running records are an excellent device for observing the student's use of strategies and to check the difficulty level of the material. This is a time-consuming procedure, so you might conduct a running record once a week and assess brief segments of text. Other assessment devices include observing students and filling out an observation checklist (an observation checklist for word-analysis strategy use can be found in Chapter 4), quizzing students on patterns and high-frequency words that have been previously taught, and evaluating writing samples.

- Keep the program structured. Students feel more secure when they have a routine to follow. However, don't be so structured that you lose sight of students' individual needs (Barnes, 1996–1997).

Instructional Routine for an Intervention Program

A typical routine for a twenty-five- to thirty-minute group session might include the following activities:

1. Rereading of a familiar book (five minutes)
2. Word study (five to ten minutes, in which a new pattern, initial consonant, or other element is presented)

3. Introduction and reading of a new book (ten minutes)
4. Writing a sentence (five minutes)
5. Taking a book home to read independently or to parents

The 10 to 30 percent of students who don't make adequate progress in an intervention program may do so in a second year of intervention. A one-on-one program known as Book Buddies II was provided for children who had been tutored during first grade but were still below grade level. After an additional year of intervention, which included twice-a-week one-on-one tutoring for forty-five minutes, all of the students were at or above grade level. Sessions included systematic instruction and practice in word recognition, comprehension, and writing. Students also took books home to read after each session (Fowler, Lindemann, Thacker-Gwaltney, & Invernizzi, 2002).

ASSESSMENT SYSTEMS

One of the best-known assessment systems for an intervention program is the Observation Survey (Clay, 1993a). Although it was created for Reading Recovery, the survey is widely used in a variety of early intervention programs. The survey includes oral reading of text in the form of running records, concepts about print, letter identification, word reading, writing, and spelling. The Bader Reading and Language Inventory (Bader, 1998) also includes a number of assessment devices for emergent literacy: Concepts about Print, Blending, Segmentation, Letter Knowledge, Hearing Letter Names in Words, and Syntax Matching (being able to match printed with spoken words). Book Buddies' (Johnston, Invernizzi, & Juel, 1998) early intervention assessment, which is also know as PALS, includes alphabet knowledge, knowledge of beginning sounds, concept of word, spelling, word-list reading, and story reading.

Measures of emergent literacy are typically included in the teacher's manual of a basal series or as a separate item. One advantage of basal criterion-referenced measures is that they are geared to the program for which they have been constructed. They are also generally accompanied by suggestions for working with students who do poorly on them.

MINICASE STUDY

Jan's performance was puzzling. Although she was a seven-year-old second-grader, she was still struggling to learn initial consonants. She had learned a series of alliterative sentences for each consonant. If you asked her the sentence for /m/, she would reply, "Mighty Mack made a muddy mess." And when she saw the letter *m*, she would say "mmm." All of this led Jan's teacher to believe that Jan had mastered initial consonants. However, Jan was unable to apply this knowledge. For instance, when Jan encountered the word *man* in a story, she responded with a very elongated "mmmm" and then said "dog."

Through rote memory, Jan had learned to associate /m/ with the letter *m* and could recite the alliterative sentence but could not manipulate individual sounds in words. Thus, when she saw the word *man,* she was unable to manipulate the sound /m/ and produce a word that began with /m/. When told, "I am going to add /s/ to *ay,* what word will I make," Jan was unable to respond.

In an informal survey, Jan was able to supply sounds for all of the consonant letters except *z* and *y*. However, this knowledge was built on a very weak foundation, one that did not include adequate phonemic awareness. Because Jan's previous program had consisted primarily of isolated drill work, it was decided to present phonemic awareness and related skills through the shared reading of easy, highly predictable children's books. After reading *Have You Seen My Cat?* (Carle, 1987) or *Brown Bear, Brown Bear, What Do You See?* (Martin, 1983), the sounds of key words in those books were discussed.

Rhymes, short poems, and word-play games were a regular part of the program. Jan was also encouraged to use invented spelling. Progress was slow and labored. However, the teacher noted that Jan responded with animation and enthusiasm to games. A colleague recommended a board game entitled *Road Racer* (Curriculum Associates). A fairly typical board game, Road Racer has a raceway composed of initial consonants and clusters. Printed on the dice—there are ten of them—are common rimes: *-at, -ame, -et.* The idea is to roll the dice and create words by combining the initial-consonant element with the phonogram. Forming words in this way involved manipulating sounds and was exactly the skill with which Jan had difficulty.

Jan's eyes lit up when the teacher introduced the game. Using a modified set of rules, the teacher read the rimes and asked Jan what sound needed to be added to make the target word. For instance, if the *et* rime turned up, the teacher read *et* and asked Jan to tell what sound would need to be added to *et* to make *pet*. Jan was far more successful with the game than she had been with any of the other devices or techniques that had been tried. She still needed hints and missed an item here and there. But, excited by the challenge of the game, she put forth maximum effort. Animated by the fun of the game and flush with success, Jan attacked her lessons with increased vigor and renewed insight into the language's sound system and was able to apply this knowledge to her reading of beginning-level books. At long last, Jan was on the roadway to literacy.

SUMMARY

Although the concept of emergent literacy recognizes that all children come to school with some experience with reading and writing, the quantity and quality of this experience varies enormously. Because of limited literacy experiences or slow progress, at-risk learners should be taught literacy skills directly in the following areas: concepts of print, phonological awareness, and letter knowledge. These are taught within the context of holistic reading and writing activities and reading aloud to students.

Concepts of print that should be taught include understanding the purpose of print and being able to identify the basic parts of a book and the basic units of print, especially letters, words, and sounds. A crucial understanding for emergent readers is being able to point to separate words as they are read aloud.

A major cause of reading disorders is a deficiency in phonological awareness. In order to read, students must be able to detect separate words, syllables, and sounds. They should also be able to note words that rhyme, and perceive beginning sounds. Playing with words, listening to rhymes, riddles, and alphabet books, and engaging in a variety of reading and writing endeavors are key activities for teaching necessary phonological skills. However, in addition to direct instruction and experiences, students apparently also need a degree of cognitive maturity in order to attain needed phonological awareness.

Letter knowledge can be presented through alphabet books, immersion in print, explicit instruction, writing, and a variety of other techniques. Students experiencing difficulty learning to read and write should be encouraged to write using invented spelling if they are unable to spell conventionally. Invented spelling, and writing in general, foster growth in phonemic awareness, concepts of print, writing, letter–sound relationships, and spelling.

A variety of early intervention programs have achieved encouraging success. The major advantages of early intervention programs include preventing the learning of erroneous concepts and eliminating the emotional damage that often accompanies failure.

There are a number of formal and informal measures for assessing emergent literacy. Two of the best known are the Observation Survey (Clay, 1993a) and the Book Buddies system, which is also known as PALS (Johnston, Invernizzi, & Juel, 1998).

APPLICATION ACTIVITIES

1. Read Marie Clay's *Reading Recovery: A Guidebook for Teachers in Training* (Portsmouth, NH: Heinemann, 1993b), which describes Reading Recovery in detail. What principles or techniques from Reading Recovery might you adapt for use in your teaching?

2. Observe a Reading Recovery or other early intervention program in your area. What are the main elements of the program? Which of these elements might you be able to use in your teaching?

3. Make a list of five children's books that might be appropriate for a shared-reading lesson.

4. Plan a shared-reading or language-experience lesson. If possible, teach the lesson and evaluate its effectiveness.

5. Analyze five samples of young children's writing. What stages are the children in? What does an analysis of their writing indicate about their knowledge of letter–sound relationships?

■ ■ ■ ■ ■

CHAPTER EIGHT

TEACHING PHONICS, HIGH-FREQUENCY WORDS, AND FLUENCY

USING WHAT YOU KNOW

Because our speech sounds can be represented by letters, we can write and read anything that can be spoken. Unfortunately, large numbers of students have difficulty learning phonics, the system of letter–sound relationships that enables them to translate printed symbols into meaningful language.

What has been your experience with phonics? What do you do when you encounter an unfamiliar name, or a word you have never seen before? How do you decipher these words? Do you know any students who have difficulty decoding words? How might they be helped? What role do you think phonics should play in a program for low-achieving readers?

ANTICIPATION GUIDE

Read each of the following statements. Put a check under "Agree" or "Disagree" to show how you feel about each one. If possible, discuss your responses with classmates.

	AGREE	DISAGREE
1. Inadequate instruction in phonics is a major cause of reading failure in the early grades.	_____	_____
2. An effective way to learn phonics is through spelling.	_____	_____
3. Vowel spellings are so irregular that instruction should focus on consonants, especially in the early stages of learning to read.	_____	_____
4. The easiest way to decipher a printed word is to decode it sound by sound.	_____	_____
5. Problem readers should learn phonics through reading rather than through formal instruction.	_____	_____
6. Students who confuse words such as *where, what,* and *when* and read one for the other need to be taught to be more careful.	_____	_____

PHONICS AND THE POOR READER

As many as one in four students experiences significant difficulty learning to read. Why? For the majority of them, it is the alphabetical nature of printed language. The average student is expected to master the basics of phonics by the end of second grade (Anderson, Hiebert, Scott, & Wilkinson, 1985). For a significant percentage of students, this is a very difficult task, one that is so poorly mastered that it remains a stumbling block to effective reading for many years or, in some cases, a lifetime. Failure to master phonics or related word-analysis skills is easily the number-one cause of reading problems. In a longitudinal study that followed fifty-four students from first through fourth grade, Juel (1994b) found that of the twenty-four children who remained poor readers through all four grades, twenty-two were poor decoders and had, in fact, failed to reach the level of decoding achievement of average second-graders.

In addition to generalized difficulty with processing words phonologically, poor readers have a variety of specific difficulties learning and using phonics. As a group, low-achieving readers are slower to learn phonics, rely on smaller units of sound, have difficulty applying phonics, tend to overrely on phonics, and fail to integrate context clues with their use of phonics (Adams, 1990).

Poor readers may also scan words less efficiently. Cohen (1974–1975) found that poor readers tend to use fewer letter cues. For instance, they may process only the word's first letter, or the first and last letters. They may fail to process the medial vowel, even though the medial vowel is known. As she notes, "One might say that the poor reader is confused with vowel sounds, but there are too many instances where it is more likely that the poor reader simply made a quick judgment based on first letter cue" (p. 647). Making judgments based on an incomplete scan could be developmental. As Cohen notes, according to the Piagetian concept of decentering, younger children make judgments based on a single perception. However, as children develop cognitively, they are able to use successive elements in a word. Responding on the basis of an incomplete scan of a word's letters could also be due to an impulsive style. Some poor readers may respond too quickly, without looking at all the letters (Gaskins, Ehri, Cress, O'Hara, & Donnelly, 1996–1997).

Example of Decoding Difficulty

As discussed in Chapter 4, it is not necessary to give a phonics test to detect decoding difficulties. Problems will show up on informal reading inventories in both the graded word lists and oral reading passages of the test. Take a look at Figure 8.1, which shows Rachel's performance on the graded word list of the Basic Reading Inventory (Johns, 1997). Pay particular attention to the untimed column. This shows the number of words that Rachel, who has just started third grade, was able to read when given time to apply decoding skills.

> Looking at word recognition on both word-list tests and oral reading passages provides a more valid assessment, because most students do better when reading words in context.

A comparison of the timed and untimed columns shows that Rachel was able to sound out only two words that she did not recognize at sight or automatically. An examination of the words missed indicates that she is able to use initial consonants to decode words but fails to use medial vowels and final consonants consistently. An examination of her performance on the oral reading passages and classroom observations confirms this conclusion

FIGURE 8.1   Performance on Word-List Test

	FLASH	UNTIMED
1. me	✓	
2. get	go	✓
3. home	here	her
4. not	no	✓
5. he	✓	
6. tree	✓	
7. girl	✓	
8. take	to	✓
9. book	boy	barn
10. milk	more	my
11. dog	✓	
12. all	✓	
13. apple	dk	dk
14. like	lick	✓
15. go	✓	
16. farm	for	fine
17. went	when	we
18. friend	dk	dk
19. about	dk	dk
20. door	do	down
Percent Correct	35	45

and also suggests that she overuses context and picture clues and underuses decoding strategies. Although she is in third grade, Rachel has failed to master rudimentary decoding skills and strategies. She needs a systematic program that follows the principles and techniques presented in this chapter.

Incidence of Deficient Decoding among Older Students

Poor decoding skills is a primary cause of poor reading, even among older students. In their study of fourth-graders who failed a state proficiency test, Valencia and Buly (2004) found that 41 percent had significant difficulty with decoding. Some 9 percent were labeled as reading disabled. They could decode single-syllable short-vowel words but needed systematic instruction in more advanced skills. Students labeled as struggling word callers and word stumblers had a fairly good grasp of single-syllable phonics but had difficulty with advanced patterns and multisyllabic words. Because their phonics skills were weak, they tended to overrely on context. Word stumblers had good language skills that enabled them to make use of context skills and so had surprisingly good comprehension. Struggling word callers, however, had limited language skills. In addition to having difficulty with the same kinds of decoding problems as word stumblers, they had poor comprehension.

A Theory of Decoding

Appendix A contains the Word Pattern Test, which assesses students' ability to read major word patterns. This test can be used to establish a starting point for phonics instruction.

In order to correct decoding deficiencies, it is necessary to understand what processes students use to decode words and then construct a theory that accounts for these processes. Instruction should grow out of the theory. Based on an extensive review of the research, Adams (1990) theorizes that the reader uses interacting cues. Using a computer analogy, she concludes that there are four processors at work: orthographic, meaning, context, and phonological, as shown in Figure 8.2. The orthographic processes letters, which are translated into speech sounds by the phonological processor. The meaning processor assigns an identity or meaning to the series of sounds translated by the phonological processor. This meaning is fed into the context processor, which constructs a continuing understanding of the text. However, communication among processors is two-way. Working in parallel fashion, the processors both send and receive information. Infor-

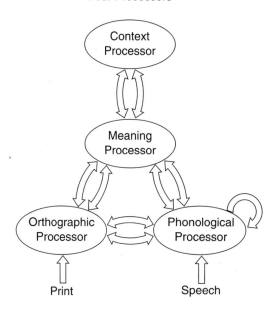

Modeling the Reading System:
Four Processors

FIGURE 8.2   Modeling the Reading System: The Four Processors

From Adams, M. J. (1990). *Beginning to read: Thinking and learning about print, A summary.* Prepared by S. A. Stahl, J. Osborn, & F. Lehr. Champaign, IL: Center for the Study of Reading, University of Illinois.

mation from context, for instance, can speed up the other three processors and vice versa. And when information from one processor is weak, the other processors work extra hard. For instance, when one encounters a word like *produce,* which can have different pronunciations, functions, and meanings, the context processor aids the meaning and phonological processors in assigning a meaning and pronunciation. Readers process most, if not all, of the letters in a word. However, at the same time, and in parallel fashion, they also use context. In keeping with this view, this text will emphasize the use of both phonics and context.

Although phonological processing is a key element in learning to read words, orthographic processing is also an essential but sometimes overlooked element. Orthographic

> Orthographic processing skill fosters rapid, fluent reading (Barker, Torgesen, & Wagner, 1992). Because they are able to recognize words faster, students with good ortho-graphic processing ability are more fluent readers.

processing is the visualization or memory of letter patterns so that students can distinguish between or spell words like *pear, pair,* and *pare.* Orthographic awareness develops from phonological processing skills (Barker, Torgesen, & Wagner, 1992). However, students may have strong phonological processing skills but weak orthographic processing ability. This can be seen in students who are good phonetic spellers but have difficulty with words that are not phonetic. Orthographic processing takes on more importance after grade 3 (Badian, 2000).

Students who lack orthographic awareness overrely on phonics and are slower in their reading. They may continue to sound out words that they have encountered many times. They are better at reading and spelling regular words (Stanovich, 1992). They tend to confuse words such as *what* and *want,* which are orthographically similar, and may continue to reverse and transpose letters longer than students who have stronger orthographic ability (Badian, 2000). Unfortunately, many struggling readers are weak in both the phonological and orthographic areas (Roberts & Mather, 1997).

HOW WORDS ARE READ

Words are read in one of four ways: decoding, analogy, prediction, or memory/immediate recognition (Ehri & Snowling, 2004). Students might decode words sound by sound (/h/ + /a/ + /t/ and then blend the sounds. Or they might decode words by sounding out the onset and then the rime (h + at). Or they might read new words by analogy (the new word *pen* is like the known word *ten*). Words are also read by prediction. Students might use the first letter and context to predict what the word might be or they might use an illustration as a clue. Memory-immediate recognition is used when the word has been encountered so many times that it is bonded in memory. Seeing the letters calls up the word. As Ehri and Snowling (2004) explain, "Knowledge of letter-sound relations provides a powerful mnemonic system that bonds the written forms of specific words to their pronunciations in memory" (pp. 436–437).

PHASES IN LEARNING TO READ WORDS

Readers' processes change as they become more skillful. From emergent literacy through mature reading, the developing reader seems to go through three phases: prealphabetic, alphabetic, and consolidated alphabetic (Ehri, 1994).

Prealphabetic Phase

In the **prealphabetic** (logographic) **phase,** readers connect certain visual aspects of a word directly with its meaning. These visual features do not involve letter–sound relationships and may not involve letter identities. The word *McDonald's* is recognized because golden arches are in the background, not because the child realizes that McDonald's starts with an *m.* The word *look* might be remembered because the *o*'s in the middle of the word look like eyes. Since the connections are arbitrary and fail to grow out of an understanding that letters represent sounds, they are easily forgotten or confused or may result in the youngster producing a synonym for the target word. The student might read *see* for the word *look.* As Ehri (1992) explains; "Because the visual cues are connected to meanings rather than pronunciation, readers may produce synonyms rather than one specific word when they read spellings" (p. 125).

> **Prealphabetic (logographic) phase:** students learn words by memorizing their shapes or other distinctive features.

Major characteristics of this phase include the following:

- Students can read a few high-frequency words.
- Students use word length, the shape of the word, or similar cues to remember words.
- Learning words at this stage requires many exposures (McCormick, 1995).
- Students' miscues are generally meaningful. Students might substitute *plane* for *jet* because the focus is on using meaning cues rather than letter–sound cues. As students reach the end of the stage, they may balk at attempting to read words they don't recognize at sight. Beginning to realize that letters represent sounds but unable to make full use of that information, students may stop responding (Biemiller, 1970).
- Not having made the connection between letters and sounds, students may spell words with random letters. *Ball* might be spelled *WOF.*
- Poor readers remain in this stage longer and may overrely on picture and meaning cues.

In a study of nonliterate adults, who knew the letters of the alphabet and a few beginning consonant correspondences, Cardoso-Martins, Rodrigues, and Ehri (2003) found that although the adults could read labels, signs, and other environmental print, they could not read these same words when they were not seen in the context of a label or sign but were simply printed in list form. Despite having seen the words many times, the adults did not recognize them out of context. They concluded that "processing of letter cues may be an unnecessary step when print is embedded in a sufficiently rich and distinctive context as is the case with most environmental print. It may be only when conspicuous nonalphabetic cues are absent that nonreaders who know letters are pushed to use their letter knowledge to perform a word reading task" (p. 353). This conclusion has implications for young novice readers as well as older novice readers. If they can get by by using picture cues, they won't bother processing the text. As the authors cautioned, "The problem with using environmental print is that the environment is much easier to read than print. More effective instruction is that which teaches students how to process letters in the spellings of words in order to read them" (p. 354).

Alphabetic Phase

As novice readers begin to learn letter identities and letter-sound relationships, they enter the **alphabetic** (letter-name) **phase** and begin to use this knowledge to make connections

Alphabetic (letter-name) **phase:** students learn words by using knowledge of letters and sounds.

between the letters in words and their sounds. They note that the *b* in *boy* stands for /b/, and that *cat* ends with a *t*, which represents the sound /t/. Novices may not make all the necessary letter–sound connections in a word. They may only associate the first or the first and last letters with speech sounds. Even so, reading is more accurate and more reliable in this stage because the connections are between letters and the sounds they represent, not between a word's meaning and an arbitrary visual feature. During the early portions of this stage, the student might use the initial consonant plus context to decode word. Confusion continues to arise, however, especially if the youngster is not using all the letters in the word. In time, most novices learn to use all of the letters in a word and use these to make more accurate and more reliable connections between letters and sounds. Switching from initial consonant plus context to the use of a more fully alphabetical strategy is characteristic of better readers. Poor readers tend to hang on to initial consonant plus context longer than good readers do (McGuinness, 1997).

Major characteristics of this phase include the following.

- Students use letter–sound relationships to decode unfamiliar words.
- Students may analyze words sound by sound: r–a–t.

Students taught by a phonics method may move to the alphabetic phase more quickly, whereas those taught by a holistic method may remain in the prealphabetic stage longer (Cohen, 1974–1975).

- Some students may begin to adopt a strategy of using known parts of a word to decode the whole word. If *fat* is not a word that they have seen in print before, they may read the *at* in *fat* and then add the *f*.
- Students can read more words.
- Students can learn words more easily because they use the relationships between a word's letters and its sounds to help them remember words.
- Students may overemphasize phonics and produce words that are graphically similar to the target words but that do not fit the sense of the selection: *bad* for *bank*. Because they are overly focused on sounding out, students may also produce nonsense words: *hep* for *help*. In time, students integrate the use of phonics and context so that they produce fewer nonwords or words that do not fit the sense of the selection (Biemiller, 1970).
- Students' spelling reflects their growing knowledge of letter–sound relationships. At first, they may use just initial consonants to spell words (*F* for *fire*). Later, they add final consonants (*FR* for *fire*) and, later still, vowel letters (*FIR* for *fire*).

Consolidated Alphabetic Phase

In the **conslidated alphabetic** (orthographic, within-word) **phase,** students use more sophisticated print units to make associations between print and sound. For instance, the reader may use final *e* as a sign that the vowel sound in *cape* is /ā/ rather than /a/. Instead of reading *goat* as /g/ + /ō/ + /t/, the reader clusters the word into longer units and may read *goat* as /g/ + /ōt/. Students' ability to learn new word patterns depends upon their understanding of the spelling system. Students who are still learning short-vowel patterns may have difficulty with long-vowel patterns. At the short-vowel phase, students understand the writing system as having a one-to-one correspondence. Each letter represents a sound. Being able to grasp long-vowel patterns means that they have to acquire a more advanced understanding of the

Consolidated alphabetic (orthographic, within-word) **phase:** students use their knowledge of patterns, rather than single letters, to read and spell.

spelling system. They must see that sounds can be signaled by patterns of letters, such as the final-*e* marker or vowel digraph for long vowels (*ripe, raid*). This is cognitively more difficult than producing a sound for each letter that one sees. Students must both look at each letter and also note the *e* at the end or the two-vowel letters and translate these into sounds. For final *e* as in *ripe*, they must process the letters from left to right, note the final *e*, and come back to the medial vowel letter. This entails carrying out two operations at the same time. Children who are not in the stage of concrete operations might have difficulty with this (Bear, personal communication, December 4, 2003).

Major characteristics of this stage include the following.

- Because they recognize natural units in words, students use longer units to decode words. The word *ranch* might be decoded as *ran–ranch* or *an–ran–ranch*.
- Students use knowledge of such orthographic features as final *e* (*cape*) or two vowels appearing together (*goat*) to decode words.
- In their spelling, students begin to use orthographic information. They add final *e* and use double vowel letters to spell vowel sounds.

According to Ehri (1994), as a student processes words, connections are created between letters and sounds. Access speed increases as a result of processing the word in print many times. Even though words are analyzed element by element, this is done so rapidly that it is virtually instantaneous (Gough, Juel, & Griffith, 1992) and so we say that we recognize words "at sight."

In time, all words, except for those we have never seen before, become "sight" words. Although words may be recognized just about instantaneously, they are learned through phonics. Through processing words phonologically, readers create bonds between a word's spelling and its pronunciation and meaning. This is true even for words such as *are* and *they*, which are only partly phonetic. As the National Reading Panel (2000) noted:

> The primary way to build a sight vocabulary is to apply decoding or analogizing strategies to read unfamiliar words. These ways of reading words help the words to become familiar. Processing letter–sound relations in the words through decoding or analogizing creates alphabetic connections that establish the words in memory as sight words. (Sec. 2, p. 99)

TYPES OF WORD RECOGNITION DIFFICULTY

Students with decoding problems fall into a number of categories. Different kinds of decoding problems often have different causes and require different kinds of instruction. The following categories are suggested by Spear-Swerling (2004).

Deficient Decoders

These students lack basic decoding skills. They need systematic instruction with lots of opportunities to apply skills. They respond to effective instruction and opportunity to practice. Deficient decoders might have been slow to learn when decoding skills were presented in the early grades. Because often there is no systematic instruction in decoding beyond second grade, they end up with missing skills.

Disabled Decoder

Despite ample instruction, disabled decoders learn new patterns extremely slowly or not at all. A fifth-grader reading on a mid-first-grade level would be an example of a disabled decoder. He might need dozens of repetitions before learning a pattern and then forget it by the next day. Disabled decoders need long-term, intensive instruction that includes techniques, such as the Orton-Gillingham or Fernald (1943) for shoring up attention/concentration and memory.

Inaccurate Decoders

Not having mastered basic decoding skills because of poor phonemic awareness or a lack of instruction or practice, inaccurate decoders misread patterns, especially those that are less common, such as the *oi* in *avoid*. They may compensate by overusing context clues and so they fail to fully analyze words. Because they fail to fully analyze words, their growth is hindered. They need systematic instruction and lots of practice. They also need to monitor for meaning.

Nonautomatic Decoders

These students have solid basic word recognition skills, but their skills are not automatic and so they read slowly and laboriously. They need lots and lots of practice with easy materials. Because they may see the purpose of reading as pronouncing words accurately rather than constructing meaning, silent reading and reading for meaning should be emphasized.

PRINCIPLES OF TEACHING PHONICS

The key to teaching phonics to poor readers is to gear instruction to the stage the students are in and to use an approach that is systematic and fits the needs of the individual learner. Ample reinforcement in the form of extensive reading is also essential. In too many programs, students are given large doses of phonics but little opportunity to apply decoding strategies. Extensive reading is required for students to incorporate strategies to the point where they become automatic. Care needs to be taken that phonics is not overemphasized, to the detriment of comprehension. Students may become so focused on sounding out words that they fail to read for meaning. Ironically, this cuts them off from context clues, a very valuable source of information about the identity of printed words.

> This text recommends early, systematic instruction in phonics along with application in context. Context speeds the use of phonics, but does not replace it.

Realizing that students are deficient in phonics, teachers may spend lengthy periods instructing students in word-analysis skills so that the students can "catch up." While direct instruction in phonics is essential for poor readers, a little phonics instruction goes a long way. A brief period of direct phonics instruction should be complemented by fairly lengthy periods of reading or other forms of application. As a rule of thumb, ten or fifteen minutes of phonics instruction a day is probably plenty.

> For those who need it, there should be some instruction in phonics every session, accompanied by opportunities to apply what was learned by reading books or other materials that incorporate the element presented.

It goes without saying that the skills taught should be those that are incorporated in the selection to be read. For instance, a good time to present the *-at* pattern would be when students are about to read a text such as a *Cat on the Mat* (Wildsmith, 1982). The skills taught should also be skills that the student needs to know.

THE CONTENT OF PHONICS: CONSONANTS

Although there are only twenty-six letters in the alphabet, there are approximately forty-one speech sounds in English. These include twenty-five consonant and sixteen vowel sounds. Many of these sounds can be spelled in more than one way. English vowels are notorious for the many ways in which they can be spelled. However, if you look at the list of consonant sounds and their spellings in Table 8.1, you can see that most have only one spelling. The consonant /b/, for instance, is regularly spelled *b* as in *baby*. Even the consonant /f/, which is one of the most variable consonant elements, is generally spelled *f;* it is only rarely spelled *ph* (photo) or *gh* (laugh). Because consonants are less variable than vowels in their spellings, they are usually presented first in most phonics programs. Coming in initial position as they do in many words, consonant letters also provide more essential and more usable cues than vowels. Also, in children's invented spelling, consonants are the first letters to appear (Read, 1971).

TABLE 8.1   Consonant Spellings

SOUND	SPELLING: INITIAL	SPELLING: FINAL	MODEL WORD
/b/	boy	tub, tube	ball
/d/	day	had	dog
/f/	five, **ph**one	life, gra**ph**	fish
/g/	gate, **gh**ost, **gu**ide	bag	goat
/h/	hen, **wh**o		hat
/hw/	**wh**en		whale
/j/	jeep, **g**iant	age, bri**dge**	jar, **g**iraffe
/k/	cap, king, **qu**it, **ch**aracter	bake, trac**k**, a**ch**e	cat, key
/l/	little	well	lion
/m/	me	am, time, hy**mn**, tom**b**	man
/n/	new, **gn**aw, **pn**eumatic		nail
/p/	page	top	pen
/r/	read		ring
/s/	side, **c**ent	bus, pass, ra**ce**	sun
/t/	tail	bat, hoppe**d**	ten
/v/	van	bra**ve**	vase
/w/	wet, **wh**eel		wagon
/y/	yes, oni**on**		yo-yo
/z/	zoo	say**s**, pri**ze**, qui**z**, **z**ebra	zoo
/ch/	church, **c**ello	ha**tch**, ques**ti**on	chair, fu**t**ure
/sh/	she, **s**ugar, **Ch**icago		shoe
/th/	think	bath	thumb
/*th*/	that	ba**the**	the
/zh/	a**z**ure, ver**si**on	gara**ge**	
/ŋ/		sing	ring

Note: "Initial" and "final" refer to words *or* syllables.

APPROACHES TO TEACHING CONSONANTS

Explicit (synthetic) **phonics:** presents phonic elements in isolation and synthesized into whole words. Thus *t* = /t/, *e* = /e/, and *n* = /n/ are taught as separate elements and then blended to form the word *ten.*

Implicit (analytic) **phonics:** presents letter–sound relationships within the context of a whole word. The correspondence *t* = /t/ is taught as "*t* represents the sound heard at the beginning of *t–en.*"

Novice readers may process words sound by sound (/h/ + /e/ + /n/), but gradually learn to chunk sounds (/h/ + /en/).

Adjust instruction for students who are not native speakers of English. Students whose first language is Spanish may have difficulty perceiving the consonant sounds /b/, /v/, /k/, /j/, /z/, /sh/, /th/, and /ch/. Spend extra time developing perception of these sounds and stress the use of context.

The two major approaches to teaching phonics are the explicit and implicit, which are sometimes termed the synthetic and analytic. In the **explicit** approach, students are taught isolated sounds and then blend the sounds together to create a word. In deciphering the word *hat,* the student would say "huh-ah-tuh" and then blend the sounds into "hat." A major problem with an explicit approach is that it distorts sounds. Stop consonant sounds, such as /b/, /d/, and /p/, cannot be spoken in isolation without distorting them (try saying *b* without making a vowel sound). In addition, blending sounds to form a word is a difficult task for many readers. Blending poses a short-term memory problem, especially if the word is a long one such as "s-t-r-a-p." By the time the student gets to the last sound, he may have forgotten the first one (National Reading Panel, 2000).

The **implicit** approach teaches phonics in the context of whole words and is the method once espoused in most of the best-selling basal systems (Stein, Johnson, Gutlophn, 1999). In an implicit approach, students are not taught that *h* makes a "huh" sound; they are told that *h* makes the sound heard at the beginning of *hat.* The major disadvantage of the implicit approach is that it is somewhat circuitous. For *m* = /m/, students are required to think about the sound they hear at the beginning of the word *moon* and abstract it from that word, which means that they must be able to segment the first sound in the word (Beck & Juel, 1995). Although it results in a distortion, it is easier to identify the sound of *m* as being "mmm."

Because it breaks down phonics into its smallest elements, explicit phonics is frequently used in corrective materials and today's basals. However, because of the distortion and the difficulty of blending, readers may not recognize the word they have sounded out. The best way to resolve this problem is to use elements of both explicit and implicit phonics. For instance, in teaching *m* = /m/, refer to *m* as the letter that stands for "mmm" as in *moon.* In this way, you are presenting the correspondence in isolation *and* in context. Students encounter the correspondence in a real word but also hear it alone. Hearing the consonant pronounced in isolation is especially important for poor readers because some students have difficulty abstracting sounds from words— detecting the /m/ in *moon,* for instance. The following sample lesson combines the best features of an explicit and an implicit approach.

■ ■ ■ ■ ■ ▬▬▬▬▬▬▬▬▬▬▬▬▬▬▬▬▬▬▬▬▬▬▬▬▬▬▬

CONSONANT CORRESPONDENCE LESSON: *s* = /s/

Step 1: Auditory perception. Hold up a series of objects or pictures of objects whose names begin with *s: saw, six, socks, seal, sandwich.* Have stu-

dents say the name of each object. Repeat the names of all the objects, emphasizing the initial sound as you do so. Lead students to see that the words all

(Continued)

begin with the same sound. Present the sound both in isolation and in the context of a word. (Although saying the sound in isolation distorts it, some youngsters have difficulty detecting a sound in the context of a word.) Say that *saw, six, socks, seal,* and *sandwich* begin with the sound /s/ as in *sun*. If any members of the class have first names that begin with *s*, ask them to raise their hands. Help the class determine whether the names actually do begin with /s/.

If students have difficulty detecting initial sounds, try asking silly questions that focus on *s*. Holding up a sock, ask, "Is this a lock? Is this a rock?" Lead students to see that *lock* and *rock* begin with the wrong sounds and must be changed to /s/ to make *sock.* Other silly questions might include the following: "Is this a wheel? (holding up a picture of a seal). Is this a bun?" (holding up a picture of the sun).

Step 2: Letter–sound integration. Write the name of each of the objects from step 1 on the board: *saw, six, socks, seal, sandwich,* and *sun.* Read each name and have students tell with which letter each of the words begins. Lead students to see that the letter *s* stands for the sound /s/ heard at the beginning of *saw, six, socks, seal, sandwich,* and *sun.* (Create a model word for *s* = /s/. A model word is one that would most likely be a part of the students' listening vocabulary and is used to illustrate a correspondence such as *s* = /s/. Most model words are easy to depict

so they can be accompanied by an illustration. A good model word for *s* = /s/ is *sun.* Place the model word along with an illustration on a consonant chart. If students forget the sound that a letter represents, the model word accompanied by its picture can be used as a reminder. Tell students that if they forget what sound *s* stands for, they can use the consonant chart to help them.)

Step 3: Guided practice. Have students read sentences that contain easy *s* words: "I see the sun." "I see Sam." With the class read labels and signs that contain *s* words, as in the examples below.

Salt
For Sale
Soda
Seven-Up

Step 4: Writing the target letter. Review the formation of *s,* upper and lowercase. Encourage students to write sentences or stories that contain *s* words.

Step 5: Application. Have students read stories and real-world materials that contain easy *s* words. Easy picture books that feature *s* words include *Have You Seen My Cat?* (Carle, 1987) and *Brown Bear, Brown Bear, What Do You See?* (Martin, 1983). If students' skills are too limited for independent or guided reading, use shared reading of "big books" or create experience or interactive stories that contain the target consonant correspondence.

OTHER CONSONANT ELEMENTS

After learning most of the initial consonant correspondences, students are introduced to consonant digraphs, final consonants, and consonant clusters.

Consonant Digraphs

Digraph: two letters that represent one sound, such as *sh* in *ship*. A *trigraph* consists of three letters that represent one sound, such as the *igh* spelling of long *i* in the word *sigh.*

Consonant digraphs (*di* = "two," *graphs* = "letter") are correspondences in which single consonant sounds are represented by two letters, as in *shore*. Note that two letters are used in *shore* to spell the initial consonant sound, but in *sure* a single consonant letter is used to spell the beginning consonant sound. Although the beginning sounds in both *shore* and *sure* have the same pronunciation, *shore* contains a digraph but *sure* does not. Common digraphs are listed in Table 8.2.

Digraphs are taught in the same way single consonant–letter correspondences are. However, you may want to point out to students that sometimes single sounds are spelled with two letters.

Final Consonants

Final-consonant correspondences are generally introduced after most initial-consonant and consonant-digraph correspondences have been taught. Final-consonant correspondences can be confusing. For instance, although initial *r, w,* and *y* represent consonant sounds, final *r, w,* and *y* are used to spell vowel sounds (*or, snow, wow, cry, holly*). Sounds represented by spellings may also change. *S* at the beginning of a word represents /s/, but it may represent /s/ or /z/ at the end of a word: *bus, has.*

Consonant Clusters

> **Cluster:** two or more letters representing two or more sounds, such as the *sc* in *scale* and the *scr* in *scream.* Clusters are also referred to as *blends.*

> A factor that is often not considered in phonics programs is motivation. Programs should be as relevant and as motivating as possible, for both the teacher and the students (National Reading Panel, 2000).

As their name suggests, **clusters** (sometimes known as *blends*) are composed of two or more letters, but unlike digraphs they represent two or more sounds, as in the *st* (/s/, /t/) in *stop* or the *spl* (/s/, /p/, /l/) in *splash.* Poor readers experience significant difficulty with clusters. Knowing the individual consonant correspondences that make up a cluster does not guarantee students will be able to decipher it. Although they may be able to read *nail* and *sail,* they may stumble over *snail.*

When teaching consonant clusters to poor readers, build on what they already know. Most clusters are composed of *s, l,* or *r* combined with other common consonant letters. A list of clusters is presented in Table 8.3. When introducing a cluster, review the known correspondences that make up the cluster. Before introducing *sp,* for instance, review initial *s* and *p.* Then use a word-building technique. Write the words *pot, pin,* and *park* on the chalkboard. Have students read each word. Then ask what letter you would have to put in front of *pot* to make the word *spot.* After adding the *s,* read the word, stressing the /s/ and /p/. Point out that *spot* begins with an *s* and *p.* Ask volunteers to read the word. Have *spin* and *spark* formed in this same way. After all the words have been read, point out that *sp* stands for the sound heard at the beginning of *spot.*

TABLE 8.2 Consonant Digraphs

DIGRAPHS	EXAMPLES
ch = /ch/	**ch**ildren, **ch**urch
ck = /k/	tra**ck**, sa**ck**
gh = /g/	**gh**ost, **gh**etto
gu = /g/	**gu**ess, **gu**est
gh = /f/	lau**gh**, rou**gh**
kn = /n/	**kn**ow, **kn**ot
ng = /ŋ/	ri**ng**, bri**ng**
ph = /f/	**ph**onics, **ph**easant
sh = /sh/	**sh**op, **sh**ell
th = /th/	**th**ink, **th**umb
th = /*th*/	**th**is, **th**at
wh = /hw/ or /w/	**wh**eel, **wh**eat
wr = /r/	**wr**ong, **wr**ite

TABLE 8.3   Consonant Clusters

	INITIAL		FINAL
L			
bl	**bl**anket, **bl**ue	ld	go**ld**, so**ld**
cl	**cl**am, **cl**oud	lf	wo**lf**, she**lf**
fl	**fl**ower, **fl**oor	lk	mi**lk**, wa**lk**
gl	**gl**ass, **gl**ad	lt	be**lt**, bo**lt**
pl	**pl**ate, **pl**ay		
sl	**sl**ide, **sl**ap		
R			
br	**br**ush, **br**ead	—	
cr	**cr**ab, **cr**ack	—	
dr	**dr**um, **dr**eam	—	
fr	**fr**og, **fr**ee	—	
gr	**gr**apes, **gr**ay	—	
pr	**pr**etzel, **pr**ize	—	
tr	**tr**ee, **tr**unk	—	
S			
sc	**sc**arecrow, **sc**out	—	
sch	**sch**ool, **sch**edule	—	
scr	**scr**eam, **scr**ub	—	
shr	**shr**ew, **shr**ink	—	
sk	**sk**unk, **sk**y		de**sk**, ma**sk**
sl	**sl**ide, **sl**ed	—	
sm	**sm**ile, **sm**ell	—	
sn	**sn**ake, **sn**eeze	—	
sp	**sp**oon, **sp**in		wa**sp**, gra**sp**
spl	**spl**ash, **spl**inter	—	
spr	**spr**ing, **spr**ead	—	
st	**st**ar, **st**and		ve**st**, ma**st**
str	**str**ing, **str**eet	—	
squ	**squ**irrel, **squ**are	—	
sw	**sw**ing, **sw**eep	—	
OTHERS			
tw	**tw**elve, **tw**ig	ct	a**ct**, effe**ct**
qu	**qu**een, **qu**ick	m	ju**mp**, la**mp**

To provide additional practice with *sp,* dictate a series of *s* and *sp* words to students. Have them write the beginning letter or letters. You might dictate words such as *soon, spoon, sank, spank, send,* and *spend.* As students write the beginnings of the words, tell them to say the sounds slowly so they can hear whether to write just an *s* or an *sp.* After students have attempted spelling the beginning of a word, write the whole word on the board and have students read it.

Students might also sort words containing *sp* or other clusters. The sort could take a number of forms. Initially, students might sort words according to whether they begin with a single consonant sound or a cluster of sounds. Students might then sort words according to which cluster they begin with.

Share-read with students selections that contain *sp* words and have students complete a variety of practice exercises. Most important of all, have students read and write stories that contain *sp*. Easy picture books that contain *sp* words include *Spot Goes to the Circus* (Hill, 1986) and *More Spaghetti I Say* (Gelman, 1977).

Confusing Consonants

Two consonant letters that offer special difficulty are *c* and *g*, because they can each represent two sounds [*c* = /k/ (*can*) or *c* = /s/ (*cent*); *g* = /g/ (*girl*) or *g* = /j/ (*gym*)]. When teaching these consonant letters, present the most frequently occurring correspondences in each pair first (*g* = /g/, *c* = /k/). Later, present the less frequently occurring correspondence (*g* = /j/, *c* = /s/). Teaching the following generalizations may also be helpful.

- The letter *c* stands for /k/ when followed by *a, o,* or *u: can, cot, cub.*
- The letter *c* stands for /s/ when followed by *e, i,* or *y: cent, city, cycle.*
- The letter *g* often stands for /g/ when followed by *a, o,* or *u: game, gone, gun.*
- The letter *g* often stands for /j/ when followed by *e, i,* or *y: general, giant, gym.* (There are a number of exceptions: *geese, get, girl, give.*)

When teaching the *c* and *g* generalizations, have students sort *c* = /k/ and *c* = /s/ words and, later, *g* = /g/ and *g* = /j/ words and discover the generalizations for themselves. An alternative to presenting the *c* and *g* generalizations is to teach students to be prepared to deal with the variability of the spelling of certain sounds. Students need to learn that letters in English, can often stand for more than one sound. After learning the two sounds for *c* and *g*, students should be taught to use the following variability strategy when they are unsure how to read a word that begins with *c* or *g*.

1. Try the main pronunciation—the one the letter usually stands for.
2. If the main pronunciation gives a word that is not a real one or does not make sense in the sentence, try the other pronunciation.
3. If you still get a word that is not a real word or does not make sense in the sentence, try using context clues, skip it, or ask for help (Gunning, 2001).

Also stress the need to read for meaning. When a group of second-graders who had been taught the *c* generalization encountered the sentence, "We went to the city to catch a train," most read it as "We went to the kitty to catch a train" (Gunning, 1988b). Had they been taught to try alternative pronunciations and to use both phonics and context, they would have a better chance to read the sentence accurately.

To help build awareness of the major sounds that letters represent, create a consonant chart similar to the one in Figure 8.3. The chart depicts major consonant letters and the

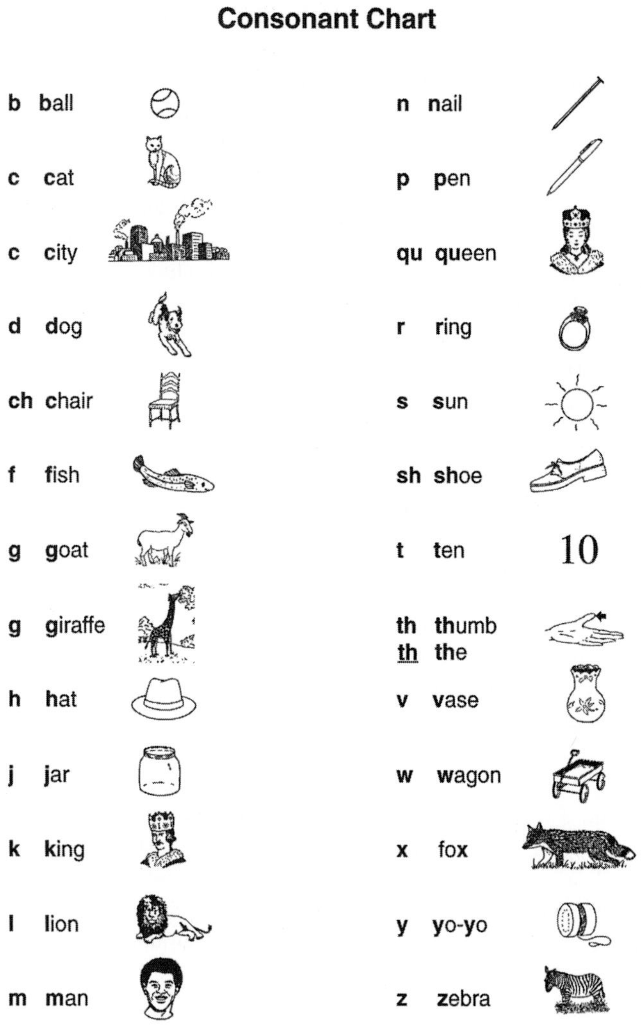

Consonant Chart

b	ball		n	nail
c	cat		p	pen
c	city		qu	queen
d	dog		r	ring
ch	chair		s	sun
f	fish		sh	shoe
g	goat		t	ten
g	giraffe		th	thumb
			th	the
h	hat		v	vase
j	jar		w	wagon
k	king		x	fox
l	lion		y	yo-yo
m	man		z	zebra

FIGURE 8.3   Consonant Chart

From: *Word Building Book A with Predictable Stories* by T. Gunning, 1996. New York: Phoenix Learning Resources. Reprinted by permission of Galvin Publications.

major sounds these letters represent. When students encounter a letter or letter combination for which they are unable to produce a sound, they can refer to the chart. The chart will be especially helpful for deciphering letters that represent multiple sounds. The chart clearly indicates, for example, that *c* represents two distinct sounds, as does *g*. After a correspondence has been introduced, add it to the chart. For students who have difficulty remembering initial-consonant correspondences, a consonant chart can be a very useful aid, one that fosters both learning and independence.

SEQUENCE OF TEACHING CONSONANTS

> **Continuant:** speech sound produced by releasing a continuous stream of breath: /f/, /y/, /h/, /l/, /m/, /n/, /r/, /s/, /v/, /w/, /sh/, /th/, /th/, /wh/, /zh/. Continuants are easier to say and detect in isolation.

> Students' progress should be continuously monitored. Phonics knowledge builds. If students fail to master initial consonants, for instance, they will only be frustrated if they are pushed ahead to consonant clusters such as *st* and *gr*.

Consonant correspondences can be taught in any order, but frequency of occurrence and ease of learning should be considered when determining which elements are taught first. Many low-achieving readers have difficulty with auditory discrimination and perception. Therefore, it is best to start with /s/, /m/, /f/, /r/, /n/, or /w/. These sounds are known as **continuants,** which means that they are articulated with a continuous stream of breath. Being articulated in this way makes them easier to detect than stop consonants. These continuants also occur with a high degree of frequency. A suggested scope and sequence for both consonants and vowels is presented in Table 8.4. The sequence is based on the frequency with which the correspondences appear and their estimated level of difficulty (Gunning, 1975).

Although consonants are typically taught before vowels in most programs, it is recommended that consonants and vowels be taught together. After presenting four or five initial-consonant correspondences, introduce *-at* or another vowel pattern and form words. If the consonant correspondences *s* = /s/, *m* = /m/, *r* = /r/, and *f* = /f/ have been taught, you can then form the words *mat, rat, sat, fat* and the sentence, "The fat rat sat on the mat." After other consonant correspondences have been introduced, gradually introduce other high-frequency patterns. If the introduction of consonants and vowels is integrated in this fashion, it will be possible to form words from elements that have been taught and also to use knowledge of both consonants and vowels to decode words.

REINFORCEMENT ACTIVITIES FOR CONSONANT CORRESPONDENCES

Reading

The best way to provide additional instruction and reinforcement with consonant correspondences is to use children's books. Alphabet books are especially appropriate for introducing and/or reinforcing consonant correspondences, as are books that are alliterative. Some books that are especially appropriate for providing practice with consonant correspondences are listed here:

Chess, V. (1979). *Alfred's alphabet walk.* New York: Greenwillow. Scenes are described with alliterative phrases.

Eastman, P. D. (1974). *The alphabet book.* New York: Random House. Each letter is accompanied by alliterative phrases.

Geisel, T. S. (1973). *Dr. Seuss's ABC.* New York: Random House. Each letter is accompanied by a humorous alliterative story.

Hofbauer, M. (1993). *All the letters.* Bridgeport, CT: Greene Bark Press. Each letter is illustrated with several objects beginning with that letter. Highly recommended.

TABLE 8.4   Sequence for Teaching Vowels and Consonants

PREPARATORY LEVEL: LETTER NAMES, PHONEMIC AWARENESS

LEVEL 1

High-frequency initial consonants

s = /s/	r = /r/	d = /d/
m = /m/	l = /l/	c = /k/
f = /f/	b = /b/	p = /p/
h = /h/	t = /t/	n = /n/

Easy long vowels
-e, -ee = /ē/ (he, me, see)
-o = /ō/ (no, so, go)

Lower-frequency initial consonants and *y*

g =/g/	r = /r/	z = /z/
w = /w/	c = /s/	x = /ks/
j = /j/	g = /j/	
j = /k/	y = /y/	

High-frequency initial-consonant digraphs

ch = /ch/	th = /*th*/
sh = /sh/	wh = /hw/ or /w/
th = /th/	

Short vowels

a = /a/	(hat)
i = /i/	(sit)
o = /o/	(not)
e = /e/	(pet)
u = /u/	(but)

LEVEL 2

Final consonants
High-frequency initial-consonant clusters
  L clusters: bl, cl, fl, gl, pl, sl
  R clusters: br, cr, dr, fr, gr, pr, tr
  S clusters: sc, scr, sk, sl, sm, sn, sp, st, str, sw
  Other clusters: tw, qu, ct, mp

Long vowels: final-*e* marker

a-e = /ā/	(brave)
e-e = /ē/	(these)
u-e = /ū/	(fuse)

Long-vowel digraphs and trigraphs

ai/ay = /ā/	(rain, hay)
ee = /ē/	(tree)
ea = /ē/	(seal)
oa = /ō/	(goat)
ow = /ō/	(crow)
igh = /ī/	(night)

LEVEL 3

r-Vowel correspondences

ar = /ar/	(star)
er = /er/	(her)
ir = /er/	(sir)
ur = /er/	(turn)
or(e) = /or/	(for, store)
air = /air/	(chair)
ear = /eer/	(dear)
eer = /eer/	(deer)

Other-vowel correspondences

au/aw = /aw/	(auto, claw)
al = /aw/	(ball, walk)
oo = /oo/	(look)
oo = /ōō/	(food)
oi/oy = /oy/	(boil, boy)
ou/ow = /ow/	(out, cow)
ue, ew = /ōō/	(true, grew)

LEVEL 4

Advanced consonant correspondences

ti = /sh/	(nation)
ssi = /sh/	(mission)
ch = /sh/	(chef)
ch = /k/	(character)

Multisyllabic patterns

Note: The teaching of consonant and vowel correspondences should be integrated. After introducing four or five consonants, introduce easy long vowels and, gradually, short vowels as additional consonants are taught.

Kellogg, S. (1987). *Aster Aardvark's alphabet adventures.* New York: Morrow. Each letter is accompanied by an alliterative story.

Laidlaw, K. (1996). *The amazing I spy ABC.* New York: Dial. Readers spy objects whose names begin with the target letter.

Moxley, S. (2001). ABCD: *An alphabet book of cats and dogs.* Boston: Little, Brown. Alliterative tale accompanies each letter.

Sorting

As noted earlier, an appealing but powerful way to help children discover basic principles of word construction is through sorting. Through sorting, children categorize words according to sound, spelling, meaning, or a combination of features. At the most basic level, pictures can be sorted according to beginning or rhyming sounds. On a more advanced level, words can be sorted according to the spelling patterns they incorporate or the meanings of the words' affixes. Through sorting, students examine each word's features and decide into which category it falls. Thus, they construct their own understanding of the underlying principles that they use to sort words. These principles are clarified and refined in discussions.

As soon as at least two correspondences have been introduced, students can sort them. When supplying correspondences for students to sort, choose ones that are distinctively different. Make letter cards for the sounds to be sorted and assemble pictures that begin with the target sounds. Place each letter card at the head of a column, say the sound each represents, and then place under it an illustration of the sound's model word. For *s*, place a *Ss* card at the head of the column and say, *"s stands for /s/, the sound that you hear at the beginning of sun."* Place a picture of the sun under *Ss* and say, *"Sun is the model word for /s/."* Follow this same procedure for the correspondence *m* = /m/ as in Figure 8.4.

Pointing to a stack of cards containing objects whose names begin with /s/ or /m/, tell students, "We're going to sort these picture cards. If the name of the picture begins with /s/ as in *sun,* we're going to put it in the *sun* column. If the name of the picture begins with /m/ as in *man,* we'll put it in the *man* column. Holding up a picture of a saw, ask, "What is this? What sound does it begin with? What column should we put it in?" Affirm or correct students' responses. "Yes, *saw* begins with the sound /s/ that we hear in the beginning of *sssun,* so we put it in the *sun* column." Sort the remaining cards in this same way. After all the cards have been sorted, have volunteers say the names of all the cards in each column and note that all the cards in the column begin with the same sound. Encourage students to suggest other words that might fit into the columns. Also have them re-sort the pictures on their own to foster speed of response. You might also add a third item to be sorted. If students seem to be using a picture card as a basis for sorting—they put *moon* under *man* because they both begin the same way—remove the picture cards as soon as they have been sorted so that they are matching the cards to the letter—*moon* is placed under the letter *m* because it begins with the sound represented by *m* (Morris, 1999).

Three correspondences should be the most that students are asked to sort. After students have mastered a group of three correspondences, drop the best-known correspondence and add a new one, or you might introduce three new correspondences.

After students have become adept at sorting cards, introduce a writing sort. In a writing sort, students write whole words or parts of them in columns headed by the target consonant sound. After sorting words beginning with /m/, /s/, or /f/, students fold their papers into three columns and head the columns: *m, s, f.* Dictate words starting with the target sounds. Students write the words in the appropriate column: *man* in the /m/ column, for instance. As you dictate the words, emphasize the initial sound. Encourage students to say the words as they write them so that they are better able to detect the word's sounds. Also encourage students to write as much of each of the words as they can, but stress the writing of the initial sounds. Correct only the errors in placing the words in the wrong column or

FIGURE 8.4   Sorting by Initial Consonant Sound

errors in writing the initial consonants. Students are held responsible only for what they have been taught, but they should be encouraged to explore letter–sound relationships and write as much of each word as they can. After students learn vowel patterns, they will be expected to spell whole words correctly in their writing sorts.

Additional Reinforcement Activities

- Using magnetic or letter cut-outs, students form *s* words.
- Students find and read *s* words in sign and food labels.
- Students create their own alphabet books.
- Students write as many *s* words as they can think of.
- Create an alphabet zoo. As a correspondence is introduced, add animals whose names begin with the target correspondence: *seal, salamander, salmon, sardine, sunfish.*
- Encourage students to use context and knowledge of *s* = /s/ to help them decode unfamiliar words that begin with *s*. However, once vowels have been introduced, encourage the use of all the word's letters and sounds.

USING A MULTISENSORY APPROACH TO LEARN
LETTER NAMES AND LETTER SOUNDS

Although he had above-average intelligence and had been taught by highly competent classroom teachers as well as a learning specialist, Nathan, a second-grader, still did not know the names of the letters of the alphabet, and in fact still could not name all the letters in his name. The teachers had tried all the usual methods for presenting the letters of the alphabet as well as a number of imaginative and motivational activities, but nothing was working. Nathan apparently has an associative learning difficulty. When students cannot seem to learn letter names and letter sounds in the normal way, try a multisensory approach. In a multisensory approach, students use their kinesthetic and tactile senses to reinforce auditory and visual senses. In addition to hearing and seeing the names of the letters of the alphabet, students say them and so get kinesthetic input and feedback and trace them, which provides tactile input and feedback. Pointing to the letter being taught, the teacher says the name of the letter and then traces it. The letter might be traced in the air, on the chalkboard, or on paper with a crayon or pencil. Slingerland (1971) recommends tracing large letters. She recommends that they be at least a foot tall, so that students feel the flow of the movements needed to form the letter. Letters are traced using the index and middle fingers. As students trace the letter, they say its name. They should trace it enough times so that the motions involved in forming the letter become automatic. Here is how the letter *m* might be introduced. The lesson is based on the Slingerland approach (1971).

MULTISENSORY LESSON

Step 1: Introducing the letter. The teacher says the name of the letter, *m,* and then has the class say the name of the letter. The teacher then calls on individuals to say the letter's name.

Step 2: Forming the letter. The teacher demonstrates the formation of the letter. As the teacher demonstrates the formation of the letter, she describes the movements she is making: down, up and around and down, up and around and down again. Students trace the letter in the air, reciting the directions for forming the word as they do so. Saying the words and tracing helps the students remember the motor movements necessary to form the letter.

Step 3: Learning the letter name. Once students have learned the movements necessary to form the letter, they begin to learn the letter name. Using a duplicated letter, students trace the letter with their fingers while saying its name. Students then copy the letter while saying its name, and, when they feel they can write the letter without looking at it, write it from memory.

Step 4: Learning the letter sound. If students can tell when two words begin with the same sound and can segment the first sound in a word, they can learn beginning-consonant correspondences. Share-read a story or a rhyme such as "The Three Little Kittens" that contains a number of /m/ words. Discuss how the words *mittens, meow,* and *mother* begin in the same way. To provide students with kinesthetic cues, demonstrate how the sound /m/ is formed. Have students note how the lips are pressed together to make the sound. Have students form the sound /m/. Going back over the nursery rhyme, note that *mittens, meow,* and *mother* all begin with the sound /m/ and are spelled with the letter *m*. Create a model word for /m/: *moon.* In practice activities, have students make the following associations.

> *Visual–auditory–kinesthetic.* Hold up the letter card. Students say its sound and the model word.

> *Auditory–visual.* Say the sound. Students, who have been given three or four alphabet

(Continued)

cards, hold up the letter card that makes the sound.

Auditory–visual–kinesthetic–tactile. Say the sound. Students write the letter that makes the sound. They say the sound as they form the letter.

THE CONTENT OF PHONICS: VOWELS

There are fewer vowel than consonant sounds. There are approximately sixteen vowel sounds in English. Table 8.5 shows twenty-one vowel sounds because these include vowels affected by *r*. Technically speaking, *r* vowels are not separate entities. However, they pose special problems for readers and so are treated as distinct elements.

Vowel correspondences are said to be irregular because a vowel sound may have a number of different spellings. However, although a vowel sound may have a dozen or more spellings, only three or four of those spellings are major. For example, long *i* has more than ten spellings: *pine, night, bayou, aisle, height, geyser, lie, coyote, dye, aye, eye* (Mish, 1993) but is most often spelled *i-e, -igh,* or *-y* as in *line, night,* or *try.* Only major spellings of vowels are presented in Table 8.5.

> Poor readers often have difficulty applying generalizations; provide practice in applying words that incorporate generalization.

> Short vowels are the most frequent (*cat, pet, hit, hot, cut*). Long vowels "say their own name" (*cake, sheep, like, boat, use*). R vowels are affected by *r* (*car, fair, for, hear, wire*). "Other" vowels fall into none of these categories (*paw, box, look, too, cow*).

> Except for the final *e*, second-graders who were observed attacking unfamiliar words made little use of phonics generalizations and rarely sounded out words letter by letter, even though half the students had been taught by an explicit phonics approach. Most sought out and used pronounceable word parts (Gunning, 1988a, 1999).

Vowel Generalizations

Although English vowel sounds can be spelled in approximately 200 ways, the great majority of vowel spellings are covered by five generalizations (Gunning, 1975). These are discussed as follows.

Short Vowels

A vowel is short when it is followed by a consonant (*bat, sit*). This generalization also applies to multisyllabic words. A vowel in a multisyllabic word is usually short when followed by two or more consonants: (*batter, bitter*). More than one word out of every four follows this generalization.

Open Syllables

A vowel is long when it comes at the end of a word or syllable: *no, na-tion, e-qual.* This generalization occurs in only about one word out of every five.

Final-*e* Markers

A vowel is long when it is followed by a consonant and a final silent-*e* marker: *cane, time.* This generalization applies to about one word in every twenty.

TABLE 8.5   Vowel Spellings

VOWELS SOUNDS	EXAMPLES	MODEL WORD
Short Vowels		
/a/	hat, batter, have	cat
/e/	ten, better, bread	bed
/i/	fit, little, remain	hit
/o/	hot, bottle, father	mop
/u/	cup, butter	bus
Long Vowels		
/ā/	made, nail, radio, hay, flavor	cake
/ē/	he, see, seal, sunny, turkey, these, neither	tree
/ī/	smile, night, pie, spider	bike
/ō/	no, hope, grow, toad, gold, roll, local	goat
/ū/	use, music	mule
Other Vowels		
/aw/	ball, walk, paw, song, caught, thought, off	saw
/oi/	joy, join	boy
/ōō/	zoo, blue, grew, fruit, group, two,	moon
/oo/	took, could, push	book
/ow/	owl, south	cow
/ə/	ago, telephone, similar, opinion, upon	banana
r Vowels		
/ar/	car, charge, heart	star
/air/	fair, bear, care, there	chair
/eer/	ear, cheer, here	deer
/ir/	sir, her, earth, turn	bird
/or/	for, four, store, floor	door

> The most frequent of the vowel sounds is *schwa,* which is the unaccented vowel sound heard in the second syllable of *sofa.*

Unstressed Syllables

A vowel is given a schwa pronunciation when it occurs in an unaccented syllable: *a-bout, di-vide.* This generalization occurs in nearly one word out of five. The problem with applying the rule is that the reader can only tell that a syllable is unstressed by pronouncing it.

Digraphs

About one out of every six vowel sounds is spelled with two or more letters (Gunning, 1975). However, digraph generalizations have been suffering from bad press for more than twenty years. At one time, there was a generalization that stated, "When two vowels go walking, the first one does the talking." As a blanket generalization, this one does not work very well. For one thing, many vowel combinations do not spell long-vowel sounds: *ou (out),* and *ea (bread),* for example. And some digraphs represent a variety of sounds. The digraph *ea,* for instance, represents at least six sounds: *bread, eat, earn, steak, dear,* and *bear.* However, a number of vowel digraphs do occur with a high degree of frequency and consistency. These include the following:

> Since *ow* might represent a long-*o* sound *(tow)* or the /ow/ sound *(cow),* students need to apply the *meaning* test. If they try one pronunciation and that does not result in a meaningful word that fits the context, they should try the other pronunciation.

ai/ay = /ā/	paid/pay	*oa* = /ō/	boat
au/aw = /aw/	cause/saw	*oi/oy* = /oi/	boil/boy
ea = /ē/	beak	*oo* = /o͞o/	soon
ea = /e/	bread	*oo* = /o͝o/	book
ew = /o͞o/	flew	*ou/ow* = /ow/	out, town
ee = /ē/	see	*ow* = /ō/	snow
ie = /ē/	field		

Although vowel correspondences are basically regular and fall, for the most part, into five spelling patterns, there are a number of exceptions. Therefore, students should be taught a flexibility strategy. They need to know that many individual vowel letters and vowel digraphs can represent more than one sound. They should also know what those vowel sounds are. Then, if they try one pronunciation and it doesn't work, they can try another.

One device that helps students deal with the variability of English spellings is a vowel-decoding chart such as the one presented in Table 8.6. The decoding chart lists spellings and then gives the vowel sounds most frequently represented by those spellings. The vowel-decoding chart lists high-frequency vowel spellings such as *ea* that may represent more than one sound. Infrequently occurring items such as the vowel spellings of *said, says,* and *friend* are not listed.

> Homographs demonstrate the need to integrate sounding out and context. You can't assign an accurate meaning and pronunciation to words such as *lead, produce, wound,* or *bow* until you see how the word is used in context.

Here is how students might use the chart. Coming across the word *own,* the student reads, "John had his own /own/ (rhymes with town) money." Realizing that /own/ is not a word and the sentence does not make sense, the reader searches for *ow* on the chart. Noting that *ow* can also have long *o* in addition to an /ow/ pronunciation, the student constructs the word *own* (/ōn/). The student sees that *own* (/ōn/) is a real word and also makes sense in the sentence. Like other strategies, this one should be modeled and reinforced with guided practice and application. As students learn alternative pronunciations for spellings, they should gradually learn to apply the flexibility strategy without the help of the chart.

APPROACHES TO TEACHING VOWELS

Vowels may be taught implicitly or explicitly, in a pattern or a word-building approach. A typical lesson includes the same five steps as a consonant correspondence lesson. In a way, vowels are easier to teach, because vowels can be pronounced in isolation without distortion. Another popular approach is to present elements in patterns or phonograms. A

TABLE 8.6 Decoding Chart for High-Frequency Variable Vowel Patterns

VOWEL SPELLING	CORRESPONDING SOUND
bead	/ē/
bread	/e/
break	/ā/
ear	/ēēr/
bear	/air/
find	/ī/
wind (moving air)	/i/
roll	/ō/
doll	/o/
wood	/oo/
food	/ōō/
lost	/aw/
most	/ō/
cow	/ow/
crow	/ō/

■ ■ ■ ■ ■ ▬▬▬▬▬▬▬▬▬▬▬▬▬▬▬▬▬▬▬▬▬▬▬▬▬▬▬

VOWEL CORRESPONDENCE LESSON

Step 1: Auditory perception. Hold up a pot, a mop, and a sock. Have students name each of the objects. Ask students what is the same about the words, *pot, mop,* and *sock.* Lead them to see that all three words have an /o/ sound. Discuss other words that have an /o/ sound: *hop, stop, clock.*

Step 2: Letter–sound integration. Write *pot, mop,* and *sock* on the chalkboard, saying each word as you do so. Point out the *o* in each word and lead students to see that the *o* makes the /o/ sound heard in *pot, mop,* and *sock.* Have students individually and as a group read the words. Discuss other words that have the sound of /o/. Ask if there is anyone in the room whose name has an /o/ sound—*Tom* or *Rob,*

for example. If so, write their names on the board. Read the names and have the class read them.

Step 3: Guided practice. Share-read a "big book," experience story, song or rhyme, or other piece that has a number of short-*o* words. Stop when you come to a short-*o* word and invite the class to read the word.

Step 4: Application. Have students read easy books such as *Who Is Who?* (McKissack, 1983), or one of Eric Hill's *Spot* books (e.g., Hill, 1986), or other pieces that contain short *o* words. Easy-to-read books that reinforce vowel correspondences are listed in Table 8.7.

major problem with a pattern approach has been the use of contrived reading material. However, patterns may be presented through an approach known as word building. This approach takes advantage of the regularity of a pattern approach, is based on the way students actually decode words, and espouses natural rather than artificial language.

Rime: the part of the word that begins with the vowel. It is the portion that rhymes. The *o* in *no,* the *ip* in *trip,* and the *eam* in *stream* are rimes.

Onset: the part of the word that precedes a vowel. It may be a consonant (*t + eam*), a digraph (*th + eme*), or a cluster (*st + eam*).

Looking at both individual letter–sound correspondences *(h-a-t)* and patterns *(h-at)* within the context of whole words helps students build a solid foundation of phonological knowledge and prepares them for using larger elements so that they become more efficient readers (Berninger, Abbott, Zook, Ogier, Lemos-Britton, & Brooksher, 1999).

Word-Building Approach

Because it actively involves students in constructing words, an effective way to introduce patterns is through a word-building approach (Gunning, 2005). In a word-building approach, beginning consonants are added to vowel patterns (*h + e = he, sh + ow = show*) and vowel–consonant patterns (*h + at = hat, g + et = get*). Research suggests that patterns have a more stable pronunciation and are easier to learn, especially when they are broken up into their onset and rime (Adams, 1990; Gluskho, 1979; Goswami, 1986, 1988; Goswami & Bryant, 1992; Santa, 1976–1977). The **rime** is the rhyming part of the word, the part that begins with a vowel (*-et*). The **onset** is the word's initial consonant or consonant combination (*g-*). From a linguistic point of view, onset and rime seem to be the natural parts of a word or syllable (Treiman, 1992). Common rimes and words containing those rimes are presented in Table 8.7.

Because some poor readers have difficulty with rimes (Bruck, 1992; Juel & Minden-Cupp, 2000), rimes are broken down into their individual sounds after being presented as wholes. After introducing the rime *-at* as a whole, the teacher should highlight its individual sounds: /a/ and /t/. In a study involving four first grades, only the two groups of struggling readers taught with an onset–rime approach were reading close to grade level by year's end (Juel & Minden-Cupp, 2000). And the students who did the best were those whose teacher broke the rimes into their individual sounds.

The word-building approach also fits the way students decipher printed words naturally. When they attack unknown words, both achieving and problem readers frequently seek out pronounceable word parts (Hardy, Stennett, & Smythe, 1973; Glass & Burton, 1973; Glass, 1976; Gunning, 1988a, 1999, McGuinness, 1997). Encountering the word *trust,* for instance, students might read it as "us-rus-trust." The word *chip* might be read as "ip-chip." The box on page 252 shows how a word-building lesson might be structured.

An interactive approach to decoding combines sounding out, meaning, and familiarity. For instance, *vat* is harder to decode than *cat* or *fat* because *vat* occurs less frequently and will not be in some students' listening vocabularies.

Adjusting Instruction.   Emilio, a fourth-grader assessed as reading on a mid-first-grade level, looked distressed. Noting weaknesses in his knowledge of short-vowel patterns, the teacher was reviewing the *-am,* *-an,* and *-ad* patterns. As the review progressed, Emilio's stress increased, even though he was able to do the activities with ease. And then the teacher caught on: the work was too easy. Emilio felt as though he was doing baby work. The teacher commented, " These patterns are too easy. Let me give you some harder ones." The teacher then began working with two-syllable words composed of familiar patterns. With some guidance, Emilio was able to read words such as *rabbit, happen, magnet,* and *address.* Emilio's self-esteem was restored and the teacher had provided a much-needed review of short-vowel patterns. Working with teenage disabled readers, Curtis and Longo (1999) used an adult literacy series. However, they noticed that *oa* words presented in the program were already known by the students, so they provided more challenging words using the *oa* element: *boast, charcoal.* When placing students, especially struggling readers

TABLE 8.7   Major Word Patterns

SHORT VOWELS

-ab	-ack	-ad	-ag	-am	-amp	-an	-and	-ang	-ank
cab	back	bad	bag	*ham	camp	an	and	bang	*bank
tab	jack	dad	rag	jam	damp	can	band	gang	sank
*crab	pack	had	tag	slam	*lamp	fan	*hand	hang	tank
	sack	mad	wag	swam	stamp	man	land	*rang	blank
	*tack	*sad	drag			*pan	sand	sang	thank
	black	glad	*flag			tan	stand		
	crack					plan			
	stack					than			

-ap	-at		-ed	-ell	-en	-end	-ent	-ess	-est
cap	at		bred	*bell	den	end	bent	guess	best
lap	bat		fed	fell	hen	bend	dent	less	nest
*map	*cat		led	tell	men	lend	rent	mess	pest
tap	fat		red	well	pen	mend	sent	bless	rest
clap	hat		shed	yell	*ten	*send	*tent	*dress	test
slap	pat		*sled	shell	then	tend	went	press	*vest
snap	rat			smell	when	spend	spent		west
trap	sat			spell					chest
wrap	that								guest

-et	-ead		-ick	-id	-ig	-ill	-im	-in	-ing
bet	dead		kick	did	big	bill	dim	in	king
get	head		lick	hid	dig	fill	him	fin	*ring
jet	read		pick	kid	*pig	*hill	skim	*pin	sing
let	*bread		sick	*lid	wig	kill	slim	sin	wing
met	spread		click	rid	twig	pill	*swim	tin	bring
*net	thread		*stick	skid		will		win	sting
pet			thick	slid		chill		chin	thing
set			trick			skill		grin	
wet			quick			spill		skin	
								spin	
								thin	
								twin	

-ink	-ip	-it		-ob	-ock	-op	-ot		-ust
link	dip	it		job	dock	cop	dot		bust
pink	lip	bit		mob	*lock	hop	got		dust
*sink	rip	fit		rob	rock	*mop	hot		just
wink	tip	*hit		sob	sock	pop	lot		*must
blink	zip	kit		*knob	block	top	not		rust
clink	chip	sit			clock	chop	*pot		trust
drink	flip	knit			flock	drop	shot		
stink	*ship	quit			knock	shop	spot		
think	skip	split				stop			
	trip								
	whip								

-ut	-ub	-uck	-ug	-um	-ump	-un	-unk	-us(s)
but	cub	*duck	bug	bum	bump	bun	bunk	*bus
cut	rub	luck	dug	hum	dump	fun	hunk	plus
hut	sub	cluck	hug	yum	hump	gun	junk	us
nut	*tub	stuck	mug	*drum	*jump	run	sunk	fuss
shut	club	struck	*rug	plum	lump	*sun	shrunk	muss
	scrub	truck	tug		pump	spun	*skunk	
			chug		thump		stunk	
					stump			

(Continued)

TABLE 8.7   Continued

LONG VOWELS

-ace	-ade	-age	-ake	-ale	-ame	-ape	-ate	-ave	-ail
*face	fade	age	bake	pale	came	ape	ate	*cave	fail
race	*made	*cage	*cake	sale	game	*cape	date	gave	jail
place	grade	page	lake	tale	*name	tape	*gate	save	mail
space	shade	rage	make	*scale	same	scrape	hate	wave	*nail
	trade	stage	rake		tame	grape	late	brave	pail
			take		blame	shape	mate		sail
			wake		shame		plate		tail
			flake				skate		snail
			shake				state		trail
			snake						

-ain	-ay		-eel	-ea	-each	-eak	-eal	-eam	-ean
main	bay		feel	pea	each	*beak	deal	team	*bean
pain	day		heel	sea	beach	leak	heal	*dream	lean
rain	*hay		kneel	*tea	*peach	peak	meal	scream	mean
brain	lay		steel	flea	reach	weak	real	stream	clean
chain	may		*wheel		teach	creak	*seal		
grain	pay				bleach	sneak	squeal		
*train	say					speak	steal		
	way					squeak			
	gray								
	play								

-eat	-ee	-eed	-eep	-eet		-ice	-ide	-ile	-ime
eat	*bee	deed	beep	*feet		*mice	hide	mile	*dime
beat	see	feed	deep	meet		nice	ride	pile	lime
neat	free	*seed	*jeep	sheet		rice	side	*smile	time
*seat	knee	weed	keep	sleet		lice	wide	while	chime
cheat	tree	bleed	peep	sweet		twice	*bride		
treat		freed	weep				slide		
wheat		speed	creep						
			sleep						
			steep						
			sweep						

-ine	-ite	-ive	-ie	-ind	-y		-o, -oe	-oke	-ole
fine	bite	dive	die	find	by		go	joke	hole
line	*kite	*five	lie	kind	guy		*no	poke	mole
mine	quite	hive	pie	*mind	my		so	woke	*pole
*nine	white	live	*tie	blind	dry		doe	broke	stole
pine		drive			fly		hoe	*smoke	whole
					*sky		toe	spoke	
					try				
					why				

-one	-ope	-ose	-ote	-oad	-oat	-ow	-old		u-e
bone	hope	hose	*note	load	boat	bow	old		use
cone	nope	*nose	vote	*road	coat	low	cold		fuse
*phone	*rope	rose	quote	toad	*goat	tow	fold		*mule
shone	slope	chose	wrote		float	blow	hold		huge
		close				glow	*gold		
		those				grow	sold		
						slow	told		
						*snow			

TABLE 8.7   Continued

OTHER VOWELS AND *r*-VOWELS

-all	-aw	-au		-oss	-ost	-ought		-oil	-oy
*ball	caw	fault		boss	cost	ought		*boil	*boy
call	jaw	*caught		loss	*lost	*bought		soil	joy
fall	paw	taught		toss	frost	fought			toy
hall	*saw			*cross		brought			
wall	claw								
small	draw								
	straw								

-oud	-our	-out	-ound	-ow	-own			-ood	-ould
loud	our	out	bound	ow	down			good	*could
*cloud	*hour	*shout	found	bow	gown			hood	would
proud	sour	scout	hound	*cow	town			*wood	should
	flour	spout	mound	how	brown			stood	
			pound	now	clown				
			*round	plow	*crown				
			sound						
			wound						
			ground						

-ook		-air	-are	-ear, ere		-ar	-ark	-ard	-art
*book		fair	care	*bear		*car	bark	*card	art
cook		*hair	hare	pear		far	dark	guard	part
hook		pair	share	there		jar	mark	hard	*chart
look		chair	scare	where		star	park		smart
took			spare				*shark		
shook			*square				spark		

-ear	-eer		-or	-orn	-ort
*ear	*deer		*or	born	*fort
dear	cheer		for	*corn	port
fear	steer		nor	torn	sort
hear			more	worn	short
near			sore		sport
year			tore		
clear			wore		

*Possible model words.

who are well aware that they lag behind their classmates, it is important to give students credit for what they know and provide them with interesting, challenging materials.

Using a Sound-by-Sound Approach

Having students build words by adding onsets to rimes is an efficient, effective approach to teaching phonics. However, at the earliest stages of learning to read, some students may have difficulty dealing with combinations of sounds. Younger students and students with poor phonological skills may need to work for a time with individual sounds (Walton, 1995). For this reason, word building presents rimes as units (*at, eep*) and as individual elements

■ ■ ■ ■ ■

WORD-BUILDING LESSON: -AT PATTERN

Step 1: Phonemic awareness and building the rime. Read a selection such as *The Cat in the Hat* (Giesel, 1957), an easy version of The Gingerbread Man, or a rhyme in which there are a number of *-at* words. Call the students' attention to the pattern words from the selection: *cat, hat, sat.* Stressing the rhyming element as you say each word, ask students to tell what is the same about the words. Lead students to see that they all have an /at/ sound as in *cat.* Ask students to listen carefully so they can tell how many sounds the word *at* has. Articulate it slowly, stretching out the sound /a/ and emphasizing the /t/ as you do so: "aaat." Tell the students to say the word *at* and listen for the sounds as they do so. Discuss how many sounds the word *at* has. Then tell students that you are going to spell the word *at.* Ask students to tell what letter would be used to spell the sound /a/ in *at.* Write *a,* commenting as you do so that it makes an /a/ sound. Have students tell what sound they hear at the end of *at.* Ask them what letter would be needed to spell /t/. Add *t,* saying /t/ as you do so. Explain that now you have the word *at.* Run your hand under each letter as you say its sound. Have several students read *at.*

> When presenting pattern words, limit the number introduced to five or six. Focus on the highest-frequency words and words that students will meet in upcoming selections.

> Nasal consonant sounds, such as /n/ and /m/, are partially absorbed by the preceding vowel. Therefore it is difficult to hear the separate sounds in *an* and *am.* When presenting the *an* and *am* patterns, present the rime as a unit. Do not attempt to say the separate sounds or have students say them.

Step 2: Adding the onset. Explain to students that you can use *at* to make other words. (Write a second *at* under the first one.) Ask students, "What do I need to add to *at* to make the word *cat*?" As you add *c* to *at,* carefully enunciate the *c* and the *at* and then the whole word. Have several students read the word. Then have students read *at* and *cat.* Then write *at* underneath *cat.* Ask students, "What do I need to add to *at* to make the word *hat*?" As you add *h* to *at,* carefully enunciate the *h* and the *at* and then the whole word. Have several students read the word. Then have students read *at, cat,* and *hat.* Introduce the words *sat* and *mat.* Then have students read all the words that have been formed. Lead students to see what is the same about the words—that they all end in *at.* Ask students if they know of any other words that rhyme with *cat.* If so, write these on the board and discuss them.

Step 3: Adding the rime. To make sure that students have a thorough grasp of both key parts of the word—the onset, which is the initial consonant or cluster—and the rime, which is the vowel and an ending consonant or cluster—present the onset or initial consonant and have students supply the rime or vowel–consonant element. Writing *c* on the board, have students tell what sound it usually stands for. Then ask them to tell what you would add to /k/ to make the word *cat.* After adding *-at* to *c,* say the word in parts, /k/–/a/–/t/, and then as a whole. Pointing to *c,* say /k/, pointing to *a,* say /a/, pointing to *t,* say /t/. Running your hand under the whole word, say "cat." Form *hat, sat,* and *mat* in this way. After all words have been formed, have students read them.

Step 4: Providing mixed practice. Realizing that they are learning words that all end in the same way, students may focus on the initial letter and fail to take careful note of the rest of the word, the rime. After presenting a pattern, mix in words from previously presented patterns and have these read. For instance, after presenting the *-at* pattern, present a list of mixed *-at* and *-an* words: *cat, can, ran, rat, pat, pan, man, mat.* Besides being a good review, this trains students to use all the word's letters in their decoding processes. Otherwise, students might say the first word in a series of pattern words and then just use the initial consonant to say the rest. If students fail to use all the letters when reading on their own, they may misread *ran* for *rat* or *can* for *cat.* Reading mixed patterns also reviews previously presented patterns.

Model Words

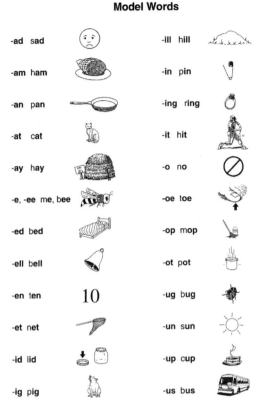

FIGURE 8.5 Model Words

From *Word Building Book A with Predictable Stories* by T. Gunning, 1996. New York: Phoenix Learning Resources. Reprinted by permission of Galvin Publications.

Keep a close relationship between the phonics you teach and the phonics students need; preview an upcoming selection and choose a new phonics element they have not mastered.

Step 5: Introducing the model word. Choose one of the pattern words to be a model word. Select a word that has high frequency, is easy, and—if possible—can be depicted. For the *-at* pattern, you might choose *cat,* which is easily illustrated. Create a model words chart for your class.

An illustrated chart of model words for short vowel patterns is presented in Figure 8.5. After a pattern has been introduced, add its model word to the chart. If students forget the pat-

tern, they can refer to the model words chart. Point out the model word *cat* and explain that it has a picture that shows the word. Tell students that if they forget how to say the model word, the picture will help them. As students encounter difficulty with *at* words, help them to look for a part of the word they can say (*at*) and, if that does not work, use the model word *cat* as an analogy word to help them decipher the unknown word. Also encourage the use of context. Students should use context to assist in the use of pronounceable word-part or other sounding-out strategies and especially when sounding-out strategies do not work. Context should also be used to make sure that the word decoded is a real word and fits the sense of the selection.

Step 6: Guided practice

- Use functional reading materials to provide practice with the pattern. Holding up an advertisement for baseball bats, ask students to tell which word says "bat." Do the same with a hat label or advertisement.

- Compose a brief experience story using *at.* Say to students; "I can use *at* words to write about some things that I have. I have a cat. I have a hat. I have a bat. (As you write each word, stress the word's sounds.)

- Have students sort *-an, -at,* and *-am* words (assuming that they have learned *-an* and *-am* patterns). They might complete a spelling sort as well as a card sort.

Step 7: Application. To apply a correspondence that was just taught, choose a selection that contains a number of words that fit the target pattern. Walk students through the selection. Discuss the title and illustrations, clarify unfamiliar concepts, point out and read to them difficult words (they should follow along with you in their books). Place particular emphasis on words that follow the pattern you just introduced. Note a sentence or caption that contains a pattern word and ask them to find the pattern word and point it out to you. Possible books include: Cameron, A. (1994). *The Cat Sat on the Mat.* Boston: Houghton. Carle, E. (1973). *Have You Seen My Cat?* New York: Scholastic. Wildsmith, B. (1986). *Cat on a Mat.* New York: Oxford.

Step 8: Spelling. cat, hat, sat, bat, mat. Learning to spell new pattern words is excellent reinforcement. Along with providing an opportunity for students

(Continued)

For students having difficulty with word building, add letters to the rimes and ask them to tell what word you made. Adding *h* to *at,* have them read *hat.* Adding *s* to *at* have them read *sat.* Also use a speech-to-print approach. Hold up the words *hat* and *ham* and ask "Which one says 'hat'?" Ask students how they know the word says "hat" and not "ham."

to apply skills, it helps them to focus on vowel sounds and patterns within words. Choose pattern words for spelling that students will most likely use in their writing. Up to five words may be chosen for the spelling lesson. To introduce the spelling lesson, explain to students that they will be learning how to spell words that use the pattern just presented. To introduce the words, give a pretest. Dictate the words and have students attempt to spell them. Say each word, use the word in a sentence, and then say each word: "Cat. My cat ran. Cat. Hat. The hat kept my head warm. Hat. Sat. She sat on the chair. Sat. Bat. I have a new baseball bat. Bat. Mat. I wiped my feet on the mat. Mat." Have students say the word, enunciating it carefully before writing it. This will help them focus on the word's sounds. After the pretest, write the correct spellings on the board, and have students check their attempts, making any corrections necessary. They should focus their studying on words that were difficult for them.

Step 9: Writing. Students compose an illustrated piece telling about a cat they know or have or a hat they would like to wear. Encourage the use of invented spelling. However, students are expected to spell pattern words correctly. (See Figure 8.6 for an overview of a word-building lesson.)

FIGURE 8.6   Steps in a Word-Building Lesson

Step 1: Build the rime. Class forms *at.*

Step 2: Add the onset. Teacher adds *c* to *at* on the chalkboard.

Step 3: Add the rime. Teacher adds *at* to *c.*

Step 4: Provide mixed practice. Teacher points to words on chalkboard as students read them: *cat, can, ran, rat, pat, pan, man, mat.*

Step 5: Introduce the model word. Teacher writes *cat* on the board next to a drawing of a cat.

Step 6: Provide guided practice. Teacher conducts shared reading with a big book.

Step 7: Apply the pattern. Students read books on their own.

Steps 8 and 9: Spell and write. Students spell pattern words and use them in their writing.

(*a-t, ee-p*). However, some students may still have difficulty with rimes. For these students, modify the approach by placing greater emphasis on the individual sounds in words. Later, as they begin to see patterns in words, place more emphasis on rimes.

For additional information on word building and other phonics programs, go to Building Literacy at http://thomasgunning.org/.

Make-and-Break Technique for Introducing or Reviewing Patterns

As an alternative to word building, or along with it, you might use the make-and-break technique to introduce patterns. In this approach, students construct, break apart, and reconstruct common word patterns (Iverson & Tunmer, 1993). Choosing the word *and,* for instance, the teacher makes the word with magnetic letters, says the word, and has the student say it. The teacher then jumbles the letters and has the student reassemble the word and say it. This is repeated until the student is able to construct and say the word with ease. The teacher then puts an *s* in front of *and,* explaining that the word now spells *sand.* The student says the word. The letter *s* is removed, and the teacher explains that the word now says *and.* The student is asked to make the word *sand,* read it, and then make the word *and.* This process is repeated with *band* and *hand.*

Whole–Part–Whole Approaches

Phonics lessons can proceed from the part to the whole or from the whole to the part. In a part–whole approach, the correspondence or pattern is presented and then is applied within the context of a whole story. However, some practitioners prefer starting with the whole, breaking the whole into parts, and reading a whole selection (Trachtenburg, 1990). Whole–part–whole approaches work especially well with students who have had negative experiences with intensive phonics programs.

Having failed with his school system's isolated phonics program, which consisted primarily of skills instruction and worksheets, James objected vehemently when his mother attempted to help him with the sheets. "I can't read those," he cried. Having been given too heavy a dose of phonics, James had learned very little about letter–sound relationships. James should be provided a holistic view of reading through the use of easy predictable books or other techniques. Once James has a sense of what reading really is, he might be presented phonics through a holistic children's book technique. To acquaint James with the *-oad* pattern, for instance, share-read with him books such as *Toad on the Road* (Schade, 1992) or *Railroad Toad* (Schade, 1994). During a rereading of the books, point out and discuss the *-oad* words. Having provided a holistic, successful experience with the *-oad* pattern, the teacher might then build the *-oad* pattern through word building or the make-and-break technique or both. Because it is nonthreatening and allows the student to generate her or his own conclusions about patterns, sorting would also be an excellent extension activity for James.

THE ROLE OF PHONOLOGICAL PROCESSING

Noting that some students were experiencing difficulty applying phonics strategies, Gaskins, Ehri, Cress, O'Hara, & Donnelly (1996–1997) revised the word-attack program so that students were taught to analyze words fully. To learn the word *will,* students noted the sounds in the word /w/, /i/, /l/ and matched these with the letters that represent the sounds *w, i, ll.*

Phonological processing provides the foundation for learning to read words. When students have a firm phonological foundation, they can make connections between the sounds in words and the word's spellings. However, when phonological awareness is weak, adequate connections are not made. Students tend to learn words as specific entities and do not generalize. For instance, after learning the *eat* pattern in *meat, seat,* and *heat,* they fail to recognize the *eat* in *wheat* and so are unable to read the word. Instruction in the *eat* pattern must be accompanied by instruction in phonological awareness. Once students can detect all the sounds in a word, they can connect them to their spellings (Harm, McCandliss, & Seidenberg, 2003). This is known as the mapping hypothesis. The mapping hypothesis holds that componential representation leads to generalization. Componential representation is the building of an awareness of the internal components of a word: the letters and the sounds represented by the letters. As Gaskins and colleagues (1996–1997) explained, the sounds and spellings in the word must be fully realized. Intervention techniques must help students become aware of the separate sounds in the words and the letters that represent them. Word building does this, as does the Benchmark program. Struggling readers might be able to read a word such as *meat* but are unable to read other *eat* words. That is because they have made a specific connection between the spelling of *meat* and the pronunciation and meaning of *meat*. However, the representation is wholistic and not componential. The student is not processing the individual sounds in the word. Poor phonological representation has led to poor orthographic representation. Intervention must help the student break the word into its component parts and connect these sounds to the appropriate letters.

THE ROLE OF DIALECT IN TEACHING PHONICS

Although he had mastered all the vowel patterns, Justin was having a great deal of difficulty with the short-*o* patterns. Having just reviewed the *-ot* pattern, the teacher was somewhat surprised when Justin, a third-grader reading on a mid-first-grade level, spelled *hot* as *hat*. Thinking that it might be a handwriting issue and that the *a* was really a poorly formed *o*, the teacher asked Justin to name the letters. "h-a-t," responded Jason. Still perplexed, the teacher asked Justin to say the word. "*Hot*," answered Justin, pointing to his head. "Like the *hot* that you wear when it is cold."

Suddenly the teacher understood. Justin had moved to the United States from Jamaica several months before. In his dialect, *hat* was pronounced /hot/; *man* as /mon/. No wonder he was struggling with short-*o* words. He had already learned to spell /hot/ as *hat*. Now the teacher was trying to tell him that it was spelled *h-o-t*. Backtracking, the teacher explained that *at* is pronounced /at/ in the United States but /ot/ in Jamaica. The teacher then explained that *hot* is a different word from *hat* and means very warm. The teacher briefly discussed dialects and suggested that if Justin heard the word *hat*, he should listen to the way the word was used and that would help him decide if the word meant very warm or something that you wear on your head. The teacher also provided auditory discrimination exercises in which Justin noted whether the teacher was saying the same word twice or two different words: *cat–cot, hat–hat, pat–pot, not–not, sat–sat, hat–hot, nat–not, rat–rot, that–that*. The teacher used *at* and *ot* words in a variety of sentences and had Justin hold up the card that spelled the word she was saying: "I am wearing my new **hat**. It is a very **hot** day. The cook made soup in a large **pot**. Do not **pat** strange dogs."

When teaching phonics it is important to be aware of your own dialect and the dialect that students speak if it is different from yours. Make adjustments in the way you introduce elements so that they fit the local dialect. For instance, in many areas, *egg* has a long-*a* pronunciation, *pen* has a short-*i* pronunciation, and *caught* has a short-*o* pronunciation so that it sounds like *cot*.

SEQUENCE FOR TEACHING VOWELS

Which vowel correspondences should be introduced first? Typically, short-vowel correspondences are taught first. These have more predictable spellings and occur with higher frequency. Most often, short-vowel sounds are spelled CVC (consonant–vowel–consonant), for example, with the vowel letter that typically represents that sound preceded and followed by a consonant (*cat, pen, tip, pot, tub*). However, this is also the type of sequence that many low-achieving readers have already encountered and have had difficulty with. You might give them a fresh start by presenting some of the easier long-vowel correspondences first.

Long vowels are easier to perceive auditorially and, if you introduce only the simplest patterns (*go, no, so; bee, see; be, he, me, we, she*), are easier to learn to read and spell. Save the final-*e* spellings (*hope, note*) and digraph-plus-final-consonant spellings (*road, coat*) until later. A suggested sequence for both vowel and consonant correspondences is presented in Table 8.4. The sequence is based on frequency of occurrence of elements and ease of learning but should be adapted to fit the particular needs of the students. The ultimate determining factor for the sequence of introduction should be the phonics knowledge that your students already possess and their need to know.

APPLICATION THROUGH READING

As students begin to learn phonics elements and decoding strategies, it is essential that they apply them by reading whole selections. For instance, students who have been introduced to long -*ee* correspondences might read *Sheep in a Jeep* (Shaw, 1986) and *Dark Night, Sleepy Night* (Ziefert, 1988). If students read materials that contain elements they have been taught, they will learn the elements better and also be better at applying them to new words (Juel & Roper-Schneider, 1985). Children's books that might be used to reinforce vowel patterns are listed in Figure 8.7.

> Beck and Juel (1995), suggest that a significant proportion of the text that first-graders read should be decodable. Most first-grade basal readers fell far below that standard (Stein, Johnson, Gutlophn, 1999; Menon & Hiebert, 1999). However, the latest basals are highly decodable.

In addition to children's books that naturally reinforce key patterns, there are books known as *decodable texts* that have been written specifically for that purpose. Decodable texts have been created to provide practice with a specific phonic element: short-*a* or short-*e* words, for instance. Depending on the skill of the author, the books may seem natural or may seem contrived and artificial. Some of the story words may not even be in the students' listening vocabularies, but are included because they incorporate the pattern being taught. Use of artificial language also makes it more difficult to make use of context clues. However, some decodable texts are well done and can be used effectively. It is suggested that you judge each title for yourself.

A First Book (Barron's). A series of five 16-page books that provide practice with short vowels.

> Although providing students with decodable text may aid word-analysis skills, it may limit vocabulary development and background building (Vinovskis, 1996).

Books to Remember (Flyleaf Publishing). A series of beautifully illustrated 30-page books that provide a review of vowel patterns.

Early Phonics Readers (Continental Press). A series of forty-eight 8-page books that cover short vowels, long vowels, and consonant clusters. CD-ROM disks that read books aloud are available.

Let's Read Together Books (Kane Press). A series of five 32-page books that focus on short vowels.

FIGURE 8.7   Books That Reinforce Vowel Patterns

SHORT-VOWEL PATTERNS

Short a

Allen, J. (1987). *My first job.* Provo, UT: Aro Publishing.

Antee, N. (1985). *The good bad cat.* Grand Haven, MI: School Zone.

Cameron, A. (1994). *The cat sat on the mat.* Boston: Houghton.

Carle, E. (1987). *Have you seen my cat?* New York: Scholastic.

Coxe, M. (1996). *Cat traps.* New York: Random House.

Flanagan, A. K. (2000). *Cats: The sound of short a.* Elgin, IL: The Child's World.

Hawkins, C., & Hawkins, J. (1983). *Pat the cat.* New York: Putnam.

Maccarone, G. (1995). *"What is THAT?" said the cat.* New York: Scholastic.

Moncure, J. B. (1981). *Word bird makes words with cat.* Elgin, IL: The Child's World.

Wildsmith, B. (1982). *Cat on the mat.* New York: Oxford University Press.

Ziefert, H. (1988). *Cat games.* New York: Puffin.

Short e

Gregorich, B. (1984). *Nine men chase a hen.* Grand Haven, MI: School Zone.

Snow, P. (1984). *A pet for pat.* Chicago: Children's Press.

Short i

Cox, M. (1997). *Big egg.* New York: Random House.

Greydanus, R. (1988). *Let's get a pet.* Mahwah, NJ: Troll.

Meister, C. (1999). *When Tiny was tiny.* New York: Puffin.

Wang, M. L. (1989). *The ant and the dove.* Chicago: Children's Press.

Wolcott, P. (1975). *My shadow and I.* Reading, MA: Addison-Wesley.

Short o

Foster, A., & Erickson, B. (1991). *A mop for pop.* New York: Barron's.

McKissack, P. C. (1983). *Who is who?* Chicago: Children's Press.

Moncure, J. B. (1981). *No! no! Word Bird.* Elgin, IL: The Child's World.

Short u

Foster, A., & Erickson, B. (1991). *The bug club.* Hauppauge, NY: Barron's.

Gregorich, B. (1984). *The gum on the drum.* Grand Haven, MI: School Zone.

Hawkins, C., & Hawkins, J. (1988). *Zug the bug.* New York: Putnam.

Lewison, W. C. (1992). *Buzzz said the bee.* New York: Scholastic.

McKissack, P., & McKissack, F. (1988). *Bugs!* Chicago: Children's Press.

Petrie, C. (1983). *Joshua James likes trucks.* Chicago: Children's Press.

Ziefert, H. (1987). *Nicky upstairs and down.* New York: Puffin.

Short-Vowel Review

Appleton-Smith, L. (1998). *Jen's best gift ever.* Lyme, NH: Flyleaf.

Boegehold, B. D. (1990). *You are much too small.* New York: Bantam.

Kraus, R. (1971). *Leo, the late bloomer.* New York: Simon & Schuster.

FIGURE 8.7   Continued

LONG-VOWEL PATTERNS

Long a

Cohen, C. L. (1998). *How many fish?* New York: HarperCollins.

Hall, K. (1995). *A bad, bad day.* New York: Scholastic.

Neasi, B. J. (1984). *Just like me.* Chicago: Children's Press.

Oppenheim, J. (1990). *Wake up, baby!* New York: Bantam.

Raffi. (1987). *Shake my sillies out.* New York: Crown.

Robart, R. (1986). *The cake that Mack ate.* Toronto: Kids Can Press.

Stadler, J. (1984). *Hooray for Snail!* New York: Harper.

Long e

Bonsall, C. (1974). *And I mean it, Stanley.* New York: HarperCollins.

Flanagan, A. K. *What a week: The sound of long e.* Elgin, IL: The Child's World.

Greene, C. (1983). *Ice is . . . whee!* Chicago: Children's Press.

Gregorick, B. (1984). *Beep, beep.* Grand Haven, MI: School Zone.

Hutchins, P. (1972). *Good night, Owl!* New York: Macmillan.

Milgrim, D. (2003). *See Pip point.* New York: Atheneum.

Shaw, N. (1986). *Sheep in a jeep.* Boston: Houghton Mifflin.

Ziefert, H. (1988). *Dark night, sleepy night.* New York: Puffin.

Ziefert, H. (1990). *Follow me!* New York: Puffin.

Ziefert, H. (1995). *The little red hen.* New York: Puffin.

Long i

Gelman, R. G. (1977). *More spaghetti I say.* New York: Scholastic.

Gordh, B. (1999). *Hop right on.* New York: Golden Books.

Greydanus, R. (l980). *Mike's new bike.* Mahtawah, NJ: Troll.

Hoff, S. (1988). *Mrs. Brice's mice.* New York: Harper.

Ziefert, H. (1987). *Jason's bus ride.* New York: Random House.

Ziefert, H. (1987). *A new house for Mole and Mouse.* New York: Puffin.

Ziefert, H. (1984). *Sleepy dog.* New York: Random House.

Long o

Armstrong, J. (1996). *The snowball.* New York: Random House.

Bauer, M. D. (2004). *Rain.* New York: Aladdin.

Buller, J., & Schade, S. A. (1998). *Pig at play.* Mahwah, NJ: Troll.

Cobb, A. (1996). *Wheels.* New York: Random House.

Daniel, C. (1999). *The chick that wouldn't hatch.* San Diego, CA: Harcourt.

Greene, C. (l982). *Snow Joe.* Chicago: Children's Press.

Hamsa, B. (1985). *Animal babies.* Chicago: Children's Press.

Kueffner, S. (1999). *Lucky duck.* Pleasantville, NY: Reader's Digest Children's Books.

McDermott, G. (1999). *Fox and the stork.* San Diego, CA: Harcourt.

Oppenheim, J. (1992). *The show-and-tell frog.* New York: Bantam.

(Continued)

FIGURE 8.7 **Continued**

Schade, S. (1992). *Toad on the road.* New York: Random House.
Ziefert, H. (1988). *Strike four!* New York: Penguin.

REVIEW OF LONG VOWELS

Matthias, C. (1983). *I love cats.* Chicago: Children's Press.
Parish, P. (1974). *Dinosaur time.* New York: Harper.
Phillips, J. (1986). *My new boy.* New York: Random House.
Ziefert, H. (1985). *A dozen dogs.* New York: Random House.

r- AND OTHER-VOWEL PATTERNS

r *Vowels*

Arnold, M. (1996). *Quick, quack, quick!* New York: Random House.
Cole, J. (1986). *Hungry, hungry sharks.* New York: Random House.
Hooks, W. H. (1992). *Feed me!* New York: Bantam.
Penner, R. (1991). *Dinosaur babies.* New York: Random House.
Ziefert, H. (1990). *Stitches.* New York: Puffin.
Ziefert, H. (1997). *The magic porridge pot.* New York: Puffin.

/aw/ *Vowels*

Brenner, B. (1989). *Annie's pet.* New York: Bantam.
Mann, P. Z. (1999). *Meet my monster.* Pleasantville, NY: Reader's Digest.
Oppenheim, J. (1991). *The donkey's tale.* New York: Bantam.
Oppenheim, J. (1993). *"Uh-oh!" said the crow.* New York: Bantam.
Rylant, C. (1989). *Henry and Mudge get the cold shivers.* New York: Bradbury Press.

/o͞o/ *Vowels*

Blocksma, M. (1992). *Yoo hoo, Moon!* New York: Bantam.
Brenner, B. (1990). *Moon boy.* New York: Bantam.
Dussling, J. (1996). *Stars.* New York: Grosset & Dunlap.
Rollings, S. (2000). *New shoes, red shoes.* New York: Orchard.
Silverman, M. (1991). *My tooth is loose.* New York: Viking.
Wiseman, B. (1959). *Morris the moose.* New York: Harper.
Ziefert, H. (1997). *The ugly duckling.* New York: Puffin.

/oo/ *Vowels*

Averill, E. (1960). *The fire cat.* New York: Harper & Row.
Brenner, B. (1989). *Lion and lamb.* New York: Bantam.
Platt, K. (1965). *Big Max.* New York: Harper.

/ow/ *Vowels*

Hays, A. J. (2003). *The pup speaks up.* New York: Random.
Hayward, L. (1988). *Hello, house.* New York: Random House.
Lobel, A. (1975). *Owl at home.* New York: Harper.
Oppenheim, J. (1989). *"Not now!" said the cow.* New York: Bantam.

Raffi. (1988). *Wheels on the bus.* New York: Crown.
Rylant, C. (1987). *Henry and Mudge under the yellow moon.* New York: Bradbury Press.
Siracusa, C. (1991). *Bingo, the best dog in the world.* New York: HarperCollins.

/oy/ Vowels

Marshall, J. (1990). *Fox be nimble.* New York: Pufffin.
Witty, B. (1991). *Noises in the night.* Grand Haven, MI: School Zone.

REVIEW OF *r* AND OTHER VOWELS

Brenner, B. (1989). *Annie's pet.* New York: Bantam.
Brenner, B. (1992). *Beavers beware.* New York: Bantam.
Hopkins, L. B. (1986). *Surprises.* New York: Harper.
Marshall, E. (1985). *Four on the shore.* New York: E. P. Dutton.
Marshall, E. (1985). *Fox on wheels.* New York: E. P. Dutton.
Milton, J. (1985). *Dinosaur days.* New York: Random House.
Rylant, C. (1987). *Henry and Mudge: The first book.* New York: Bradbury Press.

Real Kid Readers (Millbrook Press). A series of 32-page books illustrated with color photos.

Start to Read Books (School Zone). A series of 16-page books on three levels.

Wonder Books (Child's World). A series of thirty-five books reinforcing consonants and vowel patterns. Very well done.

Decodable text can be a powerful aid. Until her teacher started giving her decodable text, Cametera, a second-grader in the beginning stages of reading, was making virtually no progress (Mesmer, 1999). Even though she was being taught key patterns systematically, she wasn't learning to apply them. The text the teacher was using did not specifically reinforce the patterns that she introduced. In fact, the text contained so many patterns that Camatera was overwhelmed. When the teacher began using the Ready Readers series that reinforced patterns but managed to retain a natural flow, Camatera began making progress. The match between materials and methods made all the difference.

ADDITIONAL REINFORCEMENT FOR VOWEL PATTERNS

Sorting

Because it helps students make discoveries about printed words, sorting is one of the most valuable reinforcement activities. Students can sort vowel patterns in much the same way that they sort consonant correspondences (see Figure 8.8).

Modified Bingo

Modified bingo, which is a sorting activity in a gamelike format, may be played with just three or four columns instead of five. The heading for each column is a pattern word as in Figure 8.9.

SORTING PATTERNS BY SOUND

Step 1: Setting up the sort. Set up two or more columns as in Figure 8.8. At the head of each column, place an illustration of the pattern to be sorted. For the *-at, -an,* and *-am* patterns, you might use an illustration of a cat, a pan, and a ham.

Step 2: Explaining and modeling sorting. If students are not familiar with sorting, explain it to them. Tell them that they will be placing word cards in the *cat, pan,* or *ham* column. If a word rhymes with *cat,* it will be placed in the *cat* pattern; if with *pan,* in the *pan* column; if with *ham,* in the *ham* column. Shuffle the cards and show how you would sort them. Reading the *van* card, you would say, "Van. Let's see, does *van* rhyme with *cat*? No. The ending sound is not the same. Does *van* rhyme with *pan?* Let's see: *van–pan,* they both have the same *an* sound." Sort one or two more words or until students have caught onto the idea.

Step 3: Sorting of cards by students. Distribute the cards to be sorted. These can be cards that you have made. You could also ask students to make cards. Cards can be sorted as a group or individual activity. In a group activity, an easy way to sort cards is to place the criterion cards in the middle of a table and divide up the cards to be sorted among the students. Students then take turns placing their cards in one of the criterion columns. As students place cards, they should read the words on the cards or name the illustrations on them and explain the basis for their sorting: *hat* has an *-at* sound and rhymes with *cat.* Quickly and simply correct mistakes in sorting. For example, if a student places *tan* in the *cat* column, say that *tan* rhymes with *pan* so it goes in the *pan* column (Barnes, 1989). A very simple sort entails deciding which items are placed in a one-column sort. For instance, given some cards that rhyme with *cat* and some that don't, students could decide which ones should be placed under *cat* (Temple, Nathan, Temple, & Burris, 1993). At first, students' sorting should be guided. After they have grasped underlying principles and can sort fairly accurately, they can sort independently or with partners or in small groups.

Step 4: Discussion. If you have not already done so, discuss students' responses. The discussion should help students form a generalization about their sorting. You might ask, "Why did you put all the words in this pile?" If a student who has been working independently has missorted a word, you can take one of a number of steps (Barnes, 1989).

■ Use the missorted word as a basis for sorting. For instance, if the student placed *fence* in the long-*e* column when words were being sorted by long or short *e,* then ask the student to place all the words under *fence* that have an /e/ sound as in *fence.* Make sure, of course, that the student is reading *fence* accurately.

■ Ask the student if there are any words that she wishes to change. One problem with this approach is that an unsure student might make wholesale changes of words that are placed correctly.

■ Point to the missorted word and ask, "Why did you put that one here?" This gives students a chance to explain their reasoning and also provides the teacher with information about the student's reasoning processes so that the proper kind of assistance can be supplied. Maybe the student missorted a word because he or she was misreading it or was sorting words on the basis of spelling when they should have been sorted on the basis of sound.

Step 5: Practice. Have students sort the words again to foster mastery. As Barnes (1989) notes:

> Many teachers ask why a word sort is not mastered the first time it is attempted. The answer is that some children have difficulty generalizing new classifications cognitively. The process is not immediate. Correct and consistent sorting may take place after four or five sessions, but not after the first. (p. 301)

Step 6: Application. Have students identify words that extend the sort. If students have sorted *-at, -an,* and *-am* words, they might add words such as *Pat, Sam,* and *tan* to the sort. An excellent source of application words would be those that appear in students' reading and writing (Invernizzi, Abouzeid, & Gill, 1994).

> Because sorting involves dealing with words in isolation, students need ample opportunity to apply skills by doing lots of reading and writing.

cat	pan	ham
hat	man	jam
rat	van	Pam
bat	can	Sam
sat	fan	

FIGURE 8.8   Word Sort by Pattern

Word Bingo			
hat	**ham**	**can**	**map**
cat	**am**	**fan**	
rat		**man**	
		ran	
		van	

FIGURE 8.9   Modified Bingo

> Sorting helps students discover principles about the way the spelling system works and involves higher-level thinking skills as students categorize items.

A row must be filled out with words in the same pattern or with wild cards. Cards for all players are placed in the center of the table, and players take turns choosing cards. After selecting a card, the player reads it and looks to see if it rhymes with one of his column-heading words. If so, the player can place it in one of the squares. After placing a card, the player reads the column-heading word and all the words that have been placed in the column. This provides added practice in reading pattern words (Morris, 1999). Bingo cards can be created on a variety of levels. An early set might contain only short-*a* patterns. A later set might contain a short-*a,* short-*e,* short-*i,* and short-*o* pattern. A more advanced set might reinforce long-vowel, other-vowel, or *r*-vowel patterns.

Modified Concentration

In regular concentration, pairs of cards are shuffled and placed face down. The first player turns over a card and then tries to guess where its match might be. If the player turns over a matching card, she removes it and places the pair in front of her. The player then continues to play until she fails to make a match. Then the second player attempts to make a match. In modified concentration, cards are composed of pairs of rhyming words. Students make a match by locating the rhyming partner of the word turned over, as shown in Figure 8.10. When a player turns over a card, she must read it. She then must find its rhyming partner and read it also. Concentration requires the player to keep the rime in mind as she searches for its match. It promotes focusing on the rime that the two words share (Morris, 1999).

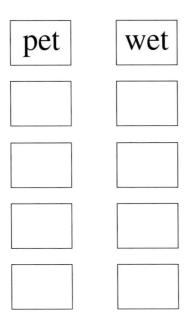

FIGURE 8.10   Modified Concentration

Little Books

One way to obtain easy-to-read books is to create your own. The books can simply contain words, or they can be illustrated with student or teacher drawings, photos, or magazine illustrations, or, if you have access to a desktop publishing system, clip art. Some patterns that might make effective little books include:

> I am _____.
> I can _____.
> The cat _____.
> I like _____.
> I play _____.
> I help _____.
> I saw _____.

You might also create caption books devoted to a topic: numbers, colors, seasons, pets, dogs, cats, birds, farm animals, cars, trucks, toys, or similar topics.

Using Writing to Reinforce Phonics

Through writing, students can make important discoveries about letter–sound relationships. Students who are at a rudimentary stage of spelling development should be allowed to use invented spelling. If a student has difficulty spelling a word, have her or him sound it out. Ask questions such as "What sound do you hear at the beginning of *bat?* What letter makes the 'buh' sound? What sound do you hear next? Say the word slowly: 'baaaat.' What sound do you hear at the end of *bat?* What letter makes that sound?"

A good way to reinforce pattern words or another element that has been introduced is to have students write a brief story using some of the pattern words. Have students write the story and then, if necessary, help the students with any words containing the target element that might have been misspelled. As always, give students credit for what they did correctly. Here is an example of how a teacher helped a student who wrote *got* for *goat.* She used the miscue as a minilesson in applied phonics:

> I see that you wrote *g-o* for the "go" sound in *goat* and that you wrote a *t* for the ending sound of *goat.* That's very good. But the *o* sound in *goat* is spelled *oa,* like this (teacher writes and carefully enunciates *goat*). The sound is /ō/ often spelled with an *oa.* If this is how I write *goat,* how might I write *boat?*

Assembling Words

When working with large groups and/or as an alternative to using magnetic letters, have the group assemble letters to make words using procedures adapted from Cunningham (1991). Letter cards can be purchased or created by cutting up file folders. To keep the letters organized, place them in separate bags, one bag for each letter.

Distribute a few letters at a time so that students are not overwhelmed with possible choices. Choose letters that reinforce familiar patterns and correspondences. To reinforce short *e,* for instance, you might distribute the following letters: *e, m, n, t, p.* Before having the words formed, tell students that they will be making words that have a short *e,* which is /e/ as in the word *ten.* Then say a short-*e* word, one that students are familiar with, and have students assemble the word with their letters. Say the word in a sentence to make sure that you and the students have the same word in mind. Also have students repeat the word. Assemble the letters to form a word for one or two examples. If students have difficulty, emphasize the separate sounds of the word: /t/, /e/, /n/. Using a larger version of the letter cards, have a volunteer form the word on the chalkboard ledge or a pocket chart.

After a word has been formed and its correct spelling demonstrated, make sure each student has formed the word correctly. Also write the word on the chalkboard. Words to be formed might include *men, ten, pen, met, net, pet.* Make sure that all the words you ask students to form are in their speaking vocabularies. After all words have been formed, discuss which ones rhyme, which ones begin with the same sound, and so forth.

Word Wall

> Because they are on the wall, the words are readily available for quick review. Troublesome words can be reviewed daily.

> On the wall, place pattern words, high-frequency words, color words, names of the months, compound words, or any other words with which students are working.

Putting words on the wall helps students to remember them. After a pattern has been introduced, place one or more of the pattern words on the wall. Arrange them alphabetically by pattern. The *-ab* pattern would be placed first, followed by the *-ack* and *-ad* patterns, and so forth. Because the words are on the wall, they can be used as a kind of dictionary. If students want to know how to spell a pattern or high-frequency word, they can find it on the wall. Review wall words periodically, using the following or similar activities.

- Find as many animal names, color words, and number names as you can.
- Pantomime an action (sit, run) or use gestures to indicate an object or other item (pan, hat, cat, pen) and have students write the word and then hold it up so you can quickly check everyone's response. Have a volunteer read the word and point to it on the word wall. Before pantomiming the word, tell what pattern the word will be in: the *cat* pattern. To make the task a bit more challenging and to get students to analyze the ending letters of patterns, tell students that the word will be in one of two patterns: the *at* or the *an* pattern.

Secret Word

Select a word from a pattern, and jot it down on a sheet of paper but don't reveal its identity (P. Cunningham & Allington, 1994). Have students number their papers 1–5. Give a series of five clues to the identity of the word. After each clue, students write down their guesses. The object of the activity is to guess the word on the basis of the fewest clues. The clues might be as follows:

1. The secret word is in the *at* pattern.
2. It has three letters.
3. It is an animal.
4. It can fly.
5. Into the cave flew the _____.

After supplying the five clues, show the secret word (*bat*) and discuss students' responses. See who guessed the secret word first.

Making Words

> "Making words" is an excellent way to review a pattern or a series of related patterns.

"Making words" is a hands-on manipulative activity in which students put together letters to create words and provides excellent reinforcement for word-building patterns. Beginning with two-letter words and extending to five-letter or even longer words, students assemble approximately a dozen words (Cunningham & Cunningham, 1992). The last word that the students assemble contains all the letters that they were given. Here's how it works. Students are given the cut-out or magnetic letters *a–d–n–s–t* and are asked to do the following.

- Use two letters to make *at.*
- Add a letter to make *sat.*
- Take away a letter to make *at.*
- Change a letter to make *an.*
- Add a letter to make *Dan.*

> To enhance the value of Making Words, focus on a few patterns.

- Change a letter to make *tan.*
- Take away a letter to make *an.*
- Add a letter to make *and.*
- Add a letter to make *sand.*
- Now break up your word and see what word you can make with all the letters (*stand*).

Poems and Verses

> Poems can reinforce a variety of patterns, ranging from simple short *a* patterns to multisyllabic ones. Some easy-to-read collections include *Surprises* and *More Surprises* (Hopkins, 1987) or *Soap Soup and Other Verses* (Kuskin, 1992).

Overusing their decoding skills or, perhaps, struggling so hard to decode words that meaning is neglected, poor readers often ignore substitutions that do not fit the sense of the sentence. Because of its rhythm and rhyme, poetry is harder to misread. The interrupted flow created by a miscue is more noticeable and more likely to be corrected. Some poor readers' mistakes seem due more to carelessness or an inexact style of reading than lack of skill. However, poetry demands an exact reading. Having students read verses is a good way for them to experience accuracy in their reading (Bloodgood & Broaddus, 1994). Poetry can also be used to promote fluency, because poetry is meant to be read over and over again.

INTERNET

Starfall at http://www.starfall.com/ features activities, stories, and film clips designed to introduce single-syllable patterns. The program has a speech component so that words can be read. It highlights words in parts so that students can hear separate sounds in words and also match letters and sounds. In a number of activities Starfall builds words much as is done in Word Building. Between the Lions at http://pbskids.org/lions/ features a number of brief film clips of songs and stories that reinforce vowel patterns. The clips are fairly sophisticated so they could be used with older as well as younger students. Words and Pictures at http://www.bbc.co.uk/schools/wordsandpictures/index.shtml is produced by the BBC, so the exercises have a distinctive British flavor, but provide imaginative reinforcement.

> Reading along with tape-recorded or CD-ROM stories can be a highly effective way to foster fluency and comprehension (Shany & Biemiller, 1995).

> Computer programs that allow students to click on unfamiliar words and obtain their pronunciations can be helpful in promoting word recognition (Olson & Wise, 1997).

Software

Because of speech capability and interactive features, phonics software has the potential to provide excellent practice. The best software titles present phonics in a functional way that motivates students. *Simon Sounds It Out* (Don Johnston), an award-winning piece of software, pronounces and helps students build words by combining initial consonants (onsets) and word patterns (rimes). Featuring an electronic tutor, it provides especially effective practice for word building. Because it pronounces and shows parts of words, it also helps develop phonemic awareness. *Tenth Planet: Exploring Literacy* (Sunburst) includes sorting activities, building words, and the writing of rhymes and songs. Programs include Letter Sounds, Vowels: Short and Long, Consonant Blends and Digraphs; Vowel Patterns; and Word Parts (working with multisyllabic words).

WORD-ANALYSIS STRATEGIES

> Some disabled readers may first read words sound by sound. They should gradually be encouraged to "chunk" sounds.

Disabled readers tend to have difficulty with the middles of words and so overrely on context and initial and final consonants (Ehri & Saltmarsh, 1995). Disabled readers also have difficulty in taking control of their learning. Even when they do know the elements in a word, they fail to use them. Corrective readers need to be taught strategies to guide them so that they analyze words fully and use what they know to analyze apparently unknown words. Tied in to the word-building instructional technique are the following key strategies: pronounceable word part, analogy, and decoding.

Pronounceable Word-Part Strategy

The word-building technique takes advantage of students' natural tendency to seek out pronounceable word parts by highlighting them. Rob, an eight-year-old struggling reader, is baffled by the word *slop* even though he knows the rime *op* and several words that begin with *sl*.

> **Pronounceable word parts:** chunks of words that lend themselves naturally to being pronounced, such as *an* or *ran* or *bran* in the word *branch.*

The teacher asks Rob if there is any part of the word that he can say. Rob looks over the word, says "op," and then says "slop." The teacher's questioning helped direct Rob to a word part that he knew. Using the known element as a base, he was able to reconstruct the entire word. This step in the strategy is known as seeking out known or **pronounceable word parts.** Later, Rob has difficulty with the word *tick.* Rob is unable to locate any pronounceable parts, so the teacher assists him by covering up the *t.* Rob reads "ick" and then "tick." Although the teacher provides help when needed, the objective is to have the student apply the strategy independently. Here is how the strategy might be taught.

■ ■ ■ ■ ■

TEACHING THE PRONOUNCEABLE WORD-PART STRATEGY

Step 1: Assessing strategy usage. Observe students as they encounter printed words whose meanings they know but that they cannot pronounce. Note the strategies they use and how successfully they are able to apply them. Discuss strategies for decoding words. Tell students that all readers, even you, run into difficult words. Ask students how they go about figuring out hard words. As you introduce strategies, build on what students know. Help them fit new strategies in with ones they are using.

Step 2: Introducing the strategy. Explain to students that words that might appear difficult often contain parts that can be sounded out. Explaining that they will be learning a strategy called pronounceable word parts, model the strategy. Show how you might look for and use a known word part to help you sound out a word. After you have worked out the pronunciation of a word, show how you would check your reconstruction by seeing if your pronunciation was that of a real word and also seeing if the word fit the context of the sentence. Explain to students that, when seeking out pronounceable word parts, there is no one way to do it. In the word *bench,* for instance, *en* might be the familiar word part for some students. For others, the familiar word part might be *ben.* Do not ask students to look for the "little word" in the big word. For one thing, many big words do not contain little words. For another, using word units might make it more difficult to pronounce the entire word. Finding *hop,* the little word in *chop,* would actually make it harder to work out the pronunciation of *chop,* since the *ch* functions as a unit.

Step 3: Guided practice for pronounceable word parts. Provide guided practice with the strategy.

Have students seek out known word parts in the following or other words that contain elements familiar to your students. Pointing to each word, ask: "Is there any part of this word that you can say?"

lunch   spend   sting   stump

As students attempt to apply the strategy, provide assistance. If they are unable to find a pronounceable word part even though the target word has one, cover up all of the word except the pronounceable word part and encourage them to say the part that is uncovered and use that part to reconstruct the whole word. For instance, if a student who knows the word *hen,* balks at *tent,* cover up all but the *en* and encourage the student to pronounce it. After *en* has been pronounced, uncover the initial *t* and have the student pronounce the *t* and then *ten.* Uncover the final *t,* have the student pronounce it, and then ask the student to read the whole word. Be sure to affirm students' efforts with specific comments: "I like the way you looked for a part of the word that you could say and then used that to help you figure out that hard word."

Do not encourage the use of the strategy with words like *of* or *you* or *wash,* or other words that are irregular and so do not lend themselves to this strategy. Encourage the use of context for these words. If it is obvious that a student cannot work out a word, tell the student the word, or ask, "Is that word _____ or _____? (you supply the target word and an option)?"

As part of your instruction, inform students that the pronounceable word-part strategy will not always work. For instance, pronouncing the *ow* in

(Continued)

knowledge or the *ash* in *squash* won't help much. Students need to learn to check their constructions to make sure they are real words that fit the context. If not, they should try alternative pronunciations.

Step 4: Application. Before students read a selection, highlight some words that you feel they may have difficulty with. If they can't pronounce them, have students seek out pronounceable word parts and see if they can construct the words' pronunciations. Emphasize the need to check to see that the word they construct is a real word and fits the story context. During reading, remind students to use the pronounceable word-part strategy if they encounter graphically unknown words. Supply help as needed. After reading, discuss words that students decoded successfully. Talk over the processes that they used to decipher the words so they become more fully aware of how the strategy works.

Step 5: Review. Review the pronounceable word-part strategy from time to time. Whenever a new word pattern is introduced, provide students with opportunities to note that pattern in words. For instance, after *-at* has been presented, have students note *at* in words such as *chat, flat, patch,* and *rattle.* Encourage students to bring to class examples of encounters with newly taught patterns and instances where they were able to work out the pronunciation of words by using the pronounceable word-part strategy.

Analogy strategy: a method in which students work out the pronunciation of a hard word by comparing it to a known word.

Explicit instruction in the use of the analogy and pronounceable word-part strategies proved to be especially effective for severely disabled readers in grades 2 through 6 (Lovett & Steinbach, 1997). In just thirty-five lessons, the program produced significant and substantial gains in decoding.

To use the analogy strategy, students must first think of a word that is like the word with which they are having difficulty and then compare the known word to the unknown one.

Analogy Strategy

Although natural, effective, and relatively easy to teach, the pronounceable word-part strategy does not always work. When it doesn't work, students should try an analogy or comparison–contrast strategy. Research suggests that the analogy or comparison–contrast strategy is relatively easy to teach (Ehri & Robbins, 1992) and is highly effective (Cunningham, 1979; Gaskins, Gaskins, & Gaskins, 1991). Here is how the **analogy strategy** works. While reading a sports story, Rob encounters the word *tame,* a word that is in his listening vocabulary but that he has never seen in print. Neither urging Rob to look for a familiar part nor covering up the *t* helps. Knowing that Rob can read the word *name,* the teacher uses an analogy strategy. She asks Rob if the word looks like any word that he knows. If Rob is unable to think of an analogy word, she may refer him to a list of analogy words known as the Model Words List (see Figure 8.5), or she might supply the analogy word. The teacher carefully prints the word *name* and immediately under it the word *tame.* She asks Rob to read the first word, which he does with ease. Noting that *tame* is similar to *name,* Rob reads it, too. If he had still been unable to read *tame,* the teacher would have used known *t* words (*to, toy*) to help him decode the initial consonant and then blend the two elements. Here is how the analogy strategy might be taught.

TEACHING THE ANALOGY STRATEGY

Step 1: Introducing the analogy strategy. Explain to students that sometimes they may not be able to find a word part that they can pronounce. Tell them that if this happens, they should try to think of a word they know that is similar. Model the strategy for them. For instance, show them how they could use the word *rain* to help decode *chain* or the word *him* to decode *trim*. Stress the need to see if the reconstructed word is a real one.

Step 2: Guided practice. Provide a number of words that may be new to students but that are analogous to known words. Have students use the known words to figure out the new ones. For instance, students might use the known words *pen* and *hit* to decipher *when, bent, spend, quit,* and *split.*

Step 3: Practice and application. Have students integrate the analogy and pronounceable word-parts strategies and apply them, as needed, to unfamiliar words in stories and articles. Post a list of model words similar to that presented in Figure 8.5 so that students can use these in case they can't think of an

analogy word. To guide students in their use of the pronounceable word-part or analogy strategy, post a set of directions for using the strategies, model their use, and provide ample opportunity for practice and application. Whenever students encounter difficulty with a word, encourage them to apply the strategies. A sample set of instructions for using the strategies is presented in the section, "How to Figure out Hard Words." You may want to reword the instructions to fit the level of your students.

Step 4: Review. Review the analogy strategy from time to time. Encourage students to bring to class examples of encounters with newly taught patterns and instances where they were able to work out the pronunciation of words by using the pronounceable word-part or analogy strategy.

Beginning readers can use an analogy strategy to decode unfamiliar words if the analogy word is present (Goswami, 1988), but they must have some phonics skills if they are to draw an analogy word from memory (Ehri & Robbins, 1992). They can use the known word *cat* to read *mat* if the word *cat* is there before them but probably would not be able to retrieve it from memory. Use of analogy becomes more common as students' store of immediate recognition words increases (Ehri & Snowling, 2004).

Decoding Strategy

Students at the very beginning stages of learning to read may not be able to spot patterns in words or use a known word to read an unfamiliar one. These students can still use a pronounceable word part. For them, the pronounceable word part might be the first sound. They might then be encouraged to read the rest of the word sound by sound and to blend the sounds together.

Context

Some words do not lend themselves to decoding or are composed of unfamiliar elements. Depending on the nature of the word and the context, students should be encouraged to use picture or verbal clues. Context should also be used as a cross-check. After students have decoded a word, they should make sure that it makes sense in the sentence.

Prompting Strategy Use

When students encounter difficult words, use a "pause, prompt, praise" approach (Tunmer & Chapman, 1999). At first, say nothing. Simply pause, and give the student a chance to work out the word on his own. (If this is during a group activity, do not allow other students to respond.) If the student is not able to decode the word, supply a prompt. Unless the word is *were, of,* or another word that has an irregular spelling or contains phonics elements with

Prompts are statements that teachers make in order to guide students to use a strategy. When students balk at a word, give them a chance to apply a strategy on their own. If they need guidance, supply a prompt.

When prompting the use of the pronounceable word-part strategy, ask students if there is any part of the word they can say. Do not ask them to "look for the little word in the big word." Often there is none, but there is usually a pronounceable word part.

Application of the pronounceable word-part strategy should be part of instruction in patterns. Once students have learned the -*en* pattern, they should be encouraged to use -*en* to help them read difficult words that contain this element.

which the student is not familiar, provide a phonics prompt. Although many programs urge the use of a context prompt such as "What would make sense here?" phonics clues are more effective and promote the transfer of word analysis skills to new words (Greaney, Tunmer, & Chapman, 1997; Tunmer & Chapman, 1999). Because it is more direct and easier to implement, prompt the pronounceable word-part strategy first. Ask, "Is there any part of that word that you can say?" If the student does not respond, provide additional assistance. For instance, if a student who has been taught the -*ee* pattern has difficulty with a word such as *sweet* and is unable to note any known parts in the word, you might cover up all but the middle *ee* and have her say what sound *ee* makes. Uncovering the *w,* have her pronounce *wee* and then, uncovering the *s,* lead her to pronounce *swee.* Uncovering the final *t,* encourage the student to pronounce the whole word.

If the student is unable to pronounce the *ee* in *sweet,* you might prompt the use of an analogy strategy. Ask the student if the word is like any word that she knows. If the student is unable to think of an analogy word, supply one. Using the model word *feet,* have her read *feet* and compare *sweet* with *feet* (cover the *sw* in *sweet* if necessary, so that she can read "eet" and then "sweet").

Some students may be slow perceiving patterns in words, such as the *an* in *plan* or the *ip* in *trip.* For these students the pronounceable word part might be the beginning consonant, or they may need to say each sound of the word individually: "p-l-a-n." If this is the case, encourage them to do so. In time, after being introduced to a number of word patterns, they should be able to perceive patterns in words.

If the student is unable to use a pronounceable word-part or analogy strategy or if the word does not lend itself to either of these strategies, prompt the use of context. Encourage the student to skip the word and read to the end of the sentence. Ask, "What word would make sense here? What word would fit?" Even when a sounding-out strategy is used, context should be used as a cross-check. After a student has used the pronounceable word-part or analogy strategy, prompt the student to see if the word is a real word and fits the sense of the sentence.

How well do the pronounceable word-part and analogy strategies work? In a series of experiments, severely disabled readers taught to use pronounceable word part and analogy strategies clearly outperformed students taught to use context (Greaney, Tunmer, & Chapman, 1997; Tunmer & Chapman, 1999). The authors recommended that "children should be encouraged to look for familiar spelling patterns first and to use context only as a backup to confirm hypotheses as to what the word might be" (p. 82).

There are two problems with the overuse of context. First, it does not work as well as decoding strategies. From context, students are only able to predict the pronunciation of about one out of every ten content words. Functions words such as *of* and *the* are 40 percent predictable (Tunmer & Chapman, 1999). Second, unless students use their phonics strategies, they will fail to develop and so their word-analysis skills will be weakened. Ironically, use of phonics skills improves students' ability to use context. When presented with a series of irregular words presented in sentence context that they had missed when they were called upon to read them in list form, students who were better decoders outperformed the poor decoders (Tunmer & Chapman, 1999). Decoding ability facilitated the use of context.

How to Figure Out Hard Words

Listed below is a series of steps that students might take when confronting a word that is unfamiliar in print.

> The pronounceable word-part strategy is listed first because it is less intrusive to the flow of reading and because it is faster and easier to apply than the analogy or contextual strategies.

1. See if there is any part of the word that I can say. If I can't say any part of the word, go to step 4.
2. Say the part of the word I know. Then say the rest of the word. If I can't say the rest of the word, go to step 4.
3. Ask: "Is the word I said a real word? Does it make sense in the story?" If not, try again or go to step 4.
4. Is the word like any word I know? Is it like one of the model words? If not, go to step 6.
5. Say the word. Is it a real word? Does it make sense in the story? If not, try again, or go to step 6.
6. Say "blank" for the word. Read to the end of the sentence. Ask myself: "What word would make sense here?"

> To foster independence, review strategy use from time to time, provide lots of practice and application opportunities, and use prompts liberally.

Students should practice saying and eventually memorize the steps of the decoding strategies. In an experiment in which low-achieving readers rehearsed the steps of a strategy by saying the steps aloud and then to themselves, they did much better than a group who were simply taught the strategy. Affirming responses so that students could see they were using the strategy successfully also increased performance (Schunk & Rice, 1993).

Balanced Use of Decoding Strategies

> An analysis of the performance of low-achieving readers suggests that those who use strategies make progress. Those who do not use strategies make very limited progress.

In addition to pronounceable word-part, analogy, decoding, and context strategies, a number of other strategies can be used to decipher words. These include using picture clues, using verbal context, using the initial letter of an unknown word, using phonics rules, using a picture glossary or picture dictionary, asking for help, or simply skipping the word altogether. Often, strategies are combined. For instance, decoding may be combined with a picture clue or context or both.

Strategy use may be inefficient or inappropriate. Using pictures clues is an early strategy that should give way to some form of using phonics clues and context. However, because they are deficient in higher-level decoding strategies, some poor readers continue to overuse picture and context clues. Because they overuse picture and context clues, they fail to develop other, more useful strategies.

Strategies should be taught directly, but careful instruction needs to be accompanied by extensive opportunities for applying strategies. After being taught a strategy, students need to be guided in its proper application. Their efforts also need to be affirmed with specific praise.

The degree to which students make progress is also a reflection of the teacher's guidance. Decoding instruction must go beyond teaching students a series of short-vowel patterns or consonant clusters. The instructor must teach students what to do when they encounter an unknown short-vowel or consonant-cluster word. That instruction cannot be limited to a few lessons or review sessions. It should include prompts that the teacher uses when the students encounter difficult words.

USING PROMPTS TO FOSTER THE USE OF BALANCED DECODING STRATEGIES

Julia, a seven-year-old second-grader reading on a primer level, misread the sentence, "The light is red now," from Eastman's (1961) *Go, Dog, Go* as "The little is red new." Analyzing the misreading, the teacher realized that while Julia had made use of initial consonants (*little* and *light* and *new* and *now* begin with the same consonant sound), she ignored other sources of information. For instance, an illustration at the top of the page clearly shows a stop light that has turned red, and in previous portions of the story, green and red lights have been mentioned. Apart from these picture and textual clues, Julia's knowledge of language should inform her that a noun will follow the article *the*. Her general knowledge of the world as well as her knowledge of language should also indicate that the sentence does not make sense as she reads it.

Julia had failed to make adequate use of all three cueing systems. Her miscues did not fit syntactically, semantically, or visually, except for the beginning sound. Through careful questioning or prompts, the teacher might lead Julia to the use of the semantic, syntactic, or phonic cueing strategies that would help her rectify her misreading. For instance, the following prompts might have been used:

> While picture clues might be fostered during the prealphabetic (logographic) and early alphabetic stages of reading, phonics and contextual clues should gradually replace them. Enlist the student's input by asking: "What would help you figure that word out?"

- Semantic: "Does that sentence make sense? What would make sense here?"
- Syntactic: "Does that sound like real language? What would sound right here?"
- Phonic: "*Little* begins with an *l*, but how does it end? How does this word end?" (teacher points to *light*) "Can you think of another word that has *i-g-h-t?* What sound does it make?" (Earlier in the story, Julia had read *night* correctly. Using this as an analogy, she might be led to work out the word *light*.) Or you could try a pronounceable word-part strategy and ask, "Is there any part of this word that you can say?"

> Poor readers often have difficulty with hard words even though these were carefully taught them. Avoid making such statements as, "You know this word. We just had it." Provide, instead, whatever prompts you feel will be most helpful.

When choosing which prompt to use and therefore which cueing system to emphasize, you need to consider a number of factors. You need to ask, "What prompt is most likely to lead to a correct response? Which prompt will provide the greatest payoff in terms of helping the student cope with difficult words in the future?" You also need to consider the student's development in reading. What strategies has she mastered? What strategies is she struggling to learn? Although the pronounceable word-part approach is frequently a good strategy to start with because it

Cross-check: the use of one strategy to verify the results of another. For instance, a student uses context to verify that the word she sounded out makes sense.

Do not pose riddle-like prompts: "It rhymes with *shoots.* You wear these on your feet" (boots). Use a prompt that leads to strategy use: "Can you say any part of that word? What would make sense here?"

To build independence, occasionally ask students to decide for themselves what strategy they might apply. Ask, "How might you figure out that word?"

To gain insight into students' strategy use, occasionally ask them to tell how they figured out a hard word. You might ask, "How do you know that word was "numb?"

If you are not sure which is the best prompt to use with a student, enlist the student's input by asking, "What would help you figure that word out?"

is simple, direct, and easy to apply, a better choice for Julia might be to supply semantic prompts. First and foremost, students need to see that reading should make sense. A semantic prompt ("What word would make sense here?") would be a reminder of that fact. Since Julia neglected to relate *light* to the known word *night,* a phonic cue might be used as a **cross-check.** After the student supplies *light* on the basis of semantic cues, ask her if *light* begins with an *l* and ends with a *t.* Ask her if she can think of another word that ends in *i-g-h-t.* If she remembers *night,* have her say the word and compare *light* to this known word.

The nature of the text being read also has an effect on strategy choice. For instance, Tiffany, a third-grader, had difficulty with the sentence, "The bear fell from the tree." Since Tiffany was stuck on *from,* she hadn't read the phrase "the tree." Noting that *from* is "irregular" and believing that having more context would aid Tiffany, the teacher requested that Tiffany reread the beginning of the sentence, say "blank" for the unknown word, read to the end of the sentence, and then see if she could tell what the word might be. After rereading the entire sentence, Tiffany had no difficulty identifying *from.* As a cross-check, the teacher asked Tiffany to tell what letters *from* begins with and what sounds these letters stand for. Noting some hesitancy and remembering that Tiffany had stumbled over other words that contained initial clusters such as *fr,* the instructor planned future lessons on clusters.

Choice of strategies is also determined, in part, by the student's cognitive processing abilities. Tiffany has difficulty remembering words and may miss the same word every time it appears in a story. In one story, Tiffany repeatedly missed the word *chance.* Hoping to provide some "hook" that would help Tiffany retrieve *chance,* the instructor asked Tiffany if there was any part of *chance* she could say. Tiffany recognized the *an,* added *ch* to it, said "*chan,*" and then was able to read *chance.* In subsequent encounters with *chance,* Tiffany was able to use this strategy when she failed to recognize the word.

Fostering Self-Correction

In reading, as in life, errors provide opportunity for growth. When a student misreads a word, don't immediately supply a correction. Let the student read to the end of the sentence or perhaps the paragraph. Often, reading additional text will indicate to the student that a miscue has been made and she will reread the text correctly. If not, supply a prompt that will lead her to self-correct: "Does that sound right? Does that make sense?"

If a student's misreading was partially correct, bring that to the youngster's attention. To confirm a student's use of context, you might say, "The word *dog* fits the sense of the sentence. Dogs do howl. But the word begins with a *w.* What word that begins with a *w* might fit there?"

Provide prompts only after a reasonable interval and when it seems likely that the student will benefit from some help, and then give only as much help as is needed to nudge the student onto the right path. Use the least intrusive prompt possible.

Sometimes, despite your careful prompting, the student is unable to make use of any of the strategies. Provide the correct response as one of two options. For example, instead of simply telling her or him that the unknown word is *goat,* ask, "Would *goat* or *got* fit here?" Then discuss why *goat* is appropriate. This "starter" prompt actively engages the student and points out strategies that she or he might use in the future.

Self-correcting is a sign of a good reader. It means the student realizes that meaning is the ultimate aim of reading. It also means that the reader actively monitors his reading to make sure that it makes sense. When students self-correct without your help, reinforce this behavior by using an affirmation prompt in which you make comments such as, "I like the way you corrected that mistake. That's what good readers do." From time to time, use an asssesment prompt to ask students how they made a self-correction or figured out a hard word: "How did you know to change *green* to *grin?* How did you figure that word out?" These questions provide insight into the processes students are using. Because students are called upon to explain what processes they are using, it leads them to a deeper understanding of the strategies and helps them generalize the strategies to other situations (Clay, 1993b). Prompts for frequently used strategies are listed in Table 8.8.

Effective Use of Strategies

Because decoding words is so difficult for them, some poor readers overuse context clues. This is especially true when they are asked to read material that is too hard for them. Other

TABLE 8.8   Word Analysis Prompts

STRATEGY	WHEN USED	PROMPT
Pronounceable word part	Unknown word contains a part student can say: *am* or *amp* in *champ*	Can you say any part of that word?
Analogy	Unknown word is like a word student knows: Unknown word *grain* is like known word *rain.*	Is this word like any word that you know?
Sound by sound	Student is unable to chunk word. Works out word sound by sound: /s/-/p/-/e/-/l spell.	Can you say the first sound, the next sound, the next sound?
Context	Student is unable to use phonics clues.	What would make sense here? Read to the end of the sentence and see what word would fit.
Monitoring	Student checks to see if the word he pronounced is a real word and fits the context of the selection. Actually, students monitor for meaning whenever they read.	Is that a real word? Does that make sense? Does that sound right?
Affirmation	Teacher wishes to reinforce the student's correct use of a strategy.	I like the way you used a part of the word that you knew to help you say the whole word.

Phonics programs for corrective readers are typically heavy on instruction and practice and light on application, with countless hours being spent on workbook pages. Actually, what corrective students need most is the opportunity to apply skills to real reading.

poor readers overuse phonics. Having poor decoding skills, they may have been drilled and skilled in phonics to such an extent that they view reading as primarily a matter of saying the right sounds. Students need to learn to balance their use of strategies. The following provide tips about what to do when students are relying too heavily on one strategy.

When Students Overuse Phonics Cues. To help students who overuse phonic cues, try the following.

- Make sure the material they read is on the appropriate level. Students should know at least 95 percent of the words. If the reader encounters too many unknown words or decodes too slowly, she or he loses the sense of the selection and will resort to the overuse of phonics.
- Stress reading for meaning. Spend extra time building background. As you build background, list key words on the board so students will be familiar with them and will be primed to read them when they are encountered in the selection. Have purposes set before the student reads.
- Stress silent reading. Oral reading can lead to a preoccupation with correct pronunciation of words rather than the construction of meaning.
- Construct a series of cloze or modified cloze exercises in which students complete stories in which words have been deleted. Demonstrate cloze by modeling how you would go about filling in the blanks. Emphasize the need to use context clues and to read beyond the blank. After doing a few exercises cooperatively, have students complete some selections on their own. Be sure to discuss the completed exercises.

When Students Overuse Context Clues. Students may overuse context cues for a variety of reasons. Their phonics skills may be weak, they may be holding onto strategies that worked with highly predictable books but are not appropriate for more mature materials, or they may not be demanding a high degree of accuracy from their reading. To build a more balanced use of phonics strategies, try the following.

- Make sure that materials are on an appropriate level of difficulty. Some students overuse context clues when they do not have the skills necessary to decode a large proportion of the unfamiliar words they encounter.
- Take several running records or informal reading inventory samples of a student's oral reading. Note whether decoding skills are adequate. If not, work to improve weak skills and teach missing ones, making sure that students have plenty of opportunity to apply skills.
- Encourage wide reading of easy materials. Poor readers often need extra practice in order for their skills to become automatic.
- Before students read a selection, review key phonics patterns that appear in the piece, so the students will be better prepared to use needed phonics skills.
- Review the phonics strategies for attacking unknown words. When students are stumped by a word, ask: "What can you do to help you figure out that word? Are there any parts that you can say? Is the word like any word that you know?"

SCOPE AND SEQUENCE OF ANALOGY
WORDS AND PATTERNS

Word building can be used with students of any age, including adults. Words in each pattern can be varied so that older readers are presented with more mature words.

Instructional and practice materials for word building are available in *Phonological Awareness and Primary Phonics* (Gunning 2000b) and *Building Words: A Resource Manual for Teaching Word Analysis and Spelling Strategies* (Gunning, 2001).

Presentation of the word patterns will vary according to the reading ability of the students and their oral language development. Younger students who are struggling with beginning reading skills would be presented with the easiest patterns: *cat, hat, fat, pet, wet.* Words introduced would be restricted to those generally known by primary-age pupils. Older students who are functioning at a beginner-reader level might also need to learn basic patterns such as *-at.* The main difference in presentation would be in choice of words to be introduced. Having more extensive vocabularies, older readers might be able to handle more difficult words within each pattern: *chat, vat, slim,* and *whim,* for instance. A suggested sequence for introducing word-building patterns is presented in Figure 8.11.

The rate of introduction of patterns will vary. In the beginning, introduce only one pattern at a time and work on it until students seem to have a firm grasp of it. As students catch onto the concept of the patterns, you may be able to present two or three at a time. This is especially true if students have some phonics skills but need a systematic review. This does not mean that all low-achieving readers should be taught all the patterns. Give students credit for what they know. They are dismayed when retaught skills that they have already mastered. An informal reading inventory, observation, and/or the Word Pattern Survey in Appendix A could be used to establish a starting point for instruction.

A MEANS TO AN END

Phonics is a means to an end. The ultimate aim of decoding is to enable students to read independently. To accomplish that goal, decoding instruction must be functional and contextual. Skills taught should be related directly to selections that students are about to read. And students should have ample opportunity to put their skills to work by reading a wide variety of children's books, periodicals, and other real-world materials.

HIGH-FREQUENCY WORDS

What are the most difficult words for reading-disabled students to learn to read? Ironically, the shortest, most frequently occurring words—**high-frequency words**—pose the most serious problem for many students. Compared to decoding *were, was,* or *where,* the words *rhinoceros* and *elephant* are a breeze. Compensating for their length by their distinctive spelling and specific meanings, *rhinoceros* and *elephant* are relatively easy to learn to read. After one or two presentations and a few encounters in a text, many students have these words mastered for life. After dozens, maybe hundreds of presentations, and countless encounters, some students still stumble over *was, were, where,* and *are.*

FIGURE 8.11   Word-Building Scope and Sequence

PREPARATORY
Phonemic awareness
Letter knowledge
Initial consonant correspondences

LEVEL 1
Easy long-vowel patterns: -*e* (he), -*ee* (bee), -*o* (no)
Short-vowel patterns

LEVEL 2
Long-vowel patterns

LEVEL 3
Other-vowel patterns: -*oy* (boy), -*ou* (out), -*ain* (pain), -*oo* (book), *oo* (soon),
and *r*-vowel patterns

> **High-frequency words,** commonly known as *sight words*, are the 200 or so most frequently occurring words in printed English.

Unfortunately, many of the most frequently occurring words in the language are abstract or lacking meaning, serving only as function words in a sentence (*the, of, with*); lack a distinctive appearance and so are easily confused with other words (*will, with, what*); and may have a spelling that gives little or no clue to their pronunciation (*one, of*).

How High-Frequency Words Are Learned

> Students who are weak in orthographic processing may have special difficulty with irregularly spelled words because they have difficulty getting a visual fix on them.

Because their spellings don't do a good job of indicating the sounds they represent, some high-frequency words, such as *of, you, was,* and *they,* don't lend themselves to a decoding approach. These words are taught in a logographic or paired-associate fashion. Students learn the words by associating the spoken words with visual features. In addition, there are other high-frequency words that do have predictable pronunciations, but they incorporate advanced phonic elements: *which, each, how.* Because these words occur with high frequency, it is difficult to read even the simplest of selections without encountering them. Therefore, they are often introduced in paired-associate or logographic fashion in the earliest stages of reading.

Novice readers can and do learn words through a sight or logographic approach. However, the number of words that they can learn in this way is limited to about forty (Gough & Hillinger, 1980). At that point, the system begins to fall apart. The learner runs out of distinctive features by which to remember each word. In addition, with many high-frequency words being similar in appearance, they are easily confused because the "visual cues selected are not

> Except for words like *of* and *one,* all words should be taught through a phonics approach so that connections are made between letters and sounds. As Torgesen (2004b) notes, a top myth in teaching reading is that if a student is a visual learner, the student should be taught through a visual approach. The truth is that decoding skills and high-frequency words must be learned phonologically.

> Using phonics to teach high-frequency words teaches students a reliable way of recognizing the words, and provides a means by which the words can be stored in memory.

unique to individual words" (Ehri, 1994, p. 326). Such words are also hard to fix in memory because the cues used to establish the associations are arbitrary. The cues have no relationship to the sounds that the letters in the words represent.

Once students have reached the alphabetic stage, high-frequency words, insofar as possible, should be taught through a phonics approach. When taught through a decoding approach, they are easier to learn and remember. Most high-frequency words are completely regular: *and, in, that, it, at, this, but.* Their pronunciations can easily be predicted from their spellings. Except for a very few words, words like *of, one, on,* and even the irregular words are mostly predictable. For most of them, the vowels are irregular: *was, from, some.* However, their initial and final letters can be used to determine beginning and ending sounds: *have, said, find, word.* Not taking advantage of these regularities deprives students of a means of learning high-frequency words. For instance, disabled and novice readers typically confuse the *wh* words: *who, what, when, where, why, which.* However, *when* is completely regular. When presenting the word *when,* help students see the familiar word part *en* in *when* by relating it to *ten* or *pen* or other known *-en* words. *Which* is also completely regular and can be related to words like *itch, pitch,* or *witch.* Although it is not completely regular, *what* can be distinguished from the other *wh* words because it ends in *t.* *Why* is also completely regular. Relate it to *by, cry,* or other words that end in *y* = /ī/. *Who,* which incorporates the less frequent correspondence *wh* = /h/ and has an irregular spelling for its vowel sound, is more problematical. One way of teaching *who* is to present it with other high-frequency words that incorporate the *o* = /o͞o/ correspondence: *do, to, two.*

Figure 8.12 shows the kinds of connections that readers might make between the spellings and sounds of regular and irregular words. The connections for *red* are straightforward. There is a connection between the letter *R* and the sound /r/, the letter and the sound /e/, and the letter *D* and the sound /d/. Similar connections are made for irregular words. Many of the connections in irregular words are between letters and the sound they typically represent. For letters that do not follow typical letter-sound rules, the readers might create exceptional connections, such as the *a* in yacht having a short-*o* pronunciation and the sound /t/ being represented as *cht.* Or the reader might remember the *ch* as being extra letters or silent letters (Ehri & Snowling, 2004).

Orthographic Processing and Learning High-Frequency Words

Orthographic ability is related to decoding ability. In the early stages of reading, students rely heavily on phonics to decode words. As decoding skills are developed and students encounter elements such as final-*e* words and vowel digraphs, orthographic or visual processing becomes an important factor. Students who have difficulty with orthographic processing may have difficulty storing advanced patterns and irregular words. Because they have difficulty with orthographic processing, they overrely on phonics, which means that their reading may

R E D
/ | \
/r/ /ɛ/ /d/

H A L* F
\   \   /
/h/ /æ/ /f/

C L O CK*
| \ \ \
/k/ /l/ /a/ /k/

C O M B*
\   \   \
/k/ /o/ /m/

S M I L E*
\ \ \ \
/s/ /m/ /ay/ /l/

Y A CH* T
\ \   \ /
/y/ /a/ /t/

D U M P
/ | \ \
/d/ /ʌ/ /m/ /p/

T O NG UE*
\ \   \
/t/ /ʌ/ /ŋ/

CH I P
/ | \
/c/ /l/ /p/

G L I S T* E N
\ \ \ \   / |
/g/ /l/ /l/ /s/ /a/ /n/

F L OA T
\ \ \   \
/f/ /l/ /o/ /t/

F L IGH T
| \ | |
/f/ /l/ /ay/ /t/

R A TT LE
\ \ \   \
/r/ /æ/ /t/ /l/

FIGURE 8.12   Connections in Memory between Letters and Sounds

From Ehri, L. C., & Snowling, M. J. (2004). Developmental variation in word recognition. In C. A. Stone, E. R. Silliman, B. J. Ehren, & K. Apel (Eds.), *Handbook of language and literacy development and disorders* (pp. 433–460). New York: Guilford Press.

be slow and laborious. They confuse letters and words that are similar in appearance, especially if the words are irregular. They frequently confuse word pairs such as *were* and *where*. Their spelling is phonetic. They spell what they hear and so have difficulty with irregular words such as *because* and *often*. They continue to misspell high-frequency words that they have encountered many times. Although weakness in orthographic processing may affect both reading and spelling, in some students it affects only spelling. These students may have sufficient orthographic memory for reading but not spelling (Orton, 1966). Students who have weak orthographic processing ability need to have many encounters with words and might need a multisensory approach to learn irregular words.

High Payoff of High-Frequency Words

> If the meanings of any of the words are unknown, discuss them. However, don't spend time developing meanings for words that are already in the students' listening vocabulary.

The High-Frequency List, which contains a number of irregular words and advanced patterns, is presented in Table 8.9 and consists of the 200 words that appear most frequently in books and other materials read by school children (Zeno, Ivens, Millard, & Duvvuri, 1995). These 200 words make up approximately 50 percent of the words in continuous text. The first word, *the,* occurs about 2 percent of the time. Because

TABLE 8.9   High-Frequency Words

1. the	41. which	81. made	121. also	161. name
2. of	42. their	82. over	122. around	162. should
3. and	43. said	83. did	123. another	163. home
4. a	44. if	84. down	124. came	164. give
5. to	45. will	85. way	125. three	165. air
6. in	46. do	86. only	126. soon	166. line
7. is	47. each	87. may	127. come	167. mother
8. you	48. about	88. find	128. work	168. set
9. that	49. how	89. use	129. must	169. world
10. it	50. up	90. water	130. part	170. own
11. he	51. out	91. little	131. because	171. under
12. for	52. then	92. long	132. does	172. last
13. was	53. them	93. very	133. even	173. read
14. on	54. she	94. after	134. place	174. never
15. are	55. many	95. word	135. old	175. am
16. as	56. some	96. called	136. well	176. us
17. with	57. so	97. just	137. such	177. left
18. his	58. these	98. new	138. here	178. end
19. they	59. would	99. where	139. take	179. along
20. at	60. other	100. most	140. why	180. while
21. be	61. into	101. know	141. thing	181. sound
22. this	62. has	102. get	142. great	182. house
23. from	63. more	103. through	143. help	183. might
24. I	64. two	104. back	144. put	184. next
25. have	65. her	105. much	145. year	185. below
26. not	66. like	106. good	146. different	186. saw
27. or	67. him	107. before	147. number	187. something
28. by	68. time	108. go	148. away	188. thought
29. one	69. see	109. man	149. again	189. both
30. had	70. no	110. our	150. off	190. few
31. but	71. could	111. want	151. went	191. those
32. what	72. make	112. lot	152. tell	192. school
33. all	73. than	113. me	153. men	193. show
34. were	74. first	114. day	154. say	194. always
35. when	75. been	115. too	155. small	195. until
36. we	76. its	116. any	156. every	196. large
37. there	77. who	117. same	157. found	197. often
38. can	78. now	118. right	158. still	198. together
39. an	79. people	119. look	159. big	199. ask
40. your	80. my	120. think	160. between	200. write

Adapted from *The educator's word frequency guide* by S. M. Zeno, S. H. Ivens, R. T. Millard, & R. Duvvuri, 1995, Brewster, NY: Touchstone Applied Science Associates.

high-frequency words play such an important role, they should be introduced periodically along with the patterns. Presented in the next section is a sample lesson for direct instruction in high-frequency words. The approach taken to introduce high-frequency words will depend, in part, on the students' stage of development and the nature of the words. Students in the alphabetic or word-pattern stages can be guided to use their knowledge of letter–sound relationships to learn high-frequency words as long as they are at least partly regular.

DIRECT TEACHING APPROACH FOR HIGH-FREQUENCY WORDS

An efficient way of presenting high-frequency words is to teach patterns that incorporate these words. Present *he, be, me, we, see;* or *at, that;* or *way, may, day.*

The direct-teaching technique is adapted from an approach devised by Bryant, Kelly, Hathaway, and Rubin (1981). It emphasizes repetition and context, and, in its adapted form, the use of phonics to help the student make solid, lasting connections between printed words and their spoken equivalents. A carefully structured, thorough technique, it has been effective with students who had considerable difficulty learning high-frequency words.

■ ■ ■ ■ ■ ▬▬▬▬▬▬▬▬▬▬▬▬▬▬▬▬▬▬▬▬▬▬▬▬▬▬▬▬▬▬▬▬▬▬▬▬▬▬

HIGH-FREQUENCY WORD LESSON

Step 1: Selecting words to be taught. Choose between four and six words for instruction. Words chosen should be ones that students will meet in a basal-reader selection, children's book, or other reading material that they are about to read. The words should also appear more than once in the piece, are important to the piece, and will probably occur in other selections. Words such as *for* and *from* that are easily confused should not be presented at the same time. Print the words on 3-by-5 cards. To avoid wasting time with words that are already known, pretest students by holding up each card and asking them to read it. Discard words known by nearly everyone. Step 2 shows how the words *old, wore, green, hat,* and *man* might be introduced.

Step 2: Presentation in isolation. First, reconstruct each word sound-by-sound or pronounceable element-by-pronounceable element so that students establish and later learn to recognize familiar parts in words. Here's how the high-frequency word *old* might be presented. Write *old* on the board. Ask if anyone can read it. If no one can, build on any knowledge of letters or letter–sound relationships that students have. If students are in the alphabetic or orthographic stage and know the letters *o-l-d* and the sounds they represent, ask students if there is any part of the word that they can say. If there are parts of the word that are familiar, have them read and use

the familiar parts to reconstruct the word. If the word is totally unfamiliar, cover it up except for its vowel and reconstruct the word sound by sound. For the word *old,* cover up the *l* and *d,* and ask students to say the sound that *o* stands for. Give help if necessary. After students read *o,* uncover the *l* and have students read *ol,* giving help as necessary. After students have read *ol,* uncover the *d,* have students say what sound it stands for, and have them read *old.* Supply assistance as needed. Then ask each student to read the word. If a student misses the word, reconstruct it with him, having the student read "o-ol-old" as you uncover the word's letters. If students are in the logographic stage, emphasize the appearance and spelling of the word, especially the first letter.

Present the word *wore* in the same way. If students are in the alphabetic or orthographic stage, begin instruction with *or* and then build the word by adding final *e* (note that this *e* does not change anything) and then *w.* For *green,* start with *ee* and add *n* so that you have formed the ending portion of the word, then *r,* and finally, *g.* For *hat,* start with *at* and add *h.* For *man,* relate it to the known word *an.* Here students read *an.* Then add *m* and have the word *man* read. After this initial presentation of the words, print them on cards, if you have not already done so, and present them once more. Continue presenting the words until students are able to read each one within one second on two consecutive presentations.

(Continued)

Step 3: Presentation in context. Present the words in phrases or short sentences. The phrases might include two or more of the high-frequency words and should be cumulative. Phrases for the words *old, wore, green, hat,* and *man,* for example, might be introduced as follows:

OLD HAT

old green hat
wore an old green hat
The man wore an old green hat.

The phrases and sentences should be presented until students can read all of them fluently.

Step 4: Application. Introduce the selection from which the high-frequency words were drawn. Discuss the title and key illustrations. Assist students in finding and reading the target high-frequency words in the selection. Have them read the entire sentence in which the target high-frequency word appears. Then, after setting a purpose for reading based on a discussion of the title, key illustrations, and high-frequency words, have students read the selection silently. During or after the follow-up discussion of the story, have students once again read the story sentences in which the high-frequency words appeared.

Step 5: Review. The next day, go over the words in isolation and in phrase and sentence context. Also provide review sessions for high-frequency words learned in previous sessions. Focus on words that continue to cause difficulty. Provide a variety of opportunities for students to apply their growing knowledge of high-frequency words by completing the practice activities presented later in this chapter. Keep in mind that the best way to build a high-frequency vocabulary is to have students read lots of easy materials. A list of books containing high-frequency words is found in Figure 8.13 (see pp. 288–289).

INDIRECT TEACHING TECHNIQUES FOR HIGH-FREQUENCY WORDS

Shared Reading

An excellent device for introducing and reinforcing high-frequency words, shared reading is a way of helping low-achieving readers read whole selections that they would not be able to read on their own. Instead of being limited to books on their reading level, which may be simplified or lacking in appeal, low-achieving readers are given access to more mature, more interesting materials.

If you are working with groups, use a big book or write the selection on the chalkboard or story paper, or show it on an overhead projector so that everyone can see the words. If working one on one, a regular-size book can be used. Introduce the text, share-read it with students, and discuss it with students in the way that was suggested in Chapter 5. During a second reading of the text, invite the students to read along with you. If the text has repeated phrases, stop as you come to these and have the students as a group or individual volunteers read them. Pay particular attention to the high-frequency words you wish students to learn. During the reading of the text, make sure that you point to each word as it is being read and that students look at the word as you point to it, so connections can be made between printed and spoken words. In addition to share-reading and highlighting them in context, also have students read high-frequency words in isolation so that they can concentrate on each word's distinguishing features. As in the direct instruction lesson, lead students to see the pronounceable word parts or letter sounds in the high-frequency words, so that they will have additional memory pegs.

As an extension, invite students to read the text with a partner or on their own. If taped versions of the text are available, also have students read along as they listen. If the text is a favorite, arrange for additional rereadings from time to time.

> **Word bank:** a collection of words that students have learned or are in the process of learning. They are used in a variety of reinforcement activities.

After students seem to have a grasp of the high-frequency words, place the words on cards and have students read them. Individual words might be recorded on 3-by-5 cards and put on rings, in envelopes, or filed in small boxes known as **word banks.** The words will then be available for sorting and other reinforcement activities. The sentences in which the high-frequency words appear might be placed on sentence strips so that students see the words in context as well as in isolation. Choose additional practice activities from those listed later in this chapter.

Singing High-Frequency Words

> Even though students have learned words through phonics, they should be given many opportunities to meet the words in the context of stories, songs, verses, etc.

As a variation on shared reading, have students sing songs that contain high-frequency words. In addition to being motivational, songs are easier to process because of repeated refrains and the element of rhyme. Sing the song or play a recorded version of it, pointing to each word as it is sung. During the second singing, have students sing along. During a third singing, you might sing the main stanzas while students sing the refrain.

As a follow-up, have students sing the words as they follow along with a taped version of the song. As they sing, they should be pointing to the words they are singing. The following sets of tapes and books are especially well done.

Down by the Bay. Raffi. New York: Crown (1987).
Kids Songs 1. N. Cassidy. Palo Alto, CA: Klutz Press (1988).
Kids Songs 2. N. Cassidy. Palo Alto, CA: Klutz Press (1989).
One Light, One Sun. Raffi. New York: Crown (1987).
Shake My Sillies Out. Raffi. New York: Crown (1987).
Wheels on the Bus. Raffi. New York: Crown (1987).

A number of children's videos use a bouncing ball to draw attention to the words of a song so that the viewers can sing along. Have students sing along with the tapes. Once they feel they know the words to the song, they can turn down the volume and then attempt to sing along. If they have difficulty, they may turn up the volume and practice some more. Sing-along tapes that you might use include the following:

Sing-Along Songs: The Bare Necessities. Walt Disney. Burbank, CA: Buena Vista Home Video.

Sing-Along Songs: Fun with Music. Walt Disney. Burbank, CA: Buena Vista Home Video.

Sing-Along Songs: Under the Sea. Walt Disney. Burbank, CA: Buena Vista Home Video.

Sing-Along Songs: Disneyland Fun. Walt Disney. Burbank, CA: Buena Vista Home Video.

Experience Stories

As explained in the previous chapter, an experience story recounts in writing an event in the students' lives, such as a trip to a farm, getting pet hamsters for the classroom, or the arrival of a baby brother. The story might also be based on a piece the students have read or a classroom discussion. Dictated by the students and written by the teacher, the experience story becomes the students' reading material. High-frequency words naturally appear in all experience stories. By choosing certain topics, you can ensure that special high-frequency words will find their way into the story. If, for instance, you want to reinforce the high-frequency words *like* and *do,* you might have the class dictate a piece on the topic, "Things I Like to Do." Because it is based on the children's experiences and written in their language, the experience story is readily understood and usually easy to read, especially for students who are still learning to speak English. Interactive stories are also an excellent device for reinforcing high-frequency words.

Individual Experience Stories. Individual experience stories are composed in much the same way as group stories. However, individual stories allow you to personalize the words being introduced. Individual stories can be illustrated and compiled into a booklet. The booklet may be taken home and, later, placed in the class library.

> **Predictable books** are easy to read because they contain elements that enable the reader to read the print: repeated phrases, rhyme, and illustrations that depict much of the print. After students have read a predictable text, cover the pictures and ask students to read the text. This gives them the experience of using phonics and context rather than relying on picture clues. You might also place words and phrases from the selection on cards or the chalkboard and have students read them.

Predictable Books

Using a technique that is a combination of shared reading and language experience, Bridge, Winograd, and Haley (1983) used predictable books to develop high-frequency vocabulary in students reading at a beginning level. **Predictable books,** as their name suggests, are texts that have repeated elements or are told in such a way that after reading or hearing a portion of the text, it is easy to predict what the rest of the text will say. Some traditional examples include *The Gingerbread Man, The Three Little Pigs,* and *Goldilocks.* Figure 8.13 lists a number of predictable books.

Predictable books build confidence because students can use illustrations and the predictability of the books to help them read the text. However, the books might be so predictable that students aren't actually processing the words but are using pictorial and verbal context to read the books. It is helpful, therefore, to have children read the text without the availability of picture clues. Here is how this might be done. Select a book that contains words that you want to teach, read the book to students, and, then reread it, encouraging students to join in. You might read a "big book" version, if available, so that students can follow along.

After several rereadings, write the story on a chart. In this version there are no illustrations, so students are forced to focus on the words. (Finding it so much easier, some poor readers read pictures instead of text, and so miss out on the opportunity to develop a high-frequency vocabulary.) With your help, if necessary, the students read the story in its chart form. Having duplicated portions of the story, cut it into sentences and distribute

CONSTRUCTING AN EXPERIENCE STORY

Step 1: Introducing the experience story. Students discuss the experience they have had. In the discussion, you draw out the children's ideas.

Step 2: Writing the experience story. Through questioning you help children frame their experience. You might say, for instance, "Let's write a story about our visit to the recycling center so that we can share it with others. What should we call our story?" Write the title that the children suggest: "Our Trip to the Recycling Center." As you write each word, say it so students match the written and spoken form. After writing the title, read it, running your hand under each word as you do so. After writing and reading the title, have students suggest a good beginning sentence, a second sentence, and so on. As with the title, read each word as you write it and then read each completed sentence. After writing the whole story, read the story once more. Ask the students if the story says what they want it to. Ask students if they want to make any changes or add any details.

Step 3: Rereading the story. Read the story once more. Invite the students to read along with you. Stop before high-frequency words that you want to reinforce and invite the class or individual volunteers to read them.

Step 4: Using sentence strips and word cards. Some students may simply memorize the story or use context to such an extent that they are not attending to the printed words. This step is designed to have them focus on the printed forms of the words. After students are familiar with the target words and sentences in the story, create tagboard strips containing the sentences. Mix up the order of the sentences and have students rearrange the sentences in correct order. If available, use a pocket chart to hold the sentence strips. If you are working with a group of students, you may want to duplicate the story and cut it into strips so that each student has a series of sentences to manipulate. Once students have arranged the sentences in their personal copies of the story, you can have a volunteer read the sentence that goes first and place the tagboard version at the top of the pocket chart and continue until all the sentences have been placed. The story is then read and checked to make sure sentences are in the right order. Students then compare their reconstructions with the one in the pocket chart. If you are working with older students and pocket charts seem too juvenile, have them rearrange ordinary strips of papers on their desks.

After students have reassembled the sentences in the story, cut the first sentence into individual words and have students reassemble it. Then proceed to the other sentences.

Step 5: Reading the experience story to others. Copy the story from the board, duplicate it, and distribute it to students. Have them read it to a partner. Once they can read the story with a degree of fluency, they may take it home and read it to their brothers and sisters, parents, and grandparents.

Step 6: Adding words to the word bank. Words that students have learned to read are added to their word banks. These words can be identified by having students underline words they can read or you can test them by putting the words on 3-by-5 cards and asking students to read them. Words that are partially known or that are not identified consistently and words that are not known but that you feel are important, could be set aside for additional instruction. You might have students keep two word banks (McCormick, 1995). Words that the student knows could be placed in a word bank entitled "Words I Can Read." Words that the student is still learning could be placed in the "Words I Am Learning" word bank.

Step 7: Providing additional practice. Review the words in the word bank on a daily basis if possible. Sorting and assembling words into sentences make excellent practice exercises. If your time is limited, you might have pairs of students test each other on their words and complete other practice activities.

FIGURE 8.13   Books Containing High-Frequency Words

LEVEL 1: PICTURE READING

Pictures illustrate all of the text. Generally one or two words label the picture: a drawing of an elephant is shown and the word *elephant* appears under it.

Bruna, D. (1984). *Animal book.* Los Angeles: Price/Stern/Sloan.
Burningham, J. (1985). *Colors.* New York: Crown.
Burton, M. R. (1989). *Tail toes eye ears nose.* New York: Harper.
Cohen, C. L. (1986). *Three yellow dogs.* New York: Greenwillow.
Hoban, T. (1972). *Count and see.* New York: Macmillan.

LEVEL 2: CAPTION

Pictures illustrate most of the text. Often, the text is a frame, which is a repeated sentence or phrase that varies by one or two words. The subject or verb varies but the rest of the sentence stays the same: The dog sat on the mat. The tiger sat on the mat. The elephant sat on the mat. The illustration may depict the part of the sentence that changes.

Brown, C. (1991). *My barn.* New York: Greenwillow.
Burningham, J. (1984). *Wobble pop.* New York: Viking.
Cameron, A. (1994). *The cat sat on the mat.* Boston: Houghton Mifflin.
Gomi, T. (1991). *Who hid it?* Brookfield, CT: Millbrook Press.
Kalan, R. (1978). *Rain.* New York: Greenwillow.
Keyworth, C. L. (1986). *New day.* New York: Morrow.
McMillan, B. (1993). *Mouse views, what the class pet saw.* New York: Holiday House.
McMillan, B. (1989). *Super super superwords.* New York: Lothrop, Lee & Shepard.
McMillan, B. (1983). *Here a chick, there a chick.* New York: Morrow.
Maris, R. (1983). *My book.* New York: Puffin.
Rathmann, P. (1994). *Good night, Gorilla.* New York: Putnam's.
Shapiro, A. L. (1997) *Mice squeak, we speak.* New York: Putnam's.
Tafuri, N. (1984). *Have you seen my duckling?* New York: Greenwillow.
Tafuri, N. (1986). *Who's counting?* New York: Greenwillow.
Wildsmith, B. (1983). *Cat on the mat.* New York: Oxford.
Wildsmith, B. (1983). *What a tail.* New York: Oxford.

EASY SIGHT-WORD LEVEL

Illustrations generally depict much or at least some of the text. There are usually 1–2 lines of text. The number of different words used in the selection ranges from 10 to 35.

Baker, K. (1999). *Sometimes.* San Diego: Harcourt.
Barton, B. (1994). *Where's the bear?* New York: Mulberry.
Beck, I. (1992). *Five little ducks.* New York: Holt.
Berenstain, S., & Berenstain, J. (1968). *Inside outside upside down.* New York: Random.
Berenstain, S., & Berenstain, J. (1968). *Bears on wheels.* New York: Random.
Carle, E. (1971). *Do you want to be my friend?* New York: Harper.
Christelow, E. (1989). *Five little monkeys jumping on the bed.* New York: Clarion.
Clarke, G. (1992). *Old McDonald had a farm.* New York: Lothrop, Lee & Shepard.
Florian, D. (1988). *A winter day.* New York: Greenwillow.
Ginsburg, M. (1972). *The chick and the duckling.* New York: Macmillan.
Gomi, T. (1977). *Where's the fish?* New York: Morrow.
Greene, C. (1982). *Snow Joe.* Chicago: Children's Press.

FIGURE 8.13 Continued

EASY SIGHT-WORD LEVEL *(continued)*

Grindley, S. (1987). *Four black puppies.* New York: Lothrop, Lee & Shepard.

Hutchins, P. (1968). *Rosie's walk.* New York: Macmillan.

Kraus, R. (1970). *Whose mouse are you?* New York: Macmillan.

Martin, B. (1967). *Brown bear, brown bear, what do you see?* New York: Holt.

Namm, D. (1990). *Little Bear.* Chicago: Children's Press.

O'Brien, J. (2001). *Farmer in the dell.* Honesdale, PA: Boyd's Mill Press.

Peek, M. (1987). *Roll over!* Boston: Houghton Mifflin.

Rascha, C. (1993). *Yo! Yes!* New York: Orchard.

Reese, B. (1979). *Little dinosaur.* Provo, Utah: Aro.

Reese, B. (1979). *Sunshine.* Provo, Utah: Aro.

Tafuri, N. (1983). *Early morning in the barn.* New York: Greenwillow.

Titherington, J. (1986). *Pumpkin pumpkin.* New York: Mulberry.

Williams, S. (1989). *I went walking.* San Diego: Harcourt.

Winder, J. (1979). *Who's new at the zoo?* Provo, UT: Aro.

Wolcott, P. (1974). *The cake story.* Reading, MA: Addison-Wesley.

them to students just as you did with the experience story. Students match the sentences to sentences on the chart. If a pocket chart is available, they might retell the story with their sentences, placing the first sentence in the first pocket and so on. Later, sentences are cut up into individual words and matched to words in the chart story. Students can then reassemble the sentence by arranging the words in the proper order.

Exemplary Teaching: Balancing Decodable Text with Predictable Books

While working with a group of five first-graders who were making very slow progress, the teacher introduced some predictable books to them and arranged for them to practice reading the books until they could read them fairly smoothly. Although it was important that they learn basic phonics patterns, it was also important that they see themselves as readers. Up to this point the teacher had been working primarily with decodable text, but had noted that the children weren't having much fun reading. They were still having a difficult time with short-*a* and short-*i* patterns. The predictable texts, with their repeated language and heavy picture support were easier to read. Learning to read these books boosted the children's self-confidence. They were quite pleased that they could take books home and read to mom, dad, grandma, grandpa, or other family members. Among the predictable books used with the five struggling readers, there was one that depicted a number of things that the main character could do: "I can read; I can sing; I can run." The book reinforced the *-an* pattern, a pattern that the children were still slow in recognizing. Another predictable book had a number of *-it* words, a pattern that was recently introduced. A judicious use of predictable books can foster both confidence and skill.

Holistic Programs

Several series of books were designed to foster reading development through the presentation of high-frequency words in predictable books written at a variety of levels: Reading Corners (Dominie Press), Little Red Readers (Sundance), and Story Box (Wright Group).

Creating Little Books

In addition to acquiring pattern books, you might create your own. The books might incorporate a particular theme: People in My Family, Foods I Like, Things I Can Do, Holidays, or a particular pattern: I can _____, I see _____, I like _____, _____ got on the bus (Johnston, Invernizzi, & Juel, 1998). You might create these on your own or recruit help from your students.

The books might be illustrated with pictures that you draw, pictures from a desktop publishing program, or student-drawn illustrations. Since instructional time is limited, be careful that students don't spend an excessive amount of time creating illustrations. You might also create open-ended books and have students complete them by placing words in the blanks. For instance, they might complete five "I can _____." or "I like _____." sentences.

Read-Along Technique

Obtain an easy book, one in which the student has an obvious interest. If the book does not have an accompanying audiotape, create one. Have the student follow along as the taped version is read. The student might read a book such as *Brown Bear, Brown Bear, What Do You See?* (Martin, 1983), which has only thirty-two different words, or *The Cake That Mack Ate* (Robart, 1986), which has just thirty different words. Start with shorter books and work up to longer ones. Students can read along with the tape until they are able to read the book on their own (Chomsky, 1978). This may require as many as twenty read-alongs. As students acquire a broader high-frequency vocabulary and begin to acquire decoding skills, fewer rereadings will be required.

> Richek, Caldwell, Jennings, & Lerner (1996) describe a student who took ten weeks to learn eight high-frequency words. The student may have had an associative word-learning problem of the type described in Chapter 6.

Using a Multisensory Technique

If students expereince serious difficulty learning high-frequency words, try using the Fernald or other multisensory technique. Multisensory techniques are explained in Chapter 14.

ADDITIONAL PRACTICE ACTIVITIES FOR HIGH-FREQUENCY WORDS

Words on the Wall

To the word wall described earlier in the chapter, add high-frequency words. You might want to separate them from the phonic pattern words, if these have been placed on the wall.

In a pantomime activity, pairs of students are given a series of five to eight words that can be pantomimed: *walk, run, fly, jump, throw.* One student pantomimes the words. The second holds up the high-frequency word being pantomimed.

When adding words to the wall, be sure to discuss any parts that students can already say or any distinctive features that the word might have and any cues that students might use to help them remember the word or distinguish it from other words: "You can tell that h-e-a-r means to listen because it has an ear in it." Also discuss the word's meaning if it is unknown or vague.

Each day, if possible, review items on the word wall. You might have students find all the animal words, for instance, or locate the opposite of *on, old,* and *dark* or note words that incorporate a newly learned pattern. When words have been mastered, remove them.

Sight-Word Commands

Create a series of cards that contain commands composed primarily of high-frequency words. When the command is displayed, the class carries it out. Commands might be just for fun, or they may be functional. Some possible commands include: Count to three. Hold up a piece of paper. Put up one hand. Put up both hands. Line up in the front of the room. Sing a song. Sit down. Stand up. Stand on one foot.

Read the Label

Label appropriate items in your class. Label the light switch with an *on* and an *off,* for example. When writing directions, try to use high-frequency words: "Put blocks here. Put toys in the box." Introduce the sign, label, or set of directions. Read it for students, pointing out each word as you do so. Then have students, as a group, read the item along with you. Also encourage individual volunteers to read the item. From time to time, review the item. Some possible functional high-frequency word signs, labels, and directions include the following:

In	Pull
Out	Walk. Don't run.
Up	Mrs. Doyle's Room
Down	Pet Corner
Push	Book Corner

Forming Phrases and Sentences

From a "big book" selection, experience story, or other source, copy a sentence that contains several high-frequency words onto oaktag. (If you are working with a large group, you might photocopy the sentences.) Cut the words apart and place them in an envelope. Have students arrange the words so they form a sentence. This builds sentence sense and comprehension while providing practice with high-frequency words.

Sorting

Using their bank of high-frequency words, have students sort their words. They might group them semantically: all the color words, all the number words, all the action words. Or they might group them structurally or phonemically: all the words that begin with *s,* or all the words that end with the *at* pattern.

Audio-Visual Aids

A high-tech approach to introducing and reinforcing high-frequency words is to use CD-ROM read-alongs. The presentation features graphics, which include animation, still pictures, or movie clips; background music and sound effects; and an oral reading of the story. As the story is being read, the text is highlighted so that the viewer can read along. If students wish, they can click on a word and have it pronounced. The viewer can even control the pacing of the reading so that the selection can be read at a slower-than-normal rate as in the Carbo recorded-book technique. CD-ROM books can be especially helpful for youngsters who are still learning to speak English.

Another piece of software, *Bailey's Book House* (Edmark), introduces a series of high-frequency words along with other beginning-level reading skills. In addition to pronouncing the words, it presents them in sentences and uses animated sequences to illustrate each word's meaning. To illustrate *in* and *out,* for example, it shows a dog in and out of a dog house. It also provides practice in using high-frequency words by helping the student compose a story.

FOSTERING FLUENCY

Although the activities described so far help to introduce high-frequency words, they also build accuracy of recognition and fluency. Before students can recognize words rapidly or automatically, they must first achieve accuracy (Samuels, 1994). Low-achieving readers may take longer to achieve accuracy than higher-achieving readers. By one estimate, students may require thirty-five or more exposures to a word before learning it, with the slowest students needing almost three times as many exposures as the brightest students (Gates, 1931). Provide ample practice, so that the words are recognized accurately. Once students can recognize words accurately, emphasize speed so that words are recognized instantaneously, and fluent reading will be fostered. Although one characteristic of fluent reading is processing words at an acceptable rate, fluency also entails reading in meaningful phrases and with appropriate expression. NAEP defines fluency as the ease or "naturalness" of reading (U.S. Department of Education, National Center for Educational Statistics, 1995). The key elements include (a) grouping or **phrasing** of words as revealed through the intonation, stress, and pauses exhibited by readers; (b) adherence to author's **syntax;** and (c) **expressiveness** of the oral reading, interjecting a sense of feeling, anticipation, or characterization. Table 8.10 describes the NAEP fluency scale. Students at levels 3 and 4 are generally considered to be fluent, and those at levels 1 and 2 nonfluent.

Model fluent reading when reading to students. Explain that, as you read, you group words into meaningful phrases and read with expression. After reading aloud to students, ask them how they enjoyed hearing the selection. Discuss things that you might have done as a reader to dramatize the selection, to convey the author's meaning, and to keep the listeners' attention (Rasinski, 2004). Discuss and demonstrate these techniques and guide students as they adopt their use.The following suggestions and activities are designed to develop rapid word recognition and fluent reading.

TABLE 8.10 NAEP Oral Reading Fluency Scale

LEVEL 4

Reads primarily in larger, meaningful phrase groups. Although some regressions, repetitions, and deviations from text may be present, these do not appear to detract from the overall structure of the story. Preservation of the author's syntax is consistent. Some or most of the story is read with expressive interpretation.

LEVEL 3

Reads primarily in three- or four-word phrase groups. Some smaller groupings may be present. However, the majority of phrasing seems appropriate and preserves the syntax of the author. Little or no expressive interpretation is present.

LEVEL 2

Reads primarily in two-word phrases with some three- or four-word groupings. Some word-by-word reading may be present. Word groupings may seem awkward and unrelated to larger context of sentence or passage.

LEVEL 1

Reads primarily word-by-word. Occasional two-word or three-word phrases may occur but these are infrequent and/or they do not preserve meaningful syntax.

Source: U.S. Department of Education, National Center for Education Statistics (1995). *Listening to Children Read Aloud, Oral Fluency 15.* Washington, DC: Author.

Wide Reading

Some low-achieving readers decode or attempt to decode every word they meet. They are able to read high-frequency words, but they are unable to read them as sight words. They seem to need to take time to sound them out. As a result, their reading is slow and laborious. These students may not have had enough time to practice newly learned skills or words, or phonics and oral reading may have been emphasized so much that they believe the purpose of reading is to pronounce written words correctly. Stress meaning by asking students to retell selections or answer questions about them, and reduce the amount of oral reading.

Fluency can also be fostered by having students read a wide variety of easy books. As they read books in which nearly all the words are known, their ability to recognize the words more quickly should increase. Students, especially if they are younger, may also be encouraged to read the same books a second, a third, or even a fourth time.

Repeated Reading

Another technique for achieving fluency is through **repeated reading** (Samuels, 1979). One way of learning high-frequency words is to read the same story over and over again. Often poor readers stumble over their text, especially when they encounter words that are

> **Repeated reading:** reading a text over and over to achieve fluency.

> Lipson and Wixson (1997) report that rereading a text is a favored activity among low-progress readers. It provides them with the opportunity to master the text.

easily confused, such as *what, where,* and *when.* Repeated reading gives them the opportunity to achieve accuracy. At the same time, through providing practice, it fosters instantaneous recognition of high-frequency words or fluency. The box that follows gives an example for presenting a lesson in introducing repeated readings. Through repeated readings, students improve in both accuracy and speed of reading. In one study, reading rate increased by about 50 percent after four readings (Rashotte & Torgesen, 1985). Gains in reading speed are most likely to transfer when there is a high overlap of words, so that the students are meeting a number of words in a new story that had been presented in a previously read selection. The sheer amount of reading also influences fluency. Students made gains when they read a number of selections on the appropriate level. Perhaps the best feature of the technique is that students enjoyed it. When the experiment was discontinued, many students requested additional repeated-reading sessions.

Repeated reading also builds students' confidence. Because they struggle with reading, below-level readers might never have had a successful reading experience. Actor and author Henry Winkler (2004), who struggled with reading, described in poignant terms how he went from one poorly understood story to the next. Undoubtedly, struggling readers have had similar experiences. Repeated reading accompanied by some coaching can help these students achieve proficient reading so that they might begin to think of themselves as readers.

REPEATED READINGS LESSON

Step 1: Introducing repeated readings. Explain the procedure to students. Tell them that they will be reading a short selection over and over again so that they will learn to read faster and better.

Step 2: Selecting a passage. Select or have the student choose short, interesting selections of approximately 100 words.

Step 3: Obtaining an initial timing. Obtain baseline data on the selections. Have the students read them orally. Time the readings and record the number of words read incorrectly. If students take more than two minutes to read the selection and make more than five errors in 100 words (not counting missed endings), the selections are too hard. If students make only one or two errors and read the selection at eighty-five words per minute or faster, the selection is too easy.

Step 4: Rereading. Go over the students' miscues with them. Help them read these words correctly. Then direct them to reread the selections until they feel they can read them faster and more smoothly.

Practice can take one of three forms: (1) reading the selection to oneself; (2) listening to an audiotape while reading the selection silently and then reading the selection without the aid of the tape; (3) reading the selection to a partner.

Step 5: Evaluating the reading. The students read the selections to you or to a partner. The number of word-recognition errors and reading speed are noted. The students are informed of their progress. A chart, as in Figure 8.14, might be constructed to show the degree of improvement. The goal is to have students read at least eighty-five words per minute. Students should practice until they reach that criterion. Word-recognition errors should also decrease. However, do not insist on 100 percent word recognition. Insisting on perfection in word reading sends the wrong message to students. It makes them think that reading is a word-pronouncing rather than a meaning-making activity. It also impedes fluency. If they are afraid of making a mistake, students will slow their reading rate (Samuels, 1979).

Repeated readings foster fluency by providing practice with easy materials. This goal can also be achieved by having students read lots of easy books.

Variations on Rereading.   Selections can be reread on a less formal basis. The evaluation may also be informal. Instead of working with a teacher, students may work in pairs. However, model the procedure first. One student reads and attempts to reach criterion while the other tracks her or his progress on the chart shown in Figure 8.14. Then they switch roles. Show students how to time the reading and count errors. To simplify the charting procedure, have students check 100-word samples only. The reader may actually read a lengthier selection, but only 100 words are used for charting progress. Students may speed through a selection to beat the clock. Encourage students to read at a normal pace. Stress that the goal is to meet the criterion, not set a world record. Occasionally, use a song or a poem instead of a typical reading selection. Because of their rhythm, some narrative poems and songs lend themselves to speedy reading.

FIGURE 8.14   Speed of Reading Chart

If you read the same words over and over, you will read faster and better. On this sheet, show how long it took you to read 100 words. Blacken one block for each 10 seconds of time you took. For the first time that you read the story, blacken the blocks under number 1. For the second time, blacken the blocks under number 2, and so on. Write down the number of mistakes that you make on the lines at the bottom.

Number of Times I Read the Story

Time (in seconds)	1	2	3	4	5	6	7	8	9	10
(2 minutes) 120										
110										
100										
90										
80										
70										
(1 minute) 60										
50										
40										
30										
20										
10										
Number of mistakes	__	__	__	__	__	__	__	__	__	__

In their study of fourth-graders who failed a state proficiency test, Valencia and Buly (2004) found that fluency was an issue for 41 percent of the students. Closer examination of a number of the students indicated limited vocabulary and language skills. Working on reading rate might not solve their problem. They might need instruction in vocabulary and language, which in turn should boost their reading rate.

Carbo Recorded-Book Method

An excellent way of providing these repeated readings is through taped stories (Carbo, 1997). However, taped stories typically move along at the pace of normal speech. This may be too rapid for the listener to match printed and spoken words. When a student reads along with a tape, the tape speed should be at about the same rate as the student can read orally. When recording books, read with expression but read slowly enough so that students can follow along. You might read the text at about 85 to 100 words per minute and then have students play it back using a tape recorder that has a speed regulator (Shany & Biemiller, 1995). As you encounter words or expressions that might be unfamiliar, pause before and after reading them so that students will have time to process the difficult words or phrases (Carbo, Dunn, & Dunn, 1986).

Record small amounts of text of from two to five minutes on each side of a tape. Gather short articles, brief chapters, poems, or other short pieces to record. In preparing audiotapes, begin the recording by announcing the title and author. Clearly describe the point where reading will start. Signal when it is time to turn a page, and announce when the reading has been completed (Carbo, Dunn, & Dunn, 1986). End each tape by briefly summarizing what you have read and setting the stage for the next tape: "Aldo's parents have agreed to get him a puppy. In the next part of the story we'll find out what kind of puppy he chooses." Similarly, on tapes that provide a continuation of a selection, summarize what has gone before and set the stage for the portion on the current tape. Produce recordings of readings with increasing length and difficulty.

Encourage students to read along with the taped selection several times, until they feel they can read it on their own. Have them attempt to read it without the tape, note difficult parts, and then have them listen to the tape once more and reread the text to brush up on parts that posed problems. Students can work alone or in pairs. If they are working in pairs, they can read to each other after practicing with the tape.

Reading poems and plays is an excellent way to build fluency. Both lend themselves naturally to repeated readings.

Reading to Others

A natural way to foster repeated readings is to have students read aloud to younger students. Practicing their performance is a natural preparation for the read-aloud. Fifth-grade struggling readers improved their fluency and achieved significant gains on standardized reading tests as a result of reading to kindergarten students (Labbo & Teale, 1990). Before reading aloud to their younger partners, the fifth-graders practiced their reading and planned ways to involve their kindergartners in a discussion of the books. Reader's theater also provides natural opportunities for reading text aloud. In addition, it focuses students' attention on meaning and interpretation (Ivey, 2000).

Buddy Reading

In buddy reading, two students who are on a similar level read together. They might read alternate pages, or if they are reading a script, take different parts. Or they might read silently and then discuss what they have read. Buddy reading might be used as a part of independent or self-selected reading. Buddy reading might even extend into reading done at home. Students might agree to read a certain number of pages each night and then discuss their reading the next day. This provides added incentive for completing reading assignments at home. Buddies won't want to let each other down (Rasinski, 2003).

Choral Reading

Besides building fluency, choral reading is a way of building a sense of community. It brings both the poorest and the best readers together in a performance in which all can be successful. Carol Tesch has her third-graders chorally read a poem each day. The poem is placed on chart paper so all can see it. Each time the poem is reread the struggling readers grow more proficient. As Tesh commented, "We'll read a poem once, twice, three times a day or even more. And each time we read their voices get stronger and more confident. Even the children who have the most difficult time in reading can read by the third time through" (Rasinski, 2003, p. 59).

Choral reading can take many forms. In its simplest form, the whole class simply reads the piece together. In refrain, one reader reads portions of the text and the other students supply the refrain. In antiphonal choral reading, students are divided into groups. One group (the boys, the left side of the class) reads the main part. The second group (the girls, the right side of the class) reads the refrain. Or the groups might read alternate stanzas. As students read, it is essential that you point to the words so they connect printed and spoken words. The piece read should also be worthy of the time spent on it. It should develop background and vocabulary, for instance.

Using Paired Reading to Help Your Students Become Better Readers (Bureau of Education and Research, 1998) provides videotaped demonstrations of paired reading used with struggling readers.

Paired Reading

Paired reading, which is also known as duolog reading (Topping, 1998), is a highly effective technique that can be used with students of any age and is easily implemented by a professional or a volunteer with a minimum of training. The teacher, a parent, or a child who is a more proficient reader teams up with a student. (Paired reading is different from partner or buddy reading, in which two students of similar reading ability read a book together). The student selects the book to be read. The book chosen should be one that would be a little too difficult for the student to read on his own. After a brief discussion of the title and cover illustration, the helper and student simultaneously read the book out loud. During this choral reading, the helper adjusts her reading rate so it matches that of the student. When the student feels that he can read a portion of the text on his own, he signals the helper by raising his left hand. When he wants the helper to resume reading with him, he raises his right hand. The helper automatically provides assistance when the student stumbles over a word or is unable to read the word within five seconds. The assistance provided should be immediate and nonjudgmental. The teacher simply says the word and has the student say it. The reading then continues. Quick correction maintains the flow of the activity (Topping, 1987, 1989). Because the helper does not provide a prompt, the helper does not need extensive training. The helper also praises the student periodically.

■ ■ ■ ■ ■ ■

EXEMPLARY TEACHING
PAIRED READING

Doctoral candidate Nancy Flanagan Knapp was investigating intervention programs when the problem she was investigating hit home (Knapp & Winsor, 1998). Her son, a first-grader, was struggling to learn to read and was falling farther behind as the year progressed. He was also becoming very discouraged. As his teacher commented, "He won't even pick up a book." In her dissertation research with second-graders, Knapp had asked them what they found to be most helpful in learning to read. Surprisingly, the favorite activity was not a school-based one but one that took place at home. Student after student mentioned having someone to read with as being especially helpful. That other person was usually a parent, a grandparent, or an older sibling.

Using the students' responses as a starting point, Knapp began reading with her son Chris, who

had finished the first-grade reading program but was unable to read on even a primer level. Chris selected books that were personally interesting to him, but the reading was a joint effort. Chris read whatever words he could and Nancy Knapp read the rest. At first Chris was only able to read a word here and there. Later he was able to read alternate pages. The two worked together every day for a full school year. Nancy modeled skills and discussed stories with him. Chris began making encouraging progress. By year's end, he was reading at the 96th percentile on a standardized reading test. His attitude also improved dramatically. Reading had become a favorite activity, and he was reading books on his own.

Tierney and Readence (2005) remind us, "Oral reading is a communication skill. It is a way of delivering information or providing entertainment to listeners, If used in this way, oral reading would seem best done for a specific purpose, and a student's performance would seem best evaluated in terms of its communicative value" (p. 244).

Alternate Reading

As an alternative to paired reading, the teacher, parent, or tutor may take turns reading the selection. At first, the teacher might do most of the reading. The student would read any words that he could. For some students this might be a few high-frequency and short-vowel words or a repeated sentence. As the student becomes more proficient, she can read larger segments. For instance, the teacher reads the first page, the student reads the second page. Or the teacher might read the difficult parts, and the pupil reads the easy parts. The teacher also supplies whatever help the student needs. For instance, if the student stumbles over a word, the teacher tells the student the word or helps the student to figure out the word. The teacher might use the pronounceable word part, analogy, or context. The teacher also explains difficult or confusing passages and discusses key events in the story from time to time. Knapp (1998) found that parents and tutors as well as teachers were able to implement this technique with a high degree of success.

Performance Reading

Repeated readings work best when there is a genuine purpose for reading. Rasinski (2003) refers to these as performance readings. Poems and nursery rhymes are designed to be read aloud. To get the proper expression, they should be read several times. Chants and

Using Technology
These sites contain scripts
and tips for RT:
Aaron Shepard's RT page at
http://www.aaronshep.com/rt/.
Readers' Theater Scripts and
Plays at http://teachingheart
.net/readerstheater.htm.
Gander Academy Readers'
Theater at http://www.cdli
.ca/CITE/langrt.htm.

cheers also lend themselves to repeated oral readings. Scripts are also designed to be read many times. In addition to prepared scripts, students might use scripts created for readers' theater.

Readers' Theater.   Since no stage or props are required and the script does not have to be memorized, readers' theater (RT) is easy to implement and highly effective in enhancing fluency, comprehension, and motivation. In **readers' theater,** participants dramatize poems, short stories, or even excerpts from historical biographies. Ready-made play scripts can be used, or participants can prepare their own. Readers' theater works especially well with low-achieving readers because it provides them with the opportunity to reread a text several times so that they become thoroughly familiar with it. It also gives them an in-depth look at a selection.

Readers' theater begins with a careful reading and discussion of the selection and is followed by the preparation of a script and its performance. The following box highlights the steps involved in readers' theater.

■ ■ ■ ■ ■ ▬▬

READERS' THEATER PERFORMANCE

Step 1: Reading the selection. The selection is read and discussed. Prereading preparation includes activating schema, building background and vocabulary, considering strategies to be used during the reading, and setting a purpose for reading.

Step 2: Preparing the script. After the selection has been discussed in much the same way as it would be in a directed reading activity, students who will reenact the piece reread the play, and discuss the characters, and perhaps create a character map (Hoffman, 1993). The teacher can let students decide who will take which parts, or he can assign parts himself. If the group includes both adept and low-achieving readers, the teacher might choose parts for the low-achieving readers that involve less reading and are easier to read. The script may be written by the teacher or by the group. Group writing is preferable, but guidance may be required. The group discusses how they want to write the script. Dialogue from the selection should remain intact. Narrative segments from the selection might be summarized, especially if they are lengthy, or they may be translated into dialogue. Additional narration may need to be composed, for the sake of clarity. Students can highlight their own dialogue with markers. Narrations can be underlined. Narrator's lines can be added as needed to introduce scenes, provide transitions, or summarize events (Hoffman, 1993).

Step 3: Interpreting the script. Once the script has been prepared, students discuss how they will portray each character: what facial expressions they will use, what gestures they will employ, and how they will use their voices to convey emotions (Tompkins & Hoskisson, 1991).

Step 4: Practicing. Students practice reading their scripts. At the end of each reading, they discuss things that each did well and what might be done to improve the performance or the script.

Step 5: Performing. The script is performed for the class. Pieces that work best for readers' theater are those that have a great deal of dialogue and a minimum of narration. Stories or even chapters from books and novels can be portrayed through readers' theater. For long works, it might be best to portray excerpts of key portions of the text.

Increasing the Amount of Reading

Fluency can also be fostered by increasing the amount of reading that students do. In one program in which students engaged in partner and echo reading of the basal text and silent reading in school and at home of self-selected books, the students gained nearly two years during the year-long program (Stahl, Heubach, & Crammond, 1997). By the end of second grade, 90 percent were reading at grade level or beyond. The students who gained the most were reading at least on a preprimer level. Apparently, students need some basic reading skill before they are ready for fluency instruction (Kuhn & Stahl, 2000).

Sometimes word-by-word reading persists despite your best efforts. If word-by-word reading persists, you might consider having students read selections in which phrases are marked so that they have practice reading in meaningful chunks. As always, stress comprehension. Don't overemphasize fluent reading, or students might focus on sounding good instead of constructing meaning.

Although fluency practice is often associated with oral reading, extensive silent reading should also produce gains in fluency. One danger of oral fluency instruction is that students will focus on saying the words rather than constructing meaning. One sign of fluency is the students' ability to read silently at a reasonable pace with adequate comprehension.

Although it is possible to build the decoding abilities of older students, even those at the lowest level of reading achievement, the extent and results of the intervention depend upon the severity of the difficulty. Students at the 30th percentile in decoding skills are readily brought up to grade level after a relatively brief period of remediation (about 60 hours). Students at the 10th percentile need about 100 hours of instruction. Although their decoding skills are brought up to grade level, their reading rate remains a bit behind. For the most severely disabled readers, those at the 2nd percentile, they need a program of about 120 hours. Although their decoding skills are brought up to the near-average range, their reading rate remains slow. Researchers (Torgesen, 2004c) speculate that because they were poor readers they read very little and so missed out on the opportunity to bring words into their immediate recognition vocabulary. Although their decoding skills have been brought up to an adequate level, they still have a limited store of immediate recognition words. There might also be neurobiological factors involved. Since these students missed out on opportunities to read, extensive silent reading of text on their level might help develop automaticity and fluency.

Closing the Gap by Providing Better Reinforcement

With the right kind of intervention, it is possible for struggling readers to catch up. In one study of first-graders, struggling readers caught up to average readers in just fifteen weeks (Menon & Hiebert, 2005). The control group had a typical basal. The intervention group was given a series of 150 little books that were designed to reinforce the phonics patterns they had been taught. However, the books were not written in the sing-song fashion characteristic of some decodable texts. The little books were carefully resequenced so that in all instances easier books were presented before more difficult books, and the books gradually became more challenging. In addition to reading books that were more carefully sequenced and did a better job of reinforcing patterns that had been taught, the intervention group read a greater variety of words. They read between 500 and 1,000 words a week. The basal group read an average of 250 words. The basal group, which devoted a full week to a selection, reread the same story several times, so they may have read as many words as the intervention group but they did this by reading the same words over and over again. Reading several books seems to be more effective than reading the same book over and over again.

AFFIRMING EFFORTS

Students, especially those who are struggling with reading and writing, need to see signs of progress. You might use a picture of a thermometer, ladder, football field, or a simple graph to represent number of words learned. On the graph, the student colors in one block for every ten words learned.

If, despite your best efforts, students cannot seem to learn high-frequency words, they may have a serious word-learning problem. They may need to be taught with a multisensory approach such as VAKT, which is described in detail in Chapter 14. To test for a serious word-learning problem, administer the Word-Learning Test in Appendix A.

MINICASE STUDY

Despite being tutored by the Title I teacher over a period of two years and having an excellent classroom teacher, Alfredo was making very limited progress. Referred to a university reading clinic, testing revealed that Alfredo, who would soon be celebrating his ninth birthday, was able to read only a dozen or so words. At school, Alfredo had been subjected to several intensive phonics programs, which obviously didn't work. The clinic instructor decided to try a more holistic approach. High-frequency words were taught in the context of easy children's books. After each session, Alfredo took home a set of five or six cards containing new words. At home he studied the words.

Despite intensive studying and completing many activities with the words, Alfredo still experienced difficulty learning new words. Often he would stumble over words such as *and* and *that,* which had been introduced and carefully reviewed. Words that were known one week were forgotten the next. Sometimes, by the end of a session, he had forgotten the words that had been taught at the beginning of the session. Encountering the words over and over again just didn't seem to help Alfredo. He seemed to need some type of mechanism that would help him remember the words.

Word building and the pronounceable word-part and analogy strategies were introduced to Alfredo. Progress was slow but steady. Encountering the word *that,* Alfredo balked and looked to the teacher for help. Realizing that the *at* pattern had been introduced to Alfredo, the teacher had Alfredo try the pronounceable word-part strategy. "Is there any part of that word you can say?" she asked. Recognizing *at,* Alfredo was then able to add *th* and say the whole word. Sometimes, Alfredo needed additional guidance. Alfredo was unable to recognize any part of the word *silly* even though he had just studied the *ill* pattern the day

Disabled readers generally do better when provided with a direct, systematic program of phonics instruction than they do with one that is embedded in the selections that they read. Further, students with the least phonological awareness seem to benefit the most from an explicit program (Foorman, Fletcher, Francis, Schatschneider, & Mehta, 1998).

before. Covering up all of the word except *ill,* the teacher asked Alfredo if he could say that word part. After Alfredo read "ill," the teacher had him add *s* and read *sill* and then read the whole word. Two pages later, Alfredo failed to recognize *silly.* However, when his teacher asked him if there was any part of the word he could say, he was able to read *sill* and then the whole word. As time passed and with lots of guidance and opportunities for application, Alfredo became more proficient at using the pronounceable word-part and other word-recognition strategies. He became more confident and began to rely on himself rather than simply giving up or asking the teacher for help. As he put more effort into his work, he learned more. Although he still had a lot of catching up to do, with the help of word building and several carefully taught and well-practiced word-recognition strategies, Alfredo had become a reader.

SUMMARY

The forty-one speech sounds of American English can be spelled in more than 200 ways. However, most consonant sounds have only one or two spellings, and most vowel sounds have only three or four common spellings. Despite this regularity, many low-achieving readers have difficulty learning how to decipher words. A program that is systematic, related to their specific needs, and that provides ample opportunity for reinforcement and application should help.

A number of approaches can be used to teach phonics: explicit, implicit, pattern, and word building. Because it combines the best features of the other three approaches and gives students a "fresh start," the word-building approach is recommended. Although consonants are typically taught before vowels, and short vowels are taught before long vowels, it is recommended that consonants and vowels be taught together and that easier long-vowel patterns be presented before short vowels.

Low-achieving readers need to be taught strategies for deciphering unknown words. These strategies include seeking out pronounceable word parts and using analogy. Context should be an integral part of any strategy that is used. Using appropriate prompts, the teacher should guide students in the use of varied but balanced strategies to decode words. Ultimately, students should apply these strategies independently.

Easy, high-frequency words, such as *was, of, the,* which are known as "sight words," are among the most difficult to learn to read. Because their spellings do not always adequately represent their sounds (*of, one*), or they are presented before students have learned the phonics elements necessary to decode them (*how, look*), they are taught through a logographic or paired-associate method. However, only about forty words can be learned in this way, because the learner runs out of ways of creating distinguishing cues, and the cues themselves are arbitrary. In actuality, most words are fully or partially regular. If feasible, high-frequency words should be learned through phonics, because this makes it possible for the student to use letter–sound cues to remember them.

A direct approach to teaching high-frequency words incorporates phonics, repetition, and reading the words in the context of real stories. Indirect approaches to teaching high-frequency words include shared reading, language experience, predictable books, and composing sentences.

High-frequency words have a high payoff in reading. The 200 highest-frequency words comprise about 50 percent of the words in running text. In order to make reading fluent, it is important that these high-frequency words be recognized immediately. Procedures that promote fluent reading include wide reading of books, rereading familiar material, performance activities, such as readers' theater and choral reading, and reading along with recorded materials.

APPLICATION ACTIVITIES

1. Examine the phonics component of two sets of materials designed for low-achieving readers. How are the phonics elements taught? Is there adequate provision for reinforcement and application?

2. Observe a beginning reader. What skills has the student apparently mastered? What skills does the student need? What strategies does the reader use to decipher difficult words?

3. Create two phonics lessons, one using the word-building approach and one using the implicit, explicit, or pattern approach. If possible, teach the lessons. Which one seemed more effective? Why?

4. Add five books to the list of predictable books suggested as being appropriate for teaching high-frequency words. If you are working with young children, choose books that would be appropriate for them. If you are working with older students, choose books appropriate for their maturity level.

5. View the video showing how oral reading fluency is assessed at http://pals.virginia.edu/PALS-Instruments/PALS-1-3.asp. What are the major elements in oral fluency? What specific oral reading behaviors led to the classification of each of the three students?

CHAPTER NINE

SYLLABIC, MORPHEMIC, AND CONTEXTUAL ANALYSIS AND DICTIONARY STRATEGIES

USING WHAT YOU KNOW

The previous two chapters have explored ways of learning single-syllable words. This chapter examines strategies for identifying polysyllabic words through syllabic, morphemic, and contextual analysis, and dictionary usage. Both phonic and syllabic analysis strategies primarily involve some form of sounding out. In this chapter, word-identification techniques that rely on meaning-based strategies are also introduced. These include morphemic analysis—which is the analysis of meaningful units of words (prefixes, suffixes, and roots)—context clues, and dictionary strategies. How useful do you find these strategies in your reading? Do you sometimes divide words into syllables in order to sound them out? Do you try to use prefixes, suffixes, and roots to help you figure out unknown words? Do you use context clues? The dictionary? How useful are these strategies to poor readers you have worked with?

ANTICIPATION GUIDE

Read each of the following statements. Put a check under "Agree" or "Disagree" to show how you feel about each one. If possible, discuss your responses with classmates.

	AGREE	DISAGREE
1. Most older low-achieving readers have been taught how to use word-analysis strategies but fail to apply them.	_____	_____
2. Except for phonics, the most valuable word-analysis strategy is the use of context clues.	_____	_____
3. In most instances, context does not provide adequate clues for the identification of a difficult word.	_____	_____

AGREE   DISAGREE

4. Using roots and prefixes and suffixes to figure out the meanings of new words is of limited value.

_____ _____

5. Because it is so difficult for struggling readers to use, the dictionary is the least useful of the word-identification strategies.

_____ _____

SYLLABIC ANALYSIS

> As students read, most automatically develop a sense of which letters occur together and patterns in words. As a result, they learn to recognize syllable boundaries (Adams, 1990). However, students who read very little or whose orthographic awareness is weak may have difficulty establishing syllabic boundaries.

As they progress through the grades, most students eventually learn phonics and may even become adept at deciphering single-syllable words. However, Shefelbine (1990) found that 15 to 20 percent of the students in the fourth- and eighth-grade classes that he tested had difficulty with multisyllabic words. Shefelbine and Newman (2000b) found that average and poor decoders were two to four times more likely than good decoders to omit syllables when reading multisyllabic words. Although students have mastered single-syllable phonics, they may have difficulty locating the known element in a polysyllabic word. For instance, *par* is a single-syllable word that appears as an element in *partial, parcel,* and *particle* but has a different identity in *parade* and *paradise.* As Shefelbine (1990) notes, "Identifying patterns of syllables requires more developed and complex knowledge of letter and spelling patterns than the knowledge needed for reading single syllable words" (p. 225). Carmen is a fairly typical example of a student who has difficulty with multisyllabic words.

Reading has never been easy for Carmen. In first grade, while most of her classmates learned sight words after just a few repetitions and seemed to catch on to phonics effortlessly, Carmen had to struggle to catch up. Now in fourth grade, Carmen has long since mastered phonics but has fallen behind once more. Despite working extra hours on her assignments, she can't seem to keep up with all the reading in science and social studies that she is required to do. Concerned, her classroom teacher administered an informal reading inventory (IRI). A copy of her performance on the IRI's word-lists test is presented in Figure 9.1 What do the test results show?

As you can see from the words she misread, Carmen has learned her phonics lessons well. She was able to read virtually all of the single-syllable words. However, she has difficulty applying her phonics knowledge to multisyllabic words. Note that Carmen was unable to read a number of multisyllabic words that should have been easy to decode. For instance, she can read *mess* and *cape* but stumbled over *escape,* which incorporates the sounds of both these words. She also misread *discover,* although she can read *miss, glove,* and *her.* And she misread *carpenter* and *passenger,* although she can easily read *car, pen, her,* and *pass.* She also had difficulty with words like *adventure* and *vacation,* which contain word parts such as *-ture* and *-tion,* which are found only in multisyllabic words. Carmen's syllabication skills, which are sometimes known as syllabic analysis, are weak. Carmen is not alone. Difficulty in decoding multisyllabic words is a major problem for many older problem readers. Why is

FIGURE 9.1   Carla's IRI Results

	FLASH	UNTIMED		FLASH	UNTIMED
1. friend	✓		1. brief	✓	
2. moment	moo	movie	2. special	dk	dk
3. squawk	✓		3. passenger	pass	passed
4. mess	✓		4. settler	✓	
5. entrance	en	enter	5. wreck	✓	
6. through	✓		6. discovery	dis	discuss
7. calm	✓		7. cause	✓	
8. glove	✓		8. invitation	dk	dk
9. carpenter	car–	carpet	9. distant	disease	✓
10. vacation	dk	dk	10. stroll	✓	
11. beast	✓		11. escape	0	exit
12. howl	✓		12. famous	✓	
13. frighten	✓		13. adventure	0	advice
14. nature	dk	dk	14. breathe	bread	breath
15. cape	✓		15. pilot	pile	✓
16. country	county	✓	16. judge	✓	
17. fruit	✓		17. claim	✓	
18. sly	✓		18. several	0	seven
19. meal	✓		19. squirt	✓	
20. absent	0	above	20. voyage	dk	dk
Totals	65	70	Totals	45	50

this so? Based on experience with single-syllable words, achieving students create syllable patterns and read long words syllable by syllable. This is done automatically as the long word is being read. Although you probably have never seen the following words, you probably have no difficulty using your knowledge of word patterns to put them into syllables: *corniculate, dimercaprol, elastomer.* Because they read less or because of a difficulty with orthographic processing, struggling readers are slower at developing patterns. Although they can read words like *car* and *soon,* they have difficulty reading the word *cartoon.* While they know the phonic elements that make up the word, they fail to see the patterns in the words and so cannot tell where one syllable ends and the next begins.

APPROACHES TO TEACHING SYLLABIC ANALYSIS

There are two major ways to teach **syllabic analysis:** through traditional rules and a pattern approach. These two approaches are not mutually exclusive and so may be used to support each other. Whichever approach is used to teach syllabication, its mission must be kept

> **Syllabic analysis:** breaking a word into syllables, pronouncing each syllable, then blending the syllables to pronounce the whole word. Used to enable people to read unfamiliar multisyllabic words.

firmly in mind. In reading, the purpose of syllabication is to break a word into smaller, more manageable units so that each of these can be sounded out, and then the units can be put back together to form a whole word. To accomplish this, it is not necessary for students to break the word at the syllable's exact boundaries. For instance, it does not make any difference whether readers divide the word *inspector* into *in-spec-tor* or *in-spect-or* or *ins-pec-tor*. As long as their analysis of the word enables them to pronounce it, that's all that counts.

Rules Approach to Syllabication

Since so many of them are poor decoders, low-achieving readers are generally discouraged by the sheer length of polysyllabic words. Seeing a long word, they immediately give up. Having a poor sense of orthographic awareness, they may have a poor sense of where one syllable ends and another begins. What they need is instruction that both builds their confidence and shows them how to handle multisyllabic words. Since they may already have been taught syllabication and failed to learn it adequately, they also need a fresh approach. Even if you are using a traditional rules approach, you can give it a new look by using animal names to illustrate generalizations as is done in the following box. If you are working with older students, you might try a sports motif.

■ ■ ■ ■ ■ ▬▬▬▬▬▬▬▬▬▬▬▬▬▬▬▬▬▬▬▬▬▬▬▬▬▬▬▬▬▬▬▬▬▬▬▬

CONCEPT OF SYLLABLES LESSON

Step 1: Introducing the concept of syllables. To introduce (or reintroduce) the concept of syllabication, say the names of some common animals, while emphasizing the separate syllables. Have students tell you how many parts the animal names have. You might also have the class clap for each syllable in a word. Say the following or similar names. If you have pictures of the animals, point to them as you say their names. Some animal names that you might use include the following:

> Animal names are used as examples of syllable generalizations to make the presentation of generalizations more interesting and memorable. Use ordinary words or another category of words, if you wish.

cat	monkey
yak	lizard
ostrich	elephant
tapir	hippopotamus

Step 2: Presenting visual syllables. Once students grasp the idea of syllables on an auditory level, write the names of the animals on the board. Point to each syllable while saying it. Have students say the syllables along with you. Start with two-syllable animal names and work up to longer syllables.

Step 3: Presenting generalizations. When students have a firm grasp of the concept of visual syllables, introduce the traditional syllable generalizations, but use the names of animals, sports teams, brand names of products, or other interesting words to make the generalizations come alive. Listed below, in approximate order of difficulty, are the major syllabication generalizations and animal names that might be used to illustrate the generalizations. You might also use an animal name to characterize each generalization. Thus, *catbird* syllables refer to compounds; *tiger* syllables refer to single consonants occurring between vowels; *rabbit* syllables refer to double consonants occurring between vowels.

Compound (catbird) words. A compound word forms separate syllables.

bobwhite	catbird
nighthawk	ricebird
killdeer	jellyfish
blackbird	glowworm

(Continued)

waxwing   ladybug
starfish   glassfish

Affix (anteater) words: Prefixes and affixes usually form separate syllables.

anteater   snowy owl
sidewinder   golden plover

Double-consonant (rabbit) words: When two consonants are placed between two vowels, the word is usually divided between the two consonants.

panda   gibbon   turkey
otter   monkey   raccoon
possum   penguin   rabbit

Single-consonant (tiger) words: When a single consonant is placed between two vowels, the consonant usually goes with the syllable to the right.

> There are a fair number of exceptions to this generalization: *robin, lizard.*

tiger   spider
tapir   zebra (*br* forms a single cluster)

Final le *(turtle) words:* Final *le* usually attaches to the preceding consonant to form a separate syllable.

turtle   beetle

Step 4: Practice and application. Practice and application should involve actually reading and/or writing words that follow the generalization that has been introduced. Having students divide words into syllables or count the number of syllables in a word is of little value, because both exercises can be performed without actually reading the words. In addition, you don't want to emphasize exact syllable division, since approximate division works just fine in most instances. The best practice and application is to have students read selections that contain words that follow the pattern that has been introduced. Other profitable practice activities are described below.

> Exact syllabic division may only be required in writing or keyboarding when dividing words at the end of a line.

- When introducing new multisyllabic vocabulary words, instead of saying the words, invite students to attempt to use their skills to pronounce them.
- Seek out books and magazines that respell words phonemically. Show students how to use the phonemic respellings. As part of the postreading discussion, have students pronounce the words or read the passages in which they appear. For instance, the Reading Rainbow book, *Dinosaur Time* (Parish, 1974) respells the names of dinosaurs and provides excellent practice for students just learning how to apply syllabication skills.
- Have the class sing song lyrics. Song lyrics are typically divided into syllables.
- Using sorting to help students discover syllable patterns. Students might sort a mixed group or open and closed syllables, for instance. The patterns in Table 9.1 (see pages 311–314) are a potential source of words to be sorted.
- To help students differentiate between open and closed syllables, have them read contrasting word pairs (*super, supper; biter, bitter; later, latter*) or complete sentences by selecting one of two contrasting words: Although the fruit looked sweet, it was (biter, bitter). We had a (super, supper) time at the park.
- Give pairs of students syllables, one on each card. Have them match up their syllables to make words.

Pattern Approach to Syllabication

> The **pattern approach** starts with a single-syllable word and shows how multisyllabic words are related to it.

Although syllabic generalizations can be useful, a more concrete method of teaching syllabication is to present high-frequency syllabication **patterns.** Presenting patterns helps students detect and learn to use pronounceable word parts within multisyllabic words. For instance, instead of presenting the open-syllable (tiger) generalization, introduce a group of long-*i*, multisyllabic words that fit the pattern. If possible, include a one-syllable known word as a contrasting element so that students can more readily identify the familiar elements in each multisyllabic word, as in the following:

tie
tiger
spider
diner
miser

> **Using Technology**
> At the Resource Room web site (http://www.resource room.net/readspell/wordlists .html), a variety of word lists for practice with both single-syllable words and multisyllabic words can be found.

Reading *tie* should help students read *tiger,* which should help them read *spider,* and so on. This is actually an extension of word building to multisyllabic words. A listing of major multisyllabic patterns is presented in Table 9.1. The patterns are sequenced in approximate order of difficulty and frequency of appearance (Gunning, 1994b). The compound word pattern is presented first because this seems to be the easiest multisyllabic pattern to learn. The schwa *a* (*above, alone*) pattern is introduced next because it occurs with a very high frequency. Several other high-frequency patterns follow: *en* (*open*), *er* (*better*), *it* (*kitten*). Short-vowel, long-vowel, and other-vowel patterns are then presented.

A LESSON IN TEACHING SYLLABICATION PATTERNS

Step 1: Teaching the patterns. Explain the importance of being able to read multisyllabic words. Tell students that you will be teaching them three patterns, *-en, o-*, and *-er,* which will help them to read hundreds of multisyllabic words.

-en *Pattern.* Write *pen* on the board and have students read it. Then write *open* directly under *pen.* Write the separate syllables of *open* in contrasting colors or underline them so students may discriminate them more easily. Say the syllables as you write them. Then have students read *open.* Contrast *pen* and *open.* Present the following words in the same way: *happen, enter, twenty, plenty.* Write the words under each other so they may be contrasted. Point out that *ten* is the model word for the *-en* pattern. Later, if students have difficulty with a word containing an *-en* syllable, encourage them to say each part of the word or as many parts as they can and then reconstruct the word. If necessary, they can use *ten* or other model words to help them.

o- *Pattern.* Write *go* on the board and have students read it. Write *ago* on the board. Write the separate syllables in contrasting colors or underline them. Say the syllables as you write them. Then have students read the word. Contrast *go* and *ago.* Present *over, broken, spoken,* and *frozen* in the same way. Point out that *no* is the model word for the *o-* pattern. Later, if students have difficulty with a word containing an *o-* syllable, encourage them to say each part of the word or as many parts as they can and then reconstruct the word. If necessary, they can use *no* or other model words to help them.

-er *Pattern.* Write *her* on the board and have students read it. Then write *under* beneath it. Write separate syllables in contrasting colors or underline them. Say each syllable as you write it. Contrast *her* and *under.* Present *ever, never, other,* and *fewer* in this same way. Later, if students, have difficulty with a word containing an *-er* syllable, encourage them to say each part of the word and reconstruct it.

(Continued)

The purpose of guided practice activities, such as combining syllables to form words, is to help students become aware of high-frequency syllables.

Step 2: Guided practice. Have students use pronounceable word parts or the model words to read the following: *stolen, token, woven, opener.* Remind them that the words they construct must be real ones. If they analyze a word and it does not seem to be real, they should try again. Also have students complete reinforcement exercises. Sample exercises include the following:

1. Form words by combining two of the three parts in each line.

wo	ven	ver
ken	spo	ker
ker	to	ken
len	ler	sto

2. Underline the word that best fits the sense of the sentence.
   a. The car locks are (frozen, chosen).
   b. The door is (open, over).
   c. Have you ever seen a four-leaf (chosen, clover)?
   d. You will need a (stolen, token) for the bus.
   e. This coat has been (frozen, woven) from fine wool.

3. Students read signs or labels that contain pattern words.
   Cocoa

Frozen Foods
Open
Buy Tokens Here
Photo Shop

4. Have students create a sentence or story using as many of the key words as they can.

Step 3: Application. Provide students with frequent opportunities to make use of this strategy by reading basal stories, trade books, periodicals, and real-world materials.

Step 4: Expansion of patterns. Expand the *en* pattern to include *tend* and *tent.* Write *ten* on the board. Then show how *-en* is a part of other words.

ten	ten
tent	tend
rodent	tender
moment	fender

One way of deciding which syllable patterns to introduce is to examine the materials students are about to read; note which multisyllabic words will probably be unknown, and then present the patterns they embody.

Step 5: Review. From time to time, review the patterns and model the process of using them. When students encounter difficult words, encourage them to seek out pronounceable word parts or use the model words to help them decode the words. Provide assistance as needed.

Pronounceable Word-Part and Analogy Strategies Applied to Polysyllabic Words

Teaching syllable patterns is a useful activity in itself. It introduces words that students may have difficulty recognizing in print. However, the true value of teaching syllable patterns is that they can be used as a basis for providing students with strategies that will enable them to decode most multisyllabic words. If students have already mastered single-syllable patterns, they can build on this knowledge to attack multisyllabic words. Basically, instruction consists of showing students how to use what they already know to attack unfamiliar words. The pronounceable word-part and analogy strategies, introduced in Chapter 8 as strategies

TABLE 9.1 Common Syllable Patterns

COMPOUND-WORD PATTERN

some	**day**	**out**	**sun**
someone	**day**light	**out**side	**sun**up
sometime	**day**time	**out**door	**sun**down
something	**day**break	**out**line	**sun**fish
somehow	**day**dream	**out**grow	**sun**light
somewhere		**out**field	**sun**beam

SCHWA-a PATTERN

a	**a**	**a**
ago	**a**round	**a**gree
away	**a**long	**a**gain
alone	**a**live	**a**gainst
awake	**a**part	**a**mong
asleep	**a**bout	**a**cross

HIGH-FREQUENCY PATTERNS

en	**o**	**er**	**ar**	**at**	**it**	**in**
p**en**	g**o**	h**er**	c**ar**	m**at**	s**it**	w**in**
op**en**	ag**o**	und**er**	g**ar**den	m**at**ter	s**it**ter	w**in**ter
happ**en**	**o**ver	**er**er	sh**ar**pen	b**at**ter	b**it**ter	w**in**dow
ent**er**	brok**en**	nev**er**	farm**er**	ch**at**ter	k**it**ten	d**in**ner
twent**y**	spok**en**	oth**er**	mark**er**	cl**at**ter	k**it**chen	f**in**ish
plent**y**	froz**en**	farm**er**	p**ar**tner	sc**at**ter	p**it**cher	

miss	**un**	**be**	**re**	**or**	**a**	**y**
miss	**un**der	**be**came	**re**mind	**or**der	**a**pay	sun**ny**
mi**ster**	**un**til	**be**side	**re**port	m**or**ning	p**a**per	sun**ny**
si**ster**	h**un**ter	**be**low	**re**ward	c**or**ner	b**a**by	fun**ny**
whi**sper**	th**un**der	**be**gin	**re**fuse	f**or**ty	f**a**mous	du**sty**
tenn**is**	h**un**dred	**be**long	**re**ceive	**be**f**or**e	f**a**vorite	sha**dy**

ey	**ble**	**i**	**ur**	**um**	**ic(k)**	**et**
turk**ey**	a**ble**	t**i**e	f**ur**	s**um**	p**ick**	l**et**
donk**ey**	ta**ble**	t**i**ger	f**ur**ry	s**um**mer	p**ic**nic	l**et**ter
monk**ey**	ca**ble**	sp**i**der	h**ur**ry	n**um**ber	att**ic**	b**et**ter
mon**ey**	bub**ble**	t**i**ny	turk**ey**	p**um**pkin	n**ick**el	l**et**tuce
hon**ey**	mum**ble**	t**i**tle	t**ur**tle	st**um**ble	p**ick**le	s**et**tle
		Fr**i**day	p**ur**ple	tr**um**pet	ch**ick**en	m**et**al

et	**im**
tick**et**	sw**im**
pock**et**	sw**im**mer
rock**et**	ch**im**ney
buck**et**	l**im**it
magn**et**	**im**prove
jack**et**	s**im**ple

(Continued)

TABLE 9.1 Continued

SHORT-VOWEL PATTERNS

ab	ad	ag	an	ang	ap	ent
cab	sad	bag	can	rang	nap	went
cabin	saddle	baggy	candy	anger	napkin	event
cabbage	paddle	dragon	handy	angry	happy	prevent
rabbit	shadow	wagon	handle	tangled	happen	cement
habit	ladder	magazine	giant		captain	invent
absent	address	magnet	distant		chapter	experiment

el	ep	es(s)	ev	ea = /e/	ea = /e/	id
yell	pep	less	seven	sweat	treasure	rid
yellow	pepper	lesson	several	sweater	measure	riddle
elbow	peppermint	address	never	weather	pleasure	middle
elephant	September	success	clever	feather	pleasant	hidden
jelly	shepherd	yesterday	every	leather	threaten	midnight
welcome	separate	restaurant	level	meadow	wealthy	

ig	il	ob	oc(k)	od	ol	om
wig	pill	rob	doc	cod	doll	mom
wiggle	pillow	robber	doctor	body	dollar	momma
giggle	silver	problem	pocket	model	volcano	comma
signal	silly	probably	chocolate	modern	follow	common
figure	building	hobby	rocket	product	holiday	comment
		gobble	hockey	somebody	jolly	promise

on	op	ot	age	ub	uc(k)	ud
monster	shop	rot	cabbage	rub	luck	mud
monument	shopper	rotten	bandage	rubber	lucky	buddy
honest	chopper	gotten	damage	bubble	bucket	study
honor	popular	bottom	message	stubborn	chuckle	puddle
concrete	opposite	bottle	baggage	subject	success	huddle
responsible	copy	robot	garbage	public	product	sudden

uf	ug	up	us	ut	uzz	
stuff	bug	pup	muss	but	fuzz	
stuffy	buggy	puppy	mustard	button	fuzzy	
muffin	ugly	supper	muscle	butter	puzzle	
suffer	suggest	upper	custom	clutter	muzzle	
buffalo	struggle	puppet	customer	flutter	buzzer	
			discuss	gutter	buzzard	

LONG-VOWEL PATTERNS

ade	aid	ail	ale	ain	ate	ea
parade	maid	mail	male	obtain	hesitate	sea
invade	afraid	detail	female	explain	hibernate	season
lemonade	raider	airmail		complain	appreciate	reason
centigrade				retain	hibernate	beaver
						eagle
						easily

LONG-VOWEL PATTERNS *(Continued)*

ea	ee	e	i = /ē/	i-e = /ē/	ide	ire
eat	bee	see	radio	magazine	side	tire
eaten	beetle	secret	easier	submarine	beside	entire
beaten	needle	fever	period	gasoline	divide	require
repeat	indeed	female	spaghetti	vaccine	decide	admire
leader	succeed	even	appreciate	limousine	provide	umpire
reader		equal	happiness	police		

ize	ise	ive	ope	one	u	y
prize	wise	drive	hope	phone	use	try
realize	surprise	arrive	antelope	telephone	music	reply
recognize	exercise	alive	envelope	microphone	human	supply
memorize	advise	survive	telescope	xylophone	museum	deny
apologize	disguise	beehive				magnify

OTHER-VOWEL PATTERNS

al	au	au	aw	oi	oy	ou
also	cause	caution	draw	point	joy	round
always	saucer	faucet	awful	poison	enjoy	around
already	author	sausage	awesome	disappointment	destroy	about
altogether	August	daughter	drawing	noisy	royal	announce
although	autumn	auditorium	crawling	avoid	loyal	amount
walrus	audience		strawberry	moisture	voyage	

ou	ow	oo	ove	u	ook	oot
mountain	power	too	prove	Sue	book	foot
fountain	tower	bamboo	proven	super	bookstore	football
surround	flower	shampoo	improve	student	workbook	footprint
compound	allow	cartoon	approve	studio	cookbook	footstep
thousand	allowance	raccoon	remove	truly	lookout	barefoot
		balloon	movements	tuna		

ood	ul(l)	ul(l)	tion	tion	sion	ture
hood	bull	full	action	question	conclusion	future
neighborhood	bulldozer	cupful	addition	mention	confusion	nature
childhood	bulletin	helpful	station	suggestion	occasion	adventure
goodness	bullfrog	careful	invention	exhaustion	explosion	creature
wooden	bully		information	indigestion	persuasion	

for decoding single-syllable words, are also effective when used to decode polysyllabic words (Cunningham, 1978, 1979). Using the knowledge they gained through studying syllabication generalizations and/or patterns and through experience coping with multisyllabic words, students should try to pronounce an unfamiliar multisyllabic word syllable by syllable. The student would pronounce the word *sudden* "sud, den, sudden." If she is unable

The key to developing strategy use is to provide many opportunities for students to apply them. For many students who have difficulty with multisyllabic words, it is partly a problem of confidence. They encounter lengthy words and give up. Students need to be encouraged to use their skills.

to pronounce the syllable as a whole, the student might pronounce the first syllable by seeking out the pronounceable word part, then go on to the second syllable, and so on. For the word *sudden,* the student might decode it as "ud-sud, en-den, sudden." Often the pronunciation of the first syllable will trigger pronunciation of the whole word, so students may pronounce it as "sud-sudden" or "ud-sud, sudden." (However, if they are unable to pronounce the first syllable, they might try their luck with a subsequent syllable. They may be able to pronounce enough syllables so that they can reconstruct the word, or pronouncing the medial or ending syllable may trigger the pronunciation of the entire word.)

If the pronounceable word-part strategy does not work, then students should try the analogy strategy. When used with multisyllabic words, this strategy works much the same way as it does with single-syllable words. However, instead of making just one comparison, it may be necessary to make two or three. Here is how it works. A student stumbling on the word *gander* uses the analogous words *fan* and *her* to sound it out. The word *locate* is sounded out by comparing its two syllables to *go* and *hate.*

The strategy does not work all the time. There are some syllables for which no analogies can be found. In addition, the pronunciation of a sound unit is often altered when it is found in a syllable, especially one that is unaccented. For instance, the *re* in *refer* is no longer analogous to *he,* because the long *e* has become a short *i* (ri-fur). Students need to be taught to make adjustments in pronunciation when applying this strategy. In making comparisons, students can think up their own analogy words or can use the analogy (model) words presented in the Word-Patterns List (Table 8.7) in the previous chapter. Here is how students might be taught the pronounceable word-parts/analogy strategy to decipher multisyllabic words.

Teaching the Strategies.   Explain why it is important to be able to read multisyllabic words. Tell students that even the most difficult words usually have some parts that they can pronounce. Show how you would use known word parts or syllables to pronounce an unfamiliar word, perhaps a name that you had never seen. Then explain that if you didn't see any pronounceable word parts, you would use a comparison strategy. That is, you would see if there were any word parts that were similar to words you know. Show, for example, how you might use the known words *pick* and *him* to pronounce *victim.*

Multisyllabic patterns should be taught early. As many as one word out or four in first-grade readers has more than one syllable (Menon & Hiebert, 2000).

As students encounter difficult multisyllabic words, help them to apply the pronounceable word-part and analogy strategies, along with context, so that ultimately they apply these strategies independently. Your aid might take the form of guiding questions such as: "Are there any parts of the word that you can say? Can you say the first part? The next part? Can you put the word together? If you don't see any parts that you know, can you see if any of the word's parts are like any words that you know? Is the first part like any word that you know? Is the second part like any word you know?" At times your guidance might need to be highly directive. For instance, if a student has been taught the *-o* pattern but has trouble with *frozen* and is unable to note any known parts in the word, you might cover up all but the *fro* and have the student say "fro" (if the student can't read *fro,* cover up all but the *o* and have the student read "o-fro"). Uncover *zen* and have the student say "zen" (if the student can't read *zen,* cover up the *z* and have the student read "*en-zen*") and then put both parts together and see if it is a real word and fits the context of the selection. If the student is unable to read *fro* or *zen,* you would use the analogy strategy and have the student compare *fro* to the model word *no* and compare *zen* to the model word *ten.* Give students as much guidance as they need, but gradually lead them to the point where they can decode independently. Listed below is a series of steps that students might take when confronting a multisyllabic word that is unfamiliar in print.

1. Say each part of the word or say as many parts as I can.
2. If I can't say a part, think of a word that is like the part I can't say and then try to say that word part. (If I can't do 1 or 2, then go to 5.)
3. Put the parts together to make a word.
4. Ask: "Is this a real word? Does it make sense in the story?" (If not, try again or go to 5.)
5. Say "blank" for the word. Read to the end of the sentence. Ask myself: "What word would make sense here?"
6. If nothing else works, I can use the dictionary or glossary.

Generalization Approach to Decoding Polysyllabic Words

Although the pronounceable word part and analogy strategies are easy to apply, students sometimes have difficulty seeing patterns in words. In these instances, they should try to use generalizations to help them decode words. After teaching a number of closed-syllable patterns, help students construct a generalization about the pattern, such as, "Syllables that end in a consonant are often short (*win-dow*)."After introducing a number of open-syllable patterns, help students construct a generalization about the pattern, such as "Syllables that end in a vowel are often long (*se-cret*)." To use generalizations to decode polysyllabic words, students should identify the first syllable by locating the first vowel and note whether the syllable is open (followed by one consonant or digraph) or closed (followed by two or more consonants). Students should say the first syllable and then proceed in this same way, syllable by syllable. After they have pronounced all the syllables, they should try to say the word, making any adjustments that are required. Prompt students as needed. If students misread an open syllable as a closed one, for instance, reading *tiny* as *tin-ny,* ask them to tell where the vowel is so they can see that the vowel should be ending the syllable and should be long (Shefelbine & Newman, 2000b). Often vowel sounds are reduced when they appear in multisyllabic words, as in *educate,* where the *u* has a schwa pronunciation. Explain to students that they should change pronunciations if necessary so they can "read the real word" (Shefelbine & Newman, 2000b). Often if the proper stress isn't given to a syllable in a multisyllabic word, it won't be a real word. Students should monitor to see if they have produced a real word, one that fits the context in which it appears. If not, they should try another pronunciation.

Implementing a Systematic Program.   On a regular basis, introduce a set of pattern words and show how these can be used to decipher multisyllabic words as in the sample lesson. It is recommended that the pattern words be introduced in sets of three. One or two sets might be introduced each week, depending on the needs of the class and the amount of instructional

> Three programs that provide instruction in the use of multisyllabic words are Megawords (Educators Publishing Service, 800-225-5750), Word Building: Book D (Phoenix Learning Resources, 800-221-1274), and the challenge level of SIPPS (Development Studies Center, 800-680-0290 X 281.

time available. A listing of pattern words was presented in Table 9.1. The patterns are listed in the order in which they might be introduced. Although there are more than 200 syllable patterns, only about 100 of these occur with a high degree of frequency. The patterns listed were chosen on the basis of frequency of occurrence and ease of learning. However, add or delete patterns to fit the needs of your students.

When should multisyllabic words be introduced? It is not necessary to wait until students have mastered all the major single-syllable patterns before presenting multisyllabic words. As soon as students have learned most of the short-vowel patterns, you may introduce multisyllabic words that are composed of patterns they have learned: *napkin, hammer, cabbage, absent, invent, address.* After students have learned long-vowel patterns, they can be introduced to multisyllabic words composed of familiar short- and long-vowel patterns: *escape, even, secret, obtain, locate.* Introducing multisyllabic words early has multiple payoffs. It provides an excellent opportunity for students to apply skills, familiarizes students with multisyllabic words at an early stage of reading, and boosts the self-confidence of older struggling readers by showing them that they can read "grown-up" words.

Additional Syllabic Analysis Programs

> For additional information about the Benchmark programs, contact http://www.benchmarkschool.com/ (phone: 610-565-3741).

There are a number of other programs for decoding multisyllabic words. In addition to Word Building, one of the most carefully constructed is the Benchmark Word Detectives program. Designed specifically for low-achieving readers, the Benchmark Word Detectives Program was developed over a period of five years at the Benchmark School (Media, Pennsylvania), a school founded to assist students in grades 1 through 8 who have serious reading disorders. Approximately twenty minutes each day is devoted to the program. The Benchmark Word Detectives program is divided into two parts, beginning and intermediate (Gaskins, Gaskins, & Gaskins, 1991; Gaskins, Ehri, Cress, O'Hara, & Donnelly, 1996–1997). In the beginning program students are introduced to a series of key words that represent high-frequency patterns. These key words are then used to help students decode unknown words. For instance, the key word *it* can be used to help students read *bit* and *mitt.* In the intermediate component, students use key words developed in the primary program to figure out multisyllabic words. Students might use the key words *grab* and *it* to decode the word *rabbit.* In all, students learn 120 key words.

Word Work Program. Designed for struggling readers in grades 4 through 8, Word Work (Wright Group/McGraw-Hill), the word study component of Fast Track, an intervention program, presents multisyllabic words by building on single-syllable patterns. For example, after short-vowel patterns are presented, two-syllable words containing short-vowel patterns are taught: *rabbit, mascot, attic, magnet.* In all, the program presents five patterns: closed *(rabbit),* open *(tiny),* silent *e (mistake),* r-controlled *(lobster),* two vowels *(teacher),* and Cle *(cable).* Vowel digraph patterns are subdivided into those that represent

EXEMPLARY TEACHING

ATTACKING MULTISYLLABIC WORDS

Megan, a student at the Benchmark School in Media, Pennsylvania, is stumped by the word *envelope*. She seeks help from her teacher, Mrs. Marjorie Downer. Instead of simply telling her the word, Mrs. Downer asks, "What did you try?" "Context," Megan responds. The question helps Mrs. Downer ascertain what strategies Megan is using. It is also a subtle reminder that the student should attempt to decode words on her own.

Seeing that context didn't help, Mrs. Downer asks Megan if she can find the first chunk in the word. Megan identifies the *e-n*. Mrs. Downer urges Megan to identify a pattern word on the wall that incorporates *e-n*. Listed on the wall are 120 pattern words that can be used by students to help them work out the pronunciation of most words.

Megan locates *ten* and uses it to help her pronounce the first syllable, *en*. Mrs. Downer then leads Megan to find the two pattern words that are analogous to the next two chunks or syllables in *envelope*. Megan uses these to pronounce the last two syllables. Putting all the chunks together, Megan is able to construct the word *envelope*. Megan then reads the word in the context of the sentence to make sure that it makes sense. While focusing on a word-analysis problem, Mrs. Downer makes sure that meaning is always paramount (Center for the Study of Reading, 1991, pp. 13–14).

long vowels *(remain)* and those that spell diphthongs or other-vowel sounds *(downtown)*. To help students determine how many syllables are in a word, a spot and dot strategy is recommended. Students spot each vowel letter or vowel digraph and place a dot over it. They then determine if the syllable is closed or open, so they can assign a short-vowel, schwa, or long-vowel pronunciation. Patterns are reinforced with decodable poems and stories. The decodable texts are stilted and the program moves fast, but it is one of the few decoding programs designed for older struggling readers.

MORPHEMIC ANALYSIS

Unless you are in the medical field, the word *hemacytometer* is probably unfamiliar to you. However, there's a good chance that you can figure it out without referring to the dictionary. The form *meter* is already familiar to you. And if you compare *hemacytometer* to *hemophilia, hemoglobin,* or *hemorrhage,* you can see that *hem* refers to blood. The root *cyt* may seem unfamiliar, but if you think of *cytoplasm* or *cytology,* that may help you infer that *cyt* means "cell," so a hemacytometer is simply a device that measures blood cells.

| **Morphemic analysis:** identification of the meaningful parts of a word to derive the meaning of an unknown word. |

Although the English language contains nearly a million words and is growing by leaps and bounds, a vast number of both its technical terms and general words have been constructed by joining roots or adding affixes to roots. **Morphemic analysis,** which is the study of meaningful word parts such as compound words, roots, prefixes, and suffixes, can help low-achieving readers recognize hundreds of words. It can also help them learn and remember words. It is easier to learn

> A **morpheme** is the smallest meaning-bearing unit in a word. The word *untimely* has three morphemes: *un-time-ly.*

chronology if you can relate it to *chronic* and *chronometer.* And if you forget what *chronology* means, you can use your knowledge of the combining-form *chron* and context to help you figure it out.

Although struggling readers do well when morphological tasks are presented orally, they do not make effective use of their knowledge of roots, prefixes, and suffixes in their reading (Champion, 1997). When tested on their knowledge of morphology, disabled readers knew only 15 percent of the prefixes, 17 percent of the roots, and 20 percent of the suffixes (Henry, 1990). With training, however, disabled readers may use their knowledge of morphology to compensate for weak phonological skills. Given training in morphology, adolescent disabled readers improved in both reading comprehension and spelling (Elbro & Arnbak, 1996). Using a morphological segmentation may help struggling readers by easing the burden on working memory, because they can concentrate on one meaningful segment at a time.

TEACHING MORPHEMIC ELEMENTS

> When presenting morphemic units, group them in some way. When teaching *mono,* also teach *uni* and other number prefixes. Present opposites. When introducing *anti,* teach *pro.* Also teach *less* and *ful* together (Dale & O'Rourke, 1971).

Morphemic elements should be taught inductively and should build on what students know. For instance, students should use their knowledge of *pedal* to derive the meaning of *pedestrian, biped, pedicure, pedometer.* By noting the use of *ped* in all five words, the students should also be able to derive a meaning for the morphemic form *ped.* Also present related forms at the same time—*podiatrist, tripod, gastropod*—so that students can see relationships among the words.

Making Connections

Make connections whenever possible. For instance, in a chapter entitled "Below and Above Earth's Surface" in an easy-to-read geography series (Lefkowitz, 1990), the following technical terms are taught: *atmosphere, stratosphere, ionosphere,* and *hemisphere.* If students are led to see the common elements in the words, they will understand them better, remember them longer, and if they forget their meanings, will be able to use morphemic units to decode the words. Lead them to see that *sphere* means *ball,* so that *atmosphere, stratosphere,* and *ionosphere* are layers of gas that form balls that surround the Earth. Note, too, the meanings of the morphemic forms: *atmo* (air), *strato* (layer), *iono* (electrically charged). When discussing *hemisphere,* lead students to see that *hemi* means "half," so a hemisphere is "half a ball."

> After students have learned a morphemic unit, show them how they can use this knowledge to derive the meanings of new words. After learning *tri,* students derive the meaning of *trifocals, trilingual,* or *trigraphs.*

The key to teaching morphemic units is to build students' awareness of these elements in words so that when they encounter a difficult word, they see if they can figure out its meaning by analyzing it morphemically. Just as you teach students to seek out pronounceable word parts when applying phonics or word building, you now teach them to seek word parts whose meanings they know. By teaching morphemics, you move students from the level of sound units to meaning units. Because of this new focus, students start noticing the meaningful components of words.

Prefixes

> A **prefix** is a morpheme placed before a word or root that changes the word's meaning, as in *unafraid* or *preview.*

Although **prefixes** are easier to learn than suffixes because there are fewer of them and their meanings are more concrete, they do not become an important factor in students' reading until they are reading second- or third-grade material. Common prefixes are listed in Table 9.2 in approximate order of difficulty.

When teaching prefixes, teach them inductively and, if possible, have students derive the meaning of a prefix through analyzing known words: *unhappy, unafraid, unknown.* When teaching *pre,* for instance, lead students to derive its meaning by discussing its effect in the following words: *preview, prepay, pretest.* In your instruction and practice activities, focus on having students develop a meta-cognitive awareness of prefixes as meaningful units. Students may not perceive *un* as being a separate element in words such as *unhappy* or *unknown,* and so, would not seek out these elements when deriving the meanings of difficult words that contain the prefix *un.*

As you introduce prefixes, inform students of prefix pitfalls (White, Sowell, & Yanagihara, 1989). The first is that many prefixes have more than one meaning. For instance, the prefix *in* can mean "not," as in *incapable* or "lack of" as in *inexperience.* Sometimes an apparent prefix is not a prefix at all. The word *indifference,* for instance, is derived from the Latin word *indifferentia.* Sometimes a prefixed word is not quite the sum of its apparent parts. The true meanings of *unbending* and *uncalled for* would be hard to infer if just the words themselves were examined. The presence of prefix pitfalls means that prefixes need to be taught with care and students need to integrate morphemic analysis and context clues.

One way to teach prefixes is to group them by families of meaning (Baumann, Edwards, Font, Tereshinski, Kame'enui, & Olejnik, 2002). Possible groups include:

■ ■ ■ ■ ■ ▬▬▬▬▬▬▬▬▬▬▬▬▬▬▬▬▬▬▬▬▬▬▬▬▬▬▬▬▬▬▬▬▬▬▬▬▬

INTRODUCING PREFIXES LESSON

Step 1: Introducing the concept of a prefix. Read the portion of the Humpty Dumpty chapter in Lewis Carroll's (1969) *Through the Looking Glass* that talks about unbirthdays. Discuss what an *unbirthday* might be and how it is different from a birthday. Also discuss what an *uncola* might be. List other *un-* words on the chalkboard: *unafraid, unhappy, unclear.* Have students tell how *un* changes the words and tell what *un* means. Note than *un* is a prefix and that prefixes are placed at the beginning of words and change the word's meaning. Note, too, that a prefix forms a separate syllable.

Step 2: Guided practice. Have students read individual words that contain the prefix *un-* and tell what each word means. Also encourage students to complete cloze (fill-in-the-blank) exercises with *un-* words or read brief passages that contain *un-* words. Students might also illustrate *un-* words (*unhappy, unlucky*) or create their own *un-* words.

Step 3: Application. Have students read materials that contain the prefix *un-.* As part of the application step, ask students to use their knowledge of *un-* to derive the meanings of new words. Encourage students to use a strategy similar to the one they used for decoding difficult words. However, instead of looking for word parts they can say, students should look for word parts they know.

Step 4: Extension. Discuss the fact that *un-* can also mean "opposite," as in *undo* and *unpack.*

TABLE 9.2   Common Prefixes

PREFIXES	MEANING	EXAMPLES
EASY PREFIXES		
un-	(not)	**un**friendly
un-	(opposite)	**un**pack
under-	(under)	**under**ground
dis-	(not)	**dis**belief
dis-	(opposite)	**dis**agree
re-	(again)	**re**read
re-	(back)	**re**pay
im-	(not)	**im**polite
in-	(not)	**in**expensive
ir-	(not)	**ir**responsible
pre-	(before)	**pre**winter
sub-	(under)	**sub**marine
tri-	(three)	**tri**color
INTERMEDIATE PREFIXES		
anti-	(against)	**anti**war
bi-	(two)	**bi**cycle
co-	(with)	**co**captain
deci-	(one tenth)	**deci**meter
en-	(forms verb)	**en**circle
ex-	(out, out of)	**ex**haust
ex-	(former)	**ex**-owner
hemi-	(half)	**hemi**sphere
inter-	(between)	**inter**state
micro-	(small)	**micro**scope
mid-	(middle)	**mid**night
milli-	(one thousandth)	**milli**meter
mis-	(not)	**mis**understanding
mis-	(bad)	**mis**behavior
mono-	(one)	**mono**rail
multi-	(many)	**multi**purpose
non-	(not)	**non**fiction
poly-	(many)	**poly**syllabic
semi-	(half, part)	**semi**sweet
trans-	(across)	**trans**oceanic
pro-	(for)	**pro**-union
sub-	(under)	**sub**way
super-	(above)	**super**sonic

- Number: *mono-, bi-, di-, tri-*
- Negative: *un-, im-, in-, il-, ir-*
- Below or part: *sub-, under-*
- Again and remove: *re-, de-*
- Before and after: *pre-, post-*
- Against: *anti-, counter-*
- Excess: *over-, super-, out-*
- Bad: *mis-, mal-*

> A **suffix** is a morpheme added to the end of a word or root that changes or adds to the meaning of the word, as in *careful* or *fearless.*

> Don't waste time with inflectional suffixes. Even if students are dropping endings, they generally learn to self-correct on their own.

Suffixes

There are two kinds of **suffixes**—inflectional and derivational. Inflectional suffixes have a grammatical function, indicating subject–verb agreement (rabbit *hops*), present participle *-ing* (*singing*), past tense *-ed* (*planned*), past participle *-en* (*written*), comparisons (*sooner, soonest*), plural *-s* (*cats*), and adverbial *-ly* (*suddenly*) functions.

Derivational suffixes either change a word's part of speech or function. Many suffixes form nouns: *-ance* (*resistance*), *-dom* (*freedom*), *-tion* (*action*). A number of others form adjectives *-(i)al* (*jovial*), *-ary* (*honorary*), *-ic* (*geographic*), *-ous* (*joyous*).

Do not spend a lot of time teaching inflectional suffixes. If students are reading for meaning and using their sense of the language, they will usually supply the necessary inflectional endings automatically. Besides, generally speaking, little or no meaning is lost if students omit inflectional suffixes as they read. Since low-achieving readers are lagging behind, you need to focus on instructional techniques that have the greatest payoff.

Derivational suffixes are another matter. They should be taught directly and reinforced periodically. When teaching students to apply knowledge of suffixes, it is also a good idea to review prefixes. Many words that have suffixes also have prefixes (White, Sowell, & Yanagihara, 1989). Derivational suffixes begin appearing in students' reading material in grade 2. The suffixes *-en, -er* can be found on that level. In grade 3, the following suffixes appear with a fair amount of frequency: *-able, -ible, -ful, -ness, -y,* and *-tion* (Gunning, 2001). A good time to teach suffixes is when students are reading on a second- or third-grade level or when suffixes are appearing in their reading material with some regularity. Suffixes are listed in Table 9.3 in approximate order of difficulty. You may want to stress the following suffixes because they occur with the highest frequency: *-er, (t)ion, -able, -al, -y,* and *-ness* (White, Sowell, & Yanagihara, 1989). Suffixes should be taught inductively, with stress placed on application. Suffixes and other morphemic elements should be taught on a systematic basis and also when there is a need.

Some suffixes have three or four or more definitions, and these definitions may be abstract. For instance, the suffix *-ic* is listed as having nine meanings in *Webster's New Collegiate Dictionary* (Mish, 1993). These definitions have been combined and simplified for Table 9.3. Because many suffixes have multiple, sometimes abstract, definitions, it is important that students see many examples of the target suffix in use. Examples need to be used to convey the sense of the suffix. For instance, seeing the suffix-containing words

TABLE 9.3   Frequently Occurring Suffixes

SUFFIXES	MEANING	EXAMPLES
EASY SUFFIXES		
-en	(made of; having)	gold**en**
-er	(one who)	farm**er**
-or	(one who)	inspect**or**
-able	(is, can be)	believ**able**
-ible	(is, can be)	vis**ible**
-ful	(full of; having)	thank**ful**
-ness	(having)	ill**ness**
-tion	(act of)	imagina**tion**
-y	(being; having)	chill**y**
INTERMEDIATE SUFFIXES		
-age	(forms nouns)	mile**age**
-al	(being; having)	accident**al**
-an, -ian	(having to do with; of)	Americ**an**, Ital**ian**
-ance	(state of)	import**ance**
-ary	(forms adjectives)	summ**ary**
-ence	(state of or quality of)	obedi**ence**
-ial	(of; having to do with)	adverb**ial**
-ian	(one who is in a field; one who)	music**ian**, guard**ian**
-ic	(of; having)	histor**ic**
-ify	(make)	terr**ify**
-ish	(having the quality of)	fool**ish**
-ist	(a person who)	motor**ist**
-ity	(state of)	activ**ity**
-ize	(make)	memor**ize**
-ive	(being)	secret**ive**
-less	(without)	hope**less**
-ment	(state of)	enjoy**ment**
-ous	(having)	danger**ous**

artistic, comic, historic, and *poetic* in the context of sentences and whole selections will do a better job of helping students understand the suffix *-ic* than will abstract definitions.

When teaching suffixes, show students how the spelling of the base word or root might be affected. Adding suffixes can change spellings in one of three ways (White, Sowell, & Yanagihara, 1989):

1. *Consonant doubling:* sunny, runner
2. *y to i:* penniless, reliable, happily, apologize
3. *Omitted final e:* hoping, activity, official, cubic

Show students that they may have to mentally restore the letters that were removed or changed when the suffix was added. Otherwise, they may not recognize the *penny* in *penniless* or the *active* in *activity*.

A **root** is the morpheme that remains after all the affixes have been removed. *Sing* is the root for *singer, singing,* and *sings.* The root is also the historical source of a word.

When presenting an affix or root, encourage students to suggest other words in the same "family" (Au, Mason, & Scheu, 1995).

Roots

The most complex of the morphemic elements is the root. A **root** is the part of a word that is left when all the affixes have been removed. It may be a word (the *help* in *unhelpfully*) or a portion of a word (the *ceive* in *receive*) (McArthur, 1992). Common roots are listed in Table 9.4. (The list contains both roots and elements known as combining forms. To avoid unnecessary distinctions, both combining forms and roots are referred to as "roots.") Although there are hundreds of roots, only the most frequently occurring and most useful elements have been included. For a more complete listing, see *The Reading Teacher's Book of Lists* (Fry, Kress, & Fountoukidis, 1997).

SOFTWARE FOR MORPHEMIC ANALYSIS

Tenth Planet's Roots, Prefixes, and Suffixes (Sunburst) provides practice with morphemic elements. Activities include composing clues and writing "Mad Blab" stories.

TABLE 9.4 Frequently Occurring Roots

ROOTS	MEANING	EXAMPLES
EASY ROOTS		
graph	(writing)	auto**graph**
tele	(distance)	**tele**scope
port	(carry)	**port**able
saur	(lizard)	dino**saur**
phon	(sound)	micro**phon**e
vid, vis	(see)	**vid**eo, **vis**ion
astro	(star)	**astro**naut
bio	(life)	**bio**graphy
INTERMEDIATE ROOTS		
aud	(hearing)	**aud**ible
auto	(self)	**auto**biography
-ology	(study of)	ge**ology**
cred	(believe)	in**cred**ible
chrono	(time)	**chrono**meter
dict	(say)	pre**dict**
duct	(lead)	con**duct**
geo	(earth)	**geo**graphy
loc	(place)	**loc**ation
manu	(hand)	**manu**al
ped	(foot)	**ped**estrian
scrib, script	(writing)	in**scrib**e, manu**script**
therm	(heat)	**therm**os

CONTEXTUAL ANALYSIS

What are a student's chances of deriving the meaning of a word from context? If reading materials on the appropriate level, students have a 15 percent chance of deriving the meanings of unfamiliar words from context (Swanborn & de Glopper, 1999). For less able readers, the odds are somewhat less. They have about a 10 percent chance of using context successfully.

> **Contextual analysis:** the use of verbal clues from a sentence or passage in order to derive the meaning of an unknown word.

For one thing, less able readers know fewer words and their knowledge of the words that they apparently know is less extensive than that of more capable readers. Their backgrounds of experience are also less fully developed. All of this makes it more difficult for them to apply skills. For instance, five out of sixteen low-achieving fifth-grade readers were unable to use context clues to arrive at the meaning of *gaucho* in the following sentence because they did not know what a cowhand is: "**Gauchos,** the cowhands of South America, learned to chase the birds on cow ponies" (Shefelbine, 1990, p. 91). One student thought that cowhands were a kind of pony; another thought that cowhands referred to the front feet of a cow. Students can't use **contextual analysis** if the target word and key words in the context clues are unknown.

Struggling readers frequently fail to make full use of available context clues. They may focus on one or two details rather than considering the whole context. For instance, one middle-school struggling reader focused on the dog's method of getting food when attempting to use context to derive the meaning of *ravenously,* and he concluded that *ravenously* means "licked."

> The satisfied Labrador had eaten *ravenously* that evening, cleaning up bowls of fresh milk and plates of food with a bottomless appetite. (Goerss, Beck, & McKeown, 1999, p. 163)

> An informal survey of difficult words in children's books and periodicals revealed the authors supplied usable context clues only about one-third of the time.

When carefully taught how to use context clues, students do improve. In one study, students nearly doubled their ability to derive the meanings of words from context (Jenkins, Matlock, & Slocum, 1989). Before instruction, they were able to use context only one time out of ten. After instruction, they were able to use context successfully nearly two times out of ten. Doubling the rate of effective context use should have a dramatic effect on students' vocabularies. For instance, it is estimated that average readers meet approximately 20,000 new words in their reading each year. If they are able to use context effectively only one out of ten times, they will become acquainted with 2,000 new words a year. However, if they double the effectiveness of their use of context, they will double the amount of new words they acquire (Jenkins, Matlock, & Slocum, 1989). The payoff is enormous. However, in order to improve students' ability to use context clues, instruction needs to be significant. Students given only limited training did not improve. The best results are also achieved when strategy instruction is combined with instruction in types of clues (Fukkink & de Glopper, 1998).

A Complex Process

Deriving the meaning of an unfamiliar word requires the following:

■ ■ ■ ■ ■

A LESSON IN TEACHING A ROOT

> Because it deals with long, difficult words, morphemic analysis is the kind of learning experience that builds students' sense of self-worth, in that it teaches them to handle the kinds of words that usually defeat them.

Step 1: Conveying the nature and importance of the element. Before presenting the element, explain to students what roots are and show how they will help them to become better readers. Place some lengthy words containing roots on the board and model the process of pronouncing the word and deriving its meaning. For instance, putting *polychromatic* on the board, explain what a root is, and underline *chrom.* Then show how you would translate the root and the affixes into their meanings (*poly* = "many," *chrom* (at) = "color," *ic* = "having") and come up with the overall meaning of the word: "having many colors." Note that words are like puzzles and often we can solve their meanings by thinking about and putting their parts together.

Step 2: Introducing the new element. Build on whatever knowledge students might have of the new element. Present words with which they are likely to be familiar. By analyzing these words, help them derive the meaning of the element. For the root *bio,* discuss *biography* and *biology* and the common item *bio.* Help them to see that *bio* means "life" or "living." Help students determine the meanings of *biographer, biohazard, biotechnology,* and *biochemistry.* Note that it is sometimes necessary to check the meanings you derive through analysis with definitions given in the glossary or dictionary.

Step 3: Guided practice. Have students read signs or articles containing *bio.* For instance, they might read a label that contains the word *biodegradable.* Or they may read a selection about *biofeedback.* After the selection has been read, have students explain what they think these *bio* words mean and how they derived these meanings.

Step 4: Application. As students encounter new words containing morphemic elements that they know, help them to apply their knowledge by using the known part or analogy strategies. For instance, when students encounter the word *biorhythm,* ask them to see if there are any parts of the word whose meaning they know. If they recognize *rhythm* but not *bio,* use an analogy strategy. Compare the *bio* in *biorhythm* to the *bio* in *biology* and *biography* and help them derive the meaning of *bio* and the whole word. After they have derived a tentative meaning, they should test it out in context to see if it fits.

> To assess students' ability to use context clues, observe them as they encounter a word whose meaning is unknown. What do they do? How successful are they at using context?

- Recognizing that a word is unknown (Nation, 2001).
- Deciding to use context to derive the meaning of the unknown word. Most use of context is virtually automatic (Rapaport, 2004). A decidedly deliberate use of context is not initiated until the reader notes that an unknown word is blocking the construction of meaning (Kibby & Wieland, 2004).
- Selecting clues to the word's meaning.
- Using the clues to compose a general meaning of the word. The reader combines text clues and background of experience to hypothesize a meaning. Background is a crucial factor because it enables the reader to make inferences about the unknown word (Rapaport, 2004). Therefore, to increase the effectiveness of students' use of context clues, it is important to model how to make inferences based on background knowledge.
- Testing the meaning of the word and changing or refining the meaning if necessary. The reader tries out the hypothesized meaning to see if it fits. If it doesn't fit, the

reader repeats the process. (Good readers revise when they find the hypothesized definition is not working out. Poor readers start all over again.) In one study, readers required five or six encounters with a word before they could derive an accurate meaning (Kibby & Wieland, 2004).

Steps for Using Context

Once they have decided to use contextual analysis here are steps that students can follow and a series of questions they can ask for deriving meaning.

Step 1: Seeking clues. Students read the entire sentence, saying "blank" for the unknown word. They then look for clues that might help them guess the meaning of the unknown word. If the clues in the sentence are inadequate, students look at earlier and later sentences.

Step 2: Combining clues. Students put all the clues together.

Step 3: Using background knowledge. Students add background knowledge to the clues they have assembled and construct a tentative definition or meaning.

Step 4: Trial substitution. Students substitute the tentative word or phrase for the unknown word.

Step 5: Checking the substitute. Students check the context to see if the substitute word or phrase fits all the cues.

Step 6: Revision. If the substitute word or phrase does not fit, students revise the substitute and try another word or phrase.

When students are attempting to use context, use prompts to guide their efforts. Because struggling readers may not be using their understanding of the text as a context clue, it is important when providing them prompts to first ask them to tell what the target section is about. Often the general sense of the passage will provide a clue as to the meaning of a word. However, students won't be able to use the overall sense of the passage if they don't comprehend it (Beck, McKeown, & Kucan, 2002). Ask students what's going on in the passage or what the passage says and then discuss what the target word might mean.

To help students learn the process, the teacher models how she goes about using context clues. The teacher also provides guided practice. During guided practice, she might ask such questions as: "What are the clues telling us? What are the clues in the sentence that contains the word telling us? Are there any clues in the sentences before the hard-word sentence? Are there any clues in the sentences after the hard-word sentence? When you put all the clues together, what does the word seem to mean?" What do I know that will help me figure out what this word means?

Stress the need to think carefully. As McKeown and Beck (2004) concluded, "For many students the most difficult part of deriving word meaning from context is the process of reasoning about how to put information together from the context and what kind of conclusions are valid to draw" (p. 24). Using think-alouds, demonstrate for students the kind of reasoning that is required in order to derive the meaning of an unknown word. Also use prompts to help students apply their reasoning skills. Here is how Angela, a middle school student, with the help of some probes by the researcher, arrived at a tentative meaning for the word *qualms,* which was contained in a selection that she was reading:

> I had a few qualms at first about how Caroline and Julia would get along together. Julia was so different from all of our school friends that I felt sort of awkward with her myself. (Duncan, 1977, p. 55)

Researcher: Talk to me. What do you think?

Angela: That maybe there are questions or how they are going to get together.

Researcher: What do you mean by questions?

Angela: Like are they going to get together or are they not. Like she's thinking in her head how is she like going to get along with her friend.

Researcher: So what does that tell you about the word *qualms?*

Angela: That she might be thinking in her head.

Researcher: What else can you tell me? (long pause before Angela responds)

Angela: Ideas.

Researcher: Keep talking.

Angela: Maybe like an uneasy feeling. (Harmon, 1998, p. 586)

Types of Context Clues

There are a number of different kinds of context clues, some being easier to use than others. Context clues, such as explicit definitions and synonyms, are easier to use than those that require making inferences (Carnine, Kame'enui, & Coyle, 1984). And, of course, the number of clues makes a difference. Some difficult words are accompanied by multiple clues. Distance also has a bearing on the use of context clues. The closer the clue is to the target word, the easier it is to use. When instructing students, especially younger ones, start with easier clues. Also, focus on words that have near, rather than distant, context clues. The next section lists some frequently occurring context clues (Sternberg, 1987).

> Periodically display a word that has such explicit context that it is possible to derive its meaning. Encourage students to use the context to construct a meaning for the word. Discuss the processes they use.

> To spotlight the use of context clues, encourage students to bring in examples of instances where they were able to use context clues to get the meaning of an unfamiliar word.

Definition.   Quite often, authors supply definitions for difficult words, especially technical terms used in science and social studies. In some instances, the definition is detailed and conceptual, far better than what might be found in a dictionary. In many cases, however, the definition is concise and appears as an appositive directly after the difficult word. An extended definition for a walker, which is a key word in the story, is provided in the following passage: "What's a walker?" Donna asks. "It's a light metal frame that helps people walk," Mrs. Price says. "It has four legs, and handles for you to hold. When you take a step, you put the walker in front of you" (Cameron, 1990, p. 16).

Synonyms.   Except for directly stated definitions, synonyms seem to be the easiest context clue. Synonyms are especially easy when they appear close to the difficult word (Carnine, Kame'enui, & Coyle, 1984). In the following sentence, a student can use the synonym *snout* to derive an approximate meaning for *proboscis:* "The housefly has a long snout or *proboscis*" (Steele, 1991b, p. 15).

Comparison–Contrast.   Comparison–contrast context clues are sometimes signaled by *not, but, however,* or *even so.* The words *even so* in the following excerpt indicate that the *lepidoptera's* ability to fly huge distances contrasts with the fact that it is *fragile,* and so suggests an approximate meaning for *fragile:* "Lepidoptera are *fragile* creatures. Even so, some of them can fly huge distances, or migrate to warmer climates" (Steele, 1991b, p. 18).

> As students encounter hard words in rich contexts and are not using clues, encourage them to do so.

Function Indicators.   Sometimes, the reader can tell what a word means by noting what the difficult word does. By noting the function of the incinerator in the following passage the reader can get a fairly clear sense of what it is: "The chassis oven, as well as the cab ovens, are heated with the help of the plant incinerator located out on the receiving dock. Freightliner burns all its scrap paper, lumber, and cardboard boxes in the *incinerator*" (Nentl, 1983, p. 35).

Example.   One or more examples of the target word are provided. This makes it possible for the reader to examine the example(s) and infer the meaning of the target word. The following passage, which includes *vegetarian,* gives a number of examples of foods that a vegetarian diet might include: "Some birds have a mostly vegetarian diet. They eat seeds, fruit, berries, nuts, grasses, shoots, waterweeds, and leaf buds" (Steele, 1991a, p. 13).

> From time to time, review and model the process of deriving the meaning of a word from context.

Experience.   The target word may label or describe a common experience. Using his background of experience, the reader can often infer meanings. Through real or vicarious experience, the reader can infer the meaning of *remote* by noting the lack of transportation and communication in the setting described in the following excerpt: "In very *remote* parts of the word there may be no roads or railroad, and the land may be covered with jungle, swamp, desert or snow. The only way that villagers or expeditions can keep in touch with the outside world is by air" (Steele, 1991c, p. 13).

Pictorial Clues.   Encourage students to use illustration clues to get the meanings of unfamiliar words. In a geography text for low-achieving readers (Abbye & Donahue, 1993), *assembly line, prairie, plateau,* and other key words are explained with pictures. When preparing students to read a passage, point out pictorial clues and stress the need to read captions to get the benefit of the clues. Often, pictorial clues are far superior to verbal ones.

USING THE DICTIONARY

Although it is an essential tool, especially for low-achieving readers, the dictionary is badly neglected. However, the dictionary is the single-most powerful source of self-help for low-

Before they use their dictionaries, encourage students to survey them so that they become familiar with the wealth of information that a dictionary contains.

achieving readers. In fact, widespread use of trade books to teach reading, the increased availability of electronic text, and the growing numbers of students who are learning English as a second language has created a greater need for dictionaries (Scott & Nagy, 1997). Once they have acquired a minimum of reading skill, low-achieving readers can use the dictionary to build their reading vocabulary.

Dictionaries vary greatly in complexity. As a practical matter, students are unable to handle dictionaries until they are able to read on a third-grade level (Halsey & Morris, 1977). It is virtually impossible to write definitions at an easier level than that. Below that level, students need to use picture dictionaries, simplified glossaries, or CD-ROM dictionaries such as *My First Incredible Amazing Dictionary* (Dorling Kindersley), which uses spoken words and illustrations to explain 1,000 words.

When choosing a dictionary, consider acquiring *Collins Cobuild New Student's Dictionary*. Cobuild is known for providing definitions that are easy to understand.

So that students will not become frustrated in their attempts to use the dictionary, obtain one that is as close to the students' reading level as possible. For an eighth-grader reading on a third-grade level, this would mean using a beginning dictionary. Along with ease of reading, also consider maturity. Select a beginning dictionary that is not obviously designed for primary students. Analyze the dictionary. Look for ease of use, definitions that are readable and understandable, and the generous use of illustrations. Or obtain an electronic dictionary that pronounces words being looked up and reads definitions.

Teaching Dictionary Skills

Instruction should be functional. Nothing is quite as dull as completing dictionary worksheets. However, students will need some direct instruction in key dictionary skills. One of the best ways to teach dictionary skills is to model the use of the dictionary. When the spelling, meaning, or pronunciation of a word is questioned in class and you are unsure of the correct answer, freely admit it and model how you use the dictionary to answer questions that you have about words.

Deriving Correct Meanings. The most difficult dictionary skill of all is to derive the correct meaning of the word being looked up. One problem is locating the correct definition. A second problem is understanding the definition. The language of definitions tends to be abstract. Even if the definition is written in understandable style, students may focus on a fragment of a definition and so misinterpret it (Scott & Nagy, 1997). In addition, when good readers go to the dictionary, they may already have a sense of the word's part of speech and may have constructed some possible meanings. Struggling readers go to the dictionary without any such expectations (Neubach & Cohen, 1988).

Encourage the use of glossaries. Because glossaries have a limited number of words and fewer definitions, they are easier to use than dictionaries.

Acquaint students with the various sources of information about a word's meaning. For instance, in the *Thorndike Barnhart Children's Dictionary* (Thorndike & Barnhart, 1998), the word *trombone* is shown in an illustration in addition to being defined. The word *triumphant* is defined, used in an illustrative phrase, and used in an illustrative sentence. The word *boycott* is defined and accompanied by a

Some dictionary definitions do not provide enough information for the reader. For instance, if the word *laser* is essential to the meaning of a passage, the reader might need to consult an encyclopedia to acquire in-depth information.

brief account of its origin. Also model the process of looking up a word. As you model the process, demonstrate to students how you use context to decide the word's part of speech and make some guesses about the word's meaning before looking it up. Show how you go about using context to select the right definition and carefully consider the whole definition, using both definitions and examples and also illustrations and word histories if available. A complex skill, dictionary usage needs explicit, sustained instruction with many opportunities to apply the skill.

Students also need multiple encounters with words so that they get a feel for how these words are used. Additionally, the traditional assignment of looking up words in the dictionary and using them in sentences should probably be eliminated. In addition to being a tedious assignment, most students are not able to use a new word in a sentence, unless it is very concrete, until they have had multiple encounters with it.

Determining the Correct Pronunciation.   For reading purposes, it is not necessary to derive the correct pronunciation of a new word. Getting the meaning is all that is needed. One young reader thought *colonel* was pronounced /kol-uh-nul/. Since she understood that the word referred to a military officer, her comprehension did not suffer. However, not knowing the pronunciation of the word, she was unable to recognize it when she heard it and so was unable to add to her knowledge of the word when it was spoken by others. In addition, had she used it in her own speech, no one would have known what she was talking about. Learning how to derive the pronunciation of a new word is an important skill.

Encourage students to take advantage of phonemically respelled words in periodicals, trade books, and texts. Students tend not to use aids such as this unless the teacher emphasizes them.

When teaching the pronunciation key, build on what students already know. Except for the symbol ŋ used in *sing* and the /zh/ symbol for the sound heard near the end of *measure,* students will be familiar with all symbols for the consonant sounds, since they do not differ from the letters used to represent their sounds. Students will also be familiar with symbols for short vowels, since they are the same. Long-vowel symbols are easy to learn because they are symbolized by a macron mark (¯). The only symbols students will have to learn are those for schwa, *r*-vowels, and the other vowels (those that are neither long nor short). Students also need to know that the pronunciation key may vary slightly from dictionary to dictionary.

After giving an overview of the pronunciation key, emphasize the familiar elements and model their use. Have students use the pronunciation key to construct pronunciations for short, straightforward words. Choose words from trade books and content-area books that they are reading. Select words whose spellings do not effectively represent pronunciations: *python, quartz, gnu, queue.* As they encounter words whose pronunciations are unknown, have students use the dictionary to reconstruct pronunciations.

As students encounter words like *route* and *tomato,* which have variable pronunciations (rōot, rout), (tə mā tō, tə ma tō), lead them to see that people in different parts of the country speak different dialects so that their pronunciations of certain words differ and they may use certain expressions and words in different ways. Discuss the fact that all dialects are equal, and that many words may be pronounced in more than one way. Thus /rōot/ and /rout/ are equally correct. The pronunciation chosen should be the one that matches the speaker's dialect.

Electronic Dictionaries

As noted earlier, one way of motivating students to use the dictionary is to obtain an electronic version. Electronic dictionaries are becoming more and more popular and are appearing as features of word processing programs, in CD-ROM software packages, and in handheld versions. One handheld device known as a Reading Pen II (http://www.quick-pen .com/) is shaped like a pen, but contains a high-resolution scanner that scans in the word, pronounces it, and displays and/or reads its definition. Apart from the novelty factor, an electronic dictionary is easier to use because it locates words more quickly and, if the dictionary has a speech component, the student does not have to use the pronunciation key. Poor readers can use this feature to have the dictionary read any words in a definition that they cannot read on their own. In addition to providing definitions, talking dictionaries can be used in any grade to help both low- and high-achieving students pronounce printed words that they are unable to decode.

> Many CD-ROM dictionaries have speech capability. Poor readers can use this feature to have the dictionary read the entry word or any words in a definition that they cannot read on their own.

Glossaries can be found in reading programs beginning in first grade and in many informational books. An especially useful type of glossary is the eGlossary, which is available on the Internet for a number of reading and content area texts. With its speech component, an eGlossary says the target word, says its definition, and reads an example sentence. The eGlossary would be especially helpful for students who are unable to pronounce the word. Because it reads the word and its meaning and an example sentence, the eGlossary would be a helpful study aid. Hearing the word spoken would foster retention. The eGlossary would also help students to go over hard words independently before reading a selection. For an example of an eGlossary, go to http://www.eduplace.com/kids/ and click on "School Books."

A Functional Tool

Knowing when to use a dictionary is just as important as knowing how to use it. When encountering a new word in their reading, students should use phonic, syllabic, and/or morphemic analysis strategies and context clues to derive the meaning and/or pronunciation of the word. If the word is not crucial to an understanding of the selection, the reader should skip it. The dictionary should be consulted only when the unknown word is essential to the meaning of the passage. Otherwise, looking up words disrupts comprehension. However, looking up problem words after reading a selection is a good idea. It is also a good idea to look up words whose meanings have been derived from context. Again, this should be done after the selection has been read. Looking up a word gives readers feedback, allows them to revise their definitions, and provides more information about the word and so is an excellent vocabulary expander and builder.

BALANCED USE OF STRATEGIES

Given the complexity of the English language and the changing needs of readers as they encounter materials of increasing difficulty, there is a need for a variety of word-analysis strategies. Phonics and syllabic analysis are required for sounding out words. Morphemic analysis and dictionary usage are essential when the meanings of words are unknown. Context is useful for identifying words that the reader cannot sound out and for deriving the meanings of unknown words. These strategies are often used in integrated fashion to support each other and as cross-checks. In a balanced program of word analysis, students need to know which strategy to use in which situation. They also need to be able to integrate strategy use.

USING THINK-ALOUDS

As they advance through the grades, struggling readers adopt strategies for dealing with unknown words. Unfortunately, these strategies may not be effective. In addition, because their strategies do not work very well, struggling readers may lack confidence in their ability to deal with unfamiliar words and may simply skip words that are difficult. Such was the case with Angela, a below-level reader in the seventh grade (Harmon, 1998). Angela generally skipped words that she did not know. And when she did attempt to derive the meaning of an unknown word, she focused on attempting to pronounce the word, a strategy that does not work if the word is not in the reader's listening vocabulary. Or she used only the immediate context in which the word appeared. She failed to consider any of the text that appeared before or after the sentence in which the word was used. Angela never considered the use of the dictionary or other reference.

One way of guiding students in the use effective strategies is to conduct a think-aloud. In a think-aloud, students stop when they come to a difficult word and then give a thought-by-thought description of what they do to try to figure out the word. The teacher does not provide instructional guidance at this point, but offers neutral prompts that encourage students to explain their thinking: Can you tell me what you are thinking? Can you tell me more?" Once you know what strategies students are using, you can then use the think-aloud as an instructional tool. You might use such prompts as: "Is there any part of that word that you can say? Are there any parts of that word that you know? Is the word like any word you know? Can you find clues to the word's meaning in other sentences or other parts of the article? Where else might you do to get help? Would a dictionary help?"

Strategies that can be used to derive the meanings of words are many and varied. The personal guidance provided in a think-aloud can help students integrate and apply strategies. Most important of all, the guidance provided can help build students' confidence in the use of word-analysis strategies and build their sense of competence. If individual think-alouds are impractical, group think-alouds may be used instead.

MINICASE STUDY

An eighth-grader, Alicia has a fifth-grade instructional level and she has a hard time keeping up with her school work. One of her difficulties is decoding multisyllabic words. Not only does Alicia have difficulty sounding out multisyllabic words, she also fails to emphasize meaning. Many of the words she sounds out are not real words. For instance, she read *tretorius* for *treacherous,* and *avication* for *aviation,* and *descrease* for *decrease.* Alicia's teacher was puzzled. Did Alicia have difficulty putting the words into syllables? Was limited vocabulary part of the problem? For instance, if Alicia did not know the meanings of *aviation, treacherous,* or *decrease,* then decoding them would not have done any good, unless she could have derived their meanings from context.

To explore these unanswered questions and determine why Alicia had difficulty with the words, her teacher went back over the items that Alicia had missed. She determined that some of the words missed were in Alicia's listening vocabulary, but some were not. Also she found that when Alicia was given a second chance and some support, she did a little better. As a result of these additional insights, a multifaceted approach was designed. Syllabication, morphemic analysis, and dictionary usage were being taught. However, they are now being taught within the context of the content-area reading that Alicia is required to complete for school.

Multisyllabic words are drawn from selections that Alicia will be reading soon in her regular assignments. When possible, words are chosen that fit into one of the multisyllabic patterns that Alicia has difficulty with: the *-ence* pattern, as in *convenience* and *confidence,* for instance. In addition, Alicia has been taught the pronounceable word-part and analogy strategies for identifying multisyllabic words. These strategies are integrated with context, and meaning is stressed so that the words Alicia constructs are real words and fit the sense of the sentence and passage.

Gradually, morphemic analysis and dictionary skills have been added to the program so that Alicia has strategies for coping with the many new words that appear in her content-area texts. Emphasis is placed on learning roots and affixes that appear in the content-area vocabulary that she is learning. Alicia also has learned to make better use of context clues and to use the glossary when necessary. Over time, Alicia is making gradual but encouraging progress.

SUMMARY

All too often, low-achieving readers have difficulty applying phonics knowledge to multisyllabic words and so need explicit instruction in this area. Approaches for teaching the decoding of multisyllabic words include traditional rules and patterns combined with word building. The strategies of seeking out pronounceable word parts and using analogy/comparison–contrast to decipher multisyllabic words should also be taught.

Low-achieving readers should be taught a number of meaning-based strategies for identifying new words. These include morphemic analysis, context clues, and dictionary skills. Morphemic analysis involves the analysis of morphemes, or meaningful units of words, such as roots, prefixes, and suffixes.

Morphemic elements should be taught inductively and should build on what students know. Morphemic elements should also be grouped in some way so that students can see relationships. Focus should be placed on teaching those elements that students have the greatest need to know and that are likely to transfer to new words they will meet. Being easier, prefixes should be taught before suffixes, but they should not be taught before students are reading on a second- or third-grade level. Roots, which are the most complex forms, should be taught last.

With instruction, low-achieving readers can double their ability to use context clues effectively. Using context is a two-stage process. In stage one, students use context and prior knowledge to construct a possible meaning. In stage two, students try out this possible meaning. Major context clues include definition, synonyms, comparison–contrast, function indicators, example, and experience.

The dictionary is an essential tool for low-achieving readers, helping students cope with difficult words and build their vocabularies. It is important that low-achieving readers use a dictionary that is on the appropriate level. Electronic dictionaries should also be introduced. Using the dictionary requires three major skills: locating the word, selecting the appropriate definition, and reconstructing pronunciation. The dictionary should be presented as a functional tool to be used as needed. Think-alouds may be used to assess students' use of word-analysis strategies and to provide guidance in their application.

APPLICATION ACTIVITIES

1. Plan a lesson teaching an element in morphemic analysis, context clues, or dictionary usage. If possible, teach the lesson and evaluate its effectiveness.

2. Examine three children's dictionaries. Pay particular attention to the way words are defined. Look up five to ten words and compare the definitions provided in terms of accuracy, completeness, and understandability. Which of the dictionaries seems most useful for low-achieving readers? Why?

3. Examine an electronic dictionary. How does it compare with a regular dictionary? In what ways might low-achieving readers find it more useful than a regular dictionary? What difficulties might they have in using it?

■ ■ ■ ■ ■

CHAPTER TEN

BUILDING VOCABULARY

USING WHAT YOU KNOW

The previous chapter discussed syllabic, morphemic, and contextual analysis, and dictionary usage, which are four key strategies for learning new words. This chapter presents principles and techniques for teaching new words and strategies for remembering them. What are some words that you have learned recently? How did you learn these words? Have you ever taken a course in vocabulary development or embarked on a program of self-study to improve your vocabulary? What techniques did you use? How effective was the program? What might be the components of a vocabulary program for low-achieving readers?

ANTICIPATION GUIDE

Read each of the following statements. Put a check under "Agree" or "Disagree" to show how you feel about each one. If possible, discuss your responses with classmates.

	AGREE	DISAGREE
1. Limited vocabulary is the major cause of poor comprehension.	_____	_____
2. Nearly all low-achieving readers have a less well developed vocabulary than do achieving readers.	_____	_____
3. Instruction in vocabulary is bound to have a positive impact on comprehension.	_____	_____
4. New words are best taught when there is a need to know them.	_____	_____
5. A certain amount of time should be set aside each day for vocabulary instruction.	_____	_____

LOW-ACHIEVING READERS AND VOCABULARY

When Valerie Anderson (Anderson & Henne, 1993) asked sixty low-achieving readers in the sixth grade what makes reading hard, the predominant response was "the words." When she asked them if they had any problems when they read, the answer was once more, "the words." When asked to tell what good readers do, the sixth-graders noted that the good readers knew the words and read fast. According to one review of the research, vocabulary deficiency is the primary cause of academic failure for disadvantaged students in grades 3 through 12 (Becker, 1977).

> Maria (1990) notes, "The reader's level of vocabulary is the best predictor of his or her ability to understand text, and the number of difficult words in a text is the best measure of its level of difficulty" (p. 111).

STAGES OF WORD LEARNING

Dale and O'Rourke (1971) list four stages of word knowledge:

1. I never saw it before.
2. I've heard of it, but I don't know what it means.
3. I recognize it in context—it has something to do with. . . .
4. I know it. (p. 3)

Another way of looking at vocabulary knowledge is to assess the depth to which a word is known or how the student can use the word. Stahl and Fairbanks (1986) and Baumann and Kaame'enui (1991) describe three degrees of word knowledge: associative-definitional, contextual-conceptual, and generative.

Associative-definitional knowledge means that the student can make an association between a word and a definition. A *monitor* is "a device used to check or control." A *nomad* is "a member of a tribe who moves from place to place to get food for cattle." Contextual-conceptual knowledge means that the student understands the "core concept the word represents and how that concept is changed in different contexts" (Stahl, 1986, p. 663). The student would understand, that although a monitor in the lobby of an apartment building and a monitor worn by a heart patient have something in common, they also have differences. Conceptual knowledge varies in depth. A student can have partial conceptual knowledge or deep conceptual knowledge. Generative knowledge means that the student can use the word appropriately in speaking or writing. As Nagy and Scott (2000) note, knowing a word is more than just being able to state a definition: "Knowing a word means being able to do things with it. . . . Knowing a word is more like being able to use a tool than it is like being able to state a fact" (p. 273).

> **Concept:** generalization formed by considering particular examples or specific characteristics of objects, actions, or states that share certain characteristics.

Before teaching new words, you must ask, "What does the student need to know about the word?" For novice readers, it may be simply a matter of learning the graphic form of a word. The word may be one that they recognize when they hear it, but they don't know its printed form. Although the word *pneumonia* may be in students' listening vocabulary, they may not recognize its printed form. When presenting a word of this type, teach only the part that is unknown. If the students know the meaning of the word, do not waste time defining it or using it in several contexts. Emphasize, instead, the *pneu* spelling of /no͞o/, which is most likely to be the unknown part of the word.

> With experience, students deepen their understandings of words stored in their lexicons. Initially, the word *cat* may refer to the family's pet. In time, it encompasses other cats, and eventually it becomes a category label for wild as well as domestic cats.

When teaching vocabulary, it helps to think in terms of **concepts.** Through their life experiences, low-achieving readers may have acquired a number of concepts for which they have no labels. For instance, students have undoubtedly seen or read about hens but might be puzzled if they encounter the word *pullet*. It will not be necessary to talk about the characteristics of a hen. Teaching should center around helping students remember that the word *pullet* means "young hen." This is an instance where you are teaching a label for a familiar concept, so the teaching should be on the associative-definitional level.

Ironically, in many instances students know the labels but not the concepts. This is especially true of abstract words such as *republic* or *democracy*, and technical words such as *ROM* and *laser*. These are words that students may have seen or heard but whose meanings may not be clear to them. And then there are words that embody new concepts and have unfamiliar labels: *osmosis, photosynthesis, introvert*. Words such as *magenta* and *pullet* can be taught in a minute or two, but a word that embodies a new concept or a new concept as well as a new label will require considerably more time and effort. These words would be presented on the conceptual-contextual level.

Teaching vocabulary also involves clarifying and deepening students' understanding of known words and helping students use new words in their speaking and their writing. See Table 10.1 for a listing of states of word knowledge and recommended instruction for each stage.

TABLE 10.1   States of Word Knowledge

STATE	INSTRUCTION
1. Knows word when hears it but does not recognize printed form.	Teach printed form.
2. Knows word's oral and written form but does not use it.	Promote generative knowledge. Give examples of its use. Clarify word. Encourage its use in a "safe" environment.
3. Knows the concept but not the label.	Teach the label and relate it to the concept.
4. Has partial knowledge of the word. May have definitional but not contextual knowledge.	Develop fuller meaning of the word. Examine the word in several contexts.
5. Recognizes the label but has no real conceptual knowledge of the concept: *republic*. Or the word may have a familiar everyday meaning but an unknown technical meaning: *energy, motion*.	Develop the concept.
6. Both the concept and the label are unknown.	Develop the concept and the label.

In addition, there are some words for which a student has partial knowledge. Students may know that a colonel is someone who is in the armed services, but may not realize that *colonel* designates a rank just below general. Or students may know a word but not use it because they are unsure of its meaning or pronunciation or both.

Adapted from: "Vocabulary Knowledge and Comprehension: A Comprehension-Process View of Complex Literacy Relationships," by M. R. Ruddell. In R. B. Ruddell, M. R. Ruddell, & H. Singer (Eds.), *Theoretical Models and Processes of Reading* (4th ed., pp. 414–417). Newark, DE: International Reading Association, 1994.

WORD KNOWLEDGE AND COMPREHENSION

Vocabulary poses a special problem for students who are still learning English. García (1991) found that more than 10 percent of the words used in a test passage were not known by Hispanic youngsters.

Although having a rich vocabulary is important in its own right, it is often taught as a means of improving comprehension. Reviewing fifty-two vocabulary studies, Stahl and Fairbanks (1986) found that average students, if given the right kind of vocabulary instruction before reading a selection, did as well as bright students on a series of comprehension tasks. The implication for low-achieving readers is obvious. Given the right kind of instruction, they may do as well as average readers. Instruction must go beyond simply supplying definitions for words. The instruction must be thorough and deep. Students must have contextual knowledge; definitional knowledge is not adequate. They should be given examples of the word used in context, unless the word is one that can be pictured. Showing a picture of a butte, for instance, would be more effective than using it in a sentence, although doing both would be better still. According to Beck and McKeown (1991), two other features are also essential if comprehension is to be improved: "fluency of access to word meanings and richness of semantic network connections" (p. 806).

If students are reading passages similar to the following, in which the boldfaced terms are new words, comprehension will likely suffer unless they can access the meanings of those words rapidly and accurately and use them to help construct the meaning of the passage. If they have only been given definitions of the words, chances are that in itself will not be sufficient to improve their comprehension of the selection. They will lack the kind of contextual knowledge needed to understand the words in their settings. And, because they were only introduced to the words once, they may forget them, or may require additional time to recall the words, either of which will hinder comprehension.

Clovis People were very successful big game hunters who first appeared in the western plains soon after the **glaciers** began to retreat. Some scientists think the Clovis people were the first American settlers and that they arrived sometime 15,000 years ago. Others think they were **descendants** of **immigrants** who arrived much earlier. Scientists may disagree about who the Clovis people were, but everyone agrees that they were **thriving** over wide areas of North and South America by 11,500 years ago. Within just a few centuries they had spread from coast to coast. Thousands of their **artifacts** have been found linking river valley to river valley from Washington State to Nova Scotia and from Alaska to the southern tip of South America. Scientists identify Clovis people by the **distinctive fluted** (grooved) spear points they made. These points are called Clovis because they were first found near Clovis, New Mexico. Clovis points have since been found all over North America and places in Central and South America. (Sattler, 1993, p. 43)

Today's explosion of knowledge is accompanied by the creation of new words. New inventions and ideas require new words.

If students have limited background and vocabulary, teaching a new word may actually involve presenting a series of related words. For instance, in teaching the word *whale,* it might be necessary to also explain the word *mammal* (Nagy & Scott, 2000). Teaching the word *atom* might involve teaching the words *electron, neutron,* and *proton* (Baker, Simmons, & Kame'enui, 1998).

Teaching vocabulary to improve comprehension, then, will require the following:

1. Teaching to contextual-conceptual knowledge. Give the word's definition, and use it in context. Discuss its meaning and help students relate the new word to known words or familiar concepts.

2. Establishing relationships. Show students or help them discover how new vocabulary words are related to each other and to words they already know. For instance, talk about ways in which descendants of immigrants might thrive and what kinds of artifacts, besides spear points, they might leave behind. Also relate the new word *thriving* to the known phrase *doing well*, and the new word *descendants* to the known phrase *children of*. This type of discussion both broadens and deepens knowledge of a word so that a student is better able to make connections between new words and known words.

3. Providing multiple exposures. At least three exposures, and preferably more, should be provided. This promotes accessibility. Ideally, these exposures should involve active manipulations of the word—completing an analogy, giving an example, supplying an opposite, relating the word to one's own experience—so that the students must think about the words (Stahl & Fairbanks, 1986).

INCIDENTAL VERSUS SYSTEMATIC INSTRUCTION

> An **incidental approach** is one in which skills are taught when the need arises.

> A **systematic approach** is one in which skills are taught on a regular, planned basis.

There are two main approaches to teaching vocabulary: incidental and systematic. In the **incidental approach,** vocabulary is taught as needed. Words likely to pose problems in a story or informational piece are taught before students read the selection. As an unknown word is encountered in class, it is discussed. The main advantage of the incidental approach is that students apply their knowledge immediately and they can see a need for learning the new words.

In the **systematic approach,** words are taught as needed, but time is also set aside for the systematic study of vocabulary. This may be a few minutes of each day or one period a week. The main advantage of the systematic approach is that vocabulary study is given more emphasis. If it is tied in with word histories, crossword puzzles, and word games, systematic vocabulary study can create an interest in words. Realistically, a systematic program of vocabulary development might cover only 400 or so words in a year's time. However, at the same time that students are learning these new words, they should also be learning strategies and habits that will foster independent word learning. As Curtis and Longo (1999) note, "They see the importance of a wider vocabulary, and become motivated to increase their vocabularies on their own" (p. 37).

■ ■ ■ ■ ■

EXEMPLARY TEACHING:
FAME (AN INTENSIVE VOCABULARY DEVELOPMENT PROGRAM)

Realizing that limited vocabularies were causing comprehension problems and poor comprehension was limiting vocabulary development in their strug- gling readers, Curtis and Longo (2001) devised an intensive vocabulary development program. Emphasis was on having students process the introduced

(Continued)

words in many contexts so that both understanding and retention would be fostered. In the presentation of the word *persistent,* notice the varied contexts and note, too, how the teacher draws out from students contexts in which the word might be used.

> A persistent person is someone who hangs in there despite difficulties. We often hear or read about people like this—people who overcame a bunch of obstacles to succeed. Like an athlete who was persistent even though he or she had injuries—they refused to give up. Can anyone think of someone they know or have heard about who was persistent, who refused to give up? . . . Could persistence ever be a negative thing? Can anybody think of a situation when someone's refusal to give up or let go might be harmful? . . . We had at least one word in an earlier unit that is related to *persistence*—can anyone think of one? The one I thought of was *endurance.* What connections do you see between *endurance* and *persistence*?

After the words were introduced, students completed unfinished sentences by providing examples of the words' meanings and then gave an example from their experience, for example, a time when they were persistent. Students then completed sentence and paragraph cloze activities as well as analogies and responded to yes/no questions that included a pair of the words studied (e.g., *persistent* and *extinguished*): Could something persistent ever be extinguished? Opportunities to use the words in conversation and writing were also provided. Topics were chosen for conversations and for writing that lent themselves to the use of the new words. Students also read selections containing the new words. The new words were incorporated into questions about the reading selection. After reading about Goodyear, for instance, students might respond to the questions: "What incidents from the article indicate that Goodyear was persistent?"

Students' progress was monitored. For each unit students were given a pretest and a posttest. Words that most students had difficulty with on the pretest were given more reinforcement. In addition to a posttest given at the end of each unit, students were assessed on their recognition of the new words in their reading and the use of the words in their speaking and writing. Teachers held conferences with students to talk over their progress and determine steps that they might take to improve. Although FAME lasted only 12 weeks, students typically gained a year in both vocabulary and comprehension.

PRINCIPLES OF VOCABULARY INSTRUCTION

Whether you use a systematic or an incidental approach to teaching vocabulary, or a combination of the two, certain basic principles form the foundation of an effective program. The first principle is to establish goals.

Establishing Goals

Establish vocabulary learning goals with your students (Baumann & Kame'enui, 1991). Include them in the goal-setting process. Ask: "Why do you want or need to learn new words?" One goal might be to build self-confidence. Another goal might be to improve reading comprehension. Still another might be to improve written and spoken expression. Students, especially ones who are academically behind, delight in learning long words. Accustomed to doing "baby" work, learning new words gives students a sense of concrete accomplishment.

Building on What Students Know

When presenting new words, build on what students know. In presenting the word *periodical,* for instance, ask students if they or their families subscribe to magazines or newspapers. Ask them where they might go if they wanted to read old magazines. See if anyone knows in what room or section of the library magazines are kept. Note that the room is often called the Periodicals Room because that is what magazines are known as. Explain that they are called *periodicals* because each magazine covers a certain period of time. Discuss what other publications might be found in the periodicals section. Have students give an example of a periodical that they read. In developing the meaning of *jubilant,* ask students to tell what kinds of things make them very happy or jubilant. After introducing both words, have students tell how a periodical might make them *jubilant.*

> Carr (1985) directed students to establish personal clues for new words. Having been introduced to the words *jubilant* and *periodicals,* students noted favorite periodicals and events that made them jubilant.

Building a Depth and Breadth of Meaning

Present a word in several contexts. Simply defining a word and supplying a single example of its use may lead to a false concept of the word's meaning. A *magnificent* sunrise may be translated as a bright sunrise. Hearing about a *magnificent* gift, a *magnificent* deed, and a *magnificent* speech should broaden the students' understanding of the word so that when they read about a *magnificent* statue, they understand that it is not a bright statue.

Creating an Interest in Words

Use joke and riddle books to help students see that words can be fun. In addition to having a few laughs, students will become more aware of words, more receptive to learning new words, and will develop a deeper appreciation of words they already know. Explore the histories of words. Investigate the histories of words like *boycott, Braille, gardenia,* and *robot.* Discuss, too, how words change and note new words that have come into the language.

Relating Words to Students' Lives

Most important of all, relate the learning of new words to students' everyday lives. As Dale and O'Rourke (1971) noted, once we are introduced to a new word, it pops up in our reading, on the TV shows that we watch, and in conversations. Encourage students to note examples of the usage of words that they have studied recently. They can write on a card the word and the context in which it was used, and share that with the class. Also have students share examples of ways in which they have used recently learned words in their writing or speaking. In relating the word *gnarled* to students' lives, seventh-grade teacher Denise Stanton used the following examples:

> Have you ever seen an elderly person who has arthritis and their hands are all twisted? That's *gnarled.* Or have you ever seen a tree trunk that the trunk itself is twisted? That's *gnarled.* (Harmon, 1998, p. 523)

Promoting Independent Word Learning

Show students how to increase and expand their vocabularies by using the tools of word learning: context, morphemic analysis, glossary, dictionary, and thesaurus. Research suggests that when students are taught how to use the tools of word learning, they acquire vocabulary at a faster rate (Baumann & Kame'enui, 1991).

TECHNIQUES FOR TEACHING WORDS

In choosing a technique, consider three factors:

1. What is the nature of the word? Is it abstract, concrete, common, rare? Is it a technical word? Does it have many meanings?
2. What background will students bring to this word? Will this be a word with which they are vaguely familiar? Do they have the conceptual background but lack the label? Do they lack the conceptual background but have the label? Do they lack both the label and the conceptual background?
3. How will the students use this word? Is it essential to the meaning of a story they are about to read? Is it a high-utility word that will appear again and again in this and other selections? Do you simply expect them to recognize it when they hear it? Will they be required to use it in their writing or speaking?

Conceptual Teaching of Key Words

> When selecting words for instruction, choose words that are essential for an understanding of key concepts, words that are probably not known by students, and words that are likely to occur in future selections.

In some selections, especially lengthy content-area pieces, twenty or more words may be unfamiliar to students. This is too large a number of new words for students to learn. An upper limit of seven is more manageable, so you must make choices. Because your overall objective in teaching words prior to the reading of a selection is to improve students' comprehension, decide, first, what you want students to comprehend and then choose the vocabulary words that they will most need to know in order to learn those ideas. For example, as a result of reading the first four pages of *Thurgood Marshall: Fight for Justice* (Bains, 1993), you might want students to learn the following concepts:

> If the number of new words in a selection is unreasonably large, you may decide that the selection is simply too difficult. It may exceed the students' instructional level.

- Thurgood Marshall was learning about the Constitution.
- Thurgood wondered why African Americans were not given equal rights that the Constitution said all Americans have.

Then go through the selection and choose those words that are needed for an understanding of the major concepts but that might pose problems for students. Emphasize high-utility words, words that are sure to occur in future reading. Listed below are words needed to understand the major concepts in *Thurgood Marshall: Fight for Justice.*

Constitution	equal protection
Fourteenth Amendment	lecture
Memorized	deny

The concepts of denying someone that which is his due, lecturing someone who has misbehaved, and studying until one knows something by heart will be in students' background of experience, but they may not be familiar with the labels for these experiences: *deny, lecture,* and *memorize.* Several of the words chosen—*Constitution, Fourteenth Amendment, equal protection*—will require building or expanding concepts.

Once the words have been chosen, you can then determine the best way to teach them. Conceptual learning needs techniques that lead students into deeper levels of processing. As Baumann and Kame'enui (1991) note, learning new concepts requires developing semantic relatedness and activating prior knowledge. This involves showing how new words are related to each other and how they relate to students' backgrounds and words they already know. When they integrate new words into their schema, readers are better prepared to use those new words to construct the meaning of a passage.

Actually, virtually all vocabulary instruction should involve some elements of semantic relatedness and prior knowledge. For example, although all children have been scolded for misdeeds, they may not have had the type of scolding that includes explaining why their actions were wrong and why they should not repeat them, a concept conveyed by the label "lecture." Unless a connection is made through discussion or some other means between the label *lecture* and the experience of being scolded, students may not truly understand what *lecture* means. It is also important to develop the concept more fully by showing how a lecture is accompanied by an explanation of why the conduct is not appropriate and why it should not be repeated.

Because most words can have many meanings, care needs to be taken that the meanings provided for the new words match those that the words have in the selections. For instance, *lecture* can mean "a speech" or "a scolding," and *deny* can mean "to say something is not true," "to disavow," or "refuse to grant." If the students access the wrong meanings, they may misinterpret a portion of the passage.

Brainstorming Techniques

One group of approaches that activates prior knowledge and helps students organize new concepts and their labels is brainstorming. In **brainstorming,** the teacher invites students to volunteer their mental associations with a word or topic. In addition to activating students' prior knowledge, brainstorming techniques provide the teacher with an opportunity to evaluate students' background of information. For instance, the teacher may not know whether students have any knowledge of the Constitution or, if they do, how extensive or accurate that information is. Brainstorming is a good way to find out. Once the teacher has some sense of the students' understanding of the Constitution, she or he "can then clear up

Brainstorming: group technique used to activate thinking by encouraging participants to volunteer whatever thoughts or associations come to mind when provided with a stimulus word.

misconceptions and make sure that new concepts and words are related to experiences that are meaningful to those particular students" (Lipson & Wixson, 1991, p. 560).

In one of its simplest forms, brainstorming can be presented through a list–group–label framework (Taba, 1967). The topic to be brainstormed is written on the board and students are invited to tell what the topic makes them think about. Writing *Constitution* on the board, for example, you would invite students to tell what comes to mind when they think of this word. All responses are listed, even those that don't seem to have any connection to the topic. After responses have been listed, the class—working together—categorizes the words into groups of three or more (a word may be placed in more than one group). After all items have been classified, they are given category labels. As they group the words and label them, students explain why certain words should be placed together and why their category name is appropriate. Since grouping or categorizing is a difficult task for many poor readers, you might model the process of categorizing and labeling items for one of the categories. As students become more proficient, they can take more responsibility for grouping and labeling.

As students supply responses, you evaluate the accuracy and extent of students' knowledge of the topic. As a member of the group, you may volunteer words during the brainstorming portion of the procedure. For instance, if students failed to mention *equal* or *equality,* you might add them to the list. Lest the number of items to be grouped grow unwieldy, limit the number of brainstormed items to twenty-five or so (Tierney & Readence, 2000a).

If you notice that the students' knowledge of the Constitution is uneven, provide them with enough of an overview of the Constitution so that they understand its basic intent, especially that it guarantees certain rights to all Americans. Since your main goal is to instruct students in essential vocabulary so that they can better understand the biography of Thurgood Marshall, you need not provide an in-depth study of the Constitution. However, if you are the reading teacher you might coordinate your lessons with those of the classroom teacher, who might undertake a study of the Constitution as part of a "Justice for All" unit.

Using Imaging and Graphic Organizers to Learn Words

Linguistic modality is not the only way of representing a word. Words can and should be represented as images (Marzano, 2004). In one study students learned words twice as well as when they created images of them as opposed to just learning a definition (Powell, 1980, as cited in Marzano, 2004). Where appropriate, have students create logographs or illustrations for their words (Beers, 2003). In a logograph, students use a symbol or drawing to illustrate the meaning of a word. Graphic organizers can also be helpful. **Graphic organizers** are semantic maps, charts, diagrams, and other visual devices that help students see and establish relationships among words. Graphic organizers seem to work espe-

Graphic organizer: diagram used to show how words or ideas are related. Graphic organizers can be used to improve vocabulary knowledge and comprehension of a passage and as a preplanning device in writing.

> **Semantic map:** places the main idea in the center and uses a series of lines and circles to show how subordinate ideas are related to it.

cially well with students who may have difficulty seeing relationships when they are only expressed verbally.

Semantic Mapping.   **Semantic mapping** is based on the list–group–label technique and combines brainstorming and graphically organizing information. After brainstorming, categorizing, and labeling, the class arranges items graphically to show their relationships. Semantic maps are also flexible. Items can be added to them during or after reading or even during subsequent lessons. Semantic maps are especially helpful to low-achieving readers who have difficulty organizing information and who may have negative associations with more verbal methods of arranging data, such as outlines. The steps in semantic mapping include announcing the topic, brainstorming, grouping and labeling, creating a map, discussing and revising the map, and extending the map. The lesson to follow describes how a fourth-grade corrective group created a map for Earth in preparation for reading *Blastoff to Earth: A Look at Geography* (Leedy, 1992).

■ ■ ■ ■ ■ ▬▬▬▬▬▬▬▬▬▬▬▬▬▬▬▬▬▬▬▬▬▬▬▬▬▬▬▬▬▬▬▬▬▬

SEMANTIC MAPPING LESSON

Step 1: Announcing the topic and inviting brainstorming responses. The teacher wrote the word *Earth* on the board and invited a student to read it. Then the teacher asked the class to tell what comes to mind when they think of the word *Earth.* Students responded with the following words: *land, water, ocean, mountains, United States, rivers, South Pole.* No one mentioned the names of any specific oceans, so the teacher asked probing questions. Students volunteered *Atlantic* and *Pacific.* No one mentioned *continents* either, so the teacher added that word. The teacher asked the students if they knew what continents are. One student explained that they are "large pieces of land," so *large pieces of land* was added to the list. When asked to name the continents, students could only think of America. The teacher explained that America is actually divided into two continents: North America and South America. Both these terms were added to the list.

Step 2: Grouping and labeling responses. Students discussed ways of grouping the words and possible titles for word groups. A preliminary map was constructed.

Step 3: Discussing and revising the map. The class discussed the map. One student remembered that Africa is a continent, and so that was added to the map. During the discussion, concepts were clarified. The teacher noted that the continent in which the South Pole is located is Antarctica, and so the map was adjusted.

Step 4: Using the map. Students used the title and cover illustration to predict what *Blastoff to Earth* might be about. Students read *Blastoff to Earth* to evaluate their predictions and find out more about Earth. The semantic map was displayed so that students could use it as a reference as they read. After students read and discussed the selection, the map was reviewed and students were invited to add additional elements. The names of the remaining oceans and continents were added, as were the names of additional land forms. During subsequent sessions, as students learned more about the Earth and its major features, they added to the map and made several other changes. Learning that Europe and Asia are considered to be one continent, they added *Eurasia* to the map. The map is presented in Figure 10.1.

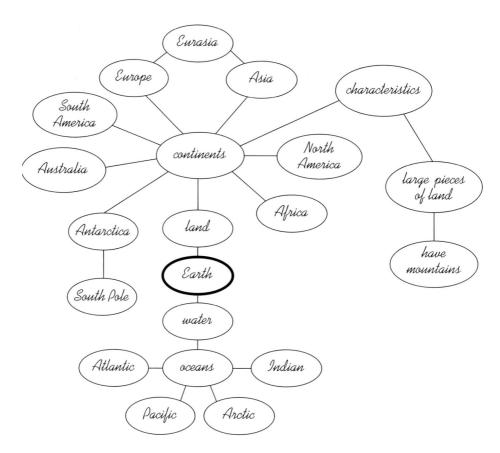

FIGURE 10.1   Semantic Map of Earth

In addition to being a prereading vocabulary-development technique, semantic maps can also be used as a way of summarizing the content of a selection or as a prewriting activity. However, in order for the technique to be of optimum value, students should participate in the creation of maps. If teachers create maps, they are the ones who sift the information and so students do not have the opportunity to organize and process the terms. According to research by Berkowitz (1986), students' performance does not show much improvement unless they have a hand in creating the maps.

Pictorial Maps.   Maps need not be verbal. They can also be visual or a combination of verbal and visual items. The words in semantic maps can be illustrated with drawings, or drawings can be used instead of words. This works especially well when working with concrete items.

> **Semantic feature analysis:** uses a grid to compare objects, people, or ideas on a number of characteristics.

Semantic Feature Analysis.   Like semantic mapping, **semantic feature analysis** (SFA), which involves comparing the characteristics of a series of related words, has been shown to be effective in improving both vocabulary and comprehension. SFA has been especially effective with poor readers and with students who have learning disabilities (Pittelman, Heimlich, Berglund, & French, 1991). Through having students assess the main features of words, SFA activates prior knowledge and helps students explore and organize relationships among words. Through eliciting the ways words in a category are the same or different, SFA helps students to establish relationships among words and to note shades of meaning. It fosters precision in word knowledge and usage.

Although it is a useful tool, SFA works best with words that have features that are either present (+) or absent (−). However, SFA can be adapted to include a graduated scale: A = always, S = sometimes, or N = never, for instance.

■ ■ ■ ■ ■ ■

SEMANTIC FEATURE ANALYSIS LESSON

Step 1: Choosing a category. Choose a topic or category. In the beginning stages, choose categories that are concrete and less complex. Tell students what the category is and ask them to give examples. In preparation for reading *Pocket Facts, Wild Animals* (Steele, 1991c), the category *mammals* is presented. Students are asked to name mammals. Prompts are provided, if necessary.

Step 2: Creating a grid. Place an outline of a grid on the board or on an overhead transparency. List "mammals" in a column on the left. Encourage students to suggest features or characteristics that at least one of the mammals possesses. Not all features have to be identified at this point. Some may be added later.

Step 3: Determining feature possession. Put a plus (+) in the block if a particular mammal possesses the feature being considered or a (−) if it doesn't. The plus need not signal that the creature always possesses the feature; it can mean that it usually

does. If the group is not sure whether the mammal does or does not possess a particular feature, put a question mark in the box. Discuss items, especially those about which students are uncertain.

Step 4: Discussion of the grid. Discuss the grid with the class. If it is missing some words or features important to the overall concept, add them. After the grid has been completed, discuss its overall significance. Have the class note major similarities and differences among the mammals. Encourage the group to sum up the ways in which mammals are the same and the ways in which they are different. Have students read *Wild Animals* to find out more about mammals.

Step 5: Extension. After students have read *Wild Animals*, discuss it and extend the grid to include mammals described in the text but not listed on the grid. The class may also want to list additional features of mammals. The completed SFA grid is displayed in Figure 10.2.

Venn diagram: uses two or more overlapping circles to compare objects, people, or ideas. The overlapping spaces are used to show commonalities. The other spaces are used to show differences.

Venn Diagrams. The **Venn diagram,** which is a device that uses overlapping circles, fosters the comparison and contrast of semantic features. In a Venn diagram, concepts are compared and contrasted. Features shared by the concepts are placed within overlapping circles. Characteristics peculiar to each concept are placed in the outer portions of the circles. A Venn diagram comparing and contrasting African and Asian elephants is presented in Figure 10.3. To make the comparisons more concrete, the diagram is illustrated with drawings of an African and an Asian elephant.

FIGURE 10.2   Semantic Feature Analysis: Mammals

	eat plants	eat meat, fish, or bugs	babies born live	lay eggs	have pouches	can run or jump	can swim	can fly	hibernate	attack people	live on land	live in water
bats	?	+	+	−	−	?	−	+	+	−	+	−
bears	+	+	+	−	−	+	+	−	+	+	+	−
elephants	+	−	+	−	−	+	+	−	−	+	+	−
foxes	−	+	+	−	−	+	?	−	−	−	+	−
giraffes	+	−	+	−	−	+	?	−	−	−	+	−
kangaroos	+	−	+	−	+	+	?	−	−	−	+	−
lions	−	+	+	−	−	+	?	−	−	+	+	−
platypuses	−	+	−	+	−	+	+	−	−	−	+	−
seals	−	+	+	−	−	−	+	−	−	−	−	+
skunks	?	+	+	−	−	+	?	−	−	−	+	−
whales	+	+	+	−	−	−	+	−	−	−	−	+

Although they may be used before reading, especially when students are reading a selection that compares and contrasts two items (electric-powered versus gas-powered cars, crocodiles and alligators, or toads and frogs), Venn diagrams probably work better as postreading organizers.

> The structured overview and the Frayer model are frequently used in content-area teaching to introduce vocabulary and can be found on pages 421–424.

Other Vocabulary-Building Devices

Other vocabulary-building devices include "possible sentences," predict-o-grams, simulations, word sorts, and the vocabulary self-collection strategy (VSS).

Possible Sentences.   Possible sentences, one of the simplest vocabulary-building techniques, may also be one of the most effective. It taps prior knowledge, arouses students' curiosity and interest, elicits predictions, fosters discussion, and helps students detect relationships among known and unknown words. As with many of the other vocabulary building

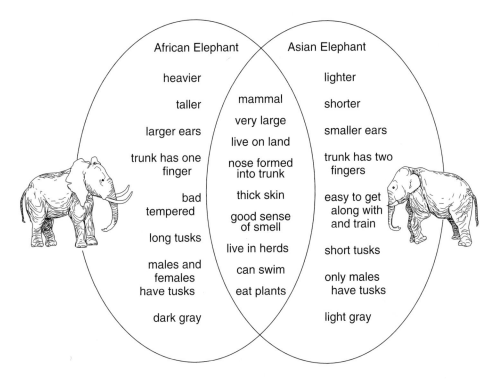

FIGURE 10.3   Venn Diagram: Comparison of African and Asian Elephants

techniques, the first step in the possible sentences technique is to determine the major concepts that you want students to learn, and then list the key vocabulary needed to learn those concepts (Moore & Moore, 1986; Moore, Readence, & Rickelman, 1989). List six to eight potentially difficult words (Stahl & Kapinus, 1991). Then choose the same number of words that are necessary to understand the key concepts, but that are easy.

> In studies with fifth-graders, use of possible sentences resulted in improved recognition of difficult vocabulary and enhanced recall of key concepts (Stahl & Kapinus, 1991).

Write the words on the board. Invite students to read them and tell what the difficult ones mean, but supply pronunciations and definitions if no one else can. Briefly discuss the words. Note that they are taken from a selection that students are about to read. Have them predict what the selection might be about. Then challenge students to create sentences in which at least two of the words from the list will be used. The sentences should be ones that might appear in the text students are about to read. Model the creation of one such sentence, explaining as you compose the statement why you think it might appear in the passage. Then have students create sentences. Note that words may be used in more than one sentence. Write students' sentences, including those that are not accurate, on the board. Stop after all the words have been used. Students then read the selection to see how accurate their sentences are. After students have completed their reading, discuss the accuracy of their sentences. Encourage them to use the text as a reference to clarify confusions, resolve disputes, or back up assertions. Edit or delete sentences that are inaccurate. Students may also expand sentences to include new information garnered from the selection. After discussing the sentences, encourage students to compose additional sentences using the words. This is especially important if students' sentences have not captured the key concepts in the selection. Since using new words in sentences is a difficult task, supply help as needed. Record the students' sentences on the board. Students may copy these sentences into their notebooks so that they have a record of key concepts contained in the selection. A possible sentences exercise completed by a group of sixth-grade low-achieving readers is presented in Figure 10.4. The exercise was written in preparation for reading the first chapter of *Ellis Island* (Reef, 1991), an easy-to-read book about the famous site.

Predict-o-Grams.   In an intriguing device called a predict-o-gram, the teacher has students group words that they believe will tell about characters, plot, setting, and other parts of a narrative (Blachowicz, 1986). Choosing words that are likely to be unfamiliar, as well as some known words, the teacher lists them on the board and discusses them with students. He then asks students to classify the words according to their prediction about how they will be used in the story. Will they be used to tell about setting, characters, problem, plot, or resolution? Students then predict the story.

> Predict-o-grams can also be used to reinforce the concept of story grammar, which is an analysis of the major parts of a story.

The predict-o-gram helps students to think about new vocabulary words in terms of a story that is to be read. It also helps students relate the words to each other. After the story has been read, students should discuss their predictions in terms of the actual content and structure of the story. They should also revise their predict-o-grams, which provides them with additional experience with the new words. The predict-o-gram for "Hungry Spider," a Trickster Tale, is shown below.

Setting	Characters	Story Problem	Plot	Resolution
house	Spider	dinner	prepare	cried
river	Turtle	invite	refresh	floated
		reluctantly	polite	surface
			disappointed	morsel
			famished	
			feast	
			pebbles	
			manners	

Simulation.   For certain abstract terms, where deep conceptual understanding is desired, you might try a simulation. For instance, to convey the concept of the Constitution, you might form cooperative learning groups and have students pretend that they were on a spaceship heading for Mars when the ship's guidance system broke down, and they ended up on a distant planet. With no hope of ever returning to Earth, they have decided to set up a new country and to draw up a set of rules for the people in this new country. After students

FIGURE 10.4   Possible Sentences with Key Words

immigrants	ocean
voyage	ships
Ellis Island	America
processed	countries
descended	pass
inspection	harbor

Students' Sentences

1. Immigrants from many countries came to America.
2. The immigrants made a long voyage by ship across the ocean.
3. After a ship docked, the immigrants were taken to Ellis Island.
4. Immigrants were processed at Ellis Island.
5. The immigrants had to pass an inspection at Ellis Island.
6. Many of us are descended from immigrants.

have completed drawing up their rules, discuss them. Lead them to see that this is what was done in 1789 in the United States. A meeting was held to set up a basic set of rules called the Constitution. Compare the rules set up by the group with the Constitution's major provisions.

Word Sorts.   As noted earlier, the word-sort technique is a categorization device that can be used to manipulate words. It can be especially useful for grouping technical terms (Tonjes, 1991). The words are placed on slips of paper or 3-by-5 cards, and the sorts can be open or closed. In a closed sort, students are given the category names. In an open sort, they must compose category names. An open sort forces students to see relationships and state what those relationships are. Listed below is a completed sort taken from *Observing the Sky* (Stott, 1991).

PLANETS	CONSTELLATIONS	COMETS
Mercury	Scorpio	Halley
Venus	Taurus	Hale-Bopp
Earth	Ursa Major	Encke
Mars	Ursa Minor	
Jupiter	Draco	
Saturn		
Uranus		
Neptune		
Pluto		

Vocabulary Self-Collection Strategy.   When students personalize their learning, they become more active and more involved learners (Blachowicz & Fisher, 2000). One device designed to foster personal selection of new words is the vocabulary self-collection strategy (VSS) (Ruddell, 1992). In the VSS, each student chooses one word to learn. The word chosen should be one that the student believes is important enough for the whole class to learn. The teacher also selects a word. Students record the sentence in which they found the word, if it is in a text, or describe the context in which they heard it if it is from a lecture, conversation, TV show, movie, song, or other source. Students tell what they think the word means in the context in which it is found. They also explain why they think the class should learn the word.

Words are discussed and defined in context. Dictionaries and glossaries may be checked to make sure that the correct pronunciation and definition have been obtained. For the teacher, the discussion offers opportunities for modeling functional use of context clues and the dictionary. The teacher adds a word and the class list is reviewed. Students choose words primarily because they seem important, useful, or are interesting. In addition to being an effective way to learn words, the SSV has the potential to turn passive students into active seekers of new words to learn. Realizing that they are responsible for selecting a word for the whole class to study, students suddenly become word conscious and begin noticing words as possible candidates for selection. As students, especially disabled readers, start attending to and thinking about words, they begin acquiring new vocabulary words at a sometimes surprising rate.

■ ■ ■ ■ ■ ■

VOCABULARY SELF-COLLECTION STRATEGY LESSON

A vocabulary self-collection strategy (VSS) lesson is initiated after the text has been read, because being familiar with the text helps students select words that are important. Here are the steps in the VSS procedure.

Step 1: Selection of words. Students select a word they would like to study. The selection process is usually done in small groups of two to five, with each group nominating one word. During the selection process, the students read the word as it is used in context, tell what they think the word means, and explain why they think the word is important to know. Some eight to ten words are nomi-

nated, and five or six are selected for the final list. If you are working with a small group of students, each student's word may be selected. The teacher may also nominate a word.

Step 2: Discussion of words. Words are listed on the board and their meanings as derived from context are discussed. If necessary, meanings are checked with a glossary or dictionary. Words selected are recorded in vocabulary notebooks or study sheets.

Step 3: Extension. Words are practiced and applied in a variety of activities.

Wide Reading. Once students are able to read challenging texts on their own, the best source of new words is through wide reading. If reading materials on the appropriate level, students have about a 15 percent chance of deriving the meanings of unfamiliar words from context (Swanborn & de Glopper, 1999). Out of 100 hard words, readers would be able to derive a suitable meaning for 15 of those words. If students read a million words at 98 percent word recognition, they would encounter 20,000 unknown words. Learning 15 percent of them means that they would pick up 300 words through their reading. Of course, if they read more and learned to make better use of context clues, they would acquire more words.

Another reason why wide reading is necessary for word learning is because readers might need to meet a word a number of times before deriving a meaning for it (Rapaport, 2004). Jenkins, Stein, and Wysocki (1984) estimate that it might require as many as six meetings before students accurately derive the meaning of a word from context and also have sufficient exposure to the word so that they remember it. One way of looking at word learning is the concept of layers of meaning. When first encountering an unfamiliar word, we might get a general impression of its meaning. With subsequent meetings of the word, we add to that general meaning and acquire a greater depth and breadth of knowledge of the word. In a sense, we learn a word bit by bit.

For free reading, students should be reading on or close to their independent levels (98 percent). Otherwise, they will be meeting too many unknown words and so won't be able to use context clues. For vocabulary development, reading informational text is especially important because these are the primary sources of an academic vocabulary (Nation, 2001).

The key to fostering reading among poor readers is to provide materials that are interesting to the students and that are on their level. These materials need not be books. They can be newspapers, magazines, or how-to manuals (see Chapter 15 for specific suggestions for motivating wide reading). Books that are particularly effective for developing vocabulary are informational books and periodical articles, especially if they define words in context or provide illustrations that depict or clarify the meaning of terms. Listening to or reading along with taped books is also a good way to build vocabulary.

Developing Vocabulary through Reading Aloud.   A rich source of vocabulary development is reading aloud. In one study, kindergarten-age children were able to pick up some new words through a single reading that involved no discussion of the new words (Senechal & Cornell, 1993). However, discussing the words results in even greater gains. Second-graders learned three out of a possible twenty words through listening to stories. With discussion and teacher explanation, the students acquired eight of the words (Elley, 1989). Since they generally do less reading, low-achieving readers, even older ones, should be read to on a regular basis. In addition to building background, this will also build vocabulary. Although a discussion or explanation of some hard words could be a natural nonintrusive aspect of reading aloud to students, care needs to be taken that you don't detract from the students' enjoyment of being read to.

To get the most out of reading aloud as a vocabulary builder, adopt a systematic approach such as that used in a technique known as Text Talk (Beck & McKeown, 2001). From each book or chapter two words were selected that were unfamiliar to students but which labeled known concepts. For younger students, these included words such as *reluctant, immense, miserable,* and *searched.* Unfamiliar words should usually be presented after the story has been read aloud. Although it is better to preteach words when students are reading on their own, it is preferable to discuss vocabulary words after a selection has been read aloud to students. If words are needed for an understanding of a selection, then they can be explained briefly as the selection is being read. This will enable students to use their knowledge of the new words to comprehend the selection.

Text Talk has six steps:

- Presenting the word in story context after an initial reading.
- Providing an easy-to-understand definition of the word.

■ ■ ■ ■ ■

EXEMPLARY TEACHING
VOCABULARY SELF-COLLECTION STRATEGY

Using the vocabulary self-collection strategy as a part of an intervention program, middle-school reading teacher Brenda Shearer (1999) saw a dramatic improvement in her students' reading achievement and attitude toward learning new words and spelling. Students selected one word per week. The class's words were discussed on Monday. During the week there were additional discussions of the words and suggestions for learning their meanings and how to spell them. The students reflected on their word study in their journals. On Fridays they were tested on their ability to spell the words and were also required to use the words in meaningful sentences.

Students enjoyed choosing words. As one student explained, "I think that we should keep picking our own words because then we will want to study them more efficiently. If we get something handed or picked out by a teacher we don't want to study something we don't like" (Shearer, 1999). Another student explained how the activity had changed his attitude toward learning new words:

> Now I often catch myself and when I listen to music or listen to someone talk, I listen to the words they say and I find myself asking what the words mean. I try to make sure I understand what it means. I find that doing this helps me understand big words when I read them in a book or a textbook or even in a magazine. (Shearer, 1999)

- Supplying examples of the use of the word in other contexts, so that the word generalizes.
- Helping students relate the word to their lives.
- Reviewing the word.
- Encouraging students to use new words in their speaking and writing and also to note examples of hearing or seeing the words.

Here is how the word *reluctant* from *A Pocket for Corduroy* (Freeman, 1978), was presented.

Step 1: The teacher introduced the word *reluctant* to label Lisa's feeling. "In the story, Lisa was reluctant to leave the Laundromat without Corduroy."

Step 2: The teacher supplied an easy-to-understand definition of *reluctant* and also asked students to say the word so that they would use the spoken representation to help store the word in memory. "*Reluctant* means you are not sure you want to do something. Say the word with me."

Step 3: The teacher provided examples of the word. "Someone might be reluctant to eat a food that he or she never had before, or someone might be reluctant to ride a roller coaster because it looks scary."

Step 4: The teacher invited students to relate the word to their lives. To assist the children, the teacher provided a frame. "Tell about something you would be reluctant to do. Try to use *reluctant* when you tell about it. You could start by saying something like 'I would be reluctant to _____.' "

Step 5: The teacher reviewed the word. As appropriate, the teacher used the word in other contexts. "I am reluctant to go outside because it is so windy."

Step 6: One key to vocabulary development is to note other contexts in which new words are used. Students were urged to be on the lookout for examples of new words in the reading that they do or on TV shows that they watch or in conversations or discussions that they hear. In an activity known as Word Wizard, new words are posted on the wall. Underneath the words, the students' names are listed. Students are given a check when they report an instance of hearing the word spoken or using the word in their writing or speaking. Students with the most checks are given an award.

Computer-Assisted Instruction

Programs or electronic texts in which students can click on an unfamiliar word and have it pronounced and/or have a definition supplied help students read texts that might be too difficult otherwise and also help build vocabulary. A number of sites on the Internet are also designed to foster vocabulary development. These include the following:

Interesting Things for ESL Students. http://www.manythings.org/
A variety of vocabulary building activities for ESL students, but may be used by all students.

Vocabulary Drill. http://www.edu4kids.com/lang1/
Good practice for using context clues.

Nanana.com. http://www.nanana.com/vocabulary.html
Provides a number of links to vocabulary sites.

Learning Network. http://www.funbrain.com/vocab/index.html
Excellent selection of vocabulary games.

TEACHING VOCABULARY TO ENGLISH LANGUAGE LEARNERS

Having had excellent instruction in both English and Spanish, Miranda, an eighth-grader, is reading on grade-level in Spanish and is fluent in English. Although her decoding skills in English reading are on grade level, she has difficulty with comprehension. Because she has had less opportunity to develop English vocabulary, Miranda's English vocabulary development is limited. Especially lacking are the higher-level words she needs to comprehend her challenging content-area texts. For Miranda and other ELL students, much of their word learning will involve learning the English equivalent of words already known in their first language. When Miranda learns the word *moon,* she need only associate it with the known Spanish word for moon, *luna.* For ELL students, word knowledge rather than pronunciation or grammar is the key concern. If you don't know the words, you have no chance of understanding what is being communicated or of communicating yourself. Miranda and other ELL students need a program of intensive vocabulary instruction, one that emphasizes acquisition of academic vocabulary.

A FULL PROGRAM OF VOCABULARY DEVELOPMENT

Although this chapter has taken a strong stand in favor of direct, systematic instruction in vocabulary, it is important to take full advantage of informal incidental opportunities to learn new words. Don't restrict vocabulary study to a set amount of time each day or week. Bring in new words that appear in daily newspapers or TV shows and encourage students to do the same. Often words that are probably unfamiliar to students dominate the news: *inflation, recession, crimes against humanity, famine, scientific breakthrough.* If appropriate, bring these to students' attention and discuss them, or better yet, encourage students to bring in new words that they encounter. Pay special attention to the words that students are learning in science and social studies and other content areas. Reinforce these in many contexts. Above all, create an interest in and enthusiasm for words. Play word games. Discuss puns and other verbal wordplay. Have a vocabulary bulletin board and a word of the day. Obtain a calendar that introduces new words. Discuss the etymologies of words and track new words coming into the language. Take full advantage of talking or CD-ROM dictionaries. Use a variety of teaching techniques. Most important, provide students with the tools for learning new words and evoke the motivation to do so.

MINICASE STUDY

As you recall from the previous chapter, Alicia is an eighth-grader who reads on a fifth-grade level. Although she has good solid average intelligence, good work habits, and a supportive family, she is struggling with reading, especially in the content areas. Although Alicia is able to decode single-syllable words, she stumbles over multisyllabic words. Instruction in multisyllabic patterns and the use of analogy and pronounceable word-part strategies improved her skill in that area. However, because of a limited vocabulary, Alicia is struggling with her science and history texts, which at this level include many advanced, technical words. Alicia's score on the Peabody Picture Vocabulary Test and her struggle with words in her content-area texts indicate that her overall vocabulary development is lagging. For instance, in her reading she did not know the meanings of words such as *haughty, sacrifices, circumference, decrease, aviation,* and *exaggeration,* words that the typical eighth-grader knows.

In addition to teaching Alicia strategies for decoding difficult words and deriving meanings of new words using context or morphemic analysis, her teacher has devised a multifaceted program for developing new vocabulary. First of all, Alicia is encouraged to read widely from self-selected magazines, newspapers, and books. Each week, she records on note cards ten new words drawn from her reading. On one side of the card, she notes the word and the context in which it appeared and what she thinks the word means. On the other side of the card, she writes the dictionary or glossary definition, thus checking her use of context. She discusses her new words with a peer partner. The two also quiz each other on the new words. In addition, Alicia is encouraged to use her new words in her speaking and writing.

Efforts are being made to build an interest in words. When the word *narcissistic* cropped up, the teacher explained the history of the word. That led to a study of words based on the names of Greek and Roman deities. When Alicia had difficulty with *transportation*, other words containing *trans* and *port* were studied.

As she has an artistic bent, Alicia was encouraged to draw diagrams and label them. For instance, when studying the parts of the brain, she copied a diagram of the brain and labeled each of the major parts. Seeing relationships among words was also stressed. When studying words from a selection, she has been encouraged to create a web, use semantic feature analysis, or use other graphic devices to help her understand how the new words were related.

Because Alicia's poor vocabulary was interfering with her comprehension of her science and history texts, an extra effort has been made to build a conceptual understanding of key terms before Alicia reads the selection. As a result, her understanding of the content-area material has been showing an encouraging improvement.

SUMMARY

Because they do not read as much as achieving readers, problem readers usually don't have as large a store of vocabulary. This deficit grows worse as low-achieving readers progress through the grades. However, because it reflects background knowledge and speeds the reading process, vocabulary is the single most important factor in comprehension. To foster comprehension, vocabulary instruction must be intensive. It must go beyond definitional knowledge to a contextual or conceptual status, should include multiple encounters, and should develop relationships.

Vocabulary instruction can be incidental or systematic or both. In the incidental approach, vocabulary is taught as needed. In the systematic approach, time is set aside for vocabulary instruction on a regular basis, so there is more focus on direct vocabulary development. Approximately 400 words can be thoroughly taught in a systematic program in a year's time.

Principles of teaching vocabulary include establishing goals, building on what students know, building depth and breadth of meaning, creating an interest in words, relating words to students' lives, and promoting independent word learning. Techniques for teaching words include conceptual teaching of key words and brainstorming techniques, such as the list–group–label and semantic mapping approaches. Graphic techniques include semantic mapping, pictorial maps and webs, semantic feature analysis, and the Venn diagram. Other vocabulary teaching techniques described in the chapter are possible sentences, predict-o-grams, word sorts, simulation, vocabulary self-selection strategy, and Text Talk. Wide reading and being read to were also discussed as ways of expanding vocabulary.

APPLICATION ACTIVITIES

1. Try using a semantic map, Venn diagram, and a semantic feature analysis on some words that you are learning. Evaluate the effectiveness of each of the devices. What are the strengths of each? What are the weaknesses?

2. Compile a bibliography of books or word games that you might use with current or future students.

3. Following the recommendations made in this chapter, plan a vocabulary-development lesson. If possible, teach the lesson and evaluate its effectiveness.

4. Read about FAME, an exemplary vocabulary program, at http://www.readingonline.org/articles/art_index.asp?HREF=/articles/curtis/index.html. How might you use elements of this program with struggling readers that you are teaching or plan to teach?

CHAPTER ELEVEN

BUILDING COMPREHENSION

USING WHAT YOU KNOW

In a sense, this chapter is the core of the text. For the most part, the previous chapters covered techniques for teaching the kinds of beginning reading and word-level skills and strategies that make comprehension possible or enhance it. Three of the chapters that follow will explore ways of applying comprehension skills and strategies to the content areas, using comprehension skills to study, and using writing to improve comprehension.

This chapter presents comprehension as an active process in which the reader constructs meaning. When you are reading, what steps do you take to foster comprehension? What are some of the reasons students might have difficulty comprehending? What steps might be taken to help them?

ANTICIPATION GUIDE

Read each of the following statements. Put a check under "Agree" or "Disagree" to show how you feel about each one. If possible, discuss your responses with classmates.

	AGREE	DISAGREE
1. A lack of background knowledge is the main cause of poor comprehension.	_____	_____
2. How much a reader comprehends depends mainly on the kinds of comprehension strategies that she uses.	_____	_____
3. Most low-achieving readers should have little difficulty learning highly effective comprehension strategies.	_____	_____
4. The fastest way to improve comprehension is to use challenging materials.	_____	_____
5. Generally speaking, comprehension deficiencies are easier to remediate than are decoding difficulties.	_____	_____

THEORIES OF COMPREHENSION

Comprehension was once seen as a passive process in which the reader's main mission was to grasp the author's message. Today comprehension is seen as an active process in which the reader plays a very active role, constructing meaning based on his or her cultural and experiential background, purpose for reading, and the overall setting. The most widely accepted description of this view of reading is schema theory. A related view of comprehension is expressed in the mental models theory of reading.

Schema Theory

The ad sitting on the kitchen table caught my eye. In a boldfaced head it was touting two books on farming. "Farm twice as effectively with half the effort!" A caption promised, "Farming made easy with these two expert guides."

The ad had been clipped by my wife, who intended to order the books. Since we don't even have a garden, much less a farm, I was puzzled by her interest in the books, until I read the rest of the ad.

What do you think the books will be about? What comes to your mind as you think about farming? My comprehension of the ad was based on my knowledge of farming. I pictured tall rows of corn, squealing pigs, bleating sheep, and a weathered barn. Even though I've never lived on a farm, I brought a fairly substantial background of knowledge to the ad. Had I grown up on a farm, I would have brought an even richer background to the ad. And that's what reading comprehension is. It isn't so much a matter of getting meaning from a selection, it's more a matter of bringing meaning to an ad, a story, or an article. Comprehension is an active constructive process that activates our schema. A **schema** is a generic concept, composed of our past experiences and our knowledge organized and filed away (Rumelhart, 1980). Schemata (the plural of schema) are based on our background of experience. We have schemata for persons, places, objects, and events. We have schemata for apple orchards, zoos, air pollution, and vacations. The richer our experiences, both real and vicarious, and the better organized they are, the richer and more useful are our schemata. In addition to our schemata based on life experiences, we also have a schemata for the way stories are told and information is presented. Our schema for stories tell us that a fable teaches a lesson, so when we read a fable we search for the moral. Our schema for informational text tells us that the main idea is often announced in the first sentence of a piece. Comprehension depends, to a large extent, on the adequacy of our schemata for world knowledge and our schemata for text. Schemata provide a framework for assimilating text information. If we are reading a mystery, our schema for mysteries tells us to look for clues. A schema helps us to make inferences. If there is a wolf in a fable, our schema for fictional wolves and fables alerts us to make the inference that the wolf will probably be intent on doing harm to someone. Schemata also help us to determine what is important in a selection. Our schema for animals might alert us to focus on their life processes. Schemata also help the reader to monitor for meaning. If a story does not proceed as expected or the information does not fit in with what the reader knows, the reader may decide to reread to make sure that he has read the passage properly (Westby, 1999). As Alexander and Jetton (2000) comment, "In essence, existing knowledge serves as the foundation of all future learning by guiding organization and representations, by serving as a basis of association with new information, and by coloring and filtering all new experiences" (p. 291).

> **Schema** (pl. schemata): abstract representation of knowledge organized and stored in memory. Schemata represent knowledge at various levels of abstraction. We can have a schema for baseball, growing tomatoes, liberty, and so on.

Comprehension is a flexible process. We may read something that conflicts with our ideas and concepts, so we must be prepared to modify our schema. And sometimes we have a schema but fail to activate it, or we activate the wrong schema, which is what I had done when I was reading the heading for the farming ad.

As I read further, I learned that the ad was about real estate farming, so I dropped my dirt farming schema and activated my schema about real estate farming. I realized that the word *farming* was being used in a figurative sense and referred to my wife's way of getting new clients. As a real estate agent, she has a farm, an area assigned to her by the broker for whom she works. Each month she sends ads to the homeowners in her farm, and occasionally she calls them. Now the ad made sense. However, had I not had indirect experience with real estate farming, I would not have had the proper schema to activate and so would have had some difficulty comprehending the ad.

Situation Models

> **Situation** or **mental model:** images or verbal representations of elements such as characters in a story or cause–effect relationships. Comprehension consists of constructing a mental model of events as they unfold.

Although schema theory provides an appropriate explanation of what happens when the reader encounters known ideas and events, it is not as satisfactory when new ideas or events are involved (McNamara, Miller, & Bransford, 1991). In a **situation** or **mental models** view of reading comprehension, readers create in their minds representations of what they have read, a representation of the situation described in the text. A situation model for fiction is the imaginary world that the reader has created and features the main characters, including their emotional or mental states, the setting, and the story situation (Graesser & Bertus, 1998). The reader keys in on the apparent main character and creates a mental model of the circumstances in which the character finds himself or herself and also keeps track of the who, when, where, and why of a story (Zwaan, Radvansky, Hilliard, & Curiel, 1998).

In expository text the situation model reflects the key information in the text and the way it is organized. The situation model for a science article would include a representation or mental sketch of the physical parts of the system, the steps in the system's process, relationships among the parts of the system and the steps in its operation, and the ways in which people might use the system.

Effective Readers

> Yuill and Oakhill (1991) found that 10 to 15 percent of the seven- to eight-year-old students in the schools where they conducted their research were adequate decoders but poor comprehenders. They failed to integrate information from text and so did not construct an adequate mental model.

Effective readers are active. Making connections is hindered if the reader is not reading actively and purposely. Successful comprehension depends in part on readers' ability to "allocate their limited attention efficiently and effectively to the most relevant pieces of information within the text and within memory" (van den Broek & Kremer, 2000, p. 7).

Another critical factor is the kind of comprehension that readers demand before moving from one sentence to the next. Good readers typically want to establish relationships between the current and previously read sentences, whereas poor readers may have a lower performance standard. They may be satisfied with simply comprehending the sentence they are currently reading or being able to pronounce all the words in the sentence. Standards of performance also depend on the goal for reading, context, motivation, interest, skill of the reader, and other factors.

One way of helping below-level readers improve their comprehension is to use causal questioning. Causal questions help readers focus on the text and raise their standard of comprehension. In causal questioning, students are asked "why" and "how" questions to help them make inferences. These questions can be asked during discussions or can be added to the text at locations where comprehension is likely to falter. This might be at points where important cause–effect relationships are being established, a reference is being made to a fact or event covered earlier in the text and that the reader may have forgotten, or where the syntax is especially difficult (van den Broek & Kremer, 2000).

Asking "why" questions helps integrate information from text with one's own background knowledge. After reading facts about skunks, students in grades 4 through 8 asked, "Why do owls prey on skunks?" and "Why are skunks awake from 3 a.m. until dawn?" (Wood, Pressley, & Winne, 1990). Asking these questions forced students to relate what they were learning to their general knowledge of the world. With this integration of world and text knowledge came a greater degree of understanding and increased retention.

CAUSES OF COMPREHENSION DIFFICULTY

Although schema deficiencies such as inadequate background and poorly developed concepts or failing to activate relevant schema can cause comprehension problems, numerous other factors can also impede understanding. As Perfetti, Marroni, and Foltz (1996) comment, "The possibilities for comprehension failure seem to be endless. Comprehension, after all, is a word that we use to cover a range of complex processes involved in language, any of which can fail" (p. 137). Reader factors that might cause a comprehension problem include lack of basic decoding skills, limited vocabulary, overuse of background knowledge or a lack or flexibility in considering new ideas, failure to read for meaning, and a lack of strategies or failure to use strategies appropriately (MacGinitie & MacGinitie, 1989; Manzo & Manzo, 1993; Maria, 1990; Pressley, 2000). These factors, of course, interact with the task, the text, the techniques being used, and the situation. A reader may be successful with some kinds of tasks and in some environments, but not with others. As you read this chapter, you will notice several instances where poor readers did just as well as good readers when given easier books. You will also notice instances in this and other chapters where poor readers performed as well as achieving readers because they employed specific strategies, a particularly effective technique was used to instruct them, or the learning situation was improved in some other way. Although reader factors are emphasized in this chapter, other major reasons for comprehension difficulties involve inappropriate texts, teaching techniques, and instructional settings.

CENTRAL ROLE OF METACOGNITION

In breakthrough research, cognitive scientists discovered that when above-average learners were given a memorization task, they spontaneously used a series of strategies such as clustering like items and using mnemonic devices (Resnick & Hall, 2003). Given the same tasks, below-average learners did not use strategies. However, when taught strategies, they learned them quickly and their performance improved significantly so that it was more in line with that of the above-average learners. However, when given the same tasks two weeks later, the below-average learners failed to use the strategies they had been taught. From this and hundreds of similar experiments, cognitive psychologists have come to the conclusion that strategies are teachable and learnable. But it isn't enough to just teach them. It is essential to teach the strategies thoroughly enough so that they are learned deeply and so that they generalize to a variety of contexts. It is also essential that students learn when, where, and under what conditions to apply strategies. This awareness of strategy use is known as metacognition. Through metacognition students take control of their learning. As cognitive psychologists Lauren Resnick and Megan Hall (2003) explain:

> Today, metacognition and self-regulatory capabilities are widely recognized as a key aspect of what it takes to be a good learner. Moreover, there is little argument that *metacognitive strategies are both learnable and teachable.* But effective strategy instruction depends on certain conditions. For example, students need to know how and why the strategies work. They need to understand that their mastery of the strategies is a developmental process and that sustained effort will produce increasing competence. They need scaffolding at first—in the form of modeling, direct teaching, and prompting—and then that scaffolding needs to be gradually removed so that students assume responsibility for using the strategies appropriately. In other words, the spontaneous and appropriate use of metacognitive strategies is teachable only if we broaden our view of teaching to include not just specific lessons, but a much broader socialization process into a learning orientation, or what Ted Sizer calls "habits of mind": a way of taking responsibility for what you know, what you can learn, and how you use it. (Principles of Learning, Forging the Link)

COMPREHENSION STRATEGIES

Strategic readers are able to use four sources of knowledge in a flexible way: (1) knowledge of a variety of appropriate strategies; (2) knowledge of one's self as a learner; (3) knowledge of the demands of the reading task, which makes it possible for the reader to select, use, monitor, and evaluate strategies; and (4) background or world knowledge (Palincsar, Winn, David, Synder, & Stevens, 1993). In addition, readers must be motivated to use their knowledge of strategies (Paris & Okra, 1986) and have confidence that they will work (Dole, Brown, & Trathen, 1996). Garner (1994) concluded that a lack of interest in the text and a lack of confidence in strategies will diminish the students' willingness to use strategies.

Intensive, step-by-step instruction is an essential element in strategy instruction. At the Benchmark School, a special school for disabled readers, students are taught one strategy at a time, with each strategy being taught, reviewed, and reinforced for nearly two months. A chart listing the steps of the strategy is displayed, and students discuss when, where, and how to use the strategy.

Strategy use is incorporated into the reading lesson. Along with building background and introducing new vocabulary, the teacher introduces or reviews a strategy that students are expected to use in their reading. After reading a selection, students discuss it and describe ways in which they used the strategy in their reading. After a strategy has been thoroughly learned, a new strategy is introduced and related to the old one so that students learn how to integrate strategies. To foster transfer, strategies are applied to a variety of materials and especially to the content areas (Gaskins, 1998).

Intensive step-by-step instruction is also the foundation of the Strategic Instructional Model (SIM) developed by the University of Kansas Center for Research on Learning and field-tested for more than twenty-five years. SIM is a highly effective approach that uses Learning Strategies Interventions to teach struggling readers. Using the strategies, students made dramatic gains. For instance, using a visualizing strategy students improved their scores on passage comprehension from 42 percent to 77 percent (Schumaker & Deshler, 1992). Similar gains were made when other strategies were used. In terms of overall performance, students taught through the SIM approach have made gains of as much as four to seven years (Fisher, Schumaker, & Deshler, 2002). Students made these gains when instruction was thorough and intensive, and they were given many opportunities for practice and application and received feedback on their performance. When instruction was minimal, gains were minimal.

> **Using Technology**
> Visit the University of Kansas Center for Research on Learning's web site at http://www.ku-crl.org/ downloads. Click on "Learning Strategies Descriptions" for more information.

Comprehension is also fostered when strategies are taught as part of a group, instead of individually. Because skilled reading involves knowing not only how to apply strategies, but when and where to apply them and which ones work best together, it is helpful to implement a procedure that involves several complementary strategies so that students can see how these work together (National Reading Panel, 2000).

> This text has organized strategies according to the cognitive processes that they demand. There is some overlapping. For instance, all strategies should involve some degree of monitoring.

There are dozens of comprehension strategies. However, they can be classified according to the cognitive operations that they incorporate: preparing, selecting and organizing, elaborating, rehearsing (studying), and monitoring. There are also affective or motivational strategies (Weinstein & Mayer, 1986).

Preparational Strategies

Preparational strategies are those that a reader uses to prepare for reading. These include activating prior knowledge, previewing a selection, predicting what might happen in a story or what information a nonfiction piece will convey, and setting a goal for reading.

Before reading a selection about acid rain, the reader asks herself or himself: "What do I know about acid rain?" If there is a prereading discussion, the teacher might activate prior knowledge. If they fail to activate prior knowledge, poor readers may not connect information in the text with what they already know. A good way to teach activating prior knowledge is through modeling. If you model the process, use a real-life example: a piece that you are reading. For instance, you might say, "I'm taking a class at night. And for homework I have to read about the brain. At first, I thought, 'This article is going to be really hard. I don't know anything about the brain.' But then I said to myself, 'Yes, I do. Let's see. I know the brain has two sides: the right hemisphere and the left hemisphere. I also know the brain has parts called *lobes* and billions of nerve cells called *neurons.*' "

> The **purpose** for reading is the information that you seek, a question to be answered, or a prediction to be assessed. A **goal** is your objective for reading. Are you reading for pleasure, to follow a set of directions, or to prepare for a test?

Setting Purpose and Goal. The **purpose** for reading might grow out of activating prior knowledge. For instance, in the example above, your activation of prior knowledge may cause you to realize that you know that the hemispheres of the brain are connected, but you aren't quite sure how they are connected. Your purpose (question to be answered) in reading might then be to find out how the hemispheres of the brain are connected. Readers also need to set a **goal** for reading. If you are reading just for your own information, your reading may be casual. If you are preparing for a test, then you would adopt a study style of reading. Your goal would be to both understand and retain what you had read. Model for students how you might set a purpose and a goal for your reading.

> Low-progress readers often lack a purpose or clear goal in reading. Discuss goals and purposes with students. Ask: "Why are you reading this? What do you hope to find out?"

Previewing. Previewing is a natural accompaniment of predicting. In previewing, the reader spends a minute or two reading the title, headings, the first paragraph or introduction, the last paragraph or summary, and scanning any illustrations, charts, graphs, or tables that accompany the piece. As readers preview, they gain an overview of the piece they are about to read. They should also activate schema, make predictions, set a purpose for reading, and create a plan for reading the piece. Should it be skimmed? Should it be read slowly and carefully? Should it be read section by section? Should it be read as a whole? A good preview can function as a framework for organizing the main ideas in a selection or as "a kind of a blueprint for constructing a mental model" (Gunning, 1996, p. 198).

> Making **predictions** depends on the students' background. Students have a more difficult time if they are reading about an unfamiliar topic, because they have little basis for predicting.

Predicting. A highly popular strategy, **predicting** forces an activation of prior knowledge. Using a prediction strategy, a reader makes an educated guess about the course of events in a story or the kind of information that will be contained in a nonfiction piece. We make predictions on the basis of what we know. Predictions can also determine our purpose in reading. We may read the selection to compare our predictions with what actually happens. It is important to use this strategy flexibly. Poor readers sometimes fail to modify their beliefs when they read information that contradicts these beliefs. These students need to be prepared to modify predictions based on information contained in the text.

Selection/Organizational Strategies

When vocabulary in a selection is difficult, as it so often is for poor readers, they must focus on decoding and process smaller units of text, perhaps only two- or three-word segments (Kletzien, 1991). Caught up in looking at individual words and details, they may fail to grasp main ideas. Selection/organizational strategies include deriving a main idea, selecting relevant details, organizing details, summarizing, and creating graphic organizers. All of these strategies involve integrating textual information in some way. Of these, deriving the main idea of a selection is the most essential. The main idea provides the underlying pattern for organizing a passage's vital details. Being able to derive main ideas is a prerequisite for summarizing, note taking, outlining, and creating graphic organizers.

> **Main idea:** what a piece of writing is all about—the gist or summary statement of the passage.

Deriving Main Ideas. Definitions of main idea vary as do the activities designed to promote grasping the main idea (Baumann, 1986). The **main idea** can be best thought of as a summary statement that subsumes all of the details in a piece of writing. The main idea of a paragraph would include what all the ideas in a paragraph are about.

In essence, constructing the main idea is a classification exercise. The reader must note similarities among the details in a paragraph and then must choose the sentence that tells about all the others (if the main idea is stated) or construct a statement that includes all the details in a paragraph (if the main idea is not stated). A good way to initiate main-idea instruction is to have students classify items, ideas, and whole sentences. For instance, young children could be asked to sort objects in a classroom and give those sorted objects a name. Students might sort toys or tools. Later, they can categorize words, indicating which word tells about all the others: *lions, elephants, whales, animals, dogs.* To foster categorizing, have students play "Twenty Questions." The student tells in which category the mystery item falls. Categories can vary depending on the age of the students. Possible categories include animals, sports, countries, food, people, sports, or hobbies. The person(s) trying to guess the identity of the item ask a series of questions, up to twenty. For the category people, the person might ask: Is it a man? Is he living now? Is he famous?

Once students have grasped the idea of categorizing, they can classify the sentences in a paragraph and tell which sentence tells about all the others. In the following paragraph, for example, students should be able to tell that the first sentence states the main idea.

> Soybeans can be eaten in many different ways. Soybean flour and oil are used to make pancakes, cookies, candy bars, soups, and many other foods. Soybean flour is used to make foods that look and taste like meat. Soybeans can also be used to make a sauce that adds flavor to foods.

After students have become adept at picking the sentence that "tells about all the others," omit the main-idea sentence from the paragraph and have them generate a main-idea statement. This is a far more difficult task, so provide guidance as needed. Also reinforce the concept of main idea by helping students use titles, topic sentences, headings, and subheads as clues to main ideas in a text. In a study by K. K. Taylor (1986), many students, but especially the poor readers, failed to use titles and topic sentences to derive main ideas in selections, even though both contained the main idea of the passage.

Eventually, students should derive main ideas from real paragraphs in real books. Start with brief paragraphs that have a clearly stated main idea in the first sentence. Then move into longer selections and include ones in which the main-idea sentence appears in the middle or end of a paragraph. Although the main-idea or topic sentence can appear anywhere in a paragraph or may even be implied, poor readers tend to select the first sentence as the topic sentence (Gold & Fleischer, 1986).

> Understanding main ideas is partly developmental. Over the years the ability to select a main idea improves. In addition, students' ideas of what is important in a selection change as they mature. Younger students select consequences of actions as being the most important element in a story, whereas older students choose the main character's goals (Stein & Glenn, 1979).

Drawing from children's books or textbooks, choose well-written paragraphs that contain topic sentences that appear in various places in the paragraph. Social studies texts might be a good source. Nearly half of the paragraphs in social studies texts contain topic sentences. However, these appear as the first sentence of the paragraph only 27 percent of the time (Baumann & Serra, 1984). As students choose topic sentences, have them verify their selections by explaining how other sentences in the paragraph support the main idea.

Apply the concept of main idea to longer pieces of writing. In a well-written science or social studies text or informational children's book, point out main ideas. Discuss the fact that just as paragraphs have main ideas, so, too, do sections of text. Show how headings often indicate the main idea of a whole section.

Implied Main Ideas. Adapting the strategies used by expert readers (Afflerbach, 1990), teach students to create main ideas by implementing the following steps:

1. Use textual cues (title, heading, major illustrations, introductory sentence) to construct a tentative main-idea statement.
2. As you read the passage, judge whether or not the sentences support the tentative main idea. If not, revise the main-idea statement.
3. After reading, judge whether all or most of the sentences support the main idea. (Often, in well-written prose, passages will contain a sentence or two that is kind of an aside, a detail that may be interesting and related to the overall topic but that does not support the main idea). If most of the sentences do not support the main idea, then see what all or most of the sentences have in common, and construct a main-idea statement that tells what they are about.

Begin with brief passages and gradually introduce longer segments of text. If possible, have students apply the steps to texts that they use in their content-area subjects. Also use writing to reinforce the concept of main ideas. Help students develop topic sentences into well-constructed paragraphs. You might use paragraph frames similar to the ones in Figure 11.1 to assist students. Once students have achieved a basic understanding of topic sentences, encourage them to compose and develop their own.

Summarizing. Summarizing is the most effective comprehension strategy of all (Pressley, Johnson, Symons, McGoldrich, & Kurita, 1989). Summarizing is a method for both improving and checking comprehension. Because it involves selecting, organizing, and restating the main details in a passage, summarizing enhances understanding and promotes retention. It also forces a self-evaluation of comprehension. If you have not comprehended a selection adequately, you will not be able to summarize it.

Summarizing is difficult. In addition to selecting the most important information, the summarizer must condense information by combining and synthesizing ideas.

Summarizing should not be confused with retelling. In a retelling, students may tell all that they know or all that they can remember. In a summary, only the important details are retold, and they are related in condensed form (Maria, 1990). One of the reasons summaries are difficult to compose is that they involve two processes: selection of important details and reduction or condensation of these details (Hidi & Anderson, 1986).

FIGURE 11.1 Paragraph Frames

FRAME 1

Some fish have names that tell what they look like.
The glassfish _____.
The pipefish _____.
The parrotfish _____.
These fish have names that really fit.

FRAME 2

Computers are one of our most useful tools. Computers are used

_____.
Computers also _____.
Computers can even _____.
Now we wonder how we ever got along without computers.

FRAME 3

My favorite day of the week is _____.
For one thing, _____.
For another, _____.
Best of all, _____.
It's too bad there aren't two _____ in every week.

Teaching Summarizing.   Although summarizing demands adequate comprehension, writing a summary involves more than just understanding a passage. It also entails using specialized written-language skills (Taylor, 1986). Because written summaries involve complex writing skills, instruction might be initiated with oral summaries. Although oral summaries are more exacting than retellings, retellings can provide solid preparation for summarizing. To make retellings more valuable, guide students so they emphasize essential details. Through careful questioning, help them highlight the most important information. Ask questions such as: "What was the most important thing that Marisol did? What three things happened to James?"

The strategies used to grasp main ideas can also form a basis for summarizing. Surveying a text provides an overview of the main ideas in a selection. Predicting also tends to make the reader focus on major events and ideas.

Use naturally occurring occasions to model summarizing. For instance, after explaining that you are summarizing, sum up a demonstration, lecture, or discussion. Summarize the main events in a story or the major details in a science or social studies article. As students catch onto the idea, ask them to summarize discussions, a current event, or a section from a story or article.

> One practical way to get students to summarize is to provide limited space for the summaries (Stahl, 2004).

Some students believe that summaries should feature the most interesting or most difficult details in a selection or sentences from the selection that are richly detailed (Taylor, 1986; Winograd, 1984). Stress the fact that summaries should feature the most essential details.

A LESSON IN WRITING SUMMARIES

Once students have some familiarity with oral summaries, present a series of steps that could be helpful in composing a written summary. As adapted from Brown and Day (1983), these include:

Step 1: Explain and show. Explain the importance and also provide several examples of summaries showing that they are a condensation of the major details in a selection.

Step 2: Find the main idea. Show students how to use the title or headings and topic sentence to get a sense of the main idea of the selection.

Step 3: Select or create a topic sentence. Show students how to choose the topic sentence or create one if the main idea is implied.

Step 4: Select details. Show students how to select essential details.

Step 5: Paraphrase, condense. Show students how to paraphrase and condense essential ideas. This involves explaining how to combine and collapse details into a more general statement. For instance, the sentence, "Maria read her science chapter and answered the questions at the end, read twenty pages of the novel the class was reading, and then worked on her social studies project" could be combined and condensed into: "Maria did her homework."

Step 6: Compare. Compare the summary with the original. Ask: Does it contain all the important information? Is the information correct?

Step 7: Check for clarity. Concerned more about content than expression, students may compose a summary that is complete and correct but poorly written. The student should go back over the summary, asking: "How does the summary sound? Is it clear? Is it easy to understand?"

To aid students in creating summaries, provide frames like those shown in Figure 11.2. Gradually wean the students from the frames so that they take over full responsibility for writing summaries. Start with brief, well-constructed passages, so that the frames will be easier to complete. However, the passage that is being summarized should have meaning to the students. It might be a passage from their science or social studies text or a trade book that explores a topic of interest. As they learn the how and what of summarizing, they should also be learning the why: summarizing will help them understand and remember information that is important to them in school or out-of-school activities. Summarizing passages from a section on which students will soon be tested is an excellent activity. Students are more likely to learn and use strategies for which they can see a genuine value (Schunk & Rice, 1987).

Utilizing Technology
The Graphic Organizer at http://www.graphic.org/index .html provides a wealth of information about these text organizers. The site features a wide variety of downloadable GO templates.

Graphic Organizers as Summaries. Graphic organizers can also be used to summarize text. Because they do not necessitate writing a paragraph, graphic organizers are easier to create than traditional summaries. Graphic organizers also do a better job of highlighting important information and showing relationships among ideas. Graphic organizers can be written in their own right or may be used in preparation for composing a written summary. Graphic organizers that might be used to create summaries include semantic maps and Venn diagrams, which were introduced in Chapter 10. A sample semantic map summarizing a brief

FIGURE 11.2   Frames for Summaries

We need fats in our diets. Fats _____. Fats also give us _____. Fats also help _____.

There are two kinds of fats. Solid fats can be found in _____. Solid fats are made from _____. Liquid fats are found in _____. Liquid fats are made from _____.

Fats can be saturated or unsaturated. Saturated fats are found mostly in _____. Unsaturated fats can be divided into two groups, _____ and _____. Unsaturated fats usually come from _____. Unsaturated fats are healthier because _____.

From *Fats,* by R. Nottridge. Minneapolis, MN: Carolrhoda Book, 1993.

The Phoenicians worked at many different trades and occupations.
1. _____.
2. _____.
3. _____.
4. _____.

From *The Phoenicians,* by P. Odik. Englewood Cliffs, NJ: Silver Burdett, 1989.

text on fruit is displayed in Figure 11.3. For additional examples of graphic organizers used with content-area texts, see Chapter 12.

Graphic organizers are only as effective as the manner in which they are made a part of the lesson. As a minimum, Merkley and Jefferies (2001) suggest following these steps when using graphic organizers:

- verbalize relationships (links) expressed by the visual
- provide opportunity for student input
- connect new information to past learning
- make reference to upcoming text
- seize opportunities to reinforce decoding and structural analysis (p. 352)

Summarizing with Somebody Wanted But So

Somebody Wanted But So is a structured way to help students summarize a narrative piece (Beers, 2003). The structure is simple. Students make four columns, one for each word. Under the **Somebody** column, the main character's name is placed. Under the **Wanted** column, students list what the main character wanted to do. This is generally a statement of the main character's goal in the story. **But** is a statement of the conflict or the problem that the main character ran into. **So** is the resolution of the outcome of the main character's efforts to achieve a goal. In some instances, students might be able to sum up the whole story with one set of statements. In other instances, they might just note a part of the story and will need to add to it. Students can add a **then** and fill in another set of **Somebody Wanted But So** statements. If there is more than one main character, students can write

FIGURE 11.3   Semantic Map

From *We Love Fruit,* by F. Robinson. Chicago, IL: Children's Press, 1992.

more than one set of statements. Initially, students might write a series of Somebody Wanted But So statements connected by *then's* and *and's*. Ultimately, they should be writing one general statement.

Elaboration Strategies

Elaboration strategies are built on preparational and organizational strategies. Information cannot be transformed, evaluated, or applied unless it has first been understood.

Using elaboration strategies, the reader transforms, judges, applies, or adds to information from the text in some way. Through elaboration, the reader may draw an inference, create a mental image, or evaluate the material that was read. Involving a higher level of comprehension and a deeper level of processing, elaboration typically improves comprehension by 50 percent (Linden & Wittrock, 1981).

Inferences.   Inferring is a main elaboration at all reading levels. Much of the information that a reader derives from text is the result of

Skilled readers are better at making inferences. Because making inferences involves additional processing and a fuller representation of the meaning of the text, this leads to better overall retention of the materials read (Yuill & Oakhill, 1991).

Possible reason for making fewer inferences include not having the relevant knowledge to make inferences, having relevant knowledge but not being able to access it, or having relevant knowledge but not realizing that it should be integrated with information from the text.

constructing inferences. Readers must go beyond what is stated explicitly, "to link up ideas in the text and to bring their general knowledge to bear on their understanding of it" (Oakhill & Yuill, 1996, p. 69). If we read "the batter struck out in the ninth inning and the game is over," we infer that baseball was being played, the batter was on the losing side, and there were two outs when the batter stepped up to the plate. The author does not have to tell us this. **Inferences** are the implied details, judgments, or conclusions that readers construct as they read. Inferences are based on readers' schemata and/or information contained in the text.

As might be expected, all readers, but especially lower-achieving ones, have difficulty making inferences (National Assessment of Educational Progress, 1986; Holmes, 1987; Wilson, 1979; Oakhill & Yuill, 1996). Why do low-achieving readers have difficulty with inferential questions? Since answering inferential questions requires combining information in the text with background or prior knowledge, having an impoverished background is one possible cause. Ironically, McCormick (1992) found that overreliance on background knowledge was a major cause of erroneous responses. In these instances readers rejected or ignored text information and used personal background knowledge to respond to questions. McCormick explains, "It may be that low-achieving students have had less access to text information because of word recognition difficulties and over time have developed a pervasive strategy of simple guessing at possible responses based on knowledge already stored in their schemata" (p. 73). Other major errors included answers that were too specific or that were only marginally related to the question. In the first instance, students were distracted by irrelevant information. In the second instance, they failed to consider all the information in the selection, focusing instead on one specific detail, rather than considering several details.

As Wilson (1979) explains, poor readers tend to give "intuitive" answers, responses rooted in personal knowledge rather than in the text. In a similar vein, Phillips (1988) and Kimmel and MacGinitie (1984) found that low-performing readers used a kind of preservative strategy in which they held firmly to an erroneous response despite conflicting evidence.

Besides providing probes and prompts, the teacher may provide additional needed information that enables students to revise or create a new concept (Cairney, 1990).

On the other hand, Oakhill & Yuill (1996) concluded that poor readers find it difficult to access relevant knowledge and integrate it with the information in the text. Poor readers may also emphasize literal comprehension and may not realize that they can and should make inferences.

Techniques designed to improve the inferencing ability of low-achieving readers need to compensate for overreliance on prior knowledge, inadequate use of text, and lack of flexibility in reasoning about what one reads. They also need to build students' confidence in their ability to draw inferences from text.

One approach that does an excellent job of incorporating these factors is Hansen and Pearson's (1982) prior knowledge prediction strategy. Although it is relatively simple to apply and teach, the strategy is powerful. After being taught the strategy, low-progress readers did just as well with inferences as did higher-achieving readers.

■ ■ ■ ■ ■ ▬▬▬▬▬▬▬▬▬▬▬▬▬▬▬▬▬▬▬▬▬▬▬▬▬▬▬

PRIOR KNOWLEDGE PREDICTION STRATEGY LESSON

Step 1: Creating questions. As with a number of successful techniques, the first step in teaching the technique is to analyze the selection to be read for two or three central ideas. For each central idea, create two questions. The first question, which is designed to activate the appropriate schema, asks students about any experiences that they may have had that might be similar to the central idea. For instance, if the central idea is "A best friend moved away," then you would create a question similar to the following: "Have you ever lost a friend because your friend moved away or you moved away?" Then you would ask a prediction question that is related to the schema activation question and the central idea. "In the story we're about to read, Jeremy's best friend is moving away. What do you think Jeremy will do?"

Step 2: Prereading discussion. In the prereading discussion, the teacher asks the schema-activation question and then the prediction question. The discussion is critical. Low-achieving readers often have difficulty activating appropriate schema. During the discussion, a student might think, "I've never had a friend move away" and so is unable to activate rele-

> Through discussions, students reveal their thought processes and help each other to learn.

vant schema. But then a student explains how he felt when his uncle and aunt moved away. He explains that they were young and had no children of their own, and had taken him many places. The discussion reminds the first youngster of how she felt when her cousin moved, so she is then able to activate the appropriate moving-away schema.

Step 3: Silent reading of selection. Students read to assess their predictions.

Step 4: Postreading discussion. The postreading discussion is also an important part of the technique. After discussing students' predictions, ask related inference questions. All too often, questions asked of low-achieving readers are restricted to the literal level. Or the higher-level questions that they are asked simply require an opinion. Inference questions should involve using both the text and prior knowledge: "How did Maria feel when her friend moved away?"

Step 5: Verifying inferences. Since low-achieving readers overrely on prior experience, it is important that they be asked to justify inferences. If a student infers that the main character in the story, Maria, is sad because her friend moved away, then the student should be asked to supply evidence from the selection that indicates Maria is sad.

Importance of Modeling. Research by McCormick (1992) suggests that low-achieving readers may have limited experience drawing inferences. It is essential that the process be explained and modeled, with lots of opportunities for guided practice and application. You might also follow a "gradual release of responsibility" model (Pearson & Gallagher, 1983). Using brief passages, you draw an inference and have students find the supporting evidence. Once they have become proficient at locating evidence, switch roles. You supply the evidence and have them draw the inferences. Ultimately, students both draw the inferences and supply the evidence. Begin with short selections and gradually work into longer ones.

Yuill and Oakhill (1991) improved the inferential comprehension of less skilled readers by modeling the process of using cues to make inferences and providing practice. For instance, after showing students how to make inferences using cues from single words, the students practiced making inferences about the sentence, "Sleepy Tom was late for school again." With the teacher's help, they inferred that Tom was a boy because Tom is a boy's name and that Tom was a student. Otherwise, he would have been called "mister." From the word *sleepy,* they inferred that he was late because he overslept and from the word *again* they inferred that this was not the first time he had been late. After working with single words in the context of sentences, the students made inferences from larger blocks of texts.

Students were then introduced to question generation. After being introduced to question words such as *who, what, where, when,* and *why,* they learned to create questions. Half of the students then created questions while the other half used their inference training to answer the student-generated queries. Student were also taught to use the question, "What happened next?", to make predictions. This was used in connection with macro-cloze. In macro-cloze a whole sentence is omitted and students predict what the missing sentence said. After students made their predictions, the omitted sentence is revealed.

> Kerry wanted cereal for breakfast.
> Hidden sentence.
> So she had to have toast instead.

> The hidden sentence was "There wasn't any left."

After relatively brief periods of instruction and practice, the less skilled readers were operating at almost the same level as their more skilled counterparts.

> **Responsive elaboration:** the teacher analyzes a student's answer to determine what reasoning processes the student is using and then, building on that analysis, elaborates the student's response.

Responsive Elaboration. Because faulty reasoning or use of inappropriate reasoning strategies is the cause of many erroneous inferences, a technique known as responsive elaboration may help students reason their way to credible inferences (Duffy & Roehler, 1987). As its name suggests, **responsive elaboration** is a teacher prompt or an elaboration made in response to a student's erroneous answer. Focus is on the process rather than the answer. Analyze the student's response and try to figure out how she or he arrived at that answer. Ask yourself, "What strategies or thought processes did the student use? What can I do to correct the process?" Here is an example of how a teacher used responsive elaboration to restructure an inference that was based on inadequate information.

Student (making erroneous inference):   Jake was a coward.

Teacher: What leads you to believe that Jake was cowardly?

Student: The story says he was so filled with fear when he saw the snake that his knees were knocking. He felt like running away even though the snake was about to bite his baby sister.

Teacher: Did he run away?

Student: Yes.

Teacher: What did he do before he ran?

Student: He picked up a big rock and threw it on the snake.

Teacher: What else did he do?

Student: He grabbed his baby sister, and then he ran.

Teacher: Would that have taken courage? The snake might still have been alive.

Student: Yes. I suppose so.

Teacher: All of us have fears, but we show courage when we overcome our fears.

QAR.   Although many low-achieving readers overrely on prior knowledge, some are textbound and respond to inferential questions with, "I can't find the answer in the book." This is especially true of younger low-achieving readers. In addition to explaining the value and purpose of inferential questions, you might try using QAR (question–answer relationship). To show students that not all answers are in the book, QAR was created to help students locate the source of answers, whether they be literal or inferential (Raphael, 1984, 1986). QAR activities are designed to help students determine whether an answer is

> To help students become more aware of the sources for answers to questions, have them create questions about a passage that are "right there," involve "putting it together," or are "on my own" or "writer and me."

1. Right there: Answer is contained within a single sentence in the text.
2. Putting it together: It is necessary to put together information from several sentences to obtain an answer.
3. On my own: The answer is part of the student's prior knowledge.
4. Writer and me: The reader must combine personal knowledge with information from the text to construct an inference.

To introduce QAR, write a paragraph similar to the following on the board. The selection and accompanying questions are designed to demonstrate the various sources of answers.

> With the sun in her eyes, the driver pulled over into the highway's slow lane and eased up on the gas. Glancing up at the large metal sign overhead, she was relieved to see that she had only two exits to go. She had started driving early in the morning, just before six a.m. Now it was nearly six p.m.

To show students where answers to questions can be found, ask questions of the following type:

- Where was the driver? (right there)
- How much farther did she have to go? (right there)
- How long had she been driving? (putting it together)
- In which direction was she heading? (writer and me)
- How do you feel after you've been in a car for a long time? (on my own)

As you discuss answers to the questions and the sources of the answers, emphasize the fact that answers are not always stated directly. During subsequent sessions, ask varied questions: some that can be answered with information in the text and some that require using background information and the text or just background knowledge. Along with discussing answers, also identify sources of answers.

Making Inferences with It Says–I Say–And So.   It Says–I Say–And So is a series of scaffolding statements that foster the drawing of inferences (Beers, 2003). As they are answering questions, students look to see what the text says (It), and then what they have to say about that (I Say), and what happens when you put what the text says and what I say together (And So). Students make four columns as shown in the chart below. Under the Question column, students write the question to be answered. Under **It says,** they write information from the text that will help answer the question. Under **I say** students think about what they know about the text information and write that. Under the **And So** column, they combine text and personal information and make an inference or draw a conclusion. Using responses to the items, students go through the process of making an inference step by step. When responses are placed on the board and discussed, students have the opportunity to see how their peers make inferences.

Question	It Says	I Say	And So
Read the question.	Find information from the text that will help you answer the question.	Think about what you know about that information.	Combine what the text says with what you know to come up with an answer.
How did the boy feel at the end of the story?	Johnathan wiped away a tear as the van pulled away. He would miss his best friend. But then he thought of the new home where he would have his very own room and a smile broke across his face.	You cry when you are sad. And you get sad when you lose your best friend. But getting your own room can make you happy. I remember how I felt when my brother moved out and I got his room.	And so that's why I think Johnathan had mixed feelings. He was sad and happy at the same time.

Start off with fairly simple questions, ones that have just one piece of information, under **It Says.** Gradually move to questions that have a number of items under **It Says** so that students need to record and consider several details.

Imaging is the process of creating visual, auditory, or other representations as one reads, listens, views, or thinks. While the verbal coding system might analyze and organize information in the form of words, the imaging system generates mental images (Sadowski, Goetz, & Fritz, 1993).

Imaging.   What might be some ways of enhancing low-achieving readers' comprehension of the following passage?

Imagine it is 140 million years ago. The oceans are warm and palmlike trees grow everywhere. Dinosaurs of all shapes and sizes roam the earth. Some of the dinosaurs are no bigger than a chicken. Others are taller than a six-story building. Some have horns and spikes. Others have duck bills and bird feet. There are no people yet. It is the middle of the Mesozoic (mez-uh-ZO-ik) Era. (McMullen, 1989, pp. 6–7)

One technique is to use imaging. In **imaging,** students create visual, auditory, or other sensory-based mental representations of characters, objects, events, or other elements in a selection. Although it is a

> When they used visualizing, low-achieving readers were better able to understand what they read and to integrate new and old information (Pressley, 1977). Poor readers don't use imaging as much as good readers, but show significant improvement after instruction (Gambrell & Bales, 1986). Images can call forth ideas and words, and words and ideas can evoke images. For instance, we can create images for justice and democracy and other abstract concepts (Sadowski, Goetz, & Fritz, 1993).

neglected technique, imaging is a powerful, easy-to-teach, easy-to-learn device that students enjoy applying. Research suggests that it increases comprehension (Sadowski, 1983, 1985) and improves comprehension monitoring (Gambrell & Bales, 1986). Students who create mental images are better at understanding what they read and detecting inconsistencies while reading than those who don't.

One advantage of imaging is that it involves the students in their texts so that they are more likely to engage in deep processing. Another is that it sparks more participation in students who are typically passive. In her use of imaging, Maria (1990) reports that many of the students who were most active in discussing their images were those who normally had little to say in class. A third advantage of imaging is that it will be a new technique for many students and so should prove to be motivational. Oakhill and Yuill (1996) found that imaging was a powerful strategy for poor comprehenders. Imaging helped them to integrate information in text in a way that they would not normally use. It was particularly helpful for inferential questions, especially when they had to infer descriptive information that was not stated explicitly. Imaging may help less able readers integrate text and use working memory more effectively insofar as it provides them with a strategy for integrating information in text. Imaging may also help poor comprehenders overcome some of the limitations they have in processing information by providing them with a more economical way of representing information from text. However, imaging may not be helpful for lengthy passages, because it may be too difficult to sustain (Yuill & Oakhill, 1991).

Imaging seems to work best with students who are eight years of age or older. Students do not seem to be able to generate images until they are at least eight (Pressley, 1977).

As with any other strategy, students should learn when, where, and why to use imaging as well as how to use it. As part of your instruction, explain why imaging is a useful strategy. Also point out that it works better with some kinds of writing than with others. Consider individual differences in the use of imagery. Some students will undoubtedly find imagery difficult to use, so you may stress the use of nonvisual strategies with them.

■ ■ ■ ■ ■ ▬▬▬▬▬▬▬▬▬▬▬▬▬▬▬▬▬▬▬▬▬▬▬▬▬▬▬▬▬▬▬▬▬▬

IMAGING LESSON

Step 1: Introducing imaging. To introduce imaging, explain what it is and why it is a valuable comprehension strategy. Then model the process. Show how you would create images of a concrete passage.

Step 2: Focusing. Encourage students to relax and clear their minds of distracting thoughts. Have students close their eyes and listen to a brief, concrete passage, forming pictures in their minds as they do. Direct students to draw pictures of their images. This fixes the images so that when the class discusses them, individual students don't forget what their original images looked like (Maria, 1990). In the beginning, you might use single sentences or very brief paragraphs. Once students have begun to grasp the idea of imaging, try using longer pieces.

Step 3: Discussing. Discuss students' images, but before doing so, talk over the fact that because each of us is a different person and has different experiences, each of us will create individual images. To show students how different people create different

(Continued)

images, compare the illustrations in different versions of classic stories, or compare illustrations of similar events or scenes from several content-area texts. When discussing students' images, use probing questions to get more detail and also to focus on important ideas. As with other activities, students can get bogged down in unimportant details.

Step 4: Guided practice. After students have caught onto the idea of creating images, ask them to create pictures of text in their minds as they read. Start off with brief concrete text and then move into longer pieces, including content-area texts. After students have read the passage and sketched their images, ask questions that focus on the main content. Also pose questions that help them to create fuller images. If the passage lends itself to it, ask questions that go beyond the visual. In addition to asking, "What did you see?," ask: "What did you hear? What did you feel? What did you touch? What did you smell?" If students have difficulty creating an image or have left out elements, encourage them to reread the passage and create an image of the piece, adding elements to their mental representation. One interesting activity is to visualize the main character of a story or a setting and then compare one's mental picture with that created by the illustrator.

Step 5: Review and application. After introducing imaging, continue to review and reinforce it. Suggest its use where it might be especially appropriate: imaging scenes, characters, or events in fiction; imaging events or scenes in history, places in geography, and processes in science. Encourage students to use drawings, even if they consist mainly of stick figures. Also encourage the creation of charts, diagrams, geographic and semantic maps, and other graphic displays to organize information that they have read. Periodically, make imaging a part of prereading activities, assignments, and discussions, so that it becomes second-nature to students.

Step 6: Assessment. Observe students as they create images. Note how well they can do the following:

- Create images from narrative text.
- Create images from informational text.
- Create images that convey the gist or main idea of a selection.
- Create images that include essential details.
- Create images that include inferred details.

REVIEWING THE STRATEGY
Learning a strategy may take a month or more. In subsequent lessons, review and extend the strategy. To review the strategy, ask the following kinds of questions.

- What strategy are we learning to use? (imaging)
- How does this strategy help us? (Helps us to picture what we have read. Helps us to remember what we read.)
- When do we use this strategy? (With fiction or informational text that can be pictured.)
- How do we use this strategy? (Review the steps of using the strategy.) Also ask students to tell about instances when they used the strategy on their own (Scott, 1998).

(This same format may be used for reviewing all of the strategies presented in this and other chapters.)

Metacognitive Awareness

Although Anna, a fifth-grader, spent thirty minutes poring over an article on the formation of rocks, she had little to show for her effort. When asked questions about the article, she was unable to respond. As she was reading, Anna wasn't really getting much meaning from the text. She didn't understand what she was reading. And she didn't realize that she didn't understand. She lacked metacognitive awareness.

All of us have difficulty with comprehension from time to time, but usually we are aware of the difficulty. We realize that our attention was diverted, and don't have the slightest idea of what we just read. Or we realize that we have gotten lost in a tangle of legalese when reading a contract. Or we don't understand the steps for installing a new piece of software. Realizing that we are not comprehending, we take corrective action: reread, get help with difficult terms, or examine a clarifying illustration. However, since they often don't realize that they are not understanding, low-achieving readers fail to take steps to repair faulty comprehension.

Metacognitive awareness is the ability to think about our cognitive processes. It is knowledge about "ourselves, the tasks we face, and the strategies we employ" (Garner, 1994, p. 717). According to Paris (1991), "As children gain experience with a task such as reading, they begin to understand their own abilities, the characteristics of a text that make reading easy or difficult, and the strategies that can be employed to aid comprehension" (p. 34).

> **Metacognitive awareness:** being conscious of one's thought processes.

In addition to being less likely to detect a comprehension problem, low-achieving readers are also less likely to choose a corrective strategy even when they do detect a problem. While achieving readers report rereading a confusing passage, poor readers are more likely to say that they would "skip it" (Garner & Reis, 1981). The four crucial areas in metacognition are (1) knowing oneself as a learner; (2) regulating; (3) monitoring; and (4) correcting (Baker & Brown, 1984; Garner, 1994).

Knowing Oneself as a Learner. Generally a student knows what his background of knowledge is and knows himself as a reader. He may realize that he is a fast, global reader with a poor background in science. Self-knowledge, however, can be faulty. A student may believe that he knows all there is to know about snakes and so fails to read with an open mind an article that contradicts his deeply held but erroneous concepts. Or the student may believe that he is dumb and that he will not learn new material no matter how hard he tries (Paris, 1991). Beaten before he starts because of a poor self-concept, the student may not exert a wholehearted effort and may not apply the strategies that he has mastered. Helping low-achieving readers know themselves as learners often involves correcting false notions and building confidence.

Regulating. Regulating means that the student exercises cognitive control over her learning. The student knows strategies and knows how, when, and where to use them. The student also knows what to read to fulfill a specific purpose. For instance, in studying for a science quiz, the student with a fast, global style will shift to a slower-paced analytic approach when she realizes that the quiz will be factual. She may choose to use a specialized study technique or simply take notes or engage in some form of self-questioning. She may focus on the textbook sections that describe areas that the teacher emphasized in class.

> **Monitoring:** mental checking of one's cognitive processes. In reading, monitoring is an awareness of whether a passage is making sense or not.

Monitoring. **Monitoring** means that the student evaluates her understanding. After each section, she may attempt to summarize what she has read or engage in self-testing by asking herself questions about what she has read. If a section doesn't make sense, she may reread it, look up difficult words in the glossary, refer to illustrations, or ask a friend, parent, or teacher for help. Imaging or summarizing can be

Poor readers' difficulty with monitoring may be caused by material that is too difficult. If they spend too much time grappling with unknown words, they may become accustomed to reading "nonsense" and do not develop the habit of monitoring for meaning.

another form of monitoring for meaning. If a student has difficulty creating images or summaries, it may be due to faulty comprehension.

Poor monitoring may also be related to poor comprehension strategies and the material's level of difficulty. In several experiments, inconsistencies and nonsense words were inserted in selections read by good and poor readers in the fourth grade. When low-achieving readers' understanding and recall of a passage was inadequate because the text was apparently too difficult, they noted fewer inconsistencies or nonsense words in the text (Paris & Myers, 1981). However, when the text was simplified, poor readers noted as many errors as the good readers. When the reading material is too difficult, poor readers are unable to make full use of the strategies they possess. If too many of the text's words are unknown, the poor reader may not comprehend well enough to see that there are inconsistencies.

Learning to monitor one's comprehension is partly developmental. In general, older students are better at monitoring than younger ones. The nature of monitoring also changes as students develop. Young students and low-achieving readers tend to focus on lower-level elements. They are concerned about processing words and sentences, whereas older readers and more competent students are more aware of their understanding of paragraphs and larger sections of text.

Correcting.   Being aware of a problem in comprehension is a necessary first step in solving that problem. The second step is correcting the problem. A number of actions can be undertaken to repair faulty comprehension. These include but are not limited to the following (Taylor, Harris, & Pearson, 1988):

- Rereading a confusing sentence or paragraph.
- Reading ahead to see if that clarifies the meaning of a passage.
- Obtaining the meaning of an unknown key word.
- Using illustrations as an aid.
- Slowing down the rate of reading.
- Using an encyclopedia or other reference to clarify a confusing concept.
- Looking back over the text to find details that one has forgotten.
- Asking oneself questions.
- Putting a confusing passage into one's own words.
- Relating ideas to one's own experience.
- Talking over the passage with a friend, a parent, or the teacher.

Instruction in Metacognition.   Instruction in metacognition should be ongoing and multifaceted, systematic and also on-the-spot as needed. Every strategy lesson should have a metacognitive aspect. Whenever students are taught a new strategy, they should also be taught how, when, and where to apply that strategy and what to do if the strategy does not work. Students, especially low-achieving readers, should be taught that reading should always make sense. Based on a review of the research, Winograd, Lipson, and Wixson (1989) constructed a plan for teaching metacognitive and other strategies.

A LESSON IN TEACHING METACOGNITIVE STRATEGIES

Step 1: Describing the strategy. The strategy is explained in detail. The teacher provides a description and examples of the strategy so that the students know what the strategy is and how it works.

Step 2: Explaining why the strategy is important. Explain and model why the strategy is valuable. Low-achieving readers may not realize that even the best readers have difficulty with comprehension at times and need to be aware of whether or not their reading makes sense. Also note that checking one's reading periodically enables the reader to clear up puzzling parts and helps the reader to remember the material longer.

Step 3: Demonstrating the strategy. Using modeling or another technique, show how you would use the strategy. Placing a brief selection on the board or an overhead, show how you pause at the end of a paragraph and ask: "Does this make sense?" Choose a tricky paragraph, one that you misread the first time, and show students how you stopped when the piece stopped making sense. You might also discuss the steps you would take to repair the comprehension gap.

Step 4: Explaining when and where to use the strategy. When teaching a strategy, be sure to note when and where it is to be used. For instance, when teaching correction strategies, note when it is appropriate to reread the sentence or the paragraph. Also point out when it might be a good idea to read ahead because the next sentence or paragraph explains the word or idea with which you were having difficulty.

Step 5: Explaining how and why to evaluate a strategy. Explain how to evaluate a strategy and why evaluation is important. For instance, explain that you need to see if rereading a sentence works, because if it doesn't you will need to use another strategy.

Steps 6 and 7: Guided practice and application. As part of instruction in metacognitive strategies, students need opportunities to try out strategies with guidance and feedback from their teachers so they can clarify misunderstandings, make necessary adjustments, and get the feel of the strategy. Be sure to affirm students' successful efforts with specific praise: "I like the way you reread that sentence when you saw that it didn't make sense" or "I like the way you used the diagram to help you understand the paragraph." They also need ample opportunity to apply the strategy to a variety of texts in a variety of situations so that the strategies become automatic, and they can see which ones work best in which situations.

> Metacognitive awareness can be developed through collaborative learning. In pairs or cooperative learning groups, students, under the teacher's guidance, discuss their use of strategies and share their thinking.

Although working with low-achieving readers, do not assume that they don't have any strategies. Before beginning instruction, find out what strategies they do use and build on those, especially if you are working with older students.

Struggling readers might not realize the mental effort that goes into constructing meaning. They might look at achieving readers and believe that they breeze their way through the text and that comprehension is something that takes place automatically for them. Struggling readers need to know that constructing meaning takes effort, but that effort pays off. They might not realize either that proficient readers reread text when it is complex or confusing. They might not even realize that you should reread if the text doesn't make sense. As Beers (2003) commented, "Rereading is probably the number one strategy independent readers use when something stumps them in text. It's probably the last strategy dependent readers use" (p. 113).

Use of Graphic Guides.   As an aid to strategy use, Paris, Cross, & Lipson (1984) used posters and slogans, such as "Be a reading detective" to remind students to use strategies as they read. A list of metacognitive strategies emphasized in the program include the following (Alverman et al.,1989, p. R8):

Think Ahead
- What is this selection about?
- What do I already know about it?
- What do I want to find out?
- What is my goal?
- How should I go about reading in order to meet my goal?

Think While Reading
- What have I read about so far?
- Do I understand it? If not, what should I do?
- What is the author saying and what do I think about it?

Think Back
- Have I learned what I wanted?
- How can I use what I read?

Informal Instruction.   In addition to formal instruction, take advantage of informal, on-the-spot opportunities to promote metacognitive awareness. Before students read a selection, ask them how they will read it—fast or slow? Also ask what they will do to check their understanding. If a selection has confusing or densely written sections, discuss ways in which those sections might be read. In the after-reading discussion, have students tell how they handled difficult or confusing portions of a selection. Ask questions that lead students to discuss their use of metacognitive strategies. "Were there any confusing passages in this article? How did you handle the confusing parts? What do you do when the selection stops making sense?"

From time to time, model metacognitive strategies that you use, and have students explain the metacognitive strategies that they use. To reinforce monitoring for meaning, have students use sticky notes to indicate passages that were difficult. Discuss those passages with students. Talk over strategies that they might use to understand the passages better.

Use of Jokes and Riddles.   Riddles are ideal for building metalinguistic knowledge because they force the listener or reader to be aware of the literal meaning and a metalinguistic aspect of a riddle. In the riddle, "Where do you take a sick horse?" (to a horspital), the key is the formation of *horspital*. In the riddle, "Why did the chicken cross the road?" (to get to the other side), the key is in the whole sentence. The listener expects the chicken to have some goal for crossing the road that goes beyond being on the other side. Riddles also require the reader to go beyond literal comprehension and so involve higher-level thinking skills. Listening to or reading riddles and discussing them has led to increased overall comprehension in struggling readers (Yuill, 1996).

IMPORTANCE OF USING APPROPRIATE MATERIALS

Regardless of what technique is used to teach comprehension strategies, it is absolutely essential that the text be on the appropriate level of difficulty. In her study of good and poor

Struggling readers often focus on low-level literacy processes. Seeing reading as getting the words right, they devote their energies to pronouncing each word correctly and neglect comprehension.

readers in high school, Kletzien (1991) found that strategy use declined as the text grew harder. Both good and poor readers used the same strategies at the independent reading level. At the instructional level the better readers demonstrated somewhat greater flexibility in the use of strategies. However, at the frustration level, poor readers "evidenced a precipitous decline in strategy usage (both in variety of strategies and in number of times strategies were used) (Kletzien, 1991, p. 79).

At the frustration level, strategy use deteriorated to a focus on small segments of text: individual words or phrases. Complaining that there were too many hard words, some of the subjects simply gave up. Explaining the drastic change in strategy use as texts grew too difficult, Kletzien (1991) commented:

> Because vocabulary and sentence structure were much more complex at this level, subjects had to work much harder at the lower-level tasks of word recognition and understanding of individual sentences, leaving less cognitive capacity available to understand the meaning of the passage as a whole and to integrate the content with what they already knew. Even subjects who reported using prior knowledge, appeared to have done so out of desperation. One subject, obviously overwhelmed by the difficulty of the material, reported, "I have no idea what this is talking about; I am just trying to remember anything I know about Africa." (p. 82)

BEYOND STRATEGIES

There is more to using strategies than knowing how, when, and where to use them. There is also an essential affective component. Just as you build on what students know in word recognition, you should also consider what they know when building comprehension strategies. Besides being an effective instructional strategy, this fosters students' self-esteem.

In typical discussions, there is an emphasis on the correctness of the answer. However, students can have the right answer for the wrong reason or the wrong answer for the right reason. Besides, the object of instruction is not to obtain answers, right or wrong; the goal is to improve students' use of strategies. When students respond correctly and the strategy or thinking process they used to obtain the response is obvious, affirm their use of the strategy: "I liked the way you used pieces of information from the story to conclude that the main character is kind." If the thinking or strategy isn't obvious, have the student explain it: "Why do you think the main character is kind?" If the student gives no response, rephrase the question or provide a probe that gives support. If the response is not fully correct, build on what the student provided. If the student responded that the main character is selfish, ask the student why she or he thinks so. (It could be a perfectly legitimate interpretation.) If the student has not considered all the evidence, encourage her or him to do so. You might say, "Let's go back to the story and take a look at the main character's actions."

If a student is unable to respond at all, even with rephrased queries, help her or him use a strategy that will lead to a response. You might say, "Let's look at what it says about the main character on p. 22." In this way, you are showing the student how to use a strategy (looking back at the text), and you are involving her in obtaining the answer. This is far better than simply supplying the answer, which leaves her no better off than she was and, in fact, may confirm or contribute to a sense of academic powerlessness.

Once the focus is shifted from task completion or getting right answers to the process of learning how to comprehend, your natural tendency will be to choose activities that foster strategy building and independence. The question that you need to keep in mind is not: "Is the answer correct?" It should be: "How I can build on what the student knows?"

In a study involving primary and middle-grade students who were low-achieving readers, Thames & Reeves (1994) found that when cognitive instruction that built on what students know was combined with self-selection of reading materials, poor readers maintained their academic self-esteem. The academic self-esteem of the members of a control group, who were taught in traditional ways, plummeted.

APPROACHES TO TEACHING STRATEGIES

Two major approaches to teaching strategies include direct explanation and transactional strategy instruction (National Reading Panel, 2000). In direct explanation (DE), emphasis is placed on explaining the reasoning process in reading and the steps for applying strategies. Strategies are taught as problem-solving procedures that help readers construct meaning. Transactional strategy instruction (TSI) also attempts to provide insight into the reasoning processes of comprehension but does so through explanation, modeling, and discussion. In TSI, teachers and students work together to create meaning from a text. Emphasis is on the interchange of ideas and interpretations among teachers and students. Although DE and TSI have construction of meaning as the ultimate goal and use many of the same procedures, TSI places more emphasis on discussion and group interpretation. In a version of TSI known as collaborative strategy instruction, disabled readers in grades 6 through 11, three-quarters of whom were reading on a third-grade level or below, gained significantly more than did a group taught using conventional approaches (Anderson & Roit, 1993). As the National Reading Panel (2000) commented:

> Teachers help students by explaining fully what it is they are teaching: what to do, how, why, and when; by modeling their own thinking processes; by encouraging students to ask questions and discuss possible answers among themselves; and by keeping students engaged in their reading via providing tasks that demand active involvement (Sec. 4, p. 125)

COLLABORATIVE STRATEGY INSTRUCTION: AN EXEMPLARY PROGRAM

From a teaching standpoint, the students looked virtually hopeless. The failures of a group of low-achieving sixth- through tenth-graders had left them apathetic and discouraged. All were operating at least two years below grade level. Their views of reading and writing were mechanistic, uninformed, and unenthusiastic (Anderson & Roit, 1993).

Taking part in an experimental program that combined strategy instruction with collaborative learning, the students made substantial progress. The key idea of the experimental program was that students have natural problem-solving abilities that they use in their everyday lives but fail to apply to reading and writing tasks. In the program, reading was presented as a problem to be solved by the group. Each group consisted of five students and a teacher. Strategies were not prescribed but were decided upon by the group. As a member of the group, the teacher was an active participant who discussed and modeled strategies, but did not dictate them.

Recognizing that these students, having been in school for a number of years, have strategies for dealing with text but might not use them, the teachers built on these strategies. Based on observations of eighty students involved in the project, the researchers compiled a list of ten strategies that students used in their everyday lives, some of which included recognizing a problem, knowing what matters, making sense, getting back on track, explaining, wrapping up experiences, and so forth; these are actually students' labels for widely used text-reading strategies, such as predicting, summarizing, and monitoring. Teachers helped students adapt and refine their everyday strategies so that they could be applied to understanding text.

Having endured criticism from themselves and others, older low-achieving readers are reluctant to talk about, or even admit, their problems with reading. Using a quality termed "cognitive empathy," teachers looked for signs that a student was struggling: a quizzical look, a sigh, a discouraged expression. Teachers capitalized on these teachable moments to show empathy and to encourage students to reveal their thinking. In the following exchange, in which a group of students are having difficulty with the term *human aging,* the teacher's role as a facilitator is demonstrated.

> This is an excellent example of responsive elaboration. In response to the students' statements, the teacher leads them to use the overall sense of the passage to obtain the correct identification of *aging.*

> Collaborative strategy instruction helped the students become aware of the strategies they already possessed and build on that knowledge. Students were active participants in their learning. They selected materials to read and identified the vocabulary words they felt might be difficult. They also discussed problems they had understanding the text.

T: I see a confused look here. Which part is confusing you?

S1: The part that says, "human again."

T: I guess it isn't really "again." Does anyone have a strategy to figure that one out? You usually have very good ones.

S2: "Agging."

T: Do you know what "agging" means?

S2: To bother?

T: I think that if I relate this word to the title, "Growing Old," that would help me to get an idea.

S1: Aging.

T: Aging. What helped you get that?

S1: After you said growing old, I looked at the title and I just remembered that someone growing old is aging. (Anderson & Roit, 1993, p. 6)

Imitating the teacher's behavior, the students soon began to show cognitive empathy toward each other. Students began giving suggestions to each other and discussing strategies that they used.

Throughout the project, the emphasis was placed on the processes used to understand text rather than on getting the right answers. "The learning goal—becoming a more active reader in order to understand text better—was clear and consistent" (Anderson & Roit, 1993, p. 28). Discussions were conversational. Instead of just asking content-specific factual questions, teachers asked and encouraged students to ask the kinds of questions that might pop up in a natural discussion of text. "What is this passage about? What is important here?" These are questions that students might well ask themselves during their reading. Although lessons might vary from day to day, and from teacher to teacher, the following box contains the steps in a typical lesson.

■ ■ ■ ■ ■

COLLABORATIVE STRATEGY INSTRUCTION LESSON

Step 1: Choose a text. Students choose a text. Each group had a library of informational pieces that students might read.

Step 2: Survey the text. Students survey the text to get an overview and look for possible problems that might hinder comprehension. At this point, students pick out vocabulary that is unfamiliar. The difficult vocabulary from the text is then discussed.

Step 3: Predict. Students decide what they think the text might be about and what they would like to learn from it.

Step 4: Read in segments. Students read the text in segments. Problems with the text are discussed.

Text is discussed in terms of purposes set initially. Students also discuss any problems they experienced comprehending the text. They talk over strategies used, which ones worked and which didn't and how they might apply what they learned about reading to other texts. During discussions, teachers might also model how they use strategies to solve reading problems. For instance, a teacher might show the group how she read to the end of a sentence to get sufficient context so that she could guess the meaning of an unfamiliar word.

THE ROLE OF REASONING

Deriving a main idea, drawing a conclusion, comparing and contrasting, making inferences, making judgments, and similar higher-level comprehension require the ability to reason. Reasoning can be developed. You can create the conditions that make your students smarter. "People can become more intelligent by living and working every day in a particular kind of environment: one that coaches them in using problem-solving skills and praises them for using the skills; one that holds them accountable for using them well because it assumes they are smart and capable. This kind of learning environment can create the beliefs and dispositions that constitute intelligence (Resnick & Hall, 2001). A key technique for developing reasoning is accountable talk.

ACCOUNTABLE TALK

One of the most powerful techniques for fostering higher-level thinking skills and improved reading and writing is through talk. But not all talk is equal. For talk to be an efficient means for learning it should be accountable (Resnick & Hall, 2001). Through accountable talk, students learn to think carefully about their responses, and base assertions on passages from a text or other sources of information. Accountable talk respects and builds on what others say. Accountable talk takes place throughout the day in teacher–student conferences, in small-group discussions, in whole class discussions, and in student presentations. Teachers develop accountable talk by explaining, demonstrating, modeling, and coaching. They elicit accountable talk through a number of questions and probes.

- They seek clarification and explanation when called for.
- They ask for proof or justification for positions or statements.
- They recognize and help clarify erroneous concepts.
- They interpret and summarize students' statements. (Resnick & Hall, 2003).

Here are some prompts that help students carry on thoughtful, accountable discussions. The prompts might be used by teachers or students.

Drawing conclusions: What conclusion might we draw from these facts?

Making within-the-text connections: What is the connection between losing the game in the first part of the story and the way Shauna treats the new kid?

Making text-to-text connections: What story that we read does this one remind you of?

Making text-to-world connections: Do you know anyone like the main character?

Clarifying: Could you explain what you mean by that? I'm not sure I understand.

Explaining: Can you tell us step-by-step how Homer's invention worked?

Predicting: What do you think will happen next? Why?

Hypothesizing: If we added salt, what do you think would happen to the freezing temperature?

Comparing: How are the twins similar in their actions?

Contrasting: How are the twins different?

Here are some prompts that might be used to facilitate a discussion.

Restating: Here is what you seem to be saying . . .

Summarizing: So far this is what the author has told us . . .

Affirming: I like the way you gave three examples to prove your point.

Including: We haven't heard from _____ yet.

Agreeing: "I agree with Justin, because . . .

Building on what others have said: I'd like to add to what Justin said.

Disagreeing: I can see how Justin came to the conclusion that the main character was unselfish. But when I think of why he did favors for others, I believe that he was just trying to get on their good side. And here is why I think that.

QUESTIONS

A key element in accountable talk is the kinds of questions that are asked. Questions are a powerful tool. We can improve students' reading performance simply by using the right kinds of questions (Hansen & Pearson, 1980). Questions also serve a multitude of purposes.

Questions can be used to evaluate, to highlight important information, to lead a student to a conclusion or to a higher level of thinking, to get a discussion going or to keep it going, to review content, or start a strategy lesson (Hyman, 1978). Questions also serve affective purposes. We can use questions to make a student feel part of a group, share feelings, or display her knowledge on a particular topic. Teachers can also use questions to trap a student who has not been paying attention. However, this is done at a price. If questions are used to embarrass or control, then they become threatening and the accepting atmosphere is corroded. Hyman (1978) recommends that the teacher handle the issue of paying attention by simply "calling for the students' attention in a straightforward way" (p. 4).

> Both good and poor readers are asked too many literal questions. About 80 percent of the questions asked in the typical reading lesson are factual (Ruddell, 1978).

Judging from research and experience, low-achieving readers have been ill served by questions. In general, they are asked lower-level questions, are given fewer prompts, and less time to respond than are achieving readers. And the teacher is more likely to call on another student "to help out" the poor reader (Allington, 1984).

Creating Questions

For Narrative Selections.   Since questions are such an important element in instruction, especially for poor readers, questioning techniques need to be planned with care. Analyzing narrative selections, Beck, Omanson, and McKeown (1982) identified the key elements in a story and constructed a map, which linked these units. The key-elements map (sometimes known simply as a story map) became a blueprint for constructing questions. The revised questions were especially helpful to the less skilled readers. The researchers found that less skilled readers had difficulty structuring the content of the story into a cohesive whole; however, responding to questions that focused on the story's main happenings significantly assisted less able readers in their attempts to create a mental map of the selection.

Creating a key elements map can be done informally by following these steps:

- List the theme, moral, starting point, or basic premise of the story.
- List the major events in the development of the plot. Include implied as well as stated events.
- List concepts or ideas that you feel students would need to know in order to understand the theme and other major elements in the story.

Prereading questions should prepare students for the theme and major plot occurrences. There should also be questions that guide students through the selection. Postreading questions should help students understand the basic facts of the story: "Who were the main characters? What happened?" Once students understand the basics of a selection, they can build on those basics and answer higher-level questions about theme, quality of story, use of literary techniques, and so forth. For an example of a simplified key elements map and questions based on the map, see Figures 11.4 and 11.5.

> When students read stories accompanied by map-based questions, their comprehension improved by 10 percent.

For Informational Pieces.   The discussion questions for an informational piece should be based on the major concepts covered in the selection. The teacher should list two to four ideas that he feels are important. Prereading questions should be designed to activate relevant schema and build background necessary to understand the article. Questions should also be posed that will help students focus on the main concepts in the selection. Post-reading questions should help students clarify and organize concepts, and relate new information to old. Once students have a grasp of basic information, they can respond to questions that involve evaluating information and applying it.

Levels of Questioning

Having had an unbalanced diet of low-level questioning, low-achieving readers need questions that involve all cognitive levels. However, this does not mean that literal questions

FIGURE 11.4   Story Elements Map

Theme (Moral):	You don't have to be big or strong to help someone.
Plot:	1. A dove saves an ant from drowning.
	2. A hunter is about to catch the dove.
	3. The ant bites the man.
	4. The dove flies free.
Needed Concepts or Ideas:	A dove is a bird.
	A fable is a story that teaches a lesson. A fable usually has animals as main characters but the animals act like people.

From Wang, M. L. (1989). *The Ant and the Dove.* Chicago, IL: Children's Press.

FIGURE 11.5   Questions Based on a Story Elements Map

BEFORE READING

Have you ever been in danger or trouble?
Have you ever been chased by a dog or lost?
Have you ever been sick? Have you ever fallen down and hurt yourself?
Who helped you? Have you ever helped anyone? Read *The Ant and the Dove.* Find out how the ant and the dove helped each other.

AFTER READING

How did the dove help the ant?
How did the ant thank the dove?
What did the ant promise to do?
What question did the dove ask?
Why did the dove ask: "What could an ant do?"
How did the ant help the dove?
What lesson does the story teach?
Is this lesson true? Have you ever known of a small person helping a big person or a child helping a grown up? Do you know what kind of story this is? What kind of story teaches a lesson and has animals that act like people?

should be neglected. Poor readers do show improvement when given low-level questions (Medley, 1977). They need to know what happened in the story or what the main facts in the article are. At that point, they are ready to be lifted to higher levels.

Questions can be classified in a number of ways. One way of arranging questions is according to the cognitive processes involved. Adapting Weinstein and Mayer's (1986) system, which was used to classify strategies, the following taxonomy evolves. The first level, comprehending, is drawn from Bloom's taxonomy (1957).

Comprehending. Students understand prose on a literal level. They can recite five facts stated in a selection, name the main characters, indicate dates and places. This level also includes having students put information in their own words.

Organizing. Students select important details from the selection and construct relationships among them. This involves identifying or constructing main ideas, classifying, noting sequence, and summarizing.

Elaborating. Elaborating entails making connections between information from the text and prior knowledge and includes a wide range of activities: making inferences, creating images and analogies, and evaluating or judging.

Monitoring. Monitoring involves being aware of cognitive processes. It involves knowing whether a selection makes sense and knowing what steps might be taken to repair comprehension.

Listed below are examples of each type of question. They are drawn from *Baseball's Best: Five True Stories* (Gutelle, 1990), an easy-to-read book that should appeal to older readers.

Comprehending. Which of the five players hit the most home runs? Which has the longest hitting streak? Which one was both a good pitcher and a good batter?

Organizing. In what ways were the five players alike? In what ways were they different?

Elaborating. Which player was most generous? Why? Which player changed baseball the most? Why? Which player was the best? Why do you think so? Picture Jackie Robinson stealing his first base in the major leagues. What do you see? What do you hear?

Monitoring. Did you find any confusing parts? Did you run into any words that you couldn't read or whose meanings you didn't know? If so, what did you do? Can you summarize each player's main accomplishments? If you forget how many home runs Hank Aaron hit or the number of games in which Joe DiMaggio hit safely, what might you do?

Atmosphere

How questions are asked is almost as important as what questions are asked. Having had negative experiences with questions, low-achieving readers need an accepting, supportive

Speaking about wait time, Hyman (1978) comments, "If the teacher does not begin to talk after each student finishes, the teacher nonverbally encourages the students to talk" (pp. 102–103).

atmosphere. Instead of being oral quizzes, discussions should be genuine opportunities to build the concepts, background, and thinking skills so necessary for comprehension.

Wait Time.   One small but very positive change that literally takes seconds to implement is to increase wait time. Typically students are given a second or less to respond to the teacher's questions. If there is no response, the teacher repeats the question, or, most often in the case of poor readers, calls on another student. After the student responds, the teacher waits less than a second before reacting to the answer (Hyman, 1978). However, Hyman (1978), Lake (1973), and Rowe's (1969) studies have shown that when the teacher increases the wait time from one second or less to three to five seconds, the following occurs:

- Fewer no responses and I don't knows
- Longer, more thoughtful responses
- Greater number of correct answers
- Greater number of alternative responses
- More evidence of reasons for answers
- Greater confidence as indicated by a tone of assurance in the voice
- Fewer responses that conveyed a "Is this what you wanted?" tone
- Greater number of responses from the lower-achieving students

Students weren't the only ones who benefited from longer wait times. Teachers demonstrated increased adaptability, asked fewer but more varied questions, and raised their expectations for slower students (Hyman, 1978).

Probes and Prompts

Questions can be used to help students focus on the topic, expand their responses, substantiate their answers, and lift students to higher levels of thought (Taba, 1965).

While establishing an encouraging atmosphere and using wait time are essential elements in a discussion, prompts and probes are also important. At times, low-achieving readers know the information requested by higher-level questions, but they have difficulty formulating their responses. This may be especially true of students who are still learning English. Prompts can help them shape their answers (Hyman, 1978).

For instance, to help students form concepts by grouping similar data, you might ask such questions as: "Which of these items go together? What do all of these have in common? What would you call all of these items?"

If students' answers are too brief, use an elaboration probe: "Would you please tell me more? Would you please explain?" If students are offering unsubstantiated opinions, use a specific probe: "You said you didn't like the story. What was there about the story that you didn't like? You said the main character was sly. What did she do that was sly?"

If a response is unclear, you might use a restating-crystallizing probe. In this probe, you restate what you believe the student said and then ask if your restatement is correct: "You seem to be saying that Roger was the cause of the family's problems. Is that right?" The purpose of a restating-crystallizing probe is to help the speaker clarify her or his thoughts. It can also be used to keep the speaker on track if she or he has gotten off the topic. You are also telling the speaker that you are paying close attention to him and that his opinions are worth hearing (Hyman, 1978).

LESSON PLANS THAT FOSTER COMPREHENSION

Questions and discussions and direct instruction in strategies designed to improve comprehension are often conducted within the framework of a lesson plan. The best known and most widely used lesson-plan formats are the directed reading activity and the directed reading-thinking activity.

> **Directed reading activity (DRA):** traditional five-step plan for conducting a reading lesson that has as its core the reading of a selection. Today the DRA is often used as part of guided reading.

Directed Reading Activity

The **directed reading activity (DRA)** has a long history in the field of reading and incorporates the following five steps: preparation, silent reading, discussion, rereading, and follow-up or extension. Updated to incorporate recent research and practice, today's DRA focuses on activating prior knowledge, strategy instruction, and emphasizes gearing activities to the major concepts and structure of the selection to be read.

The steps in the DRA, which have been modified for use with low-achieving readers, are described in the box that follows.

■ ■ ■ ■ ■

A DIRECTED READING ACTIVITY LESSON

> The preparational stage should only take about ten to fifteen minutes. Don't spend so much time preparing students that they don't have time to read.

Step 1: Preparing. In this step, you do whatever is necessary to prepare students for a successful, engrossing reading of the selection, which could be a newspaper article, a story in a basal reader, a chapter from a children's book, or an article from a magazine. As part of the preparation, introduce the selection, activate prior knowledge, build background, and develop needed vocabulary and concepts and whatever thinking skills or reading strategies might be needed to handle the selection. In general, background-building activities should remind students of what they already know about a topic, tie new information to students' background knowledge, and focus on the important ideas in the selection to be read (Adoption Guidelines Project, 1990).

Also engender interest in the selection and set a purpose question for reading. The purpose can be set in cooperation with the students. If possible, students might be involved in the selection of the piece to be read. They might also be involved in choosing the difficult vocabulary to be introduced and should discuss how the story is to be read and what strategies might work best with the piece. Because they are often alienated by past failures, poor readers need to feel involved.

Step 2: Silent reading. In general, the initial reading of a selection should be silent. The purpose of the DRA is to foster comprehension. When students read orally, they focus on pronouncing the words correctly. When students read silently, the focus is on constructing meaning. Reading silently also provides students with the opportunity to apply word-identification skills. Freed from the pressure of reading aloud, students can use pronounceable word-part, analogy, context, or other word-identification strategies to figure out difficult words.

During this portion of the lesson, observe students, note needs, and provide help to students.

Students can read the whole selection all at once or read it in sections. After each section, there is a brief discussion. Breaking up a suspenseful narrative piece into sections may lessen students' enjoyment of the selection. However, it might be wise to read a fact-packed informational piece in segments. Students may need and welcome the additional guidance provided by discussing segments of the text.

Step 3: Discussion. The discussion generally begins with students responding to the purpose question. If students read to find out how skyscrapers are built, the opening question might be: "How are skyscrapers built?" To help students get started, the question might be sliced (Pearson & Johnson, 1978), that is, broken into easier segments: "What is the first step in building a skyscraper? The second?" During the discussion, confusions are clarified and concepts are expanded. Ideas from the selection are organized and students relate new information in the story to information already in their background. Low-achieving readers may not see relationships among ideas and may have difficulty constructing a main idea from a series of details. Carefully crafted questions can help students organize and integrate information. You might also do some on-the-spot teaching. For instance, one student was unsure of the word *piles.* He wondered how piles of steel could be used to hold up a skyscraper. The class discussed the word as it was used in context: "Long, thick piles of steel are sunk into the land, down to a bed of hard rock. Those piles hold up the base of the building" (Blaine, 1986, p. 164). They concluded that *piles* had a different meaning from its ordinary use as "a heap." Checking in the dictionary, they learned that a pile is a heavy beam driven into the ground or bed of a river.

During the discussion, be alert to students' needs. For instance, you might have noticed that they had difficulty with some of the compound words that appeared in the selection: *landfill, framework.* Perhaps they also had problems keeping the sequence of events in mind. Mentally plan to review those areas during the rereading or follow-up portions of the lesson.

Step 4: Rereading. Students reread the selection for a new purpose: to obtain information they missed during the initial reading, to clarify misconceptions, to focus in on a particular aspect of the selection, for a deeper appreciation or understanding, or for a similar purpose. The rereading often offers an opportunity for a purposeful oral reading: to dramatize a portion of the selection, to read a humorous or descriptive passage, to clarify a disputed point, for instance. Although listed as a separate step, rereading often flows into the discussion stage, when you ask a student to read the sentences in which *piles* appears or the passage that explains how the crane is taken down from the top of a skyscraper, for instance. The rereading can also be an entirely separate step. For example, you may want to review strategies for comprehending sequence and have students apply these strategies as they reread the selection.

Step 5: Follow-up. The follow-up, which is an optional part of the lesson, can take many forms but should extend the main concepts or strategies stressed in the lesson or build on the lesson's content. For the skyscraper lesson, students might observe one being built and write about it, might read a book on their level about skyscrapers, or might read and discuss the poem, "Giants of the City" by Marge Blaine (1986). Whatever the activity, it should provide opportunities for further development of reading and writing skills.

The DRA differs from the text walk. Depending as it does on illustrations, a text walk is best used with heavily illustrated books. As students grow in skill, shift to the DRA or a similar format.

To create a directed reading activity, first analyze the selection to be read. Note the main ideas, concepts, or principles that you wish students to learn (if the selection is fiction, compose a key elements map). These become the focal point for your lesson. Then list the vocabulary necessary to understand the key ideas. For instance, the major ideas in "Amazing Rescue Underground" (Shea, 1992), which is written on a second-grade level but will appeal to older students, include the following:

- Jessica, a toddler, was trapped in an abandoned water well.
- A team of rescue workers saved Jessica.

After listing the major ideas, go back over the story and jot down the vocabulary words or concepts in the story that need to be known in order to comprehend the major ideas in the selection. "Amazing Rescue Underground" has more than twenty words that might be potentially difficult. However, that is far too many for students to learn at one time. The list can be narrowed down to the following six:

abandoned well	backhoe	paramedics
rescue	microphone	cable

After listing the difficult words, examine the article and determine its structure and what strategies would be needed to understand it. The piece has a dual structure. Primarily, it is sequential. It narrates and describes a series of steps taken to rescue the child. But it also has a cause–effect structure. A helpful strategy for students would be to ask: "What did the rescue workers do and why?" Drawings in the article also contribute to an understanding of the story. For instance, it mentions that a rathole rig was used to dig. Drawings depict a rathole rig better than any words could.

At this point, you are now ready to structure a preparatory discussion that will activate schema, build background and vocabulary, set a purpose, guide students in the use of reading and thinking strategies, and, last but not least, motivate the students to want to read the selection. Note how this is done in the sample DRA presented in the following box, keeping in mind that this selection could have been handled in a number of different ways.

■ ■ ■ ■ ■

DIRECTED READING ACTIVITY FOR "AMAZING RESCUE UNDERGROUND"

> The outcome of the preparing stage of the DRA is to set a purpose for reading. The purpose can be set by the teacher, by the students, or both.

Step 1: Preparing. Writing the title, "Amazing Rescue Underground," on the board, ask the class what they think the story might be about. To make sure that the class knows what *rescue* means and will recognize it in print, point to it as you say it and amplify and clarify students' responses, if necessary. Direct the class to turn to the story on p. 28 and to examine the illustration. Ask, "Based on the illustration, what do you think the story will be about?" As the illustration is being discussed, point out the cover for the abandoned well in the foreground. Write "abandoned well" on the board. As students discuss the possible content of the story, point to the vocabulary, previously written

on the board, and ask why each might be needed in a rescue at an abandoned well: *microphone,* a *backhoe, paramedics,* and a *cable.*

Assessing the students' knowledge of each term, devote as much time to each as is needed. Having built the needed vocabulary and background and activated students' prior knowledge, set a purpose for reading. Pointing out that Jessica, the child in the purple overalls, falls in the well, ask students to read to find out what steps were taken to rescue her and why. Suggest that, as students read, they use the pictures in the selection to help them understand what has happened and also to picture in their minds important scenes that are not shown.

> This is a reminder for students to use imaging as they read the story.

Step 2: Silent reading. As the students read silently, note whether they are having any difficulty. For instance, if you see that several students are trying to sound out *petroleum* and one seems stumped by *inquiries* and *ambulance,* make a note to review pronounceable word-parts and analogy strategies as applied to multisyllabic words. Also review context clues.

Step 3: Discussing. Begin the discussion with the purpose question: "What steps were taken to rescue Jessica and why?" The class talks over the steps that were taken and why each was taken. Having been engrossed in the story, they have a good sense of the sequence of events. However, there may be some confusion. For instance, some students might believe that the paramedics helped with the digging. If so, ask students to locate and read passages that clarify that point. (This is a valid purpose for orally rereading passages.) Other issues are also discussed as they come up: why the second hole had to be dug, why it had to be dug by hand, how the mother helped, how Jessica must have felt, what it was like to drill the tunnel, how long it took to drill the tunnel, what petroleum jelly is and why it was used.

Step 4: Rereading. During the discussion, you might note that the students had difficulty explaining why the rescue took two days. Have the class skim through the selection to find passages that tell why the rescue took so long. Help them calculate the time that it took to dig the tunnel. Also review strategies for figuring out some troublesome words: *petroleum, ambulance, inquiries.*

Step 5: Follow-up. Building on the words *microphone* and *paramedic,* extend students' understanding of the forms *micro* and *para.* If the class still has some questions about the rescue and they want to know what happened to Jessica since the rescue, bring in a magazine article that gives her last name. Then, with the help of the media specialist, the class might locate updates on Jessica McClure. The class might also view a made-for-TV movie of the rescue and compare the TV version with the selection they have read.

> Low-progress readers are behind and so need to have their progress accelerated. Do not spend too much time on any one story. Two days should be adequate.

Directed Reading-Thinking Activity

> **Directed reading-thinking activity (DR-TA):** form of the DRA in which students make predictions and read to verify their predictions.

Based on the DRA, the **directed reading-thinking activity (DR-TA)** places greater emphasis on student involvement. In the DR-TA, students predict what the selection might be about and then read to evaluate their predictions. Because they are more active participants in a DR-TA, students also shoulder greater responsibility for their learning. They must be able and willing to generate questions, know how to ignore irrelevant material in their quest to have their questions answered, suspend judgment, and read flexibly. They must also be able to modify their predictions if they encounter information that conflicts with their ideas (Stauffer, 1969). The DR-TA can be an especially effective technique for use with low-achieving readers because it involves them more directly and more personally in the reading process. Like the DRA, the DR-TA also has five steps.

> The DR-TA requires that students bring some background knowledge to a selection. Without adequate background, students will have difficulty making predictions.

A DR-TA LESSON

Step 1: Preparing. The preparation stage of the DR-TA is less extensive than that of the DRA. Under your guidance, students discuss the title and predict what they believe the story might be about. They then examine and discuss illustrations and tell whether or not they would change their predictions.

(Continued)

> DR-TA fosters high levels of thinking because it requires students to justify and verify predictions (Stahl, 2004). Because discussion of the text is immediate, discussions are usually on target.

Headings and the first paragraph might also be used if the title and illustration(s) are not helpful. In order to involve all students, make sure that each one makes a prediction, or at least agrees with a prediction that someone else has made. List the predictions on the board and have students say with which one they agree. After making or choosing their predictions, students read to evaluate them.

For instance, in preparation for reading the first chapter of *The Chalk Box Kid* (Bulla, 1987), you might discuss the title and have students predict what the story seems to be about. Discuss the cover illustration and encourage students to use additional information to adjust or elaborate on their predictions. Because the title and illustration provide a very limited basis for making predictions, read the initial portion of the text, down to the sentence on the second page of the story that says, "So far it was his very worst birthday." Discuss that segment of the text and have students make a final prediction as to what might happen in the first chapter. Write their predictions on the board. Make sure that everyone is involved either in making a new prediction or supporting a prediction that has already been made.

Although not typically included in a DR-TA, provision might also be made for prereading assistance with difficult vocabulary words and concepts.

Write key vocabulary words on the board and discuss each one. You might suggest to students that they use the words as an added basis for making their predictions.

Step 2: Silent reading. Students read until they are able to respond to their predictions. This might occur after a page of reading or at the end of the selection. As students read, they should be prepared to revise their predictions if necessary.

Step 3: Discussing. The discussion stage of the DR-TA is very similar to that of the DRA, except that the discussion is initiated with a consideration of students' predictions. Students evaluate their predictions. If they stayed with their original predictions, they supply reasons or details to support their positions. If they revised them, they tell how and why they did so. The discussion can also be expanded to encompass major elements in the selection just as was done in the DRA discussion.

Step 4: Rereading. Same as in the DRA.

Step 5: Follow-up. Same as in the DRA.

The DR-TA, with its emphasis on making, verifying, and revising predictions, is an excellent technique. However, it does not work well if students need extensive guidance or have such limited background for a selection that they have very little basis for making predictions. It does, however, provide a bridge from heavily teacher-directed procedures, such as the DRA, to strategies that the student applies independently, and it is an excellent device for turning passive readers into active ones.

KEEPING A VISUAL RUNNING SUMMARY

During discussions and lectures, record key information on the chalkboard. This provides visual reinforcement and provides students with a running summary of what has been presented (Greenberg, 2004). It is especially valuable for students who might have difficulty keeping past information in mind as information is introduced. It is especially helpful if the information is placed within a graphic organizer. For instance, when talking about the elements of a story, write the setting, characters' names, and other elements on a story map. This helps students see relationships. The use of graphic organizers in this way fosters increased learning (Bulgren & Scanlon, 1997/1998).

OTHER TECHNIQUES FOR BUILDING COMPREHENSION

Cloze: way of assessing comprehension by having a student fill in missing words that have been deleted from a selection. The cloze procedure can also be used as a comprehension test or as a way of estimating the difficulty level of a text.

Cloze Procedure

Short for *closure,* **cloze** is a procedure in which students read selections in which words have been deleted. Generally, every fifth, seventh, or tenth word has been removed, but other patterns of deletion are possible. As they read, students attempt to restore the omitted words. Try the following cloze exercise. As you fill in the blanks, ask yourself: "What does this task require me to do? What strategies does it require me to use? What kinds of readers would benefit from this type of activity?"

A FAMOUS AUTHOR

The only daughter of rich parents, Beatrix Potter spent most of her days by herself. There were no other _____ and boys around to _____ with. But she did _____ to draw. She spent _____ happy hours drawing pictures _____ plants and animals.

Later, _____ she was grown up, _____ sent letters to a _____ little boy. The little _____ was sick. In her _____, she told stories. One story _____ about a rabbit who _____ into trouble when he _____ into a farmer's garden. _____ little boy liked the _____. So did other boys _____ girls.

Beatrix Potter decided _____ make a book out _____ the story about the _____. Some people cautioned her _____ to. They believed she _____ only sell a few _____ and would lose a _____ of money. But Beatrix Potter _____ ahead with plans for _____ the book. As it _____ out, boys and girls _____ over the world liked _____ book. Can you guess _____ the title of Beatrix Potter's _____ is? If you said, "The Tale of Peter Rabbit," _____ are right.

Beatrix Potter _____ twenty-two other books and _____ a famous children's author. _____ books were mostly about _____, kittens, and other animals. _____ the book that boys _____ girls liked best was _____ first book. Although "The Tale of Peter Rabbit" _____ been around for close _____ one hundred years, it is _____ being read today. In fact, it is one of the best-liked children's books of all time.

Here are the words that were omitted: *girls, play, like, many, of, when, she, friend's, boy, letters, was, got, sneaked, The, story, and, to, of, rabbit, not, would, books, lot, went, publishing, turned, all, her, what, book, you, wrote, became, Her, ducks, But, and, her, has, to, still.* Check your responses. How did you do?

Because words are omitted, cloze forces us to use our background knowledge and knowledge of language to restore the missing words. Cloze also demands a close attention to meaning. You can't fill in a blank if you don't have a good grasp of what you have read.

> Degrees of Reading Power is a nationally used reading test that assesses comprehension through the use of a modified cloze.

> Cloze is an excellent device for fostering sentence-level comprehension but is not a particularly effective way to develop passage-level comprehension.

If you haven't comprehended what you have read, you have no basis for filling in the blanks. Cloze works especially well with students who overuse phonics clues, fail to use context, or fail to read for meaning.

Discussion is an essential element in the application of cloze (Jongsma, 1980). Students should justify their choices, especially if exact replacements aren't required. Explaining their responses clarifies their thinking, and it is also helpful for them to hear why others made the choices they did. Discussion also makes for a livelier lesson.

Although you might choose to accept reasonable substitutes in lieu of exact replacements, have students compare their finished products to the originals. Comparison of their choices with the words used by the author should be interesting and should help students see the importance of word choice. If you do make this kind of comparison, inform students that they are doing fine if their responses match those of the author half of the time. The standard for a cloze score at the instructional level is 44–57 percent. Table 11.1 presents the criteria for cloze levels based on exact replacements.

Before students start a cloze exercise, give them some tips for completing it. They should read the whole piece first to get an overview. During their second reading of the selection, they should read to the end of each sentence or beyond before attempting to fill in the blank. Students naturally stop at the blank, but often the words beyond the blank provide essential information. Clues may even be found in the next sentence or two. After students have filled in the blanks, they should go back and see if there are any changes they wish to make.

Tell students to ignore spelling. If students worry about spelling, they will lose their focus, and also restrict their responses to words they can spell.

Constructing Cloze Exercises.　Choose material that is interesting and on the appropriate level of difficulty. Don't use material that presents a number of new concepts, because this makes it extra hard to fill in the blanks. In classical cloze, which was originally used to assess the difficulty level of printed materials, selections were 250 words in length and every fifth word was omitted so there would be a total of 50 deletions. Having fewer deletions makes the task easier. Controlling deletions also simplifies the task. Content words, such as nouns and verbs, are more difficult to restore than structure words, conjunctions, prepositions, and articles. Deletions made at the middle or end of a sentence are also easier to restore than are deletions made at the beginning of a sentence (Rye, 1982). Deletions are also easier to restore if the clues to the deletion precede it rather than come after it.

The types of deletions you make depend on the strategies you wish to reinforce. Restoring deleted content words, especially nouns and verbs, requires comprehension of

TABLE 11.1　Criteria for Cloze

LEVEL	PERCENTAGE OF CORRECT REPLACEMENTS
Independent	> 57
Instructional	44–57
Frustration	< 44

details. Restoring structure words involves using language cues and noting relationships. Whether using classical or adapted cloze, do not delete any proper nouns or any words from the first or last sentence.

Although many students enjoy the challenge of cloze, it needs to be introduced with care. Students, especially those who are lacking in confidence, may be upset by the task if they don't understand its nature. When introducing cloze, explain the nature of the activity and tell students what it is called and why. Students respond positively when they are treated as competent individuals capable of learning mature concepts. Also model the process of filling in the blanks in a sample cloze exercise. Emphasize the need to use language as well as content clues and to go beyond the blank when necessary. Provide guided practice.

Because cloze is a fairly difficult activity, it is not recommended, in its classical form, for students reading below a third-grade level. However, students operating on a lower level can engage in modified cloze or masking.

Modified Cloze.   In modified cloze, also known as mazes, students fill in the blanks by choosing one of three or more options so that cloze becomes a multiple-choice activity. Modified cloze, although not as valuable as classic cloze, is a reasonable alternative for students who have difficulty with classical cloze because of word-retrieval problems or students who are overly concerned with spelling.

Masking.   Masking is a form of cloze that is frequently used in shared-reading situations. After an initial reading of the selection, the teacher covers predictable words with masking tape and as she or he comes to the word, asks students to predict what the covered word might be. After students make and discuss their predictions, the covered word is unmasked. This exercise is especially valuable for students who neglect context clues.

Think-Alouds

As noted in Chapter 5, think-alouds can be used to obtain additional information about the processes that a student uses in comprehension or word analysis. Think-alouds can also be used as an instructional technique. For instance, one way for you to demonstrate the thinking processes that go on as you make a prediction, summarize a story, use context to figure out a hard word, or engage in any number of reading or writing processes is to let students know your thought processes through thinking aloud. You simply tell what is going on in your head as you make a prediction: "Based on this heading, I predict that this section will tell about some helpful kinds of beetles."

When introducing think-alouds to students, first explain what they are, how they might help comprehension, and how, when, and where they might be used. Then model a think-aloud, and provide for guided and independent practice. As you model a think-aloud, stress comprehension strategies that you have previously taught, such as predicting and summarizing, and metacognitive strategies, such as checking and repairing.

Still another use of think-alouds is to have students apply them as they read a selection. They can think aloud with a partner, with the partners reading alternate paragraphs and telling each other what they were thinking about as they read. The listening partner can ask probing questions such as: "What were you thinking about? Were there any confusing parts? Were there any hard words?" The listening partner might fill out a brief think-aloud form, which can be a vehicle for discussion between the two.

Think-alouds help students become more aware of the ways in which they process text and use monitoring and other comprehension strategies. Think-alouds also allow us insight into the students' thought processes and the manner in which they are applying strategies. Therefore, think-alouds provide a unique opportunity for on-the-spot guidance. For instance, if a student admits to being confused by a passage and does not seem to know what to do about it, you can lead her or him to some possible repair strategies, asking such questions as: "What don't you understand? What is blocking your understanding? What do you need to know? What might you do to make this clear? Would rereading the sentence help? Would starting over help?"

SENTENCE-LEVEL COMPREHENSION

Students with severe comprehension problems may have difficulty understanding the simplest paragraphs. For these students, it may be necessary to start with the comprehension of single sentences. Begin by discussing and asking questions about simple sentences. Ask the student to read a sentence similar to the following and tell what it says:

> The boy ran.
> Ask: Who ran? What did the boy do?
> Expand the sentence and have the student answer questions about the expansion.
> The boy ran home.
> Ask: Where did the boy run?
> The boy ran home because it was getting dark.
> Ask: Why did the boy run home?

Gradually work up to sentences that contain embedded clauses and other complex structures. Embedded clauses are clauses that have been embedded or placed within a sentence through subordination and are one of the most complex structures, especially if the embedded clause interrupts the flow of the sentence.

> The boy who yelled to us ran home.
> Ask: Which boy ran home?

Reassembling cut-up sentences, sentence-level cloze, paraphrasing, and composing sentences are good reinforcement activities. As the student learns to comprehend single sentences, proceed to brief paragraphs and then to longer pieces. ReQuest, which is explained in Chapter 12, is also an excellent technique for use with students who have severe comprehension problems.

USING A VARIETY OF TEACHING TECHNIQUES

It is essential to use a variety of techniques when teaching comprehension to struggling readers. Often, it is necessary to present the same strategy in different ways. In addition, some techniques are teacher directed and may be appropriate for students who need structure. Others allow for more student involvement and are good for activating passive students and promoting independence. An overview of major teaching techniques is presented in Table 11.2. Additional teaching techniques, especially those that are used with expository texts, are discussed in the next chapter.

MINICASE STUDY

Although Jennifer was a nine-year-old third-grader and had no difficulty with decoding at grade level, her comprehension was poor (Sawyer, 1985). When asked to retell selections at second- and third-grade levels, Jennifer's responses were brief, very general, and involved simply stating the topic: "It's about bears and honey." She was unable to supply details about the selection and, when asked specific questions, based responses on her background knowledge and not on the text. For the most part, her responses were only marginally related to the questions.

Further testing indicated that Jennifer was able to understand simple sentences but had difficulty with complex sentences, especially those that had embedded clauses, as in "It was the first time Bill went to camp." Jennifer also had difficulty integrating information across paragraphs. In addition, Jennifer experienced problems following directions, apparently because she failed to focus on key words. Jennifer was able to organize information, but she had difficulty explaining how or why she organized it. Although she was able to categorize items correctly, she was unable to supply a category name or title.

A program of remediation focused on comprehension and, in particular, the thinking skills that are an essential element in comprehension. Instruction was initiated with materials on a late first-grade to beginning second-grade level. Activities designed to foster application of prediction strategies on the sentence level included cloze exercises (President _____ freed the slaves.) and complete-the-sentence exercises (Columbus sailed west because _____.). To foster comprehension across sentences, Jennifer was also asked to complete unfinished paragraphs (The day was dark and gloomy. Hurricane warnings were in effect and the winds were howling around the house. Suddenly, sheets of rain began to blow toward the beaches. May's father rushed in through the door and said, "_____.").

TABLE 11.2 Key Comprehension Teaching Techniques

TECHNIQUE	USES
DRA	Provides structure and guidance. Builds background and vocabulary. Teacher directed.
DR–TA	Fosters previewing and setting purposes. Stresses student involvement.
Cloze	Fosters reading for meaning and use of context. Especially effective for students who fail to read for meaning. Should only be used with students reading at least on a third-grade level.
QAR	Fosters literal and inferential comprehension by having students seek appropriate sources of information. Good for younger students.
Think-alouds	Provides insight into thought process used during comprehension. Can be used to teach any strategy and along with other techniques.

To activate Jennifer's schema and to help set a purpose for reading, semantic maps or structured overviews were suggested for use with her before she read a selection. Because Jennifer spoke mainly in short, simple sentences, activities to develop oral language were also recommended (Sawyer, 1985).

SUMMARY

According to schema theory, comprehension is an active, constructive process that activates our schemata. Comprehension can go awry if we lack the necessary schema, fail to activate it, or activate the wrong schema. The situation (mental model) view complements the schema theory of comprehension. According to the situation model point of view, readers create mental representations as they read.

Causes of poor reading comprehension are multiple and involve an interaction of reader, task, text, teaching technique, and situation. Major causes within the reader include limited vocabulary, language deficiency, deficient decoding skills, inadequate background or poorly developed schema, lack of intellectual curiosity or interest or flexibility in considering new ideas, inadequate use of thinking skills, lack of strategies, or failure to apply strategies. Overreliance on background and failure to read for meaning also cause comprehension difficulties. Although reader factors were emphasized in this chapter, teaching techniques, using appropriate texts, and the quality of the overall learning situation have a critical impact on comprehension.

One key to comprehension is the effective use of strategies. Strategies can be classified according to the cognitive processes they incorporate: preparing, selecting and organizing, elaborating, rehearsal (studying), and monitoring (metacognition).

Higher-level comprehension demands higher-level thinking skills. Accountable talk and well-chosen questions can develop both thinking and comprehension and improve attitudes. Questions should be balanced and include items from all levels: comprehending (literal level), selecting/organizing, elaborating, and monitoring (metacognition). Creating an accepting atmosphere is important to questioning. Using wait time and prompts enhances the effectiveness of questions.

The directed reading activity (DRA) is an instructional framework that incorporates the activation of schema, building of background and vocabulary, and the use of strategies and questions to build comprehension. The directed reading-thinking activity (DR-TA) is modeled on the DRA but gives the student a more active role.

Cloze, which is short for closure, is a procedure in which students read selections in which words have been deleted. As they read, students restore the deletions. In simplified versions, students use multiple-choice items to fill in the cloze blanks (mazes) or respond to one item at a time under the teacher's guidance (masking). Some severely disabled comprehenders may need help with sentence-level comprehension and understanding questions.

Another technique for teaching comprehension is think-alouds. Think-alouds can be used by the teacher to model comprehension processes. Think-alouds, when used by students, help them to become more aware of their thinking and reading processes. For students with serious comprehension problems, it may be necessary to work on understanding sentences and questions.

APPLICATION ACTIVITIES

1. Plan a lesson presenting one of the strategies described in the chapter. If possible, teach the lesson and evaluate it.

2. If you are now teaching, try using wait time and probes for a week. What changes do you notice in your students? In yourself? Ask a colleague to act as a coach and observe your performance and give you suggestions for improvement. If you are not teaching, try the technique in a small discussion group.

3. Plan a DRA or DR-TA and teach your lesson if possible. If you teach the lesson, write an evaluation of it.

4. Construct a cloze activity and try it out with a class. How did the class react?

5. Do a think-aloud with a partner on a challenging informational piece or a difficult piece of fiction. What strategies is your partner using? What strategies are you using?

CHAPTER TWELVE

READING TO LEARN AND REMEMBER IN THE CONTENT AREAS

USING WHAT YOU KNOW

Although most of the skills and strategies needed to comprehend content-area texts were introduced in the previous chapter, research shows that students often fail to transfer general skills and strategies to specific areas. A number of techniques and approaches for teaching the application of literacy skills to the content areas will be discussed. What has been your experience reading in content areas? Which subject-matter texts in your undergraduate or graduate courses did you find particularly difficult? What made them difficult? What strategies did you employ to improve your comprehension? What special difficulties might low-achieving readers experience as they attempt to read content-area material? What steps might you take to help low-achieving readers read content-area texts?

ANTICIPATION GUIDE

Read each of the following statements. Put a check under "Agree" or "Disagree" to show how you feel about each one. If you can, discuss your responses with classmates.

	AGREE	DISAGREE
1. The content-area teacher is not responsible for teaching reading or study strategies to poor readers.	_____	_____
2. The main reason that low-achieving readers have difficulty with content-area texts is because they lack general reading skills and strategies.	_____	_____
3. A major barrier to comprehension of content-area texts is a lack of background knowledge in that area.	_____	_____
4. Low-achieving readers should get most of their content-area information from lectures, discussions, experiments, and audio-visual aids, rather than from books.	_____	_____

	AGREE	DISAGREE
5. The biggest obstacle to effective studying is a lack of discipline.	_____	_____
6. Study skills are neglected at all levels of schooling.	_____	_____

THE QUIET CRISIS

Although much attention has been focused on helping struggling readers in the primary grades, there is another crisis, one that does not often make headlines and one, that unfortunately is not being addressed by national efforts. Dubbed the "quiet crisis," it refers to the inability of thousands of middle and high school students to cope with their academic texts (Schoenbach, Greenleaf, Cziko, & Hurwitz, 1999). Students hit a literacy ceiling that limits what they can do academically and later, vocationally. Not having learned to read challenging texts in their academic classes, they are unable to cope with gatekeeper reading material and so their educational and vocational futures are limited. The National Research Council (Snow, Burns, & Griffin, 1998) concluded: "The educational careers of 25 to 40 percent of American children are imperiled because they do not read well enough, quickly enough, or easily enough to ensure comprehension in their content courses in middle and secondary school" (p. 98).

Content-area teachers focus on presenting their subject matter. If they see that students are getting little from their texts, they teach around the texts. They paraphrase or summarize the text or use other methods, such as using labs, simulations, or audio-visual aids, to convey the content. As one history teacher explained, "Because you can't rely on students to read, I feel like I'm constantly summarizing the history textbook so kids don't miss the main points. I wish I didn't have to assume that role as much, but I find I do" (Schoenbach, Greenleaf, Cziko, & Hurwitz, 1999, p. 8). The teacher becomes an enabler. The students, seeing that they don't have to read the texts, stop reading assigned material. As a result, students fail to learn crucial reading skills. As they progress through the grades, the gap between the difficulty level of the text and their ability to handle it increases.

> Among the strengths students bring to the content areas are background of relevant knowledge, ability to reason, understanding of language, and ability to communicate with others (Herber & Herber, 1993).

Most of the students affected by the quiet crisis do possess solid basic reading skills. Although advanced vocabulary may pose problems, they have mastered basic decoding skills. They also have acceptable literal comprehension. What they are not prepared to deal with are the complex ideas and language structures embedded in their academic texts.

The blame for the quiet crisis has been placed, in part, on the quality of today's texts. They have been described as being dull, poorly written, biased, stuffed with facts, inaccurate, and irrelevant. While content-area texts could undoubtedly be improved, most do a decent job of presenting an overview of complex subject matter. Based on their work with reluctant and underprepared readers, Schoenbach, Greenleaf, Cziko, & Hurwitz (1999) concluded that it is the responsibility of content-area teachers to help students work through texts that are challenging and that students may see as being boring but that present key academic concepts.

CONTENT ENHANCEMENT

Using Technology
Smart Together at
http://smarttogether.org/
provides information about
Content Enhancement.

One way that students can be helped to learn content is through Content Enhancement. Content Enhancement is an approach to teaching curriculum content that is designed to assist struggling readers, but it also helps achieving readers (Fisher, Schumaker, & Deshler, 2002). Content Enhancement, which is also known as strategic teaching, is instruction "in which the teacher compensates for students' lack of strategies and models and guides students in learning how to learn" (Bulgren & Scanlon, 1997/1998, p. 293). Content Enhancement organizes and presents the curriculum in such a way that key concepts are easier to learn and more readily learned.

Here are the steps for implementing Content Enhancement as adapted from Torgesen (2004a):

Step 1: Compose two or three key questions that the unit should answer.

Step 2: Create a concept map of the key content for the unit.

Step 3: Based on an examination of the key questions and content map and the text, note the difficulties that your students, especially the struggling readers, might experience.

Step 4: Based on the potential difficulties and the nature of the material to be learned, select Content Enhancement routines.

Step 5: Based on the potential difficulties and the nature of the text, decide on key learning strategies that students will need to use.

Step 6. Incorporate the Content Enhancements and student strategies in your instruction.

Step 7. Monitor students' progress and make adjustments as necessary.

FRAMEWORK FOR TEACHING CONTENT-AREA READING

Teaching content-area reading consists mainly of applying and adapting techniques and approaches described in Chapter 11. A convenient way to look at a content-area reading lesson is to view it within the framework of a directed reading activity. A content-area reading lesson is basically an adaptation of the directed reading activity or directed reading-thinking activity. Implemented within the context of Content Enhancement, it includes establishing key ideas, preparation for reading, guided reading, rereading, extension, application, and monitoring of student progress.

Establishing Key Ideas

As noted when discussing the directed reading activity and a number of other teaching techniques, the starting point of effective instruction is to decide which key ideas or concepts you want your students to learn and then to structure questions and activities around them. Barron (1969) recommends that you analyze the selection to be read and select two to four key concepts. (Key concepts for lessons are easier to determine if you have established key questions for the unit and a concept map.) Creating key questions will give focus to your lesson and help you to determine how to prepare students for the reading of a selection and how to guide their efforts.

Preparing for Reading

Preparation for reading in the content area may take many forms but generally includes activating schema and building background, expanding vocabulary, building reasoning skills and reading strategies, establishing a purpose for reading, and motivating students. Special emphasis is placed on removing barriers to learning.

Activating Schema and Building Background.   No matter how arcane the topic, students will usually have some background knowledge to bring to it. What is important is helping students use what knowledge they have to build a bridge to the new material they are about to read. One characteristic of low-achieving readers is that even when they have relevant background knowledge, they may not realize it. An essential element in the preparation process is to help students discover what they do know about a topic. Part of helping them discover what they know is to create questions that tap into their prior knowledge. For instance, when developing the concept of representative government in preparation for reading about the Revolutionary War, you might relate this to how a class votes for a representative for the school's student council. Building on this concrete experience, lead students into a discussion about how the colonies were governed by Great Britain and had no representatives to speak for them.

> To help students relate their background of experience to content-area concepts, express the concepts in such a way that students can bring their prior knowledge to bear (Herber & Herber, 1993). A key concept such as that of representative government might be expressed as "Sometimes we let others speak for us."

Expanding Vocabulary.   Once you have established the key ideas that you wish to emphasize, choose the vocabulary words that you feel students may have difficulty with but that are essential for an understanding of the key ideas. A selection may include twenty to twenty-five or more words that you feel might be difficult for your students. Learning all those words would be overwhelming. By concentrating on those words that are most essential for an understanding of the key ideas, you limit the number of words that need to be introduced. When introducing new words, keep the number to six or seven.

Building Reasoning Skills and Strategies.   When you are analyzing the selection, note the reasoning skills or strategies required to read it. If the selection is fiction, it may demand making inferences. A social studies selection may require drawing a conclusion or making an evaluation. A description of a science process may entail imaging. Also note the structure of the piece. Readers may be able to use the structure to help them organize the information. For an article on air pollution, they may be able to use the structure to organize the information into a series of causes and effects. For a piece on regions of the United States, they may be able to organize the information in a comparison/contrast format.

Establishing Purpose and Motivating Students.   A purpose for reading should also be set. This purpose might involve questions the students have about a topic. The students should also be motivated to read. Getting them involved in setting purposes, arousing their curiosity about intriguing topics, and helping them to relate topics to their lives generate interest in reading.

Guiding the Reading

The first reading should be silent and might be guided by questions, as in the directed reading lesson, or by a prediction, as in the directed reading-thinking activity. Or you might use a study guide, an anticipation guide, or self-constructed questions. These procedures are explained later in the chapter.

Discussing the Reading

The discussion of material read might be similar to that conducted in a directed reading activity, or it might be part of a lecture on the topics covered in the text. Discussions might also take place in cooperative groups as students reflect on what they have read. Students still learning English may do better in a small discussion group. They are more likely to participate and will probably find that language is less of a barrier in a small group. These students may also benefit from the opportunity to use their home language to discuss new concepts. As Barba (1995) notes, "New knowledge can be integrated with existing knowledge only when existing knowledge (which may have been constructed in the student's native language) is restructured and students elaborate on what they already know" (p. 15).

Rereading

In the content areas, rereading is used to expand on, clarify, or organize information rather than focusing on reinforcing reading skills and strategies. By continuously monitoring students' progress, you can address problem areas.

Extending and Applying

Extension and application activities might take the form of additional reading about the topic, conducting a survey, performing an experiment, or writing an essay or report. It often involves putting the new information to use in some way.

TEXT STRUCTURE

Fostering comprehension in the content areas may also entail building an awareness of text structure. To get the most out of their reading, students need to be able to recognize and make use of narrative and expository text structures. Knowledge of text structure can also help them improve their writing skills.

Narrative Text Structure

What comes to mind as you read or hear the following passage?

> One fine afternoon Anansi the Spider was walking by the river when he saw his friend Turtle coming toward him carrying a large fish. Anansi loved to eat fish, though he was much too lazy to catch them himself. (Kimmel, 1992)

Because you are familiar with stories, chances are you expect to hear a tale in which Anansi and Turtle are the main characters. You expect the tale to have a problem that, after a series of events, will be resolved in some way. In other words, you have a schema for stories, a cognitive framework that tells you stories have characters, a setting, a problem, major events, and a resolution of the problem. If your sense of story—your **story schema**—is well developed, you may also know that a story may also have a theme or moral or may be used to explain the origin of some natural phenomenon.

> **Story schema:** the reader's concept of a story, including setting, problem, goal, characters, major episodes or plot, and resolution.

By the time they are in kindergarten, most students have a basic sense of story elements, although they cannot name or explain them. Story schema is important for comprehension. As Harris and Sipay (1990) explain, "Children use their story schemata as a framework for comprehending a story by setting up expectations for certain contents occurring in a particular sequence" (p. 566). Unfortunately, low-achieving readers may have a poorly developed sense of story. When retelling stories, they tend to omit important information about the setting, characters, and the ending, and may have difficulty with the sequence (Garnett, 1986). Poor readers have a difficult time producing a coherent summary of stories they have read. Stories that they compose tend to be made up of a series of unconnected or loosely connected events (Oakhill & Yuill, 1996). Poor readers' difficulties with stories include comprehending or retelling stories that have been read to them as well as stories that they have read. Their difficulties are also evident when they write stories. Their stories are less well structured than those of good readers when they are given a title as a prompt (Cain, 1996). However, they do better when they are given a series of illustrations that depict key events in the story, whereas good readers do not. This indicates that poor comprehenders do not have an adequate grasp of story structure. Cain (1996) concluded that poor story structure was a cause of poor comprehension.

Narrative content can be action oriented or consciousness oriented or a mixture of the two (Bruner, 1986). In action-oriented narratives, the tale is generally told from the perspective of a third-person narrator. The material usually consists of a series of episodes arranged in the order in which they took place. Little text is devoted to the psychological states of the main characters. Action-oriented stories are relatively easy to comprehend and require only an understanding of the actions being described (Westby, 1999). More complex are stories that embody the consciousness of the characters. These are often told from the perspectives of several characters and are more complex because they require an understanding of human motivation. This involves understanding the actions of others in terms of their goals and plans (Bruce, 1980). Even relatively simple stories may require complex understandings. In order to understand a trickster tale, a student must realize what deception is, recognize that false information can be given, that the intention is more important than the actual content of the message, and be able to detect deceit using cues that indicate the speaker is not telling the truth (DePaulo & Jordan, 1982). See the following Exemplary Teaching box.

■ ■ ■ ■ ■ ▬▬

EXEMPLARY TEACHING

We often associate disabled readers with decoding problems. However, there are also a large number of students whose decoding is adequate, who can pronounce all the words, but who do not understand what they have read. Sometimes their comprehension problems are quite severe. They can't seem to answer the simplest questions about a selection that seems relatively easy. One such student was Glenda, a second grader in an urban school. Glenda read "The Hen and the Apple Tree," a fable in which Wolf, disguised as an apple tree, tries to trick Hen into coming outside. However, Hen notices that the apple tree was not there the day before, and it had four furry feet, pointed ears, and a mouthful of sharp teeth. She refuses to come out and Wolf leaves in a rage. Glenda had difficulty constructing a story map of the fable. In fact, despite all the clues provided, Glenda did not realize that the tree was not a real tree but was Wolf disguised as a tree.

Discussion revealed several areas of need. Glenda apparently did not have a schema for fables. Her teacher, Thomas Christopher, began reading and discussing fables to the group. Glenda, a good decoder, also seemed to believe that the mark of a good reader was how you sounded. She did not realize that meaning is reading's bottom line. Christopher deemphasized oral reading and began stressing meaning. Glenda was also inexperienced at making inferences. Christopher began teaching the students strategies for making inferences. Realizing that he had not given Glenda much before-reading guidance, Christopher began providing more preparation for reading. During the preparation periods, he emphasized building and activating schema. He also broke the reading into shorter segments. As the year progressed, Christopher introduced other key comprehension strategies, such as monitoring for meaning, summarizing, and questioning.

Fostering the comprehension of narratives requires being aware of the students' level of knowledge of narratives. One way of assessing a student's comprehension of narrative schema is to ask the student to retell a familiar story or to create a story based on a wordless picture book (Westby, 1999). Ask questions that probe the depth of students' understanding of a story: "How did Jan feel in the story? Why do you think she felt that way? What might she do to make up for her embarrassing mistake?" Students with poorly developed story schema will retell stories as a series of isolated incidents or will have information about isolated incidents but will have difficulty creating a coherent story. They will have a difficult time making inferences about the characters' goals and motivation. They will also have difficulty inferring emotions and characteristics and predicting outcomes (Westby, 1999).

Developing a Sense of Story.   The best way to develop a sense of story is to read to students and discuss stories with them. After hearing and discussing many stories, they naturally aquire a series of expectations about what takes place in a story. If your students lack a strong sense of story, start out by reading brief action stories told in relatively simple language. As students' comprehension of stories becomes more advanced, read stories that emphasize the development of characters and that provide insight into motivation and emotions. As you discuss stories, you might also highlight the most important elements in a story, asking questions such as:

> Where did the story take place?
> Who were the most important characters in the story?
> What did Anansi plan to do?
> How did Turtle trick Anansi?
> How do you think Anansi felt after he discovered that he had been tricked?
> Why didn't Warthog believe Anansi?
> What did Anansi learn?
> What lesson do you think the story teaches?

| **Story map:** graphic display showing the major elements in a story. Often the focus is on the plot. |

Questions should be geared to the key elements of the story. These help students form a solid sense of story. One way to make sure questions are keyed to the major elements in a story is to create a key elements map (Beck, Omanson, & McKeown, 1982). The creation of a key elements map is described in Chapter 11. Student versions of key elements maps, which are also known as **story maps,** can be used to enhance low-achieving readers' comprehension (Cunningham & Foster, 1978; Fitzgerald & Spiegel, 1983). A sample student story map is presented in Figure 12.1.

Questions as well as the type of story being read should be geared to the students' level of story knowledge. As Westby (1999) notes, "Children with limited narrative abilities frequently do not enjoy listening to or reading complex stories" (p. 193). If students have difficulty retelling a story or responding to questions about a story that you have read to them, try selecting less complex stories.

Writing also helps develop a sense of story. Students might begin by imitating a simple, predictable pattern, such as the one in *Millions of Cats* (Gág, 1928). In time, they can try more complex patterns. As students develop a sense of story, they can also take a deeper look at theme, more complex plots, and more realistic characterization. Composing group stories provides reluctant writers with support and also models the process for them.

Wordless picture books or a series of illustrations can also be used as a prompt for a story. The advantage of using a series of illustrations is that this helps structure the story for the student.

In addition to story knowledge, students must also know the language of stories in order to be able to read and write stories. As you read stories to students and discuss and write stories with them, highlight the language of storytelling.

FIGURE 12.1   Story Map

Setting:	*By the river*
Characters:	*Anansi*
	Turtle
	Warthog
Problem:	*Anansi wanted a fish.*
Main Happenings in Story:	*Anansi asked Turtle to teach him to fish.*
	Anansi made a net.
	Anansi put the net in the river.
	Anansi caught a fish and cooked it.
	Turtle ate the fish.
	Anansi asked Warthog for justice.
	Warthog did not believe Anansi.
Outcome:	*Spiders learned how to weave nets.*

> **Story grammar:** shows how the major parts of a story are interrelated. A story grammar might include setting, problem, goal, characters, major episodes, and resolution.

Other Techniques for Developing a Sense of Story.   Techniques that involve the use of **story grammar** to predict and build comprehension are the probable passages, predict-o-gram, and story impressions techniques. Probable passages is similar to possible sentences and predict-o-gram, which were discussed in Chapter 10. In probable passages, students use their inferential skills to predict which vocabulary words tell about which story grammar category: setting, characters, problem, resolution, or ending. Once they have placed vocabulary words in story grammar categories, students predict what the story might be about. This can be done orally, or students might create a written probable passage that summarizes the story. In addition to fostering a sense of story grammar, comprehension, and vocabulary knowledge, probable passages also promote summarizing skills.

Story impressions also use vocabulary from the story to activate students' story schema. Story impressions are designed specifically for corrective readers, and have been shown to be an effective technique for fostering improved comprehension (McGinley & Denner, 1987). In story impressions, students use a series of words and phrases from a selection to reconstruct the story. Words and phrases that offer useful clues are chosen. Although students are encouraged to structure a story that is as close as possible to the actual story, faithfulness to the original tale is not the essential factor in students' achievement. The ability to use the clues to construct a logical tale is the main factor in improved comprehension. To present story impressions, try the following steps.

A LESSON IN DEVELOPING STORY IMPRESSIONS

Step 1: Developing a set of story impressions. First, read the whole story. Then reread it and select words that highlight characters, setting, and key elements of the plot. Whenever possible, use the exact words from the story. Use single words, or phrases limited to three words. Choose ten to fifteen clues and arrange them in order. Use arrows to show that one element leads to another.

Step 2: Explaining story impressions. Explain the purpose of story impressions and how it works. Have the title of the story read and tell students that clues from the story are listed on the board. Explain that they will be using the clues to create a story and then they will read the actual story to compare what they have written to what the author has created.

Step 3: Reading the clues. Read the clues with students. Discuss any words that may be unfamiliar. Encourage students to think about the kind of story that might be created based on the words listed.

Step 4: Creating a story impression. After discussing the clues, you and the class create a story impression based on the clues. Students may add words and phrases not presented. Focus on creating a story that is interesting and logical. After the story has been composed and written on the board, discuss it, and encourage students to evaluate it and make revisions if needed.

Step 5: Reading of author's story. Direct students to read the author's story and compare their version with the author's story.

Step 6: Discussing the story. Discuss the author's story. Compare the author's and students' versions. As students become proficient in this technique, they might create and discuss story impressions in small cooperative learning groups. Story impressions can also be used as part of the writing program (McGinley & Denner, 1987). They provide excellent practice in constructing narrative pieces.

A list of story impression clues based on Edgar Allen Poe's "The Tell-Tale Heart" and a low-achieving reader's construction of a story based on the clues is presented in Figure 12.2.

Expository Text Structures

We organize information from our reading according to the structure of the ideas in a selection. The main idea is at the top of the structure. Supporting details are organized around the main idea.

What makes the following paragraph easy or hard to read?

Skin has four important jobs. One, it keeps harmful bacteria out of your body. Two, it keeps the water in your body from drying up. The outer layer of skin is waterproof. And oil glands in the skin produce oils that keep the skin moist. Three, skin regulates the temperature of your body. Layers of fat in the skin help to keep you warm. Sweat glands in the skin let the body give off moisture through the skin. This helps you cool off. Four, skin is the sense organ of touch. (Bledsoe, 1990, p. 185)

The paragraph, which was taken from *Fearon's Biology,* a text for below-level readers, is well structured. It has a main idea, announced in the first sentence, followed by a listing of four details. By using the structure of that paragraph, the student can better understand its content. In fact, the structure provides a map of the information presented in the paragraph. Using that map should improve the encoding of the information. Students will know that they will be looking for four items as they read the paragraph. The structure also helps the readers organize the information: one main idea and four details. Knowing

FIGURE 12.2 Story Impressions (Prereading) Activity Based on Poe's "The Tell-Tale Heart"

STORY IMPRESSIONS GIVEN TO A CLASS	A REMEDIAL EIGHTH-GRADER'S STORY GUESS WRITTEN FROM THE STORY IMPRESSIONS
house ↓ old man ↓ young man ↓ hatred ↓ ugly eye ↓ death ↓ tub, blood, knife ↓ buried ↓ floor ↓ police ↓ heartbeat ↓ guilt ↓ crazy ↓ confession	There was a young man and his father, an old man. They lived in a house on a hill out in the bouniey's. The old man hated his son because he had an ugly eye. The young man was asleep in his bedroom when he was awakened by screaming. He went to the bedroom and saw his father laying in the tub. There was blood everywhere and a knife through him. The young man found a tape recording hidden behind the door on the floor. He turned it on there was screaming on the tape. The young man started to call the police, but then he stopped and remembered what his mother had told him. She had told him that he had a split personality. So he called the police and confessed to being crazy and killing his father. His heartbeat was heavy as he called.

From William J. McGinley & Peter R. Denner (1987, December) "Story Impressions: A Prereading/Writing Activity," *Journal of Reading, 31*(3) 248–253. Reprinted with permission of William McGinley and the International Reading Association.

the structure, the student will be better able to take notes, create a semantic map, or outline the paragraph.

Typically, young and low-achieving readers fail to use text structure as a reading strategy. For younger readers this may be due, in part, to a lack of experience with expository text. For older low-achieving readers it may reflect a lack of knowledge about text structure strategy or simply failure to use this strategy. Using the text structure strategy, good readers seek the author's main idea and then relate the details to that main idea. The students then create a mental representation of the text that reflects the text structure (problem–solution, cause–effects, for instance). When recalling the text, they retrieve the major idea first and then the details. Poor comprehenders, on the other hand, do not organize information and simply encode a passage as a list of unrelated items. As Meyer, Brandt, and Bluth (1980) comment: "The reader has no focus and simply tries to remember something from the text" (p. 80). The result is a "list-like collection of descriptions about the passage topic with no attempt to interrelate them" (p. 80).

Types of Expository Text Structure.   Expository texts are organized in a variety of ways. Major types of organization are listed below.

Time Sequence.   This structure is a listing, but time order is indicated. Signal words include *after, at last, before, finally, later, long ago, then, today, tomorrow, yesterday,* and the names of specific days, times, and dates. Time sequence is frequently found in fiction and in history texts.

> Ferdinand Magellan, A Portuguese captain, was commissioned to sail in search of the Far East in 1519. He sailed across the Atlantic Ocean and reached the coast of South America. He then journeyed south, to the southern tip of South America. There he found a waterway that became known as the Strait of Magellan. The stormy waters led from the Atlantic to the Pacific Oceans. Magellan had found the water route around the new world. (King & Napp, 1998, p. 39)

Enumeration/Description.   This structure also may present details in a simple list, provide a series of descriptive details, or give a series of examples. No cause–effect, time, or other relationships are used. The structure may be cued by words such as *for example, one, two,* and other number words. Enumeration/description is frequently found in fiction and social studies but may also be found in science.

> The coral snake lives in the southern United States. It usually lives in a damp, cool spot under fallen leaves, and looks for lizards or other snakes to eat. (Scott, 1993, p. 23)

Explanation/Process.   This structure explains how something works or is done, such as how a laser disk player works, how plants make food, how a President is elected, how rocks are formed, or how we hear. Explanation/process passages dominate scientific writing.

> Knowledge of text structure can be used to organize in one's mind information that one has read and can also be used to structure information that one is writing.

> In conduction, heat is moved along by molecules bumping into one another. Suppose you put a spoon in a cup of hot coffee. The top of the spoon doesn't touch the coffee at all. Yet it will soon be hot. This is because of conduction. The coffee heats the bottom of the spoon. The hot molecules on the bottom of the spoon bump into other spoon molecules. This warms them up. In turn, these molecules warm up the next ones up the spoon. The heat moves right on up to the tip of the spoon. (Bledsoe, 1994, p. 199)

Comparison/Contrast.   This structure focuses on similarities and/or differences, using cue words such as *although, but, however, similar, different, on the one hand, on the other hand.* Comparison/contrast structures are frequently found in social studies texts but are also found in science writing.

Rabbits are much like rodents. There are two big differences. Rabbits have four cutting teeth while rodents have only two. Also rabbits have very strong back legs. These make rabbits very good hoppers and leapers. (Bledsoe, 1988, p. 165)

Problem/Solution. In this type of structure, a problem is presented and then its solution specified.

Kids in the U.S. throw away more than four billion little drink boxes a year. Drink boxes can sit for 300 to 400 years in a landfill. As an answer to this problem some cities and school systems have drink-box recycling programs. If there isn't a drink-box recycling program in your area, ask your student council to start one. Better yet, try filling a Thermos or sports bottle with juice instead of buying drink boxes—and urge your friends to do the same. (Lowery & Lorbiecki, 1993, p. 17)

Cause/Effect. In this structure, a cause is described and then its effects are presented. In a variation the effect or effects are presented and then the causes are given.

Fishing, hunting, and trapping are one cause of animal extinction. Another cause is the clearing away of plant life. Animals that lived in these places die because their homes have been destroyed. (Bledsoe, 1988, p. 247)

> Newspaper articles often follow a journalist structure (Simonsen, 1996). The main idea of the article is highlighted in the first paragraph, and the details follow in the remaining paragraphs.

Although a piece of writing may have a predominant structure, most combine two or more organizational patterns. The following piece is composed primarily of a comparison/contrast pattern that compares plant and animal cells, but the pattern flows naturally into an enumeration/description pattern as cell walls are described and the function of chloroplasts is explained.

Plant and animals cells have a few important differences. First, plant cells have cell walls. The cell wall is outside the membrane. It is harder and stronger than the membrane.
Plant cells usually have bigger vacuoles than animal cells. This is because plant cells must store a lot of water. Often, however, animals cells have more vacuoles than plant cells.
The most important difference is that plant cells have something called chloroplasts. Chloroplasts store a green coloring. This green coloring traps sunlight. Plants use the trapped sunlight to make their food. (Bledsoe, 1994, p. 43)

Older students and better readers are more aware of organizational patterns and make more effective use of them. However, text structure can be taught to poor readers and has resulted, in some studies, in both improved comprehension and improved writing (Gordon, 1990). Instruction seems to be most effective when both reading and writing are involved (Horowitz, 1985).

Teaching Text Patterns

To teach text structures, start with the easiest pattern. For younger children, the time-sequence pattern seems easiest (Englert & Hiebert, 1985). For older students, the comparison/contrast pattern seems to be the best choice for initial instruction (Meyer & Rice, 1984).

To teach a time-sequence pattern, begin with everyday activities. Compose a list of the day's activities, or recount a recent trip in an experience story. Include and emphasize time signal words: *next, after, soon.* Next, read a brief, well-structured selection with the class. Using a think-aloud procedure, show how you would use cue words and the sense of the selection to determine the structure of the passage and, in turn, use the structure to improve comprehension (Gordon, 1990).

Discussing the time-sequence passage about Magellan, you might say, "The first sentence tells me that Magellan started out in 1519. This paragraph looks like it will have a time-sequence order. Yes, here it says he sailed across the Atlantic and then went south. This is definitely a time-sequence passage. As I read this passage, I'll try to keep the events in order."

"You can tell a time-sequence passage by the way the events happen one right after another and also because there are words that signal time order. Dates such as *1519* signal time order. Can you find other words that signal time order?" The class would discuss the role that *then, finally,* and *at last* play in cueing time order.

Under your guidance, have students read brief, well-structured time-order passages. Help them pose questions that take advantage of the structure of the passage. When discussing the selection, ask a question that incorporates time structure. For instance, for the Magellan passage, you might ask students to trace in order the main parts of Magellan's journey around the world. Asking how many ships or men took part in the journey are valid questions but don't take advantage of the structure of the passage, which is what you are emphasizing.

Have students compose graphic organizers that show the structure of the piece. For time-sequence passages, you might use a timeline or a series of boxes as in Figure 12.3, which show time order. For explanation/process, show the steps in the explanation or process in a series of boxes. For comparison/contrast, you might use a Venn diagram (see p. 349). For enumeration/description, you might use a semantic map or web (see p. 346).

To reinforce the use of signal words, cut up a passage that incorporates cue words and have students reassemble it as in the following exercise. Select a passage similar to the one shown, in which putting the passage back together again would be difficult without cue words.

Have you ever wondered how dolphins are trained?

Next, the dolphin is taught to look at the trainer.

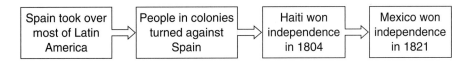

FIGURE 12.3 Sequence Chart

At last, the dolphin is taught to do easy tricks like taking a bow.

First of all, a dolphin has to be trained to eat dead fish, because in the wild, dolphins eat only live fish.

Have students compose time-order pieces. You may want to have them use well-structured passages as models or supply frames as in Figure 12.4. Starting with simplified sequence patterns, Cudd and Roberts (1989) report using frames as early as the second half of first grade.

If you do use frames, gradually phase them out so students are creating their own pieces. Also encourage the use of signal words; but as students grow in writing skill, lead them to see that the overuse of signal words can produce prose that is wooden. After students have a fairly good grasp of one pattern, introduce another. (For more information on using text structures in writing, see Chapter 13.)

Encourage students to use their knowledge of patterns in their studying as well as in their reading and writing. For instance, when taking notes, students should take advantage of the text pattern so that major historical events are listed in order and effects are listed under causes or vice versa.

> **Structural organizer:** helps students take advantage of the organization of a selection in order to enhance comprehension and retention.

Using the Structural Organizer.   The structural organizer can be a powerful technique for guiding students in the use of text organization as a reading strategy. In one study, ninth-graders who used a structural organizer recalled 77 percent more than did those who read as they usually did (Slater, Graves, & Piche, 1985). A **structural organizer** is a study or reading guide in which the organization of the text is briefly explained and a partially completed outline or other organizer is supplied. The reader is told how and why to finish the outline. Figure 12.5 shows a structural organizer.

Using Headings and Subheads.   Show students how heading and subheads reflect the organization of text. Before reading, they provide an overview of topics covered and a guide to learning. After reading, they can be used as a summary of what was read and an aid to locating information (Dickson, 2004a). Model for students how you survey a selection to get an overview of the information being presented. Using a think-aloud, demon-

FIGURE 12.4   Frame for an Explanation/Process Sequence Paragraph

_____ is easy. First, you_____.
The next step is to _____.
Then you _____.
Finally, you _____.
Just four simple steps, and you're finished.

FIGURE 12.5   Sample Structural Organizer

Chapter 15: How We Use the Land

In this chapter, which talks about using land, William Lefkowitz, the author, uses two types of writing patterns: main idea and details and cause and effect. Read the section to answer the cause-and-effect and main idea questions:

Why is there a limited amount of usable land? (p. 175, par. 1)

Causes for Limited Amount of Usable Land

1. _____
2. _____
3. _____
4. _____
5. _____

What are the seven major uses of land in the United States? (pp. 176–177)

Seven Major Uses of Land

1. _____
2. _____
3. _____
4. _____
5. _____
6. _____
7. _____

What are the three causes of shrinking farmland in the United States? (pp. 180–181)

Three Causes of Shrinking Farmland

1. _____
2. _____
3. _____

Exercise based on W. Lefkowitz, *Fearon's United States Geography*. Belmont, CA: Fearon Education, 1990.

strate how you make use of the titles, headings, and subheads. Demonstrate how you use these aids to activate background knowledge and predict the content of the selection. After you get an overview of the selection, you use each of the subheads as a guide to the particular section that you are reading. Provide activities in which students survey a section and discuss what they believe the section will be about. Have them read specific sections, using subheads as a guide. Discuss how the subheads helped them comprehend the section.

INSTRUCTIONAL TECHNIQUES
FOR FOSTERING LEARNING FROM TEXT

There are numerous techniques for fostering comprehension in general reading and in the content areas. It is important to have a variety of techniques, as this sparks interest. Some techniques are especially effective in building background, whereas others can be effective in activating schema, creating interest, or organizing information. Some are teacher directed; others are more student centered. The well-prepared reading teacher has knowledge of a variety of techniques but, more important, knows which techniques work best in which situations. As you read about each technique, think of its advantages and disadvantages and the situations in which it might work best. Techniques have been grouped according to when they would most likely be used: before, during, or after reading.

Before-Reading Techniques

The purpose of before-reading teaching techniques is to help students get an overview of the selection to be read, to activate prior knowledge, build background knowledge and vocabulary, set goals, and establish strategies for reading and reasoning. Before-reading techniques feature the anticipation guide, structured overview, and Frayer model. In the previous chapter, the directed reading activity and directed reading-thinking activity were presented as devices to prepare students to read. The initial portions of these techniques may also be used to prepare students for reading a content-area selection.

Anticipation Guide.   At this point, you should be fairly familiar with the anticipation guide. It has appeared at the beginning of each chapter in this book. An anticipation guide consists of a list of three to six controversial or debatable statements. Students respond to the statements by indicating whether they agree or disagree with them.

Anticipation guides force students to think about a subject before they read about it. While activating their prior knowledge, it may also bring to the fore erroneous concepts that they have about a topic. Low-achieving readers tend to hold onto beliefs even when they are contradicted in print (Lipson, 1984; Maria & MacGinitie, 1987). Anticipation guides, by bringing forth erroneous beliefs, make these easier to deal with. Here are the steps for creating and using an anticipation guide (Head & Readence, 1986).

> Anticipation guides have the potential to spark a lively discussion and interest in the topic. This activates prior knowledge and fosters motivation for active reading.

■ ■ ■ ■ ■ ▬▬▬▬▬▬▬▬▬▬▬▬▬▬▬▬▬▬▬▬▬▬▬▬▬▬▬▬▬▬

STEPS FOR INTRODUCING AN ANTICIPATION GUIDE

Step 1: Identifying major concepts. Note two or three major ideas that you wish students to learn.

Step 2: Determining students' background. Considering students' general store of knowledge and beliefs and content of the selection to be read, what

misunderstandings might they have about the topic? Jot these down.

Step 3: Creating the guide. Write three to six statements that encompass key concepts. Compose statements that tap areas in which students have misconceptions or doubts. Do not compose statements about areas in which students have no knowledge, because they won't be able to say whether they agree or disagree. The best kinds of statements are those for which the students have enough information so they can respond, but not so much that they won't be acquiring new information as they read. Be careful not to write statements that are really true–false items and that do not require students to assess their knowledge, beliefs, and opinions (Head & Readence, 1986).

Step 4: Introducing the guide. Explain the guide. It may be placed on the board or on sheets of paper. Read the directions and the statements orally and ask students to respond to each statement by checking "Agree" or "Disagree." Students may work independently or in small groups. Small groups may be more effective in getting students to consider their ideas on the topic, including misconceptions.

Step 5: Discussing responses. Discuss each statement. You might have students raise their hands to indicate if they agree or disagree. Have students explain their reasons. Try to elicit at least one agree and one disagree statement for each item so students are better able to evaluate both sides of an issue. The discussion should help students open their minds as they consider their beliefs in relationship to the beliefs of others. The discussion should also motivate students to want to read, so they can evaluate their beliefs.

Step 6: Reading the text. Restate the gist of students' responses. Then have them read the selection to evaluate their answers.

Step 7: Discussing the text. Students can discuss the text and their responses to the original statements once more, this time in the light of having read the selection. They can talk over how reading the text had an impact on their original responses.

Extended Anticipation Guide.   The extended guide adds a second part in which readers indicate whether they have found support in the text for their responses (Duffelmeyer, Baum, & Merkley, 1987). If they did not find support, they rewrite in their own words information from the text that conflicts with their beliefs. Because the extended anticipation guide requires the student to paraphrase information that conflicts with a misconception, it should be more effective in motivating students to revise erroneous information.

Structured Overview.   In order to study how students read content materials, Barron (1979) took on the role of a student in a high school biology class, a subject in which he had little background. Overwhelmed by a long list of unfamiliar technical terms, he wondered how he would cope with all the new words. The solution was not long in coming.

> Later that evening, as I attempted to read the chapters associated with the unit, a simple fact began to dawn on me. All the vocabulary words were related in some way. I started to arrange the words in a diagram to depict relationships, occasionally adding terms from the two preceding units. Gradually, much of the content with which I had been struggling became clear. (pp. 172–173)

Out of this experience was born the structured overview. A structured overview builds on what students already know. It shows how new words in a selection that students are about to read or a unit that they are about to study are related to words that are familiar to them. For instance, students can better understand the word *mollusks* when they realize that the term includes clams, snails, scallops, oysters, and octopuses. The original structured overview was very much teacher directed and followed a series of six steps as outlined in the following box.

A LESSON IN TEACHING A STRUCTURED OVERVIEW

Selecting key concepts helps you decide what is important and provides a rationale for selecting the words that you wish to present.

Step 1: Selecting key concepts. Read over the selection or unit to be read and select two to four concepts or ideas that you wish to emphasize. In introducing a unit on mollusks, for example, the teacher decided that she wanted to stress the following ideas (the lesson is drawn from an easy-to-read science text by Gottlieb, 1991).

- Mollusks are soft-bodied invertebrates and fall into one of three main groups.
- Snails are mollusks that have one valve.
- Clams and oysters have two valves.
- Octopuses, squid, and cuttlefish have no valves.

Step 2: Selecting related vocabulary. Analyze the vocabulary in the selection and choose words that you feel would be needed to understand the key ideas.

cuttlefish	squid	clam
mollusk	coquinas	scallops

invertebrate	shell	oysters
univalve	snail	tentacles
valveless	gills	bivalve

Step 3: Arranging words. Arrange the words so that you show relationships.

Step 4: Inserting known words. Add words that the students already know, so they can relate new words to known words.

Step 5: Checking the overview. Look over the overview. Are relationships shown clearly? Is the overview easy to understand? A completed overview is shown in Figure 12.6.

Step 6: Introducing the overview. Place the overview on an overhead projector, chart paper, or on the board. Point to the word *mollusks* and tell students that they will be reading about mollusks. Ask them what they can tell about mollusks by examining the overview. Discuss the fact that mollusks are invertebrates and so have no backbone. Talk over the three main kinds of mollusks and examples of each. Clarify any concepts that seem confusing. Make any changes to the overview that seem necessary.

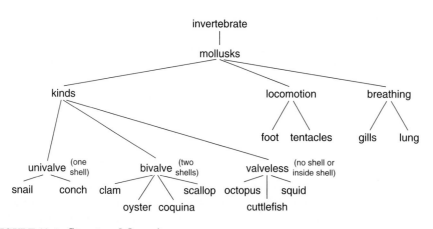

FIGURE 12.6   Structured Overview

Keep the overview in a prominent place so that, as students read about mollusks, they can refer to the overview. As students learn more about mollusks, encourage them to add to the overview. You may want to add sections that contain key words that refer to movement, obtaining oxygen, obtaining food, or other vital activities.

Revised Structured Overview. The original structured overview is teacher directed and works well when students have little background to bring to a topic. In the revised structured overview, students are more actively involved. Barron (1979) found that when students played a role in constructing an overview, they learned more.

The revised overview begins with brainstorming (Estes & Vaughn, 1985). Place the key concept on the board and discuss it. A concept such as *mollusks* would probably not work well for a prereading structured overview, because students might have little background to bring to the concept. However, you might use a more familiar concept such as *clam* or *octopus* or *snail.* As the students respond, probe and supply prompts, asking questions such as "What sea animals are like clams? What are some land animals, besides turtles, that have shells?"

After listing on the board what students know, you might add some of your own items, especially if key concepts were omitted. You and the class can then group items that go together and devise a title or category name for them. The items are then arranged in a structured overview. Again, at this point, you should feel free to add important concepts or vocabulary that have not been mentioned. You should also review the overview and tie it in with the students' purpose for reading the selection. The students might use the overview to predict what the selection will be about. Students might add to the overview after they have read the selection.

The Frayer model works best with high-level, complex concepts that have a hierarchical organization.

Frayer Model of Conceptual Development. Because they are small, crawl on the ground, and have a somewhat similar appearance, spiders, insects, mites, and ticks are often lumped together. Even students who know that spiders are not insects are surprised to learn that neither are ticks or mites. A procedure that has been used successfully to teach concepts to low-achieving readers in both social studies and science is the Frayer model of conceptual development (Peters, 1979).

A carefully thought-out, systematic procedure, the Frayer model develops concepts through discovering relevant attributes, considering irrelevant attributes, and noting examples and nonexamples. The concept is also placed within a hierarchy so the students see superordinate, coordinate, and subordinate categories. This allows students to see how the concept fits in within an overall conceptual scheme. Seeing all these relationships, students learn concepts better because they have more semantic cues. Here is how the concept of *insects* might be taught.

■ ■ ■ ■ ■ ▬▬▬▬▬▬▬▬▬▬▬▬▬▬▬▬▬▬▬▬▬▬▬▬▬▬▬▬▬▬▬

FRAYER MODEL LESSON

Step 1: Brainstorming the concept. In order to involve students and find out what they know about the topic, write the topic word on the board and ask students to tell what comes to mind when they hear, for example, the word *insect.* List students' responses on the board.

(Continued)

Through seeing superordinate, coordinate, and subordinate categories, students can better grasp how key concepts are interrelated.

Step 2: Discussing examples of the concept. From the information listed on the board, note examples of insects. If there are few examples, list additional ones.

Step 3: Discussing relevant characteristics. Talk over what insects have in common—six legs and three body parts.

Step 4: Arranging concepts in a hierarchy. Show where insects fall in the hierarchy. Show superordinate categories. Insects are arthropods. Arthropods are invertebrates. Invertebrates are animals. Then show coordinate categories. Insects belong in the same group of arthropods as do crustaceans, arachnids, chilopods, and diplopods. Discuss subordinate categories: Coleoptera (beetles), Lepidoptera (butterflies and moths), Hymenoptera (ants, bees, wasps), Diptera (flies).

Step 5: Discussing common characteristics. Help students decide what the relevant characteristics of an insect are, that is, three pairs of legs and three body parts.

Step 6: Discussing irrelevant characteristics. Discuss irrelevant characteristics of insects: color, size, whether they have eyes, the climate in which they are found.

Step 7: Discussing nonexamples. Discuss why a spider, a scorpion, a tick, a mite, or a centipede is not an insect.

Step 8: Testing the concept. Provide the students with examples and nonexamples of creatures and have them tell whether they are insects and explain their responses. An example of Frayer's model is shown in Figure 12.7.

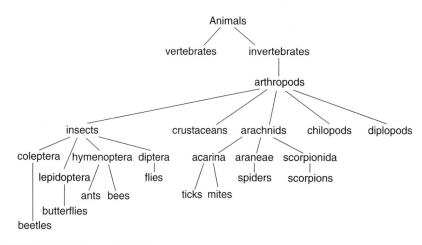

FIGURE 12.7   Frayer Model

During-Reading Techniques

As students read content-area texts, they hone in on critical information, information that answers the purpose question that was established for their reading. Students distinguish between relevant and irrelevant information or between important and unimportant details.

They organize information, using main ideas that they have recognized as they read or constructed. They make inferences about causes; visualize settings, characters, and processes; generate questions; summarize; predict; integrate new information with old; and modify schema if necessary. They also make use of heads and subheads, charts, photos, drawings, other graphical features, and the overall organization and layout of the chapter or section being read. In addition, they monitor for meaning and use correction strategies, such as rereading, as necessary.

In general, adept readers use many of the strategies highlighted in the previous chapter. In addition, they employ a strategy introduced earlier in this chapter: using chapter organization and text structure to enhance comprehension. The techniques that promote the use of during-reading strategies include frame questions, study guides, glosses, and think-alouds.

One key to learning the content of a subject matter is to know the questions to ask. The questions help determine what information is most important and how that information is organized.

Frames: categories of information that reflect the structure of content-area text (Armbruster & Anderson, 1981). A history frame, reflecting the content area's concern with causes and effects, may detail the causes of the Revolutionary War.

Frame Questions. In a sense, each content area attempts to answer a series of questions. Much of science is devoted to asking questions about mechanisms, processes, systems, and theories. For instance, the following questions are regularly asked about major systems of the body: What are the parts of the system? Where is the system located? How does the system work? What is the system's function? What are some signs that the system is not functioning properly? In geography, frequently asked questions include: Where is it? What are its major physical characteristics? How was it formed? How is it changing? History is concerned with questions of time and causes and effects. **Frames** are visual representations of the answers to implied or explicit content-area questions (Armbruster & Anderson, 1981). Frames reflect the structure of the content area. For instance, a history frame, reflecting the content area's concern with causes and effects, may detail the major causes of the Revolutionary War. One way to take advantage of the frame organization is to construct a frame matrix.

Frame Matrix. As its name suggests, the frame matrix has two major aspects: a *frame,* which highlights essential categories of information—such as location, area, population, climate—and the *matrix,* which allows the comparison of two or more elements in terms of the frames or categories (see Figure 12.8).

To construct a frame matrix, seek out the important categories of information for a topic. Then note how each category might be subdivided. If you are familiar with a topic, you might set up a tentative frame and then verify it by checking the text that students are about to read (Armbruster, 1991). You might also check the topic in an encyclopedia. Encyclopedias often organize their articles around major topics or questions.

Possible frame questions for a chapter or a book on weather disasters might include: What is it? What are its main characteristics? What causes it? What damage does it do? How is it forecast? What are the signs of it? How can you protect yourself against it? What are some of the most notorious ones?

FIGURE 12.8   Frame Matrix

Countries of North America			
	Canada	Mexico	United States
Location	Northern North America	Southern North America	Central North America
Area	3,851,809 sq miles (9,976,186 sq km)	761,600 sq miles (1,972,547 sq km)	3,536,341 sq miles (9,159,123 sq km)
Population	31 million	101 million	285 million
Climate	Temperate-Cold	Warm	Varies
Income per person	$23,300	$8,500	$21,181

In a study of states, possible frame questions might include: What is its name? Where is it? How big is it? How many people does it have? What is the average income of its people? What are its main industries? What are its natural resources? What is its capital?

A frame matrix helps students see relationships. Students can see at a glance what entities are being compared and what the major categories of information are. Making comparisons is facilitated because categories being compared are lined up side by side. The matrix also makes it obvious when information is missing (Heiman & Slomianko, 1986).

> Frame matrices work best as a study guide and are effective when comparisons are being made or when the focus is on key categories of information.

> **Study guide:** written set of questions or other activities designed to assist students in their reading of a segment of content-area text.

Study Guides.   **Study guides** come in many shapes and sizes, and may take a variety of forms and serve a number of purposes. One recent text discusses nearly twenty varieties of study guides (Wood, Lapp, & Flood, 1992). Study guides lead students through the reading and thinking processes necessary to acquire the key concepts in the text (Maxworthy, 1993).

Content Guides.   One of the simplest guides is the content guide. Low-achieving readers often find a fact-packed content-area text to be overwhelming. Through questions, statements, matching items, sentence-completion exercises, and the completion of graphic organizers, a content guide leads students to the significant content in the

> Originally designed to pro-vide guidance as secondary students read their content-area texts, study guides can be particularly effective when used with low-achieving readers.

chapter. As an additional aid, the pages on which the essential infor-mation is located are generally noted.

Pattern Guides. Pattern guides make use of the structure of text. Not-ing the pattern of a piece of writing (time-sequence, cause–effect, problem–solution) enhances comprehension because it gives the reader a plan to follow. In most pieces of extended writing, however, the author uses several patterns. In the section covered by the Pattern Guide in Figure 12.9, the author used both a problem–solution and a cause–effect pattern.

> **Gloss:** form of study guide in which segments of the text are clarified through notes, usually placed in the margin.

Glossing. Glossing is a promising technique for helping low-achieving readers cope with the complexities of content-area texts. The normal interaction or transaction in reading is between reader and author. Gloss-ing places the teacher in the interaction as an expert adviser (Stewart & Cross, 1991).

A **gloss,** which is similar to a study guide, is a series of notes or suggestions designed to improve a student's reading of a passage. The notes and suggestions are written on a

FIGURE 12.9 Pattern Guide

Read Chapter 32: Living in Communities, pp. 229–234

Problems:

What was Borneo's main problem?

_____

_____

_____

What was the second problem?

_____

_____

_____

Solutions:

How was the first problem solved?

_____

_____

How was the problem solved?

_____

_____

Cause and Effects

What were the unwanted effects of using chemicals? Fill in the boxes to show what happened when chemicals were used.

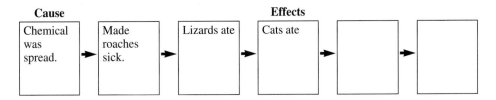

From L. J. Bledsoe, *Biology, The Kingdom of Life.* Castro Valley, CA: Quercus, 1988.

sheet of paper lined up with the text as shown in the sample gloss in Figure 12.10. The gloss may contain definitions of difficult terms, an explanation of a difficult concept, a paraphrase of a confusing sentence, a suggestion to tap prior knowledge, or a suggestion that may in some other way enhance comprehension or metacognition. The notations in the gloss might consist of a statement, a question, a brief paragraph, or even a fill-in-the-blank or complete-the-statement activity.

Various kinds of questions might be included: those that help the student tap prior knowledge or integrate new information with old, those that help the student set a purpose

---

Directions: Read "Proclamation of 1763," in *United States History,* pp. 97–99. As you read, use this gloss: A proclamation (prok-luh-MAY-shun) is a government order. Remember that the Treaty of Paris gave England all French land east of the Mississippi, except for New Orleans. England also got Florida from Spain.

SECTION 1   THE PROCLAMATION OF 1763

British control of America was firmly established with the Treaty of Paris. However, the real hold that Great Britain had on colonies was weak. New and different laws were passed in an effort to control trade. Colonial merchants and shippers found other ways of getting around those laws. Then new events affected the **relationship** between Great Britain and the colonies.

> **Relationship**
> Two or more things or groups connected in some way

WHAT WAS THE PROCLAMATION OF 1763?

> **This is the main idea of this section. As you read, ask yourself: What events caused problems between Great Britain and the colonies?**

The first problem was caused by an event that took place in the spring of 1763. Great numbers of colonists settled in the Ohio Valley, west of the Appalachian Mountains. An Ottawa chief, Pontiac, knew that more American Indian land was in danger of being lost to British settlers. Chief Pontiac organized several American Indian nations and attacked colonial forts with some success.

To avoid further trouble with the American Indians, King George III signed the Proclamation of 1763. This act ordered all settlers to leave the Ohio Valley and return to the established colonies. It did not allow any more people to make new settlements west of the Appalachians. It said that no traders could enter the area without approval of the king.

The colonists were opposed to the new law. They had fought in the long French and Indian War. Now the law was saying that no one could go west. Many colonists felt that the king didn't really care about protecting them from the American Indians. They felt its real purpose was to prevent them from developing the new land. They also felt that they could fight their own battles with the American Indians. The Proclamation of 1763 was the first of several new controls to be forced on the colonies.

> **Chief Pontiac led a rebellion of American Indians against colonial forts beginning in 1763.**

> **Why were the colonists against the law?**

FIGURE 12.10   Sample Gloss

for reading, those that help a student use an essential comprehension or word-recognition strategy, those that help a reader check her or his understanding of the text (Richgels & Hansen, 1984).

Designed to integrate content and process, glosses typically include activities that focus on both. A gloss may also be designed to focus on a particular area, such as difficult vocabulary, or a particular strategy, such as using the organization of the passage. A gloss can also be used to make a text more readable. All too often, there is a gap between the reading ability of low-achieving readers and the difficulty level of the text. Steps that might be taken in preparing a gloss to make the text more accessible include the following:

- Give the reader an easy-to-read overview of the text.
- Highlight the most important information.
- Paraphrase in more understandable language essential segments that may be too difficult for students to read on their own.
- Give the meanings of essential vocabulary.
- Gloss photos, drawings, and charts, and other graphic pieces of information. Even if the text is virtually indecipherable for students, they can learn from the diagrams and other illustrations and from the gloss that you provide.
- Provide an easy-to-read summary of the most important information.

■ ■ ■ ■ ■ ▬▬▬▬▬▬▬▬▬▬▬▬▬▬▬▬▬▬▬

CREATING A GLOSS

If a text is far too difficult, create a gloss that directs students to portions that they can comprehend: illustrations and captions, for instance. Through discussions or summaries of the text, present key ideas that are not explained by illustrations and captions.

Step 1: Examine the text. Decide which two or three concepts you would like students to learn. Note the difficult vocabulary that will be needed to understand the key concepts. Note also the organization of the passage and the main strategies that might be used to understand the passage, such as inferring, summarizing, evaluating, and imaging.

Step 2: Write the gloss. Keeping in mind the students' prior knowledge and command of strategies, decide which elements you would like to empha-

size, and write a gloss accordingly. Focus on a few elements. Limit your gloss to one or two items per page. Students find it difficult and tiresome to cope with too many items (Stewart & Cross, 1993). This also makes the task less burdensome for you.

Step 3: Consider and refine. Line up a sheet of paper with the text and print your gloss next to the target text. If this is a duplicated sheet, write your gloss directly in the margin and photocopy the page. As you write your gloss, imagine that you are with your students as they are studying. Think of the questions they might have about the material, the words they might stumble over, and the elements they might find confusing. Imagine, too, what you might say to help them read purposefully and strategically, monitoring for meaning as they progress through the passages. Let the answers to those questions guide your construction of a gloss. A sample gloss is presented in Figure 12.10.

Allow students who are still acquiring English to discuss new concepts in a small discussion group in their own language. This will allow them to use their old knowledge to help them understand new knowledge.

After-Reading Techniques

After reading content-area material, students should engage in some activity that will help them integrate the information they have just read with what they already know. Students should also evaluate new information and apply it in some way, if possible. The directed reading and directed reading-thinking lessons, which were presented in the previous chapter, include provision for after-reading activities. Other techniques that incorporate after-reading techniques are reflection, graphic postorganizers, and extending and applying.

Reflection.   Simply comprehending content-area text is not enough. Readers must integrate it with their own knowledge and retain it. One of the best ways to accomplish this dual goal is to reflect upon one's reading. Although reflective reaction can take place within a whole-class discussion, it works better in a small-group setting. Students have more opportunity and are more willing to talk when there are just a few of them. Students need a topic or series of questions on which to focus. If students have completed a study, anticipation, or other guide, then that can become the basis of their discussion. Cooperative learning of the type involved in reflection encourages them to clarify and expand their thinking as they explain their responses. As mentioned previously, small discussion groups are especially helpful for students who are still learning English.

Graphic Postorganizer.   If a structured overview was presented as a prereading activity, it can also be used as a graphic postorganizer. All that needs to be done is to replace some of the terms with blanks. After having read the selection, the students can then fill in the blanks.

Once students grasp the concept of structured overviews or graphic postorganizers, they can construct their own. Students are given index cards containing key words from the selection read (or they can copy the words from the board). They are also given blank cards so they can add their own words. Meeting in small groups, students arrange the words to form a graphic postorganizer.

Students discuss items as they decide how to place them. The teacher circulates and gives guidance as needed. After the groups have completed their postorganizers, the class as a whole then constructs one organizer. The key element in this procedure is to encourage students to discuss why elements are arranged in a certain way. Not surprisingly, it is apparent that the more students are involved, the more they learn. Postorganizers, with student involvement, result in more learning than do teacher-directed structured overviews (Moore & Readence, 1984).

Extending and Applying.   Students can extend and apply content-area reading in a variety of ways. They can read trade books or periodicals that elaborate on and extend information presented in the text. They can conduct experiments, surveys, and observations. They can seek information from nonprint sources: interviews and audiovisual materials. They can keep a journal of observations, write letters to the editor, create posters or ads, write plays, or compose reports. Students can also apply what they have learned to their own lives. As an application of information learned in health units, for instance, they can change their diets and get more sleep and exercise. After an ecology unit, they can take steps to increase recycling and decrease waste.

KWL provides students the opportunity to learn from each other and also gives the teacher insights into the students' level of knowledge about a topic.

KWL Plus: A Before-, During-, and After-Reading Technique

The widely used KWL Plus (What We Know, What We Want to Find Out, What We Learned, What We Still Want to Know) technique incorporates before-, during-, and after-reading strategies. KWL grew out of teachers' search for a more effective instructional approach. In this instance, Ogle (1989) and her colleagues were seeking a way to "build active personal reading of expository text" (p. 206). The teachers wanted an approach that involved all students, including the one-third who were typically passive. The technique would be one that stresses activating prior knowledge, would help counter erroneous concepts, and would help students relate new information to their background of knowledge. As Ogle and Blachowicz (2002) explain, "Rather than having teachers teach content by "pouring in" dry, distilled data, students should begin with what they already know and have experienced and then ask their own questions to guide their learning" (p. 261).

The plus in KWL Plus means that students complete a semantic map or other graphic organizer and write a summary.

Group Brainstorming.   KWL begins with brainstorming a topic. In preparation for reading an article about the Pacific Ocean, you might write the word *ocean* on the board and have students tell what they know about oceans. You would then write words and phrases volunteered by students. Writing on the board what some students know and what some students want to learn provides a model for struggling readers so that they will be better prepared to write what they know and want to learn on their individual sheets (Ogle & Blachowicz, 2002). Conflicting information may be offered. If so, this can be posed as a question to be answered. For instance, if students disagree about the number of oceans, one of the items under "What we want to find out" would be "How many oceans are there?" "The group discussion is the catalyst for raising questions that students might not have formulate on their own. It is these questions and the diversity of ideas and knowledge that capture the students' interest and propel their desire to read and learn. Once students have framed their inquiry around their knowledge and questions, they are stimulated to read the text materials in an active way and to keep notes of their learning and new questions (Ogle and Blachowicz, 2002, p. 262). Students might also work in pairs so that they can help each other. Based on the class discussion, the teacher can adapt the lesson. She might find out that students have so little background information that reading a particular selection would be too difficult or that they would need extensive preparation before reading it (Ogle & Blachowicz, 2002).

Individual Brainstorming.   After the group brainstorms, students individually list on their KWL Plus sheets what they know about the topic. (The KWL Plus forms contain four columns—What We Know, What We Want to Find Out, What We Learned, What We Still Want to Know—and a space for noting categories of information that are expected to be addressed in the text that will be read. A sample KWL Plus sheet is shown in Figure 12.11). The group brainstorming helps students activate their background knowledge and so aids them in assessing what they know about the topic. Because you have listed the group's ideas on the board, spelling should not be a barrier for students who have difficulty in this area.

FIGURE 12.11   KWL Plus Sample

Name _____ Date _____

Topic _____

What we know	What we want to find out	What we learned	What we still want to learn
H Dolphins live in the sea.	Are dolphins fish?	Dolphins are mammals. Have to breathe air. Give milk to babies. Are warm blooded.	
C Dolphins can swim fast.	Do dolphins have enemies?	Orca whales and sharks.	
C Dolphins are smart.	How do dolphins protect themselves?	Swim away from danger. Bulls make circle and bump enemies.	Are dolphins found in all oceans?
F Dolphins eat fish.	How do dolphins find food?	Use clicking sounds that bounce off sea animals and come back to them.	Are there different kinds of dolphins?
C Dolphins can be taught to do tricks.	How are dolphins trained to do tricks?	No answer	How are dolphins trained to do tricks?

Categories of Information

Where Dolphins Live
What They Eat
How They Look
What Their Main Characteristics Are
How They Care for Their Young
What Their Living Habits Are
How They Get Food

From R. A. Morris, *Dolphins*. New York: Harper, 1975.

Categorizing.   After completing their lists, students are asked to categorize what they know. They can use a single letter or abbreviation to indicate categories: *l* for location of ocean, *s* for size of oceans, *c* for creatures who live in the ocean, and so forth. If students are not familiar with categorizing, discuss which of the ideas that have been listed on the board should be grouped together and what their group names might be. You might also model the process of categorizing and constructing category names.

> If you wish to simplify KWL, both categorizing and antici-pating may be omitted. Although they are recom-mended by Ogle (1989), most teachers do not use them.

Anticipating.   As an optional step, after completing the classification activity, students anticipate the categories of information that might be presented in the article they are about to read. Ask students to tell what topics the author will probably cover in the article, asking, "If you were the author, what would you tell about the oceans? What main topics would you write about?" Anticipating categories should help students organize information as they read. On their sheets, students record the categories that they believe the author will probably address.

Questioning.   The final activity in the prereading stage involves posing questions. Students tell what they want to find out. As in the brainstorming portion of the lesson, this is both a group and an individual endeavor. Throughout the lesson, note areas of partial, conflicting, and missing information; through discussion, help students consider these areas and, later, pose questions about them. After asking the class to tell what they want to find out, list their questions on the board. If the questions do not cover the essentials, probe in order to lead students to create additional questions. Ogle cautions that the text should not be read until "some real questions to guide the reading, have emerged from the group" (1989, p. 214). On their KWL sheets, students list the questions that are most important to them. If they wish, students can simply copy the group's questions. However, with experience, students tend to personalize their list of questions.

> As students note the answers to their questions, they might also list information that they weren't looking for but that is valuable and interesting.

Reading.   Students read the selection to get the answers to their questions. New information is written in abbreviated form under the "What we learned" column. If questions are not answered or if new questions arise, these can be noted in a fourth column, "What we still want to know."

After Reading.   After students have completed their reading, the article is discussed. Students talk over what they learned. Information is elaborated and clarified. Comparing what students said they knew and what they learned provides an opportunity to correct misconceptions, if they still exist. Information students learned is written on the board. This models note taking and gives students a chance to revise their notes. Students also discuss questions that they still have about the topic.

If the information is important, students might also create a semantic map that depicts major details graphically, or they might prepare an information map, which uses frame questions and is described in Chapter 13. If the students wish, they might also pursue any unanswered questions or new ones that may have cropped up. As part of their discussion, they can talk over possible sources of information for their unanswered questions.

Graphic Organizer for Retelling (GO! Chart)

An excellent device for integrating a number of strategies is the Graphic Organizer for Retelling (GO! Chart) (Benson & Cummins, 2002). The Go! Chart is ninety inches wide and is composed of six columns: Predictions/preview, Vocabulary, Understandings, Interpretations, Connections, and Retelling (organizing). In the first column students' predictions, which are based on previewing, are recorded. Based on their preview and predictions, students are asked to predict what vocabulary will be used in the selection. This is recorded in the second column. In the third column, Understandings, students tell what they noticed in the selection or what they learned. In the fourth column, Interpretations, students draw conclusions and make inferences about their reading. In the fifth column, Connections, students make connections between what they have read and their own experiences or a previously read selection. For the last column, Retelling, students select a graphic organizer to represent the elements of a story or main ideas of a nonfiction selection.

■ ■ ■ ■ ■

SAMPLE KWL PLUS LESSON

BEFORE READING

Step 1: Brainstorming. In preparation for reading *Dolphins* (Morris, 1975), a mature-appearing paperback written on a second-grade level, encourage students to brainstorm the topic of dolphins. Writing the word *dolphins* on the board, ask, "What do you know about dolphins?" List students' responses on the board. If one student says that dolphins are fish and another says they are not, ask each student to explain her or his reasoning. The class might decide to make the classification of dolphins one of the things they want to find out. After the group brainstorms, students write down in the first column what they know about dolphins.

Step 2: Categorizing. Information is categorized and students discuss the kinds of topics the book might present. They might decide that the book will tell where dolphins live, what they eat, how they look, what their main characteristics are, how they care for their young, what their living habits are, how they get food.

Step 3: Discussing what you want to find out. Students then discuss what they want to find out. They might want to find out whether dolphins are fish, how they get food, whether they have enemies, how they protect themselves, how they learn to do tricks, and how smart they are. The class's questions are listed on the board or a large sheet of paper. Students list their individual questions on their sheets.

DURING READING

Step 4: Discussing what you found out and what you still want to learn. The class reads and notes what they found out and what they still want to learn. They see that the author gives information about the birth and care of a young dolphin, which was not an area in which they were seeking information.

The class might also construct a semantic map highlighting information that they acquired about dolphins.

AFTER READING

Step 5: Discussing, rereading, and seeking additional information. Students discuss what they learned. If there is still a bit of confusion about whether the dolphin is a fish or a mammal, reread the section of the text dealing with that subject. To further clarify the matter, you might discuss with the class the characteristics of mammals. Students might note questions that were not answered: How smart are dolphins? How are they trained? The class may also have wanted to know whether dolphins are found in all oceans and how many different kinds of dolphins there are. The class discusses where that information might be found.

In collaborative discussions, there is more focus on processes, as the teacher explains her thinking and provides evidence or justification (Palincsar, 2003). The teacher also pays more attention to the processes that students use to compose their responses.

OUTSTANDING COLLABORATIVE APPROACHES

Working collaboratively with the teacher and other students has proved to be a powerful technique for improving the comprehension of low-achieving readers. Three of the most carefully documented and highly effective of the collaborative techniques are ReQuest, reciprocal teaching, and Questioning the Author. ReQuest, which is easier to implement, can be used along with or as a stepping stone to reciprocal teaching.

ReQuest

ReQuest was designed so that teacher and student would discuss one sentence at a time; however, some users have analyzed whole paragraphs as a unit, rather than single sentences.

Although he had excellent word-recognition skills, William's comprehension was just about nil. Even when the task was reduced to reading short, easy paragraphs, William's comprehension barely improved. At that point, William's teacher decided to try ReQuest (Manzo, 1969; Manzo & Manzo, 1993). ReQuest is a rock-bottom technique that approaches comprehension at the sentence level but that activates even the most passive student.

INTRODUCING ReQuest

Step 1: Prepare to read. You and the student read the title and first sentence of the selection. You might also look at any illustrations or other graphic elements that may be part of the introduction.

Step 2: Explain. Explain to the student that she may ask as many questions about the first sentence, title, and illustrations as she can. The student is told to ask the kinds of questions that a teacher might ask.

Step 3: Set a purpose for reading. The student asks questions, and you answer them. Then you ask questions about the first sentence, title, and illustrations. The objective of your questions is to model questioning behavior, to orient the student to the material, and to provide background for setting a purpose for reading.

Step 4: Continue questioning. Questioning proceeds as in step 3. First, the student asks questions about the next sentence. Then you do. As the two of you move through the selection sentence by sentence, you ask questions that involve putting together information from several sentences. ReQuest continues until a purpose for reading is established but lasts no longer than ten minutes. Usually this entails going through a paragraph or two. The concluding question is "What do you think the rest of the selection will be about?"

Step 5: Student continues reading. The student reads the rest of the selection silently for the purpose or prediction that has been established. The student is encouraged to read flexibly and to adjust her purpose for reading, if necessary.

Step 6: Discuss the selection. The ReQuest procedure can be used with any subject, in any grade, but seems to work best with informational text. However, Maria (1990) reports using ReQuest successfully with narrative material. ReQuest has also been used with students in such a way that the paragraph rather than the sentence is used as the basis for analysis.

"The greatest strength of ReQuest seems to be in that it gets students to overcome some of the subtle liabilities that tend to inhibit questioning—such as having to admit ignorance, and not knowing how to frame questions, and simply not realizing what it is that they don't know" (Manzo & Manzo, 1993, p. 317).

ReQuest requires both teachers and students to construct questions and answers about single sentences. The teacher is the master craftsperson, the student, an apprentice. In the procedure, the teacher models both asking and answering questions. Although initially designed to be a corrective one-on-one technique, ReQuest may be adapted for group use.

However ReQuest is used, Manzo and Manzo (1993) caution that teachers should model higher-level questioning. Students tend to construct the same kinds of questions that have been asked in their classes. Unfortunately, many of these are on a low level. Manzo suggests that the teacher do two things to improve the level of questioning: "(1) Try to ask the types of questions that you would hope someone might ask you; and (2) try to ask questions that reflect the highest objectives of your teaching as well as more literal or reconstructive ones" (p. 317).

Reciprocal Teaching

In a sense, reciprocal teaching (RT) is both an expansion and extension of the ReQuest procedure. Designed for use with small groups, reciprocal teaching also involves students as active participants and, like ReQuest, uses a teacher–apprentice model. Incorporating four powerful comprehension strategies—questioning, summarizing, predicting, and clarifying—**reciprocal teaching** has had a great deal of success with corrective readers of various levels, including at-risk students in college (Brown & Palincsar, 1986, Hart & Speece, 1998; Rosenshine & Meister, 1994). Because it is a complex technique, it is recommended that it be used for an extended period of time.

Reciprocal teaching: fosters the development of key strategies—predicting, questioning, summarizing, and monitoring—within a teacher-guided cooperative learning framework.

Although reciprocal teaching is an outstanding example of cooperative learning, the teacher is very much an active participant. A key element in reciprocal teaching is scaffolding on which the teacher supports the learners, much as a master craftspersons supports apprentices. The student apprentices take on greater responsibility as they acquire increased expertise.

The focus of the lesson is a brief text. At first, the teacher conducts the lesson. Later, a student is appointed to be a teacher. The student-teacher makes a prediction based on the title and illustration, or the beginning of the selection being read. (If the class has read a segment of the selection, then the prediction is based on what has been read.) A segment is then read silently by the group. After the segment has been read, the student-teacher generates and poses one or more questions. Questioning is a highly effective strategy because it requires students to determine essential information, create a question, and self-check their comprehension by seeing if they can answer the question. Just as with summarizing, students can ask questions at many levels. Initial questions may simply require recall of facts or details. More advanced questions require inferring, drawing conclusions, or evaluating. After the questions have been discussed, the student-teacher summarizes the selection. Summarizing is an essential skill because it requires students to determine essential information, paraphrase it, and integrate or synthesize it (Palincsar, 2003). Summarizing can take place on many levels from single paragraph, to section, to whole selection. When starting out with reciprocal teaching, students typically summarize at the paragraph level. With instruction

■ ■ ■ ■ ■

EXEMPLARY TEACHING
USING ReQuest

Although Josh's word recognition was adequate, his comprehension was extremely poor, especially when he was required to read informational texts. As a result of his woefully inadequate comprehension, Josh, a sixth grader, was failing science. Informal reading inventory results confirmed Josh's poor comprehension. Although word recognition was adequate up through sixth-grade level, Josh's comprehension was poor at every level from the third grade up.

Using a think-aloud, the reading specialist determined that Josh's goal in reading was to complete the assignment. He was not seeking meaning from his reading. A very passive reader, he had few strategies and simply plunged into his text without previewing, activating schema, or setting a specific purpose. Once he started reading, Josh did not monitor to see if the text made sense. Nor did he stop at key points in the chapter or at the end to summarize what he had read. When queried, Josh was unable to answer a single question about the section on rocks that he had read as part of a think-aloud. The read-

ing specialist also noted that the text was a bit too difficult for Josh. Because Josh's comprehension was so poor, the reading specialist tried ReQuest with him. Intrigued by the idea of creating questions for the teacher, Josh's comprehension improved while he was working directly with the teacher but deteriorated when he read on his own. Focusing on short segments, the teacher adapted the procedure so that it included the whole text. As Josh's comprehension improved, the teacher began gradually increasing the length of the selections and decreasing the amount of direct guidance. The teacher also began introducing previewing, predicting, self-questioning, and other strategies.

Because the science text was too difficult for Josh, easy-to-read trade books that explored the same concepts as the science texts were used. The teacher also provided lots of opportunities for Josh to engage in hands-on activities and use audiovisual aids to build background. As Josh became a more active and a more strategic reader, his grasp of content-area material improved.

and practice, they begin to summarize longer sections of text. At the end of the discussion, the student-teacher makes a prediction about the upcoming segment. Predicting is a difficult skill because it requires hypothesizing about what will occur in the future (Graesser & Bertus, 1998). To predict well, students must use background knowledge as a basis for reasoning about what is likely to occur. Predicting also involves the use of text structure as students use headings and subheads as an aid to forecasting (Palincsar, 2003). Predicting, of course, also provides students with a purpose for reading: to assess their prediction.

At any time during the discussion, students can ask for clarification if there is a word they don't know or if any other aspect of the story is puzzling. Poor comprehenders typically fail to realize that they don't understand what they are reading. Clarifying is a way to show them how to monitor for meaning and to take steps to repair faulty comprehension. Clarifying is especially effective for students who glance over the words and make the sounds that correspond to the symbols but don't get the words' message. As part of clarifying, students need to note when the words fail to make sense and ways in which they might repair comprehension by rereading, using illustrations, using the glossary, and so on (Palincsar, 2003). Members of the groups are also given a chance to ask questions that might have occurred to them as they read. If students are struggling readers, the teacher might read the text aloud.

In introducing reciprocal teaching, the purpose of the technique is explained and students are taught how, when, where, and why to use each of the four strategies: predicting, questioning, summarizing, and clarifying. One of the strengths of the procedure is that strategies are modeled and monitored in the context of actual reading. In the beginning the teacher's efforts will be very direct, as she or he explains and models strategies. Later, as students become increasingly more expert in the use of strategies, the teacher can function as a coach, make corrections and adjustments, provide useful suggestions, and urge students onward.

> At first, the teacher may have to create summaries, predictions, and questions for students to imitate. Gradually, students should begin to generate questions, predictions, and summaries.

Direct instruction, plenty of practice, and gradual release of responsibility are at the heart of the success of reciprocal teaching (Brown & Palincsar, 1986). Note in the sample dialog in Figure 12.12 how the teacher worked with a small group of low-achieving readers. Student A is the leader for this segment. The teacher is T.

Questioning the Author

> Like RT, QTA is also a collaborative technique. Instead of using strategies to construct meaning, students respond to a series of queries. Queries are questions designed to prompt students to use the text and their background knowledge to construct meaning.

One technique that is especially effective in helping struggling readers comprehend content-area text is Questioning the Author (QTA) (McKeown, Beck, & Sandora, 1996). In most approaches, students, including the poorest readers, are essentially left on their own to make sense out of texts that are stuffed with facts and loaded with technical terms. In Questioning the Author, students and teacher construct meaning cooperatively in an ongoing fashion. Instead of having struggling readers become overwhelmed by being asked to read and understand a large segment of text, perhaps even a whole chapter, the class reads a small segment, collaboratively constructs meaning, and then moves on to the next segment. The segment read and discussed provides a solid foundation for the comprehension of the next segment. With discussion distributed throughout the reading of the selection, instead of just at the end, students have many opportunities to discuss and clarify complex ideas and integrate information. Although it was originally designed for use with informational text, QTA has also been used to help struggling readers understand complex literacy pieces (Sandora, Beck, & McKeown, 1999).

> Ultimately, students should incorporate these QTA queries into their reading. QTA lends itself to deeper discussion and more critical analysis. It seems well suited for social studies texts in which ideas are discussed.

The core of QTA lessons is a series of queries. Queries are designed as collaborative inquiries that provide general guidance as students construct meaning. They are different from the usual kinds of questions asked at the end of the reading, which are often designed to assess students' grasp of the material. Initiating queries are used to get the meaning-making discussion started and include: "What is the author trying to say here? What is the author's message? What is the author trying to tells us?" Follow-up queries are designed to help the students extend and deepen their understanding. If a passage did not seem clear, the teacher might ask, "What did the author mean here? Did the author explain this clearly?" Questions could also be asked that help connect ideas that had been read previously. "How does this connect to what the author told us before? How do these two ideas fit together?" Other kinds of questions lead students to seek reasons. "Does the author tell

FIGURE 12.12 Sample Reciprocal Teaching Dialog

Can Snakes Sting with Their Tongues?

No—snakes' tongues are completely harmless. They're used for feeling things and for sharpening the snakes' sense of smell. Although snakes can smell in the usual way, the tongue flickering in the air picks up tiny particles of matter. These particles are deposited in two tiny cavities at the base of the nostrils to increase the snakes' ability to smell.

1. A: Do snakes' tongues sting?
2. K: Sometimes.
3. A: Correct.
       This paragraph is about do snakes sting with their tongue, and different ways that the tongue is for and the senses of smell.
4. T: Are there any questions?
5. C: Snakes' tongues don't sting.
6. T: Beautiful! I thought, boy, I must have been doing some fast reading there because I missed that point. A, could you ask your question again?
7. A: Do snakes' tongues really sting?
8. T: Now, A, since you have asked the question, can you find in that paragraph where the question is answered?
9. A: No, snakes' tongues are completely harmless.
10. T: So we'll try it again. Can you generate another question that you think a teacher might ask?
11. A: What are the tongues used for?
12. T: Good!
13. L: The sense of smell.
14. T: Is that correct? A, do you disagree? Yes.
15. A: That answer was right, but there are other things that the tongue can do.
16. L: But she only said tell one, she didn't say tell all of them.
17. T: O.K.
18. B: It is used to pick up tiny particles.
19. T: O.K. I think that this is an important point. You have the basic concept which is correct, O.K., but what the question really is saying is, is it used for smell? O.K.?
20. B: They are used for feeling things for sharpening snakes' sense of smell.
21. T: O.K. They are used for sharpening the snakes' sense of smell. Are they used for smelling? That's the point we aren't clear on.
22. L: In my answer I said it is for the sense of smell.
23. T: This is fine; this is what the technique is all about. What it means is not that you are right or wrong or good or bad. What it says is that we have just read something and have had a disagreement about what it says. We need to work it out.
24. A: My prediction is that they will now talk about the different things about snakes. Where they live, and what they eat and stuff like that.

From: A. Brown & A. Palincsar, *Reciprocal Teaching of Comprehension Strategies: A Natural History of One Program for Enhancing Learning,* (Tech. Rep. 334), Table 5. Champaign, IL: University of Illinois, 1985.

us why? Why do you think the author included this information?" Questions might also help students see how what they are learning relates to their background knowledge: "How does this fit in with what you know?"

To keep discussions on track and constructive, the teacher uses six Question-the-Author moves: marking, turning back, revoicing, modeling, annotating, and recapping.

Marking. The teacher highlights a student's comment or idea that is important to the meaning being built. The teacher might remark, "You are saying that some good things came out of the Great Depression. It led to Social Security, unemployment insurance, and regulation of banks." Or the teacher might simply say, "Good point!"

Turning back. The teacher turns students' attention back to the text so that they can obtain needed information, correct a misreading, or clarify a point. "Yes, I agree the stock market collapse was a main cause of the Great Depression. But what were some other causes? What does the author tell us about some things that were happening years before the stock market collapsed?"

Revoicing. The teacher helps students express clearly what they are trying to say. "So what you're telling us is that the people who grew up during the Depression worked extra hard and saved money because they were afraid there might be another Depression."

Modeling. The teacher demonstrates how she might go about creating meaning from text. She might show how she rereads a confusing passage, makes an inference, or summarizes a section. The teacher might say, "As I was reading this passage, I realized that it didn't make sense, so I read it again." or "Here's how I used the diagram to figure out how supply and demand works."

Annotating. The teacher supplies information that is missing from a discussion but that is important for understanding key ideas. It could be information that the text failed to mention. "The author tells us that businesses were making a lot of money because they didn't pay their workers much. What the author didn't say was that low wages were one cause of the Depression. Because of low wages, workers didn't have the money to buy the goods that the factories were making. Factories began losing money and had to close down."

Recapping. The teacher highlights essential points and summarizes. "Now we understand that there were a number of causes of the Great Depression and that some of those causes had been building for years."

Steps in a Questioning the Author lesson are listed below.

QUESTIONING THE AUTHOR LESSON

Step 1. Analyze the text and decide what you want students to know or understand as a result of reading the text. List two or three major understandings.

Step 2. Note any potential difficulties in the text that might hinder students' comprehension. This could include unfamiliar vocabulary, confusing concept, or needed background information.

Step 3. Divide the text into readable segments. A segment might be a single sentence or paragraph or sev-

eral paragraphs. A segment will generally encompass one major idea.

Step 4. Based on the understandings you wish students to attain and the possible difficulties posed by the text, plan your queries. Queries should be planned for each segment.

Step 5. Introduce the selection. Introduce unfamiliar vocabulary and other blocks to comprehension in a particular segment before that segment is read.

Step 6. Students read the first segment silently.

Step 7. Students and teacher discuss the first segment and construct meaning.

Step 8. Students go on to the next segment.

Step 9. At the conclusion, the class, with the teacher's guidance, summarizes what has been read.

In the following excerpt from a Questioning the Author lesson, note how students construct meaning and the depth of their thinking. The class has just read a text segment about the presidency of James Buchanan, which stated that many people believed that he liked the South better than the North because he said that owning slaves should be a personal choice. The teacher began the discussion by posing a general query. After a student responded, the teacher asked a follow-up question.

Teacher: This paragraph that Tracy just read is really full of important information. What has the author told us in this important paragraph?

Laura: They think that Buchanan liked the South better because he said that it is a person's choice if they want to have slaves or not, so they thought that he liked the South better than the North.

Teacher: Okay. And what kind of problem did this cause Buchanan when they thought that he liked the South? What kind of problem did that cause?

Janet: Well, maybe less people would vote for him because like in Pennsylvania we were against slavery and might have voted for him because he was from Pennsylvania. But now since we knew that he was for the South, we might not vote for him again.

Jamie: I have something to add on to Janet's 'cause I completely agree with her. We might have thought that since he was from Pennsylvania and Pennsylvania was an antislavery state, that he was against slavery. But it turns out he wasn't.

Teacher: Just like someone whom you think is your best friend, and then all of a sudden you find out, oh, they're not. (McKeown, Beck, & Sandora, 1996, pp. 113–114)

At this point, students read and then discuss another text segment.

CONTENT KNOWLEDGE

Throughout this text the emphasis has been on the processes of reading and writing, especially the teaching techniques and strategies used in learning text. However, process and content must be integrated. Content shapes the techniques and strategies that we and our students use. It is difficult to make inferences in areas in which we have limited knowledge. Noting main ideas is easier when we are acquainted with a subject and have a sense of what the subject's major and minor issues are. The process is somewhat circular. The more students know, the more they are prepared to learn. The more they know, the better they can apply strategies. The better they apply strategies, the more they learn. Use of strategies increases knowledge, which fosters more effective use of strategies.

TEXTBOOKS IN THE CONTENT AREAS

The amount students learn is also dependent on the quality and appropriateness of their textbooks. All too often texts in the content areas are too difficult for low-progress readers. Many content-area texts are written a year or more above grade level (Chall & Conard, 1991; Kinder, Bursuck, & Epstein, 1992).

If the regular text is simply far too difficult for students, consider obtaining a text that is written on a simpler level. A list of some easy-to-read language arts, social studies, science, and math texts is presented in Table 12.1. You might also use easy-to-read trade books that cover the topics you wish to explore (see Appendix B). Because easy-to-read texts may be less detailed than the regular texts, you might want to supplement the information in the text with discussions, use of audio-visual aids, and other activities. For students with severe reading problems, consider using recorded versions of the text. Students who are unable to read their texts because of a documented reading disability may qualify for books recorded for the blind. Talking Books, a service sponsored by the National Library Service for the Blind and Physically Handicapped (Library of Congress, Washington, DC 20542), provides for individuals who are blind, who have physical disabilities, or who have organic reading disabilities, taped versions of periodicals and popular books, including children's titles. Recording for the Blind and Dyslexic (20 Roszel Road, Princeton, NJ 08540), a private organization, provides recorded versions of school textbooks for students with reading problems.

> Readabilitities of 5,500 textbooks, including basal readers, in current use are available at www.tasaliteracy.com.

> Beginning in 2007–2008, science assessment will be required in each of the following grade ranges: 3–5, 6–9, and 10–12.

Adapting Texts

Another possibility is to adapt the textbook, a procedure that may result in significant gains for low-achieving readers (Lovitt, Rudsit, Jenkins, Pious, & Benedetti, 1986). Adapting an entire text would be a monumental undertaking. Choose only those chapters that contain the most essential concepts and focus on the most important information in the chapter. Adapting a text to make it easier is more than just substituting easy words for hard words or short sentences for long ones. One reason informational texts are so difficult is that they try to cover too much and end up being a dense recitation of facts. One way of making a text easier is to expand on key concepts and omit or eliminate nonessential details. Here are some suggestions for adapting text.

Signal main ideas. Use headings and topic sentences to announce key concepts. Also provide a brief preview, perhaps in the form of a graphic organizer, and a concise summary.

Develop key concepts fully. Do not introduce extraneous details, even though they may be interesting.

Use signal words to foster cohesiveness. Use lots of *buts, ands, on the other hands,* and other words that help show relationships among ideas.

Use straightforward language patterns. Avoid passives and long, involved sentences.

TABLE 12.1 **Easy-to-Read Content-Area Texts**

TEXT	PUBLISHER	GRADE LEVEL	READING LEVEL
Language Arts			
Basic English Composition	AGS	6–12	3.8
Pacemaker Curriculum English Composition	Globe Fearon	5–12	3–4
American Literature	AGS	9–12	3.5–4.0
Pacemaker Curriculum World Literature	Globe Fearon	6–12	3–4
Science			
Biology	AGS	6–12	3.5
Concepts and Challenges in Earth Science	Globe Fearon	6–12	5–6
Physical Science	AGS	6–12	3.5
Wonders of Science	Steck-Vaughn	7–12	2
Social Studies			
America's Story	Steck-Vaughn	5–10	2–3
Pacemaker Curriculum World History	Globe Fearon	6–12	3–4
United States History	AGS	6–12	3.8
World History	AGS	6–12	3.8
Math			
Algebra	AGS	9–12	3.5
Essential Math Skills	Phoenix		5–6
Pacemaker Curriculum Pre-Algebra	Globe Fearon	6–12	3–4
Practical Arithmetic Series	Globe Fearon	6–12	3–4

Use fewer pronouns than you normally would. That way students will not become confused wondering what the pronoun's antecedent is.

Use concrete language and give lots of examples.

> The teacher of low-achieving readers needs to increase their access to information by making their texts more accessible and by providing sources of information that do not require reading.

Directed Listening-Thinking Activity

Another option for handling a text that is too difficult is to use the format of a directed listening-thinking activity (DL-TA) to read it to students (Gillet & Temple, 1994). Similar in structure to the directed reading-thinking activity, except that students listen instead of read (Stauffer, 1969), the directed listening-thinking activity is presented in the following box.

DIRECTED LISTENING-THINKING ACTIVITY

Step 1: Making predictions. Under your guidance, students survey and discuss the title, headings, and illustrations of the chapter or section to be read. You read the titles and headings to students. Based on the survey and discussion, students predict what the content of the selection might be. Predictions are written on the board.

Step 2: Listening to the selection. As you read, the students listen. Stop periodically to involve students in modifying predictions, summarizing text, asking questions about the text, evaluating what is being read, relating new information to old information, noting hard words and key terms, and using diagrams, charts, graphs, and other illustrative materials. During your oral reading, you can model the use of effective strategies and gradually lead students to use those same strategies as they listen, so

they learn how to summarize, question, and monitor for meaning.

Step 3: Discussion. Students discuss the selection in light of their predictions. Discuss how the content differed from students' predictions. Provide needed elaborations and explanations and clarify confusing concepts. Note how the information relates to the students' background of knowledge and how they might apply information in the text. After the selection has been discussed, you might guide students as they dictate a summary of the material presented. Write their dictated summary on the board and review it with them. It can be copied by students into their notebooks or you can duplicate it so that students have material to read and study on their own. A dictated summary is found in Figure 12.13.

FIGURE 12.13   Student-Dictated Summary of a Content-Area Selection

How Plants Make Food

Green plants make their own food. They use sunlight to do this. The light causes a gas called carbon dioxide to combine with water. When water and carbon dioxide combine, they form sugar. The plants use this sugar to grow and stay well. Using light to make food is called photosynthesis (foh•tuh•SIN•thuh•sis).

By making food, plants help us to breathe. When water and carbon dioxide combine, oxygen is made. We need oxygen to breathe. Without plants, we would have no air to breathe. Plants keep us alive.

Hands-on Inquiry Approach

In the typical science text, the student reads about a concept and then performs an experiment. In an inquiry approach, the experiment comes first and is used to introduce concepts and important information. Students observe the experiment and then discuss the science concepts and related information illustrated by the experiment. Vocabulary for these science concepts is introduced at this time. Vocabulary and concepts are easier to learn because they are based on students' hands-on experiences. The teacher might lead the students to compose a written summary of the unit's major concepts. This summary, which might include illustrations, could be used instead of the text or as an introduction to the text. Once they are familiar with the major concepts covered and related technical vocabulary, students will be in a better position to handle the text.

■ ■ ■ ■ ■ ▬▬▬▬▬▬▬▬▬▬▬▬▬▬▬▬▬▬▬▬▬▬▬▬▬▬▬▬▬▬

EXEMPLARY TEACHING
HANDS-ON LEARNING

> If audio-visual materials and easy trade books are available and there are varied opportunities for observation and hands-on experiences, the poor reader will have greater access to content-area information.

Particulary because they have failed with books and paper-and-pencil tasks, low-achieving readers often appreciate hands-on experiences. Taking advantage of the opportunities offered by her seaside home, one literacy specialist enlivened a unit on sea creatures by bringing in specimens from Long Island Sound. A youngster who normally couldn't think of a word to write had no difficulty recording his observations of the live crab that his teacher brought in. As he examined the crab, he had lots of questions, the main one being, "Will the crab pinch me with its claws?" Questions led to the reading of a nonfiction book on sea creatures. Since that book didn't answer all of the youngster's questions, other texts were consulted.

When the teacher brought in a lobster, the youngster wanted to know how a lobster was different from a crab. At the teacher's suggestion, the youngster recorded his observations. With the help of his teacher, a chart was constructed comparing the two creatures. Again, books on sea creatures were consulted to supply information not provided by observation. As the weeks passed, the chart grew, as did the student's knowledge of sea creatures and his ability to read for information, take notes, create charts, and summarize information. Poems and fiction books related to the theme were also read, and sea songs were read and sung.

TEACHING LITERATURE

In teaching literature to low-achieving readers, a key question is which works will be introduced. Often, as students move up through the grades, there is an expectation that certain literary works will be introduced. In fifth grade this might be *And Now Miguel*. In seventh grade it might be *Treasure Island*. In twelfth grade, *The Great Gatsby* might be assigned. In some instances, the class may have an anthology that consists primarily of selections written on grade level or above. Because of their reading problems, low-achieving readers may have difficulty reading some literary selections. The issue is one of providing students with quality literature that they can understand and appreciate. There are several ways of accomplishing this goal.

Choose selections that students can read. Not all pieces of literature are equally difficult. In American literature, for instance, Hemingway is easier to read and understand than Faulkner. A number of the classics are surprisingly easy to read. Table 12.2 provides estimated readabilities for a number of well-known works. The readability scores factor in only sentence complexity and difficulty of vocabulary. Background of experience, conceptual development, and emotional maturity are essential elements in understanding a piece of literature and need to be considered along with readability estimates.

Other measures that can be taken to make literary works accessible to low-achieving readers include the following.

TABLE 12.2 **Sampling of Easy-to-Read, High-Quality Books**

BOOK	READING LEVEL
Fritz, J. (1958). *The Cabin Faced West.* New York: Coward-McCann.	4–5
George, J. (1959). *My Side of the Mountain.* New York: Scholastic.	4
Goodall, J. (1988). *My Life with the Chimpanzees.* New York: Simon & Schuster.	5–6
Hamilton, V. (1985). *The People Could Fly: American Black Folktales.* New York: Knopf.	3–4
Hamilton, V. (1967). *Zeeley.* New York: Macmillan.	4–5
Hemingway, E. (1952). *The Old Man and the Sea.* New York: Scribner.	4–5
Kumgold, J. (1953). *And Now Miguel.* New York: Harper.	4
Lowry, L. (1989). *Number the Stars.* Boston: Houghton Mifflin.	5–6
Mowat, F. (1961). *Owls in the Family.* Boston: Little, Brown.	5–6
O'Dell, S. (1986). *Streams to the River, River to the Sea.* Boston: Houghton Mifflin.	3
Paterson, K. (1977). *Bridge to Terabitha.* New York: Avon.	4
Paulsen, C. (1987). *Hatchet.* New York: Simon & Schuster.	4
Saroyan, W. (1943). *The Human Comedy.* New York: Harcourt, Brace, Jovanovich.	4–5
Steinbeck, J. (1939). *The Grapes of Wrath.* New York: Bantam.	5–6
Uchida, Y. (1978). *The Journey Home.* New York: Atheneum.	5
Voight, C. (1982). *Dicey's Song.* New York: Fawcett.	5
Yepp, L. (1977). *Child of the Owl.* New York: Harper.	5

Provide extra support. If the selection is challenging but not overwhelming, build background and vocabulary, provide glosses or other study guides, and read difficult portions to the students.

Use audio-visual aids. Use filmstrips, taped recordings, videocassettes, or CD-ROM versions of the works. If students simply can not handle the reading, read the piece to them or obtain taped versions of the work. Many of the classics are available on audio tapes. Students might read along as they listen to a taped reading of the text. Even though students will not have to decode the words, they will still need assistance with comprehension and appreciation, so working with vocabulary, concepts, background, and esthetic elements will be essential.

Abridged versions work well for some authors. Because he was paid by the word, Dickens tended to use more words than necessary. *David Copperfield* and *Tale of Two Cities* can be acceptably abridged.

Use abridged or adapted versions. Abridged versions are simply shortened versions. The author's language has not been simplified. Literacy Volunteers of New York has abridged and added explanatory notes to a wide variety of contemporary literature and popular pieces, including Jane Goodall's *In the Shadow of Man* (1992), Alice Walker's *The Temple of My Familiar* (1992), and excerpts from classic American plays. The texts also provide brief overviews of the pieces to be read, suggestions for reading them, and a biography of the author. Just sixty-four pages in length, these paperbacks have a mature, appealing format. Although they are designed for adult new readers, some, if selected with care, can be used with secondary school students.

Adaptations of literary works are more controversial than abridgements, because adaptations involve changing and possibly distorting the author's words. If the issue is one of having students read an altered version of the original versus not reading it at all because it is too difficult, you may decide to use an adaptation. Selected sources of adapted and abridged classics are presented in Table 12.3.

Personal Response

> The reader's stance is on a continuum from *efferent* to *esthetic*. Reading directions to assemble a bicycle would be efferent. Reading a poem about death could be highly esthetic if it evoked strong emotion.

Reading literature, of course, involves much more than just understanding the words or the ideas. For instance, a class that reads a genuinely humorous story, such as O'Henry's "The Ransom of Red Chief" and does not laugh, did not understand the story, even though they may be able to give you a detailed account of the plot. When literature is read, the emphasis should be on an esthetic reading, on evoking a personal response from the reader. Eliciting a genuine reader response involves setting up situations in which students feel encouraged to respond freely. First of all, selections should be chosen that lend themselves to reader response. Second, activities and questions should be geared to a personal response. Questions that encourage readers to relate some aspect of the selection to their own lives are especially helpful. In discussions of the piece, emphasis should be on personal response and interpretation. Small-group discussions work especially well, because students are more likely to share honestly and openly in such a setting. Struggling readers are more likely to do their best when they can relate what they are reading to their own lives.

TABLE 12.3 Adapted and Abridged Classics

ADAPTED TEXT(S)	PUBLISHER	DESCRIPTION
Globe's Adapted Classics	Globe Fearon	Classics from American and English literature. Reading levels: 3–4 to 7–8
Lake Illustrated Classics	Lake	British and American classics are presented in illustrated strips. Reading level: 4
Longman Classics	Longman	Classics in British and American literature. Reading levels: 3–6
Pacemaker Classics	Globe Fearon	Classics from English and American literature. Audiotapes are available. Reading levels: 3–4
Phoenix Everyreaders	Phoenix	Presents classics from American and British literature. Reading level: 4

Self-Selection

One element that fosters response is reader selection. If possible, readers should have a choice in at least some of the pieces they read. This need not be a fully open choice. You might have them choose which of three novels they would rather read, for instance. Students become more involved when they are part of the selection process.

Sheltered English

Sheltered English: the practice of teaching subject-matter content in English to English language learners who have learned conversational English but not academic language.

Because of the integration of language arts, reading, writing, listening, and speaking reinforce each other. Increasingly, reading and writing are used to build oral language skills among English learners. Instead of using isolated drills on syntax and vocabulary and contrived conversations, English learners now develop English speaking skills by reading quality literature or content-area materials and discussing it and writing about it. Known as **sheltered English,** bilingual immersion, or cognitive academic language learning, the approach blends content and language development (Gersten & Jiménez, 1994). A major advantage of integrating second language acquisition and content exploration is that it fosters the development of both everyday and academic language as well as higher-level thinking skills. In sheltered instruction, teachers make a special effort to make content instruction understandable to all students, including those who are still acquiring academic English. This is something that conscientious teachers have always done. However, sheltered instruction has a second component. While presenting content, the teacher also takes steps to foster language development. Colburn and Echevarria (1999) comment that sheltered classes are "distinguished by careful attention to students' needs related to learning another language" (p. 36). In a sense, content and language objectives are combined. Some steps that they take include the following.

- Make the input as comprehensible as possible. Use simple sentence structures and understandable vocabulary. Speak slowly but distinctly and use gestures freely. Pantomime actions and demonstrate processes. Avoid idioms and jargon.
- Make directions as clear as possible. Show students what to do in addition to telling them. If possible, model the process for them.
- Whenever possible, use the visual to reinforce the verbal. When introducing a new word, show a picture of it if possible, and write it on the board. When mentioning a place, write its name on the board and show it on a map.
- Use audio-visual aids whenever possible. Use timelines, graphs, videos, and film clips on CD-ROM.
- Use realia such as nutrition labels, menus, job applications, and bank deposit slips.
- Use brainstorming, quick-write, and similar techniques to tap prior knowledge.
- Use demonstrations and skits to make the language as meaningful as possible.
- Emphasize hands-on activities, drawings, webs, and maps, so that students can use techniques that are less language dependent to deepen and express their knowledge.

- Modify use of text. If necessary, read portions of the text with students or do a text-walk as was explained in Chapter 7. Obtain texts that use a simpler language and more visuals.
- Encourage students to discuss content in their native language.
- Provide opportunities for students to talk over ideas. This could be in whole-class discussions, in pairs, or in small groups.
- Check students' understanding of the material frequently, by asking questions about the material covered. Ask students to retell what they have learned or explain the significance of what they have learned.
- When assessing, allow students to demonstrate their knowledge in multiple ways. Where possible, include ways that do not rely heavily on language. These might include conducting an experiment, drawing a diagram, or completing a project.

READING TO LEARN AND REMEMBER

> Successful studying requires metacognition in addition to a command of useful study strategies. Students must know how and when to use strategies.

Adequate comprehension is a prerequisite for retaining ideas and information but does not guarantee it. That requires studying. Knowing how to study is a complex task, which is both cognitive and affective. Studying involves the interaction of the ability, background knowledge, and motivation of the student; the nature of the course, its content, materials, task requirements, and teacher expectations; and the students' perception of the course and its requirements (Nist & Simpson, 2000). As Kletzien and Bednar (1988) note, students need to take control of their studying. This, in turn, involves four variables: knowing oneself as a learner, setting goals, assessing tasks, and employing thinking processes and strategies.

Know Oneself as a Learner

Low-achieving readers often have a poor opinion of themselves as learners. Having failed in the past, they may see themselves as not being able to study adequately. They may even have given up trying to experience success in their school work. Too often, students attribute a lack of success to a lack of ability. If failure is attributed to lack of ability, students have little recourse but to give up trying. They may lack a sense of self-efficacy. The students need to see a connection between success and hard work and a link between high achievement and working smart. The assessment task also has to be moderated so that it allows for a successful performance. If tests are so hard that low-progress readers have little chance of passing them, they will soon give up trying.

> When giving an assignment, purposes should also be made clear: to learn about the two major types of trees, deciduous and evergreens, for instance.

Setting Goals

All too often the student's only goal is to complete the assignment. The focus should be on learning rather than on task completion. Students need a goal for reading: to read for enjoyment, to learn how to perform a task, or to learn and remember material for a test. The goal will help determine the nature of the task.

Analyze the study demands that are made of students by you and other teachers in your school. Also consider tasks, such as taking phone messages, that students engage in outside of school.

Assessing Tasks

The task includes the type of material to be read, its difficulty, and its length. The goal also has a bearing on the task. Reading J. D. Salinger's *The Catcher in the Rye* for pleasure is a much different task from reading it for a test. Reading directions so that one can plant a tree requires a different kind of reading than reading about trees in order to pass an objective test.

Applying Thinking Processes and Strategies

Once students have a clear idea of their learning goal (what they hope to be able to do), their purpose for reading (questions to be answered), and the task, they are in a better position to determine what thinking processes are involved in learning the material and then selecting strategies that incorporate those processes. Thinking processes and strategies include those that help the student prepare for the reading (surveying, predicting), those that foster comprehension during reading (summarizing, inferring, imaging, judging), and those that aid retention (taking and studying notes, creating and studying graphic organizers, using mnemonic devices). Students need to ask themselves, "What do I need to do to learn this material?"

While reading a chapter on the effects of World War II and realizing that there will be an essay test on the chapter, the student might decide that selecting and organizing is required because she will have to provide essential information in an organized fashion. The student might then choose a strategy that involves creating a semantic map. If the student believes that she will be called upon to make critical judgments, then she might select an elaboration strategy, one that requires making judgments as she reads and reflecting after reading. There are a number of popular strategies for studying textbooks. These include but are not limited to underlining, outlining, taking notes and completing study guides or graphic organizers, and the venerable SQ3R.

AIDS TO STUDYING

Successful studying requires more than simply comprehending, because it bears the extra burden of retrieval. If you cannot remember information, it does not matter whether you understood it or not when you first read it. However, as a practical matter, understanding is a key component of information retrieval. Material that is well understood is easier to understand. As Memory and Moore (1992) note, there are three time-honored aids to studying: principles, organization, and association.

Principles

The best way to promote both comprehension and retrieval of information is by teaching **principles.** If students understand the principles behind certain actions, events, or processes, they are better able to understand new information and to retrieve it later on. For instance, readers who understand the principle of supply and demand will be better able to understand why prices fell during the Great Depression. They will also be better able to under-

Principles: generalizations or rules that underlie events, concepts, or processes.

stand how the loss of jobs caused a drop in demand, and the drop in demand, in turn, caused even more jobs to be lost.

In human biology, students are faced with learning that arteries are thick and elastic and carry oxygen-rich blood away from the heart, but veins are thin and less elastic and carry blood laden with carbon dioxide to the heart. The difference between veins and arteries seems arbitrary and so is difficult to remember (Bransford, 1994). However, if a principle is invoked or an explanation supplied, then the information becomes more meaningful and easier to remember. If the reader is told that arteries are thicker and more elastic because blood is pumped through the arteries in forceful spurts and therefore arteries must be elastic so that they can expand and contract as they push the blood forward, readers are better able to remember which is thicker and more elastic, a vein or an artery. The readers are able to use a principle to help them remember whether a vein or an artery is more elastic and thicker, rather than relying on sheer memory or some mnemonic device.

The moral is clear. Make learning as meaningful as possible. If the selection provides a principle, the teacher should make sure that it is emphasized. If the underlying principle has not been stated, then help students discover it. Bransford (1994) discusses a content-area selection that describes various types of shelters that Native Americans constructed but does not explain why some were permanent while others were easily disassembled, and some had slanted roofs while others did not. Again, the information would be arbitrary until the teacher helped the students discover the principles behind the construction of the dwellings: living habits, climate, and availability of materials.

If neither the teacher nor the text makes the material meaningful, then the student needs to seek underlying principles. One of the study strategies that students need to be taught is how to make information meaningful.

One way of helping students retain principles is to have them apply them (Memory & Moore, 1992). For instance, after explaining why dwellings are built in different ways, you might ask students to survey the construction of homes in their area and discuss why they were built that way. You might ask such questions as: "Why do homes in cold areas have sharply pitched roofs? Why are homes in warm places painted in light colors?" In order to build knowledge of principles, you need to ask a lot of "why" questions—after, of course, basic facts have been established.

Organization

> **Organization:** the manner in which ideas, events, processes, or other items are related.

The second-best comprehension and memory aid is **organization.** If students see the organization of a passage—main idea/details, cause/effect, or comparison/contrast—they are better able to see major ideas and cluster or chunk information. By grouping the following animals into categories—dogs, horses, cows, and cats—you will find that you can learn them faster and recall them more easily than if you just tried to memorize them as listed.

Collie	Manx	Siamese	Morgan
Holstein	Bulldog	Jersey	Pomeranian
Calico	Clydesdale	Beagle	Guernsey

Ayrshire	Tabby	Brown-Swiss	Bloodhound
Palomino	Arabian	Appaloosa	Persian

Questions and graphic organizers that mirror the organization of the selection help students cluster information. Previewing helps students detect the organization of a selection. The headings, for instance, may provide an outline of the chapter (Memory & Moore, 1992). Certain study techniques, such as outlining, and using graphic organizers, also help students detect the organization of a piece.

Organizational Study Strategies

A number of study strategies can help students organize information. In these strategies, some form of noting and recording major ideas is advocated. The organizational strategy featured in this chapter is SQ3R.

SQ3R

> **SQ3R:** five-step study technique: survey, question, read, recite, review.

The oldest and the most widely advocated system for learning from text is **SQ3R,** which stands for Survey, Question, Read, Recite, Review. Devised by Francis Robinson (1970) in the 1940s and updated over the years, SQ3R is based on sound psychological principles of learning, with the five steps to be implemented as follows.

■ ■ ■ ■ ■ ▬▬▬▬▬▬▬▬▬▬▬▬▬▬▬▬▬▬▬▬▬▬▬▬▬▬

STEPS IN SQ3R

> Activating prior knowledge has been added to SQ3R to update it (Vacca & Vacca, 1986).

Step 1: Survey. Survey the chapter to obtain an overview of what you are about to read and to see what you already know about the topic. Read the title, introductory paragraph or overview, headings and subheads, and summary. Predict what the section is about. Activate prior knowledge. Ask yourself: "What do I know about this topic?"

Step 2: Question. Turn each heading into a question. The heading "Fruits Protect Seeds" is transformed into the question, "How do fruits protect seeds?" If you are taking notes, you might jot the question down.

Step 3: Read. Read the section to answer the question that you posed. Reading to answer a question keeps your focus active and purposeful.

Step 4: Recite. When you come to the end of a section, recite. See if you can answer the question that you posed: "How do fruits protect seeds?" This step is metacognitive. It forces you to check your comprehension. If you cannot answer the question, go back over the section and find the necessary information. Recitation may be oral or written. A written recitation can later be used as notes for study. Use two-column notes, putting the question on the left and the answer on the right. If you record your responses, make sure they are very brief so the procedure doesn't become time-consuming and tiresome. Also, refrain from taking notes until you have read the entire section.

Step 5: Review. After the entire assignment has been completed, review what you have read. This will help you see the overall significance of what you have read, organize information, and integrate new information with prior knowledge. In addition to deepening your understanding of the material, it will help you remember it. Some authors suggest inserting a sixth step, an R for reflection. After reading, you might think over what you have read (Pauk, 1984).

For more information on mnemonic strategies, see Mastropieri, M. A. and Scruggs, T. E. (1989). *Teaching students ways to remember.* Cambridge, MA: Brookline.

When taught and applied properly, SQ3R has been shown to be an effective study technique. However, it does take low-achieving readers longer to learn to use the technique (Caverly & Orlando, 1991), and it should be taught early, before students have a chance to pick up ineffective study habits (Early & Sawyer, 1984).

When teaching SQ3R, build on what students already know about reading and studying. Chances are they are already being taught to survey and generate questions and read to answer those questions. Also begin with easy, well-structured content materials. Although you can teach SQ3R in a few sessions, learning to apply the technique may take months.

You might have conferences with students periodically to discuss their application of SQ3R. At that time you might go over their SQ3R notes. Since studying is idiosyncratic, allow individual adaptations of SQ3R.

Association

Association: link between ideas, processes, events, or other items.

Although principles and organization are powerful study aids and should be used if at all possible, simple **associations** can also be helpful, especially if the material to be learned is arbitrary. Memory devices have been successful throughout the ages to help learners better remember facts, terms, and similar types of information.

Associational Strategies

Mnemonics: strategies such as rhymes and acronyms that rely on creating artificial rather than meaningful associations.

How many days are there in May or September? Most of us, when asked that question, resort to the rhyme, "Thirty days hath September, April, June, and November." We can't use understanding because there is no particular principle for determining that, except for February, some months have thirty days and some thirty-one. Rather than resorting to brute memory, we use a **mnemonic.** Levin (1993) states that a mnemonic strategy "involves a transformation of otherwise difficult-to-remember material into something more memorable" (p. 236).

Most of the association devices explored in this section incorporate mnemonic devices. Mnemonic devices have a long history. Many of the traditional nursery and other rhymes are mnemonic devices designed to help school children in bygone years memorize important facts.

Acronyms

Acronym: word formed from the first letters in a series of words, as in ZIP (Zone Improvement Program) code.

In an **acronym,** each letter stands for a word. A word is made up of the first letter of each of the words to be memorized. The best-known example is probably HOMES, for the names of the Great Lakes: Huron, Ontario, Michigan, Erie, and Superior. In recalling the names of the Great Lakes, students use HOMES as a mnemonic aid: the letter *h* reminds them that the name of one of the Great Lakes begins with an *h,* the letter *o* reminds them that the name of another of the Great Lakes begins with an *o*, and so on. Another well-known acronym is ROY G. BIV, which helps retrieve the colors of the spectrum: *r*ed, *o*range, *y*ellow, *g*reen, *b*lue, *i*ndigo, and *v*iolet.

Rhymes

> The key-word strategy, which was presented earlier as a device for learning the meanings of new words, is an example of a mnemonic or associative strategy.

Rhymes are another mnemonic device that have been used for hundreds of years to aid students' memories. When the associations between the pieces of information to be learned are arbitrary and no meaningful connections can be constructed, rhymes are used to assist memory. Two of the best-known rhymes include the one indicating how many days each month has, and the one used to help with the spelling of words containing adjacent *i* and *e:*

Thirty days hath September,
April, June, and November.
February hath twenty-eight alone,
And all the rest have thirty-one.

Use i *before* e *except after* c.
Or when sounded as a
As in neighbor *and* weigh.

Acrostics

> **Acrostic:** sentence or rhyme or series of words in which the first letter in each word stands for a word or spells out a word.

An **acrostic** is a sentence or rhyme in which the first letter of each word stands for the first letter in a series of words to be memorized. For instance, the sentence, "My Very Educational Mother Just Served Us Nine Pizzas" could be used to help recall the names of the planets: Mercury, Venus, Earth, Mars, Jupiter, Saturn, Uranus, Neptune, Pluto (Richardson & Morgan, 1997, p. 322).

STUDY HABITS

Poor or ineffective study habits are a major cause of failure. A large proportion of students have inefficient study habits. When students are asked how they would study a section of expository text in order to recall as much as they could, most typically respond that they would simply reread the material or just concentrate. Some will admit to having no strategy for remembering the material. A first step in helping students who have become discouraged or have given up is to show them that they can learn. In a number of studies cited in earlier chapters, low-achieving readers achieved higher grades when they were taught effective strategies.

To determine how best to break the cycle of failure, survey the students. Find out how they study for tests. Find out which subjects or which kinds of tests are most troublesome and plan a program of intervention. Enlist the aid of the subject-matter teacher.

> Students may not be aware of how much studying is required in order to learn a list of new words or several concepts thoroughly. They may need to learn a criterion for adequate performance.

Metacognitive Aspects of Studying

Students also need to know what to study: all of the chapters covered? Selected portions of the chapters, handouts, notes? They also need to know whether the test is cumulative. Will it cover all the information from the beginning of the term, or just the information for the last unit or since the last major test?

In addition to knowing what to study, students need to know how, when, where, and how long to study. A student should know his or her personal best time to study. Some may do better studying early in the morning. Others are at their best at night. Some prefer an informal environment; others do their best work at a desk. Some students need lots of structure. Others like to have choices about when, where, and how they study (Carbo, Dunn, & Dunn 1986). Help students become aware of the conditions under which they study best. These should be conditions that are comfortable but that also result in improved performance. When students get high grades on a test, you might discuss with them how they went about studying for that particular test.

Overcoming Obstacles to Studying

Teachers should also help students discover impediments to study: (1) lack of self-discipline, (2) lack of time, (3) boredom, (4) lack of perseverance, and (5) distractibility. Work out with students ways of overcoming these obstacles.

Lack of Discipline.   Set a routine. Study at the same time and the same place. The place should be free of distractions, although if the student works better with background music, that should not be considered a "distraction." Break large tasks into smaller, more manageable ones. Instead of tackling a whole chapter, break it up into three-page or five-page sections. Start with the easiest and most enjoyable task, to build a sense of accomplishment. Use rewards such as a ten-minute break for every fifty minutes of studying. Or you might encourage students to keep a chart showing number of minutes spent studying each night. At the end of each week, give the students checks or stars for completing their charts. The best motivator is success. If students do well after studying, they will have an incentive for studying harder. Counseling may be in order for students who cannot seem to make themselves study.

Lack of Time.   Have students chart how they spend their time during a typical day. By analyzing the time spent, determine when might be the best time to study. Also select a place to study. If students live in a crowded apartment, they might decide to study in school or at the local library, or to study early in the morning while everyone else is still in bed.

Boredom.   Show students how to set goals and become active learners. Tell them to use self-testing to challenge themselves, and to tackle boring tasks in short but concentrated segments.

Lack of Perseverance.   Begin with short periods of study, perhaps just ten minutes. Gradually build up to longer periods. Also use self-rewards. Try beginning with the easiest or most interesting task.

Distractibility. To aid in avoiding distractions, use self-talk: "I will read three pages. I will concentrate on my reading. I will ask myself questions about what I have read. If I can answer the questions, I will reward myself and take a break." Stress with these students that brief periods of focused study are better than long periods interrupted by internal and external distractions.

Creating Study Plans

Help students devise individual study plans. These plans might include when and where the students plan to study. Plans should be long term and short term. If students have long-term projects, they might indicate how they plan to complete those projects. In the beginning, students might evaluate their study sessions by using a form such as the study log shown in Figure 12.14, reflections they have written in a learning log, or through discussions. The evaluation should include what study tasks the students undertook, what study strategies they used, and approximately how much time they spent on each task. They should also report any problems they had and assess the effectiveness of their study efforts. This will help students gain a greater awareness of what it means to be an effective learner. Students will also be able to see which strategies work best and how much time tasks take.

FIGURE 12.14   Study Log

Name _____

STUDY TASK	DATE, TIME, AND PLACE OF STUDYING	TIME SPENT STUDYING	STUDY METHOD USED (OUTLINE, SQ3R, ETC.)	QUESTIONS, DIFFICULTIES, COMMENTS	RESULTS (TEST GRADES, QUIZZES, CLASS DISCUSSION)
Read chapter about kinds of rocks	*1–6* *7–8:10*	*1 hr, 10 min*	*Frame*	*Many hard words*	*Quiz—90*
Read chapter on WWI.	*1–6* *8:30–9*	*30 min*	*SQ3R & Review notes*	*Many names & dates*	
Study for test on WWI	*1–7* *7–7:50*	*50 min*			*Test—C Knew causes of war but not names & dates*

PREPARING FOR TESTS

The best time to start preparing for a test is the first day of class. Grasping material from the start is essential, as is organizing it and reviewing it from time to time. Using two-column or three-column notes, creating information maps, and other organizers are good ways to prepare for a test. Note taking should be geared, in part, to the type of test the student will be taking. If the test will be an objective one, for instance, then more attention should be paid to essential details.

Students should also learn the value of periodic review. Spaced review is also generally better than massed review, especially when facts or processes are being studied. Spaced review means that students space out their studying over a period of days or weeks. In massed review, students study for lengthy periods of time. Cramming is a form of massed review.

Students should also study the material in the same way that they will be expected to demonstrate their knowledge of it. If they will be asked to identify the parts of a frog in a lab practicum, then they should practice doing just that. Or if they will be asked to write essay questions, they should create skeletal answers to possible essay questions.

In their study of standardized test taking among elementary school students, Calkins, Montgomery, and Santman (1998) found that many of the students did not know how to take a test. Among the flaws in the students' test taking, they found:

- Not reading or following directions
- Using a casual reading style that was more suitable for reading a novel
- Not making educated guesses
- Not realizing that it was possible and even desirable to look back over a passage to find the answer to a question
- Not checking answers
- Using personal knowledge rather than text knowledge

As an experienced test taker, model how you go about taking a test. Explain your thinking processes as you read and follow directions. Show how you go about eliminating distractors when you are not sure of an answer. Model the process of checking answers and pacing yourself. Invite successful test takers to discuss their strategies. Provide extra coaching for students whose responding style lowers their scores: those who work too rapidly and fail to check answers as well as those who work too slowly and are overly concerned with making a mistake. If the test has a high ceiling and has advanced items, provide students with strategies for reading difficult passages and answering tough questions. Also explain the correction factor. On some tests, students lose points for wrong responses, and so are better off leaving an answer blank if they have no idea which of the options is correct. However, if they can eliminate more than one of the options, the odds of getting the right answer will be in their favor. If there is no penalty for guessing, students should make their best guess.

A strategy such as QAR adapted to test taking should be effective in helping students decide whether the answer is right there, so that if they don't recall it, they can go back over the passage and find it, or whether it's an author-and-me question, so they have to make an inference based on information contained in the passage.

Probe low-scoring students to find out how they handle difficult passages. Do they give up? Do they make random guesses? Or do they try to make as much sense out of the passages as they can and, when all else fails, match up unknown words in the answer options with the same words in the selection? Students need to know that they can sometimes answer questions correctly even when they don't know every word in the passage.

Test preparation must be ethical. Obviously, giving students examples from the actual test is wrong. However, it is also unethical to raise students' scores without also increasing their underlying knowledge and skill. As assessment expert Popham (2000) states, "No test preparation practice should increase students' test scores without simultaneously increasing student mastery of the assessment domain tested" (p. 82). The aim of test preparation should be to instruct students so that they have the test-taking skills they need so that their performance will reflect their true state of knowledge and/or skill. In fact, teachers are remiss if they do not help students attain the level of test-taking competence that will allow them to demonstrate what they truly know. See pp. 487–488 for suggestions for teaching students to create written responses to test questions.

MOTIVATING STUDENTS TO PUT FORTH NEEDED EFFORT

Summarizing, questioning, and imaging and other reading strategies take more effort than simply glancing over the page. As Irene Gaskins (2003) comments, "Implementing strategies almost always entails more effort than students are accustomed to putting forth when they read" (p. 149). Therefore, it is essential that students see the payoff for the extra effort. Explain to students that their grades are almost sure to improve if they use appropriate strategies. Tell them that research studies show that students' marks on quizzes increase by 30 or 40 points after learning strategies (Fisher, Schumaker, & Deshler, 2002). A more direct approach is to teach one-half of the class a strategy and then give a quiz to the whole class and compare how students do.

MINICASE STUDY

Carmen's teacher, noting her low grades, discussed her performance with her and arranged for Carmen to obtain specialized help from the reading teacher. Through an informal interview and by using a think-aloud as Carmen demonstrated how she studied for quizzes, the reading teacher determined that Carmen was not studying efficiently or effectively. She had virtually no study skills and no specific goal, except to obtain passing grades.

The first thing the specialist did was to help Carmen set specific learning goals for each reading assignment. She also helped Carmen set up a study schedule and determine the best time and place to study.

Noting that Carmen seemed to lack confidence and did not give herself credit for what she did know, the specialist used KWL Plus with her. Discussing what she knew and deciding what she wanted to learn helped Carmen personalize her learning. As Carmen's comprehension and sense of personal involvement grew, the specialist introduced SQ3R. Emphasis was placed on preparing for the types of questions that the teacher typically asked in classroom recitations and written tests.

Carmen was also instructed in the use of text structure to help her comprehend and organize key ideas in science and social studies, the two areas in which she was having most difficulty. As Carmen progressed, the reading teacher helped her construct frame maps based on her SQ3R notes. The reading teacher also showed Carmen how to use frames to prepare for quizzes and tests.

Carmen's grades gradually improved. As Carmen began to see rewards for studying, she put more effort into her work, and by year's end she was passing all subjects.

SUMMARY

From 25 to 40 percent of middle and high school students have difficulty reading their content-area textbooks. With its technical vocabulary, greater density of ideas, increased demands on conceptual knowledge, and more complex organizational patterns, content-area reading can be overwhelming for students who have marginal reading skills. In addition to being overstuffed with facts, many content-area texts are written on a level beyond the grade for which they were intended. Teachers of below-level readers can seek easier texts, use trade books written on the appropriate level of difficulty, provide additional assistance with the text, use glosses, use taped versions of the text, make greater use of sources of information that do not require reading, and use hands-on activities. Texts can also be adapted, but this is time consuming.

Content Enhancement organizes and presents the curriculum in such a way that key concepts are easier to learn and more readily learned and so fosters understanding. Teaching students how to use text structures also fosters comprehension. Other instructional techniques that can be employed to foster comprehension in the content areas can be categorized as those that are used before, during, or after reading. Before-reading techniques feature the anticipation guide, structured overview, and the Frayer model. During-reading techniques feature frame questions and study guides, including glosses. After-reading techniques include reflecting, graphic postorganizers, applying, and extending. KWL is an approach that encompasses before-, during-, and after-reading techniques. Collaborative techniques that incorporate several highly successful comprehension strategies are ReQuest, reciprocal teaching, and questioning the author.

Dealing as it does with material that is predominantly narrative, literature books are somewhat easier to comprehend than are social studies or science texts. In addition, teachers of low-achieving readers have a wider range, in terms of difficulty level, of literature texts from which to choose. For low-achieving readers, teachers may choose texts that are of high quality but are less demanding to read.

In order to study effectively, students must know themselves as learners. They must be able to size up a learning task, set reasonable goals, and have a solid grasp of effective study strategies.

There are three approaches to studying: principles (understanding), organization, and association. The most widely used study strategy is SQ3R: survey, question, read, recite, review, to which a sixth step, reflect, is sometimes added. SQ3R is an organizational strategy. Other organizational study strategies include various forms of note taking.

Associational memory devices include mnemonic approaches: rhymes, acronyms, and acrostics.

Poor study habits are a major cause of academic failure. Assessing students' study strategies and habits, building students' knowledge of self as a learner, instructing, coaching, and counseling are techniques that can help to improve students' study habits. Ultimately, however, students must take responsibility for their own learning.

Motivation to study stems, in part, from seeing that one's studying pays off in the form of higher grades. Knowing how to take tests is a functional life skill for students. Students need to know that a study plan for an objective test will be different from a study plan for an essay test.

APPLICATION ACTIVITIES

1. Examine texts written for low-achieving readers. Analyze the texts. What makes them easy to read? What are the major disadvantages and advantages of using easy-to-read texts?

2. Construct a study guide or a gloss. If possible, introduce it and arrange for a group of students to use it.

3. Try out SQ3R with some material that you wish to learn. Use it for at least five sessions. Assess its effectiveness. What are its advantages? What are its disadvantages?

4. Teach one of the study strategies covered in this chapter to a disabled reader or a group of low-achieving readers. Assess the effectiveness of the lesson.

5. Read and try out the suggestions made in Oczukus, L. D. (2003). *Reciprocal teaching at work, Strategies for improving reading comprehension.* Newark, DE: International Reading Association.

CHAPTER THIRTEEN

BUILDING WRITING STRATEGIES

USING WHAT YOU KNOW

Beset by difficulties in organizing their ideas and frequently handicapped by poor spelling and illegible handwriting, low-achieving readers find writing even more difficult than reading. The process approach, with its emphasis on the message as opposed to the mechanics, is a powerful tool for teaching disabled writers and will be emphasized in this chapter. However, focus will also be placed on presenting strategies that have proved to be effective with low-achieving readers and writers.

How do you feel about writing? What kinds of writing do you find relatively easy? What kinds do you find difficult? What strategies or routines do you use to help you write? How would you go about helping low-achieving writers?

ANTICIPATION GUIDE

Read each of the following statements. Put a check under "Agree" or "Disagree" to show how you feel about each one. If possible, discuss your responses with classmates.

		AGREE	DISAGREE
1.	Good writers are born, not made.	_____	_____
2.	If you can say it, you can write it.	_____	_____
3.	The more planning you do beforehand, the better the writing.	_____	_____
4.	The hardest part of writing is revising.	_____	_____
5.	The major problem that struggling readers and writers have with writing is spelling.	_____	_____

EXTENT OF WRITING PROBLEMS

How many students have writing problems? Based on the 2002 National Assessment of Educational Progress writing assessment, at grades 4, 8, and 12, the percentages of students performing below the basic level of writing achievement were 14, 15, and 26 percent,

> Writing is both more complex and more abstract than talking. When people talk to each other, they are aided by cues to start, to stop, to continue, to clarify, or to elaborate. When composing, writers are on their own (Bereiter & Scardamalia, 1982).

respectively (see Table 13.1) (Persky, Daane, & Jin, 2003). They have such limited writing skills that they lack even partial mastery for the writing demanded by their grade level. Students do better on narrative writing than informative, and better on informative than persuasive tasks.

THE CHANGING NATURE OF THE WRITING PROCESS

As students mature as writers, the nature of their writing changes. Inexperienced writers use a knowledge-telling process, in which writing is similar to telling a story orally or providing an oral explanation. It requires "no greater amount of planning or goal setting than ordinary conversation" (Bereiter & Scardamalia, 1982, p. 9). Beginning writers use a "what next" strategy, in which they write from one sentence to the next without having an overall plan for the whole piece (Dahl & Farnham, 1998). The sentence currently being written provides a springboard for the next sentence. Over time, writers acquire the ability to transform knowledge, in which they develop and revise their thoughts as they write so that writing becomes a way of exploring and learning. As more experienced writers compose, their writing affects their thinking, and their thinking affects their writing. Instead of merely summarizing thoughts, writers reconsider old ideas and draw new conclusions, which are reflected in their writing. To develop thinking abilities, writing activities should go beyond merely requiring students to retell or summarize. They should involve comparing, contrasting, concluding, and evaluating, so that students can reshape and transform their knowledge. Struggling writers, often because of poorly developed skills, get stuck in the knowledge-telling stage of writing. Asked to respond to a narrative poem or short story, struggling writers frequently resort to providing a plot summary. If the story is a challenging one, they might use all their mental energies to understand the story, so they are unable to evaluate it at the same time. Or they might not have a schema for the kind of writing that requires a critical analysis. When faced with challenging tasks, even experienced writers resort to using knowledge telling. The knowledge-telling strategy is adopted because the task is so challenging for the writers that they are unable to go beyond simply recording content. The problem with knowledge telling is that the writers do not provide their own interpretations, and voice or distinctive style is lacking.

One form of knowledge telling is a copying strategy. Using a copying strategy, students simply retell what they have read or heard. They may paraphrase or use their own

TABLE 13.1   Writing Levels for a National Sample of Students: 2002

GRADE	BELOW BASIC	BASIC	PROFICIENT	ADVANCED
4	14	84	58	2
8	15	84	54	2
12	26	78	51	2

From H. R. Persky, M. C. Daane, & Y. Jin, *NAEP 2002 writing report card for the nation and the states.* Washington, DC: U.S. Department of Education, 1999.

words. Copying could be more of a reading than a writing issue. It may mean that the reader is still constructing the meaning of the passage and so is dependent on the author's words in order to say what the passage means. If the author's ideas are difficult to understand, writers may solve the problem by retelling these ideas in the author's words (Collins, 1998). Once students have a clear understanding of an idea, they can start integrating it with their own ideas. Paraphrasing, of course, is a highly useful writing strategy, as is imitating the styles of accomplished writers. Struggling writers need to be taught strategies that build on copying. Students need to be taught how to paraphrase, imitate, and integrate.

As with developing reading skills, the emphasis in writing instruction is on building on what students know. And that means digging deeply. When working with problem writers, it is easy to be stopped cold by surface features and go no further. You need to look beyond awkward wording, dysgraphic handwriting, bizarre spellings, random use of capital letters, and look into the message the students are attempting to convey and the processes they are using. The process approach to writing emphasizes composing and revising and puts mechanics in perspective so that they don't become the be-all and the end-all of writing instruction.

> **Writing process:** model of teaching writing that views writing as being composed of planning, composing, revising, editing, and publishing.

The five elements in the **writing process** are prewriting, composing, revising, editing, and publishing. Although these elements are listed separately, they operate in a circular or recursive fashion. Before I write, I plan and prepare, but actually I am composing in my head as I plan, and as I write I might revise and even edit and also plan what comes next. I might do much of my planning after I have started writing. I may not even know what I'm going to write until I have actually written it. Fiction writers report being motivated to write so they can see how the story comes out. With this type of writing, characters often take on a life of their own.

Prewriting

> **Prewriting:** part of the writing process that includes all the things a writer does before composing, including selecting a topic and planning.

Prewriting consists of all those things that a writer does to prepare for writing. It may take ten minutes, or it may be an idea that someone has been mulling over for ten years. The core of prewriting is topic selection. If students are going to invest time and energy and put themselves into their writing, they must have a sense of personal involvement in their writing. The best topics are those that students select for themselves because they have a personal interest in them and about which they know a great deal or want to explore. However, this does not mean that students should get bogged down in biographical narratives. Struggling writers need to acquire a command of the major types of writing. They need to be able to write explanatory and persuasive pieces. However, they should be encouraged to write a persuasive piece about an issue that touches their lives or explain a process that is of interest to them.

Modeling Topic Selection.   Since underachieving writers may have limited experience in selecting topics, model the process for them. For instance, if the students are writing about famous Americans as part of a biography unit, list some of the people you might want to

> Teachers who lack confidence in their underachieving writers often supply them with topics and then wonder why their finished products are brief and devoid of creativity.

write about. List four or five names on the board and think-aloud your reasons for your choices, as in the following example:

Martin Luther King
Sally Ride
Roberto Clemente
Thomas Edison
Tiger Woods

Give an honest appraisal of which one you would like to write about. You might give the pros and cons of each topic, saying, "I know Martin Luther King worked hard for justice and equal rights and Sally Ride was the first women astronaut, Roberto Clemente was an outstanding baseball player and tried to help poor people, and Tiger Woods may be one of the best golfers ever, but I'm most interested in Thomas Edison. He went on to become one of the most famous inventors of all time, but I heard that he had trouble with school. I'd like to find out more about his growing-up days and write about that."

Sources of topics are endless. Students can write about their everyday lives: what they have seen, heard, or read about in class or outside of school. The topic might be a class trip, an interesting project, being the new boy or girl in class, the school principal, a guest speaker, a piece of information in a science or social studies book, or an article in *Sports Illustrated for Kids.*

Research is another possibility. Students can explore topics about which they have

> Notebooks provide their owners with the opportunity to collect ideas and information over a period of time before setting out to write. Choosing a topic becomes a matter of selecting ideas that have had time to ripen.

limited knowledge but which interest them: they can explore and write about how to take care of a new puppy, how to grow tomatoes, or how CD-ROM works. They can find out more about sharks, deserts, or the stars. They can write to their favorite basketball player or pop singer. They can interview their grandparents to find out about life in the 1960s, or talk to a dietitian about eating the right kinds of foods. You might also encourage students to talk to family members and friends about possible topics and to keep a notebook or file of possible subjects. A writer's notebook should be a place to generate ideas, explore topics, or jot down observations (Calkins & Harwayne, 1991).

If students are really stuck for a topic, you might suggest some sure-fire generic topics. For instance, play the song, "My Favorite Things" or read the book *Honey, I Love and Other Poems* (Greenfield, 1978) and talk over your favorite things or the things that you love. Then have students make a list of their favorite things and develop it into an autobiographical piece.

Reading is also a rich source of topic ideas. A brief article about bird watching or seeing-eye dogs may motivate students to explore this topic and report on their findings. In their notebooks, students might also record favorite passages, realistic characters, unusual settings, imaginative phrases, and humorous or wise expressions that might become the basis for future writing.

Planning.   After a topic has been selected, students gather and organize information. This is a crucial step for underachieving writers. Their compositions are typically very brief,

> Drawing can be a rehearsal for writing. Moore and Caldwell (1991) devised a program in which students drew story boards showing characters, setting, story events, and main ideas before composing their pieces.

suggesting that they lack adequate content knowledge or they were unable to make use of the knowledge they do have (Graham & Harris, 1993). They may not realize how much information they have on a topic or may have difficulty organizing it and putting it in written form. To help students make use of information that they already possess, drawing and brainstorming are effective techniques. Drawing helps younger students encapsulate their ideas. When they write in response to a drawing they have created, the drawing provides them a stable prompt for suggesting what details they might develop. Because it taps another dimension, drawing also helps older students retrieve details that they may not have thought of. After J. L. Olson (1987) encouraged her students to draw illustrations of their subjects before writing about them, the detail in their written pieces increased markedly. An essential element in the procedure was discussion. Olson discussed students' drawings with them before they began writing. This helped them translate into words the details recorded in their drawings.

Students may have a number of ideas that they wish to express, but they might not know how to organize them. Completing a semantic map or a preplanning sheet will help them organize their thoughts. However, they should be encouraged to add new ideas or details as they write. Since writing is, in part, a discovery process, writers often think up new ideas as they write.

Brainstorming.   An effective technique for helping students access details is to have them brainstorm the topic. The stimulus for brainstorming can be the topic or a single word. Model the process, emphasizing that in brainstorming you come up with as many ideas as you can think of. Students are then encouraged to brainstorm. Urge them to listen to ideas expressed by others, because that may help them think of other ideas.

Rehearsal.   A valuable planning technique is to provide students with time to mull over their topics. Before they begin composing, professional writers may have rehearsed the piece they are about to write for days or weeks or even years. When they sit down at their desks, they are ready to write. They have already shaped the piece in their minds. Encourage students to **rehearse** topics. Try giving them previews of writing assignments a day or so ahead of time, so that they have time to think over possible topics and how they might develop them.

> **Writing rehearsal:** practice of mentally composing a piece before actually writing it down.

Audience.   An important part of planning is considering the audience. Novice writers have a difficult time adjusting their writing for an outside reader. They believe that if they can understand it, so can anyone who happens to read it. To help build audience awareness, discuss the concept of audience before students start writing. Ask such questions as: "For whom are you writing? Who will read your piece? What will you need to tell your readers so they will understand your piece?"

In the past, much of the writing that students did in school was for the teacher. Students wrote to complete an assignment or to be evaluated. This limited the range of students' writing. In today's schools, students write real pieces for a variety of audiences.

Approaches to Prewriting.   The amount of time and effort devoted to prewriting will depend, in part, on your approach to writing or the nature of the particular writing task (Collins, 1998). Some teachers take a write-it-now, fix-it-later approach, in which the focus of instruction is on revising first drafts to incorporate key features. The other approach is to supply a maximum of prewriting instruction so that students include key features in their first drafts. Neither approach is more effective than the other. However, getting it right the first time can be a confidence builder and allows more opportunity for refinement or fine-tuning.

Composing

> Simple narrative writing is less complex than expository or persuasive writing. As Bruner (1986) explains, there are two types of thinking: narrative and logical-scientific. Narrative thinking is more basic. Students have much more experience with narrative than they do with logical-scientific thinking, which is more complex and abstract.

> **Composing:** act of writing. The focus should be on getting one's thoughts down, rather than creating a finished, error-free piece on the first attempt.

Disabled writers may be hindered by poor spelling ability, labored handwriting, possible difficulty in retrieving the right words to express their thoughts, and a negative association with writing, so they may scrawl only a sentence or two before calling it quits. The first order of business when working with low-progress writers is to emphasize content over mechanics. Stress with these students that the important thing in a first draft is to get one's thoughts down and not to worry about spelling, punctuation, capitalization, handwriting, or the appearance of the paper until later. Tell students to spell as best they can. You might show them examples of first drafts in which the author may have used one or two letters to represent whole words or used invented spelling (see Chapters 5 and 7 for more information on invented spelling). Explain that there will be plenty of time to check spelling, punctuation, and capitalization, but that will come later.

Model the **composing** process for students and show them some rough drafts that you have written in which wholesale changes were later made. If students need more convincing, invite reporters from the local newspaper or other professional writers to talk to the class about how they write their first drafts. If labored handwriting is a serious problem, you might try having students dictate their pieces or use a word processor if they have adequate keyboarding skills.

As students compose, they may reach a point where they can't seem to continue. Encourage them to seek additional information, or they may have a conference with a peer, with you, or with a writing group. These conferences serve some of the same functions in eliciting more writing that speaker–listener interactions in conversations do. They help elicit output. It is also a good idea to circulate around the room as students write, providing support for students or brief miniconferences to help them access additional information. If students are still stuck, they might consider putting the piece aside and coming back to it later, or trying another topic.

> **Writing conferences:** meetings between student and teacher or student and peer editor for the purpose of discussing the student's writing.

Writing Conferences.   The ultimate purpose of **writing conferences** is to help students discover that they have something to say (Murray, 1989). Through careful questioning and responding, the teacher affirms the students' efforts. Through the conference, students discover and

Graves (1983) comments: "Listening is hard work. . . . It isn't easy to put aside personal preferences, anxieties about helping more children, or the glaring, mechanical errors that stare from the page. I mumble to myself, 'Shut up, listen, and learn!' " (p. 100).

clarify what they plan to do with their pieces and explore processes that might be used to attain their goals.

Conference questions are of three general types: opening, following, and process (Graves, 1983). Opening questions are ice-breakers designed to start the flow of the conference. These are open-ended, non-threatening inquiries: "How is it going? What are you writing about? Where are you now in your piece?" Following questions are designed to maintain the flow. Often, they are simply restatements or summaries, in question form, of what the student has told you: "You're having difficulty getting started?" or "Your team lost the championship game and you feel you're to blame?" or "You like your new school but miss your old friends?" As their name suggests, process questions focus on the writing process itself. Process questions might be of a general nature: "What do you think you'll do next? What do you want to do with this piece? Where will you start? What part do you like best? Is there a part you aren't happy with?" Or the questions can be more specific: "What happened after this? Can you explain this? As a reader, I'd like to know more about this. What can you do to make your beginning stronger? Can you think of a different way to say this?" (Turbill, 1982). Process questions help students become aware of the strategies they are using so they can exert greater control over them. After students have solved a writing problem or finished a piece, you might ask questions that will lead them to reflect and comment on the processes they have used: "Your new ending is more interesting. How did you go about writing it?" (Graves, 1983).

Process questioning should also help you discover the writer's strengths and weaknesses, the strategies the writer is using, and ways in which you might build upon the writer's knowledge and strategies. In his work with struggling writers, Collins (1998) asked students to tell what made writing hard and to ask for help whenever they had questions about their writing or when they were encountering difficulty. This helped him to discover underlying writing problems and allowed him to suggest useful strategies.

■ ■ ■ ■ ■

EXEMPLARY TEACHING
FOCUSING IN ON KEY EVENTS

For struggling writers, a common flaw is failure to focus on a key event or even what Calkins and Oxenhorn (2003) term a small moment. Instead they attempt to recount all the events of a day or experience. Here is how teacher Lois Burdett used a conference to help a student hone in on an important event. "Here you told me your hamster died, but then you went right into your shopping trip at Kmart. How did you feel when your hamster died? Who buried it? Where did you bury?" (Spandel, 2005, p. 233). Responding to her teacher's queries, the writer described in vivid terms a description of the pet's last moments and how she touched its body to see if she could detect any signs of life. She followed with a description of her tears as she realized her pet was gone. She describes her rush into the basement to break the sad news to her dad. The piece ends with a description of the burial and the marker that contained the hamster's name and e-mail address. A few well-thought-out questions by the teacher transformed a dull recounting of a day's events into a poignant piece.

Revising: procedure in the writing process in which the writer reviews what has been written and makes changes in content and expression.

Revising

Real **revising** means taking a fresh look at what you have written and asking yourself such basic questions as: "What am I trying to say here? Have I said what I want to say? Have I said all that I want to say? Is my writing clear? Is it as fresh and vivid as I can make it? Does it sound right? Does it feel right? Do all the parts fit?" Over time and with experience and feedback, students will develop an ear for their prose. An inner voice will tell them that something is amiss, that the piece doesn't sound or feel right. Accomplished writers spend a large proportion of their time revising. Their revising is also more global. They consider the whole piece as they revise and may rework it so it does what they want it to do. However, with relatively brief instruction, inexperienced writers can also be taught to revise globally (Hayes, 2000).

There's a saying among writers that "There's no such thing as bad writing; there's only bad revising." Most writers revise and revise and revise some more.

To help students gain a sense of what it means to revise, model the process. Show them how you add or delete details, rewrite sentences, move elements around, change words. However, focus on those aspects of revising that your students can handle. In the past, students were reluctant to revise because it meant recopying the entire piece. Demonstrate to students shortcuts they can take. Show them how they can use copy-editing marks: arrows to move elements, carets to add. They can cross out items or even manually cut and paste elements. If possible, demonstrate how a word processor might be used in the revision process. One of the advantages of using word processors is that the mechanics of revising are made so much simpler.

As students look over their rough drafts, encourage them to see whether they have any questions about what they wrote. Have them put themselves in the readers' place and ask: "Will the readers understand what I'm trying to say? Have I told the readers enough? Will the readers want to know more?" Often, the major problem with disabled writers' pieces is that they haven't told enough. They have supplied a few barebone facts without elaborating. Or they have written "hodge-podges of anything-I-can-think-of-that relates-to-this-topic pieces" (Calkins & Oxenhorn, 2003, p. v) instead of focusing on a key moment or incident (see Exemplary Teaching: Focusing in on Key Events).

When modeling the revising process, focus on one or two key items that the class as a whole seems to need. For instance, if students are not including enough details in their pieces, demonstrate adding information. Also alert students to the fact that revisions can sometimes be less effective and less clearly written than the original. Encourage students to reread their piece after they have revised it to make sure the revised version sounds better than the original.

Revising should be cumulative. After students have mastered one revising strategy, introduce a second. For instance, after students have learned to add details to flesh out a piece of writing, you might find that they need to work on interesting beginnings. As students revise, they can focus on writing interesting beginnings but should also be responsible for making sure that they included sufficient detail. You might have students compose a revision checklist and add elements as these are taught. See also the Revision Think Sheet in Figure 13.7, later in the chapter.

When revising, struggling readers and writers tend to focus on surface features such as capitalization and spelling. Guide them in looking for and reworking substantive elements such as using examples to develop a topic and using colorful adjectives. During the process, emphasize things that students have done well so that they have something to build on.

In writing narratives, struggling readers often fail to develop their characters. They fail to show why they acted the way they did or how they were feeling (Newcomer & Barenbaum, 1991). In preparing students to write narratives, read aloud to them or have them read selections in which the characters' motivations and emotions are developed. Discuss how the characters' motivations and emotions are revealed. Using these as models, have the class compose a group narrative in which motivation and emotion are revealed and then have students write their own pieces. As you conference with students, ask them why the characters were acting in a certain way and what they were thinking and feeling.

In writing expository text, struggling readers and writers often fail to develop their topics. They may give just one example or one reason or one detail. Just as with narratives, discuss model paragraphs and, later, longer pieces that are well developed. Note in particular how the authors developed their ideas and have students follow suit in a group story and then individual pieces. During prewriting, composing, and revising, emphasize the development of the topic.

Editing

Up until this point, the focus has been on the content of the piece. Emphasis was rightfully placed on composing rather than on the mechanics of writing. In this final step, students edit their pieces for mechanical errors. Normally, in the **editing** process, all errors are corrected. Since disabled writers tend to make an excessive number of errors, you may choose to focus on just one or two areas of concern. However, if pieces are to be published, then you may want to have all errors corrected.

> **Editing:** process of making corrections in a written piece. Often there is a focus on mechanical errors rather than on making changes in content.

As with the other conventions in writing, capitalization, punctuation, and usage should be taught directly and related to the writing that students are doing. To decide which elements to teach, examine students' first drafts to see what is needed. Focus on one element, capitalization of proper names, or question marks, for instance.

Editing Strategies.   Once you have analyzed students' errors, discuss with them the kinds of mistakes they make. Keeping in mind any error patterns that you note, teach them strategies for minimizing errors and detecting those that do crop up. If students mix up the order of the letters in words, have them slowly and carefully read the piece exactly as it is written, so that *turly* is read as *turly* and the student can note that the word is misspelled. If students omit endings, have them check the endings of words. If students omit syllables, have them pronounce each syllable in any multisyllabic words they have written. Also, students might circle any words that they feel might be misspelled.

Skills Lessons.   While group skills lessons should be taught on a regular basis, also provide instruction as needed on an informal basis. Whether taught as part of whole-group direct instruction or a repair-it-on-the-spot basis, skill instruction works best if it is taught when needed. As students edit, it is helpful if they have a checklist to help them. Checklists can be generic, or they can be individualized and geared to the needs of specific students. A sample editing checklist is presented in Figure 13.1. For older students, you might provide them with a mnemonic strategy for editing, such as SCOPE:

S   Spelling: Is the spelling correct?

C   Capitalization: Are the first words of sentences, proper names, and proper nouns capitalized?

O   Order of words: Are the words in the right order?

P   Punctuation: Does each sentence end with a period, question mark, or exclamation mark? Are commas and apostrophes placed where needed?

E   Express complete thought: Is each sentence complete? Does each sentence have a subject and a predicate? (Bos & Vaughn, 1994)

Publishing

Writing real pieces for real people is an essential element in the writing process. Writing for a real audience changes the nature of students' writing. For instance, several studies of poor writers in the intermediate and secondary grades found that these students expressed themselves effectively when writing on their own to peers or family members. Ironically, many of these same students had been judged to be poor writers on the basis of performance on school-related writing tasks (Dyson & Freedman, 1991).

> **Publishing:** part of the writing process in which students share their writing in some way. The piece could be printed in a booklet or newspaper, or it could be read or dramatized.

Developing as a writer requires getting a response to one's writing. One of the advantages of **publishing,** or making public one's writing, is that it invites feedback. Without feedback, the writer has no way of gauging whether or not her or his work was understood and enjoyed by the audience. Response from others also helps students learn to see their writing as others see it, which builds a sense of audience. Through audience reaction writers can see which parts of their pieces are most effective and which parts may need clarifying or elaborating.

GUIDED WRITING

Just as students benefit from structured guidance in reading, they also do better when given guidance as they write. Although some skills can be taught to the whole class, students' spe-

FIGURE 13.1   Editing Checklist

1. Is the piece clear?
2. Are the sentences complete?
3. Does each sentence end with a period, question mark, or exclamation point?
4. Is the first word of each sentence capitalized?
5. Are the names of people (George, Uncle Fred) and places (New York, U.S., Main Street) capitalized?
6. Are all the words spelled correctly?

cific needs can be targeted more effectively if they are members of small groups. Instead of being grouped by reading level, students are grouped by reading and writing level. Just as with oral language acquisition, students' understanding of the writing process and ability to write develops over time and with experience. Students' concepts of writing and abilities become deeper, more complex, and broader. Although the development of writing is not a linear process, it may be helpful to think of students' writing as occurring in overlapping stages.

Writing level is determined by analyzing sample written pieces or portfolios. Instruction is geared to the students' level of development. Guidelines for determining students' stages of writing are listed in Figure 13.2. The stages were devised for grades 1, 3, and 5 but can be adapted for any grade. Within each stage there may be a range of performance. The stages consider topic development, awareness of audience, use of language, including sentence structure and word choice, and surface features or use of mechanics.

The teacher meets with one or two groups each day and conducts a writing process or strategy lesson. Students are grouped by their level of development and are given instruction geared to their stage. For the emergent writer, the focus of instruction might be ways to develop a topic more fully. Prewriting activities might include brainstorming or webbing details to support a topic. For the experimenting writer, the focus of instruction might be on creating interesting beginning sentences. Prewriting activities might include looking at model beginnings and brainstorming possible beginning sentences. Engagement is emphasized. Students who are genuinely interested in a topic and want to share their ideas and stories with others will put more into their writing and will begin to write with voice. Students share their work, and, as they progress, they learn to peer edit. Guided writing geared to students' needs has the power to increase students' writing proficiency dramatically (Davis, Jackson, & Johnson, 2000).

Modeling Writing

One way of guiding students' writing is to model the process. For instance, you might recount an interesting incident from a time when you were their age. One teacher wrote about a time that she was frightened when she discovered a bullfrog in her room. After recounting the incident, show the class how you might go about writing about it. Think aloud as you write, so that students can gain some insight into the process. You might also enlist the class's help by asking for suggestions for details that might be added or for the spellings of words. Also model the processes of revising and editing. After rereading and discussing the completed story, brainstorm topics that the class might write about. Referring back to the model story and how the details made it come alive, discuss details that they might include in their stories. They might make a list of these details or depict them in an illustration.

STRATEGIC WRITING INSTRUCTION

Strategic writing instruction also provides needed guidance. Strategic writing instruction, which can be integrated with guided writing, has four steps:

1. Identifying a strategy worth teaching
2. Introducing the strategy by modeling it

FIGURE 13.2 Developmental Stages/Scoring Guidelines

STAGE 1: THE EMERGING WRITER

Little or no topic development, organization, and/or detail.
Little awareness of audience or writing task.
Errors in surface features prevent the reader from understanding the writer's
message.

STAGE 2: THE DEVELOPING WRITER

Topic beginning to be developed. Response contains the beginning of an
organization plan.
Limited awareness of audience and/or task.
Simple word choice and sentence patterns.
Errors in surface features interfere with communication.

STAGE 3: THE FOCUSING WRITER

Topic clear even though development is incomplete. Plan apparent although ideas
are loosely organized.
Sense of audience and/or task.
Minimal variety of vocabulary and sentence patterns.
Errors in surface features interrupt the flow of communication.

STAGE 4: THE EXPERIMENTING WRITER

Topic clear and developed (development may be uneven). Clear plan with
beginning, middle, and end (beginning and/or ending may be clumsy).
Written for an audience.
Experiments with language and sentence patterns. Word combinations and word
choice may be novel.
Errors in surface features may interrupt the flow of communication.

STAGE 5: THE ENGAGING WRITER

Topic well developed. Clear beginning, middle, and end. Organization sustains the
writer's purpose.
Engages the reader.
Effective use of varied language and sentence patterns.
Errors in surface features do not interfere with meaning.

STAGE 6: THE EXTENDING WRITER

Topic fully elaborated, with rich details. Organization sustains the writer's purpose
and moves the reader through the piece.
Engages and sustains the reader's interest.
Creative and novel use of language and effective use of varied sentence patterns.
Errors in surface features do not interfere with meaning. (Georgia Department of
Education, 2000)

From Georgia Department of Education, *Developmental stages/scoring guidelines for writing.*
Atlanta, GA: Author, 2000. Reprinted with permission from Georgia Department of Education.

3. Helping students try out the strategy with workshop-style teacher guidance
4. Helping students work toward independent mastery of the strategy through repeated practice and reinforcement (Collins, 1998, p. 65.)

To identify a strategy worth teaching, examine students' writing and discuss their writing with them. Note their struggles. Select a strategy that would seem to be of most assistance to them. Some strategies that have been of help to struggling writers include: creating webs, drawing, talking over a story or expository piece before writing it, listing supporting details or examples, brainstorming, and using models. The strategy can be introduced through teacher modeling, to a whole class, a small group, or an individual. After the strategy has been introduced, it is essential that students have the opportunity to try it out in a workshop-style situation. At this point, the teacher and student work together to implement the strategy. As they work they make necessary adaptations, and the student personalizes the strategy so that the strategy is co-constructed by teacher and student. One student, for instance, personalized topic sentence and supporting details by noting that paragraphs have a lead sentence and following sentences (Collins, 1998). Using his personalized strategy helped him to write a coherent, well-developed paragraph. Repeated practice and application to other situations lead to independent mastery of the strategy.

WRITING WORKSHOP

The writing workshop is a way of providing students with the opportunity to try out newly introduced strategies under the teacher's guidance (Collins, 1998). Through individual or small-group conferences, the teacher can help students adapt and implement strategies that were taught in whole-class or guided writing sessions. A flexible structure, the workshop generally includes whole-class instruction, guided writing, time to write while individual and small-group conferences are held, and sharing time. If possible, the writing workshop should be held every day. Daily writing keeps the writer connected to the piece that he is developing. If several days pass without engagement with the piece, the writer loses the flow of the writing. Whole-class instruction might cover the structure of a persuasive piece or the format of a business letter if that is what the class is working on. Writing time follows and may last for thirty minutes or longer. During writing time, students work on their writing, have peer or teacher conferences, or meet in small groups to discuss their writing. Guided writing lessons tailored to the needs of small groups of students are held at this time. At the end of the writing time, the class meets as a whole and individual students share their pieces. Listeners are encouraged to offer affirming comments and positive suggestions or to ask questions about any portion of the piece that was not clear. By asking questions, responding students are suggesting to the writer parts of the piece that might be expanded or clarified.

The writing workshop needs to be well organized. Necessary supplies should be available. Student works in progress should be kept in folders. Charts of students' progress and needs should be maintained.

■ ■ ■ ■ ■

EXEMPLARY TEACHING
WRITING STRATEGY INSTRUCTION

When Margarita, a ninth-grader, was assigned to summarize and evaluate a newspaper article, she used a strategy adopted by many struggling writers. She simply retold the article and copied many of the article's details (Collins & Collins, 1996). When questioned about the strategies that she used, she replied that she knew she needed facts and so simply went back to the article and got them. Deciding that Margarita needed strategy instruction that would help her go beyond the author's words and do some interpretive and evaluative writing, Kathleen Collins suggested a read–think–summarize–interpret strategy in which the writer would read the article carefully, maybe several times, summarize what was said, and then interpret

what was said. To help students go beyond summarizing to interpreting, Kathleen Collins decided to use DEN (Double-Entry Notebook). To use DEN, students create two columns. In the first column they summarize or record what they have read. In the second column they react to or reflect on what they have read.

Kathleen modeled using double-entry notes to the class. She then had students apply the strategy under her guidance. Using double-entry notes, Margarita wrote a longer essay that included more details and that was the product of Margarita's construction and interpretation. Margarita found DEN to be helpful because "It helped me write down what I'm thinking about while I'm reading."

THE ROLE OF RUBRICS

Rubrics are more than just scoring guides. Rubrics have the power to improve instruction. They also serve as "instructional illuminators." As Popham (2000) notes, "Appropriately designed rubrics can make an enormous contribution to instructional quality" (p. 292). Well-constructed rubrics specify the essential tasks that the students must complete or the key elements that must be included in order to produce an excellent piece of work. This helps both the teacher and the student focus on key skills. In order to be effective, rubrics should be concise. They should contain only three to six evaluative criteria; otherwise, both student and teacher get lost in details. Second, each evaluative criterion must encompass a teachable skill. For instance, evaluative criteria for a persuasive piece might include use of examples and/or reasons to advance a position, effective organization, use of persuasive language, and correct use of mechanics. All of these criteria are teachable. Rubrics should also be brief, clear, and easy to use.

In a program known as Reading to Write (Wolf & Gearhart, 1994), teachers used a rubric-based feedback form to provide practical suggestions to individual students. Designed to be used with narrative writing, the rubric and feedback form focus on seven areas: theme, character, setting, plot, communication, convention, and writing process. Because their writing was tied in with their literature study, students had learned about theme, character, setting, plot, and the communication of a story through the reading and discussion of numerous narrative selections. After using the rubric to assess students' writing, the teachers filled out a feedback form, which contained the same seven categories and empty boxes where comments could be made. Teachers were asked to make specific comments in at least one area. One comment would be a commendation in which the student was told what he had done well: "Great description of the cabin. I had no trouble picturing it in my mind." The second comment was a recommendation for improving the next draft or the next piece of writing: "You told how Noah saved his life by tricking the bear. But you didn't say or show how he felt when the bear got very close to him or how he felt when the bear finally left." Feedback forms were given out during conferences. The commendation and recommendation were given orally and explained to the student, and the form was then stapled to the student's written piece. Guidelines for providing feedback included:

- Be specific—tie your remark explicitly to the child's story.
- Be clear and considerate—write in language the child can understand.
- Limit your comments to one commendation and one recommendation—avoid a jumbled list. You can use the rubric to guide your choice for a commendation and recommendation.
- Tie your remarks to what you have tried to accomplish in your instruction—if you are working on a particular genre, what features do you expect to find in the child's writing? Use key examples from the professional literature you used in your instruction to provide background and models.
- Keep the developmental perspective in mind—where has this child been and where do you want to guide him/her next? (p. 24)

The assessment is particularly effective because it is closely tied to what students are reading and writing and because it leads to specific praise so students know what they are doing well. Because of specific suggestions for improvement, they also know what they can do better.

If possible, students should become involved in constructing rubrics. Involvement in constructing the rubric leads to better understanding of what is expected of them. In one study, students involved in rubric creation used them to assess their writing and that of their peers. As a result of creating and using rubrics, their writing showed a significant improvement (Boyle, 1996).

WRITING PROGRAMS FOR LOW-ACHIEVING READERS AND WRITERS

Although the research on the writing of low-achieving readers sometimes paints a picture of students who have little knowledge of the writing process (Englert et al., 1988), intervention research by a number of experts portrays a very hopeful scene. In one study, neutral examiners assessed pieces written by achieving and low-achieving readers and could not tell which were which. Incredibly, the pieces written by the low-achieving readers had the same high quality as those written by the achieving readers. What wrought this magic? A carefully conceived program known as Cognitive Strategy Instruction in Writing (CSIW), which makes generous use of scaffolding (Dixon, Carnine, & Kame'enui, 1993).

Cognitive Strategy Instruction in Writing

Cognitive Strategy Instruction in Writing focuses on using text structures to improve writing and features "conspicuous strategies." Through modeling and think-alouds, the teacher demonstrates and makes visible the writing process and the strategies used in her or his own

When students first wrote information pieces using CSIW, their topics tended to deal with everyday activities. In time, they used their newly acquired writing skills to compose subject-matter pieces.

writing (Dixon, Carnine, & Kame'enui, 1993; Raphael & Englert, 1990). Using modeling, coaching, discussion, and other techniques, the teacher focuses on the following features of process writing: topic selection, purpose (the kinds of questions the text might be expected to answer), identification of audience, brainstorming, use of text structure, grouping ideas, using key or signal words, revising, editing, and publishing. The instructional program is broken down into four phases: text analysis, modeling the writing process, guiding students, and providing opportunities for independent writing (Raphael & Englert, 1990).

A key feature in Cognitive Strategy Instruction in Writing is the use of Think Sheets. The following lesson explains how Think Sheets are used.

TEACHING CSIW

Step 1: Analyzing the text. Since low-achieving readers show little awareness of text structure, either in their reading or their writing, examining text structures is emphasized. Samples from basals, trade books, periodicals, or content-area texts can be used to illustrate a particular structure. It is also a good idea to use examples written by students, perhaps from previous years. As you analyze the text, which can be written on the board or chart or on an overhead, point out and discuss the following:

- The topic of the text
- Its purpose
- The kinds of questions the reader might expect the text to answer
- The audience
- The text structure itself
- Signal words that might be used in the text structure

You might also note some areas in which the piece might be improved. Perhaps there is a part that is not clear, or a step may have been omitted from a process. Or signal words might be used to improve the comprehensibility of the piece.

Step 2: Modeling the writing process. After analyzing and discussing the text, demonstrate the composing of an informational piece by writing one yourself. If a new game is to be introduced to the class, you might write a how-to piece explaining how the game is to be played. As you go through the

process, think aloud, so the class can see how you plan and compose a piece. Make explicit your sense of audience, your purpose for writing, strategies you might use to help your planning, such as listing the steps in a process and indicating needed materials. Also talk about the text structure that you plan to use, why you are using that structure, and what might be some signal words that could be used to "glue" the structure together. Later, after a discussion with students, model the revising and editing processes.

Think Sheets: scaffolds that prompt students to use writing strategies that they have been taught recently. Think Sheets are gradually phased out, as students take fuller responsibility for their writing.

Step 3: Introducing Think Sheets. As you model the process, introduce the concept of Think Sheets. These are prompts that help students plan, organize, revise, and edit their pieces. Each type of writing or text structure should have its own Think Sheet. Although sample Think Sheets are presented here, it should be emphasized that Think Sheets can take a variety of forms and should be tailored to meet the needs of your students.

Think Sheets might provide prompts for the following (Dixon, Carnine, & Kame'enui, 1993):

- Who is my audience?
- What is my goal?

- What do I know about this topic?
- What can I tell the readers at the beginning to get them interested?
- What do I need to tell my audience so they will understand what I am trying to say?
- How can I group my ideas? (steps in a process, similarities or differences in a comparison/contrast piece, reasons in a persuasive piece, solution to a problem, causes of a problem, etc).
- What signal words might I use? (*first, then, because, and, but, however, moreover,* etc.).
- What might be a good ending sentence? (sum up, leave with a thought or question).

Depending on how much help students need, separate Think Sheets might be used for each major phase of the writing project. The Think Sheet in Figure 13.3 provides an example of prompts that a student might use to plan a piece. After completing a Plan Think Sheet, the student might then work on an Organize Think Sheet (Figure 13.4), which answers such questions as: What is being explained? What materials, etc., are needed? What are the steps?

Once both the Plan and Organize Think Sheets have been completed and discussed, students write their rough drafts. When students write their rough drafts, they write them on colored paper. This is a reminder that they are writing an initial draft, one that must be revised before being copied onto white paper.

The last two major think sheets are the Self-Editing and Revision Think Sheets. Self-Editing Think Sheets are filled out by students before they submit their pieces for peer

FIGURE 13.3   Plan Think Sheet

Author's Name _____   Date _____

Topic: _____

Who: Who am I writing for?

_____

_____

What: What do I want to tell my readers?

_____

_____

_____

_____

How: How can I organize my ideas?

_____ Explanation   _____ Problem/Solution

_____ Comparison/Contrast   _____ Other

_____ Main Idea/Details

Adapted from C. S. Englert, T. E. Raphael, & L. M. Anderson, *Cognitive Strategy Instruction in Writing Project.* East Lansing, MI: Institute for Research on Teaching, 1989.

FIGURE 13.4   Organize Think Sheet (Explanation)

Author's Name _____   Date _____

What is being explained? _____

_____

What materials are needed? _____

_____

What are the steps?

First, _____

Next, _____

Third, _____

Then, _____

Finally, _____

Adapted from *Cognitive Strategy Instruction in Writing Project.* C. S. Englert, T. E. Raphael, L. M. Anderson. East Lansing, MI: Institute for Research on Teaching, 1989.

editing. The Self-Editing Think Sheets have three concerns (see Figure 13.5). After asking writers to tell what they like best, the Self-Editing Think Sheet requests that writers reexamine their pieces and note any parts that they might want to change. Writers are then asked to list any questions that they have for their editors. After having conferences with peer editors, students use the Revision Think Sheet to complete a plan for revising the piece.

The Revision Think Sheets ask students to note their plans for revision because the researchers found that, unless they make specific plans, students tend to simply recopy their papers, making only a few surface revisions, despite having gone through self-editing and peer-editing procedures (Raphael, Englert, & Kirschner, 1989). When carefully monitored and guided, peer editing also provided students with a sharpened sense of audience, which in turn may lead to more substantive revisions. When a peer editor states that he would like to know more about a topic and that a part of a piece is not clear, then the writer is more likely to add information and clarify. A Revision Think Sheet is shown in Figure 13.6.

After writing three pieces with decreasing amounts of assistance, students are asked to write a final piece on their own.

Guiding Students.   Students write several pieces under your guidance. Students are asked to use the text structure being studied but are free to write on any topic that makes use of that structure. The first paper may be composed by a group. The second paper can be written by individual students, but the students receive extensive teacher and peer support. A third paper is also written by individual students, but the students take increased responsibility for their work. However, peer or teacher support is provided as needed (Dixon, Carnine, & Kame'enui, 1993). Gradually, students learn to write pieces that incorporate two or more text structures.

FIGURE 13.5   Self-Edit Think Sheet (Explanation)

Author's Name _____   Date _____

1. After rereading my paper, what do I like best?

_____

_____

2. Did I tell what was being explained?

_____

_____

3. Did I tell what materials were needed?

_____

_____

4. Did I write down all the steps?

_____

_____

5. Is each step clearly explained?

_____

_____

6. Did I use signal words?

_____

_____

7. What parts do I want to change?

_____

_____

8. What questions do I have for my editor?

_____

_____

Adapted from C. S. Englert, T. E. Raphael, & L. M. Anderson, *Cognitive Strategy Instruction in Writing Project.* East Lansing, MI: Institute for Research on Teaching, 1989.

In using CSIW, it should be kept in mind that the heart of the program is the modeling and careful guidance that the teacher provides and the guided sharing in which the students engage. The Think Sheets are simply helpful scaffolds that prompt students to use strategies they might not have been able to apply without some guidance or that they may have overlooked. In time, students should be helped to incorporate the strategies prompted by the Think Sheets so that they are able to use the strategies on their own, without the reminders.

FIGURE 13.6   Revision Think Sheet

SUGGESTIONS FROM MY EDITOR

What suggestions has your editor given you?

1. _____

2. _____

3. _____

4. _____

5. _____

6. _____

Decide on the suggestions you want to use. Put an X next to all the suggestions you would like to use in revising your paper.

MY IDEAS FOR REVISING MY PAPER

Now decide on any other changes that you might like to make. Ask yourself:

Is there any way I can make my paper more interesting?

_____

_____

Is there any way I can make the paper clearer or easier to understand?

_____

_____

RETURNING TO YOUR DRAFT

On your draft, make all the changes you think will make your paper better. Use ideas from the list above, from your self-edit think sheet, and any other ideas you have for your paper. When you are ready, you can write your final copy.

Adapted from C. S. Englert, T. E. Raphael, & L. M. Anderson, *Cognitive Strategy Instruction in Writing Project.* East Lansing, MI: Institute for Research on Teaching, 1989.

Harris and Graham's Strategy Instruction

> Strategy instruction is tied to students' goals. Once students have formulated a goal for their writing, they are taught a strategy that helps them to reach that goal.

> Review sessions are essential. These remind students of the steps in a strategy and provide opportunities for fine-tuning and adapting strategy use.

Strategy instruction is also the centerpiece of a writing program for disabled writers devised by Harris and Graham (1992). However, the Harris–Graham program is broader than CSIW. Whereas CSIW focused on text structure, the Harris–Graham program includes a wide range of strategies and emphasizes the setting of goals. A goal may involve any aspect of writing, from content to overall organization to mechanics. A student's goal might be to increase the length of her writing, include more suspense in a story, use questions for opening sentences, use more picturesque language, spell every word correctly, or use complex sentences 25 percent of the time (Harris & Graham, 1992). Setting goals might be done on the basis of observing the students at work, discussing the students' past work, or asking the students to tell what aspect of their writing they would most like to improve. Listed in the following box are suggested steps for strategy instruction as adapted from Harris and Graham (1992).

■ ■ ■ ■ ■

A LESSON IN TEACHING WRITING STRATEGIES

> Strategy instruction is tied to students' goals. Once students have formulated a goal for their writing, they are taught a strategy that helps them to reach that goal.

Step 1: Introducing strategies and setting goals. Help students set individual or group goals. Once goals have been decided, explain what strategy instruction is. Explain that almost any operation that improves writing can be taught as a strategy. Discuss with students the strategies you use when you write. In collaboration with the students, you decide which strategy might be introduced to help them reach their goals. For instance, if the students have difficulty generating content and if their goal is to write more elaborated pieces, brainstorming might be chosen as a strategy to be presented.

Stage 2: Preskill development. Students are taught any skills needed to understand and apply the strategy about to be taught. For instance, if students are going to be taught how to use paragraph patterns to organize their writing, they would first need to be taught how paragraphs are organized.

Stage 3: Discussing the strategy. Explain the strategy, its steps, its value, and when and where it might be used. A very basic strategy that you might teach students is how to develop a paragraph using examples. You might have students examine pieces of writing in which examples are used to develop a topic. Discuss the paragraphs and the value of using examples to writing convincing pieces. Discuss when and where examples might be used. Have students tell how they might use the strategy in their writing.

Stage 4: Modeling the strategy. Model the strategy using any prompts, charts, mnemonics, or other aids that students might find helpful. For instance, you might write a piece telling why you think your cat is smart. Model the process of writing the piece. Note the steps that you use in writing your piece:

State the topic.
Write examples to prove the topic sentence.
Explain each example,
Add an interesting ending.
Take a look at the piece to see if you have used convincing examples.

Step 5: Providing scaffolding. Use think sheets, mnemonics, visual displays, or other devices to prompt students so that they follow all the steps. As incorporated into Stage 4, the mnemonic prompt for using examples is SWEAT. "With a little SWEAT, you can write an interesting piece." Using the mnemonic, students memorize the steps in the strategy.

Stage 6: Collaborative practice. Students try out the strategy. During conferences, emphasize the strategy that has just been taught. Provide feedback and guidance. Feedback should be specific, "I like the way you used SWEAT to help you put three exciting examples in your piece."

> Review sessions are essential. These remind students of the steps in a strategy and provide opportunities for fine-tuning and adapting strategy use.

Stage 7: Application. Students apply the strategy on their own. However, review sessions are held to refine strategy use and to foster transfer.

CRISS Writing Strategies

Using writing as a means of learning is emphasized in CRISS (*CR*eating *I*ndependence through *S*tudent-owned *S*trategies), an exemplary program designed to help students learn content-area materials. Highly successful with low-achieving readers and writers, the writing component of CRISS stresses direct instruction and plenty of support for the learners. One form of support is the use of a series of highly structured writing formats including framed paragraphs, opinion/proof paragraphs, and RAFT, a procedure that focuses on four major aspects of writing (Santa, Havens, & Maycumber, 1996). CRISS writing strategies can be taught within the framework of the Lesson in Teaching Writing Strategies.

> Framed paragraphs should be presented in such a way that, over time, they require more and more input from students until, ultimately, students don't need to use them anymore.

Framed Paragraphs. The most highly structured form of writing is the framed paragraph. Framed paragraphs provide the main idea of the piece, indicate how many details the piece will contain, supply transition words, and may even provide a conclusion. While providing a maximum of support, framed paragraphs show students ways of organizing their ideas. A sample frame paragraph is shown in Figure 13.7. Also refer to the Exemplary Teaching Lesson to see how one teacher made use of her version of framed paragraphs.

> The opinion/proof format can be used with other kinds of writing: cause/effect, problem/solution, main idea/details.

Opinion/Proof. If students seem to need extra support for their writing, you might have them try an opinion/proof piece. The opinion/proof is a basic type of writing in which students back up an opinion with evidence or reasons. Opinion/proof pieces can be used in connection with informational text or as the basis for developing a piece on any topic.

To structure an opinion/proof piece, the student divides a sheet of paper in two. The opinion is placed in the left-hand column. The proof

---

EXEMPLARY TEACHING
BUILDING ON INTERESTS

Discouraged by years of perceived failure, Jason, a seventh-grader, decreed that he would no longer write. No more essays or book reports. Not even journal entries. He couldn't write, and that was that. Capitalizing on Jason's interest in baseball, his corrective specialist, Carigan-Belleville (1989), asked him how his team had done on the previous Saturday. After discussing the game with him, she asked if he would give her three reasons why his team deserved to win. After Jason did so, she suggested that he put that in writing, using the following format:

> Question: Who won Saturday's baseball game?

> Five-sentence paragraph:

1. Topic sentence (answer to the question)
2. Reason #1
3. Reason #2
4. Reason #3
5. Conclusion (restate topic sentence in different words) (pp. 57–58)

Although the format might have hindered the free expression or creativity of some young writers, it was just what Jason needed. Using clear cues and a highly structured format, Jason was able to write a paragraph successfully.

Later, Jason started using story starters such as "If I had more money. . . ." Jason also began writing in his journal. In addition, Carigan-Belleville arranged for Jason to dictate his stories into a tape recorder, using the taped versions as a kind of rehearsal for the written pieces. Jason's willingness and ability to write improved significantly. As a side benefit, Jason also became more interested in reading.

FIGURE 13.7   Frame Paragraph

Starting a Coin Collection

If you want to start a coin collection, follow these steps.

First, _____.

Next, _____.

Then, _____.

Finally, _____.

Once you've followed these steps, you'll have a hobby that you can enjoy for many years to come.

---

is placed to the right. Once the opinion has been stated and the proof written down, the student can then develop his piece. As students write their pieces, they should be encouraged to elaborate so that the piece they write is not just a restatement of the outline. They also need to compose a conclusion. A sample opinion/proof piece is shown in Figure 13.8.

> **RAFT:** structured approach to writing that helps students focus on four key elements: *r*ole of the writer, *a*udience, *f*ormat, and *t*opic.

RAFT.   When writing essays for content-area subjects, students often turn in pieces that lack clarity and depth, two flaws that are occasioned by an assignment that is too general and too vague (Santa, Havens, & Maycumber, 1996). **RAFT** is an approach that sharpens the writing by helping the student focus on four elements: *r*ole of the writer, *a*udience, *f*ormat, and *t*opic. RAFT pieces can be written from the student's viewpoint, but quite often they are not.

FIGURE 13.8   Opinion/Proof Paragraph

OPINION	PROOF
Basketball is the best sport.	Basketball has a lot of action.
	Basketball can be played just about anywhere.
	Basketball can be played inside or outside.
	You don't need a lot of equipment to play basketball.
	You don't need a lot of people to play basketball.
	Anyone can play basketball.

In my opinion basketball is number one. Basketball has lots of action. There's no standing around like there is in baseball. You can also play it just about anywhere. You don't need a huge field. All you need is a hoop. And you don't need a lot of fancy equipment. All you need is a ball. And you don't need to get together a crowd of people before you can play. You can play with any number from two to ten. You can even shoot some hoops on your own. You can't beat basketball. It's the champion of sports.

R   Role of the writer. The writer can be a historical figure, a scientist, the President, a rock star, lawyer, police chief, or even an animal or inanimate object.

A   Audience. Typically students write for the teacher, so their pieces tend to be bland. The audience could be a judge, a legislator, future generations, the people of the world, a historical figure, a sports star, parents, or whomever else the writer wants to address.

F   Format. The piece can be a letter to the editor, an essay, a news story, a TV script, a diary entry, a speech, a memo, or whatever format seems appropriate.

T   Topic. The statement of the topic is accompanied by a strong verb so that it is an expression of the writer's purpose: **demand** a refund for a faulty product, **persuade** a radio station to let the town's teens have an hour show each week, **convince** an investor to back your new invention.

To introduce RAFT, explain its purpose and components and model writing a RAFT piece. Once students understand RAFT, brainstorm possible topics. The topics might fall under a general theme. For instance, if you are studying immigration, have students suggest possible RAFT pieces: a ship owner composing an ad to persuade Italian peasants to sail to America, an Irish teen describing in a letter to his parents his or her first few days in Boston, an editorial writer hailing the newcomers.

In time, students should create their own RAFT topics. They should also go through all the stages in the writing process, including revising, editing, and publishing, as well as preplanning and composing. Refer to the minicase study at the end of the chapter to see how RAFT was used to help an extremely reluctant writer.

Collaborative Strategy Approach

Less structured and more student-centered than the three previously presented systems, the collaborative strategy approach combines instruction in writing strategies and text models. Students' writing is related to their reading. After completing a selection, students note the kinds of information covered in the text and the text's structure. Students then decide how they might use the kinds of structure and information presented in the text in their own writing. For instance, if the author used a problem–solution organization in a selection the students have read, the students would talk over problems they have and possible solutions. Using the selection they have read as a model, they then compose a problem–solution piece (Anderson & Henne, 1993).

> At the beginning of the Collaborative Strategy Instruction study, students were reluctant to write. At the end of the four-month period, the students were writing four to six double-spaced, typed pages (Anderson & Henne, 1993).

A key element in the approach is the use of a teaching segment known as *writer's craft*. From a selection that has just been read, students examine, discuss, and use a stylistic device. Stylistic devices include writing interesting topic sentences; paragraphing; elaborating by supplying causes, effects, reasons, examples, or descriptions; using a vivid vocabulary; developing character using dialogue; using signal words to indicate time-order or other relationships; and using any of a variety of other stylistic devices.

> Writer's craft consists of strategies and so can be taught within the framework of the Lesson in Teaching Writing Strategies explained earlier in this section.

Why the Programs Work

Although the programs for low-achieving readers and writers vary in the way they are organized and implemented, they have several essential procedures in common. All three incorporate direct instruction and emphasize strategies and writing process. All four provide additional support in the form of frame paragraphs, planning sheets, mnemonic reminders, or collaborative instruction and discussion.

All of the programs also met with encouraging success. This success presents a clear message. When low-achieving readers and writers are provided with a carefully planned, thoroughly implemented, supportive program of writing instruction, they improve, sometimes dramatically. Students respond positively to techniques or strategies that make it easier for them to apply their skills.

USING WRITING TO CLOSE THE GAP

Writing is a powerful tool for closing the gap that exists between students who are members of a minority group and/or are economically disadvantaged and students who are members of majority groups and the middle class. In 90/90/90 schools 90 percent or more of the students are eligible for free and reduced lunch, are members of ethnic minority groups, but 90 percent of students meet academic standards in reading or another area (Reeves, 2003). In 90/90/90 schools expository writing is emphasized. Elementary students are required to produce acceptable pieces of writing once a month; secondary students, once a quarter. Programs are schoolwide and include a common rubric. Guidance is thorough and ongoing.

The rubric is geared to students' grade level and English proficiency. A five-sentence piece might be satisfactory for a young English learner, whereas an older native speaker might be required to write a three-page piece. Students are expected to meet the rubric's proficiency standard. They are required to revise and edit as much as necessary in order to produce a proficient piece. Writing assignments are not treated as work samples to be graded but as opportunities to build essential reading and writing skills.

MOTIVATING RELUCTANT WRITERS

Understandably, low-achieving readers and writers frequently are extremely reluctant to write. If they do write, often it is just a sentence or two composed entirely of words that they can spell. Three kinds of writing that are especially effective for helping students overcome their reluctance to engage in composing are writing aloud, written conversation, and journal writing.

Writing Aloud

In writing aloud, the teacher and the students create an experience story together. Although the teacher scribes the story, the students make suggestions about both content and form. The teacher invites the students to help her write a story. Based on the teacher's prompts, they make suggestions about details that might be added. They also help with the mechanics. The teacher might ask them to help her spell a word or ask what kind of punctuation mark is needed at the end of a sentence. Using her knowledge of what the students know and what they need to know, she might decide that this is a good opportunity to reinforce the *-ed* ending. Writing *wait,* she might ask them what needs to be added to *wait* to make *waited.* Emphasizing that the first copy is a draft, the group rereads it and revises and edits it during subsequent sessions (Dorn, French, & Jones, 1998).

Although they are often used with young children to reinforce beginning reading skills, group-composed selections are an excellent technique for modeling the composition of both narrative and expository pieces at all levels. They give students, especially those who are struggling, guided practice in writing.

Written Conversation

> **Written conversation:** writing-improvement technique in which a teacher and student talk to each other on paper. Instead of speaking words to each other, they write them.

An effective technique for promoting fluency is arranging for the student to talk to someone on paper. A **written conversation** is generally between the teacher and the student. You and student sit side by side. You might initiate the conversation by posing a written question that helps the student describe an event or idea: "How is your basketball team doing this year?" After the student reads your question, she or he responds in writing. You reply with another written question and the student answers it with a written response. Sitting at a round table, you might carry on a written conversation with a small group of students. While one student responds to your written query, you can write a note to a second student. As students grow in proficiency, they can converse in writing with each other. The activity could also be extended into writing letters or leaving e-mail messages (Rhodes & Dudley-Marling, 1988).

Written conversations work well with problem writers because you gear your writing to each student's level of reading and writing proficiency and also take into consideration each student's interests. In addition, through modeling good writing, you provide scaffolding so students can move up to higher levels of writing performance. Written conversations are also nonthreatening. Although a written conversation can be as brief as a single sentence, output generally increases as a result of using this device. Written conversations also have a positive effect on reading (Rhodes & Dudley-Marling, 1988).

Journal Writing

> **Journal:** daily record of events, thoughts, ideas, or feelings.

Journal writing allows students to respond to their world in a personal way. In their journals, they can react to something they have learned in school, discuss an exciting TV show or a Little League game in which they played a key role, or describe the acquisition of a new pet. Through journal writing or the use of writer's notebooks (discussed earlier in the chapter), students can explore topics and techniques. It helps them discover that the events in their lives are worth writing about. Journal writing promotes fluency and exploration. Because journal writing is personal, it should not be subject to revision or correction. Focus should be on the message, not the mechanics.

WRITING INSTRUCTION FOR ELL STUDENTS

Because their vocabulary, knowledge of grammatical structures, and organizational patterns are generally less well developed, English language learners will need more intensive instruction in writing. To foster writing, it will be necessary to build vocabulary and syntax. Before students write a sequence piece, for instance, introduce words that signal sequence: *first, next, at last.* When writing a how-to piece, introduce words and phrases used to explain: *first you; then you; after that; be careful to* (Calkins, 2003). ELL students might be able to express themselves better in writing than speaking.

An excellent way to familiarize ELL students with syntactical patterns is to engage in written conversation with students or to use dialogue journals. A written conversation can be very informal. You might write a note that asks students a question, such as: What is your favorite book? Or What are your favorite TV shows? Students can use key words in the question to formulate a reply. In your response, include a question or cue that leads to additional writing. You might also model a response. Note the following interchange:

T: What do you find hardest about living in a new country?

S: I find the hardest thing is trying to talk to people.

T: When I lived in Mexico for a summer, I also found that talking to people was the hardest thing for me to do. I was afraid that people would laugh at the way I said the words. What makes talking to others the hardest thing for you?

Another way of structuring language experience stories is to select topics in such a way as to control syntax. Experience stories may be written so that they focus on declarative sentences, questions, or another syntactical element. An experience story in which students write about things they like or can do would focus on statement sentences. An experience story on favorite animals could be structured in such a way that it includes both a question and a statement: What is my favorite animal? My favorite animal is ____. Other stories might reinforce more complex patterns: I like Saturdays because ____.

Language experience is flexible. Students can write on any topic and in virtually any format. Since the language experience is also written in the student's native language, it can be geared to the student's level of English language development.

PREPARING FOR ASSESSMENT PROMPTS

One writing skill that struggling writers need to learn is how to respond to an assessment prompt. In writing workshop, students have the luxury of time to preplan, compose, and revise. Often they select their own topic. All that is changed when they must respond to an assessment prompt. Because time is limited, they might be tempted to rush through the assigned piece. However, they should take a moment or two to read and reread the prompt carefully to be sure they understand what the prompt is asking for. They should also take a moment or two to jot down a brief but tentative outline or map (Spandel, 2005). To prepare students for writing to a prompt, group struggling writers according to writing needs. In preparation for writing to a prompt, struggling writers should become familiar with the rubric that will be used to assess the prompt. They should have some experience writing to similar prompts. Show students how you would go about writing to a prompt. Do a think-aloud, so that they get insight into the thought processes involved. Model how you would preplan, compose your piece, and revise and edit. As a cooperative venture, have the group of struggling writers respond to a prompt. After students have responded, discuss their work in light of the rubric. Praise what is effective and provide suggestions for improvement. Provide guided writing instruction in terms of writing needs. In her program to prepare students for constructed responses on high-stakes tests, Boyles (2002) recommends two aids: an answer organizer and the answer frame. In the answer organizer you lay out step-by-step what students are to do: write the topic sentences first, add three supporting details, write a concluding sentence. Answer frames provide even more assistance than answer organizers do. In the answer frame, you fill in a portion of the answer and have students finish it. Do not spend an excessive amount of time on writing to prompts. Once students are familiar with writing to a prompt, added practice will have a diminishing effect. Students will be better off engaged in the regular writing program. As Fletcher and Portalupi (2001) note, a writing workshop properly implemented should prepare students for whatever writing assessment they encounter:

> Your students need time to write their hearts out; to explore many different subjects; to write deeply about a single one. They need to write for the fun of it, and at times they need coaches by their sides stretching them to write with more precision and craft.
> It boils down to this: Your students will perform fine on these tests as long as you provide them with regular opportunities for writing in the workshop. (p. 110)

THE NEED FOR A BALANCED PROGRAM

Writing is a complex task that has three interacting major components: generating appropriate content in sufficient quantity, organizing the content, and using appropriate grammatical and mechanical elements (Collins, 1998). Underachieving writers have problems in all three areas. An effective way to help underachieving writers develop needed proficiency is to teach writing through a balanced process and strategy approach. Students who report using elements of the process approach, especially planning and composing more than one draft, outperform those who don't (Greenwald, Persky, Campbell, & Mazzeo, 1999). For struggling writers, however, co-construction of key strategies also needs to be an essential component of the program. If workshops fail to provide effective strategy instruction, students may spend most of their time writing about what they know and using familiar forms of writing, usually personal narrative. Writing about familiar topics in familiar forms hinders struggling readers' progress (Collins, 1998). Struggling writers need more opportunities to learn different forms and explore new topics, not fewer.

SPELLING

Spelling can be a twofold problem. If a student is spending an excessive amount of time trying to figure out how to spell words, then less cognitive energy is left for composing the

> To individualize spelling instruction, have students work with a partner on seven or eight high-frequency words each week.

piece. Deficiency in the lower-level process of physically producing text can impede the higher-level processes of composing a message or an imaginative tale. Poor spelling may inhibit the writer in another way. A writer who is ashamed of her poor spelling may not look beyond the spelling to the story she is trying to tell and so may restrict her writing to words that she can spell. What is needed is a three-pronged approach. In addition to providing systematic instruction in spelling and extra support, focus on the content of the writing so that the student doesn't let spelling restrict her writing or, worse yet, begin to equate poor spelling with poor writing.

Spelling is harder to learn than decoding skills. Given the same amount of instruction, struggling readers learn more than twice as much phonics as they do spelling. Spelling is especially difficult to learn if students have difficulty with phonological or orthographic processes or both. If students have difficulty with phonological processes, sounds may not be adequately represented in the mind's ear. Thus students may omit a sound or confuse a sound while spelling a word. They have particular difficulty with sounds that are hard to detect, such as the second sound in a cluster: the *t* in *stop* or the *r* in *brave*. They also have difficulty with sounds such as /l/, /r/, /m/, and /n/ when they are in the middle of a word or at the end. The inflectional endings *s* and *ed* also pose problems and are frequently omitted (Moats, 1995). If the student has difficulty with orthographic processes, letters representing sounds may not be adequately represented in the mind's eye, especially when these letters comprise irregular, infrequent, or complex spellings. The student will then have difficulty retrieving the correct spelling of an irregular or advanced pattern word from memory (Berninger et al., 1999). These students lack what Gentry (1997) terms the "spelling gene." They have serious difficulty visualizing words, which is the main characteristic of average and good spellers. Although there are a small number of students who experience difficulty learning to spell because of poor orthographic processing ability, this doesn't mean that they can't improve their spelling. As Apel, Masterson, and Niessen (2004) warn, "Frequently, students and adults are heard to say, 'I'm just not a good speller, as if to imply that they have no control over their spelling abilities and that their spelling proficiency can never change'" (p. 644). This becomes a self-fulfilling prophecy. One element in a program for struggling spellers should be to build their sense of self-efficacy.

If students have a weaknesses in their phonological system, their spellings may not contain all the sounds in a word. Thus, *treasure* might be spelled *tessar*. However, if their phonological system is functioning well but there are weaknesses in the orthographic system, the word's sounds may be represented phonetically, but they may not be spelled accurately. *Treasure* might be spelled *trezur*.

Correct spelling requires being able to use phonological processes, orthographic processes, spelling rules, such as when to double the final consonant of a word, and a knowledge of roots, prefixes, and suffixes. Students may also use an analogy process, so that they use their knowledge of a known word such as *chance* to spell a word such as *trance* that they may have never written before. When analyzing spelling errors, ask the following questions:

- Is the student able to use knowledge of sound–spelling relationships to spell words?
- Is the student applying spelling rules?
- Is the student able to use orthographic knowledge or visual sense to spell words that cannot be spelled strictly phonetically?

- Is the student able to use an analogy strategy to spell words?
- Is the student able to use morphemic analysis to spell words?
- Is the student able to use meaning clues, so that when spelling a word such as *magician* he uses his knowledge of the word *magic*?
- Are some apparent misspellings due to faulty handwriting?
- Is the student making careless errors? (Bos & Vaughn, 1994)

Teaching Spelling

A program for teaching spelling should be individualized, since students' abilities in spelling vary greatly. The program should be based on the student's current level of functioning in spelling and an analysis of the kinds of errors made. In a study in which one group of struggling third graders were given a second-grade spelling program, they outperformed the third graders on a spelling test made up of second-grade words and did as well on the test made up of third-grade words, even though they had not been taught these words. The researchers concluded that the experimental group learned more about the spelling system because instruction was pitched to their level of understanding as opposed to the third-grade comparison group, who were being taught "over their heads" and so did not learn as much (Morris, Blanton, Blanton, Nowacek, & Perney, 1995). To find a student's current level of spelling ability, administer the Spelling Inventory from the *Classroom Reading Inventory* (Silvaroli & Wheelock, 2001), the Gentry Spelling Grade Level Placement Test (Gentry, 1997), or the Spelling Placement Inventory in Chapter 2. The student's instructional level is the highest level at which between 50 and 75 percent of the words are spelled correctly. However, the student's level of spelling tells only part of the story. Also analyze the types of errors students make to get a sense of the kinds of processes the students are using to spell words.

> One characteristic of struggling readers is their reluctance to take risks with their writing. The stories they write are restricted by the words they know how to write rather than by the story they want to tell or the feelings and ideas they would like to express (Dorn, French, & Jones, 1998).

Note, too, the stage of spelling at which the student is operating. As discussed in Chapter 5, research conducted by Henderson (1990) and his colleagues (Templeton & Bear, 1992) indicates that students' spelling develops in stages. By knowing what stage a student is in, the teacher can build on that knowledge and teach spelling more effectively. The Elementary Spelling Inventory, which can be found Chapter 5, can be used to estimate students' spelling stage.

It is also a good idea to note what kinds of strategies students use to help them spell words correctly. Do they attempt to visualize it? Do they try to go through it sound by sound? Do they use rules or knowledge of word structure? Does writing it out seem to help them? See, too, if they attempt to correct misspelled words in their written pieces. If they do, what strategies do they use? This information can be obtained through observation and through interviews with the students.

Words chosen for spelling instruction should be those that students need in their writing. If students are about to write about football, the spelling words might include *football, sports, kickoff, score, quarterback, half-time,* and similar words. High-frequency words should also be presented. In order to help students see patterns in words, it will also be helpful to present high-frequency patterns (a listing of patterns can be found in Table 8.7 on pp. 249–251.

When introducing new words to poor spellers, use active teaching procedures, such as the test-study-test method. In this method, students take a pretest, study the words they missed, and then take a retest. It is also important to teach students a strategy for studying words. A popular strategy, which emphasizes seeing the word in the mind's eye, is the Fitzgerald method (Fitzgerald, 1951).

1. Look at the word carefully.
2. Say the word to yourself.
3. Close your eyes and picture the word.
4. Cover up the word and write it.
5. Check the spelling.
6. If the word is misspelled, repeat steps 1–5.

Sorting.   A valuable activity for fostering a conceptual understanding of spelling is word sorting, especially if the sorting is geared to the students' level of spelling development. If students are in the alphabet stage and are having difficulty deciding whether words that begin with a /k/ sound are spelled with a *c* or a *k*, then they might engage in sorting activities in which they categorize words according to whether they begin with a /k/ sound, regardless of spelling, and then sort /k/ words according to their spelling. Instead of memorizing rules about the use of *c* and *k* to spell /k/, students form their own generalizations.

In the word-pattern stage, students can, through sorting, form generalizations about the use of final *e* and digraphs to spell long-vowel sounds. In the syllabic stage, students might, through sorting, form a generalization about when to double the final consonant when adding *ing* or *ed*. In the morphemic analysis stage, students might discover when to use the prefixes *im, in, ir,* and *un.* As they group words and construct understandings that they would not have developed if they had just looked at words individually, students develop a deeper understanding of the spelling system, and, in the process, become better decoders as well as better spellers.

Help students see the meaning connections in spelling. One fourth grader failed to see the relationship between *nature* and *naturally* even when it was pointed out to her, and another fourth grader thought that the presence of *round* in *surround* was merely a coincidence (Hughes & Searle, 1997). A word such as *granddad* is easier to spell if the student goes beyond the sound pattern, which could lead to spelling the word *grandad,* and thinks about the meaning in which *grand* is added to *dad* to form the word *granddad.* Word sorts can help students describe some of the principles that underlie such perplexing decisions as when to use the *ible* versus when to use *able* spelling or when to use the *ir, im, in,* or *il* prefix. At this stage students should focus on or even spell the base word first and then add prefixes or suffixes. For instance, students will not compose misspellings such as *realy* or *unecessary* if they focus on *real* and *necessary* as the base words and then add the suffix *ly* or the prefix *un* (Snowball & Bolton, 1999).

In addition to conceptual understanding, all students, but especially poor spellers, need lots of practice. Often students will spell a word correctly on a test but misspell it when writing a letter or story. This may indicate a lack of fluency. The student may not have had enough practice with the word (Trathen, 1995). Moreover, some words just seem to be especially troublesome. Students might keep an alphabetical list of troublesome words in a small spelling notebook for handy reference (Roswell & Chall, 1994).

The first word that students should be taught to spell is their names. Sadly, some older disabled may not have learned to spell their last names. As a practical matter, students should also be taught to spell their addresses and other words that are important to them. Spelling can also be tied to the phonics patterns they are learning. Select the most useful words from the phonics patterns that they are studying. In general, students should only be taught to spell words that they can read. Patterns are especially useful elements because once students can spell one pattern word, they can build on that knowledge to spell other words in that pattern. For instance, once students can spell *ten,* they should be able to learn to spell *men, pen,* and other words fairly easily. To show students how to use their knowledge of one word to spell other words, ask, "If you can spell *ten,* then what others can you spell?" (Snowball & Bolton, 1999). Lead them to see that *men* and other *en* words are spelled just like *ten* except for the first letter. Using this same principle of building on what students know, show them how if they can spell a base word, they can spell its inflected forms. If they can spell *help,* they can spell *helps, helping,* and *helped.*

Poor spellers may have a poor visual sense of how words should be spelled, so use mnemonic devices, overpronunciation, and overlearning to help them learn to spell words, especially those that are not very predictable. The mnemonic for *friend* might be "*friend* has an *i* and an *end* at the end." In overpronunciation, students articulate sounds that are normally not spoken but are represented in the spelling of the word, saying dif-FER-ence, av-ER-age, in-TER-est. Overlearning entails studying a tricky word even after its correct spelling has been learned.

If they have poor visual memory, students will probably have difficulty with homophones, such as *hair* and *hare* and *hear* and *here.* Inability to distinguish between pairs of homophones is a characteristic of students who have weak orthographic processing ability. Use mnemonic devices to compensate for students' weak ability in this area. The *air* messed up my h*air.* You h*ear* with your *ear.* In their spelling notebooks, students might have a special section for homophones. To help students discriminate and remember the spellings of homophones, they might draw illustrations of the homophones and write an illustrative sentence.

Just as students are shown how to use word-analysis strategies when they encounter difficult words, they should also be taught how to use spelling strategies when they are attempting to spell a difficult word. Possible spelling strategies include best spelling, think how it sounds, think how it looks, try it out, analogy, think of its parts, use a rule, use a reference, and ask for help (Wilde, 1992; Snowball & Bolton, 1999).

Using best spelling, students spell the word as best they can and later check the accuracy of the spelling. This strategy is particularly effective when students are writing and don't want to interrupt the flow. Using think how it sounds, students deliberately articulate each sound in the word and attempt to write the word sound by sound. This works especially well when the word to be spelled is highly predictable. Using think how it looks, the student attempts to visualize the word. This is effective for high-imagery words or words such as *one* and *of* that don't lend themselves to a think-how-it-sounds strategy. In try it out, which is a form of think how it looks, students "have a go" at a word. They write the word, and if it doesn't look right, they write it again, and perhaps even a third or fourth time, and then choose the version that looks correct. Students should not erase words that they believe might be misspelled. Otherwise, they won't be able to compare possible spellings to see which one looks correct.

Using the think-of-its-parts strategy, students think of the base word and then think of the affixes that are being added. For instance, when spelling *comedian,* students might have a sense that it should be written with two *ms* (*commedian*). However, thinking of the base and the prefix that was added (*comedy + ian*) should help them resist this impulse. For the use-a-rule strategy, students might drop the final *e* (*baking*) or double the final consonant (*hopped*) or try another useful spelling generalization. In the use-a-reference strategy, students use spelling notebooks, a dictionary, a list of spelling words that have been posted, a spell checker, electronic speller, their texts, or some other helpful source. If all else fails, students can ask for help from a friend, a teacher, or a parent.

Teach strategies directly. However, match strategies to the stage that students are in. Students in the alphabetic or letter-name stage should use a sound-it-out strategy. Students in the morphemic analysis stage might use think-of-its-parts strategies. Model the use of the strategies. For instance, as you write on the board, model the process of sounding out a word by stretching out its sounds or attempting to visualize the word or trying out spellings.

Also use prompts for spelling, in the same way that you use prompts for decoding. Prompts should be geared to the student's level of spelling development and the nature of the word being spelled. Some prompts that can be used are listed in Table 13.2. Some of the prompts direct students to use a particular strategy to spell a word. The proof prompt reminds students to proofread their work, the affirmation prompt reinforces students' use of a particular strategy and encourages future use of that strategy, the assessment prompt helps you to find out more about the spelling processes the student is using.

Don't make spelling an all-or-nothing activity. This can be discouraging to struggling learners. Give students credit for the part of the word that they spell correctly. If the student spells the word *wrinkle* as *rinkle,* he has shown a fairly advanced knowledge of the spelling system. Show the student how much he knows and then show him what he needs to add. By showing students what is correct and then moving to what needs correcting, we show students how to look at misspellings. "They need to realize that they have not missed the *whole* word but rather just a part of it—in effect, they already *know* most of the word" (Templeton & Morris, 1999, p. 110).

Most students who have difficulty learning to spell apparently follow the same developmental course as other students, but do so at a slower pace. Disabled spellers tend to be several years behind students who have average spelling ability. However, they respond to systematic instruction and do fairly well with phonetically regular words but may need additional work with words that are not strictly phonetic (Worthy & Invernizzi, 1990). Because of this it is doubly important that these students be provided with words that are at their level. It may also be a good idea to give them fewer words per session and more practice.

If poor spellers have a weakened phonological system, emphasis should be placed on detecting sounds in words. At the earliest levels, emphasize the individual sounds of words and their spellings, especially when dealing with such items as clusters *(stand)*, which are difficult to detect. When introducing a word such as *stand,* help students focus on each sound in the word. Say each sound, /s/, /t/, /a/, /n/, /d/, and have students say them with you. If students have an orthographic weakness, they should visualize the word or use a mnemonic to help them remember the tricky part: *piece* has a *pie* in it. Students with severe spelling problems, whether they are due to phonological or orthographic problems or both, might trace the

TABLE 13.2   Spelling Prompts

STRATEGY	WHEN USED	PROMPT
Best spelling	Student hesitates while writing a piece because she is unsure of the spelling of a word.	Spell the word as best you can and check it after you have finished writing.
Think how it sounds	Student is having difficulty spelling a word that has a predictable spelling.	Say the word slowly. Stretch it out. What sound do you hear first? What sound do you hear next? And so on.
Think how it looks	Student is having difficulty spelling a word that contains letters that are not directly predictable from its sounds.	Can you picture the word? Can you see it in your mind? How does it look?
Try it out	Student is not sure how to spell a word.	Try writing the word. Does it look right? If not, try writing it again.
Analogy	Student is having difficulty spelling a word that sounds and looks like a word that she can spell.	Is the word like any word that you know how to spell? How do you spell *(known word)*? How do you spell *(unknown word)*?
Think of its parts	Student is having difficulty writing a long word.	Think of the word's parts. How would you write the first part? The second part?
Using a rule	Student is not sure how to spell a word to which a rule applies.	What rule might help you spell this word?
Use a reference	Student is unable to spell a word, and none of the other situations applies.	Where might you find the correct spelling of that word?
Proofing	Student has misspelled words in her written piece.	Do the words have all their sounds? Do they look right?
Affirmation	Teacher wishes to reinforce the student's correct use of a strategy.	I like the way you stretched the word out and thought about each of its sounds.
Assessment	Teacher wants to see what strategies the student is using.	How did you figure out how to spell that word?

word to help them remember its spelling. Students in the alphabetic stage might say each sound as they trace each letter. However, students in the word-pattern stage and beyond are beginning to chunk words and see patterns in words. They might say the word or each syllable as a whole as they trace it. Steps for a tracing technique that has been adapted from Fernald (1943) are listed below.

STEPS FOR TRACING SPELLING WORDS

Step 1. Students say the word as a whole.

Step 2. Students in the alphabetical stage say each sound as they trace the word. If learning *dig,* the student says, "dig, /d/, /i/, /g/, dig." If in the word-pattern stage students say the whole word or say the word syllable by syllable. For the word *nation* the student says, "nation, na, tion, nation," and traces the word or syllable as he says it. The student continues to trace the word until he believes he can write it from memory

Step 3. The student writes the word from memory and checks his spelling with the correct spelling. If the student can write the word correctly twice, then he goes to the next word. If not, he continues to trace.

Tracing and saying words focuses students' attention and helps them to become aware of the separate sounds or sound patterns in a word. Tracing can also be a helpful technique for students who have poor visual memory for words. Struggling readers and writers also need to be provided with words on their spelling level, not their reading level. Spelling generally lags behind reading, especially as students move into the middle grades. A student reading on a third-grade level may still be struggling with second-grade spelling. Struggling readers should also be encouraged to use a spell checker.

Individualizing Spelling Instruction. Just as in reading, struggling spellers need instruction that is geared to their level of spelling development. Even though they may be older and the rest of the class is doing advanced words, disabled spellers may need to learn such a basic strategy as stretching out the sounds of a word. Students operating on this level also need simple consonant–vowel–consonant words rather than the multisyllabic words that classmates may be learning to spell. One way of individualizing spelling is to have students create spelling journals. On the inside cover of their journals, students write or paste a list of the steps for studying spelling words. In the rest of the journal students write words to be learned. These can be dictated words from the word or syllable patterns they are learning, high-frequency words, words that they need to write a piece they are currently working on, special-interest words, or words from subject-matter areas. A good source of words is those that they have had difficulty with in their writing. Words to be learned are written in the left-hand column of notebook pages, which have been divided into columns as shown in Figure 13.9. In a second column, students rewrite the word but circle parts of the word that are difficult. This might be the *ph* in *phone* or the *ean* in *ocean.* Student might write a mnemonic aid to help them remember the tricky part of the word. The mnemonic aid could be provided by the teacher or created by the student. Five columns can be drawn to the right of the list of spelling words. These can be used to check daily quizzes.

Electronic Aids

Students should be shown how to use the spell checkers incorporated into most of today's word processing programs. Hand-held electronic spelling aids such as *Spelling Ace* (Franklin) and *Elementary Spelling Ace* (Franklin) might also be introduced. When users type in misspelled words, these devices use data about typical patterns of phonetic misspellings to help the learner locate the correct spelling of the misspelled word. They also

FIGURE 13.9   Sample Page from Spelling Notebook

WORDS	HARD PARTS	HELPFUL HINTS	QUIZZES			
receive	*rec<u>ei</u>ve*	*<u>i</u> before <u>e</u> except after <u>c</u>*				
heart	*h<u>ea</u>rt*	*An <u>ear</u> can hear a h<u>ear</u>t beat.*				
build	*b<u>ui</u>ld*					

Use of word processing software is widespread. At least one student in every three completes a rough draft or final copy on a computer (Greenwald, Persky, Campbell, & Mazzeo, 1999).

feature spelling games and have the capacity to store words for later review.

The Role of Writing

Frequent opportunities to write play an essential role in the development of spelling skills and strategies. Writing provides a reason for learning to spell, along with opportunities for students to apply their skills.

HANDWRITING

Because writing makes heavy demands on memory, discrimination, perception, and fine-motor skills—areas in which low-achieving readers are often weak—reading problems are frequently accompanied by deficiencies in handwriting. Because instructional time is limited and handwriting seems a less vital skill than reading, handwriting instruction may be condensed or neglected. However, if it is taught as a functional part of the overall language arts program, handwriting can reinforce a number of skills necessary for reading. For instance, Benjamin has a poor sense of directionality, frequently reverses letters, and, on occasion, forgets what a letter looks like. Good handwriting instruction will help Benjamin proceed in consistent fashion from left to right and top to bottom. A focus on proper letter formation will also help him to commit to memory the shapes of letters. This should help reduce mirror images of letters and help him to remember letter forms. If it is tied in with phonics instruction and composing activities, handwriting can be used to reinforce and extend writing and reading instruction. Last but not least, legible handwriting can build self-esteem. Although students' reading difficulty may go undetected, handwriting is on display for teachers, parents, and peers to see. Legible handwriting can be a source of pride. And as a practical matter, stu-

Previously, students were taught letter formation and then taught to write. Today, students are urged to write as best they can. As they experience what writing is and have a need to form letters, then letter formation is introduced.

Preventing Academic Failure (Bertin & Perleman, 1999) is an excellent source of handwriting and spelling activities for struggling spellers.

One technique that has been used to help struggling writers express themselves is interactive writing (p. 192). A small-group interactive writing activity can be completed in ten to fifteen minutes. Possible topics include a retelling of a story, an account of a class trip, a weather report, a menu, a list of favorite foods or activities, or a news account.

In one study, explicit instruction in handwriting and spelling for students having difficulty in those areas resulted not only in better handwriting and more accurate spelling but also improved writing performance (Graham, 1999).

dents are often judged, rightly or wrongly, on the quality of their handwriting. All other things being equal, neatly written papers receive higher grades than barely legible ones. See Chapter 5 for suggestions for assessing writing.

It is not unusual to find older students who are still not sure how to form all the letters of the alphabet. A program for students who have not mastered handwriting skills should be systematic and functional. Approximately ten to fifteen minutes a day should be devoted to handwriting instruction. As with other types of learning, instruction should build on what students know. In addition to being able to form letters, students should use proper spacing between words, have consistent slant, align the letters, create lines that are smooth, and create letters that are consistent in size. Students should also learn to evaluate their handwriting.

Instruction should have a kinesthetic base so that students get a feel for how letters should be produced. When presenting letters, have students write them in the air and trace them on their desks before they use a pencil to form them. As students write letters, they should recite the movements necessary to make the letter. In forming a lowercase manuscript *t*, the student might say, "Stroke down, stroke across." Periods of short instruction work best. Ten or fifteen minutes of instruction per day is adequate. However, handwriting skills can be applied during spelling, writing workshop, or whenever students are writing.

In addition to being able to write legibly, students also should be able to write quickly enough that they can copy material from the board, take notes, or complete writing assignments within a reasonable amount of time. Writing that is labored will hamper students' progress.

If students fail to respond to instruction or if their difficulties seem to be rooted in physical problems, consult with the occupational therapist. Occupational therapists assist children who have difficulty performing functional tasks, including handwriting. Signs that a student may need specialized help include inconsistent use of the left or right hand for writing or drawing, avoidance of writing tasks, difficulty copying from the board, illegible handwriting, difficulty maintaining proper posture or grip, and failure to profit from instruction (Vreeland, 1998). If the student does have difficulty copying, have the student's vision checked. The student may have difficulty with far vision or may experience strain when switching from far-point (looking at the board) to near-point (writing on his paper) tasks.

MINICASE STUDY

One student in George Rusnak's class had had such bad experiences with writing that when asked to write, he responded, "Fail me if you want, I won't write!" Wisely, Rusnak decided to take two important steps: find out why the student's attitude toward writing was so negative and provide a structure that would help the student feel that he could be successful.

Rusnak started off the writing unit by asking, "What are your experiences with writing?" As students related their experiences with writing, most of which were negative,

Rusnak talked over some of the bad experiences he had had when he was a student and how he coped with them.

Rusnak then introduced RAFT to support the students' attempts to write. To get students started, Rusnak provided them with an intriguing writing activity.

> *Role*—worm in an apple
> *Audience*—farmer
> *Format*—persuasive letter
> *Topic*—explaining to farmer why he shouldn't take the worm's apple

This lighthearted assignment was followed by one in which students took the role of a historical character and was related to the students' study of history. The piece had to be factual but affective. The student's personal involvement had to be evident. Supported and motivated through three drafts, the youngster who would rather fail than write transformed a 72-word empty letter into a 423-word, superbly written piece. A writer was reborn (Rusnak, 1994).

SUMMARY

On a nationwide assessment, from 14 to 26 percent of students were unable to write on a basic level. Effective instruction for struggling writers combines balanced instruction in writing strategies with the process approach to writing. The five elements in the writing process are prewriting, composing, revising, editing, and publishing. Prewriting includes topic selection and planning. An important component of the planning process is considering one's audience. Composing is the creation of the written piece. When composing, students should focus on the message rather than the mechanics. Rehearsing what one plans to write can aid the composing process. Revising is an essential but often neglected part of the writing process. True revising involves taking a fresh look at what one has written and making substantive changes, if necessary. Editing involves checking and correcting mechanical errors. Publishing is an important element in writing because it provides the student with a genuine purpose for writing and helps the student gain a sense of audience. Although they are presented separately, the elements in the writing process overlap, and several may occur simultaneously.

Instruction in writing is carried out through modeling, formal and informal lessons, guided writing, strategy instruction, and conferences. A major purpose of writing conferences is to help students discover that they have something to say. A second major purpose is to discover difficulties that students may be having and help them overcome those difficulties.

Exemplary writing programs for low-achieving readers and writers include CSIW (Cognitive Strategy Instruction Writing), Collaborative Strategy Instruction, the Harris–Graham program, and CRISS writing. Although the details of implementation vary, the programs all provide direct instruction in the use of strategies and support in the form of planning sheets, mnemonics, frames for writing, and/or discussion.

Journals, logs, and writer's notebooks provide opportunities for disabled writers to apply their skills in a personal way. Freewriting and conversational writing also promote fluency in written expression.

Instruction for ELL students should include development of the language required by the writing activity. A language experience approach is particularly appropriate for ELL students. A writing program should include an appropriate amount of instruction and practice in writing to assessment prompts but this should not be overdone.

Although the focus in writing is on the message, mechanics are also important. Spelling instruction should be individualized, since students' achievement in spelling varies considerably. In addition, disabled writers need both formal and informal instruction in the mechanics of writing, with emphasis on those elements for which a need is demonstrated. Low-achieving readers and writers may also need special help with handwriting.

APPLICATION ACTIVITIES

1. Observe a guided writing class or writing workshop in action. Note the organization of the class and the major activities in which the students are engaged. What do you like best about the class? How might it be improved?

2. Design a planning sheet similar to those created in CSIW, or plan a strategy lesson similar to those described by Harris and Graham. If possible, present the planning sheet or strategy and evaluate its effectiveness.

3. Use RAFT, opinion/proof, or another structured writing device to write a piece. Evaluate the effectiveness of the device. How might these structured devices help low-achieving writers? How might they be inhibited by them?

4. Design a rubric for scoring a piece of writing that your students have written or will write. Try out the rubric. Revise it in the light of any shortcomings that you note. Also select from your students' writing anchor pieces that illustrate each of the rubric's categories.

■ ■ ■ ■ ■

CHAPTER FOURTEEN

SEVERE PROBLEM CASES, STUDENTS ACQUIRING ENGLISH, AND OLDER STUDENTS

USING WHAT YOU KNOW

Most low-achieving readers will learn to read if taught by the methods described in previous chapters. However, about one low-achieving reader in 100 has such a severe difficulty learning to read words that she or he may need to be taught through special word-learning techniques. Two of the best-known word-learning techniques are the VAKT (Visual, Auditory, Kinesthetic, Tactile) and the Orton–Gillingham approaches, both of which involve tracing or writing words. Word Building, an approach described in Chapter 8, has also been used successfully with students who have severe reading problems.

Both VAKT and the Orton–Gillingham approaches have been in use for a number of years. Because they are tedious for both student and teacher, they are also somewhat controversial. However, because both techniques have been used successfully with students with the most serious reading problems, it is important that you have an understanding of them. You may have students with whom you wish to try the techniques because everything else you have attempted has failed. Even if you decide not to use the techniques, you should be aware of them because they are in fairly widespread use. If, for instance, you are a classroom teacher and the LD teacher is using the Orton–Gillingham approach with one of your students, you can better support the program if you know something about it. In addition, many of the "new" corrective techniques are built on either VAKT or Orton–Gillingham. Portions of Reading Recovery, for instance, are based on VAKT (Clay, 1993b), and dozens of techniques are based on Orton–Gillingham. You will be in a better position to assess a new technique if you understand the principles on which it is based.

Teens and adults who have reading and writing problems often bring with them a long history of failure and may have a can't-do attitude. It is important that they see themselves as competent learners and adopt a can-do outlook. Students who are still acquiring English and are struggling with reading and writing face the dual task of learning a new language and overcoming reading and writing difficulties.

What is your experience with students who have severe reading problems? Have you ever taught or known students who couldn't seem to learn new words no matter how carefully they were taught? Have you worked with older problem readers or students whose struggle to learn to read and write is compounded by their struggle to master a new language?

ANTICIPATION GUIDE

Read each of the following statements. Put a check under "Agree" or "Disagree" to show how you feel about each one. If possible, discuss your responses with classmates.

	AGREE	DISAGREE
1. If taught properly, all students can learn to read.	_____	_____
2. Word-learning techniques that use tracing are successful because they establish additional connections in memory.	_____	_____
3. Generally speaking, learning words sound by sound or part by part is a better approach for low-achieving readers than learning them as wholes.	_____	_____
4. The older a low-achieving reader is, the harder she or he is to teach.	_____	_____
5. If possible, students who are still acquiring English should be taught to read in their native language.	_____	_____

THE NEED FOR SPECIALIZED TECHNIQUES

A small percentage of low-achieving readers, approximately one reader in 100 (McCormick, 1994), seem to have such extreme difficulty learning printed words or letter–sound relationships that they may need to be taught through specialized programs. One such student is Martha.

Although she had high-average intelligence, eight-year-old Martha was making very little progress in reading. Because Martha was experiencing difficulty learning to read new words, she was referred to a nearby university reading clinic. Despite intensive one-to-one instruction, she made very limited gains. Martha seemed to forget the high-frequency words she was taught soon after they were introduced. After a year of supplementary instruction, Martha was only reading on a primer level. She was able to read only nine of twenty first-grade high-frequency words on an informal reading inventory word-list test.

VAKT TRACING TECHNIQUE

The struggle to learn to read was taking its toll on Martha. A vivacious youngster on the playground, she was quiet and subdued during her reading lessons. She seemed discouraged and was putting forth less and less effort. Feeling somewhat desperate, her teacher decided to try a technique that she had recently learned in her corrective reading methods

Both the Fernald and VAKT techniques use visual, auditory, kinesthetic (sense of movement), and tactile senses to help the student concentrate on the words being learned. Use of various modalities may help students produce representations in memory that are more detailed and more lasting. Use of multiple modalities may also create more connections so that words are stored and retrieved more easily (Moats & Farrell, 1999).

An essential element in Martha's success was the enthusiasm of her teacher, who made learning interesting and fulfilling and affirmed Martha's successes.

class: the VAKT (Visual–Auditory–Kinesthetic–Tactile) tracing technique (Johnson, 1966). **VAKT** is an adaptation of the **Fernald** tracing technique (Fernald, 1943), which is estimated to be the most widely used approach for teaching severely disabled readers (Tierney & Readence, 2000a). VAKT is a language-experience approach. As students attempt to write letters to relatives, summarize selections that have been read to them, describe experiences they have had, label diagrams, or make written observations about scientific experiments, they learn the words they don't know by seeing, saying, hearing, and tracing them (VAKT) or, in later stages, by seeing, hearing, and saying them (VAK). Although most words are learned in a writing context, some words from reading selections may also be learned through VAKT or VAK.

Long touted by experts in the field of reading difficulties (Clark & Uhury, 1995; Clay, 1993b; Fernald, 1943; Johnson, 1966; Johnson & Kress, 1966; Manzo & Manzo, 1993; Roswell & Chall, 1994), the tracing technique worked as promised. Revived by her initial success and the support of her sensitive teacher, Martha was soon learning new words with enthusiasm. Within just four weeks, she learned to read more than fifty words, which was nearly as many words as she had learned in two full years of schooling.

A technique of last resort, VAKT is recommended only for students who have serious word-learning problems. While most students have no difficulty learning to read by seeing and hearing, a small percentage of the population has such a serious difficulty learning to associate printed symbols with the words they represent that they need special methods that use kinesthetic (sense of movement) and tactile (sense of touch) as well as visual and auditory stimulation. In her guidebook on Reading Recovery for teachers, Clay (1993b) advises using a tracing approach with students who are not learning words by visually analyzing them or by reconstructing them with magnetic letters. "If visual analysis and word reconstruction do not produce good results, introduce tracing and add the feel of the movements to the child's sources of information" (p. 56). Because it is a method quite different from those typically used, VAKT can offer students a sense a getting off to a fresh start.

Signs of Need

The major sign that VAKT is needed is failure to learn or remember printed symbols despite adequate ability and opportunity. A candidate for VAKT stands out because he is very slow to learn printed words and, even after apparently learning them, soon forgets them. Jonathan, when tested at age twelve, knew fewer than half the words on a primer list. Awilda had to trace the word *where* twenty-five times before learning it, and then was unable to recognize it when she encountered it in a story minutes later. There may also be signs of stress associated with reading. Obviously distressed when her teacher handed her a book, one gifted student who had a serious word-learning problem blurted out, "Excuse me! We're not going to read, are we?"

Prerequisites for VAKT

Although designed for students who have the severest reading problems, VAKT does have a number of prerequisites (Johnson & Kress, 1966). The child must be able to hear, see, say, and trace the words. A child with a profound hearing loss cannot use the technique. In addition, the learner needs enough phonological awareness so that she or he can detect separate syllables in a word. Since the technique also involves tracing and writing letters, the child should also know how to form most of the letters of the alphabet.

> The purpose of the introductory stage of VAKT is to acquaint the student with procedures for using the technique and to demonstrate that this technique will enable him to learn.

Introductory Stage of VAKT

VAKT works, in part, because both the teacher and learner believe in it (Johnson & Kress, 1966). The purpose of the introductory stage is to show the student how the technique works and, more important, to convince the student that she or he can learn to read words by using it.

In introducing the technique, you will need the following equipment:

- A dictionary
- A large black crayon
- A number of strips of 4-inch × 12-inch paper
- A stapler
- A recording sheet

Establishing Rapport. As you establish rapport, find out whether the student is left-handed or right-handed. The teacher and student should be seated side by side, and the student should be able to observe the teacher as she or he traces new words. A right-handed teacher working with a right-handed learner sits to the student's right. You should also determine whether the student uses cursive or manuscript handwriting. Although Fernald (1943) and Johnson and Kress (1966) recommend cursive because there is smoother flow and better sense of the wholeness of words written in cursive, manuscript is preferred by some because it matches the print that students will read.

Once you have established rapport with the learner, explain the technique. Tell the student that she will be using a new way to learn to read and spell words, one that a lot of bright students just like herself have used. Invite the student to suggest a word that she would like to learn. Tell the student that it can be a long word or a difficult word, any word that she would like to learn. One student requested that he be taught how to spell his last name. Up until that time, he had been using an initial to signify his surname. The student was ten years old.

Using the Dictionary. Except for proper names, all new words are looked up in the dictionary. This ensures that accurate syllabic division is obtained and familiarizes the student with the dictionary. Involve the student in the task by asking the student what letter the word begins with and where it might be found in the dictionary. The student may also be asked to turn to the section in the dictionary where the word might be found. If she is looking up the

FIGURE 14.1 **Model Word Prepared by Teacher**

MANUSCRIPT	CURSIVE
<u>di</u>nosaur	*dinosaur*

word *tiny,* the student locates the *t*'s and not the word *tiny* itself, since this would involve knowing how to spell the word and would also be too time-consuming.

Before looking up the word, ask the student how many parts (syllables) it has. Then look up the word and tell the student whether she is right or wrong. Alerting the student to watch carefully, you say the word and write it in blackboard-size script on a strip of 4-inch × 12-inch paper placed horizontally. Say each syllable as you initiate the writing of the syllable. If you are using cursive, cross *t*'s and dot *i*'s from left to right and then say the whole word once more. Also underline the separate syllables (as in Figure 14.1) if the word is multisyllabic. With your index and ring fingers, trace the word. Continue demonstrating the tracing technique until the student feels that she can do it.

> Martha had to trace the word *dinosaur,* one of her introductory words, twenty-five times before she was able to write it correctly. However, as time went on, she required fewer tracings to learn words.

Student Tracing.   The student traces the word until she feels she can write it from memory. Tracing should be conscientious and accurate. Unless the student is totally involved in the process, it will not work. Do not allow any inaccurate tracings. Inaccurate tracing includes faulty tracing of the individual letters. For reference, have a cursive or manuscript chart available. If the student begins to trace a manuscript *b* by going around and up, stop the student and show her how to trace it. The tracing should be accompanied by an explanation, "When I trace *b*, I start at the top, come straight down, and then go up and around." In addition to seeing that tracings are accurate, make sure that the student

- Says the whole word
- Says a syllable as she or he begins to trace the syllable
- Dots *i*'s and crosses *t*'s after tracing the whole word (If the student is using manuscript writing, the *i*'s are dotted and the *t*'s crossed as they are formed.)
- Says the whole word again

If the student skips a step or fails to follow the procedure exactly, stop her immediately. A major aim of VAKT is to establish correct habits, so you want to avoid reinforcing erroneous responses. The student may ask for a demonstration if her tracing procedures are not accurate, or may undertake additional tracings. Or you may suggest additional tracings or demonstrations if you feel these are needed.

> When tracing words, Martha tended to say them sound by sound: /m/-/y/-/s/-/e/-/l/-/f/. However, in VAKT, words are pronounced syllable by syllable: /my/-/self/.

Writing from Memory.   Once the student feels that she knows the word, she writes it twice from memory. With the teacher's copy turned over, the student writes the word in normal-size script across the top of a second strip of 4-inch × 12-inch paper positioned vertically. The student compares her or his copy with the model copy. If it is correct, the student covers her writing with a third sheet of 4-inch × 12-inch paper and writes the target word once more. If the word is again written correctly, the student copy is dated and stapled to the teacher's copy. It is then filed in a box that has alphabetic dividers. If the student has difficulty, she may be asked to trace the word again.

Keeping Records. Records should be kept of words learned and number of demonstrations and tracings. (The symbols used to record the student's performance are presented in Figure 14.2.) These records provide an ongoing means for monitoring progress and can also be used as a basis for deciding when to move into another stage. The record displayed in Figure 14.3 shows that the word was presented in the introductory stage and indicates that the teacher demonstrated the tracing five times. The student traced the word correctly seven times in succession, then wrote the word from memory incorrectly twice in a row, but finally wrote the word correctly twice in a row.

Students remain in the introductory stage until they have mastered the tracing procedures. Some students may enter Stage 1 after tracing just one or two words. Others may need additional experience and should not be rushed.

Stage 1 of VAKT

In terms of tracing procedures, Stage 1 is identical to the introductory stage. The major difference is in the source of the words to be learned. Words learned in the introductory stage are chosen by the student. Words to be learned in Stage 1 are those the student needs to know for her writing.

> As used in VAKT, the language-experience approach has an added step. After being scribed by the teacher and read by the teacher and student, the teacher dictates to the student, who then scribes the story.

VAKT is the word-learning component of a language-experience approach. The student may be composing a letter, a set of instructions, a shopping list, an account of a trip she has taken, or a summary of an experiment. After the experience has been discussed and organized, the student dictates what she plans to write. The teacher records the student's dictation. After the story has been recorded, the teacher then dictates it back to the student.

FIGURE 14.2   VAKT Symbols

d   demonstration tracing

| accurate tracing

Γ   partial tracing—student was stopped because of faulty procedures

✓   correct writing of word from memory

✓   incorrect writing of word from memory

FIGURE 14.3   VAKT Record

dinosaur (1)   *d d d d d* | | | | | | | ✔ ✔ ✔ ✔

Any words that the student is unable to write are presented, traced, and written from memory just as in the steps of the introductory stage.

Here is how Martha, the student taught at a university literacy center, was helped as she composed an experience story. Martha told about going swimming in a pool, which the teacher wrote down and then read back to her.

> When I go swimming, I walk in the water first. Then I swim under the water. I hold my breath and get the diving sticks from my mom. Sometimes I get the sticks at nine feet. I like to do this because it is fun.

Now that the story was composed, Martha began the physical writing of it. Following the teacher's oral reading of the first sentence, Martha was able to write the first three words "When I go," but asked for help with *swimming*.

Teacher: How many syllables do you hear in swimming?
Martha: (after some hesitation) Two?
Teacher: We'll check and see. Do you know where in the dictionary it might be?
Martha: In the middle.
Teacher: Open to it.

> Because it is based on student-dictated stories, VAKT can be used with disabled readers of all ages, including adults.

After opening to *s,* Martha handed the dictionary to the teacher, who located the word and reported: "Here it is. You were right. Swimming has two syllables. Watch me while I write it for you."

After some demonstrations and several practice tracings, Martha was able to write the word correctly twice. Although Martha was able to write a few words such as *I, go, when, the, my, get, at, to,* and *do,* she needed to trace most of the words in the story.

At the end of each session, words that had been learned by tracing were underlined. After the session, the selection was typed so Martha would have the opportunity to see it in print. Newly learned words—those that had been underlined—were typed in list form. On the following day, Martha read the words that had been put in list form and the portion of the experience story that had been typed. Words that Martha forgot were practiced once more. When Martha missed a previously learned word, she retrieved it from the file—which provided incidental practice with initial consonants and alphabetical order—traced it, and again rewrote it twice from memory. The additional spelling attempts were dated and stapled to the original attempts.

When the student reads the previous day's words typed in list form, the student's performance is noted just as on the word-list test of an informal reading inventory. Performance is recorded on a photocopy. If the student cannot read the words in isolation, she or he is given the opportunity to read them in the context of the experience story. A sample experience story with words underlined is shown in Figure 14.4.

FIGURE 14.4 Sample VAKT Story

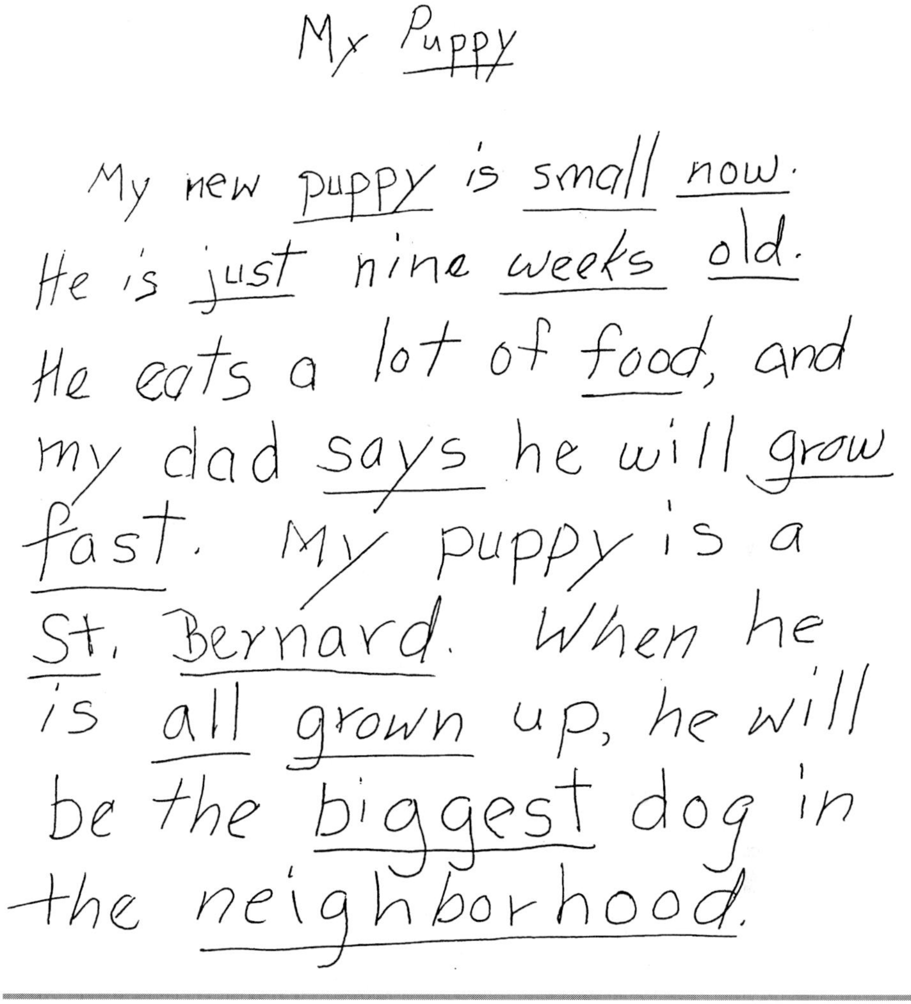

My Puppy

My new puppy is small now. He is just nine weeks old. He eats a lot of food, and my dad says he will grow fast. My puppy is a St. Bernard. When he is all grown up, he will be the biggest dog in the neighborhood.

In addition to tracing and using new words in stories, numerous opportunities should be provided for the student to read newly learned words in other contexts. These contexts might include rhymes, poems, songs, recipes, and similar pieces. Target words should be mixed with known words so that the student is almost sure to be successful (Johnson & Kress, 1966).

Moving from One Stage to Another

As students gain skills and learn words with greater ease, they move to more advanced stages. Signs that students are ready to move to a more advanced stage include fewer repetitions and less reliance on the word-learning technique that is characteristic of that level. Signs that a student in Stage 1 is ready to move into Stage 2 include needing fewer tracings before learning a word and learning an increasing number of words with no tracing at all. The student demonstrates the ability to learn words by looking, saying, and hearing rather than by looking, saying, hearing, and tracing. If students in Stage 1 say they can learn a word without tracing it, give them the opportunity to do so. Have them simply look at the word and say it. As they near the completion of Stage 1, students may use VAKT with some words and VAK with others. The transition from Stage 1 to Stage 2 is made when students can learn all their new words without the use of tracing.

Stage 2 of VAKT

Stages 1 and 2 are the same, except that in Stage 2 the student is not required to trace. Since there is no tracing in Stage 2, 4-inch × 6-inch cards may be used instead of sheets of 4-inch × 12-inch paper. Instead of tracing the word, the student studies it from the card.

STEPS IN STAGE 2 OF VAKT

Step 1: Identify. The word to be learned is identified. The student asks for the word or makes an error as she or he attempts to write it.

Step 2: Analyze the word. You ask how many parts or syllables the word has. The student checks the word file to see if the word is there. If not, you and the student find it in the dictionary. Note how many syllables the word has and inform the student.

Step 3: Review the word. If the word is in the file box, review the word. If the word is not in the file box, say the word, say each syllable as you write each sylla-

ble, and, after having written each syllable, say the word as a whole. Syllables are underlined.

Step 4: Say the word. The student studies the word by saying it as a whole, saying each syllable, and saying it as a whole once more.

Step 5: Spell the word. The student attempts to spell the word correctly twice on a second card, which is held vertically.

Step 6: Use the word. The student writes the word in the story.

Stage 3 of VAKT

In Stage 3, the student uses the dictionary rather than teacher-written copy as a model. If the word is not in the file box, the student, with the teacher's help, if necessary, locates the word in the dictionary and checks syllabication. The student studies the word from the dictionary, saying it as a whole, in syllables, and then as a whole. When the student feels that she or he has mastered the word, the student writes it twice on a 4-inch × 6-inch card held vertically. If new, the word is then written on the front of the card held horizontally and is filed. The word is then written in the story. Stage 3 is discontinued when the student no longer seems to need it.

Need for a Total Approach

VAKT is just one part of a total program for students who have severe reading problems. While the focus of the explanation of VAKT has been on mechanical procedures, the

> Along with VAKT, Martha used Word Building, read a variety of children's books, and composed stories using invented spelling.

approach includes providing opportunities for investigating topics of interest, composing experience stories, reading children's books, participating in discussion groups, and doing all the things that might be done in an exemplary classroom.

VAKT should also be combined with a systematic word-analysis program such as Word Building. Initial patterns to be taught might be those that the student needs in her or his writing. For instance, noting the word *might* and *night* in a story, the teacher might initiate a study of the *-ight* pattern. Johnson (1966) cautions that VAKT and VAK are not substitutes for the development of word-analysis skills. However, the sight words learned in VAKT may become the basis for teaching phonics and other word-recognition skills.

> Loudon and Arthur (1940), Pickary (1949), and Bartlet and Shapiro (1956) report successful use of VAKT. Meyer (1978) cites sixteen additional sources of support for it.

As with any technique, the heart of VAKT is in the quality of the teaching. VAKT works best when the teacher carefully observes the student's learning strategies and builds on what he knows. If the student is using initial consonants, for instance, build on that strength. When that student is hesitant about writing a word, ask him to tell how he thinks it might begin. Also have the student use his knowledge of initial consonants to help locate words being looked up in the dictionary.

The overall program should be both systematic and incidental. Using Word Building or another phonics program, gradually introduce needed word-analysis elements. However, also take advantage of opportunities that arise naturally. For instance, if the student dictates a story about a time when she and some friends had to start rowing to shore when the motor on their boat conked out, but they got a tow from a passing Coast Guard boat, then do a spontaneous study of the *ow* and *oa* spellings of long *o*.

Adapted VAKT

Classical VAKT emphasizes the wholeness of words. When tracing single-syllable words, the student says it as a whole and does not break it into its constituent sounds. Multisyllabic words, however, are broken down into separate syllables. Research suggests that struggling readers, especially in the beginning stages, benefit by noting the separate sounds in words and also seeing the words as a whole. The following adaptation of VAKT has been tried out with struggling readers and has been found to be effective.

First, the teacher shows how many sounds are in a word and which letters represent those sounds. The teacher says the word, checks its spelling in a dictionary, writes the word while saying each sound, and then says the whole word. The teacher says the whole word, underlines each letter or letter group that represents a sound, says each sound while underlining it, and then says the whole word. The teacher demonstrates tracing by saying the whole word, saying each sound while tracing the letter(s) that makes that sound, and saying the whole word. The student says the whole word, says each sound while tracing the letter that makes that sound, and says the whole word. Learning the word *stop,* the students would say, "stop, /s/, /t/, /o/, /p/, stop." For words in which some sounds are spelled with two letters, the teacher puts one line under both letters to show that they represent just one sound: <u>sh</u>-<u>o</u>-<u>p</u>. An irregular word such as *laugh* would be written: <u>l</u>-<u>au</u>-<u>gh</u>. Multisyllabic words are traced in syllables just as in classical VAKT.

Multisensory processing results in multiple memory traces, with the kinesthetic and tactile modalities reinforcing visual and auditory pathways (Hulme, 1981).

VAKT also strengthens phonemic awareness.

Why Is VAKT Effective?

In addition to establishing a kinesthetic and tactile link and focusing attention, VAKT provides structure and support, builds on what the student knows, instills confidence, and has high expectations for the student. VAKT also forces the student to note all the letters in a word (Gates, 1927). The technique removes the association of failure by providing students with a method they have never seen before. It is also firmly grounded in language development and the student's interests. Speaking of multisensory techniques, Moats and Farrell (1999) commented, "Most likely it is not simply the multimodal nature of such practice that explains its power but the mediating effect of various sensory and motor experiences on attention and recall" (p. 15).

ORTON–GILLINGHAM APPROACH

Orton–Gillingham approach: specialized word-learning technique that uses intensive synthetic phonics reinforced by tracing.

A no-nonsense, highly structured skill-and-drill synthetic phonics technique, the **Orton–Gillingham Approach** presents the isolated sounds of letters and then builds these individual sounds into words "like bricks into a wall" (Gillingham & Stillman, 1983, p. 40).

In a typical drill, the teacher shows the letter and the student supplies its sound. The teacher says a sound and the student names the letter. The teacher says a sound and the student writes the letter that represents that sound. After the sounds of the letters *a, b, f, h, i, j, k, m, p, t* have been taught, they are blended together to make words: *bat, hat, jab, it.* To avoid distorting consonant sounds, the student is encouraged to pronounce the first two sounds together, /ba/ and then add the final sound /t/.

After learning to read a few words, spelling is initiated. The teacher says the word. The student repeats it, names its letters, *m-a-n,* writes each letter as he says it, *m-a-n,* and then reads the word: *man.*

Later on, this spelling technique will be used to teach nonphonetic or sight words. As in the VAKT technique, students use their kinesthetic and tactile senses. They say and write the words. However, there is a crucial difference. As you will recall, in the VAKT technique the student says each word or syllable as a whole as she or he traces it. In the Orton–Gillingham approach the student says the letter name as she or he writes the letter, so that the association is between the name of the letter and its form. This is done, according to Gillingham and Stillman (1983), because words like *laugh* do not lend themselves to being pronounced letter sound by letter sound. One of the problems inherent in a letter-by-letter or sound-by-sound approach is that it fails to take advantage of the regularities that can be found in an approach that uses patterns.

Although apparently in widespread use, the Orton–Gillingham approach, in order to embody current research and practice, needs to be modified in the following ways:

- Start where the student is. Pretest the student with an informal reading inventory or similar instrument and begin instruction at the point where the student has difficulty.

- Encourage wide reading. Students do learn to read by reading. However, make sure that students are given books on the appropriate level.
- Orton–Gillingham advocates skill and drill on isolated phonics exercises. Phonics instruction should be functional and contextual. Skills taught should be those that are needed, and are best taught when students are about to apply them in reading or writing.
- The Orton–Gillingham technique requires learning a series of phonics generalizations. Eliminate or simplify the teaching of rules, except for the ones suggested in Chapter 8. Students make very limited use of rules when attacking unfamiliar words (Gunning, 1988b, 1999).

OTHER ORTON-BASED APPROACHES

Although the Gillingham–Stillman approach is perhaps the best known of the Orton-based approaches, there are a number of other approaches that grew out of Orton's work. All have in common systematic instruction in synthetic phonics and the use of visual, auditory, and kinesthetic modalities. However, one major difference is the connections that are emphasized. In the Gillingham–Stillman approach, students say the name of each letter as they trace it. In some Orton-based approaches, students say the sound of each letter as they trace. Which works better? Sheffield (1991) has tried both and claims that both work well. However, she believes that making the connection between the sound and the letter yields faster progress in reading, but the student who makes the connection between the letter and its name does better in spelling.

> **Using Technology**
> The Wilson Reading System can be accessed at http://www.wilsonlanguage.com/w_wrs.htm. This web site provides information about the Wilson program.

The Wilson Reading System grew out of Barbara Wilson's experience teaching adult struggling readers at Massachusetts General Hospital. Designed originally for older students, the Wilson System is now used in grades 3 and up. However, younger students use level A workbooks, while older students use Level B.

The program is highly structured and is designed specifically as a remedial program for students in grades 3 and beyond who have decoding problems. Although the program includes some work on comprehension and development of background and vocabulary, its main focus is on building decoding skills. A typical lesson starts with a card drill in which students review previously presented sounds by saying the sound shown on the card. A new pattern or card is then introduced. Students practice the new element by reading words and sentences containing the new element. They are then given a quick drill in which the teacher pronounces a sound and the student names the letter that represents that sound. This is followed by reviewing or teaching students how to spell the element introduced and the dictation of words, sounds, and sentences. Students then read a passage designed specifically to reinforce the patterns taught so far. The lesson ends with the teacher's reading of a literature selection to build the student's background and vocabulary and acquaint him with good literature. Active participation and manipulatives are key elements in the program. The program also introduces multisyllabic words early on. After students learn several single-syllable patterns, they learn multisyllabic words that incorporate those patterns: *limit, happen.*

Like other programs that use highly controlled vocabulary, the reading material tends to be contrived: "Tim sat in the shop. A mom and a tot came in. The mom got gum for the tot." Other widely used Orton–Gillingham-based approaches include Recipe for Reading (Traub & Bloom, 1975), Slingerland (Slingerland, 1971), Alphabetic Phonics (Educators Publishing Service) and Project Read (P.O. Box 20631, Bloomington, MN 55420, phone 800-450-0343).

ADAPTED WORD BUILDING

| If students have difficulty with Word Building, assess their phonemic awareness. Inadequate phonemic awareness can make learning phonics more difficult. |

An adapted form of Word Building has been used with encouraging success with severely disabled readers and is highly recommended. As described in Chapter 8, Word Building focuses on the learning of patterns. Although patterns are presented as both individual sounds, /a/ + /t/, and as patterns, /h/ + /at/, the emphasis is on the pattern as a unit. For most students, this is an efficient, effective way to learn phonics. However, if students are having difficulty learning patterns, adapt the technique so that they learn individual letter sounds. When presenting the -*at* pattern, for instance, point out the separate sounds in *at:* /a/ + /t/. If students have difficulty using pronounceable word parts—if they cannot pronounce the *ap* in *map,* for instance—then see if they are able to process the word sound by sound. In other words, if the student is struggling, make whatever adjustments are necessary. Although decoding a word sound by sound distorts speech sounds and is burdensome, it may be a necessary procedure for some students.

In most cases the use of a sound-by-sound approach will be temporary. As students become proficient in recognizing individual sounds in words or patterns, they will grow in their ability to perceive larger elements in words. Eventually you should be able to present new elements through patterns, and students will be able to decode unfamiliar words by using pronounceable word parts.

If you adapt Word Building, Benchmark, or another word-learning system and students are still struggling, use VAKT along with the phonics system. A major drawback of using VAKT is that it is so time-consuming. If time is an issue, shorten VAKT by adapting the writing portion. Instead of having the student dictate a paragraph, help her or him construct an oral sentence as is done in Reading Recovery (see Chapter 7). So that the tracing portion of the approach will reinforce the pattern being taught in Word Building, encourage the student to dictate a sentence using one or more of the pattern words. After studying the -*et* pattern, a student might dictate a sentence similar to the following: "I took my pet to the vet."

After the student has dictated the sentence, dictate it back to him and have the student write it just as in the VAKT approach. Words with which the student has difficulty should be traced. At the conclusion of the session, copy the sentence onto a strip of tagboard as in Reading Recovery. It can then be cut up and taken home to be read for practice. The segmented sentence should be reassembled and read the next day. Here is how a sample lesson using adapted Word Building might be taught.

SAMPLE ADAPTED WORD-BUILDING LESSON

Step 1: Presentation of pattern. Present pattern. (See detailed lessons in Chapter 8.)

> VAKT should be added to Word Building only if the student is having difficulty learning words taught through a Word Building approach. If Word Building with adapted VAKT is not successful, try classical VAKT.

Step 2: Creation of pattern sentence. Have student create a sentence using one or more pattern words and dictate that sentence to you.

Step 3: Writing of sentence by student. Dictate the sentence to the student and have the student write it. Have the student trace any words that are difficult.

Step 4: Tracing of words (Stage 1). The student says the whole word, traces and says each syllable, and then says the whole word. The student continues tracing the word until he feels he can write it from memory.

Step 5: Writing the word from memory. Turning the tracing copy over, the student says the whole word, says each syllable as he writes each syllable, on a strip of 4-inch × 12-inch paper placed vertically, and then says the whole word. The student checks the spelling of the word, covers the word that he has just written, and writes the word a second time and once again checks it for accuracy. The correctly written words are dated, stapled to the tracing copy, and filed alphabetically.

Step 6: Writing the word in the sentence. The student writes the new word in the sentence and reads it. As in VAKT, keep a record of demonstrations and tracings and words learned each time. The sentence can be written on tagboard and cut up for practice reading at home.

Step 7: Application of word patterns. Word patterns taught should be applied. A list of easy trade books that can be used for the application phase are presented in Figure 8.7 on p. 258. Crossword puzzles, riddles, jokes, signs, and ads can also be used to reinforce the pattern.

Classical VAKT is designed to help students learn a basic store of words that they can read immediately. Phonics skills also need to be taught. The adapted version of VAKT recommended for use with Word Building is designed to reinforce patterns being taught. The reason sentences are written, rather than whole stories, as in VAKT, is to simplify the approach and make it easier to use and less time-consuming. However, if possible, VAKT should be used as described earlier in the chapter.

A TOTAL PROGRAM

The special word-learning techniques discussed in this chapter are just one part of a total program for low-achieving readers. Writing and wide reading and content-area learning should also be a part of the low-achieving reader's program. An integrated program that builds on the student's strengths is best. Because students are probably well aware of their difficulties with reading and writing, attempts should be made to recognize and foster abilities that they have in athletics, the arts, or other areas. Although specialized word-learning techniques require one-on-one instruction, low-achieving readers can be part of a group or the whole class for other learning activities.

WORKING WITH OLDER PROBLEM READERS: TEENS AND ADULTS

Although this text stresses prevention and early intervention, it is never too late to teach someone to read and write. Having endured a childhood that was long on sharecropping but short on schooling, Ruby S. Williams was virtually illiterate as she passed into an adulthood that included working as a domestic and raising fourteen children (Sack, 1995). At the age of 84, motivated by a desire to read the Bible, she enrolled in a program that provided her with a tutor. Working several nights a week with a tutor for a period of a year, she reached her goal.

Assessing Older Learners

Older severely disabled readers can and do learn to read. In one study, disabled readers in grades 5 and 6 made just as much progress as disabled readers in grades 2, 3, and 4, and in some instances the older students made even more progress than their younger counterparts (Lovett & Steinbach, 1997).

Having had negative experiences with tests in the past, older students generally abhor tests. Assessment should be as informal and as limited as possible and might consist primarily of the administration of an informal reading inventory. In administering an informal reading inventory, use one such as the Classroom Reading Inventory (Silvaroli & Wheelock, 2001), or the Bader Reading and Language Inventory (Bader, 1998), both of which have forms designed for older students. An inventory such as the Reading Evaluation Adult Diagnosis (Colvin & Root, 2000), which was designed specifically for adults, can also be used. Or you might construct an inventory using the kinds of materials the learner might be expected to meet: a shopping list, a menu, a set of directions, selections that gradually increase in difficulty from a series of work manuals. Using this type of material will be far less threatening.

Because older problem readers generally are very sensitive about their difficulty, it is important that assessment and instruction sessions be nonthreatening and positive.

As you work with older problem readers, explain the purpose of any assessment device that you administer. Also inform them of the results in a positive, constructive way. Highlight strengths and any steps that might be taken to help them with their difficulty. Most important of all, focus on the older student's strengths. Build on the older learner's background of experience and any special skills that she or he may have developed.

Programs for Older Problem Readers

In general, the principles and procedures for teaching older problem readers are the same as those for teaching younger problem readers. However, it is doubly important that instruction be tied to the learner's goals. Find out from the student why she or he wishes to improve in reading and writing. For Mrs. Williams, it was the desire to read the Bible. For others it might be the desire to read to their children or to obtain a better job. For older students in school, it might be the desire to pass or to graduate. Or they may want to learn how to read the manual that prepares them for the state driver's license test. Students might bring to class the actual materials that they want to read: a newspaper article, a letter from a friend, a form for school or work, or a text from a content-area class. And you might help them with any literacy tasks that they wish to master: filling out a job application or writing a thank-you note.

Because older problem readers have probably been given an overdose of skill-and-drill material, start with an approach that is holistic and use materials that reflect real life:

If students are on a beginning reading level, you might build a high-frequency reading vocabulary or initial decoding skills by using easy functional-level materials, such as signs or food labels (Roswell & Chall, 1994).

signs, labels, menus, newspapers, magazines, novels, or stories on the appropriate level. Do not use children's picture books, easy readers from a basal series, or other materials that are demeaning to students. Trade books that might be used with older problem readers are listed in Appendix B. As you can see, there are lots of materials at second-grade level and up. However, there are few materials written below a second-grade level that would be suitable for older learners. If you are working with older beginning readers, you might want to try a language-experience approach.

Since language-experience stories are based on the reader's experiences, they match the reader's maturity level and should also be of interest to the learner. Topics chosen should reflect the needs and interests of the learner. They can be autobiographical or might be related to a hobby, the learner's work, or an interest the learner wishes to explore.

Middle school and high school problem readers may have difficulty with their high school texts. If possible, obtain easy-to-read texts. Another possibility is to use the Directed Listening-Thinking Activity (DL-TA) with their texts as explained in Chapter 12. The DL-TA has been used with good success by older students who have serious reading problems (Gillet & Temple, 1994). As noted in Chapter 12, most textbooks have been taped and are available free of charge from Recording for the Blind and Dyslexic for those students who have a documented difficulty with reading. Variable-speed tape recorders are available for purchase from this same source.

Girls and Boys Town Program.   Although it was created for underachieving adolescents who are residents of Girls and Boys Town, a facility that primarily serves troubled youths, the FAME reading program has been used successfully in public schools throughout the United States (Curtis & Longo, 1999). Students entering the program are typically reading two or three years below grade level, but some may be functioning five or more years below their grade placement. The average gain is close to two years for each year in the program. A developmental approach is used. Students are provided with instruction that matches the stage of reading they are in, and they are given materials that are on their instructional level. Instruction is based on a thorough assessment and continuous monitoring of progress. Depending on the student's stage of development, the following areas are emphasized: decoding, vocabulary, comprehension, and study skills. For students at an early stage of development, decoding skills are emphasized. For more advanced students, comprehension and study skills are stressed.

Using Technology
Girls and Boys Town can be accessed at http://www.girls andboystown.org/pros/training/education/FAME_program.asp. This web site provides added information about Reading for FAME.

Reading for FAME is available for purchase, but training is required.

Students are taught in small groups by well-trained teachers. The teachers employ a variety of effective instructional and management techniques. Students are active partners in their learning. Teachers discuss their reading problems with them, explain what they are teaching and why, and keep them informed about their progress on a regular basis. They also clearly explain what is expected of them.

The teachers stress the positive. Realizing that they are working with students who have a history of failure, teachers provide a structured environment where students know what is expected and are encouraged to take risks. Students know why they are in the program and what they will be able to do when they complete it. So that students know what to expect, a schedule of activities is placed on the board each day. Generally, three to five activities are planned for each class period. Students are willing to engage in difficult activities because they can see from the schedule that the activity won't last too long. Activities are often motivational and include games and working on the computer.

Commercial Materials

Commercial programs for older problem readers come in a variety of shapes and sizes. A sampling of reading programs that can be used with middle school and high school students is presented in Table 14.1. Programs designed for adults are listed in Table 14.2.

WORKING WITH BILINGUAL LEARNERS

Currently, there are more than five million elementary and secondary school students who are still learning English (Padolsky, 2004). Some of these students come to school speaking no English at all. Others have varying degrees of proficiency in English. The largest segment of these students speak Spanish as their home language. As a group, Latino

---

EXEMPLARY TEACHING
WORKING WITH STRUGGLING READERS ON THE SECONDARY LEVEL

Working with struggling readers on the secondary level, reading specialist Cynthia Fischer emphasizes affective as well as cognitive factors (Fischer, 1999–2000). After assessing below-level readers and noting the literacy process they use, she confers with them. They must show at least a minimum of motivation and commit to a five-day-a-week program. Because she complements her instruction with volunteer tutors, much of the instruction is one on one. Since students vary widely at the secondary level, instruction is tailored to their needs. In addition, the individual attention boosts their self-esteem. The program includes instruction in key strategies at the students' reading level. Content-area texts are used so that students can see an immediate payoff for their efforts. Since wide reading is a key element in any reading improvement program, students spend substantial amounts of time reading self-selected materials. Although Fischer has a library of materials for students, she keeps some money aside so she is able to acquire additional books or periodicals when there is nothing suitable for a particular student. For homework, students are required to read a book of their choosing and keep a running account in their notebook of plot and character development or main ideas.

In addition to content-area and self-selected reading, students read to kindergarten children once a week. During the week they practice with the book they plan to read aloud. Again, this provides valuable reading practice and also builds the struggling readers' self-concept.

Since the tutors help out only two days a week, Fischer works with groups of three or four students three days a week. During this time she introduces strategies that all need, conducts book shares, or provides writing opportunities. Students' writing is published in a newsletter. The newsletter also features such items as accounts of students reading to kindergarten children and suggestions for outside reading. The newsletter motivates students to write and also affirms their efforts.

Students gain an average of 2.2 years during the school year. And they also stay in school. Only about 1 percent of the students who take part in the program drop out.

TABLE 14.1   Literacy Programs for Secondary School Students

TITLE	PUBLISHER	INTEREST LEVEL	GRADE LEVEL	OVERVIEW
Contemporary Reader	Jamestown	7–12	2.5–5	Features informational selections and comprehension exercises.
Fast Track	McGraw-Hill	4–8	1–5+	Covers both decoding and comprehension.
High Point	Hampton Brown	6–12	1–8+	Includes decoding, comprehension, and oral and written language. Especially appropriate for ELL.
Focus on Reading	SRA	7–12	2.5–6.0	Fictional and informational selections, some by well-known writers. Comprehension and vocabulary exercises.
Great Series	Steck-Vaughn	6–12	2–4	Each text features great escapes or great rescues or other events. Comprehension and vocabulary exercises.
High Noon Reading	High Noon	3–12	1–4+	Features systematic instruction in decoding and comprehension.
Inroductory Word Detective Program for Grades 5 and Above	Benchmark School	5–12	2–4+	Designed to develop decoding skills of older struggling readrers.
Language!	Sopris West	1–12	1–9	Features decoding, comprehension, spelling, oral language, and writing.
Learning System 100	Harcourt	9–12	1–10	Includes decoding, comprehension, vocabulary, oral language, and writing. Computer-based program.
Reading 180	Scholastic	1–12	1–9	Features decoding, comprehension, vocabulary, written and oral English. Computer-based program.
Reading Advantage	Great Advantage	5–10	2–6	Features comprehensive vocabulary and word study.
Reading Skills for Life	American Guidance Service	6–12	1–6	Includes worktexts, easy readers (at lower levels) and extra practice activities on CD-ROM.
Reading XL	Scholastic	6–10	4–9	Includes reading of trade books as well as anthologies.
Soar to Success	Houghton Mifflin	6–8		Features cooperative groups, reading of trade books, and teaching of comprehension strategies.

TABLE 14.2 Literacy Programs for Adults

NAME OF PROGRAM	PUBLISHER	LEVELS	OVERVIEW
Challenger	New Readers Press	1–8	Focuses on building reading vocabulary and comprehension. Book 1 provides a compressed overview of basic decoding. Also has a writing series.
Directions	Steck-Vaughn	2–6	Four-book series builds comprehension and vocabulary.
Laubach Way to Reading	New Readers Press	1–4	Uses a strong phonics approach and a variety of materials.
Reading for Today	Steck-Vaughn	1–6	Features fiction, informational pieces, and life-coping skills for adults. Includes decoding, comprehension, and writing.
Voyager	New Readers Press	1–8	Includes decoding, comprehension, and writing designed for adults.

students read significantly below average and have a higher dropout rate (Williams, Reese, Campbell, Mazzelo, & Phillips, 1995). Techniques recommended throughout this text should be effective when working with English learners. However, special provision must be made for language and cultural variations. A program for English learners should emphasize the building of English language skills, especially **academic language.** If at all possible, initial reading instruction should be in the student's native language. Students who are literate in their native language can transfer these skills to reading English once they learn English. A firm foundation in their native language enables students to learn a second language (Ramirez, 1992). Learning to read builds upon students' vocabulary, ability to manipulate language, familiarity with rhyme and alliteration, and awareness of environmental print. In addition, students use their knowledge of language to help them decode difficult words and to self-correct. Students with limited command of English lack these resources for learning to read in English. As the Committee on Preventing Reading Difficulties in Young Children (Snow, Burns, & Griffin, 1998) concluded:

> **Academic language:** words used to label key concepts in the content areas and also abstract words commonly used in instruction.

> It is clear that initial reading instruction in the first language does no harm, and it seems likely from research findings and from theories about literacy development that initial reading instruction in the second language can have negative consequences for immediate and long-term achievement. The conclusion leads us to urge initial literacy instruction in a child's native language whenever possible and to suggest that literacy instruction should not be introduced in any language before some reasonable level of oral proficiency in that language has been obtained. (p. 238)

As students acquire English, they first learn everyday conversational skills. Conversational English is contextualized and supported by such nonverbal aids as gestures, pointing to objects as you talk about them, and pantomiming. On average, it takes about two years for students to become relatively proficient in everyday English. However, being decontextualized and more abstract, the language of school, in which procedures and concepts are explained, may take five or more years to acquire (Cummins, 1994). When teaching English learners, make sure that they understand the language of instruction. Depending on the level and topic being covered, carefully explain such terms as *sounds, letters, beginning, ending, consonant, vowel, title, author, illustrations, setting, characters, main idea, conclusion, summarize, planning, revising,* and *editing,* and use them consistently. Interchanging the terms *artist* and *illustrator,* for instance, could be confusing. Avoid figurative language and idioms: *beat around the bush, has a big heart, turn over a new leaf* (Gersten & Jiménez, 1994). Use demonstrations, illustrations, or real objects whenever possible. When introducing the correspondence *b* = /b/, for instance, show a button, ball, and bag or pictures of these objects as you talk about words that begin with /b/.

When working with English learners, stress content rather than form. When acquiring a language, content is learned first and then is followed by form. Olivares (1993) suggests:

> When asking students to answer questions or give explanations orally, teachers should attend to what students are saying rather than to how they are saying it. Interrupting the message to correct a language error will discourage students from participating and remove the focus from how well they are mastering the content. (p. 44)

Also provide prompts that encourage students to clarify or expand responses. Make comments such as, "That's interesting. I'd like to hear more about that. Can you explain that? Can you tell us more? So what happened next?"

Special Comprehension Strategies for Bilingual Readers

For bilingual students, reading and comprehending in their weaker or nondominant language is more difficult. Fortunately, successful bilingual readers do use a repertoire of strategies to aid them. One of the major obstacles is vocabulary. If they have recently learned to speak English, chances are that they will encounter a greater number of unknown words than will their same-age English-speaking counterparts. One strategy that students can use is to seek out cognates. A Spanish-speaking student who does not recognize the word *carnivorous,* searches her vocabulary and notes that it is similar to the Spanish word *carnivoro* (Jiménez, García, & Pearson 1995). Another strength that bilingual students may possesses is that they are more metacognitively aware. Learning a second language has provided them with greater insights into language on an abstract level. They also use their native language as a source of help by activating prior knowledge in both languages and by translating when encountering a difficult passage, especially when they are in the earlier stages of learning English. Transferring prior knowledge, translating passages into their native language, and reflecting on text in their native or stronger language has the potential for improving comprehension (Jiménez, 1997).

Even though English learners may have a rich background of knowledge, the background may not match the background required for the reading of a particular selection. For instance, they may come from a culture where parents, teachers, and other authority figures are treated more formally and so they may have difficulty comprehending a selection such as *Help I'm Trapped in My Teacher's Body* (Strasser, 1993), in which student–teacher relationships are more casual.

Selecting Materials

Just as when selecting texts for native speakers of English, choose books and other materials that are on the English learners' reading and interest levels. However, also seek books that have illustrations that support the text and that use straightforward, predictable language. Carefully chosen materials can foster language development. For instance, books with repetitive patterns such as *Brown Bear, Brown Bear, What Do You See?* (Martin, 1983) can provide practice with two basic sentence patterns, the question and the statement. English learners can model a discussion or a piece of writing on the patterns found in *Brown Bear.* However, be sure to seek out materials that are culturally relevant. Books that contain expressions in the students' native language are especially desirable. Bilingual students find the use of their native language reassuring, even just occasional use (Jiménez, 1997). A number of books are written primarily in English but include some Spanish expressions. One simply written picture book, *Subway Sparrow* (Torres, 1993), which tells about a bird trapped on a subway car, includes text in English, Spanish, and Polish, thus providing an excellent opportunity for interaction among youngsters from three linguistic communities. Some books that contain a significant number of words or expressions in Spanish include:

> Geeslin, C. (1998). *On Ramon's farm.* New York: Atheneum.
> Gershator, D., & Gershator, P. (1995). *Bread is for eating.* New York: Holt.
> Soto, G. (1998). *Big bushy mustache.* New York: Knopf.
> Soto, G.(1987). *Cat's meow.* New York: Scholastic.
> Winther, B. (1998). *Plays from Hispanic tales.* Boston: Plays.
> Zamorano, A. (1997). *Let's eat.* New York: Scholastic.

Using Technology
The Official Gary Soto web site (http://www.garysoto.com/) lists a number of books that have Spanish expressions.

If students can read in another language, they should be urged to continue reading materials in that language.

Some English learners have essential concepts that they are unable to express in English because they lack the English words that label these concepts. For instance, on the beginning reading level, counting books and books that name colors may help English learners learn the names of numbers or colors in English. There are also concept books that provide the names of farm animals (*Big Red Barn,* Brown, 1989), farm implements (*Tractor,* Brown, 1995), vegetables (*Growing Vegetable Soup,* Ehlert, 1987), tools (*Tools,* Morris, 1992a) and many other items.

Reading real-world materials, such as signs, menus, advertisements, announcements, phone books, and job applications, should be an integral part of the program. The youngest students need to know how to decipher common signs such as *in, out, open, up, down, closed, men, women, exit, emergency exit, office, nurse.* Older students need to know how to read and fill out job applications.

Although voluntary reading is widely advocated for providing opportunities to apply skills, wide reading also builds listening and speaking skills in a second language. When provided with classroom libraries of interesting books, middle-grade students in Fijian schools showed impressive gains in reading and oral language skills (Elley & Mangubhai, 1983).

Adapting Instruction

Krashen (1996) recommends voluntary reading of easy books to build vocabulary and the ability to handle complex grammatical constructions. Cho and Krashen (1994) cite the case of Karen, an adult English learner who, as a result of reading an easy series of books, gained five years in reading ability, going from a second- to a seventh-grade level.

English learners who are experiencing difficulty with literacy should be taught to read and write in their first language. Learning to read and write in one's native language is far easier, and the skill of reading and writing in one language transfers to other languages (Filmore & Valdez, 1986). Learning to read in a second language, of course, makes greater demands on a student. In addition to learning decoding and comprehension skills and strategies, students must also deal with unfamiliar words and sentence structures (Chamot & O'Malley, 1994). Before presenting a selection, you may want to analyze the text for sources of possible difficulty and confusion. Some possible problem areas include the following.

Syntax. Does the selection contain sentence structures such as passives or contractions with which the student might have difficulty?

Semantics. Does the selection use terms, figures of speech, or idiomatic expressions that might pose problems for the English language learner (ELL)?

Culture. Are there cultural items, such as might appear in a story about foods or sports, that might be unfamiliar to the ELL reader?

Krashen (1996) advocates comprehensible input for developing English. This includes learning language in classes, in informal conversations, through voluntary reading, and through sheltered English.

To foster both reading and oral language skills, allow lots of time to discuss stories. Also establish an accepting atmosphere and use prompts. Students may have ideas that they wish to contribute but may have difficulty formulating them. Also paraphrase responses and encourage students to expand upon them (Gersten & Jiménez, 1994). For instance, if a student answers, "Because he was afraid" to the question, "Why did the little boy hide?" You might rephrase that as, "Yes, the little boy hid because he was afraid." To expand the response, you might ask such questions as: "Where did the little boy hide? What was he afraid of? What are some things that make you afraid?"

Sometimes teachers misinterpret students' lack of fluency in English as reflecting a low level of knowledge or ability. It is important that literacy programs for English learners foster higher-order cognitive processes, lead to higher levels of student involvement, and enable students to engage in extended discourse (Gersten & Jiménez, 1994).

Although many formal tests are available for assessing students' language proficiency, observing students as they converse with friends and respond to discussions in class will provide some sense of their grasp of language. However, it is important that you observe them in several situations. Students might talk more freely in informal situations but might be more inclined to use academic language when responding in class. The listening-capacity test of an informal reading inventory can be used as a rough gauge of students' ability to understand language. The highest level at which students can answer 75 percent of the questions is the approximate level at which they can understand English and the level at which they should be able to read with understanding if they have adequate decoding skills (Crawford, 1982).

MINICASE STUDY

When he was accepted for instruction at the Fernald School (a special school for students with severe reading problems) of the University of California at Los Angeles, fourteen-year-old John was described as being "defeated, troubled, and angry" (Berres & Eyer, 1970). A behavior problem since kindergarten, John howled like a wolf and rolled on the floor when asked to sit in the back of the room because of his distracting behavior.

Despite having average intelligence, John was reading on a first-grade level. Not surprisingly, he avoided academic tasks, and when the teacher offered him a book he "broke out into a cold sweat" (p. 34).

The first order of business was to deal with John's perception of himself. John had to learn to see himself as a capable student and act like a learner. Because John was hyperactive, he was given tasks of brief duration, was allowed to choose activities, and was encouraged to run around the school track or spar with a punching bag whenever his excess energy seemed too much to handle.

Instruction capitalized on John's main interest. He wanted to be a plumber and often helped his father, who was a plumber. Plumbing supply catalogs, invoices, and sales slips were used to foster John's literacy skills.

Because of John's severe word-learning difficulty, the Fernald (VAKT) tracing technique was used with him. This was tied into his interest in plumbing. The first word that John learned was *tools*. He planned to use the word to fill out an order blank.

Because of the novelty of the Fernald technique and because it was helping him learn words that he wanted to write, John responded favorably to the approach. John remained in Stage 1 for seven months. During that period he built up enough reading vocabulary that he was able to begin reading easy books. John enjoyed high-interest, low-readability books because they didn't seem "babyish."

In John's second year, he expressed a desire to read Edgar Allan Poe's tales of horror. Given extra help by the teacher, John did surprisingly well with a collection of Poe's stories. As John experienced success, his inappropriate behavior faded away. After three years at the Fernald School, John was reading at an eighth-grade level. He had gained the literacy skills and confidence he needed to attend high school.

SUMMARY

About one student in 100 has a serious word-learning problem and may need to be taught through specialized word-learning techniques. Two of the best known and most widely used word learning techniques are VAKT (Fernald) and Orton–Gilligham.

VAKT, which is based on the Fernald tracing technique, advocates using visual, auditory, kinesthetic, and tactile senses to learn words. Using these four senses may forge connections that will help the student remember new words. VAKT also fosters fuller attention and concentration and builds confidence. Classical VAKT can be adapted to strengthen phonological processing and to make it easier to implement.

The Orton–Gillingham approach is a highly structured, intensive phonics method that makes use of a form of tracing known as S.O.S. (Simultaneous Oral Spelling), in which students name the letters as they write words. A number of programs are based on the Orton–Gillingham approach. Some involve having students say the individual sounds of words as they trace the words.

Specialized word-learning techniques should be presented within the context of a total program. Wide reading of appropriate-level texts and writing are highly recommended. Word Building, adapted if necessary, can also be used with students who have serious word-learning problems.

With their history of failure, older poor readers and writers may feel too discouraged to try. Help them see that they are competent learners. Build on their strengths and construct a program that addresses their needs but uses appropriate materials and ties in with their personal goals.

Problem readers and writers who are still acquiring English face the double burden of acquiring a second language and overcoming their literacy difficulties. If possible, they should be taught to read and write in their native language. Acquisition of reading and writing in English is far easier if the students can read and write in their own language. Oral language and reading and writing skills are best acquired in the context of learning content. The language-experience approach and cooperative learning are especially appropriate for students who are still acquiring English.

APPLICATION ACTIVITIES

1. Read Fernald's (1943) classic text, *Remedial Techniques in Basic School Subjects* (New York: Macmillan), or the annotated version published by Pro-Ed (Idol, 1988). What kinds of suggestions did Fernald make that are still valid today?

2. If possible, observe the use of Fernald (VAKT), the Orton–Gillingham, or a program based on the Orton–Gillingham approach. How did the student respond to the program? What are the strengths of the program? What might be its weaknesses?

3. With a partner, try out the tracing component of VAKT. Follow the steps exactly and make sure you have the proper equipment: a dictionary, stapler, large black crayon, and slips of 4-inch × 12-inch paper.

4. Try out Word Building in its adapted form, if necessary, with a student who has a serious word-learning problem. How does the student respond to the techniques? What are the strengths and weaknesses of the program?

5. Read "Teaching Older Readers How to Read," by J. Horowitz (*The Reading Teacher, 54,* 24–26, 2000). What suggestions does Horowitz have for teaching older nonreaders?

CHAPTER FIFTEEN

ORGANIZATION OF EARLY INTERVENTION AND CORRECTIVE PROGRAMS

USING WHAT YOU KNOW

Corrective instruction is changing. From an isolated skills emphasis in a resource room, instruction is becoming more balanced and more collaborative. There is greater coordination between the corrective specialist and the classroom teacher and, increasingly, corrective instruction is taking place in the classroom. In addition, corrective programs typically include writing as well as reading.

With what corrective reading or writing programs are you familiar? What are the components of the program? How effective is the program? What do you think should be the components of an exemplary corrective program?

ANTICIPATION GUIDE

Read each of the following statements. Put a check under "Agree" or "Disagree" to show how you feel about each one. If possible, discuss your responses with classmates.

	AGREE	DISAGREE
1. Corrective instruction has been proven to be effective.	_____	_____
2. Except for the most severe cases, the classroom teacher should have major responsibility for the instruction of her or his pupils.	_____	_____
3. Small-group corrective instruction is more practical than one-on-one teaching.	_____	_____
4. Students in the earliest grades should be given the highest priority for corrective instruction.	_____	_____
5. Although top-down approaches might work well with achieving students, corrective students need a skills approach.	_____	_____

524

THE CHANGING FACE OF INTERVENTION

Given the requirements of (NCLB), the nature of corrective instruction is changing. Since the goal of NCLB is that all students will meet proficiency standards in reading, there is a growing effort to help struggling readers. Although there has been an emphasis on early intervention, there has also been a widespread increase in intervention at the upper elementary and secondary levels. There is also a growing realization that meeting the goals of NCLB will take an all-out effort by the school, parents, and the community at large. Early results indicate that NCLB has resulted in getting additional help for groups of students who have been left behind but that include a disproportionate number of struggling readers and writers: poor children, minority children, and students with disabilities. There is evidence that these groups are doing better (Jennings, 2003, 2004).

Emphasis on Prevention

Currently there is a demand for effective research-based literacy programs so that problems can be prevented. Today's literacy programs incorporate differentiated instruction. Literacy programs contain instructional suggestions and materials for struggling readers as well as for achieving readers and for ELL students.

Today emphasis is on prevention of difficulties and early intervention based on predictive assessments. If students do fall behind, assistance is being provided in a more timely fashion. There is also a focus on accelerating the progress of students who are behind. Torgesen (2004c) recommends a layered approach to intervention in which there are three tiers. Each tier provides more intensive instruction. The aim of Tier I is to prevent difficulties. It consists of a well-planned program of literacy instruction that lasts for at least 90 minutes a day. Tier II, which is designed for students who start to fall behind, consists of small-group intensive instruction. It is in addition to the main program and supplants and supports it for an added 30 minutes a day. Progress is monitored at least once a week. Tier III is designed for students who have not responded to Tier I and Tier II. Since they haven't responded to Tier 1 or Tier II, they should be given a diagnostic assessment. A program based on that assessment should be implemented. They might need instruction that is more structured or which provides more reinforcement. If their learning difficulty is serious enough, they might need one-on-one instruction and might need an approach such as VAKT.

Allington (1994) stresses the need for enhancement of classroom instruction. "The primary role of special program funds and personnel would be to enhance the quality of classroom literacy instruction available to children finding learning to read and write difficult" (p. 25).

A Better Classroom Program

Actually, the best way to attack the problem of reading and writing deficiency is to create a highly effective program for the whole school. This will minimize the number of students who need extra help. And it will also build the skills of the students who have been remediated.

If students are placed in a special program, that program should be coordinated with the classroom program. The intervention teacher may use intensive phonics, VAKT (Fernald), or some other specialized technique. Through discussions and careful planning, the specialist and classroom teacher can create programs that are mutually supportive. For instance, classroom teachers may schedule extra reading of books that contain short vowels because that is being taught in the corrective program. On the other hand, if the classroom teacher is presenting short vowels, the corrective teacher may provide complementary instruction, perhaps through Word Building. Both should agree, too, on which strategies the student will use to attack new words and in what order these strategies should be applied: pronounceable word part, analogy, and context, for instance. They may decide to have the student seek out pronounceable word parts and reconstruct the word by building on those or use an analogy strategy.

Collaboration

Collaboration entails having classroom teachers and resource personnel work together. Collaboration may be between the teacher and the specialist, and also between specialists from different disciplines.

Collaboration is the key to providing the best possible program for low-achieving readers and writers. In a **collaboration,** the reading specialist works with the student's teacher(s), other specialists and administrators, parents, and the student to plan, implement, and monitor a program. Collaboration is especially important in reading and writing instruction. The classroom teacher should be involved in every phase of the program, from assessment through instruction. During assessment it is essential to obtain information about the student from the teacher. The teacher can shed light on the students' work habits, ability to get along with others, and strengths and weaknesses in a variety of academic areas, not just reading and writing. Specialists working with the classroom teacher should decide on the best program for the student.

Increasingly, specialists are functioning as coaches to help classroom teachers improve their programs so that literacy problems will be prevented or ameliorated in the classroom.

Organizing to Assist Struggling Readers and Writers

The role of the literacy specialist is changing, from a corrective teacher whose mission is to work with students with severe reading problems, to a consultant involved with all aspects of the literacy program.

Helping all the struggling readers who need it requires making optimum use of time and resources and calls for the full efforts of the school staff and the wholehearted cooperation of parents and the community at large. A first step toward bringing everyone together is to set up a literacy committee. In addition to setting up a core program, there should be intervention programs for those who fail to make adequate progress. Insofar as struggling readers are concerned, the committee sets up guidelines for intervening, guidelines for diagnosis, guidelines for monitoring students' progress, and guidelines for professional development. The committee, in consultation with literacy and learning specialists, would also decide on intervention programs and materials. Perhaps, most important of all, the committee would evaluate the effectiveness of the program and, based on student data, recommend changes.

Grade-Level Meetings.   Increasingly, teachers are working together to help struggling readers and writers. One device that fosters teacher-to-teacher collaboration is grade-level meetings, which should be held once a week or once every two weeks. At these meetings,

■ ■ ■ ■ ■ ▬▬▬▬▬▬▬▬▬

EXEMPLARY TEACHING
COLLABORATION AND COORDINATION

Programs for struggling readers are most effective when they are coordinated with the classroom program. Although pleased with the progress of the majority of her students, first-grade teacher Dodie McGill always felt a bit frustrated at the end of each school year. There were always a handful of students who still had not made what she felt was adequate progress. When she noticed the gains made by students in Reading Recovery, which had just been implemented in her school, Partee Elementary School in Gwinnett County, Georgia, she and the other first-grade teachers began to discuss with the Reading Recovery teachers how instruction might be improved for all students.

Adopting the name Reading Express, the group created a collaborative structure that would benefit all students. For one hour each day, the Reading Recovery teacher met with a whole first-grade class. During that time the Reading Recovery teacher taught and modeled key strategies. That way both teachers and student learned the strate-

gies. The teacher also demonstrated a book introduction, guided reading, and taking and using running records. Classroom teachers were able to adapt successful Reading Recovery techniques and use them in their classrooms.

As a result of the collaboration, first-grade teachers achieved a better understanding of their students' literacy development and were able to improve the quality and effectiveness of their program. Because first-grade teachers were now using, in adapted form, many of the techniques used in Reading Recovery, there was a greater continuity between the Reading Recovery and the classroom program. As a result, students were better able to extend the gains they made in Reading Recovery. And students who were not chosen for Reading Recovery but were still a bit behind had the benefit of more effective instruction and better materials. As a result, the first-graders' reading achievement rose dramatically (Kinnucan-Welsch, Magill, & Dean, 1999).

the focus should be on student achievement. For teachers, grade-level meetings provide an excellent opportunity to discuss underachieving students and elicit suggestions from peers for assisting them. Inviting the literacy and learning disabilities teacher and other specialists fosters collaboration. If the literacy and learning disabilities specialist attend, they could provide their expert advice.

Study Groups.   Study groups might meet once a month or more often, if they also wish to foster collaboration as teachers learn together. In a study group, participants choose a topic to investigate and then seek out information through reading professional books or journals, attending conferences, or inviting experts to provide presentations.

Review Conferences.   In review conferences, teachers and administrators collaborate. Each classroom teacher meets with the principal and specialists to review students' progress. The group examines formal test data, progress monitoring results, and informal assessment data; it might also look at portfolios. Suggestions are made for students who aren't making adequate progress and also for ways that the classroom program might be improved.

COMPONENTS OF AN INTERVENTION PROGRAM

Goal: general statement of what students are expected to learn. One source of goals/ objectives is the English Language Arts Standards (International Reading Association and National Council of Teachers of English, 1996).

Although the corrective program should be an integral part of the regular program, it should also have certain key elements. These elements are explored in the following section.

Goals

A clear statement of **goals** is the first step in creating an effective program. A statement of philosophy is also helpful. From the statement of general goals should flow specific **objectives.** Successful programs have overall goals and specific objectives, and concrete ways of determining whether goals and objectives have been met. As a practical matter, the goals of a corrective program are often tied, at least in part, to the state's or local school district's standards. This is especially true if the attainment of these standards is assessed by high-stakes tests.

Objective: specific statement of what students are expected to learn. Instructional objectives should be stated in terms that students can understand.

Selecting Students

A major practical concern of intervention programs is selecting pupils who need special help and scheduling instruction. A basic principle of selection is to choose those students who have the greatest need. In some circumstances, laws and regulations govern the selection process. Students are chosen for a learning disabilities (LD) class on the basis of discrepancy guidelines and/or failure to respond to intervention. In the past, students falling below a certain cutoff-point—the twenty-third percentile of a standardized reading test, for example—were chosen for Title I programs. Current Title I regulations call for using assessment measures that are aligned with standards established by the states. Under this plan, students who fail to meet criteria set by the state are selected for Title I programs. Reading Recovery and a number of other early intervention programs simply select the lowest-achieving students. This might be the lowest-achieving 20 percent or the neediest three students in a class. The response to intervention approach to assessment is cutting down on the number of students recommended for special education placement and is securing instructional help sooner for struggling readers (Torgesen, 2004d). However, the intervention programs vary in effectiveness so that response to intervention is somewhat subjective. As a practical matter, it helps to consider all three factors: discrepancy, low achievement, and response to intervention.

Because of the fallibility of tests and other assessment instruments, it is wise to use more than one selection device.

Take care when interpreting measures used with students who have not had an equal opportunity to learn. As McGill-Franzen (1994) notes, the role of prior knowledge or experience on assessment devices is "often grossly underrated" (p. 19).

Screening Devices.   Numerous assessment devices can be used to select students for a program. The selection devices chosen will depend on the goals of the program, the philosophy of reading, and the corrective or intervention procedures. A program that emphasizes letter–sound relationships will probably include a measure of phonics. One that includes writing will probably assess writing.

Group tests, whether norm-referenced or criterion-referenced, might be used as a screening device to identify students who may need intervention or a corrective program. They should not be used as the sole selection device, however. Group tests, because of the guessing factor, can provide erroneous information for individuals. Portfolios, observations, and individual tests, together with recommendations by professionals, should also be used in the selection process.

Curriculum

The corrective strand of the program should be coordinated with the school's language arts curriculum. The program, however, should be based on evidence that it is effective and that it follows evidence-based principles.

The curriculum for a corrective program should reflect the school's philosophy of reading, goals or standards, the nature of the program, and the students' needs. The curriculum should also be balanced and mesh with what is being done in the classroom. Although the specific needs of the student or group should be addressed, the program should not be too narrow. For instance, if a child has difficulty with word identification, there should be an emphasis on word-level skills and strategies. However, these need to be applied within the context of real reading, lest you create a competent decoder who fails to read for meaning or dislikes reading. Too broad a program, on the other hand, might result in one that is unfocused and so is ineffective.

Instructional Approaches

The core of an intervention or corrective program is the instructional approach. The program planner has many decisions to make. Will the program use direct instruction? Will it use holistic approaches? Or will it use some type of combination of the two? Will there be an emphasis on application of skills and strategies? Will voluntary reading be fostered? Will specialized word-learning techniques, such as VAKT, be used with students who have severe reading problems? Will process writing be part of the program? Will a highly structured writing approach, such as CSIW, be used? The instructional activities should fit in with the philosophy and overall goals of the program. Above all, the instructional components should also consider the strengths and needs of the students.

Instructional Schedule

The number of sessions will vary depending upon the severity of the difficulty.

Scheduling students for fewer than two sessions a week is probably not worthwhile. There would be a lack of continuity and too much forgetting because of the lapse of time between sessions. Five sessions a week is ideal, but may be impractical if there are a large number of students who need help.

For a program to make a difference, a significant amount of time is needed. Based on an analysis of a number of studies, Guthrie, Seifert, and Kline (1978) concluded that a minimum of fifty hours of corrective instruction is required for sustained gains. In the Boulder Project (Hiebert, 1994) and Early Intervention in Reading (Taylor, Strait, & Medo, 1994), two corrective programs for at-risk first-graders, many students needed a full year before showing adequate progress, and about one in four needed a second year of extra help.

Typical Corrective Session

Strategies taught through corrective instruction should be those the student can apply in his regular classroom.

Time is limited in a corrective class, so it is important for sessions to be well planned and energetic. The typical session lasts from thirty to fifty minutes and might include three to seven students. The greater the need of the students, the smaller the group should be. A daily session might include review of past material, introduction or extension of a skill or strategy, reading of a new selection, discussion and extension of the selection, and writing, if time allows. There might also be time for reading of a selection by the teacher or an activity chosen by the student.

Discontinuing Students

After students have been discontinued, meet with them periodically to make sure that they are having success and are able to apply strategies they learned.

According to Harris and Sipay (1990), one practice that can negate the effects of a corrective reading program is setting arbitrary time limits for corrective instruction, with the result that students are discontinued from the program too soon. Harris and Sipay (1990) suggest using two criteria to determine if students are ready to be discontinued: Is the student able to meet the reading demands of the regular classroom? Does the student read voluntarily? If the reading demands of the classroom are too great, the student may be overwhelmed unless he is given extra help. If the student does not read on her own, improvement may cease. After students have been discontinued, they should be given follow-up support.

Organizational Patterns

How should low-achieving readers be organized for instruction? One-on-one teaching? Small group? Whole class with supplementary instruction? The organizational pattern to be followed depends on the nature of the student's difficulty, the resources available, and the policies and philosophy of the local school district.

The question of how many is too many in a corrective group depends on the severity of the students' difficulties. The greater the needs, the smaller the group should be.

One-on-One and Small-Group Instruction.   As can be seen from the dramatic results achieved by Reading Recovery, one-to-one tutoring by expert teachers provides the most effective instruction. While one-on-one instruction works best for the neediest students, it is not always possible to supply because of resource limitations. The next best organization pattern is the small group. In one study, Title I professionals teaching small groups found three to be a workable number. In a review of studies of successful corrective programs, Guthrie, Seifert, and Kline (1978) found that the ratio of students to teacher was no higher than four to one. Apparently as ratios grow higher, the teacher's efforts are stretched too thin. Based on the research, then, three to four seems to be the optimum number for small group instruction.

Small Groups versus Whole Class Instruction

Struggling readers do better when taught in small groups and when they are grouped according to common needs (National Reading Panel, 2000; Juel & Minden-Cupp, 2000;

Foorman & Torgesesen, 2001). In small groups students' needs can be met more easily, they have opportunity to respond, and the teacher is better able to assess their progress and adjust instruction accordingly.

Guided Reading. One way of providing small-group instruction is through guided reading. Guided reading is a framework within which the teacher supplies whatever assistance or guidance students need in order for them to read successfully (Fountas & Pinnell, 1996). Guided reading is used with individuals or groups who are on approximately the same level of reading development. Selections are provided that match the students' level of development. The amount of guidance provided varies depending on the students' abilities and the complexity of the selection to be read. For beginning readers, the guidance might consist of going through the text page by page and discussing the selection and highlighting unfamiliar expressions, unknown concepts, and difficult words. Although designed for all students, guided reading is a way of ensuring that struggling readers are given materials and instruction that is on their level.

Joplin Plan Grouping. The more groups the teacher has, the less time there is to spend with each group. One way of reducing the number of groups is to use the Joplin plan. In this plan, which is used in Success for All, students are redistributed for reading instruction according to their reading levels. One teacher may take the lowest-level readers, another the second-lowest, and so on. Special education teachers, the reading specialist, and other resource personnel might also work with groups. This reduces the overall group size. The reading specialist, special education teachers, and others who have special expertise in reading might be assigned the most disabled readers.

Reading workshop: students choose their own books, respond to their reading in a dialog journal, and meet individually or in groups with the teacher to discuss their reading.

Reading Workshop. In a **reading workshop,** which is a form of individualized reading, students choose their own books and read at their own pace. Using dialog journals, the students respond to their reading and carry on a written conversation about their reading with their teacher (Atwell, 1987). Conferences may be held to discuss books, monitor students' progress, and provide on-the-spot instruction if needed. If individual conferences are too time-consuming, then group conferences can be held. During conferences, the teacher notes common needs and at the appropriate time provides whole-class instruction if the entire class seems to need the skill. Or the teacher assembles an ad-hoc group composed of those students who apparently need instruction in the skill. Reading workshop is an excellent way of providing low-achieving readers with appropriate level materials and personalized instruction. Individualized and small-group instruction works especially well when an inclusion model is being implemented and several professionals are working in the classroom simultaneously.

Catching Up

Summer can be an excellent time for struggling readers to catch up. All too often, however, struggling readers, because reading is difficult, don't read over the long summer months and fail to maintain the gains they made during the school year. Summer school programs

For primary grade students Torgesen (2004c) recommends an additional 30 to 60 minutes a day of instruction for students who have fallen behind.

that are well planned, have small classes, good teachers, conscientious evaluation, and parental involvement are especially effective (Cooper, Nye, Kelly, & Greathouse, 1996). Saturday, before-school, and after-school programs are also good bets for providing additional instruction.

Retention

The annual retention rate in the nation's schools has hit 15 percent (National Association of School Psychologists, 2003). It is estimated that 30 percent or more of students are retained at least once before ninth grade. Despite the widespread use of retention, it is not an effective tool for closing the gap and, in fact, contributes to it. Although students who have been retained may do somewhat better, those gains fade after two or three years. Underachieving students who have been promoted do just as well as comparable underachieving students who have been held back. Moreover, students who have been retained are more likely to have social and emotional problems and to drop out of school. In fact, retention is the best predictor of future dropout.

Need for an Extended Program

Although prevention is preferable to remediation, there is a need for specialized reading and writing instruction throughout all the grades. Moreover, as students pass through the grades and the demands of reading change, different types of reading or writing difficulties may surface. The student who had a word-identification problem that was successfully remediated in grade 1 may evidence a comprehension difficulty in grade 3 or 4 when the comprehension of informational text of a more technical nature is required. In addition, students whose reading and writing abilities were adequate in the elementary grades may encounter difficulties in secondary school. The corrective reading/writing program must be a multifaceted one so that it can meet a variety of demands.

Pacing

Pacing: rate at which instruction is provided, and the rate at which students are guided through materials. Ironically, students most in need of an accelerated pace are often the ones who are provided with a slower-moving program in which expectations are set low (McGill-Franzen, 1994).

Pacing is crucial in a program of remediation. **Pacing** is the rate at which students are introduced to new learning and move through materials. The ideal is to accelerate students' progress so that they can catch up with their classmates and so profit from instruction in the regular program. Having caught up, they should not need corrective services, except perhaps for some follow-up or short-term intervention from time to time. Energized teaching, careful sequencing of tasks, not wasting time on activities that have little or no payoff, and promoting independence so that students can extend their learning promote accelerated progress. Involving parents and emphasizing out-of-school reading helps, too (Goldenberg, 1994).

Accelerated pacing does not mean pushing children beyond their limits or exerting undue pressure. Students' progress should be monitored to make sure that the pace is appropriate.

Monitoring

> Struggling readers should probably be monitored with an IRI, running record, or similar device at least once a month.

A key element in successful programs is monitoring of progress. In addition to the use of ongoing monitoring devices, Success for All conducts more formal assessments every eight weeks. Using measures designed specifically for the program, assessments are used to determine who needs tutoring, to change reading groups, to indicate needed changes in programs, and to determine other needs, such as the need for a hearing check or family intervention. The essential ingredient in a monitoring program is making changes when they are needed.

Involving Parents

> Parents of low-achieving readers should be involved in every step of the process. They can supply information about the student's strengths and needs that otherwise might not be revealed to the school.

Parents need to know the nature of their child's difficulty. It is helpful if they are informed that many bright children have reading difficulties. There should be an ongoing dialog between the parents and the school to inform the parents of the student's progress, enlist the parents' help, and answer questions. If, because of illness, death, divorce, neglect, or some other difficulty, it is not possible to involve parents, then the substitute caregiver or a willing relative should be involved (Comer, 1988).

Working with a disabled reader can be slow and intense and sometimes frustrating. These students may need a great deal of repetition and often show no sign today of what they seemed to know yesterday. Progress can be painstakingly slow. Lacking training and objectivity, parents may not be well equipped to teach their children. However, they can help in other essential ways. First, they can provide love and support and see to it that the child comes to school well rested, fed, and with all the necessary equipment. They can also supply encouragement. Knowing that their youngster, who had a serious word-learning problem, would have difficulty in school, the parents of one reading-disabled youngster played up his strengths. They enrolled him in arts and crafts and sports activities—areas in which he showed ability—so that he could experience success. An easy-to-implement but highly effective technique that parents might use to help their children is paired reading, which is explained in Chapter 7.

Family Literacy

> **Family literacy:** all the types of reading and writing in which a family engages, as well as attempts to foster increased ability in reading and writing within the family.

One special way of working with parents who have problems with reading and writing is by helping them with their own literacy difficulties so they can better help their children. Parents who are not proficient readers and writers may not realize the essential role they play in the literacy development of their children and so may fail to support their children's literacy learning efforts.

A **family literacy** program can take many forms. Parents and children may attend sessions held after school or during the summer. The parents and children may be given separate programs, or the program might be coordinated in such a way that the parents spend some of the time working directly with their children. In other versions, just the parents attend sessions, but they are taught reading and writing skills, which they pass on to their children. Now able to read on a basic level, parents are then able to read storybooks to their children or help out with homework. In a third version, parents are taught ways to foster their children's reading and writing skills by reading to them, talking with them, or supervising homework. As they learn ways to help their children, their own literacy skills improve.

Parents may need extensive guidance in the use of techniques to help foster their children's literacy development. For instance, while working with parents from diverse cultures, Paratore (1995) found that it was not enough to provide parents with storybooks and demonstrations on how to read to children. The parents needed many opportunities to observe read-aloud sessions as well as opportunities to practice reading aloud and discuss their read-aloud sessions.

Leadership

An effective program of remediation and intervention requires leadership. Support from the administration is essential. However, the program also needs expert day-to-day guidance. In helping staff work with low-achieving readers and writers, the literacy specialist can provide assistance in a number of ways. Ideally, decisions are made in collaboration with the staff, perhaps in the form of a literacy committee. The staff should work together on the following:

- Construction of a mission statement and goals for the intervention/corrective program
- Selection of students needing additional help
- Construction of curriculum for low-achieving readers
- Selection of approaches and techniques to be used
- Selection of materials
- Construction of a parental-involvement component
- Providing instructional suggestions and program changes for individual students and groups
- Construction or selection of monitoring and assessment components
- Construction of a professional development component
- Decisions about when students are ready to be discontinued
- Coordination of the efforts of all professionals

The Role of Test Preparation

Study after study has shown that when struggling readers are given a well-planned intervention program, test scores rise. It isn't necessary to institute a program of test practice. In fact, implementing extensive programs of test preparation may actually limit students' progress. Test prep programs often focus on lower-level skills. However, there are steps that can be taken to make sure that test results reflect the genuine gains that your students have made. The most effective step is to integrate key content and skills that are tested into your curriculum. In her study of high-performing versus low-performing schools, Langer (2004) found that schools in which teachers incorporated test skills into the curriculum outperformed schools that focused on test preparation. Higher-performing schools used tests to examine their language arts programs. They analyzed the tests so as to note which skills and strategies were being assessed and then revised their programs to include assessed skills. It is important that struggling readers be taught in systematic fashion to answer questions that demand higher-level thinking and/or constructed response. Some time, but not an excessive amount, was spent instructing students in test-taking skills and in familiarizing them with the test format (Langer, 2004).

WORKING WITH THE ADMINISTRATION

Buehl and Stumpf (1999) recommend that struggling readers be served within the context of the total school reading program. Programs that provide remedial instruction only have met with disappointing results.

Working with the administration is crucial. In virtually every study of effective schools, administrative support is a critical element (Hoffman, 1991). Your first order of business should be to discuss your program with the key administrators. They will be more likely to support your program if they understand it, and if it makes sense to them. When you meet with administrators, be prepared to answer any questions that they have. Make sure that you are able to explain your program clearly, have a valid rationale for your program, and can buttress your claims with research or achievement results. Also be aware of any other schools in the area that might have similar programs. Once you initiate a program, be sure to document students' performance.

PROFESSIONAL DEVELOPMENT

The most essential element in any program of remediation and assessment is the quality of instruction. Successful programs provide ongoing professional development, including follow-up, active supervision, and feedback. They also have a clearly stated approach, philosophy, and a full description of instructional procedures. When the change in a corrective program is significant, then the inservice should be substantial. Many of the exemplary procedures and programs discussed in this text took months or even years to implement fully. Even relatively minor changes should be given adequate time and attention. An introduction of a new procedure should be accompanied by follow-up sessions, a plan for its gradual implementation, feedback, and coaching (Radencich, Beers, & Schumm, 1993).

TUTORS

While there is no substitute for one-on-one instruction by highly trained professionals, volunteer tutoring can achieve remarkable results and may be the best alternative when funds are lacking. According to an extensive review of the research by Cohen, Kulik, and Kulik (1982) and Wasik (1998), one-on-one tutoring works better than small-group instruction. Further, when older low-achieving readers tutored younger low-achieving readers, the tutors often improved as much as or even more than the tutees. In a recent study, the following factors were felt to be the foundation for effective tutoring (Juel, 1991, 1994a).

- Caring, supportive attitude. Tutors showed that they cared. Many also were able to empathize with their students because they themselves remembered struggling with reading and writing when they were in the primary grades.
- Teaching the system. The tutors showed students how words are deciphered, how comprehension is achieved. They helped them gain insight into the process, the "tricks of the trade."
- Breaking down word recognition and spelling into small steps. Tutors dealt with individual sounds and letters so the students could see how words were composed.
- Reinforcement. Tutors provide ample verbal and nonverbal praise and affirmation.

Tutoring programs work best when the tutors are trained and provided with ongoing support and professional supervision. The tutors need to know that they are on the right track and that their efforts are paying off. They also need praise and affirmation.

Peer Tutoring

Using Technology
For information about PALS, consult their web site at http://kc.vanderbilt.edu/kennedy/pals/.

Peer tutoring typically has a double payoff. Both tutor and tutee learn. Peer tutoring can be set up on an informal basis so that achieving students can help students who are struggling or who lack information on a topic or those having difficulty applying a certain skill. Or you can make use of structured peer tutoring programs, such as Class Wide Peer Tutoring (CWPT), which has been validated in several scientific studies (Greenwood, Abbott, & Tapia, 2001) or Peer-Assisted Learning Strategies (PALS), which is a version of classwide peer tutoring (PALS, 2004.)

NCLB Mandated Tutoring

If you are in a school that fails to make adequate yearly progress under NCLB, you may be required to offer parents the opportunity to have their children tutored by a qualified provider. Although the provision may seem punitive to the schools designated, it is a way to obtain extra services for students who need it. To optimize the benefits of this service, explore the available programs and determine the relative advantages of each. Make sure that the programs and procedures for participating in them are fully explained to parents. For resources and suggestions for setting up and maintaining a supplemental tutoring program, refer to Tutors for Kids at www.tutorsforkids.org.

MATERIALS

All too often, low-achieving readers end up with materials that are too difficult for them. The first step in teaching reading to underachieving readers is to match students and books. As Fry (1977a) explains,

> Before you begin teaching reading to a child, or a whole class for that matter, you must assess reading abilities in order to provide reading material at the proper level of difficulty. This is important, for a mismatch in reading material can result in disinterested readers.

Material that is too difficult is frustrating and breeds failure, which in turn often causes a dislike of reading. (p. 5)

Marie Clay (1993b), one of the creators of Reading Recovery, insists that students be given materials that are on the appropriate level of difficulty. Emphasis in Reading Recovery is on teaching students to use a balance of strategies, which include context and phonics, to read unfamiliar words. However, if too many words are unknown, students are unable to use context because they are not able to derive enough meaning from the passage. If they are unable to use context, they may overrely on phonics or picture clues.

Comprehension also suffers when the material is too difficult. When high school students reading below their grade level were given material on their instructional level, they used a variety of strategies. However, when these same below-level readers were given material on their frustration level, use of comprehension strategies plummeted, and a number of students simply gave up (Kletzien, 1991). Research by Berliner (1981), Gambrell, Wilson, and Gantt (1981), and Nation (2001) suggests that students make the most progress when reading materials in which no more than 2 to 5 percent of the words are unknown.

The first step in making the match involves finding out what level of material the student is able to read. This can be done by administering an individual or group reading inventory as was explained in Chapter 4. It is also helpful to obtain information about the reader's background of knowledge in terms of the book about to be read (Chall & Dale, 1995). An easy book on ice hockey could be difficult if the student knows nothing about the sport. The second step in making the match is finding material on the appropriate level of difficulty and the appropriate level of maturity. This is not an easy task. By and large, most books are written for children of average or above-average reading ability (Gunning, 1998c). Finding appropriate books for older low-achieving readers can be challenging. However, if you know what to look for and where to look, the task is manageable.

> **Readability:** ease with which a book or other piece of written material can be understood.

Readability: The Other Half of the Match

Publishers of school materials generally provide reading levels for their texts. Using a formula or subjective leveling scale, they estimate that the material is at a third-, fifth-, or eighth-grade level, which means that the average third-, fifth-, or eighth-grader should be able to read it. Some publishers of children's books also supply **readability** levels. If no readability level is indicated for a book that you wish to use, you might estimate readability through the use of a **readability formula** or rating scale.

> **Readability formulas** predict the ease of reading of a particular piece of writing based on the objective assessment of such factors as the sentence length and familiarity of vocabulary.

New Dale–Chall Readability Formula. One of the most carefully validated of the readability formulas is the New Dale–Chall Readability Formula (Chall & Dale, 1995). The New Dale–Chall can be used to estimate the difficulty level of material from grade 1 through grade 16, but is most valid for materials in the range from grade 3 to grade 12. The New Dale–Chall's estimate of difficulty is based on average sentence length and the number of words not found on the Revised Dale List. The Revised Dale List is a compilation of 3,000 words known by most fourth-graders.

> Aspects noted on the New Dale–Chall worksheets are prior knowledge expected of the reader, vocabulary and concepts used in the text, overall organization, and use of headings and other features that affect the ease of reading the text.

Primary Readability Formula.   Designed to estimate the readability of materials with a difficulty level of grade 1 through grade 4, the Primary Readability Formula (Gunning, 2000a) complements the new Dale–Chall and also takes into consideration subjective factors.

Fry Readability Graph.   Easy to use and extending from grades 1 through 17, the Fry Readability Graph is the most popular of the formulas. The Fry Graph bases its estimate on two factors: sentence length and number of syllables in a word. Number of syllables in a word is a measure of vocabulary difficulty. In general, the more syllables a word has, the harder it tends to be. A syllable count is used because it is faster to count syllables than it is to look up words on a list. The Fry Readability Graph (Fry, 1977b) is presented in Figure 15.1.

> A distinct advantage of the Flesch–Kincaid is that it is bundled into Microsoft Word and other popular word processing programs.

Flesch–Kincaid Readability Estimate.   A revision of the Flesch formula that yields grade levels, the Flesch–Kincaid's readability estimate is based on the number of syllables in a word and average sentence length (Kincaid, Fishburne, Rogers, & Chissom, 1975). It also correlates rather closely with the Fry Graph (Fusaro, 1988).

There are three readability formulas that are too complex for hand calculation: the Degrees of Reading Power, the Lexile, and the Atos.

> Computer software that can be used to apply the DRP formula is available from Touchstone Associates.

Degrees of Reading Power.   The Degrees of Reading Power (DRP) measures sentence length, number of words not on the Dale List, and average number of letters per word (TASA, 1999). Most readability formulas report their estimates in grade-equivalent scores, such as 3.4 or 2.7. However, the Degrees of Reading Power reports its levels in DRP units. Table 15.1 translates DRP units into grade-equivalent scores.

The Lexile Framework (MetaMetrics).   The Lexile Framework is somewhat similar to the DRP system. Scores are reported in lexile units. Reading material at a mid-first-grade level has a lexile score of 200. The most difficult material has a lexile rating of 2000. Table 15.1 translates lexile units into grade-equivalent scores. The Lexile Framework measures the difficulty of text using sentence length and frequency of word usage.

ATOS (Advantage-TASA Open Standard).   ATOS uses number of words per sentence, characters per word, and average grade level of words and analyzes the entire text to estimate the readability of books and provides a grade-level equivalent.

> Making a match between the reader and the book requires teacher judgment. The teacher evaluates a text in terms of students' background of knowledge, interests, and purpose for reading.

Subjective Factors

Except for the New Dale–Chall and the Primary Readability Index, readability formulas measure only difficulty of vocabulary and length of sentences. There are, of course, other factors that should be considered when choosing books for a student. For informational texts, these factors include use of graphics, page layout, clarity of writing style, abstractness, and density of concepts. These are factors that do not lend themselves to measurement by a formula. The subjective Readability Index,

FIGURE 15.1 Fry Readability Graph

This is a readability formula intended to help you determine the approximate difficulty or readability level of most written material.

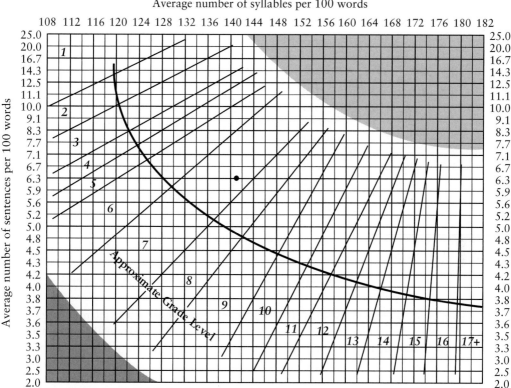

Average number of syllables per 100 words

Directions: Randomly select 3 one hundred word passages from a book or an article. Plot average number of syllables and average number of sentences per 100 words on graph to determine the grade level of the material. Choose more passages per book if great variability is observed and conclude that the book has uneven readability. Few books will fall in gray area but when they do grade level scores are invalid.

Count proper nouns, numerals and initializations as words. Count a syllable for each symbol. For example, "1945" is 1 word and 4 syllables and "IRA" is 1 word and 3 syllables.

Example:	Syllables	Sentences
1st Hundred Words	124	6.6
2nd Hundred Words	141	5.5
3rd Hundred Words	158	6.8
Average	141	6.3

Readability 7th Grade (see dot plotted on graph)

From Edward Fry, Rutgers University Reading Center, New Brunswick, N.J. 08904. For further information and validity data, see the *Journal of Reading,* December 1977.

TABLE 15.1   Comparison of Readability Levels

GRADE EQUIVALENT	DRP SCORE	LEXILE	GUIDED READING	DRA	READING RECOVERY
Caption			A–B	A–2	1–2
Preprimer 1			C	3	3–4
PP2			D	4	5–6
PP3	34–36		E	6–9	7–8
Primer	37–39	200–300	F	10–12	9–10
1	40–43	300–400	G–I	11–16	11–17
2a	44–45	400–500	J–K	17–20	18–20
2b	46–47	400–500	L–M	21–22	
3	48–49	500–700	N–P	23–28	
4	50–51	700–800	Q–S	30–38	
5	52–53	800–900	T–V		
6	54–55	900–1000	W–X		
7	56–57	1000–1100	Y		
8	58–59	1000–1100	Z		
Adult Periodicals					
Professional Journals					

which includes subjective factors, such as prior knowledge and reader interest is presented in Table 15.2. Assessing both subjective and objective factors should provide you with the optimum information for judging the suitability of a text, and enable you to make appropriate matches.

Holistic Estimate of Readability

The Qualitative Assessment of Texts (Chall, Bissex, Conard, & Harris-Sharples, 1996) helps you take a look at key elements in a text and plan activities that help students better understand the text.

An alternative to using formulas is to judge the material holistically, by comparing it with a series of model passages or a series of benchmark books written on a range of difficulty levels. The rater decides which passage the material is most like. If it is most like the third-grade passage, then it is estimated to be on a third-grade level of difficulty. The most carefully developed of these instruments is the Qualitative Assessment of Texts (Chall, Bissex, Conard, & Harris-Sharples, 1996).

Leveling Books

Although traditional formulas provide reasonably accurate estimates of the difficulty levels of most reading materials, they don't work at the beginning levels. Formulas don't consider such factors as usefulness of illustrations and number of lines per page, which are major determinants of the difficulty level of beginning materials. Formulas do indicate with reasonable accuracy that materials are on a first-grade level. However, first-grade reading encompasses a wide range of material, including counting or color books that have just one or two easy words per page as well as books such as the Frog and Toad or Henry and Mudge

TABLE 15.2 Subjective Readability Index

TEXT FACTORS

CONTENT	Low				High
Familiarity of concepts	1	2	3	4	5
Concreteness of concepts	1	2	3	4	5

STYLE

Clarity of writing	1	2	3	4	5
Elaboration of key concepts	1	2	3	4	5
Ease of vocabulary	1	2	3	4	5
Simplicity of sentences	1	2	3	4	5
Use of anecdotes	1	2	3	4	5
Relates text to students' background	1	2	3	4	5

ORGANIZATION

Use of heads, subheads	1	2	3	4	5
Focus on major ideas	1	2	3	4	5
Logical flow of ideas	1	2	3	4	5
Exclusion of irrelevant material	1	2	3	4	5

FEATURES THAT ENHANCE COMPREHENSION

Chapter overview	1	2	3	4	5
Summary	1	2	3	4	5
Questions	1	2	3	4	5
Graphics	1	2	3	4	5
Phonemic respellings	1	2	3	4	5
Definitions provided in text	1	2	3	4	5
Glossary	1	2	3	4	5

Total
(The higher the total, the easier the text)

READER FACTORS

Background of knowledge	1	2	3	4	5
Vocabulary	1	2	3	4	5
Overall reading ability	1	2	3	4	5
Interest	1	2	3	4	5
Motivation	1	2	3	4	5
Study/work habits	1	2	3	4	5

Total
(The higher the number, the better the reader)

series that contain brief chapters and may contain a thousand words or more. Fountas and Pinnell (1996, 1999, 2001) have compiled a list of leveled books for students in grades 1 through 6. Lists of leveled books can be found in Gunning, 2000a and Gunning 2005.

SOURCES OF INFORMATION ABOUT THE READABILITY OF BOOKS

Leveled Books: Portland Public Schools Database lists titles, Reading Recovery levels, and readability levels of 1,108 books ranging in difficulty from beginning readers to advanced elementary (http://teachers.pps.k12.or.us/curriculum/literacy/leveld_books/.

Assessing a book's reading level can be time-consuming. Fortunately, a number of references supply readability information on books. *Best Books for Building Literacy for Elementary School Students* (Gunning, 2000a) provides readability estimates for 1,000 books. Readability estimates for more than 40,000 books can be found in Advantage Learning System's Accelerated Reading Catalogs or on-line at www.renlearn.com. Readabilities of more than 12,000 books can be found in an easy-to-use piece of software known as *BookLink* (TASA, 2000) (TASAliteracy.com). Lexile levels can be found at the Lexile Framework, at http://www.lexile.com. Approximately 25,000 books have been provided with lexile levels. *Matching Books to Readers: Using Leveled Books in Guided Reading, K–3* (Fountas & Pinnell, 1999) lists according to estimated grade levels titles for more than 7,000 books for students in grades 1 to 3. *Guided Reading* (Fountas & Pinnell, 1996), lists titles of more than 3,500 books for students in grades 1 to 3. *Guiding Readers and Writers Grades 3–6* (Fountas & Pinnell, 2001) lists 1,000 titles.

VOLUNTARY READING

Although this text features dozens of techniques designed to help low-achieving readers and writers move up the literacy ladder, the key to success to any reading improvement program lies in fostering voluntary reading. Unfortunately, low-achieving readers, who start out having difficulty with reading, read less. Because they read less, they fall further behind. In first grade, good readers have been observed reading three times as much as poor readers (Allington, 1983). Stanovich (1986) calls this the "Matthew effect," which is essentially the poor getting poorer and the rich getting richer. "The very children who are reading well and who have good vocabularies will read more, learn more word meanings, and hence read even better" (p. 381). By the middle grades, the difference in the time spent reading between the best and the poorest readers might be tenfold.

Even slight increases in time spent reading lead to gains (Anderson, 1996). Students show significant gains when they engage in as little as ten minutes of free reading a day (Fielding, Wilson, & Anderson, 1986).

Include in your collection books of jokes, riddles, puns, and songs. Also feature heavily illustrated books. Reluctant readers can start on these fast reads and move up to more substantive works.

No matter how fine a library your school has, it is important that you also have books close at hand. Students are far more likely to borrow books if they are readily available. The classroom library should be as extensive and diverse as you can make it. Because they are inexpensive and have a mature look, paperbacks are recommended, especially for older students. However, also include hardcover books. Include, too, young people's magazines and newspapers. *Sports Illus-*

trated for Kids, which is written on a fifth-grade level, is highly popular with young people who like sports. Even if the text is a little difficult, they can get help from the photos in this generously illustrated periodical. Be sure to feature *Know Your World Extra, Scholastic Action,* and other periodicals designed for low-achieving readers. A listing of easy-to-read periodicals is presented in Figure 15.2. For an extensive listing of young people's magazines, see *Magazines for Kids and Teens* (Stoll, 1997).

TECHNOLOGY FOR THE READING/WRITING PROGRAM

Technology plays a dual role for low-achieving readers and writers. Through computers, CDs, and videocassettes, traditional topics can be presented in new and more interesting ways. Through computer simulations, students can be more deeply involved in their learning. As both hardware and software become more sophisticated, the amount of interaction between student and material can be increased. In addition, with some programs, students are able to obtain help with background information and vocabulary, receive additional instructions, have segments read aloud, or branch into an easier portion.

LeapPad

LeapPad books feature an electronic pen that speaks. On phonics books, the pen can be directed to speak the whole word, the individual sounds in the word, or the letters in the words. At higher levels, the pen speaks whole words, phrases, or the whole story. It can also be used to define difficult words. By passing the pen over illustrations of a story's characters, the reader-listener can get added information about the character, which should enhance story comprehension. LeapPad has materials ranging from pre-K to grade 5 and includes programs for ELL students.

Computers as Literacy Tools

Increasingly, computers are becoming literacy tools. They can help with the organization, composition, analysis, and dissemination of information. Through adaptive technology, computers can be used to compensate for difficulties in reading and writing. Talking word processing programs, such as *Dr. Peet's Talk/Writer* (Hartley), *Special Writer Coach* (Tom

---

FIGURE 15.2 High-Interest, Low-Readability Periodicals

Action. New York: Scholastic.
  Reading levels 4–5. Interest levels grades 7–12. Twice monthly.
Know Your World Extra. Stamford, CT: Weekly Reader Corp.
  Reading levels 3–4. Interest levels grade 5 through high school. Twice monthly.
News for You. Syracuse, NY: New Reader's Press.
  Reading levels 4–6. Interest levels secondary and adult. Weekly.

> Using technology also does wonders for the self-esteem of problem learners. Using high-tech tools can provide a first-class boost to youngsters who often feel like second-class learners.

Snyder), and *Write Out Loud* (Don Johnston) are especially helpful for students who have difficulty reading or writing. By hearing their piece read back to them, they will be more likely to note awkward expressions, missing *-ing* and *-ed* endings, and omitted words. Even the best writers read over glaring errors, but will probably recognize them if they hear them read aloud. *Co-Writer* (Don Johnston) helps students construct sentences and make spelling and word choices by predicting what word might come next. It lists the words and will also read them. The student then chooses the word that seems most suitable, or he can reject all the choices.

CD-ROM software that reads texts to students provides struggling readers access to text that they might not be able to read on their own and also provides practice for building fluency. For instance, *Start to Finish Books* (Don Johnston) is a series of high-interest books designed for students from age nine to seventeen. Books are written on a second- to third-grade level. Students can have the whole book read aloud or can have individual words pronounced.

Using the Internet

Because many Internet sites include illustrations and film clips, the poor reader is assisted. Even greater assistance is provided by talking Web browsers. Many computers and computer programs have a built-in text-to-speech feature. CAST eReader (http://www.cast.org/) is one such Web browser that reads Web pages out loud. Speed of reading can be regulated, and there is a note-taking feature. Awesome Talkster http://www.awesome library.org/Awesome_Talking_Library.html combines a browser, directory, search engine, and text-to-voice technology. Students can have whole pages read to them, or they can select the text they wish to have spoken. Awesome Library is accessible to all computers. Awesome Talkster is only accessible to PCs.

TEACHER TOOLS

Technology provides a number of tools for the teacher. For instance, using *Wynn Reader* (Arkenstone), the teacher can make adaptations in electronic text. Text can be added, deleted, or simplified. Study aids, such as highlighting, listing, voice notes, and a built-in dictionary are available. *Worksheet Magic Plus* (Teacher Support Software) allows teachers to quickly and easily create fifteen different kinds of practice activities, including crossword puzzles and word searches. *Inspiration* (Inspiration Software, Don Johnston) can be used to make graphic organizers. The software includes thirty-five graphic organizer templates and 1,250 pieces of clip art.

Assistive Technology

One of the latest developments in **assistive technology** is the appearance of voice-activated computers. Using a voice-recognition device, the computer responds to speech, so the student does not have to type in a story. Two of the best-known programs are Dragon Dictate

> **Assistive technology:** use of devices to assist people who have a physical disability or learning problem to perform tasks that would otherwise be difficult or impossible for them.

> For the Mac PC, the text-to-speech feature can be found in Universal Access (in Systems Preferences) along with other adaptations for persons with disabilities.

> **Using Technology**
> The Univeristy of Oregon web site at http://ces.uoregon.edu/intersect/default.html has suggestions for creating and using digital materials; it also has links to many sources of digital books.

> **Using Technology**
> Traditional Stories Online Texts can be accessed at http://falcon.jmu.edu/%7Eramseyil/tradelec.htm. This web site features fairy tales and myths.

(ScanSoft) and Via Voice (ScanSoft). (Students would need training in the use of the programs.) Commands can also be spoken rather than typed. The program can be used by students whose ability to spell is very limited and by students who are physically unable to type.

For students who have serious reading problems, reading systems such as the Kurzweil 3000 system or Read and Write Gold (Text Help) are available. These typically consist of a scanner, optical character recognition (OCR) software, a word processing program, and a speech synthesizer. The text that the student wishes to read is scanned into the word processing program. Once scanned in and analyzed by the OCR software, it is read aloud by the computer's voice synthesizer. Anything that can be scanned in can be read. The reader will have to supply the occasional word that the scanner's software is unable to pronounce or that it mispronounces. OCR software continues to increase in both accuracy and ease of use.

Additional information about assistive technology and software is available from national, regional, and local sources. One of the best overall sources is Alliance for Technology Access (http://www.ataccess.org/), which provides links to a large number of sites.

Using ebooks

Because they are in a digital format, ebooks have a number of advantages. For one thing, they can be read by a screen reader or a talking word-processing program. This makes them accessible to struggling readers. To make them even more accessible, ebooks can be linked to a dictionary so that students can readily get help with difficult words. A third advantage is that the text can be added to or altered. You might add explanatory notes or illustrations or even rewrite difficult portions. Ebooks are readily available on the Internet from a number of sources. The International Children's Digital Library (ICDL) features a collection of multicultural ebooks in dozens of languages for children ages 3–13. Other extensive sources of digital books include project Gutenberg (http://www.promo.net/pg/) and the University of Virginia (http://etext.lib.virginia.edu/). The University of Virginia has a Young Readers collection of public domain texts.

> Online Children's Stories can be accessed at http://www.acs.ucalgary.ca/%7Edkbrown/stories.html. This web site has links to a wealth of stories, songs, and poems.

Technology and ELL Students

Technology can be especially helpful to ELL students. Using text-to-speech software, ELL students can have words pronounced and stories read. If words are unfamiliar, students can obtain their meanings and pronunciations in an electronic dictionary. Some text-to-speech programs are multilingual. Students can find the equivalent of an English word in their native tongue. Or the student can use translation software such as http://babelfish.altavista.com/ to have passages translated from English into their native language or from their native language into English.

EVALUATION

Each student needs to be evaluated in terms of the goals established for her or him. Students may spend years in an intervention program and make little progress. When students make limited progress, the situation needs to be examined and changed.

Programs should also undergo periodic evaluation. Programs need to be evaluated in terms of their overall goals and objectives. If one goal is to increase in-class corrective instruction, then that should be assessed. If another goal is to set up an early intervention program to help the lowest achieving 20 percent of first-graders, then that should be assessed too.

Data gathered for evaluation should be broad-based and should include a variety of assessment devices. Gathering data is only a part of evaluation. The data is then used to make a judgment about the effectiveness of the reading program. The question to be asked is: To what extent were the goals of the program met? Once a judgment has been made, the next step in the evaluation program is to make necessary changes. If the intervention or corrective program is not reaching enough students or fails to remediate a high proportion of them, then the program needs to be analyzed and revamped. The components of an effective literacy program are listed in Figure 15.3. Above all else, a successful program for low-achieving readers and writers requires caring, well-trained professionals, the firm belief that low-achieving readers and writers can learn, and a willingness to affirm and build upon the unique gifts that each student possesses.

SUMMARY

Given the requirements of NCLB, the nature of corrective instruction is changing. Since the goal of NCLB is that all students will meet proficiency standards in reading, there is a growing effort to help struggling readers at all levels. Key elements in the effort have been to intervene early and to provide added instructional time. There has also been greater cooperation among professionals and more emphasis on professional development, including coaching, grade-level meetings, and study groups. The role of literacy and learning specialists has been changing from an emphasis on providing intervention to one of consulting and coaching.

Components of a remedial reading/writing program include goals, student selection, curriculum, instructional approaches, instructional schedule, organizational patterns, pacing, materials, monitoring, grouping, involving parents, leadership, professional development, and evaluation. Goals should be clearly expressed and based on a statement of the overall philosophy of the program. Students needing assistance are generally selected on the basis of a discrepancy between potential achievement, failure to reach a certain level of achievement, and/or failure to respond to intervention. Because of the possibility that any one test or other assessment device may yield erroneous results, students should be selected on the basis of several assessment devices.

FIGURE 15.3   Components of an Effective Literacy Program

Goals
    Clearly stated
    Based on a statement of philosophy
    Translated into specific objectives
Selection of Students
    Based on discrepancy between achievement and potential
    Based on failure to achieve a set standard
    Based on a variety of selection devices
    Based on response to intervention
Organization
    Uses one-to-one instruction
    Uses small group instruction
    Makes provision for students who need extended instruction
    Attempts to implement an inclusion model
Pacing
    Accelerates students' progress
    Proceeds at a rate that is challenging but not overwhelming
    Promotes out-of-school reading
Monitoring
    Monitors progress on an ongoing basis
    Uses several devices for monitoring
    Adjusts program as necessary
Grouping
    Uses various grouping patterns
    Does not use patterns that stigmatize low-achieving readers
    Uses cooperative grouping
Involving Parents
    Explains program to parents
    Keeps parents informed of child's progress
    Involves parents in supporting the child's efforts
Leadership
    A designated person or group is responsible for planning, supervising, and monitoring the
    program.
Professional Development
    Provision is made for ongoing professional development.
    Professional development is based on achievement data and tied in to students' performance.
    Professional development includes grade-level meetings, study groups, and coaching.
Volunteers
    Parents and other volunteers from the community tutor students or act as aides.
    Volunteers are instructed, supervised, and affirmed.
Evaluation
    Program is evaluated in terms of its goals.
    Evaluation is broad-based and uses many sources of assessment information.
    Evaluation is used to improve the program.

The curriculum for a program for low-achieving readers and writers should be broad-based but should mesh with the school's overall curriculum. The daily instructional schedule should include provision for instruction, guided practice, and independent application and should feature varied activities. Students can be discontinued from the program when they are able to meet the demands of the regular classroom and are reading on their own.

Although one-on-one remedial instruction is highly effective, small-group intervention, if carefully planned, can also achieve significant results. Modifications and additional assistance are provided as needed when struggling readers are instructed within the context of the whole class. While short-term intervention succeeds with most students, a small percentage need extensive, long-term assistance. Programs that are properly paced are more successful.

Ongoing monitoring so that appropriate adjustments can be made is also an important ingredient. Although there are many ways of grouping students, heterogeneous and cooperative grouping foster increased achievement in low-achieving readers and writers. Whole class instruction, if used, should be supplemented with small-group instruction or reading or writing workshop or some other form of individualization.

Parents should be informed of any difficulties their children are experiencing in acquiring literacy skills. They should also be involved in supporting their children's efforts.

Leadership and professional development are also important components of an effective program. An often-untapped source of additional assistance is the volunteer tutor. Tutors should be trained, supervised, and affirmed.

One of the most important instructional decisions that a teacher makes is matching the reader with appropriate materials. Subjective assessment should be used along with objective formulas to obtain the most valid assessment of the difficulty level of texts. If low-achieving readers do not read voluntarily, they have little chance of making satisfactory progress. Key components of a voluntary reading program include obtaining easy-to-read materials that match students' interests, making students feel like readers, and stressing the value of voluntary reading.

Technology can assist low-achieving readers by providing them with materials that are interesting, instructive, and interactive. Technological tools and adaptive technology can help students compensate for learning difficulties.

Programs should be evaluated in terms of their goals. Evaluation should include consideration of a variety of assessment information and should lead to improvement of the program.

APPLICATION ACTIVITIES

1. Observe a successful intervention program in your locality. What are the outstanding features of the program? What provision is made for Tier III students? These are students who did not do well in the intervention program.

2. Read the following selection, which contains information about a number of early-intervention programs. What are some similarities in the programs? What are some differences? What do the programs suggest about early intervention? Tierney, R. J., & Readence, J. E. (2005). Intervention programs for "at risk" students. In Tierney, R. J., & Readence, J. E. (Eds.), *Reading strategies and practices* (6th ed.) (pp. 126–159). Boston: Allyn & Bacon.

3. Create a list of suggestions in a resource booklet that can be given to parents whose children are enrolled in an intervention program. Focus on providing ways in which parents can affirm their children and support their efforts in nonthreatening ways.

4. Use the Fry Graph or the Primary Readability Formula (available in the Instructor's Manual) to estimate the readability level of the content-area text or a trade book that your class is reading or might read. How does your assessment compare with that supplied by the publisher?

5. Using one of the resources listed in the chapter, locate five high-interest, low-readability books. What makes them easy? With whom might you use them?

■ ■ ■ ■ ■ ▬▬▬▬▬▬▬▬▬▬▬▬▬▬▬▬▬▬▬▬▬▬▬▬▬▬▬▬▬▬▬

INFORMAL ASSESSMENT MEASURES

WORD-LEARNING TEST

Name of Student _____   Date _____

Grade _____

Word-Learning Test

Directions: Ask the student to read the following words until she or he misses at least seven of them, or use seven words that the student missed on a word-list or similar test. Write these words on cards and teach them to the student. Follow the instructions following the test.

both   _____
few   _____
much   _____
eight   _____
think   _____
great   _____
year   _____
found   _____
large   _____
sure   _____
learn   _____
group   _____
word   _____
come   _____
front   _____
hold   _____
gone   _____
talk   _____
dark   _____
warm   _____

Teaching Presentation

Present the seven words chosen to be test words. Hold the word so that the student can see it readily. After you say it, have the student say it. Shuffle the word cards and present them in the same way a second time.

Testing Trials

Present each word and ask the student to read it. If the student gives a correct response, say, "Yes, that's correct. The word is _____." If the student gives an incorrect response, say, "No, that is not correct. The word is _____." Put the correct responses in a separate pile. Note the correct responses on the Learning Trials sheet. Do not record incorrect responses. Shuffle all the cards after each trial. Continue presenting testing trials until the student gets all the words correct on two consecutive trials or until the student has had ten learning trials. If the student has not gotten all seven words within ten trials, note the number correct. To check long-term retrieval, give a single test trial one hour later and then twenty-four hours later.

Name of Student _____   Date _____

Examiner _____

LEARNING TRIALS

WORD	1	2	3	4	5	6	7	8	9	10
1.										
2.										
3.										
4.										
5.										
6.										
7.										

RESULTS

Number of trials _____

	Words Known	Symbols for Correct Response
Immediate (first test)	_____	✓
At end of 60 minutes (first retest)	_____	C
Next day (second retest)	_____	+

Comments _____

_____

_____

_____

Name _____   Total Number Correct _____

Date _____   Estimated Level _____

WORD PATTERN SURVEY

1. go _____	21. game _____	41. spark _____	61. through _____
2. me _____	22. tree _____	42. stair _____	62. straight _____
3. see _____	23. wide _____	43. shore _____	63. enough _____
4. I _____	24. road _____	44. curl _____	64. clue _____
5. no _____	25. use _____	45. steer _____	65. edge _____
6. hat _____	26. goat _____	46. park _____	66. strong _____
7. wet _____	27. save _____	47. purse _____	67. suit _____
8. sit _____	28. wheel _____	48. clear _____	68. thought _____
9. hop _____	29. mine _____	49. storm _____	69. flood _____
10. fun _____	30. cute _____	50. charge _____	70. breathe _____
11. ran _____	31. chain _____	51. chalk _____	71. calm _____
12. men _____	32. speak _____	52. brook _____	72. clothes _____
13. win _____	33. slide _____	53. crown _____	73. knock _____
14. got _____	34. toast _____	54. join _____	74. soft _____
15. bug _____	35. blind _____	55. should _____	75. fault _____
16. drop _____	36. plane _____	56. stew _____	76. tough _____
17. jump _____	37. steel _____	57. bounce _____	77. height _____
18. sand _____	38. drive _____	58. crawl _____	78. laugh _____
19. ship _____	39. broke _____	59. broom _____	79. earth _____
20. lunch _____	40. price _____	60. pound _____	80. brought _____

Directions: Give one copy of the survey to the student and keep one for marking. Mark each response + or – . Start with the first item for all pupils. Say to the student, "I am going to ask you to read a list of words to me. Some of the words may be hard for you, but read as many as you can." Stop when the student gets five in a row wrong. The survey tests four levels. Each level has twenty items as follows: 1–20, easy long-vowel and short-vowel patterns; 21–40, long-vowel patterns; 41-60, *r*-vowel and other-vowel patterns /aw/, /o͞o/, /oo/, /ow/, /oy/; 61–80, irregular and low-frequency patterns. Students are proficient at a level if they get 80 percent or more correct at that level. Students should be instructed at a level if they get more than 4 out of 20 wrong at that level.

Name _____   Score _____

Date _____

SYLLABLE SURVEY

1. sunup	_____	26. opposite	_____
2. inside	_____	27. message	_____
3. ago	_____	28. success	_____
4. open	_____	29. struggle	_____
5. under	_____	30. repeat	_____
6. farmer	_____	31. recognize	_____
7. finish	_____	32. survive	_____
8. mistake	_____	33. appreciate	_____
9. thunder	_____	34. antelope	_____
10. morning	_____	35. creature	_____
11. reward	_____	36. audience	_____
12. famous	_____	37. pleasant	_____
13. mumble	_____	38. spaghetti	_____
14. spider	_____	39. information	_____
15. chicken	_____	40. voyage	_____
16. rocket	_____	41. confusion	_____
17. magnet	_____	42. neighborhood	_____
18. distant	_____	43. studio	_____
19. prevent	_____	44. allowance	_____
20. museum	_____	45. microphone	_____
21. several	_____	46. auditorium	_____
22. building	_____	47. available	_____
23. probably	_____	48. disappointment	_____
24. modern	_____	49. bulletin	_____
25. monument	_____	50. moisture	_____

Directions: **Give one copy of the survey to the student and keep one for marking. Mark each response + or − . If possible, write down each incorrect response for later analysis. Start with the first item for all pupils. Say to the student, "I am going to ask you to read a list of words. Some of the words may be hard for you, but read as many as you can." Stop when the student gets five in a row wrong. A score of 45 or more indicates that the student is able to decode multisyllabic words. A score between 40 and 44 indicates some weakness in decoding multisyllabic words. A score below 40 indicates a definite need for instruction and practice in decoding multisyllabic words. A score of 5 or less suggests that the student may be deficient in basic decoding skills. Give the Word Pattern Survey.**

From T. Gunning (1994). *Teacher's Guide for Word Building, Book D.* New York: Phoenix Learning Resources. Reprinted by permission of Galvin Publications.

■ ■ ■ ■ ■ ▬▬▬▬▬▬▬▬▬▬▬▬▬▬▬▬▬▬▬▬▬▬▬▬▬▬▬

HIGH-INTEREST, LOW-READABILITY BOOKS

TITLE	PUBLISHER	READING LEVEL	INTEREST LEVEL
HIGH-INTEREST, LOW-READABILITY SERIES FOR YOUNGER STUDENTS			
African American Biography Series Features brief biographies of a variety of African Americans.	Enslow	3	3–5
Amanda and Oliver Pig Series Tales of growing up in a warm, loving family.	Dial	1	1–3
Amelia Bedelia Series Because she takes figurative language literally, Amelia Bedelia is always engaged in humorous situations.	Harper	1	1–3
Animal Adventures Portrays wolves, manatees, moose, whooping cranes, bobcats, and other interesting animals.	Perfection	1–2	2–6
Arthur Series Arthur, the chimp, experiences the joys and difficulties of childhood.	Harper	1–2	1–3
Boxcar Children Mysteries Having made their home in a boxcar, the Aldens solve a variety of mysteries.	Penguin	2	2–5
Cam Jansen Detective Series Cam solves a variety of mysteries.	Penguin	2	2–4
Commander Toad Series Humorous adventures in space.	Putnam	2	2–4
Fox Series Although he is a wily creature, Fox usually ends up being outfoxed in good-humored fashion.	Dial, Penguin	1–2	1–3
Henry and Mudge Series Young boy enjoys his oversized dog.	Bradbury	1	1–3
Historical Moments Portrays ancient Egypt, pirates, the Wild West, and Jesse Owens.	Perfection Learning	2	2–6

Historical Moments—American Revolution Six fictional texts portray key moments in the Revolution.	Perfection Learning	2	2–6
Historical Moments—The Civil War A series of six informational and fiction texts covers several aspects of the Civil War.	Perfection Learning	1–3	2–6
Historical Moments—Early America/Settling the Colonies A series of six fiction texts portrays life in early America.	Perfection Learning	1–2	2–6
Historical Moments—Settling the West Six fictional texts portray the Alamo, the Pony Express, the Chisholm Trail, and other key events in the settling of the West. A seventh book portrays Kit Carson.	Perfection Learning	2	2–6
Historical Toys Gives the history and current uses of bicycles, kites, marbles, and other toys.	Perfection Learning	2	2–6
Kids of Polk Street School Elementary school youngsters have a series of adventures as they encounter the problems of growing up.	Dell	2–3	2–4
Kooties Club Mysteries Preteens investigate a series of mysteries including a Ben Franklin ghost and "I Love Elvis" signs.	Perfection Learning	2	2–6
Magic School Bus Series Ms. Frizzle uses a magic school bus to take her class on unusual but scientifically informative field trips.	Scholastic	3	3–5
Max Series With his flying umbrella, Max is a very unusual but funny detective.	Harper	1	1–3
Morris Series A lovable moose, Morris becomes involved in a series of humorous escapades.	Harper	1	1–3
Nate the Great Detective Series By making judicious use of clues, Nate finds missing objects and solves other everyday mysteries.	Dell	2	2–4
Rookie Biography Series Basic, easy-to-read biographies of a variety of noteworthy individuals.	Children's Press	2	2–4
Rookie Read-About Science Series Brief, well-illustrated explorations of varied science topics.	Children's Press	1	1–3
Troll Easy-to-Read Mysteries Mysteries solved include finding missing animals and lost objects.	Troll	2	2–4

TITLE	PUBLISHER	READING LEVEL	INTEREST LEVEL
HIGH-INTEREST, LOW-READABILITY SERIES FOR OLDER STUDENTS			
Adventures Features a variety of exciting adventures in 32-page paperback format.	Steck-Vaughn	3	5–10
Asteroid 7 Jones, Morga, and Gold are partners in a "flex" mine operation on Asteroid 7 (part of the asteroid belt orbiting the sun between Jupiter and Mars).	High Noon	2	5–9
BesTellers Features a variety of tales of mystery, suspense, and adventure involving young adults.	Globe/Fearon	1–4	9–12
Brains and Parker McGoohan Teens travel in time machine to meet famous scientists of the past.	High Noon	3	6–12
Capstone High-Interest, Low-Readability Books Includes a variety of nonfiction with a focus on topics interesting to upper elementary and middle school students.	Capstone	3–4	3–9
Chapter Books Pairs fiction and nonfiction books.	Perfection	1–4	2–6
Chapter 2 Books Includes a variety of fiction books.	Perfection	1–3	4–6
Double Fastbacks Features fifty-four 64-page fast-paced novels dealing with romance, mystery, crime, sports, horror, spies, and strange occurrences. Some Fastbacks are accompanied by tapes.	Globe/Fearon	4–5	9–12
The Ecology Kidds Series Dr. Kidd and her teenage twins solve ecology mysteries.	High Noon	2	5–10
Encounters Series Adventure series deals with a variety of problems teens deal with: drugs, running away, and work.	EMC Publishing	3–4	8–12
Fact Meets Fiction Pairs of 96-page books, one factual and one fictional, deal with science, natural disasters, shipwrecks, and animals.	Sundance	4–5	7–12
Fastbacks Features seventy-four 32-page fast-paced novels dealing with romance, mystery, crime, sports, horror, science fiction, and spies.	Globe/Fearon	4–5	9–12

Fearon's Amazing Adventures Features eight novels that tell tales of escape and survival.	Globe/Fearon	3	7–12
Fearon's Flights of Fantasy Features eight novels that transport readers to other times and other places.	Globe/Fearon	3	9–12
Fearon's Freedom Fighters Includes 80-page biographies of M. L. King, Nelson Mandela, César Chavez, Fannie Hammer, and Malcolm X.	Globe/Fearon	3–4	7–12
Four Corners Corina and Zack, co-workers at the Park Museum, encounter adventure and mystery as they travel to faraway places.	High Noon	2	5–10
High Adventures Features a series of ten intriguing adventures.	High Noon	3–4	6–12
History's Mysteries Features the disappearance of Amelia Earhart, the Roanoke mystery, and other famous mysteries of the past.	Crestwood House/ Simon & Schuster	5–6	4–8+
Illustrated Classics Includes seventy-two classics in heavily illustrated format. Read-along cassettes available.	AGS (American Guidance Services)	3.8–4.8	6–12
Incredible Histories Includes such high-interest topics as famous hoaxes, haunted castles, missing treasure, and impossible quests.	Crestwood House/ Simon & Schuster	5–6	4–8+
Informational Books: Environmental Disasters Avalanches, hurricanes, oil spills, earthquakes, fires, floods, volcanoes, and tornadoes are among the disasters explored.	Perfection Learning	3–4	4–8
Informational Books: Moments in History Explorers, the Civil War, famous trials, the American Revolution, Ancient Egypt, pioneer days, World War II, the early settlers, and communications are among the topics discussed.	Perfection Learning	3–5	4–8
Informational Books: Relationships Explores caring for young children, making friends, and taking care of pets.	Perfection Learning	2	4–8
Informational Books: Thrills and Adventure Stunt pilots, gorillas, sled dog racing, kayaking, sea monsters, Bigfoot, climbing mountains, exploring caves, and making movies are among the topics explored.	Perfection Learning	2–4	4–8
Informational Books: Unsung Heroes Includes overcoming tragedy, helper dogs, and minibiographies of outstanding women.	Perfection Learning	3–4	4–8
The Kirkwood Kids Middle school youngsters have a series of adventures.	Perfection Learning	3–4	4–7

Lake Classics	Lake Education	3	6–12
Features a variety of classic short stories from American, British, and world literature. Available on audiotape.			
Meridian Books	High Noon	3–4	7–12
Teens experience a series of mysteries and adventures.			
Movie Monsters	Crestwood House/ Simon & Schuster	3–5	4–8+
Monster movie scripts are rewritten.			
Mysteries	Steck-Vaughn	2–3	5–10
Features a variety of modern-day mysteries in 32-page paperback format.			
The Mystery of . . .	Crestwood House/ Simon & Schuster	5–6	4–8+
Features Bigfoot, the Lock Ness monster, and other famous real-life mysteries.			
Novels: Adventure	Perfection Learning	2	4–8
Features tales of danger and survival.			
Novels: Contemporary Fiction	Perfection Learning	2	4–8
Includes fictionalized biographies of César Chavez, Langston Hughes, Albert Einstein, Socrates, Martin Luther King, and Queen Lili'Uokalani.			
Novels: Contemporary Fiction	Perfection Learning	2	4–8
Features tales of humor and magic.			
Novels: Historical Fiction	Perfection Learning	2–3	4–8
Series of twenty-one texts including tales of shipwrecks, World War II, moving West, escaping slavery, and adapting to a new family.			
Novels: Humor	Perfection Learning	2	4–8
Features tales of growing up and troubled family relationships.			
Novels: Mystery	Perfection Learning	2–3	4–8
Features tales of ghosts, mystery places, and sightings of Bigfoot in New York's Central Park.			
Novels: Sports	Perfection Learning	2	4–8
Features tales of stolen bases (literally) and time travel.			
Passages Novels: Contemporary	Perfection Learning	3–6	6–8
Teens encounter variety of conflicts in a series of mysteries and adventures by Ann Schraff.			
Passages Novels: Historical	Perfection Learning	3–6	6–12
Teens play a role in the Gold Rush, colonization, the Great Depression, World War I, immigration, the Civil Rights Movement, the Civil War, World War II, and other historical eras.			
Passages Novels: Suspense	Perfection Learning	3–6	6–12
Includes tales of ghosts, disappearing people, and a tiger attack during a field trip.			
Perspectives	High Noon	3–4	6–12
Includes twenty tales of adventure.			

Postcards from America
    Four teens have adventures as they visit cultural
    landmarks in America.
	High Noon	2	5–9+

Postcards from Europe
    Four teens have adventures as they visit cultural
    landmarks in Europe.
	High Noon	2	5–9+

Postcards from South America
    Four teens have adventures as they visit cultural
    landmarks in South America.
	High Noon	2	5–9+

Reading Success Paperbacks
    Features Bill Cosby, Michael Jordan, and other
    celebrities.
	High Noon	3–4	6–12

Retold Program: Classics Anthologies Features retold myths from around the world.	Perfection Learning	6	6–12

Retold Program: Myths and Folktales
    Features retold American, British, and world classic
    short stories. Also includes retold novels: *Frankenstein,
    Huckleberry Finn, The Red Badge of Courage, Treasure
    Island*, and *A Tale of Two Cities*.
	Perfection Learning	6	6–12

The Riddle Street Mystery Series
    Meg, a reporter, and Tom, a photographer, team up to
    solve mysteries.
	High Noon	1	4–8+

Rigby PM Features a variety of nonfiction books.	Harcourt Achieve	2–6	4–8
Saddleback Classics Series includes sixteen classic novels.	Sundance	4	5–12

Science Fiction
    Features a variety of science fiction tales in 32-page
    paperback format.
	Steck-Vaughn	4	5–10

The Scoreboard Series High schoolers overcome obstacles in five major sports.	High Noon	2	9–16+

Silverleaf Novels
    Middle school students encounter stepparents, divorce
    problems, and difficulties with friends and teachers.
	Perfection Learning	3.5	4–7

Sound Out Chapter Books
    The set contains six books, three of which focus on
    short vowels and three that include words with both
    short and long vowels. These 32-page books portray a
    series of adventures that includes a forest fire, a lost tug,
    a robbery, and survival at sea.
	High Noon	1	7–11+

SporTellers Young athletes encounter obstacles.	Globe/Fearon	2–3	9–12

Sports Immortals
    Features Babe Ruth, Jackie Robinson, Babe Didrickson,
    and other sports greats from the past.
	Crestwood House/
	Simon & Schuster
		5	5–10+

Starting Gate Each book in this five-book series contains four short stories on contemporary topics. Starting with 101 basic sight words, each story adds a handful of new words to the students' reading vocabulary. By the time all five books have been completed, a new vocabulary of 315 words has been introduced.	High Noon	1–4	6–12
Start-to-Finish: Classic Adventures Includes *The Adventures of Huckleberry Finn, Treasure Island, Red Badge of Courage,* and stories by Edgar Allan Poe, Jack London, Mark Twain, Shakespeare, and tales of Sherlock Holmes. Available on audiotape and CD-ROM.	Don Johnston	3	6–12
Start-to-Finish: Nick Ford Mysteries Nick Ford solves a series of mysteries.	Don Johnston	3	6–12
Start-to-Finish: Step into History Features biographies of Rosa Parks, Frederick Douglass, Harriet Tubman, and César Chavez. Available on audiotape and CD-ROM.	Don Johnston	3	6–12
Summit Features a variety of fiction.	Perfection	3–7	5–12
Take Ten Novels Series of five 56-page novels in each of the following categories: mystery, adventure, thrillers, chillers, disaster, and sports.	Sundance	4	7–12
Thrilloglogy Twelve 48-page minianthologies, each including three tales of horror or science fiction.	Sundance	5	7–12
Timeless Classics: Author and Short Story Collections Features tales by Edgar Allan Poe, Mark Twain, Shakespeare, Washington Irving, Jack London, Rudyard Kipling, Louisa May Alcott, and tales of Sherlock Holmes.	Perfection Learning	2–3	4–8
Timeless Classics: Cultural and Historical Tales Features tales of Africa, America, China, ancient civilizations, and the Civil War.	Perfection Learning	2–3	4–8
Timeless Classics: Fables, Folktales, and Legends Includes Greek mythology, Aesop's fables, and fairy tales.	Perfection Learning	2–3	4–8
Tom and Ricky Mystery Series Two fourteen-year-olds solve a variety of mysteries. Series features nine 5-book sets. Some of the titles are available in Spanish and English.	High Noon	1–2	4–8+
Trailblazers Portrays life on the trails in a series of fictionalized accounts of courage, adventure, and hardship.	High Noon	2	4–9
Uptown, Downtown Series Vesey, a high schooler, encounters a series of difficulties and adventures in an urban setting.	Globe/Fearon	2–3	9–12

Individual Titles

BOOK'S AUTHOR, YEAR AND TITLE	NO. OF PAGES	READING LEVEL	INTEREST LEVEL
HIGH-INTEREST, LOW-READABILITY BOOKS FOR YOUNGER STUDENTS			
Adler, D. A. (1997). *Lou Gehrig, the luckiest man.* Harcourt, Brace. An outstanding baseball player, Lou Gehrig set a record for most consecutive games played that stood for more than fifty years.	30	3	4–5
Ballard, R. (1993). *Finding the Titanic.* Scholastic. Robert Ballard explains how the *Titanic* sank and how he found it and explored it.	48	3	4–5
Bancroft, H., & Van Gelder, R. G. (1997). *Animals in winter,* HarperCollins. Animals have a variety of ways of coping with winter.	32	1	2–3
Batten, M. (1998). *Baby wolf.* Grossett & Dunlap. Follows a baby wolf as it is born and grows into a young adult.	48	1	2–3
Blume, J. (1971). *Freckle Juice.* Bantam Doubleday Dell. Andrew uses a "secret formula" to acquire freckles.	40	3	3–4
Brenner, B. (1978). *Wagon wheels.* Harper. Two African American boys head West.	32	1	2–4
Brown, M. (1983). *Spooky riddles.* Random House. Features easy-to-read riddles that involve scary creatures.	38	1	2–3
Bulla, C. R. (1975). *Shoeshine girl.* Crowell. Because of her troublesome ways, an angry ten-year-old Sarah is sent to live with her kindly but wise Aunt Ida during the summer.	84	2	4–6
Byars, B. (1977). *The pinballs.* HarperCollins. Abandoned by her parents and living in a foster home, Carlie thinks of herself as a pinball with no control over her life.	136	4	5–7
Byars, B., & Truesdale, S. (1985). *The Golly sisters go West.* HarperCollins Heading West in a covered wagon to put on shows, the Golly sisters have a series of humorous misadventures and misunderstandings.	64	1	2–3
Chardiet, Bernice, & Maccarone, G. (1990). *The best teacher in the world.* Scholastic. Bunny feels very proud when Ms. Darcy, the best teacher in the world, chooses her to deliver a note to Mrs. Walker. Unable to find Mrs. Walker and too embarrassed to ask for help, Bunny fails to deliver the note.	29	1	2–3
Cole, J. (1986). *Hungry, hungry sharks.* Random House. Provides interesting information about sharks.	48	2	2–4+
Cole, J., & Calmeson, S. (1995). *Yours till banana splits.* Morrow. Features dozens of autograph rhymes.	64	3	5–6

Cosby, B. (1998). *Money troubles.* Scholastic. After working hard to buy a telescope, Little Bill decides to donate his money for the homeless and the hungry.	34	3	3–5
Demuth, P. (1996). *Johnny Appleseed.* Grossett & Dunlap. Heading West as a young man, John Chapman began planting apple seeds and soon came to be called Johnny Appleseed.	32	1	2–3
Donnelly, J. (1987). *The Titanic lost and found.* Random House. Portrays in words and pictures the sinking of the *Titanic.*	48	3	4–5
Donnelly, J. (1988). *Tut's mummy lost . . . and found.* Random House. Describes the death of King Tut, the preparations made for his burial, and his burial in a pyramid.	48	3	4–5
Dorros, A. (1987). *Ant cities.* HarperCollins. Explains how ants live and work together.	32	2	3–4
Flynn, G. (2000). *Venus and Serena Williams.* The Child's World. Chronicles the sisters' rise to fame in the world of tennis.	24	4	5–7
Fowler, A. (1996). *The biggest animal on land.* Children's Press. With photos and texts, provides an overview of elephants.	32	1	2–3
Fritz, J. (1993). *Just a few words Mr. Lincoln.* Grossett & Dunlap. Asked to speak at the new cemetery for the war dead at Gettysburg, Lincoln wrote a short speech in which he urged that the United States "have a new birth of freedom." Although just 271 words long, Lincoln's Gettysburg Address became one of the most famous speeches of all time.	48	3	4–5
Giovanni, N. (1985). *Spin a soft song* (Rev. ed.). Farrar, Strauss & Giroux. Although written for African American children, the poems have a universal appeal.	57	3	5–6
Hall, K., & Eisenberg, L. (1986). *Buggy riddles.* Puffin. Presents a series of easy riddles on the theme of bugs.	48	1	2–3
Hall, L. (1973). *Barry, the bravest Saint Bernard.* Random House. Barry helped rescue people lost in the St. Bernard Mountain Pass in Switzerland.	48	3	4–5
Hayward, L. (1988). *Hello, house!* Random House. Brer Rabbit tricks fox.	32	P	1–3
Hayward, L. (1989). *Baby Moses.* Random House. Because Moses is in danger from Egypt's pharaoh, Moses's mother puts him in a basket and places the basket in the river.	32	1	2–3
Hayward, L. (1997). *Cave people.* Grossett & Dunlap. Describes the Neanderthals and tells how they lived.	48	2	3–4
Hopkins, L. B. (Ed.) (1992). *Questions, poems of wonder.* HarperCollins. Easy-to-read poems that ask questions.	64	2	3–4
Ingoglia, G. (1992). *Awesome animals.* Golden. Portrays the flying snake, vampire bat, and other intriguing animals.	48	2–3	2–4+

Kallen, S. (1996). *Mutts.* Abdo Consulting Group. Describes mutts and their major characteristics.	24	3	4–5
Kessler, L. (1982). *Old Turtle's baseball stories.* Yearling Books. Old Turtle spins some amazing baseball yarns.	55	1	1–3
Kramer, S. (1997). *Wagon train.* Grossett & Dunlap. Portrays life in a wagon train headed west in 1848.	32	2	3–6
Kunhardt, E. (1987). *Pompeii . . . buried alive.* Random House. Uses words and pictures to explain how the ancient town of Pompeii was buried under ash and lava and is now a tourist attraction because many buildings were preserved.	48	3	4–7
Levinson, N. S. (1992). *Snowshoe Thompson.* HarperCollins. Wanting to mail a letter to his dad, who has gone to search for gold in California, Danny is told that it will be impossible to get over the mountains until spring. But Snowshoe Thompson makes a pair of skis and promises to deliver the mail.	64	1	2–3
Lundell, M. (1995). *A girl named Helen Keller.* Scholastic. Deafened and blinded by a high fever, little Helen Keller became a wild child until Anne Sullivan began teaching her.	48	2	3–4
McKie, Roy (1979). *The joke book.* Random House. Features a number of knock-knock and other jokes.	48	2	3–4+
Milton, J. (1985). *Dinosaur days.* Random House. Portrays major dinosaurs and discusses their disappearance.	48	1	1–3
Milton, J. (1996). *Mummies.* Grossett & Dunlap. Explains why pharaohs were buried in pyramids and how their bodies were mummified.	48	3	4–5
O'Connor, J. (1986). *The teeny tiny woman.* Random House. A ghost retrieves a bone taken from the top of its grave.	32	1	3
O'Connor, J. (1992). *Comeback! Four true stories.* Random House. Features the stories of four star athletes who made amazing comebacks after serious physical injuries.	48	3	4–5
Parish, P. (1974). *Dinosaur time.* Harper. Describes the major dinosaurs in very simple language.	32	1	1–3
Peck, R. N. (1982). *Banjo.* Knopf. While seeking a reclusive mountain man who was to be the subject of their report, two boys fall to the bottom of a dangerous deserted mine.	80	3	5–7
Penner, L. R. (1995). *Sitting Bull.* Grossett & Dunlap. Although named Slow as a boy, because he did everything very slowly, he was renamed Sitting Bull when he proved himself in battle.	48	2	3–4
Penner, L. R. (1996). *Twisters.* Random House. Describes tornadoes, waterspouts, dust devils, and hurricanes, and the damage they can do.	46	3	4–5
Phillips, L. (1998). *Monster riddles.* Puffin. A collection of easy-to-read riddles about vampires, ghosts, and other monsters.	42	2	3–4

Prelutsky, J. (1997). *The beauty of the beast.* Knopf.
    A variety of poems about ants, cats, birds, dogs, fish, sharks,
    lizards, toads, and other creatures. Science tie-in: study of
    animals.
	10	3	4–6

Recht, L. (1991). *Dinosaur babies.* Random House.
    Explains how baby dinosaurs grew up and how they were
    cared for.
	32	1	1–3

Robinson, F. (1995). *Recycle that!* Children's Press.
    Explains that we are using lots of resources to make products,
    but we could save some of our resources by recycling
    materials or reusing items.
	32	1	2–3

Royston, A. (1998). *Truck trouble.* Dorling Kindersley.
    Follows John as he prepares his tractor trailer and makes
    deliveries.
	32	1	2–4

Ruepp, K. (1997). *Horses in the fog.* North-South.
    Trapped on a sand bar during a sea fog, Charlie uses a trick
    taught to her by an elderly fisherman to find her way back to
    shore as high tide starts moving in.
	64	3	3–6

Rylant, C. (1992). *Best wishes.* Richard C. Owen.
    Writer Cynthia Rylant explains how her childhood dreams
    have come true.
	32	3	4–5

Rylant, C. (1997). *Poppleton everyday.* Scholastic.
    Poppleton, the pig, gets seasick looking at the stars, makes
    many demands as he buys a grown-up bed, and finds that
    sailing is not relaxing when a storm comes up and flips you
    into the water.
	48	1	2–3

Sachar, L. (1995). *Wayside School gets a little stranger.* Avon.
    After being closed for 243 days, Wayside School reopens and
    is stranger than ever.
	168	3	4–6

Schwartz, A. (1985). *All of our noses are here and other noodle tales.*
    HarperCollins.
    Although noodle families are kind and loving, they have very
    little brain power and do foolish things such as believing that
    the people they see in a mirror are another family.
	64	1	2–3

Dr. Seuss (1976). *The cat's quizzer.* Random House. Asks a series of humorous questions and a few sensible ones.	62	2	3–4

Shea, G. (1997). *First flight: The story of Tom Tate and the Wright
    brothers.* HarperCollins.
    Tom Tate, a young boy, observes the Wright brothers as they
    conduct their flying experiments and finally become the first
    people to fly.
	48	2	3–5

Shuter, J. (1997). *The ancient Egyptians.* Heinemann.
    Explains major categories of ancient Egyptian civilization:
    origins, importance of the Nile, farming, government, trade,
    gods and goddesses, mummies, pyramids, everyday life,
    houses, children, and medicine.
	32	3	4–5

Shuter, J. (1997). *The ancient Greeks.* Heinemann. Well-illustrated and easy to read description of ancient Greece.	32	3	4–5
Smith, C. (1997). *How to draw cartoons.* Gareth Stevens. Shows how to use basic shapes to draw cartoon figures.	24	2	3–4
Smith, J. L. (1998). *Wizard and Wart in trouble.* HarperCollins. Using magic, Wizard turns ants into butterflies, a flood into whipped cream, and ice zings into trees.	48	1	2–3
Stadler, J. (1984). *Hooray for Snail.* Dutton. A slow base runner, Snail has to hit the ball to the moon to get a home run.	32	P	1–3
Stadler, J. (1988). *Cat at bat.* Dutton. Comic drawings illustrate a series of humorous rhymes.	32	P	1–3
Stadler, J. (1991). *Cat at bat is back.* Dutton. Sequel to *Cat at bat.*	32	P	1–3
Storad, C. J. (1998). *Tarantulas.* Lerner. Describes physical characteristics, behavior, enemies, and habitats of tarantulas.	48	3	4–5
Wells, R. E. (1997). *What's faster than a speeding cheetah?* Whitman. Compares the speed of a human with that of an ostrich and then shows increasingly faster creatures and objects.	29	3	4–5
Wroble, L. A. (1997). *Kids in colonial times.* Rosen. Provides an overview of life in colonial times.	24	3	4–5

HIGH-INTEREST, LOW-READABILITY BOOKS FOR OLDER STUDENTS

Adler, C. S. (1999). *Winning.* Clarion. To maintain a friendship, eighth-grader Vicky is challenged to cheat at tennis.	156	5	7–8
Avi. (1980). *Man from the sky.* Knopf. A young boy aids in the capture of a thief who parachutes from the sky.	40	2	4–6+
Bailer, D. (1999). *Touchdown: Great quarterbacks in football history.* Random House. Features biographies of six of the greatest pro quarterbacks of all time.	48	4	5–9
Balgassi, H. (1997). *Tae's sonata.* Clarion. A homesick Korean girl is assigned to work on a school project with one of the school's most popular boys.	123	4	7–8
Berends, P. (1973). *The case of the elevator duck.* Random House. Gilbert tracks down the owner of a duck left on an elevator in a housing project.	54	3	4–6+
Blatchford, C. H. (1998). *Going with the flow.* Carolrhoda. When he transfers to another school in mid-year, Mark misses his old friend and is embarrassed because his teacher calls attention to his deafness.	40	3	5–8

Boulais, S., & Marvis, B. (1998). *Tommy Nunez.* Mitchell Lane. Although he got in a number of minor scrapes when he was growing up and quit school, joining the Marines helped Tommy Nunez turn his life around.	32	4	5–12
Bunting, E. (1981). *The waiting game.* Lippincott. Three best buddies, who are seniors in high school and members of the football team, make plans for the future.	56	4	6–12
Bunting, E. (1984). *Someone is hiding on Alcatraz Island.* Houghton Mifflin. Danny hides from gang members.	40	3	5–8+
Byars, B. (1970). *Summer of the swans.* Viking. Sara's fourteenth summer is moody and difficult.	142	4	5–9
Coerr, E. (1977). *Sadako and the thousand paper cranes.* Bantam Doubleday Dell. A victim of the "atomic bomb disease," Saddako was an eleven-year-old girl who tried to ward off leukemia by making a thousand paper cranes.	64	4	5–7
Coville, B. (1993). *Aliens ate my homework.* Minstrel. Set upon by bullies at school, life changes for sixth-grader Rod Albright when visitors from outer space enlist his aid in tracking down an escaped criminal.	179	4	5–6
Dolan, E. (1983). *Great mysteries of the air.* Dodd, Mead. Recounts strange disappearances and other mysteries.	127	4	4–6+
Donnelly, J. (1987). *The Titanic lost and found.* Random House. Portrays in words and pictures the sinking and finding of the *Titanic.* Also describes steps taken to make ships safer.	48	3	5–8
Donnelly, J. (1988). *Tut's mummy lost . . . and found.* Random House. Describes the death of King Tut, the preparations made for his burial, and his burial in a pyramid. Also describes the search for and discovery of King Tut's tomb.	48	3	5–8
Dubowski, M. (1998). *Titanic: The disaster that shocked the world!* Dorling Kindersley. Heavily illustrated, depicts the sinking of the *Titanic.*	48	4	5–9
Gantos, J. (1994). *Heads or tails: Stories from the sixth grade.* Farrar Strauss & Giroux. In this slightly off-center collection of short stories, Jack has a series of misadventures.	151	4	5–6
Gutman, B. (1988). *Rookie summer.* Turman. Bobbie has a difficult time handling the pressures of the big leagues.	78	4	7–12
Gutman, B. (1988). *Smitty.* Turman. Smitty, an outstanding female high school basketball player, struggles against the system as she plays for the boys' team.	78	4	7–12

Hesse, K. (1996). *The music of dolphins.* Scholastic.   180   3+   8–12
    Raised by dolphins from the age of four, Mila, a teenager, is studied by scientists. Several brief segments are relatively difficult to read. However, most of the book is on a third-grade level.

Kehret, P. (1988). *The winner.* Turman.   78   4   7–12
    Bart helps rescue his kidnapped girl friend.

Kehret, P. (1996). *Small steps: The year I got polio.* Whitman.   179   5   6–12
    In 1949, at the age of twelve, Peg Kehret was paralyzed from the neck down by polio.

Mathis, S. B. (1997). *Running girl: The diary of Ebonee Rose.*
    Harcourt Brace.   60   4   5–7
    Ebonee writes about her dream of following in the footsteps of the great African American track stars.

Mills, C. (1997). *Losers, Inc.* HarperCollins.   150   4   5–6
    Both academically and athletically, sixth-grader Ethan Winfield falls far short of the accomplishments of his older brother, Peter.

Molzahn, A. B. (2001). *Sammy Sosa.* Capstone Press.   48   4   5–8
    Highlights the life of Dominican-born home-run hitter.

Park, B. (1995). *Mick Harte was here.* Random House.   88   4   5–7
    Phoebe learns to cope with her brother's sudden death and to honor his memory.

Paulsen, G. (1987). *Hatchet.* Simon & Schuster.   64   4   6–9
    Tormented by a secret that led to his parents' divorce, thirteen-year-old Brian Robeson crash-lands deep in the Canadian wilderness while on his way to visit his father.

Paulsen, G. (1993). *Amos gets famous.* Dell.   68   5   6–8
    While trying to impress Melissa, Amos becomes involved in a series of slapstick misadventures. Part of a series featuring Amos and Dunc.

Paulsen, G. (1994). *Mr. Tucket.* Delacorte.   166   4   5–8
    While heading West on a wagon train, fourteen-year-old Francis Tucket is captured by Pawnee Indians.

Paulsen, G. (1995). *Danger on Midnight River.* Bantam Doubleday
    Dell.   53   4   5–7
    On a trip into the woods, thirteen-year-old Daniel saves the boys who snubbed him at school.

Paulsen, G. (1997). *Grizzly.* Bantam Doubleday Dell.   53   5   5–7
    Justin McCallister goes after a grizzly bear after it kills his pet lamb, but is lucky to escape with his life.

Paulsen, G. (1998). *My life in dog years.* Delacorte Press.   137   4   5–12
    Writer Gary Paulsen describes nine dogs and the effects they have had on his life.

Pitts, P. (1988). *Racing the sun.* Avon.   148   4   6–7

Life changes for Brandon when his Navajo grandfather comes
to live with him.

Platt, K. (1981). *Dracula, go home!* Dell.	87	2	4–7+

Larry notices that one of the guests at his aunt's inn looks like
Dracula.

Shea, G. (1992). *Amazing rescues.* Random House.	48	3	7+

Rescued are a girl grabbed by an alligator, an unconscious
skydiver, and a child trapped in a well.

Spinelli, J. (1996). *Crash.* Knopf.	162	4	6–7

Rough-and-tumble seventh-grader Crash Coogan faces life the
way he plays football: head-on.

Stolz, M. *Explorer of Barkham Street.* HarperCollins.	179	4	5–8

A reformed bully, thirteen-year-old Martin Hastings has
difficulty making and keeping friends.

Strasser, T. (1994). *Help! I'm trapped in the first day of school.* Scholastic.	114	4	5–7

Having fallen in with a pal who delights in making life
miserable for others, Jake Sherman has an unsatisfactory first
day of school. But then he gets the opportunity to make up for
his mistakes as he relives the first day of school, time after
time after time.

Strasser, T. (1996). *Hey, Dad, get a life!* Holiday House.	164	4	5–9

After his death, Mr. Halkit returns and helps his daughters,
Kelly and Sasha, with chores and homework.

Wulffson, D. (1989). *More incredible true adventures.* Cobblehill/Dutton.	110	4	4–8+

The roof of a jet that is ripped off in mid-flight, a camper who
is attacked by a grizzly, and similar true adventures are
portrayed dramatically.

SAMPLE ASSESSMENT REPORT

Reading Report

Student:	James Lawlor (not his real name)
Evaluator:	Thomas G. Gunning, Ed.D.
Dates of Evaluation:	5–1–05, 5–2–05
Student's Birthdate:	4–20–95
School:	P. T. Barnum Elementary School
	501 North St.
	South Haven, CT
Grade:	3
Parents:	Mildred and Frank Lawlor
Address:	127 Whale St.
	South Haven, CT
Phone:	123–4567

REASON FOR REFERRAL

James Lawlor is a ten-year-old, third-grade student at the P. T. Barnum School in South Haven, Connecticut. James was referred for testing by Mr. Alvarez, his teacher. Mr. Alvarez is concerned because James is struggling with both reading and writing and is operating well below grade level.

OBSERVATIONS

During the two-day test period, James was very cooperative and worked very hard on the many tasks that were presented to him. He never said or showed that he was either tired or bored with the tests. In fact, on some of the tests that had to be ended because of a time limit, James expressed a desire to continue. On other tasks that were concluded because he had missed a number of items, James said that he wanted to try again or study the items so that he could do better.

James also frequently inquired about his performance on a number of the tests. He asked such questions as: "How am I doing? How many did I get right? Did I fail that test?"

Although the frequent inquiring about performance suggests a certain amount of anxiety, James did not exhibit any overt signs of feeling anxious, except on those tests that demanded reading. On the silent-reading selections of the Basic Reading Inventory, for instance, James's performance was accompanied by a great deal of lip movement, audible vocalization, and finger pointing. These signs of anxiety were present even when the material being read was well within James's capacity.

Of all the tests that were given, James seemed to enjoy most the one that required him to put blocks together to form a series of increasingly complex designs and the one that entailed putting a puzzle together. These tests were a part of the Weschler Intelligence Scale for Children–Revised. James' best performance was on that part of the Weschler Intelligence Scale for Children–Revised that required him to explain what he would do in certain social situations and that asked him to explain why certain social rules and conditions were necessary. His poorest performance was on a test that entailed connecting a series of numbers with their corresponding symbols.

James's favorite subject in school is math. He likes math because it is "easy." He liked reading least of all, but he feels that he does "okay" in reading. He said that he feels that some words are long, the books have too many hard words, and they are boring. He feels that reading would be easier if he knew the words. James doesn't have a favorite book or author and doesn't read at home. James's favorite activities are playing sports and building models. He plays on Little League baseball and Midget football teams.

James wants to be a builder when he grows up. He said it would be fun to build houses. He understands that this occupation demands training and the ability to follow instructions. James's mother said that his brothers and he have helped their father with a number of projects and that James is a good worker.

CASE HISTORY

A case history was obtained from Mrs. Mildred Lawlor, James's mother, who was openly cooperative and responsive to all questioning. The Lawlor family includes fifteen-year-old John, thirteen-year-old Lawrence, ten-year-old James, Mrs. Mildred Lawlor, and Mr. Frank Lawlor. The family appears to be closely knit and cooperative. As an example, while the father has been recuperating from injuries resulting from work, the three boys have been cooking meals and taking care of minor repairs under the father's direction. Mrs. Lawlor is employed full-time as a practical nurse. Mrs. Lawlor noted throughout the course of the interview that John's maturational development seemed to lag behind that of her other children almost from the very beginning. She cited that James sat by himself at the age of 11½ months, walked at 2 years, and talked at 2½ years. At the present time, however, she believes that James exhibits physical coordination skills that surpass those of his brothers when they were at this age. He especially enjoys participation in team sports such as baseball, basketball, and football.

SCHOOL HISTORY

James's formal education began at the age of 5½, when he attended kindergarten in the South Haven Public Schools. Because James was still not reading at the end of first grade, he repeated the grade. During his second year in first grade, James was given help twice a week by the school's Title 1 teacher. Assistance was increased to four days a week in second grade. Despite increased assistance, progress has been minimal. James's current teacher reports that James is cooperative and works hard, but lately has been beginning to show signs of avoidance when asked to read and write. Mr. Alvarez reports that James becomes restless during reading time, often asks to leave the room, and can't seem to focus on the selection the group is reading.

CLASSROOM OBSERVATIONS

James is in a class in which reading of basals is combined with the reading of trade books. Because James and several other students would have difficulty reading the third-grade basal on their own, they follow along as the teacher reads the selection to them. Meanwhile, the other class members read the basal on their own. For a twenty-minute period each day, the classroom teacher also provides special instruction and materials for James and the other students in his group. They are given material that they can read on their own and additional instruction in decoding strategies.

Because this group has a limited store of words that they can recognize immediately, the teacher is currently supplying instruction in this area. The words that the teacher presents are drawn from a children's book that the students are about to read. The books used with this group are easier than the basal reader. However, even in this group James is struggling. He is much slower to learn the new words and forgets them more easily. Although James was able to read each of the new words correctly when they were presented on the blackboard, he stumbled over them when he encountered them in the selection. The teacher told James that "he knew the word" and reminded James that they had just studied it, but that didn't help James. When James missed a word, the teacher suggested that he use context; but there were so many words in the selection that James didn't know, he was unable to use context.

After the lesson, the teacher requested a conference with the observer. He confessed to being baffled by James. He couldn't understand why the techniques he was using weren't meeting with success. He was especially distressed because James seemed to forget words so quickly. The observer and teacher discussed James's difficulty remembering printed words and decided to use a word-building approach because James didn't seem to do well with a sight approach. It was also decided to teach James pronounceable word-part and analogy strategies in addition to context strategies and to give James easier materials.

A follow-up observation revealed that the recommendations seemed to be working. Even in the easier book, James had to struggle with some of the words, but, because he knew most of the words, he was better able to use context. He also seemed more confident and more willing to take risks. According to the teacher, James also found the pronounceable word–part and analogy strategies to be helpful. As the teacher explained, James no longer had to rely solely on memory, which often failed him. During the session, James was able to decode the word *chimney* by reading the pronounceable word-part *im,* adding *ch* to make *chim,* and then using context to figure that the word must be *chimney.*

ASSESSMENT RESULTS

Physical

The Keystone Telebinocular was administered by the school nurse in order to assess James's visual functioning. James is functioning within the normal limits. The Maco Audiometer was used as a screening device to measure James's hearing capacity. The results seem to indicate that his capacity to hear is within the normal range.

James was given a physical at the walk-in clinic at South Haven General Hospital. James had been complaining of stomach pains. Unable to find a physical cause, the examining physician suggested that James might be experiencing stress but has scheduled a follow-up exam. Other than complaints of stomach distress, James is apparently in good health.

Academic Aptitude

The Weschler Intelligence Scale for Children Revised (WISC-R) was administered by the school psychologist in preparation for a conference on James's reading difficulty. The Weschler Intelligence Scale for Children Revised is an individually administered intelligence test that consists of a series of verbal subtests and a series of performance subtests. The verbal section of the test is subdivided into five areas designed to measure the child's ability to deal with verbal tasks in a variety of situations. The performance section, which also contains five subtests, assesses the child's ability to function in situations that are less verbal in nature. James's overall score on the WISC-R test fell within the average range. His score on the verbal section was much higher than his score on the performance part and indicates that he is "bright normal." James did particularly well on verbal subtests that required him to define words, use social judgment, and use his general fund of knowledge. However, he had difficulty reciting a series of numbers forwards and backwards. His score on the performance section indicates that he is "average." However, James scored well below average on the subtest that measured his ability to make new associations and to work rapidly and accurately by requiring him to connect a series of numbers with their corresponding symbols.

Memory

The Word Sequences and Design Sequences subtests of the Detroit Test of Learning Aptitude (Third Edition) were administered in order to assess James's ability to pay attention, concentrate, and use auditory or visual memory to remember a series of words or designs. Although James did somewhat better on the tasks requiring him to remember a series of designs, his performance on both tasks was well below his expected level of achievement. Performance was similar to his below-average ability to recite numbers forwards and backwards on the WISC-R.

Rapid Automatized Naming

A portion of the Rapid Automatized Naming Tests (R.A.N.) was administered in order to assess how fast and how accurately James could name a series of letters and numbers. On the letters and numbers subtests, James's performance was similar to that of the average five-year-old. The results suggest a slowness and lack of automaticity in recognizing and naming letters and numbers.

Reading

The Word-Lists portion of the Basic Reading Inventory (sixth ed.) was administered, with the following results:

GRADE LEVEL	FLASH SCORE	UNTIMED SCORE
Preprimer	75	85
Primer	60	75
First	30	40
Second		
Third		
Fourth		
Fifth		

The results of the Graded Words List of the Basic Reading Inventory (sixth ed.) indicate that James's ability to recognize words immediately, without taking time to figure them out, is adequate only at the preprimer (beginning first-grade) level. When given time to figure out words that he wasn't able to recognize immediately, James was only able to read five additional words correctly. James was able to figure out three-letter words that began with a single consonant and ended with a single consonant (*top, pet, hen, met*) but had difficulty with words that began with two or more consonants (*truck*) or that had complex vowel spellings (*brave, hurry, front*).

The passages section of The Basic Reading Inventory was also administered. The Basic Reading Inventory is an individual reading test. It is designed to indicate the level of reading material a student can profitably handle with instruction in a classroom or small-group setting. It also indicates the level of material that a student can read without any assistance, and the level of material that would be very difficult for him to handle, even with assistance. The Basic Reading Inventory also gives information about the student's oral reading, his ability to analyze and sound out words in context, and his ability to understand what he had read. The passages portion of the Basic Reading Inventory yielded the following results:

READING LEVEL	GRADE
Independent	Preprimer
Instructional	Primer
Frustration	First
Hearing Capacity	Fifth

According to the results of this test, James can read preprimer (beginning first-grade) material without any assistance. His comprehension and ability to read the words are nearly perfect at this level. However, because he had difficulty reading several of the words in the selection at the primer (middle-first-grade) level, James would need the teacher's assistance with material at this level. James missed so many words at the end-of-first-grade level that this material would be too difficult for him even with the teacher's help.

Even at the easiest level, James's oral reading was slow and laborious. During silent reading, James moved his lips, and he vocalized several of the words. As the selections grew more difficult, his vocalizations became more frequent and more audible. James seemed to recognize few words automatically and needed time to attempt to sound out most of the words. However, he was attempting to read for meaning. Often, when he misread a high-frequency word such as *when* or *are,* he would self-correct his miscue (word misread) when he saw that it didn't fit the sense of the sentence. When James's miscues were analyzed, most fit the context. However, often the miscue was graphically quite different from the expected response. James was using context but failed to integrate his use of context with phonics cues. Because of his apparently weak deciphering skills, he was overrelying on context.

James's comprehension of the selections that he read was perfect. However, because of deficient decoding skills, he was restricted to first-grade material. When selections were read to him, James was able to comprehend material on a fifth-grade level. This suggests that if James had adequate decoding skills, he would be able to read fifth-grade-level material.

Writing

Writing was assessed by examining James's portfolio and asking him to write a letter telling about himself. James has written on a variety of topics, but the content of his written pieces lacks elaboration. For instance, in his letter he told that he works with his father on Saturdays, but he didn't tell what kinds of things he did. James also has difficulty with format and mechanics. He didn't use standard letter form and did not capitalize names or use end punctuation consistently. He also was reluctant to write any word that he couldn't spell.

Phonics

The Word Pattern Survey was administered in order to assess James's ability to use phonics to decipher words. James had no difficulty reading three-letter, short-vowel patterns (*wet, sit, hop, fun*) but had problems with long-vowel patterns (*game, road, wheel*). He also had difficulty with words that contained consonant clusters at the beginning or end of the word (*drop, jump*).

Word Learning

Because James had significant difficulty reading printed words, a number of additional tests and procedures were used to obtain further information in this area.

Assisted Testing of Words List.   After the Word-Lists subtest was completed, portions of the subtest were readministered under assisted-testing conditions. James was given another opportunity to read some of the easier words that he had missed. If he missed a word again, he was given assistance. The idea was to see how much help and what kind of help he would need in order to be able to read the words. For instance, James was able to read the *il* and *en* in *children* when the teacher asked him if there were any parts of the word he could read. After pronouncing *il* and *en* in *children,* he was able, with a little coaching, to construct the word *children.* Given this same kind of assistance, James was also able to read *silver* and *smell.*

Word-Learning Test.   The Word-Learning Test was given to assess James's ability to learn to read new words. In this test, the student is presented seven words that were previously missed. Each word is printed on a card and shown to the student, who is asked to say the word. If he is unable to read the word or misreads it, the examiner tells the student the word. After all seven words have been presented, they are shuffled and presented again. After 10 trials, James knew just four of the words. The next day James knew just one of the words. His performance was similar to that of other students who have serious word-learning problems.

Visual-Auditory Learning Subtest.   The Visual-Auditory Learning subtest of the Woodcock-Johnson Cognitive Abilities Battery was administered. This subtest assesses the student's ability to link spoken words with printed symbols. This task is similar to what is required when a student learns sight words. James's performance was equal to that of the average four-year-old.

Spelling

According to the Elementary Spelling Inventory, James is operating in the early word pattern stage. James is able to spell regular short-vowel words such as *hat, pet, hit, lot,* and *cut* correctly and is ready to learn long-vowel patterns, such as *late, made, hope, boat,* and *bean.*

ADDITIONAL TESTING

Trial Teaching

Because James did poorly on the Word-Learning Test, which presented words in sight-word style, James was taught seven words using a word-building approach, in which the student builds words by adding a consonant to the vowel portion of the word (*g* + *ate*). For a period of fifteen minutes, magnetic letters and other devices were used to help James learn the words. Several sentences using the words were constructed, so that James could see the words in context. At the end of fifteen minutes, James was able to read all seven of the words. The next day, after a brief review, James was able to read all seven again.

SUMMARY

James appears to have at least average academic ability. His ability to define words and use social judgment and general knowledge suggest that his true academic ability might be above average. In addition, he is able to understand fifth-grade-level material when it is read to him. This suggests that his ability to comprehend language is equal to that of the average fifth-grader. This is the level of reading that James might be expected to achieve if he were not held back by poorly developed decoding skills. However, James did have difficulty with tasks that involve paying attention and concentrating and remembering a series of numbers, words, or pictures. James also was slow in naming letters and numbers. James' poorest performances were on those tests that required him to associate printed words or wordlike symbols with spoken words or to associate numbers with symbols. Apparently because of poor memory and underlying processing abilities, James has significant difficulty learning to read words. Learning new words is a struggle for him, and he soon forgets them. However, James does do better when a phonics rather than a sight approach is used.

Insofar as his reading ability is concerned, James is able to read preprimer (beginning-first-grade) material on his own. However, he needs assistance with any reading selections that are on a primer (middle-first-grade) level. Reading material on an ending-first-grade level and beyond is, at this time, so taxing for James that he would not be able to handle it. However, when material is read to James, he is able to understand selections on the fifth-grade level. James is reading well below his capacity. James's spelling and writing are also well below grade level and significantly below James's capacity.

James's low level of achievement in reading is apparently caused by his lack of a store of words that he recognizes instantly or at sight, his limited knowledge of phonics or word patterns, and his lack of strategies that he might use to figure out hard words.

RECOMMENDATIONS

Because James seems to learn best through a sounding-out approach, a systematic program of phonics should be taught. The program known as Word Building is recommended because James had some success with this in his trial teaching lesson. In Word Building, the student learns patterns by assembling them: adding *b* + *ake* to construct *bake,* *c* + *ake* to make *cake,* and so on. James should also be taught a series of strategies for deciphering hard words. These strategies should include looking for parts of the word he can say and then using known parts to build the word, thinking of a known word that is like the hard word, and using context to figure out the word.

James also needs to be given reading material that is on his level. Books that have too many unknown words are discouraging and don't provide James with the opportunity to apply his reading skills. In fact, James needs as much opportunity as possible to read books and other materials that are easy for him. In addition to showing him that reading need not be a struggle, reading easy books will provide practice in recognizing words so that the speed and ease with which he reads improves. Because James expressed an interest in animals and sports, he might enjoy books such as the following, which are on a primer (middle-first-grade) level:

Kick Pass and Run. Leonard Kessler.
Oliver. Syd Hoff.
A Dog Named Sam. Janice Poland.

Old Turtle's Riddle and Joke Book. Leonard Kessler.
The Day the Teacher Went Bananas. James Howe.
Dinosaur Time. Peggy Parish.
If the Dinosaurs Came Back. Bernard Most.

Games might also be used to reinforce James' ability to decode vowel patterns. One possible choice is Road Racer (Curriculum Associates). Puzzles, riddles, songs, verses, and poems that incorporate patterns should also be motivating.

Writing might also be used to reinforce James's word-analysis skills. Because James's spelling ability is limited, he should be encouraged to use invented spelling so that he can give full expression to his ideas. He would also profit from the language-experience approach, in which he discusses an experience, dictates a story, and then reads the dictated story. This technique can also be used to explore topics in which James is interested. The teacher or an aide can read aloud to James books and articles that are too difficult for James to read on his own. The information is discussed and then summarized in an experience story. Also take judicious advantage of tape-recorded books, talking software, electronic talking dictionaries, and other technology that might assist James with reading and writing tasks that otherwise would be too difficult for him.

Because of his low level of reading ability, James is restricted in the range of books that he can read. In order to continue building James's excellent background of knowledge, James should be read to in the classroom and at home. Another way of building on James's excellent background of information is to involve him in activities that don't require reading and writing. In class discussions, for instance, make it a point to call on James. Also encourage James to engage in art, sports, and other activities that don't require reading and writing, so that he experiences a sense of achievement.

James's parents can help by focusing on the things that James does well. They should encourage him to engage in activities that he enjoys, such as playing sports and helping his father. The parents might also continue to read to James and provide books that are on his reading level and in which he is interested. The parents should continue to build his background of information by taking him to the zoo, museums, and other places and discussing topics of interest with him.

REFERENCES

PROFESSIONAL REFERENCES

Aasved, H. (1989). Eye examinations. In H. Gjessing & B. Karlsen (Eds.), *A longitudinal study of dyslexia* (pp. 192–209). New York: Springer-Verlag.

Abrams, J. C. (1988). A dynamic-developmental approach to reading and related learning disabilities. In S. M. Glazer, L. W. Searfoss, & L. M. Gentile (Eds.), *Reexamining reading diagnosis: New trends and procedures* (pp. 29–47). Newark, DE: International Reading Association.

Adams, M. J. (1990). *Beginning to read: Thinking and learning about print.* Cambridge, MA: MIT Press.

Adoption Guidelines Project (1990). Comprehension I: The directed reading lesson. In Adoption Guidelines Project, *A guide to selecting basal reading programs.* Champaign, IL: University of Illinois, Center for the Study of Reading.

Afflerbach, P. (1990). The influence of prior knowledge on expert readers' main idea construction strategies. *Reading Research Quarterly, 25,* 31–46.

Alegria, J., & Morais, J. (1991). Segmental analysis and reading acquisition. In L. Rieben & C. A. Perfetti (Eds.), *Learning to read: Basic research and its implications* (pp. 135–148). Hillsdale, NJ: Lawrence Erlbaum.

Alexander, J. C. (1998). Reading skill and context facilitation: A classic study revisited. *The Journal of Educational Research, 91,* 314–318.

Alexander, P. A., & Jetton, T. L. (2000). Learning from text: A multidimensional and developmental perspective. In M. L. Kamil, P. B. Mosenthal, P. D. Pearson, & R. Barr (Eds.), *Handbook of reading research, Volume III* (pp. 285–310). Mahwah, NJ: Erlbaum.

Allen, J., Michalove, B., & Shockley, B. (1993). *Engaging children, community and chaos in the lives of young literacy learners.* Portsmouth, NH: Heinemann.

Allington, R. (1983). The reading instruction provided readers of differing reading ability. *Elementary School Journal, 83,* 548–559.

Allington, R. L. (1984). Oral reading. In P. D. Pearson, R. Barr, M. L. Kamil, & P. Mosenthal (Eds.), *Handbook of reading research* (pp. 829–863). New York: Longman.

Allington, R. L. (1994). The schools we have: The schools we need. *The Reading Teacher, 48,* 14–29.

Allington, R. L., & Walmsley, S. E. (1995). No quick fix: Where do we go from here? In R. A. Allington & S. A. Walmsley (Eds.), *Rethinking literacy in America's elementary schools* (pp. 253–264). New York: Teachers College Press.

Alvermann, D., Bridge, C. A., Schmidt, B. A., Searfoss, L. W., Winograd, P., Paris, S. G., Priestly, M., & Santeusanio, R. D. (1989). *Heath Reading.* Lexington, MA: Heath.

Alvermann, D. E., & Phelps, S. F. (1994). *Content area and reading and literacy: Succeeding in today's diverse classrooms.* Boston: Allyn & Bacon.

American Academy of Ophthalmology (1984, 1990). *Vision.* Chicago: American Academy of Ophthalmology.

American Academy of Pediatrics (1996). Vision screening. *Pediatrics 98,* 153–157.

American Academy of Pediatrics (1998). Learning disabilities, dyslexia, and vision: A subject review. *Pediatrics, 102,* 1217–1219.

American Academy of Pediatrics (2000). Clinical practice guideline. Diagnosis and evaluation of the child with attention deficit/hyperactivity disorder. *Pediatrics, 105,* 1158–1170.

American Psychiatric Association (1994). *Diagnostic and Statistical Manual of Mental Disorders* (4th ed.). Washington, DC: American Psychiatric Association.

American Psychiatric Association (2000). *Diagnostic and statistical manual of mental disorders* (4th ed., text revision). Washington, DC: American Psychiatric Association.

Anderson, R. C. (1990, May). *Microanalysis of classroom reading instruction.* Paper presented at the Annual Conference on Reading Research, Atlanta, GA.

Anderson, R. C. (1996). Research foundations to support wide reading. In V. Greaney (Ed.), *Promoting reading in developing countries* (pp. 55–77). Newark, DE: International Reading Association.

Anderson, R. C., Hiebert, E. H., Scott, J. A., & Wilkinson, I. A. G. (1985). *Becoming a nation of readers: The report of the Commission on Reading.* Washington, DC: National Institute of Education.

Anderson, V., & Henne, R. (1993). *Collaborative, integrated reading and writing strategy instruction.* Paper presented at the annual meeting of the National Reading Conference, Charleston, SC.

Anderson, V., & Roit, M. (1993). Planning and implementing collaborative strategy instruction for delayed readers in grades 6–10. *The Elementary School Journal, 94,* 121–137.

Anyon, J. (1980). Social class and the hidden curriculum of work. *Journal of Education, 162*(1), 67–92.

Apel, K., Masterson, J. J., & Niessen, N. L. (2004). Spelling assessment frameworks. In C. A. Stone, E. R. Silliman, B. J. Ehren, & K. Apel (Eds.), *Handbook of language and literacy development and disorders* (pp. 644–660). New York: Guilford Press.

Applebee, A. N., Langer, J. A., & Mullis, I. V. S. (1988). *Who reads best? Factors related to reading achievement in grades 3, 7, and 11.* Princeton, NJ: Educational Testing Service.

Armbruster, B. B. (1991). Framing: A technique for improving learning from science texts. In C. M. Santa & D. C. Alvermann (Eds.), *Science learning: Processes and applications* (pp. 104–113). Newark, DE: International Reading Association.

Armbruster, B. B., & Anderson, T. H. (1981). *Content area textbooks* (Technical Report 23). Champaign, IL: University of Illinois, Center for the Study of Reading.

Arnold, N. (2003). *Washington alternate assessment system technical report on standard setting for the 2002 portfolio* (Synthesis Report 52). Minneapolis, MN: University of Minnesota, National Center on Educational Outcomes. Available at http://education.umn.edu/nceo/OnlinePubs/Synthesis52.html

Athey, I. (1985). Reading research in the affective domain. In H. Singer & R. B. Ruddell (Eds.), *Theoretical models and processes of reading* (3rd ed., pp. 527–557). Newark, DE: International Reading Association.

Atwell, N. (1987). *In the middle.* Portsmouth, NH: Boynton/Cook.

Au, K. H., Mason, J. M., & Scheu, J. A. (1995). *Literacy instruction for today.* New York: HarperCollins.

Baddeley, A. (1992). Working memory. *Science, 255,* 556–559.

Bader, L. A. (1998). *Bader Reading and Language Inventory* (3rd ed.). Upper Saddle River, NJ: Prentice Hall.

Bader, L. A., & Wiesendanger, K. O. (1986). University based reading clinics: Practices and procedures. *The Reading Teacher, 39,* 698–702.

Badian, N. A. (1997). Dyslexia and the double deficit hypothesis. *Annals of Dyslexia, 47,* 69–87.

Badian, N. A. (1999). Reading disability defined as a discrepancy between listening and reading comprehension: Longitudinal study of stability, gender differences, and prevalence. *Journal of Learning Disabilities, 32,* 138–148.

Badian, N. A. (2000). *It's not just phonological awareness! The importance of orthographic processing in reading.* Paper presented at the 27th Annual Conference on Dyslexia and Related Reading Disorders, New York.

Bain, A. M. (1991). Handwriting disorders. In A. M. Bain, L. L. Bailet, & L. C. Moats (Eds.), *Written language disorders: Theory into practice* (pp. 43–64). Austin, TX: Pro-Ed.

Baker, L., & Brown, A. L. (1984). Megacognitive skills and reading. In P. D. Pearson, R. Barr, M. L. Kamil, & P. Mosenthal (Eds.), *Handbook of reading research* (pp. 353–394). New York: Longman.

Baker, S., Gersten, R., & Scanlon, D. (2002). Procedural facilitators and cognitive strategies: Tools for unraveling the mysteries of comprehension and the writing process and for providing meaningful access to the general curriculum. *Learning Disabilities Research & Practice, 17,* 65–77.

Bandura, A. (1977). Self-efficacy: Toward a unifying theory of behavioral change. *Psychological Review, 84,* 191–215.

Barba, R. H. (1995). *Science in the multicultural classroom: A guide to teaching and learning.* Boston: Allyn & Bacon.

Barker, T. A., Torgesen, J. K., & Wagner, R. K. (1992). The role of orthographic processing skills on five different reading tasks. *Reading Research Quarterly, 27,* 335–346.

Barnes, B. L. (1996–1997). But teacher you went right on: A perspective on Reading Recovery. *The Reading Teacher, 50,* 284–292.

Barnes, W. G. W. (1989). Word sorting: The cultivation of rules for spelling in English. *Reading Psychology, 10,* 293–307.

Barr, R., Blachowicz, C., & Wogman-Sadow, M. (1995). *Reading diagnosis for teachers: An instructional approach* (3rd ed.). New York: Addison-Wesley.

Barr, R., & Dreeben, R. (1991). Grouping students for reading instruction. In R. Barr, M. L. Kamil, P. Mosenthal, & P. D. Pearson (Eds.), *Handbook of reading research, Volume II* (pp. 885–910). New York: Longman.

Barr, R. D., & Parret, W. H. (2001). *Hope fulfilled for at-risk and violent youth: K–12 programs that work* (2nd ed.). Boston: Allyn & Bacon.

Barron, R. F. (1969). The use of vocabulary as an advance organizer. In H. L. Herber & P. L. Sanders (Eds.), *Research in reading in the content areas: First year report* (pp. 29–39). Syracuse, NY: Syracuse University Reading and Language Arts Center.

Barron, R. F. (1979). Research for classroom teachers: Recent developments on the use of the structured overview as an advanced organizer. In H. L. Herber & J. D. Riley (Eds.), *Research in reading in the content areas: Fourth report* (pp. 171–176). Syracuse, NY: Syracuse University Reading and Language Arts Center.

Bartlet, D., & Shapiro, M. B. (1956). Investigation and treatment of a reading disability in a dull child with severe psychological disturbances. *British Journal of Educational Psychology, 26,* 180–190.

Bartoli, J., & Botel, M. (1988). *Reading/learning disability: An ecological approach.* New York: Teachers College Press.

Baumann, J. F. (1986). The direct instruction of main idea comprehension ability. In J. F. Baumann (Ed.), *Teaching main idea comprehension* (pp. 133–178). Newark, DE: International Reading Association.

Baumann, J. F. (1989). *Reading assessment: An instructional decision-making perspective.* Columbus, OH: Merrill.

Baumann, J. F., Edwards, E. C., Font, G., Tereshinski, C., Kame'enui, E. J., & Olejnik, S. F. (2002). Teaching morphemic and contextual analysis to fifth-grade students. *Reading Research Quarterly, 37,* 150–173.

Baumann, J. F., & Kame'enui, E. J. (1991). Research on vocabulary instruction: Ode to Voltaire. In J. Flood, J. M. Jensen, D. Lapp, & J. R. Squire (Eds.), *Handbook of research on teaching the English language arts* (pp. 604–632). New York: Macmillan.

Baumann, J. F., & Serra, J. K. (1984). The frequency and placement of main ideas in children's social studies textbooks: A modified replication of Braddock's research on topic sentences. *Journal of Reading Behavior, 16,* 27–40.

Bear, D., & Barone, D. (1989). The elementary spelling inventory (with error guide). *Reading Psychology, 10,* 275–292.

Bear, D. R., Invernizzi, M., Johnston, F., & Templeton, S. (1996). *Words their way: Word study for phonics, vocabulary, and spelling instruction.* Upper Saddle River, NJ: Merrill.

Bear, D. R., Invernizzi, M., Templeton, S., & Johnston, F. (2004). *Words their way: Word study for phonics, vocabulary, and spelling instruction* (3rd ed.). Upper Saddle River, NJ: Pearson.

Beaver, J. (1997). *Developmental reading assessment resource guide.* White Plains, NY: Celebration Press.

Beck, I. L., & Juel, C. (1995). The role of phonics in learning to read. *American Educator, 19*(2), 21–25, 39–42.

Beck, I. L., & McKeown, M. G. (1991). Conditions of vocabulary acquisition. In R. Barr, M. L. Kamil, P. Mosenthal, & P. D. Pearson (Eds.), *Handbook of reading research, Volume II* (pp. 789–814). New York: Longman.

Beck, I. L., & McKeown, M. G. (2001). Text talk: Capturing the benefits of read-aloud experiences for young children. *The Reading Teacher, 55,* 10–20.

Beck, I. L., McKeown, M. G., & Kucan, L. (2002). *Bringing words to life: Robust vocabulary instruction.* New York: York.

Beck, I. L., McKeown, M. G., & Omanson, R. C. (1987). The effects and uses of diverse vocabulary instructional techniques. In M. G. McKeown & M. E. Curtis (Eds.), *The nature of vocabulary acquisition* (pp. 147–163). Hillsdale, NJ: Lawrence Erlbaum.

Beck, I. L., Omanson, R. C., & McKeown, M. G. (1982). An instructional redesign of reading lessons: Effects on comprehension. *Reading Research Quarterly, 17,* 462–481.

Becker, W. C. (1977). Teaching reading and language to the disadvantaged—What we have learned from field research. *Harvard Educational Review, 47,* 518–543.

Beers, K. (2003). *When kids can't read: What teachers can do—A guide for teachers 6–12.* Portsmouth, NH: Heinemann.

Benson, V., & Cummins, C. (2000). *The power of retelling, developmental steps for building comprehension.* Bothell, WA: Wright Group/McGraw-Hill.

Bereiter, C., & Scardamalia, M. (1982). From conversation to composition: The role of instruction in a developmental process. In R. Glass (Ed.), *Advances in instructional psychology, Volume 2* (pp. 1–64). Hillsdale, NJ: Lawrence Erlbaum.

Berkowitz, S. J. (1986). Effects of instruction in text organization on sixth-grade students' memory for expository text. *Reading Research Quarterly, 21,* 161–178.

Berliner, D. C. (1981). Academic learning time and reading achievement. In J. T. Guthrie (Ed.), *Comprehension and teaching: Research reviews* (pp. 203–226). Newark, DE: International Reading Association.

Berninger, V. (1990). Multiple orthographic and phonological codes: Keys to instructional interventions for developing word identification. *School Psychology Review, 19,* 518–533.

Berninger, V. W., Abbott, R. D., Zook, D., Ogier, S., Lemos-Britton, Z., & Brooksher, R. (1999). Early intervention for reading disabilities: Teaching the alphabet principle in a connectionist framework. *Journal of Learning Disabilities, 32,* 491–503.

Berres, F., & Eyer, J. T. (1970). Cases from full-time remedial students: John. In A. J. Harris (Ed.), *Casebook on reading disability* (pp. 25–47). New York: David McKay.

Bertin, P., & Perleman, E. (1999). *Preventing academic failure: A multisensory curriculum for teaching, reading, spelling, and handwriting in the elementary school classroom.* White Plains, NY: Monroe Associates.

Betts, E. A. (1946). *Foundations of reading instruction.* New York: American Book Company.

Beverstock, C. (1991). *Your child's vision is important.* Newark, DE: International Reading Association.

Biemiller, A. (1970). The development of the use of graphic and contextual information as children learn to read. *Reading Research Quarterly, 6,* 75–96.

Biemiller, A. (1977–1978). Relationships between oral reading rates for letters, words, and simple text in the development of reading achievement. *Reading Research Quarterly, 13,* 223–253.

Biemiller, A. (1994). Some observations on acquiring and using reading skill in elementary schools. In C. K. Kinzer & D. J. Leu (Eds.), *Multidimensional aspects of literacy research, theory, and practice. Forty-third Yearbook of the National Reading Conference* (pp. 209–216). Chicago: National Reading Conference.

Biemiller, A. (2001). Teaching vocabulary: Early, direct, and sequential. *American Educator, 25,* 25–28.

Biemiller, A., & Slonim, N. (2001). Estimating root word vocabulary growth in normative and advantaged populations: Evidence for a common sequence of vocabulary acquisition. *Journal of Educational Psychology, 93,* 498–520.

Bisson, S. A., Phillips, S. A., Creamer, S. M., & Baker, T. K. (1999). Shared Reading, books, and audiotapes: Supporting diverse students in school and at home. *The Reading Teacher, 52* 430–444.

Bjorklund, B., Handler, N., Mitten, J., & Stockwell, G. (1998). *Literature circles: A tool for developing students as critical readers, writers, and thinkers.* Paper presented at the 47th Annual Conference of the Connecticut Reading Association, Waterbury, CT.

Blachman, B. A. (2000). Phonological awareness. In M. L. Kamil, P. B. Mosenthal, P. D. Pearson, & R. Barr (Eds.), *Handbook of Reading Research, Volume III* (pp. 483–502). Mahwah, NJ: Erlbaum.

Blachowicz, C. L. Z. (1986). Making connections: Alternatives to the vocabulary notebook. *Journal of Reading, 29,* 643–649.

Blachowicz, C. L. Z., & Fisher, P. (2000). Vocabulary instruction. In M. L. Kamil, P. B. Mosenthal, P. D. Pearson, & R. Barr (Eds.), *Handbook of Reading Research, Volume III* (pp. 503–523). Mahwah, NJ: Erlbaum.

Blaine, M. (1986). Giants of the city. In J. Stanchfield & T. Gunning (Eds.), *Wings* (New Directions in Reading) (pp. 162–169). Boston: Houghton Mifflin.

Bloodgood, J., & Broaddus, K. (1994). *Working with severe reading problems: Remediation.* Paper presented at the annual meeting of the International Reading Association, Toronto, Ont.

Bloodgood, J. W. (1999). What's in a name? Children's name writing and literacy acquisition. *Reading Research Quarterly, 34,* 342–367.

Bloom, B. (Ed.). (1957). *Taxonomy of educational objectives.* New York: McKay.

Bond, G. L., Tinker, M. A., Wasson, B. B., & Wasson, J. B. (1994). *Reading difficulties: Their diagnosis and correction* (7th ed.). Boston: Allyn & Bacon.

Bos, C. S., & Anders, P. L. (1990). Effects of interactive vocabulary instruction on the vocabulary learning and reading comprehension of junior-high learning disabled students. *Learning Disability Quarterly, 13,* 31–42.

Bos, C. S., & Vaughn, S. (1994). *Strategies for teaching students with learning and behavior problems* (3rd ed.). Boston: Allyn & Bacon.

Bowers, P. G., Sunseth, K., & Golden, J. (1999). The route between rapid naming and reading progress. *Scientific Studies of Reading, 3,* 31–53.

Boyle, C. (1996). *Efficacy of peer evaluation and effects of peer evaluation on persuasive writing.* Unpublished master's thesis, San Diego State University, San Diego, CA.

Boyles, N. (2002). *Teaching written response to text: Constructing quality answers to open-ended comprehension questions.* Gainsville, FL: Maupin House.

Bradley, J. M., & Thalgoot, M. R. (1987). Reducing reading anxiety. *Academic Therapy, 22,* 349–358.

Brady, S. (1986). Short-term memory, phonological processing, and reading ability. *Annals of Dyslexia, 36,* 138–153.

Brady, S. A. (1991). The role of working memory in reading disability. In S. A. Brady & D. P. Shankweiler (Eds.), *Phonological processes in literacy: A tribute to Isabelle Y. Liberman* (pp. 129–151). Hillsdale, NJ: Lawrence Erlbaum.

Bransford, J. D. (1994). Schema activation and schema acquisition: Comments on Richard C. Anderson's remarks. In R. B. Ruddell, M. R. Ruddell, & H. Sanger (Eds.), *Theoretical models and processes of reading* (4th ed., pp. 483–495). Newark, DE: International Reading Association.

Bricklin, P. M. (1991). The concept of "self as learner": Its critical role in the diagnosis and treatment of children with reading disabilities. *Reading, Writing, and Learning Disabilities, 7,* 201–217.

Bridge, C. A., Winograd, P. N., & Haley, D. (1983). Using predictable materials vs. preprimers to teach beginning sight words. *The Reading Teacher, 36,* 884–891.

Bristow, P. S., Pikulski, J. J., & Pelosi, P. L. (1983). A comparison of five estimates of reading instructional level. *The Reading Teacher, 37,* 273–279.

Broaddus, K., & Bloodgood, J. (1999). "We're supposed to already know how to teach reading": Teacher change to support struggling readers. *Reading Research Quarterly, 34,* 426–451.

Broderick, P. (1998, September 1). Pediatric vision screening for the family physician. *American Family Physician.* Available online at http://www.aafp.org/afp/980901ap/broderic.html

Brown, A. L., & Day, J. D. (1983). Macrorules for summarizing text: The development of expertise. *Journal of Verbal Learning and Verbal Behavior, 22*(1), 1–14.

Brown, A. L., & Palincsar, A. (1986). *Reciprocal teaching of comprehension strategies: A natural history of one program for enhancing learning* (Technical Report 334). Champaign, IL: University of Illinois, Center for the Study of Reading.

Bruce, B. (1980). Plans and social actions. In R. Spiro, B. Bruce, & W. Brewer (Eds.), *Theoretical issues in reading comprehension* (pp. 367–384). Hillsdale, NJ: Erlbaum.

Bruck, M. (1992). Persistence of dyslexics' phonological awareness deficits. *Developmental Psychology, 28,* 874–886.

Bruck, M., & Treiman, R. (1992). Learning to pronounce words: The limitations of analogies. *Reading Research Quarterly, 27,* 374–388.

Bruner, J. (1986). *Actual minds, possible worlds.* Cambridge, MA: Harvard University Press.

Bryant, N. D., Kelly, M. S., Hathaway, K., & Rubin, E. (1981). *A summary of directions for the "LD-Efficient" teaching manual.* New York: Research Institute for the Study of Learning Disabilities, Teachers College, Columbia University.

Bryant, P., & Bradley, L. (1985). *Children's reading problems.* Oxford, England: Basil Blackwell.

Buehl, D., & Stumpf, S. (1999). *High School Reading Task Force Report.* Madison, WI: Madison Metropolitan School District.

Buehl, D., & Stumpf, S. (2000). *Developing middle school and high school programs for struggling readers.* Paper presented at the annual meeting of the International Reading Association, Indianapolis, IN.

Bulgren, J. A., & Scanlon, D. (1997/1998). Teachers' instructional routines and learning strategies that promote understanding of content-area concepts. *Journal of Adolescent & Adult Literacy, 41,* 292–302.

Burcham, B., Carlson, L., & Milich, R. (1993). Promising school-based practices for students with attention deficit disorder. *Exceptional Children, 60,* 174–180.

Burns, P. C., & Roe, B. D. (2002). *Burns/Roe informal reading inventory: Preprimer to twelfth grade* (6th ed.). Boston: Houghton Mifflin.

Bus, A. G., & van Ijzendoorn, M. H. (1999). Phonological awareness and early reading: A meta-analysis of experiential training studies. *Journal of Educational Psychology, 91,* 403–414.

Bush, C., & Huebner, M. (1979). *Strategies for reading in the elementary school* (2nd ed.). New York: Macmillan.

Butkowsky, I. S., & Willows, D. M. (1980). Cognitive-motivational characteristics of children varying in reading ability: Evidence for learned helplessness in poor readers. *Journal of Educational Psychology, 72,* 408–422.

Byrne, B., & Fielding-Barnsley, R. (1995). Evaluation of a program to teach phonemic awareness to young children: A 2-year and 3-year follow-up and a new preschool trial. *Journal of Educational Psychology, 87,* 488–503.

Byrne, B., Fielding-Barnsley, R., & Ashley, L. (2000). Effects of preschool phonemic identity training after six years: Outcome level distinguished from rate of response. *Journal of Educational Psychology, 92,* 659–667.

Cain, K. (1996). Story knowledge and comprehension skill. In C. Cornoldi & J. Oakhill (Eds.), *Reading comprehension difficulties: Process and intervention* (pp. 167–192). Mahwah, NJ: Erlbaum.

Cairney, T. H. (1990). *Teaching reading comprehension: Meaning makers at work.* Philadelphia: Open University Press.

Calkins, L. (2003). *Units of study for primary writing: A yearlong curriculum* (K–2). Portsmouth, NH: Heinemann.

Calkins, L., Montgomery, K., & Santman, D. (1998). *A teacher's guide to standardized reading tests.* Portsmouth, NH: Heinemann.

Calkins, L. M., & Oxenhorn, A. (2003). *Small moments: Personal narrative writing.* Portsmouth, NH: Heinemann.

Calkins, L. M. (1994). *The art of teaching writing* (2nd ed.). Portsmouth, NH: Heinemann.

Calkins, L. M., & Harwayne, S. (1991). *Living between the lines.* Portsmouth, NH: Heinemann.

Campbell, R. (1998). Looking at literacy learning in preschool settings. In R. Campbell (Ed.), *Facilitating preschool literacy* (pp. 70–83). Newark, DE: International Reading Association.

Cappella, E., & Weinstein, R. S. (2002). Turning around reading achievement: Predictors of high school students' academic resilience. *Journal of Educational Psychology, 93,* 758–771.

Carbo, M. (1997). *What every principal should know about teaching reading: How to raise test scores and nurturing a love of reading.* Syosset, NY: National Reading Styles Institute.

Carbo, M., Dunn, R., & Dunn, K. (1986). *Teaching students to read through their individual learning styles.* Boston: Allyn & Bacon.

Cardoso-Martins, C., Rodrigues, L., & Ehri, L. (2003). Place of environmental print in reading development: Evidence from nonliterate adults. *Scientific Study of Reading, 7,* 335–355.

Carigan-Belleville, L. (1989). Jason's story: Motivating the reluctant student to write. *English Journal, 78,* 57–60.

Carlson, N. R. (1993). *Psychology: The science of behavior* (4th ed). Boston: Allyn & Bacon.

Carnegie Corporation (1994). *Starting points: Meeting the needs of our youngest children.* New York: Carnegie Corporation.

Carnine, D., Kame'enui, E. J., & Coyle, G. (1984). Utilization of contextual information in determining the meaning of unfamiliar words. *Reading Research Quarterly, 19,* 188–204.

Carr, E. M. (1985). The vocabulary overview guide: A metacognitive strategy to improve vocabulary, comprehension and retention. *Journal of Reading, 28,* 684–689.

Carroll, J. B. (1977). Developmental parameters in reading comprehension. In J. T. Guthrie (Ed.), *Cognition, curriculum and comprehension* (pp. 1–15). Newark, DE: International Reading Association.

Casbergue, R. M., & Greene, J. F. (1988). Persistent misconceptions about sensory perception and reading disability. *Journal of Reading, 31,* 196–203.

Castiglioni-Spalton, M., & Ehri, L. C. (2003). Phonemic awareness instruction: Contribution of articulatory segmentation to novice beginners' reading and writing. *Scientific Studies of Reading, 7,* 25–52.

Catts, H. W., & Kamhi, A. G. (1999). Defining reading disabilities. In H. W. Catts & A. G. Kamhi (Eds.), *Language and reading disabilities* (pp. 50–72). Boston: Allyn & Bacon.

Caverly, D. C., & Orlando, V. P. (1991). Textbook study strategies. In D. C. Caverly & V. P. Orlando (Eds.), *Teaching reading and study strategies at the college level* (pp. 86–165). Newark, DE: International Reading Association.

Celano, M. P., & Geller, R. J. (1993). Learning, school performance, and children with asthma: How much at risk? *Journal of Learning Disabilities, 26,* 23–37.

Center, Y., Wheldall, K., Freeman, L., Outhred, L., & McNaught, M. (1995). An experimental evaluation of Reading Recovery. *Reading Research Quarterly, 30,* 240–263.

Center for Research on Learning at the University of Kansas (2000). *The learning strategies curriculum.* Available at www.ku-crl.org

Center for the Study of Reading (1991). *Manual for the Benchmark program* [video cassette]. Urbana, IL: University of Illinois.

Centers for Disease Control and Prevention (2004). *Fast stats A to Z: Asthma.* Available at http://www.cdc.gov/nchs/fastats/asthma.htm

Chall, J. S. (1996). *Stages of reading development* (2nd ed.). San Diego: Harcourt.

Chall, J. S., Bissex, G. L., Conard, S. S., & Harris-Sharples, S. H. (1996). *Holistic assessment of texts: Scales for estimating the difficulty of literature, social studies, and science materials.* Cambridge, MA: Brookline.

Chall, J. S., & Conard, S. S. (1991). *Should textbooks challenge students? The case for easier or harder books.* New York: Teachers College Press.

Chall, J. S., & Dale, E. (1995). *Readability revisited: The new Dale-Chall Readability Formula.* Cambridge, MA: Brookline.

Chall, J. S., Jacobs, V. A., & Baldwin, L. E. (1990). *The reading crisis: Why poor children fall behind.* Cambridge, MA: Harvard University Press.

Chamot, A. U., & O'Malley, J. M. (1994). Instructional approaches and teaching procedures. In K. Spangerberg-Urbschart & R. Pritchard (Eds.), *Kids come in all languages: Reading instruction for ESL students* (pp. 82–107). Newark, DE: International Reading Association.

Champion, A. (1997). Knowledge of suffixed words: A comparison of reading disabled and nondisabled readers. *Annals of Dyslexia, 47,* 29–55.

Chase, C. H. (1996). A visual deficit model of developmental dyslexia. In C. H. Chase, G. D. Rosen, & G. F. Sherman (Eds.), *Developmental dyslexia: Neural, cognitive, and genetic mechanisms* (pp. 127–158). Baltimore: York Press.

Chase, C., & Stein, J. (2003). Visual magnocellular deficits in dyslexia. *Brain, 126,* 2.

Chicago Public Schools (2000). *How to create a rubric from scratch.* Available at http://intranet.cps.k12.il.us/Assessments/Ideas_and_Rubrics/Create_Rubric/create_rubric.html

Cho, K., & Krashen, S. D. (1994). Acquisition of vocabulary from the Sweet Valley Kids series: Adult ESL acquisition. *Journal of Reading, 37,* 662–667.

Chomsky, C. (1978). When you still can't read in third grade: After decoding, what? In S. J. Samuels (Ed.), *What research has to say about reading instruction* (pp. 13–30). Newark, DE: International Reading Association.

Cioffi, G., & Carney, J. J. (1983). Dynamic assessment of reading disabilities. *The Reading Teacher, 36,* 764–768.

Clark, D. B., & Uhury, J. K. (1995). *Dyslexia: Theory and practice of remedial instruction* (2nd ed.). Parkton, MD: York Press.

Clay, M. M. (1985). *The early detection of reading difficulties* (3rd ed.). Auckland, NZ: Heinemann.

Clay, M. M. (1991). Introducing a new story book to young readers. *The Reading Teacher, 45,* 264–272.

Clay, M. M. (1993a). *An observation survey of early literacy achievement.* Portsmouth, NH: Heinemann.

Clay, M. M. (1993b). *Reading Recovery: A guidebook for teachers in training.* Portsmouth, NH: Heinemann.

Cohen, A. S. (1974–1975). Oral reading errors of first grade children taught by a code emphasis approach. *Reading Research Quarterly, 10,* 616–650.

Cohen, P. A., Kulik, J. A., & Kulik, C. (1982). Educational outcomes of tutoring: A meta-analysis of findings. *American Educational Research Journal, 19,* 237–248.

Colburn, A., & Echevarria, J. (1999). Meaningful lessons. *The Science Teacher, 66*(2), 36–39.

Cole, M. L., & Cole, J. T. (1989). *Effective intervention with the language impaired child* (2nd ed.). Salem, MA: Aspen.

Collins, J. L. (1998). *Strategies for struggling writers.* New York: Guilford Press.

Collins, K. M., & Collins, J. L. (1996). Strategic instruction for struggling writers. *English Journal, 85,* 54–61.

Colvin, R. J., & Root, J. H. (2000). *Reading evaluation adult diagnosis: An informal inventory for assessing adult student reading needs and progress.* Syracuse, NY: Literacy Volunteers of New York.

Comer, J. P. (1988). *Maggie's American dream: The life and times of a black family.* New York: New American Library.

Comfort, R. L. (1994). Understanding and appreciating the ADHD child in the classroom. In C. Weaver (Ed.), *Success at last: Helping students with AD(H)D achieve their potential* (pp. 63–74). Portsmouth, NH: Heinemann.

Community Update. (2001). Reading by leaps and bounds. *Community Update, 86,* 4. Available at http://www.ed.gov/G2K/community/01-04.pdf

Cooper, H., Nye, B. C., Kelly, L. J., & Greathouse, S. (1996). The effects of summer vacation on achievement test scores: A narrative and meta-analytic review. *Review of Educational Research, 66,* 227–268.

Cox, A. R. (1992). *Foundations for literacy: Structures and techniques for multisensory teaching of basic written English skills.* Cambridge, MA: Educators Publishing Service.

Crawford, A. N. (1982). From Spanish reading to English reading: The transition process. In M. P. Douglass (Ed.), *Claremont Reading Conference Yearbook* (pp. 159–165). Claremont, CA: Claremont Reading Conference.

Crawford, A. N. (1993). Literature, integrated language arts, and the language minority child: A focus on meaning. In A. Carrasquillo (Ed.), *Whole language and the bilingual learner* (pp. 61–75). Norwood, NJ: Ablex.

Cudd, E. T., & Roberts, L. (1989). Using writing to enhance content area learning in the primary grades. *The Reading Teacher, 42,* 392–404.

Cummins, J. (1994). The acquisition of English as a second language. In K. Spangenberg-Urbschat & R. Pritchard (Eds.), *Kids come in all languages: Reading instruction for all ESL students* (pp. 36–62). Newark, DE: International Reading Association.

Cunningham, J. W., Erickson, K., Spadorcia, S. A., Koppenhaver, D. A., Cunningham, P. M., Yoder, D. E., & McKenna, M. C. (1999). Assessing decoding from an onset-rime perspective. *Journal of Literacy Research, 31,* 391–414.

Cunningham, J. W., & Foster, E. O. (1978). The ivory tower connection: A case study. *The Reading Teacher, 31,* 365–369.

Cunningham, P. (1991). *Phonics they use: Words for reading and writing.* New York: HarperCollins.

Cunningham, P. M. (1978). Decoding polysyllabic words: An alternative strategy. *Journal of Reading, 21,* 608–614.

Cunningham, P. M. (1979). A comparison/contrast theory of mediated word identification. *The Reading Teacher, 32,* 774–778.

Cunningham, P. M., & Allington, R. L. (1994). *Classrooms that work: They can all read and write.* Boston: HarperCollins.

Cunningham, P. M., & Cunningham, J. W. (1992). Making words: Enhancing the invented spelling-decoding connection. *The Reading Teacher, 46,* 106–115.

Cunningham, P. M., Hall, D. P., & Defee, M. (1991). Non-ability grouped, multi-level instruction: A year in a first-grade classroom. *The Reading Teacher, 44,* 566–571.

Curtis, M. E., & Longo, A. M. (1999). *When adolescents can't read: Methods and materials that work.* Boston: Brookline Books.

Curtis, M. E., & Longo, A. M. (2001, November). Teaching vocabulary to adolescents to improve comprehension. *Reading Online, 5*(4). Available at http://www.readingonline.org/articles/art_index .asp?HREF=curtis/index.html

Dahl, K., & Farnham, N. (1998). *Children's writing, Perspectives from research.* Newark, DE: International Reading Association & National Reading Conference.

Dale, E., & O'Rourke, J. (1971). *Techniques of teaching vocabulary.* Chicago: Field.

Daneman, M., & Carpenter, P. A. (1980). Individual differences in working memory and in reading. *Journal of Verbal Learning and Verbal Behavior, 19,* 450–466.

Davis, G., Jackson, J., & Johnson, S. (2000, May). Guided writing: Leveling the balance. Paper presented at the annual meeting of the International Reading Association, Indianapolis, IN.

DeBruin-Parecki, A., Paris, S., & Seidenberg, J. (1997). Family literacy: Examining practice and issues of effectiveness. *Journal of Adolescents & Adult Literacy, 40,* 596–605.

DeFord, D. E. (1997). Early writing: Teachers and children in Reading Recovery. In S. L. Swartz & A. F. Klein (Eds.), *Research in Reading Recovery* (pp. 148–172). Portsmouth, NH: Heinemann.

DeFord, D. E., Lyons, C. A., & Pinnell, G. S. (1991). Introduction. In D. E. DeFord, C. A. Lyons, & G. S. Pinnell (Eds.), *Bridges to literacy: Learning from Reading Recovery* (pp. 1–8). Portsmouth, NH: Heinemann.

DeNavas-Walt, C., Proctor, B. D., & Mills, R. J. (2004). U.S. Census Bureau, Current Population Reports, P60-226, *Income, poverty, and health insurance coverage in the United States: 2003.* Washington, DC: U.S. Government Printing Office. Available at http://www.census.gov/hhes/www/poverty03.html

Deno, S. L., Fuchs, L. S., Marston, D., & Shin, J. (2001). Using curriculum-based measurement to establish growth standards for students with learning disabilities. *School Psychology Review, 30,* 507–524.

DePaulo, B., & Jordan, A. (1982). Age changes in deceiving and deceit. In R. Feldman (Ed.), *Development of nonverbal behavior in children* (pp. 140–180). New York: Springer-Verlag.

Dickinson, D. K. (2001). Putting the piece together: The impact of preschool on children's literacy development in kindergarten. In D. K. Dickinson & P. O. Tabors (Eds.), *Beginning literacy with language: Young children learning at home and at school* (pp. 175–203). Baltimore: Brookes.

Dickinson, D. K., McCabe, A., & Clark-Chiarelli, N. (2004). Preschool-based prevention of reading disability. In C. A. Stone, E. R. Silliman, B. J., Ehren, & K. Apel (Eds.), *Handbook of language and literacy development and disorders* (pp. 209–227). New York: Guilford Press.

Dickinson, D. K., & Smith, M. W. (1994). Long-term effects of preschool teachers' book reading on low-income children's vocabulary and story comprehension. *Reading Research Quarterly, 29,* 104–122.

Dickson, S. V. (2004a, July). Adaptations for struggling readers in the content areas: Teacher-to-Teacher Initiative Summer Workshop. Available at http://www.ed.gov/teachers/how/read/list.jhtml

Dickson, S. V. (2004b, July). *Targeted instruction for struggling readers: A framework for providing remedial reading instruction. Teacher-to-Teacher Initiative Summer Workshop.* Available at http://www.ed.gov/teachers/how/read/list.jhtml

Dixon, R. C., Carnine, D., & Kame'enui, E. (1993). Tools for teaching diverse learners: Using scaffolding to teach writing. *Educational Leadership, 51*(3), 100–101.

Dole, J. A., Brown, K. J., & Trathen, W. (1996). The effect of strategy instruction on the comprehension performance of at-risk students. *Reading Research Quarterly, 31,* 62–88.

Donahue, P., Daane, M., & Grigg, W. (2003). *The nation's report card, reading highlights for 2003.* National Assessment of Educational Progress, National Center for Educational Statistics. Available at http://nces.ed.gov/pubsearch/pubsinfo.asp?pubid=2004452.

Donahue, P. A., Voelkl, K. E., Campbell, J. R., & Mazzeo, J. (1999). *NAEP 1998 reading report card for the nation and the states.* Washington, DC: U.S. Department of Education.

Donahue, P. L., Finnegan, R. J., Lutkus, A. D., Allen, N. R., & Campbell, J. R. (2001). *The nation's report card: Fourth-grade reading 2000.* Washington, DC: U.S. Department of Education.

Dorn, L. J., French, C., & Jones, T. (1998). *Apprenticeship in literacy: Transitions across reading and writing.* York, ME: Stenhouse.

Duffelmeyer, F. A., Baum, D. D., & Merkley, D. J. (1987). Maximizing reader-text confrontation with an Extended Anticipation Guide. *Journal of Reading, 35,* 654–656.

Duffy, G. G., & Roehler, L. R. (1987). Improving reading instruction through the use of responsive elaboration. *The Reading Teacher, 40,* 514–520.

Duffy-Hester, A. (1999). Teaching struggling readers in elementary school classrooms: A review of classroom reading programs and principles for instruction. *The Reading Teacher, 52,* 480–495.

Dunn, L., & Dunn, M. (1997). *Peabody Picture Vocabulary Test-III.* Circle Pines, MN: American Guidance Services.

DuPaul, G. J., & Eckert, T. L. (1996). Academic interventions for students with attention-deficit/hyperactivity disorder: A review of the literature. *Reading and Writing Quarterly: Overcoming Learning Difficulties, 14,* 58–82.

Durrell, D., & Catterson, J. (1980). *Durrell analysis of reading difficulty.* San Antonio, TX: Psychological Corporation.

Durrell, D. D. (1980). Letter–name value in reading and spelling. *Reading Research Quarterly, 16,* 159–163.

Dyson, A. H., & Freedman, S. W. (1991). Writing. In J. Flood, J. M. Jensen, D. Lapp, & J. R. Squire (Eds.), *Handbook of research on teaching the English language arts* (pp. 754–774). New York: Macmillan.

Early, M., & Sawyer, D. J. (1984). *Reading to learn in grades 5 to 12.* New York: Harcourt Brace Jovanovich.

Early Childhood-Head Start Task Force (2002). *Teaching our youngest: Guide for preschool teachers and child care and family providers.* U.S. Department of Education, U.S. Department of Health and Human Services. Available at http://www.ed.gov/teachers/how/early/teachingouryoungest/index.html

Ehri, L. C. (1983). A critique of five studies related to letter–name knowledge and learning to read. In L. M. Gentile, M. L. Kamil, & J. S. Blanchard (Eds.), *Reading research revisited* (pp. 143–153). Columbus, OH: Merrill.

Ehri, L. C. (1992). Reconceptualizing the development of sight word reading and its relationship to reading. In P. B. Gough, L. C. Ehri, & R. Treiman (Eds.), *Reading acquisition* (pp. 107–143). Hillsdale, NJ: Lawrence Erlbaum.

Ehri, L. C. (1994). Development of the ability to read words: Update. In R. B. Ruddell, M. R. Ruddell, & H. Singer (Eds.), *Theoretical models and processes of reading* (4th ed., pp. 323–358). Newark, DE: International Reading Association.

Ehri, L. C., & Robbins, C. (1992). Beginners need some decoding skill to read words by analogy. *Reading Research Quarterly, 27,* 12–26.

Ehri, L. C., & Saltmarsh, J. (1995). Beginning readers outperform older disabled readers in learning to read words by sight. *Reading and Writing: An Interdisciplinary Journal, 7,* 295–326.

Ehri, L. C., & Snowling, M. J. (2004). Developmental variation in word recognition. In C. A. Stone, E. R. Silliman, B. J. Ehren, & K. Apel (Eds.), *Handbook of language and literacy development and disorders* (pp. 433–460). New York: Guilford Press.

Ekwall, E. E., & Shanker, J. L. (2000). *Ekwall/Shanker reading inventory.* Boston: Allyn & Bacon.

Elbro, C., & Arnbak, E. (1996). The role of morpheme recognition and morphological awareness in dyslexia. *Annals of Dyslexia, 46,* 209–240.

Elbro, C., Borstrøm, I., & Petersen, D. K. (1998). Predicting dyslexia from kindergarten: The importance of the distinctiveness of phonological representations of lexical items. *Reading Research Quarterly, 33,* 36–60.

Elkonin, D. B. (1973). Reading in the USSR. In J. Downing (Ed.), *Comparative reading* (pp. 551–579). New York: Macmillan.

Elley, W. B. (1989). Vocabulary acquisition from listening to stories. *Reading Research Quarterly, 24,* 174–187.

Elley, W. B., & Mangubhai, F. (1983). The impact of reading on second language learning. *Reading Research Quarterly, 19,* 53–67.

Englert, C. S., & Hiebert, E. H. (1985). Children's developing awareness of text structures in expository materials. *Journal of Educational Psychology, 76,* 65–75.

Englert, C. S., Raphael, T. E., Anderson, L. M., Anthony, H. M., Fear, K. L., & Gregg, S. L. (1988). A case for writing intervention: Strategies for writing informational text. *Learning Disabilities Focus, 8,* 98–113.

Enz, B. (1989, May). *The 90 percent success solution.* Paper presented at the annual convention of the International Reading Association, New Orleans, LA.

Estes, T., & Vaughn, J. (1985). *Reading and learning in the content classroom* (2nd ed.). Boston: Allyn & Bacon.

Eylon, B., & Linn, M. C. (1988). Learning and instruction: An examination of four research perspectives in science education. *Review of Educational Research, 58,* 251–301.

Farr, R., & Carey, R. F. (1986). *Reading: What can be measured?* Newark, DE: International Reading Association.

Farr, R., & Farr, B. (1990). *Integrated assessment system.* San Antonio, TX: Psychological Corporation.

Fernald, G. M. (1943). *Remedial techniques in basic school subjects.* New York: McGraw-Hill.

Ferreiro, E. (1986). The interplay between information and assimilation in beginning literacy. In W. H. Teale & E. Sulzby (Eds.), *Emergent literacy* (pp. 15–49). Norwood, NJ: Ablex.

Feurstein, R., Rand, Y., & Hoffman, M. B. (1979). *The dynamic assessment of retarded performers: The Learning Potential Assessment Device—Theory, instruments, and techniques.* Baltimore: University Park Press.

Fielding, L., & Roller, C. (1992). Making difficult books accessible and easy books acceptable. *The Reading Teacher, 45,* 678–685.

Fielding, L. G. (1996). Choice makes reading instruction child centered. In C. Roller (Ed.), *Variability, not disability: Struggling readers in a workshop classroom* (pp. 43–55). Newark, DE: International Reading Association.

Fielding, L. G., Wilson, P. T., & Anderson, R. C. (1986). A new focus on free reading: The role of trade books in reading instruction. In T. E. Raphael (Ed.), *The contexts of school-based literacy* (pp. 149–160). New York: Random House.

Filmore, L. W., & Valdez, C. (1986). Teaching bilingual learners. In M. E. Wittrock (Ed.), *Handbook of research on teaching* (pp. 648–685). New York: Macmillan.

Fischer, C. (1999–2000). An effective (and affordable) intervention model for at-risk high school readers. *Journal of Adolescent & Adult Literacy, 43,* 326–335.

Fisher, J. B., Schumaker, J. B., & Deshler, D. D. (2002). Improving the reading comprehension of at-risk adolescents. In C. C. Block & M. Pressley (Eds.), *Comprehension instruction: Research-based best practices.* New York: Guilford Press.

Fitzgerald, J. A. (1951). *A basic life spelling vocabulary.* Milwaukee, WI: Bruce.

Fitzgerald, J. (1999). What is this thing called "balance"? *The Reading Teacher, 53,* 100–107.

Fitzgerald, J., & Spiegel, D. (1983). Enhancing children's reading comprehension through instruction in narrative structure. *Journal of Reading Behavior, 15,* 1–17.

Five, C. L. (1992). *Special voices.* Portsmouth, NH: Heinemann.

Fletcher, R., & Portalupi, J. (2001). *Writer's workshop.* Portsmouth, NH: Heinemann.

Flynt, E. S., & Cooter, R. B., Jr. (Eds.). (1995). *Flynt–Cooter inventory for the classroom.* Scottsdale, AZ: Gosuch Scarisbrick.

Foorman, B. R., Fletcher, J. M., Francis, D. J., Schatschneider, C., & Mehta, P. (1998). The role of instruction in learning to read: Preventing reading failure in at-risk children. *Journal of Educational Psychology, 90,* 37–55.

Foorman, B. R., & Torgesen, J. (2001). Critical elements of classroom and small group instruction promote reading success in all children. *Learning Disabilities Research & Practice, 16,* 203–212.

FOSS—Full Option Science System. (2004). *Frequently asked questions about the FOSS program: How is reading integrated into the FOSS program?* Available at http://lhsfoss.org/faq.html#b2

Fountas, I., & Pinnell, G. S. (1996). *Guided reading: Good first teaching for all children.* Portsmouth, NH: Heinemann.

Fountas, I., & Pinnell, G. S. (1999). *Matching books to readers: Using leveled books in guided reading, K–3.* Portsmouth, NH: Heinemann.

Fountas, I., & Pinnell, G. S. (2001). *Guiding readers and writers grades 3–6.* Portsmouth, NH: Heinemann.

Fowler, A. E. (1991). How early phonological development might set the stage for phonological awareness. In S. A. Brady & D. P. Shankweiler (Eds.), *Phonological processes in literacy: A tribute to Isabelle Y. Liberman* (pp. 97–117). Hillsdale, NJ: Lawrence Erlbaum.

Fowler, M. C., Lindemann, L. M., Thacker-Gwaltney, S., & Invernizzi, M. (2002). *A second year of one-on-one tutoring: An intervention for second graders with reading difficulties* (CIERA Report #3-019). Ann Arbor, MI: University of Michigan School of Education.

Frith, U. (1986). A developmental framework for developmental dyslexia. *Annals of Dyslexia, 36,* 69–81.

Fry, E. (1977a). *Elementary reading instruction.* New York: McGraw-Hill.

Fry, E. (1977b). Fry's readability graph: Clarifications, validity, and extension to level 17. *Journal of Reading, 21,* 242–252.

Fry, E. B., Kress, J. E., & Fountoukidis, D. L. (1997). *The reading teacher's book of lists* (4th ed.). Englewood Cliffs, NJ: Prentice-Hall.

Fuchs, L. S. (2003). Assessing intervention responsiveness: Conceptual and technical issues. *Learning Disabilities Research & Practice, 81,* 172–186.

Fuchs, L. S., & Fuchs, D. (1997). Use of curriculum-based measurement in identifying students with learning disabilities. *Focus on Exceptional Children, 30,* 1–16.

Fuchs, L. S., Fuchs, D., & Deno, S. E. (1982). Reliability and validity of curriculum-based informal reading inventories. *Reading Research Quarterly, 18,* 6–26.

Fukkink, R. G., & de Glopper, K. (1998). Effects of instruction in deriving word meaning from context: A meta-analysis. *Review of Educational Research, 68,* 450–469.

Furth, H. G. (1970). *Piaget for teachers.* Englewood Cliffs, NJ: Prentice-Hall.

Fusaro, J. (1988). Applying statistical rigor to a validation study of the Fry Readability Graph. *Reading Research and Instruction, 28,* 44–48.

Galvin, G. A. (1981). Uses and abuses of the WISC-R with the learning disabled. *Journal of Learning Disabilities, 14,* 326–329.

Gambrell, L. B. (2000, May). *Motivation matters: Fostering full access to literacy.* Paper presented at the annual meeting of the International Reading Association, Indianapolis, IN.

Gambrell, L. B., & Bales, R. J. (1986). Mental imagery and the comprehension monitoring performance of fourth- and fifth-grade poor readers. *Reading Research Quarterly, 21,* 454–464.

Gambrell, L. B., Wilson, R. M., & Gantt, W. N. (1981). Classroom observations of good and poor readers. *Journal of Educational Research, 24,* 400–404.

Ganske, K. (1993). *Developmental spelling analysis: A qualitative measure for assessment and instructional planning.* Barboursville, VA: Author.

Ganske, K. (2000). *Word journeys: Assessment-guided phonics, spelling and vocabulary instruction.* New York: Guilford Press.

García, G. E. (1991). Factors influencing the English reading test performance of Spanish-speaking Hispanic children. *Reading Research Quarterly, 26,* 371–392.

García, G. E., Pearson, P. D., & Jiménez, R. T. (1994). *The at-risk situation: A synthesis of reading research.* Champaign, IL: University of Illinois, Center for the Study of Reading.

Gardner, H. (1983). *Frames of mind: The theory of multiple intelligences.* New York: Basic Books.

Gardner, H. (1999). *Intelligence reframed.* New York: Basic Books.

Garner, R. (l994). Metacognition and executive control. In R. B. Ruddell, M. R. Ruddell, & H. Singer (Eds.), *Theoretical models and processes of reading* (4th ed., pp. 715–732). Newark, DE: International Reading Association.

Garner, R., & Reis, R. (1981). Monitoring and resolving comprehension obstacles: An investigation of spontaneous text lookbacks among upper-grade good and poor comprehenders. *Reading Research Quarterly, 16,* 569–582.

Garnett, K. (1986). Telling tales: Narratives and learning disabled children. *Topics in Language Disorders, 6*(2), 44–52.

Gaskins, I. W. (1998, May). *What research suggests are ingredients of a grades 1–6 literacy program for struggling readers.* Paper presented at International Reading Association convention, Orlando, FL.

Gaskins, I. W. (2003). Taking charge of reader, text, activity, and context variables. In A. Sweet & C. Snow (Eds.), *Rethinking reading comprehension* (pp. 141–165). New York: Guilford Press.

Gaskins, I. W., Ehri, L. C., Cress, C., O'Hara, C., & Donnelly, K. (1996–1997). Procedures for word learning: Making discoveries about words. *The Reading Teacher, 50,* 312–327.

Gaskins, R. W., Gaskins, J. C., & Gaskins, I. W. (1991). A decoding program for poor readers and the rest of the class, too! *Language Arts, 63,* 213–225.

Gates, A. I. (1927). *The improvement of reading: A program of diagnostic and medical methods.* New York: Macmillan.

Gates, A. I. (1931). *Interest and ability in reading.* New York: Macmillan.

Gathercole, S. E., & Baddeley, A. D. (1990). Phonological memory deficits in language disordered children: Is there a causal connection? *Journal of Memory and Language, 29,* 336–360.

Gentile, L. M., & McMillan, M. M. (1987). *Stress and reading difficulties: Research, assessment, intervention.* Newark, DE: International Reading Association.

Gentry, J. R., & Gillet, J. W. (1993). *Teaching kids to spell.* Portsmouth, NH: Heinemann.

Gentry, R. (1997). *My kid can't spell.* Portsmouth, NH: Heinemann.

Georgia Department of Education (2000). *Developmental stages/scoring guidelines for writing.* Atlanta, GA: Georgia Department of Education.

German, D. J. (1992). Word-finding intervention for children and adolescents. *Topics in Language Disorders, 13*(1), 33–50.

German, N. (1986). *National College of Education Test of Word Finding.* Allen, TX: DLM Teaching Resources.

Gersten, R., & Jiménez, R. T. (1994). A delicate balance: Enhancing literature instruction for students of English as a second language. *The Reading Teacher, 47,* 438–449.

Geschwind, N. (1972). Disconnection syndromes in animals and man. In N. Geschwind (Ed.), *Selected papers on language and the brain* (pp. 106–236). Boston: Reidel.

Gibson, E. J. (1965). Learning to read. *Science, 148,* 1066–1072.

Gibson, E. J., Gibson, J. J., Pick, A. D., & Osser, H. (1962). A developmental study of the discrimination of letter-like forms. *Journal of Comparative and Physiological Psychology, 55,* 897–906.

Gibson, E. J., & Levin, H. (1974). *The psychology of reading.* Cambridge, MA: MIT Press.

Gilger, J. W., & Wise, S. E. (2004). Genetic correlates of language and literacy impairment. In C. A. Stone, E. R. Silliman, B. J, Ehren, & K. Apel (Eds.), *Handbook of language and literacy development and disorders* (pp. 25–48). New York: Guilford.

Gillet, J. W., & Temple, C. (1994). *Understanding reading problems: Assessment and instruction* (4th ed.). New York: HarperCollins.

Gillingham, A., & Stillman, B. (1983). *Remedial training for children with specific disability in reading, writing, and penmanship* (7th ed.). Cambridge, MA: Educators Publishing Service.

Glass, G. G. (1976). *Glass analysis for decoding only: Teacher's guide.* Garden City, NY: Easier to Learn.

Glass, G. G., & Burton, E. H. (1973). How do they decode? Verbalizations and observed behaviors of successful decoders. *Education, 94,* 58–65.

Glazer, S. M. (1991). Behaviors reflecting emotional involvements during reading and writing activities. *Reading, Writing, and Learning Disabilities, 7,* 219–231.

Gluskho, R. J. (1979). The organization and activation of orthographic knowledge in reading aloud. *Journal of Experimental Psychology: Human Perception and Performance, 5,* 674–691.

Goerss, B. L., Beck, I. L., & McKeown, M. G. (1999). Increasing remedial students' ability to derive word meaning from context. *Reading Psychology, 20,* 151–175.

Gold, J., & Fleisher, L. S. (1986). Comprehension breakdown with inductively organized text: Differences between average and disabled readers. *Remedial and Special Education, 7,* 26–32.

Goldenberg, C. (1994). Promoting early literacy development among Spanish-speaking children: Lessons from two studies. In E. H. Hiebert & B. M. Taylor (Eds.), *Getting reading right from the start* (pp. 171–200). Boston: Allyn & Bacon.

Goldman, S. R., Varma, K. O., & Sharp, D. S. (1999). Children's understanding of complex stories: Issues of representation and assessment. In S. R. Goldman, A. C. Graesser, & P. van den Broek (Eds.), *Narrative comprehension, causality, and coherence: Essays in honor of Tom Trabasso* (pp. 135–160). Mahwah, NJ: Erlbaum.

Goodman, K. S. (1969). Analysis of oral reading miscues: Applied psycholinguistics. *Reading Research Quarterly, 5,* 9–30.

Goodman, K. S. (1974). Miscue analysis: Theory and reality in reading. In J. E. Merritt (Ed.), *New horizons in reading* (pp. 15–26). Newark, DE: International Reading Association.

Goodman, K. S. (1982). Revaluing readers and reading. *Topics in Learning and Learning Disabilities, 1*(4), 87–93.

Goodman, K. S., & Goodman, Y. M. (1978). *Reading of American children whose language is a stable rural dialect of English or a language other than English.* Detroit: Wayne State University Press (ERIC Document Reproduction Service No. ED 182 465).

Goodman, Y. S. (1992). Through the miscue window. In K. S. Goodman, L. B. Bird, & Y. M. Goodman (Eds.), *The whole language catalog: Supplement on authentic assessment* (pp. 20–21). Santa Rosa, CA: American School Publications.

Gordon, C. J. (1990). Contexts for expository text structure use. *Reading Research and Instruction, 29*(2), 55–72.

Gordon, W. C. (1989). *Learning and memory.* Belmont, CA: Brooks/Cole.

Goswami, U. (1986). Children's use of analogy in learning to read: A developmental study. *Journal of Experimental Child Psychology, 42,* 73–83.

Goswami, U. (1988). Orthographic analogies and reading development. *Quarterly Journal of Experimental Psychology, 40,* 239–268.

Goswami, U. (2000). Phonological and lexical processes. In M. L. Kamil, P. B. Mosenthal, P. D. Pearson, & R. Barr (Eds.), *Handbook of reading research, Volume III* (pp. 251–267). Mahwah, NJ: Erlbaum.

Goswami, U., & Bryant, P. (1992). Rhyme, analogy, and children's reading. In P. B. Gough, L. C. Ehri, & R. Treiman (Eds.), *Reading acquisition* (pp. 49–63). Hillsdale, NJ: Lawrence Erlbaum.

Gottlieb, J. (2004, March 9). North End's school success studied. *The Hartford Courant,* B1 and B7.

Gough, P. B., & Hillinger, M. L. (1980). Learning to read: An unnatural act. *Bulletin of the Orton Society, 30,* 179–196.

Gough, P. B., Juel, C., & Griffith, P. L. (1992). Reading, spelling, and the orthographic cipher. In P. B. Gough, L. C. Ehri, & R. Treiman (Eds.), *Reading acquisition* (pp. 35–48). Hillsdale, NJ: Lawrence Erlbaum.

Graesser, A. C., & Bertus, E. L. (1998). The construction of causal inferences while reading expository texts on science and technology. *Scientific Studies of Reading, 2*(3), 247–269.

Graham, S. (1999). Handwriting and spelling instruction for students with learning disabilities: A review. *Learning Disability Quarterly, 22,* 78–98.

Graham, S., & Harris, K. R. (1993). Teaching writing strategies to students with learning disabilities: Issues and recommendations. In L. J. Meltzer (Ed.), *Strategy assessment and instruction for students with learning disabilities: From theory to practice* (pp. 271–292). Austin, TX: Pro-Ed.

Graves, D. H. (1983). *Writing: Teachers and children at work.* Exeter, NH: Heinemann.

Graves, D. H. (1991). All children can write. In S. Stives (Ed.), *With promise: Redefining reading and writing to "special" students* (pp. 115–125). Portsmouth, NH: Heinemann.

Greaney, K., Tunmer, W. E., & Chapman, J. W. (1997). Effects of rime-based orthographic analogy training on the word recognition skills of children with reading disability. *Journal of Educational Psychology, 89,* 645–661.

Greenberg, S. (2004, August). *Using assessment to inform instruction.* Paper presented at the Reading First Summer Institute, Cromwell, CT.

Greenwald, E. A., Persky, H. R., Campbell, J. R., & Mazzeo, J. (1999). *NAEP 1998 writing report card for the nation and the states.* Washington, DC: U.S. Department of Education.

Greenwood, C. R., Abbott, M., & Tapia, Y. (2001). *CWPT-LMS blueprint.* Juniper Gardens Children's Project, University of Kansas. Available at http://www.lsi.ku.edu/jgprojects/cwptlms/html2002/ProjectInfo/blueprint.htm

Grigg, W. S., Daane, M. C., Jin, Y., & Campbell, J. R. (2003). *The nation's report card: Reading 2002.* Washington, DC: U.S. Department of Education, Institute of Education Sciences, National Center for Education Statistics. Available at http://nces.ed.gov/nationsreportcard/

Grissmer, D. W., Flanagan, A., Kawata, J., & Williamson, S. (2000). *Improving student achievement: What NAEP state test scores tell us.* Santa Monica, CA: Rand.

Gunning, T. (1975). *A comparison of word attack skills derived from a phonological analysis of frequently used words drawn from a juvenile corpus and an adult corpus.* Unpublished doctoral dissertation, Temple University, Philadelphia.

Gunning, T. (1982). Wrong level test: Wrong information. *The Reading Teacher, 35,* 902–905.

Gunning, T. (1988a, May). *Decoding behavior of good and poor second grade students.* Paper presented at the annual meeting of the International Reading Association, Toronto, Ont.

Gunning, T. (1988b). *Teaching phonics and other word attack skills.* Springfield, IL: Charles C Thomas.

Gunning, T. (1994a). *Word Building: Beginnings.* New York: Phoenix Learning Systems.

Gunning, T. (l994b). *Word Building Book D.* New York: Phoenix.

Gunning, T. (1994c). *Word building book D.* New York: Phoenix Learning Systems.

Gunning, T. (1996). *Creating reading instruction for all children* (2nd ed.). Boston: Allyn & Bacon.

Gunning, T. (1998a). *Best books for beginning readers.* Boston: Allyn & Bacon.

Gunning, T. (1998b). Primary Reading Passages Inventory. In T. Gunning (Ed.), *Best books for beginning readers* (pp. 155–184). Boston: Allyn & Bacon.

Gunning, T. (1998c, December). *An analysis of the characteristics of the best-selling children's books.* Paper presented at the annual meeting of the National Reading Conference, Austin, TX.

Gunning, T. (1999, December). *Decoding behavior of good and poor second-grade students.* Paper presented at the annual meeting of the National Reading Conference, Orlando, FL.

Gunning, T. (2000a). *Best books for building literacy for elementary school children.* Boston: Allyn & Bacon.

Gunning, T. (2000b). *Creating literacy instruction for all children* (3rd ed.). Boston: Allyn & Bacon.

Gunning, T. (2000c). *Phonological awareness and primary phonics.* Boston: Allyn & Bacon.

Gunning, T. (2000d, May). *The primary readability index revised: Using subjective and objective factors to level books for primary grade students.* Paper presented at the annual meeting of the International Reading Association, Indianapolis, IN.

Gunning, T. (2001). *Building words: A resource manual for teaching word analysis and spelling strategies.* Boston: Allyn & Bacon.

Gunning, T. (2005). *Creating literacy instruction for all students.* (5th ed.). Boston: Allyn & Bacon.

Guthrie, J. (2003a). *Classroom contexts in engaged reading: An overview.* Available at http://www.cori.umd.edu/Research/Papers/Classroom.htm

Guthrie, J. T. (2004b, May). *Classroom practices promoting engagement and achievement in comprehension.* Keynote presentation at Reading Research 2004, Reno, NV.

Guthrie, J. T., Seifert, M., & Kline, L. W. (1978). Clues from research on programs for poor readers. In S. J. Samuels (Ed.), *What research has to say about reading instruction* (pp. 1–12). Newark, DE: International Reading Association.

Halsey, S., & Morris, E. (1977). *Macmillan beginning dictionary.* New York: Macmillan.

Hansen, J. (1987). *When writers read.* Portsmouth, NH: Heinemann.

Hansen, J., & Pearson, P. D. (1980). *The effects of inference training and practice on young children's comprehension* (Technical Report 166). Urbana, IL: University of Illinois, Center for the Study of Reading.

Hansen, J., & Pearson, P. D. (1982). *Improving the inferential comprehension of good and poor fourth-grade readers* (Report No. CSR-TR-235). Urbana, IL: University of Illinois, Center for the Study of Reading (ERIC Document Reproduction No. ED 215-312).

Harcourt Educational Measurement (2000). *Some things parents should know about testing: A series of questions and answers.* Available at http://www.hbem.com/library/parents.htm

Hardy, M., Stennett, R. G. F., & Smythe, P. C. (1973). Word attack: How do they figure them out? *Elementary English, 50,* 99–102.

Harm, M., McCandliss, B. D., & Seidenberg, M. S. (2003). Modeling the successes and failures of interventions for disabled readers. *Scientific Studies of Reading, 7,* 155–182 .

Harmon, J. W. (1998). Vocabulary teaching and learning in a seventh-grade literature-based classroom. *Journal of Adolescent and Adult Literacy, 41,* 518–529.

Harris, A. J., & Sipay, E. R. (1985). *How to increase reading ability* (8th ed.). New York: Longman.

Harris, A. J., & Sipay, E. R. (1990). *How to increase reading ability* (9th ed.). New York: Longman.

Harris, K. R., & Graham, S. (1992). *Helping young writers master the craft: Strategy instruction and self-regulation in the writing process.* Cambridge, MA: Brookline Books.

Harste, J. C., Short, K. G., & Burke, C. (1988). *Creating classrooms for authors: The reading-writing connection.* Portsmouth, NH: Heinemann.

Hart, B., & Risley, T. R. (1995). *Meaningful differences in the everyday experience of young American children.* Baltimore, MD: Brookes.

Hart, E. R., & Speece, D. L. (1998). Reciprocal teaching goes to college: Effects for postsecondary students at risk for academic failure. *Journal of Educational Psychology, 90,* 670–681.

Hayes, J. R. (2000). A new framework for understanding cognition and affect in writing. In R. Indrisano & J. R. Squire (Eds.), *Perspectives on writing: Research, theory, and practice* (pp. 6–44). Newark, DE: International Reading Association.

Haywood, H. C. (1993, November). *Interactive assessment: Assessment of learning potential, school learning, and adaptive behavior.* Paper presented at the Ninth Annual Learning Disorders Conference, Cambridge, MA.

Haywood, H. C., Brown, A. L., & Wingenfeld, S. (1990). Dynamic approaches to psychoeducational assessment. *School Psychology Review, 19,* 411–422.

Head, M. H., & Readence, J. E. (1986). Anticipation guides: Meaning through prediction. In E. K. Deshner, T. W. Bean, J. E. Readence, & D. W. Moore (Eds.), *Reading in the content areas* (2nd ed., pp. 229–234). Dubuque, IA: Kendall/Hunt.

Heiman, M., & Slomianko, J. (1986). *Methods of inquiry.* Cambridge, MA: Learning Associates.

Helen Keller International (2000). *Childsight in the United States.* Available at http://www.child sight.org/

Helen Keller International (2004). *Child Sight faces.* Available at http://childsight.org/faces/index.htm

Henderson, E. H. (1990). *Teaching spelling.* Boston: Houghton Mifflin.

Henderson, E. H., & Templeton, S. (1986). A developmental perspective of formal spelling instruction through alphabet, pattern, and meaning. *Elementary School Journal, 86,* 305–316.

Henry, M. K. (1990). Reading instruction based on word structure and origin. In P. G. Aaron & R. M. Joshi (Eds.), *Reading and writing disorders in different orthographic systems* (pp. 25–49). Dordrecht, Netherlands: Kluwer Academic Publishers.

Henry, M. K. (1989). Children's word structure knowledge: Implications for decoding and spelling instruction. *Reading and Writing, 1,* 135–152.

Herber, H. L., & Herber, J. N. (1993). *Teaching in content areas with reading, writing, and reasoning.* Boston: Allyn & Bacon.

Herman, P. A., Anderson, R. C., Pearson, P. D., & Nagy, W. E. (1987). Incidental acquisition of word meanings from expositions with varied text features. *Reading Research Quarterly, 22,* 263–284.

Hidi, S., & Anderson, V. (1986). Producing written summaries: Task demands, cognitive operations, and implications for instruction. *Review of Educational Research, 56,* 473–493.

Hiebert, E. H. (1994). A small-group literacy intervention with Chapter 1 students. In E. H. Hiebert & B. M. Taylor (Eds.), *Getting reading right from the start* (pp. 85–106). Boston: Allyn & Bacon.

Hiebert, E. H., & Taylor, B. M. (2000). Beginning reading instruction: Research on early interventions. In M. L. Kamil, P. B. Mosenthal, P. D. Pearson, & R. Barr (Eds.), *Handbook of reading research, Volume III* (pp. 455–482). Mahwah, NJ: Erlbaum.

Hoffman, J. V. (1991). Teacher and school effects in learning to read. In R. Barr, M. L. Kamil, P. Mosenthal, & P. D. Pearson (Eds.), *Handbook of reading research, Volume II* (pp. 911–950). New York: Longman.

Hoffman, L. (1993, October). *Using readers' theatre in the general English classroom: Motivating reluctant readers and writers.* Paper presented at the annual meeting of the Connecticut Reading Association, Waterbury, CT.

Holliday, W. G. (1991). Helping students learn effectively from science text. In C. M. Santa & D. E. Alvermann (Eds.), *Science learning: Process and applications* (pp. 38–47). Newark, DE: International Reading Association.

Holmes, B. C. (1987). Children's inferences with print and pictures. *Journal of Educational Psychology, 79,* 14–18.

Horowitz, J. (2000). Teaching older nonreaders how to read. *The Reading Teacher, 54,* 24–26.

Horowitz, R. (1985). Text patterns. *Journal of Reading, 28,* 534–542.

Hugdahl, K. (1993). Functional brain asymmetry, dyslexia, and immune disorders. In A. M. Galbruda (Ed.), *Dyslexia and development: Neurological aspects of extra-ordinary brains* (pp. 133–154). Cambridge, MA: Harvard University Press.

Hughes, M., & Searle, D. (1997). *The violent "e" and other tricky sounds: Learning to spell from kindergarten through grade 6.* York, ME: Stenhouse.

Hulme, C. (1981). *Reading retardation and multi-sensory teaching.* London: Routledge & Kegan Paul.

Hulme, C., & MacKenzie, S. (1992). *Working memory and severe learning difficulties.* Hillsdale, NJ: Lawrence Erlbaum.

Hultquist, A. M. (1997). Orthographic processing abilities of adolescents with dyslexia. *Annals of Dyslexia, 47,* 89–104.

Hyman, R. T. (1978). *Strategic questioning.* Englewood Cliffs, NJ: Prentice-Hall.

Idol, L. (Ed.). (1988). Reprint of Fernald, G. M. (1943). *Remedial techniques in basic school subjects.* Austin, TX: Pro-Ed.

Ilg, F., & Ames, L. B. (1964). *School readiness.* New York: Harper & Row.

Impara, J. C., Plake, B. S., & Spies, R. A. (Eds.) (2003). *The fifteenth mental measurements yearbook.* Lincoln, NE: University of Nebraska Press.

International Reading Association (1999). *High stakes assessments in reading: A position statement of the International Reading Association.* Newark, DE: International Reading Association.

International Reading Association (2000). Teaching all children to read: The roles of the reading specialist: A position statement of the International Reading Association. *The Reading Teacher, 54,* 115–119.

International Reading Association (IRA) & National Council of Teachers of English (NCTE) (1996). *Standards for the English language arts.* Newark, DE: IRA & NCTE.

Invernizzi, M., Abouzeid, M., & Gill, J. T. (1994). Using students' invented spellings as a guide for spelling instruction that emphasizes word study. *The Elementary School Journal, 95,* 155–167.

Invernizzi, M., Rosemary, C., Juel, C., & Richards, C. R. (1997). At-risk readers and community volunteers: A 3-year perspective. *Scientific Studies of Reading, 1,* 277–300.

Irwin, P. A., & Mitchell, J. N. (1983). A procedure for assessing the richness of retellings. *Journal of Reading, 26,* 391–396.

Iverson, S., & Tunmer, W. W. (1993). Phonological processing skills and the Reading Recovery program. *Journal of Educational Psychology, 85*(1), 112–126.

Ivey, G. (1999). Reflections on teaching struggling middle school readers. *Journal of Adolescent and Adult Literacy, 42,* 372–381.

Ivey, G. (2000, May). *Dispelling myths associated with struggling middle school readers.* Paper presented at the Annual Meeting of the International Reading Association, Indianapolis, IN.

Jackson, M. D. (1980). Further evidence for a relationship between memory access and reading ability. *Journal of Verbal Learning and Verbal Behavior, 19,* 683–694.

Jenkins, J. R., Matlock, B., & Slocum, T. A. (1989). Approaches to vocabulary instruction. *Reading Research Quarterly, 24,* 215–235.

Jenkins, J. R., Stein, M. L., & Wysocki, K. (1984). Learning vocabulary through reading. *American Educational Research Journal, 21*(4), 767–787.

Jennings, J. (2003). *From the capital to the classroom: Year 2 of the No Child Left Behind Act.* Available at http://www.cep-dc.org/nclb/

Jennings, J. (2004, August). *Statement on Phi Delta Kappa/Gallup poll on education.* Washington, DC: Center on Education Policy. Available at http://www.ctredpol.org/pubs/pdkpoll35/jennings_pdk35_statement.htm

Jiménez, R. T. (1997). The strategic reading abilities and potential of five low literacy Latina/o in middle school. *Reading Research Quarterly, 32,* 224–243.

Jiménez, R. T., García, G. E., & Pearson, P. D. (1995). Three children, two languages, and strategic reading: Case studies in bilingual/monolingual reading. *American Educational Research Journal, 32*(1), 31–61.

Jobe, F. W. (1976). *Screening vision in schools.* Newark, DE: International Reading Association.

Johns, J. L. (2001). *Basic reading inventory* (8th ed.). Dubuque, IA: Kendall/Hunt.

Johnson, D. (1993). *Diagnostic teaching: Implications for intervention.* Paper presented at the Ninth Annual Learning Disabilities Conference, Cambridge, MA.

Johnson, D. J., & Myklebust, H. R. (1967). *Learning disabilities: Educational principles and practices.* New York: Grune & Stratton.

Johnson, J. F. (2002). High-performing, high-poverty, urban elementary schools. In B. Taylor & P. D. Pearson

(Eds.), *Teaching reading: Effective schools, accomplished teachers* (pp. 89–114). Mahwah, NJ: Erlbaum.

Johnson, M. S. (1966). Tracing and kinesthetic techniques. In J. Money (Ed.), *The disabled reader: Education of the dyslexic child* (pp. 147–160). Baltimore: The Johns Hopkins Press.

Johnson, M. S., & Kress, R. A. (1966). *Eliminating learning problems in reading disability cases.* Unpublished paper, Temple University, Philadelphia.

Johnson, M. S., Kress, R. A., & Pikulski, J. J. (1987). *Informal reading inventories* (2nd ed.). Newark, DE: International Reading Association.

Johnston, F. (1999). *Reply 1A.* Available at http://www.readingonline.org/articles/words/forum.html

Johnston, F. R., Invernizzi, M., & Juel, C. (1998). *Book Buddies: Guidelines for volunteer tutors of emergent and early readers.* New York: Guilford Press.

Johnston, P., & Allington, R. (1991). Remediation. In R. Barr, M. L. Kamil, P. Mosenthal, & P. D. Pearson (Eds.), *Handbook of reading research, Volume II* (pp. 984–1012). New York: Longman.

Johnston, P. H. (1992). *Constructive evaluation of literate activity.* New York: Longman.

Johnston, P. H. (2000). *Running records: A self-tutoring guide.* Portland, ME: Stenhouse.

Joint Task Force on Assessment (1994). *Standards for the assessment of reading and writing.* Newark, DE: International Reading Association & Urbana, IL: National Council of Teachers of English.

Jongsma, E. (1980). *Cloze instruction research: A second look.* Newark, DE: International Reading Association.

Jorm, A. F. (1983). *The psychology of reading and spelling disabilities.* London: Rutledge & Kegan Paul.

Juel, C. (1991). Cross-age tutoring between student athletes and at-risk children. *The Reading Teacher, 45,* 178–186.

Juel, C. (1994a). *Building a community of readers: University, community, and school partnerships.* Paper presented at the annual meeting of the International Reading Association, Toronto, Ont.

Juel, C. (1994b). *Learning to read and write in one elementary school.* New York: Springer-Verlag.

Juel, C. (1996). What makes literacy tutoring effective. *Reading Research Quarterly, 31,* 268–289.

Juel, C., Griffith, P. L., & Gough, P. B. (1986). Acquisition of literacy: A longitudinal study of children in first and second grade. *Journal of Educational Psychology, 78,* 243–255.

Juel, C., & Minden-Cupp, C. (1999). *Learning to read words: Linguistic units and strategies* (Ciera Report 1-008). Ann Arbor, MI: Center for the Improvement of Early Reading Instruction, University of Michigan School of Education.

Juel, C., & Minden-Cupp, C. (2000). Learning to read words: Linguistic units and instructional strategies. *Reading Research Quarterly, 35,* 458–492.

Juel, C., & Roper-Schneider, D. (1985). The influence of basal readers on first-grade reading. *Reading Research Quarterly, 20,* 134–152.

Juel, C., & Minden-Cupp, C. (1999). Learning to read words: Linguistic units and strategies. *Reading Research Quarterly, 35,* 458–492.

Kaderavek, J. C., & Sulzby, E. (1999). *Issues in emergent literacy for children with language impairments* (Ciera Report 2-002). Ann Arbor, MI: Center for the Improvement of Early Reading Instruction, University of Michigan School of Education.

Karweit, N. L., & Wasik, B. A. (1994). Extra-year kindergartens and transitional first grades. In R. L. Slavin, N. L. Karweit, & B. A. Wasik (Eds.), *Preventing school failure: Research, policy, and practice* (pp. 102–121). Boston: Allyn & Bacon.

Kelleher, K. J., McInerny, T. K., Gardner, W. P., Childs, G., & Wasserman, R. C. (2000). Increasing identification of psychosocial problems: 1979–1996. *Pediatrics, 105,* 1313–1321.

Kephart, N. C. (1966). *The slow learner in the classroom* (2nd ed.). Columbus, OH: Merrill.

Kibby, M. (1995). *Practical steps for informing literacy instruction: A diagnostic decision-making model.* Newark, DE: International Reading Association.

Kibby, M. W., & Wieland, K. (2004). *How readers think during vocabulary acquisition: Findings from the verbal protocols of good readers when encountering unknown words in context with applications to instruction.* Paper presented at the International Reading Association convention, Reno, NV.

Killgallon, P. A. (1942). *A study of relationships among certain pupil adjustments in language situations.* Unpublished doctoral dissertation. University Park, PA: Pennsylvania State University.

Kimmel, S., & MacGinitie, W. H. (1984). Identifying children who use a perseverative text processing strategy. *Reading Research Quarterly, 19,* 162–172.

Kincaid, J. P., Fishburne, R., Rogers, R. L., & Chissom, B. S. (1975). *Derivation of new readability formulas (Automated Readability Index, Fog Count, and Flesch Reading Ease formula) for Navy enlisted personnel* (Branch Report 8-75), Chief of Naval Training, Millington, TN.

Kinder, D., Bursuck, B., & Epstein, M. (1992). An evaluation of history textbooks. *The Journal of Special Education, 25,* 472–491.

Kinnucan-Welsch, K., Magill, D., & Dean, M. (1999). Strategic teaching and strategic learning in first-grade classrooms. *Reading Horizons, 40*(1), 3–21.

Kintsch, W. (1994). Text comprehension, memory, and learning. *American Psychologist, 49,* 294–303.

Klenk, L., & Kibby, M. W. (2000). Re-mediating reading difficulties: Appraising the past, reconciling the present, constructing the future. In M. L. Kamil, P. B. Mosenthal, P. D. Pearson, & R. Barr (Eds.), *Handbook of reading research, Volume III* (pp. 667–690). Mahwah, NJ: Erlbaum.

Kletzien, S. B. (1991). Strategy use by good and poor comprehenders reading expository text of differing levels. *Reading Research Quarterly, 26,* 67–86.

Kletzien, S. B., & Bednar, M. R. (1998). A framework for reader autonomy: An integrated perspective. *Journal of Reading, 32,* 30–33.

Knapp, N. F. (1998, December). *The reading apprenticeship intervention and its effect on reading skills and attitudes of delayed primary readers.* Paper presented at the 48th Annual Meeting of the National Reading Conference, Austin, TX.

Knapp, N. F., & Winsor, A. P. (1998). A reading apprenticeship for delayed primary readers. *Reading Research and Instruction, 38*(1), 13–29.

Koskinen, P. S. (1999). Shared reading, books, and audiotapes: Supporting diverse students in school and at home. *The Reading Teacher, 52,* 430–444.

Koskinen, P. S., Blum, I. H., Bisson, S. A., Phillips, S. M., Creamer, T. S., & Baker, T. K. (1999). Shared reading, books, and audiotapes: Supporting diverse students in school and at home. *The Reading Teacher, 52,* 430–444.

Koskinen, P. S., Blum, I. H., Palincsar, A. S., Collins, K. M., Marano, N. L., & Magnusson, S. J. (2000). Investigating the engagement and learning of students with learning disabilities in guided inquiry science teaching. *Language, Speech, and Hearing Services in Schools, 31,* 240–251.

Krashen, S. (1996). *Effective second language acquisition.* Torrance, CA: The Education Centre.

Kratcoski, A. M. (1998). Guidelines for using portfolios in assessment and evaluation. *Language, Speech, and Hearing Services in the Schools, 29,* 33–40.

Krehbiel, C., & Jones, C. (2004, July). *Feedback: A powerful tool for raising student achievement in language arts.* Summer Workshop Presentation, Montgomery County, MD. Available at http://www.ed.gov/teachers/how/tools/initiative/summerworkshop/krehbiel/index.html

Kuhn, M., & Stahl, S. (2000). Teaching children to learn word meanings from context: A synthesis and some questions. *Journal of Literacy Research, 30,* 119–138.

Labbo, L. D., & Teale, W. H. (1990). Cross-age reading: A strategy for helping poor readers. *The Reading Teacher, 43,* 362–369.

Lake, J. H. (1973). The influence of wait time on the verbal dimensions of student inquiry behavior. *Dissertations Abstracts International, 34,* 6476A (University Microfilms NO. 74-08866).

Landauer, T., & Dumais, S. (1997). A solution to Plato's problem: The latent semantic analysis theory of acquisition, induction, and representation of knowledge. *Psychological Review, 104,* 211–240.

Langer, J. A. (2004). Beating the odds: Teaching middle and high school students to read and write well. In R. B. Ruddell & N. J. Unrau (Eds.), *Theoretical models and processes of reading* (5th ed., pp. 1040–1082). Newark, DE: International Reading Association.

Learning Media (1991). *Reading in junior classes.* Wellington, New Zealand: Ministry of Education.

Learning Media (1994). *Books for Ready to Read classrooms.* Katonah, NY: Richard C. Owen.

Leslie, L., & Allen, L. (1999). Factors that predict success in an early literacy intervention project. *Reading Research Quarterly, 34,* 404–424.

Leslie, L., & Caldwell, J. A. (2001). *Qualitative reading inventory* (3rd ed.). Boston: Allyn & Bacon.

Levin, J. R. (1993). Mnemonic strategies and classroom learning: A twenty-year report card. *The Elementary School Journal, 94,* 235–244.

Levin, J. R., Johnson, D. D., Pittelman, S. D., Levin, K. M., Shriberg, L. K., Toms-Bronowski, S., & Hayes, B. L. (1984). A comparison of semantic and mnemonic-based vocabulary-learning strategies. *Reading Psychology, 5*(2), 1–15.

Levy, B. A., Abello, B., & Lysynchuk, L. (1997). Transfer from word training to reading in context: Gains in reading fluency and comprehension. *Learning Disability Quarterly, 20,* 173–188.

Liberman, A. M., & Mattingly, I. G. (1989). A specialization for speech perception. *Science, 243,* 489–494.

Liberman, I. Y., Shankweiler, D., Fischer, F. W., & Carter, B. (1974). Explicit syllable and phoneme segmentation in the young child. *Journal of Experimental Child Psychology, 18,* 201–212.

Lindamood, C. H., & Lindamood, P. C. (1975). *The A.D.D. program: Auditory discrimination in depth.* Allen, TX: DLM Teaching Resources.

Lindamood, P., & Lindamood, P. (1998). *The Lindamood phoneme sequencing program for reading, spelling, and speech: LIPS.* Austin, TX: Pro-Ed.

Linden, M., & Wittrock, M. C. (1981). The teaching of reading comprehension according to the model of generative learning. *Reading Research Quarterly, 17,* 44–57.

Lipson, M. Y. (1984). Some unexpected issues in prior knowledge and comprehension. *The Reading Teacher, 37,* 760–764.

Lipson, M. Y., & Wixson, K. K. (1997). *Assessment and instruction of reading disability: An interactive approach* (2nd ed.). New York: HarperCollins.

Lipson, M. Y., & Wixson, K. K. (1991). *Assessment and instruction of reading disability: An interactive approach.* New York: HarperCollins.

Livingstone, M. (1999). The magnocellular/parietal system and visual symptoms in dyslexia. In D. D. Drake (Ed.), *Reading and attention disorders: Neurological correlates* (pp. 81–92). Baltimore, MD: York Press.

Loudon, B., & Arthur, G. (1940). An application of the Fernald method to an extreme case of reading disability. *Elementary School Journal, 40,* 599–606.

Lovegrove, W. J., & Williams, M. C. (1993). Visual temporal processing deficits in specific reading disability. In D. M. Willows, R. S. Kruk, & E. Corcos (Eds.), *Visual processes in reading and reading disabilities* (pp. 311–329). Hillsdale, NJ: Lawrence Erlbaum.

Lovett, M. W., Borden, S. L., DeLuca, T., Lacerenza, L., Benson, N. J., & Brackstone, D. (1994). Treating the core deficits of developmental dyslexia: Evidence of transfer-of-learning following phonologically and strategy-based reading training programs. *Developmental Psychology, 30,* 805–822.

Lovett, M. W., & Steinbach, K. A. (1997). The effectiveness of remedial programs for reading disabled children of different ages: Does the benefit decrease for older children? *Learning Disability Quarterly, 20,* 189–210.

Lovitt, T. C., Rudsit, J., Jenkins, J., Pious, C., & Benedetti, D. (1986). Adapting science materials for general and learning disabled seventh graders. *Remedial and Special Education, 7*(1), 31–39.

Luria, A. R. (1970). The functional organization of the brain. *Science, 153,* 66–78.

Lyons, C. (1995, December). *An analysis of the literacy behaviors of hard to accelerate Reading Recovery students.* Paper presented at the annual meeting of the National Reading Conference, New Orleans, LA.

Lyons, C. (2000). *Reading Recovery in the United States: More than a decade of data.* Available at http://readingrecovery.org/rr/rrusa.htm

MacArthur, C. A., Graham, S., & Schwartz, S. (1991). Effects of a reciprocal peer revision strategy in special education classrooms. *Learning Disabilities Research and Practice, 6,* 201–210.

MacGinitie, W., & MacGinitie, R. (1989). *Manual for scoring and interpretation of the Gates-MacGinitie reading tests* (3rd ed.). Chicago: Riverside.

Macías, R. F. (2000). *Summary report of the survey of the states' limited English proficient students and available educational programs and services, 1997–1998.* Washington, DC: National Clearinghouse for Bilingual Education.

Maclean, M., Bryant, P., & Bradley, L. (1987). Rhymes, nursery rhymes, and reading in early childhood. *Merrill-Palmer Quarterly, 33,* 255–281.

Manis, F. R., Seidenberg, M. S., & Doi, L. M. (1999). See Dick RAN: Rapid naming and the longitudinal prediction of subskills in first and second graders. *Scientific Studies of Reading, 3,* 129–157.

Manning, G. L., & Manning, M. (1984). What models of recreational reading make a difference? *Reading World, 23,* 375–380.

Manzo, A. V. (1969). The ReQuest procedure. *Journal of Reading, 13,* 123–126.

Manzo, A. V., & Manzo, U. C. (1993). *Literacy disorders: Holistic diagnosis and remediation.* Fort Worth, TX: Harcourt Brace Jovanovich.

Manzo, A. V., Manzo, U. C., & McKenna, M. C. (1995). *Informal reading-thinking inventory.* Fort Worth, TX: Harcourt Brace Jovanovich.

Maria, K. (1990). *Reading comprehension instruction: Issues and strategies.* Parkton, MD: York Press.

Maria, K., & MacGinitie, W. (1987). Learning from texts that refute the reader's prior knowledge. *Reading Research and Instruction, 26,* 222–238.

Martin, M. (1995). Spelling in the kindergarten. Paper presented at the annual meeting of the International Reading Association, Anaheim, CA.

Martinez, M., Roser, N. L., & Strecker, S. (1999). "I never thought I could be a star": A Readers' Theatre ticket to fluency. *The Reading Teacher, 52,* 326–334.

Marzano, R. J. (2004). The developing vision of vocabulary instruction. In J. Baumann & E. Kame'enui (Eds.), *Reading vocabulary: Research to practice* (pp. 118–138). New York: Guilford Press.

Marzano, R. J., Gaddy, B. B., & Dean, C. (2000). *What works in classroom instruction.* Aurora, CO: Mid-Continent Research for Education and Learning.

Mason, J. M., & Au, K. H. (1990). *Reading instruction for today* (2nd ed.). Glenview, IL: Scott, Foresman.

Maxworthy, A. G. (1993). Do study guides improve text comprehension? *Reading Horizons, 34,* 137–150.

McArthur, T. (Ed.) (1992). *The Oxford companion to the English language.* New York: Oxford University.

McBride-Chang, C., Wagner, R. K., & Chang, L. (1997). Growth modeling of phonological awareness. *Journal of Educational Psychology, 89,* 621–630.

McCandliss, B., Beck, I. L., Sandak, R., & Perfetti, C. (2003). Focusing attention on decoding for children with poor reading skills: Design and preliminary tests of the word building intervention. *Scientific Studies of Reading, 7,* 75–104.

McCormick, S. (1987). *Remedial and clinical reading instruction.* Columbus, OH: Merrill.

McCormick, S. (1992). Disabled readers' erroneous responses to inferential comprehension questions. *Reading Research Quarterly, 27,* 54–93.

McCormick, S. (1994). A nonreader becomes a reader. *Reading Research Quarterly, 29,* 157–176.

McCormick, S. (1995). *Instructing students who have literacy problems* (2nd ed.). Englewood Cliffs, NJ: Prentice-Hall.

McCormick, S. (1999). *Instructing students who have literacy problems* (3rd ed.). Upper Saddle River, NJ: Prentice-Hall.

McGill-Franzen, A. (1994). Compensatory and special education: Is there accountability for learning and belief in children's potential? In E. H. Hiebert & B. M. Taylor (Eds.), *Getting reading right from the start* (pp. 13–35). Boston: Allyn & Bacon.

McGinley, W. J., & Denner, P. R. (1987). Story impressions: A prereading/writing activity. *Journal of Reading, 31,* 248–253.

McGregor, K. K. (2004). Developmental dependencies between lexical semantics and reading. In C. A. Stone, E. R. Silliman, B. J. Ehren, & K. Apel (Eds.), *Handbook of language and literacy development and disorders* (pp. 302–317). New York: Guilford Press.

McGuinness, D. (1997). Decoding strategies as predictors of reading skill: A follow-up study. *Annals of Dyslexia, 47,* 117–150.

McKenna, M. C., Kear, D. J., & Ellsworth, R. A. (1995). Children's attitudes toward reading: A national survey. *Reading Research Quarterly, 30,* 934–956.

McKeown, M. G., & Beck, I. L. (2004). "Direct and rich vocabulary instruction," In J. Baumann & E. Kame'enui (Eds.), *Reading vocabulary: Research to practice* (pp. 13–27). New York, Guilford Press.

McKeown, M. G., Beck, I. L., & Sandora, C. A. (1996). Questioning the author: An approach to developing meaningful classroom discourse. In M. F. Graves, P. van den Broek, & B. M. Taylor (Eds.), *The first R: Every child's right to read* (pp. 97–119). New York: Teachers College Press & International Reading Association.

McNamara, T. P., Miller, D. L., & Bransford, J. D. (1991). Mental models and reading comprehension. In R. Barr, M. L. Kamil, P. Mosenthal, & P. D. Pearson (Eds.), *Handbook of reading research, Volume II* (pp. 490–511). New York: Longman.

Meares, O. (1980). Figure/ground, brightness contrast and reading disabilities. *Visible Language, 14,* 13–29.

Medley, D. M. (1977). *Teacher competence and teacher effectiveness: A review of process-product research.* Washington, DC: American Association of Colleges for Teacher Education.

Meisel, S. J. (1998). *Assessing readiness* (Ciera Report 3-002). Ann Arbor, MI: Center for the Improvement of Early Reading Instruction, University of Michigan School of Education.

Mellor, B., & Simons, M. (1991). As we see it: An interview with Kenneth S. & Yetta M. Goodman. In K. S. Goodman, L. B. Bird, & Y. M. Goodman (Eds.), *The whole language catalog* (pp. 100–101). Santa Rosa, CA: American School Publishers.

Meltzer, L. (1993). *Assessment of learning disabilities: The challenge of evaluating the cognitive strategies and processes underlying learning.* Paper presented at the Ninth Annual Learning Disorders Conference, Cambridge, MA.

Memory, D. M., & Moore, D. W. (1992). Three time-honored approaches to study: An update. In E. K. Dishner, T. W. Bean, J. E. Readence, & D. W. Moore (Eds.), *Reading in the content areas: Improving classroom instruction* (3rd ed., pp. 326–340). Dubuque, IA: Kendall/Hunt.

Menon, S., & Hiebert, E. F. (1999). *Literature anthologies: The task for first-grade readers* (Ciera Report 1-009). Ann Arbor, MI: Center for the Improvement of Early Reading Instruction, University of Michigan School of Education.

Menon, S., & Hiebert, E. H. (2005). A comparison of first graders' reading acquisition with little books or literature-based basal anthologies. *Reading Research Quarterly, 40,* 12–38.

Menyuk, P. (1991). Linguistics and teaching the language arts. In J. Flood, J. M. Jensen, D. Lapp, & J. R. Squire (Eds.), *Handbook of research on teaching the English language arts* (pp. 24–29). New York: Macmillan.

Merkley, D. M., & Jefferies, D. (2001). Guidelines for implementing a graphic organizer. *The Reading Teacher, 54,* 350–357.

Mesmer, H. A. (1999). Scaffolding a crucial transition using text with some decodability. *The Reading Teacher, 53,* 130–142.

Metametrics (2000). *About Lexile.* Available at http://www.lexile.com/

Metsala, J. L. (1999). The development of phonemic awareness in reading-disabled children. *Applied Psycholinguistics, 20,* 49–58.

Meyen, E. L., & Skrtic, T. M. (1988). *Exceptional children and youth: An introduction.* Denver, CO: Love.

Meyer, B., Brandt, D., & Bluth, G. (1980). Use of top-level structure in text: Key for reading comprehension of ninth-grade students. *Reading Research Quarterly, 16,* 72–103.

Meyer, B. J. F., & Rice, G. E. (1984). The structure of text. In P. D. Pearson, R. Barr, M. L. Kamil, & P. Mosenthal (Eds.), *Handbook of reading research* (pp. 319–351). New York: Longman.

Meyer, C. A. (1978). Reviewing the literature on Fernald's technique of remedial reading. *The Reading Teacher, 31,* 614–619.

Meyer, L. A. (1991). Are science textbooks considerate? In C. M. Santa & D. E. Alvermann (Eds.), *Science learning: Process and applications* (pp. 28–37). Newark, DE: International Reading Association.

Miles, T. R., & Miles, E. (1999). *Dyslexia a hundred years on* (2nd ed.). Philadelphia: Open University Press.

Miller, G. A. (1956). The magical number seven plus or minus two: Some limits on our capacity for processing information. *Psychological Review, 63,* 81–97.

Mish, F. C. (1993). *Webster's tenth new collegiate dictionary.* Springfield, MA: Merriam-Webster.

Moats, L. C. (1995). *Spelling: Development, disabilities, and instruction.* Baltimore: York Press.

Moats, L. C., & Farrell, M. L. (1999). In J. R. Birsh (Ed.), *Multisensory teaching and basic language skills* (pp. 1–18). Baltimore: Paul H. Brookes.

Monti, D., & Cicchetti, G. (1996). *TARA: Think-aloud reading assessment.* Austin, TX: Steck-Vaughn Berrent.

Moore, B. H., & Caldwell, H. (1991). Drama and drawing for narrative writing in primary grades. *Journal of Educational Research, 87,* 100–110.

Moore, D. W., & Moore, S. A. (1986). Possible sentences. In E. K. Dishner, T. W. Bean, J. E. Readence, & D. W. Moore (Eds.), *Reading in the content areas: Improving classroom instruction* (2nd ed.) (pp. 174–179). Dubuque, IA: Kendall/Hunt.

Moore, D. W., & Readence, J. E. (1984). A quantitative and qualitative review of graphic organizer research. *Journal of Educational Research, 78,* 11–17.

Moore, D. W., Readence, J. E., & Rickelman, R. J. (1989). *Prereading activities for content area reading and learning* (2nd ed.). Newark, DE: International Reading Association.

Moore, R. C., & Aspegren, C. (2001). Reflective conversations between two learners: Retrospective miscue analysis. *Journal of Adolescent and Adult Literacy, 44,* 492–503.

Morgan, W. P. (1896). A case study of congenital word blindness. *British Medical Journal, 2,* 1378.

Morris, D. (1992). Concept of word: A pivotal understanding in the learning-to-read process. In S. Templeton & D. R. Bear (Eds.), *Development of orthographic knowledge and the foundations of literacy: A memorial festschrift for Edmund H. Henderson* (pp. 53–77). Hillsdale, NJ: Lawrence Erlbaum.

Morris, D. (1999). *The Howard Street tutoring manual: Teaching at-risk readers in the primary grades.* New York: Guilford.

Morris, D., Blanton, L., Blanton, W. E., Nowacek, J., & Perney, J. (1995). Teaching low-achieving spellers at their "instructional level." *Elementary School Journal, 96,* 163–178.

Morris, D., Bloodgood, J. R., Lomax, R. G., & Perney, J. (2003). Developmental steps in learning to read: A longitudinal study in kindergarten and first grade. *Reading Research Quarterly, 38,* 302–328.

Morris, D., Shaw, B., & Perney, J. (1990). Helping low readers in grades 2 and 3. *Elementary School Journal, 91,* 133–150.

Morrow, L. M. (1994). *Literacy development in the early years* (2nd ed.). Boston: Allyn & Bacon.

Moustafa, M. (1995). Children's productive phonological recoding. *Reading Research Quarterly, 30,* 464–476.

Murphy, J. M. (1996). *A follow-up study of delayed readers and an investigation of factors related to their success in young adulthood.* Unpublished doctoral dissertation, University of Pennsylvania, Philadelphia.

Murphy, L. L., Plake, B. S., Impara, J. C., & Spies, R. A. (2002). *Tests in print VI.* Lincoln, NE: University of Nebraska Press.

Murray, B. A., Stahl, S. A., & Inez, M. G. (1993). *Developing phonological awareness through alphabet books.* Paper presented at the annual meeting of the National Reading Conference, Charleston, SC.

Murray, D. M. (1989). *Expecting the unexpected: Teaching myself—and others—to read and write.* Portsmouth, NH: Boynton/Cook.

Myers, J., & Lytle, S. (1986). Assessment of the learning process. *Exceptional Children, 53,* 138–144.

Myers, S. (2000, March). *Language symposium.* Paper presented at the 27th Annual Conference on Dyslexia and Related Reading Disorders, New York.

Nagy, W. E. (1988). *Teaching vocabulary to improve reading comprehension.* Newark, DE: International Reading Association.

Nagy, W. E., & Anderson, R. C. (1984). How many words are there in printed English? *Reading Research Quarterly, 19,* 304–330.

Nagy, W. E., & Scott, J. A. (2000). Vocabulary processes. In M. L. Kamil, P. B. Mosenthal, P. D. Pearson, & R. Barr (Eds.), *Handbook of reading research, Volume III* (pp. 269–284). Mahwah, NJ: Erlbaum.

Nathenson-Mejia, S. (1989). Writing in a second language: Negotiating meaning through invented spelling. *Language Arts, 66,* 516–526.

Nation, P. (2001). *Learning vocabulary in another language.* Cambridge, England: Oxford University Press.

National Assessment of Educational Progress (1986). *The reading report card: Progress toward excellence in our schools—Trends in reading over four*

national assessments, 1971–1984. Princeton, NJ: Educational Testing Service.

National Association of School Psychologists (2003). *Position statement on student grade retention and social promotion.* Available at http://www.nasponline .org/information/pospaper_graderetent.html

National Center on Student Progress Monitoring (2004). *Common questions on progress monitoring.* Available at http://www.studentprogress.org/progresmon .asp#3

National Dissemination Center for Children with Disabilities (2004). *Deafness and hearing loss.* Available at http://www.nichcy.org/pubs/factshe/fs3txt .htm

National Reading Panel (2000). *Report of the National Reading Panel.* Washington, DC: Author.

Nelson, J. S., Epstein, M. H., Bursuck, W. D., Jayanthi, M., & Sawyer, V. (1998). The preferences of middle school students for homework adaptations made by general education teachers. *Learning Disabilities Research and Practice, 13,* 109–117.

Neubach, A., & Cohen, A. (1988). Processing strategies and problems encountered in the use of dictionaries. *Dictionaries, 10,* 1–19.

Neuman, S. B. (1999). Books make a difference: A study of an access to literacy. *Reading Research Quarterly, 54,* 286–311.

Neuman, S. B., & Celano, D. (2001). Books Aloud: A campaign to "put books in children's hands." *The Reading Teacher, 54,* 550–557.

Neville, D. (1965). The relationships between reading skills and intelligence test scores. *The Reading Teacher, 18,* 257–262.

Newcomer, P. L., & Barenbaum, E. M. (1991). The written composing ability of children with learning disabilities: A review of the literature from 1980 to 1990. *Journal of Learning Disabilities, 24,* 578–593.

Nicholson, T. (1999). Literacy in the family and society. In G. B. Thompson & T. Nicholson (Eds.), *Learning to read: Beyond phonics and whole language* (pp. 1–22). Newark, DE: International Reading Association.

Nist, S. L., & Simpson, M. L. (2000). College studying. In M. L. Kamil, P. B. Mosenthal, P. D. Pearson, & R. Barr (Eds.), *Handbook of reading research, Volume III* (pp. 645–666). Mahwah, NJ: Erlbaum.

Oakhill, J., & Yuill, N. (1996). Higher-order factors in comprehension disability: Processes and remediation. In

C. Cornoldi & J. Oakhill (Eds.), *Reading comprehension difficulties: Process and intervention* (pp. 69–92). Mahwah, NJ: Erlbaum.

O'Connor, R. (2000). Increasing the intensity of intervention in kindergarten and first grade. *Learning Disabilities Research and Practice, 15,* 43–54.

O'Connor, R. E, & Bell, K. M. (2004). Teaching students with reading disability to read words. In C. A. Stone, E. R. Silliman, B. J, Ehren, & K. Apel (Eds.), *Handbook of language and literacy development and disorders* (pp. 481–498). New York: Guilford Press.

O'Connor, R. E., Bell, K. M., Harty, K. R., Larkin, L., Sackor, S., & Zigmond, N. (2002). Teaching reading to poor readers in the intermediate grades: A comparison of text difficulty. *Journal of Educational Psychology, 94,* 474–485.

Oetting, J. B., Rice, M. L., & Swank, L. K. (1995). Quick incidental learning (QUIL) of words by school-age children with and without SLI. *Journal of Speech and Hearing Research, 38,* 434–445.

Office of Elementary and Secondary Education (2000). *The reauthorization of the Elementary and Secondary Education Act (ESEA).* Available at http://www.ed.gov/legislation/ESEA/

Ogle, D., & Blachowicz, C. L. Z. (2002). Beyond literature circles: Helping students comprehend informational texts. In C. C. Block & M. Pressley (Eds.), *Comprehension instruction: Research-based best practices* (pp. 259–274). New York: Guilford Press.

Ogle, D. M. (1989). The know, want to know, learn strategy. In K. D. Muth (Ed.), *Children's comprehension of text* (pp. 205–223). Newark, DE: International Reading Association.

Olivares, R. (1993). *Using the newspaper to teach ESL learners.* Newark, DE: International Reading Association.

Olson, H., Mead, B. R., & Payne, D. (2002). *A report of a standard setting method for alternate assessments for students with significant disabilities.* Synthesis Report 47. Minneapolis, MN: University of Minnesota, National Center on Educational Outcomes. Available at http://education.umn.edu/nceo/OnlinePubs/Synthesis26.htm

Olson, J. L. (1987). Drawing to write. *School Arts, 87*(1), 25–27.

Olson, R. K., & Wise, B. W. (1997). Reading on the computer with orthographic and speech feedback: An overview of the Colorado remediation project.

Reading and Writing: An Interdisciplinary Journal, 4, 107–144.

Orton, J. (1966). The Orton-Gillingham approach. In J. Money (Ed.), *The disabled reader: Education of the dyslexic child* (pp. 119–145). Baltimore: The Johns Hopkins Press.

Orton, S. T. (1937). *Reading, writing, and speech problems in children.* New York: Norton.

Padolsky, D. (2004). *Ask NCELA, No. 1 Q: How many school-aged English language learners (ELLs) are there in the U.S.?* Office of English Language Acquisition, Language Enhancement & Academic Achievement for Limited English Proficient Students (OELA), National Clearinghouse for English Language Acquisition & Language Instruction Education Programs. Available at http://www.ncela.gwu.edu/expert/faq/01leps.htm

Palincsar, A. M. (2003). Collaborative approaches to comprehension instruction. In A. Sweet & C. Snow (Eds.), *Rethinking reading comprehension* (pp. 99–114). New York: Guilford Press.

Palincsar, A. S., & Brown, A. L. (1986). Interactive teaching to promote independent learning from text. *The Reading Teacher, 39,* 771–777.

Palincsar, A. S., & Klenk, L. (1992). Fostering literacy learning in supportive contexts. *Journal of Learning Disabilities, 25*(4), 211–225, 229.

Palincsar, A. S., Magnusson, S. J., Collins, K. M., & Cutter, J. (2001). Promoting deep understanding of science in students with disabilities in inclusion classrooms. *Learning Disabilities Quarterly, 2,* 15–32.

Palincsar, A. S., Winn, J., David, Y., Snyder, B., & Stevens, D. (1993). Approaches to strategic reading instruction reflecting different assumptions regarding teaching and learning. In L. J. Meltzer (Ed.), *Strategy assessment and instruction for students with learning disabilities: From theory to practice* (pp. 247–292). Austin, TX: Pro-Ed.

PALS (Peer-Assisted Learning Strategies) (2004). *About PALS.* Available at http://kc.vanderbilt.edu/kennedy/pals/about.html

Paratore, J. R. (1995). Implementing an intergenerational literacy project: Lessons learned. In L. M. Morrow (Ed.), *Family literacy, connections in schools and communities* (pp. 37–53). Newark, DE: International Reading Association.

Paris, S. (1993). *Classroom assessment for reading strategies, metacognition, and motivation.* Paper presented at the Ninth Annual Learning Disorders Conference, Cambridge, MA.

Paris, S. G. (1991). Assessment and remediation of metacognitive aspects of children's reading comprehension. *Topics in Language Disorders, 12*(1), 32–50.

Paris, S. G., Cross, D. R., & Lipson, M. Y. (1984). Informed strategies for learning: A program to improve children's reading awareness and comprehension. *Journal of Educational Psychology, 76,* 1239–1252.

Paris, S. G., & Myers, M. (1981). Comprehension monitoring, memory, and study strategies of good and poor readers. *Journal of Reading Behavior, 13,* 5–22.

Paris, S. G., & Okra, E. (1986). Children's reading strategies, metacognition, and motivation. *Developmental Review, 6,* 25–56.

Paris, S. G., Wasik, B. A., & Turner, J. C. (1991). The development of strategic readers. In R. Barr, M. L. Kamil, P. Mosenthal, & P. D. Pearson (Eds.), *Handbook of reading research, Volume II* (pp. 609–640). New York: Longman.

Pauk, W. (1984). The new SQ3R. *Reading World, 23,* 386–387.

Pauk, W. (1989). *How to study in college* (4th ed.). Boston: Houghton Mifflin.

Paul, T. D. (1996). *Patterns of reading practice.* Madison, WI: Institute for Academic Excellence.

Pearson, P. D., & Gallagher, M. C. (1983). The instruction of reading comprehension. *Contemporary Educational Psychology, 8,* 317–345.

Pearson, P. D., & Johnson, D. D. (1978). *Teaching reading comprehension.* New York: Holt, Rinehart & Winston.

Perfetti, C. A. (1992). The representation problem in reading acquisition. In P. B. Gough, L. C. Ehri, & R. Treiman (Eds.), *Reading acquisition* (pp. 145–174). Hillsdale, NJ: Lawrence Erlbaum.

Perfetti, C. A., Beck, I., Bell, L., & Hughes, C. (1988). Phonemic knowledge and learning to read are reciprocal: A longitudinal study of first grade children. In K. E. Stanovich (Ed.), *Children's reading and the development of phonological awareness* (pp. 39–75). Detroit: Wayne State University.

Perfetti, C. A., Marroni, M. A., & Foltz, P. W. (1996). Sources of comprehension failure: Theoretical perspectives and case studies. In C. Cornoldi & J. Oakhill (Eds.), *Reading comprehension difficulties: Processes and interventions* (pp. 137–165). Mahwah, NJ: Erlbaum.

Perrin, J. (1990). The learning styles project for potential dropouts. *Educational Leadership, 48*(2), 23–24.

Persky, H. R., Daane, M. C., & Jin, Y. (2003). *The Nation's report card: Writing 2002* (NCES 2003–529). Washington, DC: U.S. Department of Education, Institute of Education Services, National Center for Education Statistics.

Peters, C. (1979). The effect of systematic restructuring of material upon the comprehension process. *Reading Research Quarterly, 11,* 87–110.

Philliber, W. W., Spillman, R. E., & King, R. E. (1996). Consequences of family literacy programs for adults and children: Some preliminary findings. *Journal of Adolescent and Adult Literacy, 39,* 558–565.

Phillips, L. M. (1988). Young readers' inference strategies in reading comprehension. *Cognition and Instruction, 5*(3), 193–222.

Phillips, L. M., Norris, S. P., Osmond, W. C., & Maynard, A. M. (2002). Relative reading achievement: A longitudinal study of 187 children from first through sixth grades. *Journal of Educational Psychology, 94,* 3–13.

Pickary, J. A. (1949). An adult nonreader. In W. S. Gray (Ed.), *Classroom techniques in improving reading* (pp. 115–117) *(Supplementary Educational Monographs, No. 79).* Chicago: University of Chicago Press.

Pinnell, G. S., & Fountas, I. C., (1998). *Word matters.* Portsmouth, NH: Heinemann.

Pinnell, G. S., & McCarrier, A. (1994). Interactive writing: A transition tool for assisting children in learning to read and write. In E. H. Hiebert & B. M. Taylor (Eds.), *Getting reading right from the start* (pp. 149–170). Boston: Allyn & Bacon.

Pinnell, G. S., Pikulski, J. J. Wixson, K. K., Campbell, J. R., Gough, P. B., & Beatty, A. S. (1995). *Listening to children read aloud.* Washington, DC: U.S. Department of Education, National Center for Education Statistics.

Pittelman, S. D., Heimlich, J. E., Berglund, R. L., & French, M. P. (1991). *Semantic feature analysis: Classroom applications.* Newark, DE: International Reading Association.

Pollack, M., & Arenson, K. W. (2000, May 17). Bulletin board: Free eyeglasses for students. *The New York Times,* p. B8.

Popham, W. J. (2000). *Modern educational measurement: Practical guidelines for educational leaders.* Boston: Allyn & Bacon.

Powell, W. R. (1971). The validity of the instructional reading level. In R. E. Liebert (Ed.), *Diagnostic viewpoints in reading* (pp. 121–133). Newark, DE: International Reading Association.

Prescott, J. O. (2003, January/February). The power of reader's theater: An easy way to make dramatic changes in kids' fluency, writing, listening, and social skills. *Scholastic Instructor.* Available at http://teacher.scholastic.com/products/instructor/readerstheater.htm

Pressley, M. (1977). Imagery and children's learning: Putting the picture in developmental perspective. *Review of Educational Research, 47,* 585–622.

Pressley, M. (2000). Comprehension instruction in elementary school: A quarter-century of research progress. In B. Taylor, M. F. Graves, & P. van den Broek (Eds.), *Reading for meaning: Fostering comprehension in the middle grades* (pp. 32–51). New York: Teachers College Press.

Pressley, M., Johnson, C. J., Symons, S., McGoldrick, J. A., & Kurita, J. A. (1989). Strategies that improve children's memory and comprehension of what is read. *Elementary School Journal, 89,* 3–32.

Quenemoen, R., Thurlow, M., Moen, R., Thompson, S., & Morse, A. B. (2003). *Progress monitoring in an inclusive standards-based assessment and accountability system* (Synthesis Report 53). Minneapolis, MN: University of Minnesota, National Center on Educational Outcomes. Available at http://education.umn.edu/NCEO/OnlinePubs/Synthesis53.html

Radencich, M. C. (1995). *Administration and supervision of the reading/writing program.* Boston: Allyn & Bacon.

Radencich, M. C., Beers, P. G., & Schumm, J. S. (1993). *A handbook for the K–12 resource specialist.* Boston: Allyn & Bacon.

Ramirez, J. D. (1992). Executive summary of the final report: Longitudinal study of structured English immersion strategy, early-exit and late-exit transitional bilingual education programs for language-minority children. *Bilingual Research Journal: The Journal of the National Association for Bilingual Education, 16,* 1–62.

RAND Reading Study Group (2004). A research agenda for improving reading comprehension. In R. B. Ruddell & N. J. Unrau (2004). *Theoretical models and processes of reading* (5th ed.) (pp. 720–754). Newark, DE: International Reading Association.

Rapaport, W. J. (2004, May). *What is "context" in contextual vocabulary acquisition? Lessons learned from artificial intelligence and verbal protocol of good readers when they encounter unknown words*

in context. Paper presented at the International Reading Association Convention, Reno, NV.

Raphael, T. E. (1984). Teaching learners about sources of information for answering questions. *The Reading Teacher, 28,* 303–311.

Raphael, T. E. (1986). Teaching question-answer relationships, revisited. *The Reading Teacher, 39,* 516–522.

Raphael, T. E., & Englert, C. S. (1990). Writing and reading: Partners in constructive meaning. *The Reading Teacher, 43,* 388–400.

Raphael, T. E., Englert, C. S., & Kirschner, B. W. (1989). Acquisition of expository writing skills. In J. M. Mason (Ed.), *Reading and writing connections* (pp. 261–290). Boston: Allyn & Bacon.

Rashotte, C. A., & Torgesen, J. K. (1985). Repeated reading and reading fluency in learning disabled children. *Reading Research Quarterly, 20,* 180–188.

Rasinski, T. C. (1999). Making and writing words. *Reading Online,* an electronic journal of the International Reading Association. Available at http://www.readingonline.org/articles/words/rasinski_index.html

Rasinski, T., & Padak, N. (1996). *Holistic reading strategies: Teaching children who find reading difficult.* Englewood Cliffs, NJ: Merrill.

Rasinksi, T. V. (2003). *The fluent reader: Oral reading strategies for building word recognition, fluency, and comprehension.* New York: Scholastic.

Rasinksi, T. V. (2004, August). *Using assessment to guide instruction focusing on fluency.* Paper presented at the Reading First Summer Institute, Cromwell, CT.

Ratner, N. B. (1993). Atypical language development. In J. B. Berko (Ed.), *The development of language* (pp. 325–368). New York: Macmillan.

Read, C. (1971). Pre-school children's knowledge of English phonology. *Harvard Educational Review, 41,* 1–34.

Reading Recovery Council of North America (2000). Descubriendo la lectura: *Reading Recovery in Spanish.* Available at http://readingrecovery.org/rr/dll.htm

Reading Recovery Council of North America (2000). *Phonological awareness and Reading Recovery.* Available at http://readingrecovery.org/rr/phon.htm

Reeves D. (2002). *Ideas for improving high school reading and academic success.* Center for Performance Assessment. Available at http://www.makingstandardswork.com/ResourceCtr/index.php

Reeves, D. (2003). *High performance in high poverty schools: 90/90/90 and beyond.* Center for Resource Assessment. Available at http://www.makingstandardswork.com/ResourceCtr/fullindex.htm

Reitsma, P. (1989). Orthographic memory and learning to read. In P. G. Aaron & M. Joshi (Eds.), *Reading and writing disorders in different orthographic systems* (pp. 51–73). Dordrecht, The Netherlands: Kluwer.

Resnick, L. B. (1999, June 16). Making America smarter. *Education Week on the Web, 18.* Available at http://www.edweek.org/ew/vol-18/40resnick.h18

Resnick, L. B., & Hall, M. W. (2001). *The principles of Learning: Study tools for educators* [CD-ROM, version 2.0). Pittsburgh, PA: University of Pittsburgh, Learning Research and Development Center, Institute for Learning. Available at www.instituteforlearning.org

Resnick, L. B. , & Hall, M. W. (2003). *The principles of learning: Study tools for educators.* (CD-ROM version 3.1). Pittsburgh, PA: University of Pittsburgh, Learning Research and Development Center. Institute for Learning.

Rhodes, L. K., & Dudley-Marling, C. (1988). *Readers and writers with a difference: A holistic approach to teaching learning disabled and remedial students.* Portsmouth, NH: Heinemann.

Rhodes, L. K., & Nathenson-Mejia, S. (1992). Anecdotal records: A powerful tool for ongoing literacy assessment. *The Reading Teacher, 45,* 502–509.

Riccio, C. A., & Hynd, G. W. (1996). Neuroanatomical and neurophysiological aspects of dyslexia. *Topics in Language Disorders, 16,* 1–13.

Richardson, J. S., & Morgan, R. F. (1997). *Reading to learn in the content areas* (3rd ed.). Belmont, CA: Wadsworth.

Richek, M. A., Caldwell, J. S., Jennings, J. H., & Lerner, J. W. (1996). *Reading problems: Assessment and teaching strategies* (3rd ed.). Boston: Allyn & Bacon.

Richek, M. A., List, L. K., & Lerner, J. W. (1989). *Reading problems: Assessment and teaching strategies* (2nd ed.). Boston: Allyn & Bacon.

Richek, M. A., & McTague, B. K. (1988). The "Curious George" strategy for students with reading problems. *The Reading Teacher, 42,* 220–226.

Richgels, D. J., & Hansen, R. (1984). Gloss: Helping students apply both skills and strategies in reading content texts. *Journal of Reading, 27,* 312–317.

Rist, R. (1970). Student social class and teacher expectations: The self-fulfilling prophecy in ghetto education. *Harvard Educational Review, 40,* 411–451.

Robeck, M. C., & Wallace, R. R. (1990). *The psychology of reading: An interdisciplinary approach* (2nd ed.). Hillsdale, NJ: Erlbaum.

Roberts, R., & Mather, N. (1997). Orthographic dyslexia: The neglected subtype. *Learning Disabilities Research and Practice, 12,* 236–250.

Robinson, F. P. (1970). *Effective study* (4th ed.). New York: Harper & Row.

Rochman, H. (1984). Booktalking the classics. *School Library Journal, 30,* 44.

Roller, C. (1996). *Variability, not disability: Struggling readers in a workshop classroom.* Newark, DE: International Reading Association.

Rosenberger, P. B. (1992). Dyslexia—Is it a disease? *The New England Journal of Medicine, 326* (3), 192–193.

Rosenblatt, L. M. (1978). *The reader, the text, and the poem: The transactional theory of the literary work.* Carbondale, IL: Southern Illinois University Press.

Rosenblatt, L. M. (1994). The transactional theory of reading and writing. In R. B. Ruddell, M. R. Ruddell, & H. Singer (Eds.), *Theoretical models and processes of reading* (4th ed.) (pp. 1057–1092). Newark, DE: International Reading Association.

Rosenshine, B., & Meister, C. (1994). Reciprocal teaching: A review of the research. *Review of Educational Research, 64,* 479–530.

Rosner, J. (1975). *Helping children overcome learning difficulties.* New York: Walker.

Rosner, S., Abrams, J., Daniels, P., & Schiffman, G. (1991). Dealing with the reading needs of the learning disabled child. *Journal of Learning Disabilities, 14,* 436–448.

Roswell, F., & Chall, J. (1992). *Diagnostic assessments of reading.* Itasca, IL: Riverside.

Roswell, F. G., & Chall, J. S. (1994). *Creating successful readers: A practical guide to testing and teaching at all levels.* Chicago, IL: Riverside.

Roswell, F. G., & Natchez, G. (1989). *Reading disability: A human approach to evaluation and treatment of reading and writing difficulties* (4th ed.). New York: Basic Books.

Roth, K. J. (1981). Reading science texts for conceptual change. In C. M. Santa & D. E. Alvermann (Eds.), *Science learning: Process and applications* (pp. 48–63). Newark, DE: International Reading Association.

Routman, R. (1991). *Invitations: Changing as teachers and learners K–12.* Portsmouth, NH: Heinemann.

Rowe, M. B. (1969). Science, silence, and sanctions. *Science for Children, 6*(6), 11–13.

Rowell, C. G. (1992). *Assessment and correction in elementary language arts.* Boston: Allyn & Bacon.

Ruddell, M. R. (1992). Integrated content and long-term vocabulary learning with the vocabulary self-collection strategy. In E. K. Dishner, T. W. Bean, J. E. Readence, & D. W. Moore (Eds.), *Reading in the content areas: Improving classroom instruction* (3rd ed.) (pp. 190–196). Dubuque, IA: Kendall/Hunt.

Ruddell, M. R. (1994). Vocabulary knowledge and comprehension: A comprehension-process view of complex literacy relationships. In R. B. Ruddell, M. R. Ruddell, & H. Singer (Eds.), *Theoretical models and processes of reading* (4th ed., pp. 414–447). Newark, DE: International Reading Association.

Ruddell, R. B. (1978). Developing comprehension abilities: Implications from research for an instructional framework. In S. J. Samuels (Ed.), *What research has to say about reading instruction* (pp. 108–120). Newark, DE: International Reading Association.

Rumelhart, D. (1980). Schemata: The building blocks of cognition. In R. J. Spiro, B. C. Bruce, & W. F. Bruner (Eds.), *Theoretical issues in reading comprehension* (pp. 33–58). Hillsdale, NJ: Lawrence Erlbaum.

Rumelhart, D. E. (1985). Toward an interactive model of reading. In H. Singer & R. B. Ruddell (Eds.), *Theoretical models and processes of reading* (3rd ed., pp. 722–750). Newark, DE: International Reading Association.

Rusnak, G. (1994). *Instructional conversations in the writing process.* Paper presented at the annual reading conference of the International Reading Association, Toronto, Ont.

Rutherford, F. J., & Ahlgren, A. (1990). *Science for all Americans.* New York: Oxford University Press.

Rutter, M., & Yule, W. (1975). The concept of specific reading retardation. *Journal of Child Psychiatry and Psychology, 16,* 181–197.

Rye, J. (1982). *Cloze procedure and the teaching of reading.* London: Heinemann.

Sack, K. (December 31, 1995). 84-year-old finds the joy of reading a good book. *The New York Times,* p. 16.

Sadowski, M. (1983). An exploratory study of the relationship between reported imagery and the comprehension and recall of a story. *Reading Research Quarterly, 19,* 110–123.

Sadowski, M. (1985). The natural use of imagery in story comprehension and recall: Replication and extension. *Reading Research Quarterly, 20,* 658–667.

Sadowski, M., Goetz, E. T., & Fritz, J. B. (1993). Impact of concreteness on comprehensibility, interest, and memory for text: Implications for dual coding theory and text design. *Journal of Educational Psychology, 85,* 291–304.

Salvia, J., & Ysseldyke, J. E. (1998). *Assessment in special and remedial education* (7th ed.). Boston: Houghton Mifflin.

Samuels, S. J. (1979). The method of repeated reading. *The Reading Teacher, 32,* 403–408.

Samuels, S. J. (1994). Toward a theory of automatic information processing in reading revisited. In R. B. Ruddell, M. R. Ruddell, & H. Singer (Eds.), *Theoretical models and processes of reading* (4th ed., pp. 816–837). Newark, DE: International Reading Association.

Sandora, C., Beck, I., & McKeown, M. (1999). A comparison of two discussion strategies on students' comprehension and interpretation of complex literature. *Journal of Reading Psychology, 20,* 177–212.

Santa, C. (1988). *Creating independence through student-owned strategies* (2nd ed.). Dubuque, IA: Kendall/Hunt.

Santa, C. M. (1976–1977). Spelling patterns and the development of flexible word recognition strategies. *Reading Research Quarterly, 12,* 125–144.

Santa, C. M., Abrams, L., & Santa, J. L. (1979). Effects of notetaking and studying on the retention of prose. *Journal of Reading Behavior, 11,* 247–260.

Santa, C., M., Havens, L. T., & Maycumber, E. M. (1996). *Creating independence through student-owned strategies* (2nd ed.). Dubuque, IA: Kendall/Hunt.

Santa, C. M., & Høien, T. (1999). An assessment of Early Steps: A program for early intervention. *Reading Research Quarterly, 34,* 54–79.

Sawyer, D. J. (1985). *Language problems observed in poor readers.* Boston: College Hill Press.

Sawyer, D. J. (1987). *TALS Test of Awareness of Language Segments.* Rockville, MD: Aspen.

Scanlon, D. (2002). PROVEing what you know: Using a learning strategy in an inclusive classroom. *Teaching Exceptional Children, 34,* 48–54.

Scanlon, D., Deshler, D. D., & Schumaker, J. B. (1996). Can a strategy be taught and learned in secondary inclusive classrooms? *Learning Disabilities Research and Practice, 11,* 41–57.

Scanlon, D. M., & Vellutino, F. R. (1997). A comparison of the instructional backgrounds and cognitive profiles of poor, average, and good readers who were initially identified as at risk for reading failure. *Scientific Studies of Reading 1*(3), 191–215.

Schiffini, A. (1999). *Successful strategies for your older struggling readers.* Torrance, CA: Staff Development Resources.

Schlagal, R. (1992). Patterns of orthographic development into the intermediate grades. In S. Templeton & D. Bear (Eds.), *Development of orthographic knowledge and the foundations of literacy: A memorial Festschrift for Edmund H. Henderson* (pp. 31–52). Hillsdale, NJ: Lawrence Erlbaum.

Schoenbach, R., Greenleaf, C., Cziko, C., & Hurwitz, L. (1999). *Reading for understanding.* San Francisco: Jossey-Bass.

Schumaker, J. B., & Deshler, D. D. (1992). Validation of learning strategy interventions for students with learning disabilities: Results of a programmatic research effort. In B. N. Y. Wong (Ed.), *Contemporary intervention research in learning disabilities: An international perspective* (pp. 22–46). New York: Springer-Verlag.

Schunk, D. H., & Rice, J. H. (1987). Enhancing comprehension skill and self-efficacy with strategy value information. *Journal of Reading Behavior, 19,* 285–302.

Schunk, D. H., & Rice, J. M. (1993). Strategy fading and progress feedback: Effects on self-efficacy and comprehension among students receiving remedial services. *The Journal of Special Education, 27,* 257–273.

Scott, J. A., & Nagy, W. E. (1997). Understanding the definitions of unfamiliar words. *Reading Research Quarterly, 32,* 184–200.

Scott, T. (1998, May). *Using content area text to teach decoding and comprehension strategies.* Paper presented at the Annual Meeting of the International Reading Association, Orlando, FL.

Searl, H. M. (2004, July). *Examining student work: A protocol for improving reading instruction.* Teacher-to-Teacher Initiative Summer Workshop. Available online at http://www.ed.gov/teachers/how/read/list.jhtml

Seligman, M. E. P. (1975). *Helplessness.* San Francisco: Freeman.

Semel, E., Wiig, E., & Secord, W. A. (1995). *Clinical evaluation of language fundamentals.* Orlando, FL: Psychological Corporation.

Senechal, M., & Cornell, E. J. (1993). Vocabulary acquisition through shared reading experiences. *Reading Research Quarterly, 28,* 360–374.

Shand, M. (1993). *The role of vocabulary in developmental reading disabilities* (Technical Report 576). Urbana, IL: Center for the Study of Reading.

Shany, M. T., & Biemiller, A. (1995). Assisted reading practice: Effects on performance for poor readers in grades 3 and 4. *Reading Research Quarterly, 30,* 382–395.

Shapiro, E. S. (1996). *Academic skills problems: Direct assessment and intervention.* New York: Guilford Press.

Shaywitz, B. A., Pugh, K. R., Jenner, A. R., Fulbright, R. K., Fletcher, J. M., Gore, J. C., & Shaywitz, S. E. (2000). The neurobiology of reading and reading disability (dyslexia). In M. L. Kamil, P. B. Mosenthal, P. D. Pearson, & R. Barr (Eds.), *Handbook of reading research, Volume III* (pp. 229–249). Mahwah, NJ: Erlbaum.

Shaywitz, S. (2003). *Overcoming dyslexia: A new and complete science-based program for reading problems at any level.* New York: Knopf.

Shaywitz, S. E. (2000, March). *The science of reading: Why some very smart people may have trouble reading.* Paper presented at the 27th Annual Conference on Dyslexia and Related Reading Disorders, New York.

Shaywitz, S. E., & Shaywitz, B. A (2000). Dyslexia: From epidemiology to neurobiology. In D. D. Drake (Ed.), *Reading and attention disorders: Neurological correlates* (pp. 113–128). Baltimore: York Press.

Shaywitz, S. E., Shaywitz, B. A., Fletcher, J. M., & Escobar, M. D. (1990). Prevalance of reading disability in boys and girls: Results of the Connecticut Longitudinal Study. *Journal of the American Medical Association, 268,* 998–1002.

Shearer, B. (1999). *The vocabulary self-collection strategy (VSS) in a middle school.* Paper presented at the 49th Annual Meeting of the National Reading Conference, Orlando, FL.

Shefelbine, J., & Newman, K. K. (2000a). *SIPPS (systematic instruction in phoneme awareness, phonics, and sight words) manuals.* Oakland, CA: Developmental Studies Center.

Shefelbine, J., & Newman, K. K. (2000b). *SIPPS Challenge Level,* (2nd ed.). Oakland, CA: Developmental Studies Center.

Shefelbine, J. L. (1990). Student factors related to variability in learning word meanings from context. *Journal of Reading Behavior, 22,* 71–97.

Sheffield, B. B. (1991). The structured flexibility of Orton-Gillingham. *Annals of Dyslexia, 41,* 41–54.

Siegel, L. (1998). The discrepancy formula: Its use and abuse. In B. K. Shapiro, P. J. Accardo, & A. J. Capute (Eds.), *Specific reading disability: A view of the spectrum* (pp. 123–135). Timonium, MD: York Press.

Silvaroli, N. J., & Wheelock, A. (2001). *Classroom reading inventory* (9th ed.). New York: McGraw-Hill.

Simmons, J. (1990). Portfolios as large-scale assessment. *Language Arts, 67,* 262–268.

Simmons, J. (1990). Portfolios as large-scale assessment. *Language Arts, 67,* 262–268.

Simon, H. A. (1986). The role of attention in cognition. In S. L. Friedman, K. A. Klivington, & R. W. Peterson (Eds.), *The brain, cognition, and education* (pp. 105–115). Orlando, FL: Academic Press.

Simonsen, S. (1996). Identifying and teaching text structures in content-area classrooms. In D. Lapp, J. Flood, & N. Farnan (Eds.), *Content-area reading and learning instructional strategies* (pp. 59–73). Boston: Allyn & Bacon.

Sinatra, R. C., Berg, D., & Dunn, R. A. (1985). Semantic mapping improves reading comprehension of learning disabled students. *Teaching Exceptional Children, 17,* 310–314.

Singer, H. (1977). IQ is and is not related to reading. In S. Wanat (Ed.), *Issues in evaluating reading* (pp. 43–55). Arlington, VA: Center for Applied Linguistics.

Skjelfjord, V. (1976). Teaching children to segment spoken words as an aid in learning to read. *Journal of Learning Disabilities, 9,* 297–306.

Slater, W. H., Graves, M. F., & Piche, G. L. (1985). Effects of structural organizers on ninth grade students' comprehension and recall of four patterns of expository text. *Reading Research Quarterly, 20,* 189–202.

Slavin, R. E., & Madden, N. A. (2000). *Success for All Foundation: Our history.* Available at http://www.successforall.net/about/history.htm

Slavin, R. E., Madden, N. A., Dolan, L. J., & Wasik, B. A. (1996). *Every child, every school: Success for all.* Thousand Oaks, CA: Corwin Press.

Slavin, R. E., Madden, N. A., Karweit, N. L., & Dolan, L. (1990). Success for all: First-year outcomes of a comprehensive plan for reforming urban education. *American Educational Research Journal, 27,* 255–278.

Slavin, R. E., Madden, N. A., Karweit, N. L., Dolan, L. J., & Wasik, B. A. (1994). Success for All: Getting reading right the first time. In E. H. Hiebert & B. M. Taylor (Eds.), *Getting reading right from the start* (pp. 125–148). Boston: Allyn & Bacon.

Slingerland, B. H. (1971). *A multi-sensory approach to language arts for specific language disability children: A guide for primary teachers.* Cambridge, MA: Educators Publishing Service.

Smith, D. D. (1998). *Introduction to special education: Teaching in an age of challenge* (3rd ed.). Boston: Allyn & Bacon.

Smith, M. K. (1941). Measurement of the size of general English vocabulary through the elementary grades and high school. *General Psychological Monographs, 24,* 311–345.

Smith, S. D., Brower, A. M., Cardon, L. R., & DeFries, J. C. (1998). Genetics of reading disability: Further evidence for a gene on chromosome 6. In D. D. Drake (Ed.), *Reading and attention disorders: Neurological correlates* (pp. 63–74). Baltimore: York Press.

Snow, C. E., Burns, S. M., & Griffin, P. (1998). *Preventing reading difficulties in young children.* Washington, DC: National Academy Press.

Snowball, D., & Bolton, F. (1999). *Spelling K–8: Planning and teaching.* York, ME: Stenhouse.

Snyder, L. S., & Godley, D. (1992). Assessment of word-finding disorders in children and adolescents. *Topics in Language Disorders, 13,* 15–32.

Spandel, V. (2005). *Creating writers through 6-trait writing assessment and instruction* (4th ed.). Boston: Allyn & Bacon.

Spear-Swerling, L. (2004). A road map for understanding reading disability and other reading problems: Origins, prevention, and intervention. In R. B. Ruddell & N. J. Unrau (Eds.), *Theoretical models and processes of reading* (5th ed.), pp. 517–573). Newark, DE: International Reading Association.

Spear-Swerling, L., & Sternberg, R. J. (1996). *Off track: When poor readers become "learning disabled."* Boulder, CO: Westview Press.

Speece, D. (2003a). *Progress monitoring assists decision making in a response-to-instruction framework.* National Center on Student Progress. Available at www.studentprogress.org

Speece, D. (2003b, December). *Responsiveness-to-Intervention Symposium.* The National Research Center on Learning Disabilities. Kansas City, MO. Available online at http://www.nrcld.org/html/sympo sium2003/speece/speece4.html

Spring, C., & French, L. (1990). Identifying children with specific reading disabilities from listening and reading discrepancy scores. *Journal of Learning Disabilities, 23,* 53–58.

Stahl, K. A. D. (2004). Proof, practice, and promise: Comprehension instruction in the primary grades. *The Reading Teacher, 57,* 598–609.

Stahl, S. A., Duffy-Hester, A. M., & Stahl, K. A. D. (1998). Theory and research into practice: Everything you wanted to know about phonics (but were afraid to ask). *Reading Research Quarterly, 33,* 338–355.

Stahl, S. A., & Fairbanks, M. M. (1986). The effects of vocabulary instruction: A model-based meta-analysis. *Review of Educational Research, 56,* 72–110.

Stahl, S. A., Heubach, K. M., & Crammond, J. G. (1997). *Fluency-oriented reading instruction.* Athens, GA: National Reading Research Center, University of Georgia. Reading Research Report 79, (ED405554).

Stahl, S. A., & Kapinus, B. A. (1991). Possible sentences: Predicting word meanings to teach content area vocabulary. *The Reading Teacher, 45,* 36–43.

Stahl, S. A., Stahl, K. A., & McKenna, M. C. (1998, December). *How do phonological awareness, spelling, and word recognition relate to each other?* Paper presented at the Annual Meeting of the National Reading Conference, Austin, TX.

Stanovich, K. E. (1986). Matthew effects in reading: Some consequences of individual differences in the acquisition of literacy. *Reading Research Quarterly, 21,* 360–407.

Stanovich, K. E. (1991). Discrepancy definitions of reading disability: Has intelligence led us astray? *Reading Research Quarterly, 26,* 7–29.

Stanovich, K. E. (1992). Speculations on the causes and consequences of individual differences in early reading acquisition. In P. B. Gough, L. C. Ehri, & R. Treiman (Eds.), *Reading acquisition,* pp. 307–342. Hillsdale, NJ: Lawrence Erlbaum.

Stanovich, K. E., & Cunningham, A. E. (1992). Studying the consequences of literacy within a literate society: The cognitive correlates of print exposure. *Memory & Cognition, 20,* 51–68.

Stanovich, K. E., & Siegel, L. S. (1994). Phenotypic performance profile of children with reading disabilities: A regression-based test of the phonological-core

variable-difference model. *Journal of Educational Psychology, 86,* 24–53.

Stauffer, R. G. (1969). *Directing reading maturity as a cognitive process.* New York: Harper & Row.

Stein, J. F. (1996). Visual system and reading. In C. H. Chase, G. D. Rosen, & G. F. Sherman (Eds.), *Developmental dyslexia: Neural, cognitive, and genetic mechanisms* (pp. 107–125). Baltimore: York Press.

Stein, M., Johnson, B., & Gutlophn, L. (1999). Analyzing beginning reading programs: The relationship between decoding instruction and text. *Remedial and Special Education, 20,* 275–287.

Stein, N., & Glenn, C. G. (1979). An analysis of story comprehension in elementary school children. In R. Freedle (Ed.), *New directions in discourse processing, Volume II* (pp. 53–120). Norwood, NJ: Ablex.

Sternberg, R. J. (1985). *Beyond IQ: A triarchic theory of intelligence.* Cambridge, England: Cambridge University Press.

Sternberg, R. J. (1987). Most vocabulary is learned from context. In M. G. McKeown & M. E. Curtis (Eds.), *The nature of vocabulary acquisition* (pp. 89–105). Hillsdale, NJ: Lawrence Erlbaum.

Sternberg, R. J. (1996). *Successful intelligence: How practical and creative intelligence determine success in life.* New York: Penguin.

Stewart, R. A., & Cross, T. L. (1991). The effect of marginal glosses on reading comprehension and retention. *Journal of Reading, 35,* 4–12.

Stewart, R. A., & Cross, T. L. (1993). A field test of five forms of marginal gloss study guides: An ecological study. *Reading Psychology, 14,* 113–139.

Stewig, J. W., & Nordberg, B. (1995). *Exploring language arts in the elementary classroom.* Belmont, CA: Wadsworth.

Sticht, T. G., & James, J. H. (1984). Listening and reading. In P. D. Pearson, R. Barr, M. L. Kamil, & P. Mosenthal (Eds.), *Handbook of reading research* (pp. 293–317). New York: Longman.

Stieglitz, E. L. (1997). *The Stieglitz Informal Reading Inventory* (2nd ed.). Boston: Allyn & Bacon.

Stoll, D. R. (1997). *Magazines for kids and teens.* Newark, DE: International Reading Association.

Stone, C. A. (2004). Contemporary approaches to the study of language and literacy development: A call for the integration of perspectives. In C. A. Stone, E. R. Silliman, B. J., Ehren, & K. Apel (Eds.), *Handbook of language and literacy development and disorders* (pp. 3–24). New York: Guilford Press.

Strock, M. (2004). *Autism spectrum disorders (Pervasive developmental disorders).* NIH Publication No. NIH-04-5511, National Institute of Mental Health, National Institutes of Health, U.S. Department of Health and Human Services, Bethesda, MD. Available online at http://www.nimh.nih.gov/publicat/autism.cfm

Stuart, M., & Colthheart, M. (1990). Does reading develop in a sequence of stages? *Cognition, 30,* 139–181.

Sulzby, E. (1989). Assessment of writing and of children's language while writing. In L. Morrow & J. Smith (Eds.), *The role of assessment and measurement in early literacy instruction* (pp. 83–109). Englewood Cliffs, NJ: Prentice-Hall.

Sulzby, E., & Barnhart, J. (1992). The development of academic competence: All our children emerge as writers and readers. In J. W. Irwin & M. A. Doyle (Eds.), *Reading/writing connections: Learning from research* (pp. 120–144). Newark, DE: International Reading Association.

Sulzby, E., & Teale, W. (1991). Emergent literacy. In R. Barr, M. L. Kamil, P. Mosenthal, & P. D. Pearson (Eds.), *Handbook of reading research, Volume II* (pp. 727–757). New York: Longman.

Swanborn, M. S. L., & de Glopper, K. (1999). Incidental word learning while reading: A meta-analysis. *Review of Educational Research, 69,* 261–285.

Swanson, H. L., & Alexander, J. E. (2001). Cognitive processes as predictors of word recognition and reading comprehension in learning-disabled and skilled readers. *Journal of Educational Psychology, 89,* 128–158.

Swanson, H. L., & Alexander, J. E. (2001). Cognitive processes as predictors of word recognition and reading comprehension in learning-disabled and skilled readers. *Journal of Educational Psychology, 89,* 128–158.

Taba, H. (1965). The teaching of thinking. *Elementary English, 42,* 534–542.

Taba, H. (1967). *Teacher's handbook for elementary social studies.* Reading, MA: Addison-Wesley.

TASA (1999). *Degrees of Reading Power.* Brewster, NY: Touchstone Applied Science Associates.

TASA (2000). *Booklink.* Brewster, NY: Touchstone Applied Science Associates.

Taylor, B., Harris, L. A., & Pearson, P. D. (1988). *Reading difficulties: Instruction and assessment.* New York: Random House.

Taylor, B. M. (1992, May). *Early intervention in reading: Supplemental instruction for low-achieving readers provided by first-grade teachers.* Paper presented at the annual meeting of the International Reading Association, Orlando, FL.

Taylor, B. M., Strait, J., & Medo, M. A. (1994). *Early intervention in reading: Supplemental instruction for groups of low-achieving students provided by first-grade teachers.* In E. H. Hiebert & B. M. Taylor (Eds.), *Getting reading right from the start* (pp. 85–106). Boston: Allyn & Bacon.

Taylor, D., & Dorsey-Gaines, C. (1988). *Growing up literate, learning from inner-city families.* Portsmouth, NH: Heinemann.

Taylor, K. K. (1986). Summary writing by young children. *Reading Research Quarterly, 21,* 193–208.

Taylor, S. E., Klein, L. C., Lewis, B. P., Gruenewald, T. L., Gurung, R. A. R., & Updegraff, J. A. (2000). Biobehavioral responses to stress in females: Tend-and-befriend, not fight-or-flight. *Psychological Review, 107,* 411–429.

Temple, C., Nathan, R., Temple, F., & Burris, N. A. (1993). *The beginnings of writing* (3rd ed.). Boston: Allyn & Bacon.

Templeton, S., & Bear, D. (1992). A summary and synthesis: "Teaching the lexicon to read and spell." In S. Templeton & D. Bear (Eds.), *Development of orthographic knowledge and the foundations of literacy: A memorial festschrift for Edmund H. Henderson* (pp. 333–352). Hillsdale, NJ: Lawrence Erlbaum.

Templeton, S., & Morris, D. (1999). Theory and research into practice: Questions teachers ask about spelling. *Reading Research Quarterly, 34,* 102–112.

Thames, D. G., & Reeves, C. K. (1994, May). *Preventing the progression of negative attitudes among poor readers.* Paper presented at the Annual Meeting of the International Reading Association, Toronto, Ont.

Thorndike, E. L., & Barnhart, C. L. (Eds.) (1998). *Thorndike-Barnhart children's dictionary.* Glenview, IL: Scott Foresman-Addison-Wesley.

Thorndike, R. L., & Hagen, E. P. (1977). *Measurement and evaluation in psychology and education* (4th ed.). New York: Wiley.

Tierney, R. J., & Readence, J. E. (2000a). Intervention programs for "at-risk" learners. In R. J. Tierney & J. E. Readence (Eds.), *Reading strategies and practices: A compendium* (5th ed.), (pp. 126–159). Boston: Allyn & Bacon.

Tierney, R. J., & Readence, J. E. (2000b). *Reading strategies and practices: A compendium* (5th ed.). Boston: Allyn & Bacon.

Tierney, R. J., & Readence, J. E. (2005). Intervention programs for "at-risk" learners. In R. J. Tierney &

J. E. Readence (Eds.), *Reading strategies and practices: A compendium* (6th ed., p. 244). Boston: Allyn & Bacon.

Tompkins, G. E., & Hoskisson, K. (1991). *Language arts: Content and teaching strategies.* New York: Merrill.

Tonjes, M. J. (1991). *Secondary reading, writing, and learning.* Boston: Allyn & Bacon.

Topping, K. (1987). Paired reading: A powerful technique for parent use. *The Reading Teacher, 40,* 608–609.

Topping, K. (1989). Peer tutoring and paired reading: Combining two powerful techniques. *The Reading Teacher, 42,* 488–494.

Topping, K. (1998). Effective tutoring in America Reads: A reply to Wasik. *The Reading Teacher, 52,* 42–50.

Torgensen, J. (1994). *Research based approach to prevention of reading disabilities.* Paper presented at the New York Branch of the Orton Dyslexia Society, Twenty-First Annual Conference, Language and Medical Symposia on Dyslexia, New York.

Torgesen, J. K. (2000). Individual differences in response to early interventions in reading: The lingering problem of treatment resisters. *Learning Disabilities Practice, 15,* 55–64.

Torgesen, J. K. (2004a, May). *Adolescnt literacy, reading comprehension, & the FCAT.* Paper presented at the CLAS Conference, Naples, FL. Available at http://www.fcrr.org/science/pptpresentations.htm

Torgesen, J. K. (2004b, April). *Immediate intensive interventions: Their critical role within a whole school program to prevent reading difficulties.* Paper presented at the Regional Leadership Meeting, sponsored by the Eastern Regional Reading First Technical Assistance Center, April 2004. Available at http://www.fcrr.org/science/pptpresentations.htm

Torgesen, J. K. (2004c, June). *Struggling readers: What works for intermediate level students.* Paper presented at the Pennsylvania Summer Reading Conference, State College, PA. Available at http://www.fcrr.org/science/pptpresentations.htm

Torgesen, J. K. (2004d, August). *Using data and interventions to improve outcomes in early literacy skills.* Paper presented at the Second Annual Literacy Conference, Atlantic City, NJ. Available at http://www.fcrr.org/science/pptpresentations.htm

Torgesen, J. K., Alexander, A. W., Wagner, R. K., Rashotte, C. A., Voelher, K. K. S., & Conway, T. (2001). Intensive remedial instruction for children with severe reading disabilities: Immediate and long-term outcomes from two instructional approaches. *Journal of Learning Disabilities, 34,* 33–58, 78.

Torgesen, J. K., & Hecht, S. A. (1996). Preventing and remediating reading disabilities: Instructional variables that make a difference for special students. In M. F. Graves, P. van den Broek, & B. M. Taylor (Eds.), *The first R: Every child's right to read* (pp. 160–188). Newark, DE: International Reading Association.

Torgesen, J. K., Wagner, R. K., & Rashotte, C. A. (1997). Prevention and remediation of severe reading disabilities: Keeping the end in mind. *Scientific Studies of Reading, 1,* 217–234.

Torgesen, J. K., Wagner, R. K., Rashotte, C. A., & Herron, J. (2004). *Summary of outcomes from first grade study with Read, Write, and Type and Auditory Discrimination in Depth instruction and software with at-risk children.* Tallahassee, FL: Florida Center for Reading Research. Available at http://www.fcrr.org/science/technicalreports.htm

Trachtenburg, P. (1990). Using children's literature to enhance phonics instruction. *The Reading Teacher, 43,* 648–654.

Trathen, W. (1995). *What is the effect of children's orthographic knowledge on their ability to learn and retain new orthographic structures?* Paper presented at the 45th Annual Meeting of the National Reading Conference, New Orleans, LA.

Traub, N., & Bloom, F. (1975). *Recipe for reading.* Cambridge, MA: Educators Publishing Service.

Treiman, R. (1992). The role of intrasyllabic units in learning to read and spell. In P. B. Gough, L. C. Ehri, & R. Tremain (Eds.), *Reading acquisition* (pp. 65–106). Hillsdale, NJ: Lawrence Erlbaum.

Troia, G. A. (2004). Phonological processing and its influence on literacy learning. In C. A. Stone, E. R. Silliman, B. J. Ehren, & K. Apel (Eds.), *Handbook of language and literacy development and disorders* (pp. 271–301). New York: Guilford Press.

Tunmer, W. E., & Chapman, J. W. (1999). Teaching strategies for word identification. In G. B. Thompson & T. Nicholson (Eds.), *Learning to read: Beyond phonics and whole language* (pp. 74–102). Newark, DE: International Reading Association.

Turbill, J. (1982). *No better way to teach writing!* Rozelle, Australia: Primary English Teaching Association.

Uhry, J. K., & Ehri, L. (1999). Ease of segmenting two- and three-phoneme words in kindergarten: Rime cohesion or vowel salience? *Journal of Educational Psychology, 91,* 594–603.

U.S. Department of Education, National Center for Educational Statistics (1995). *Listening to children read aloud: Oral fluency, 15.* Washington, DC: Author. Available at http://nces.ed.gov/pubs95/web/95762.asp

U.S. Department of Education (2002). *Twenty-second annual report to Congress on the implementation of the Individuals with Disabilities Education Act.* Washington, DC: Author. Available at http://www.ed.gov/about/reports/annual/osep/2002/index.html

Vacca, R. T., & Vacca, J. L. (1986). *Content area reading* (2nd ed.). Boston: Little, Brown.

Valencia, S., & Buly, M. R. (2004). Behind test scores: What struggling readers really need. *The Reading Teacher, 57,* 520–531.

van den Broek, P., & Kremer, K. E. (2000). The mind in action: What it means to comprehend during reading. In B. Taylor, M. F. Graves, & P. van den Broek (Eds.), *Reading for meaning: Fostering comprehension in the middle grades* (pp. 1–31). New York: Teachers College Press.

Vandervelden, M. C., & Siegel, L. S. (1997). Teaching phonological processing skills in early literacy: A developmental approach. *Learning Disabilities Quarterly, 20,* 63–81.

Vandervelden, M. C., & Siegel, L. S. (1995). Phonological recoding and phoneme awareness in early literacy: A developmental approach. *Reading Research Quarterly, 30,* 854–876.

Vellutino, F. R. (1987). Dyslexia. *Scientific American, 256*(3), 34–41.

Vellutino, F. R. (2003, December 2). *Response to intervention as a vehicle for distinguishing between reading disabled and non–reading disabled children: Evidence for the role of kindergarten and first-grade intervention.* Paper presented at the National Research Center on Learning Disabilities Responsiveness-to-Intervention Symposium, Kansas City, MO. Available at http://www.nrcld.org/html/symposium2003/vellutino/vellutino9.html

Vellutino, F. R., Fletcher, J. M., Snowing, M. J., & Scanlon, D. M. (2003). Specific reading disability (dyslexia): What have we learned in the past four decades? *Journal of Child Psychology and Psychiatry, 45,* 2–40.

Vellutino, F. R., & Scanlon, D. M. (1985). Verbal memory in poor and normal readers. In D. B. Gray & J. F. Kavanaugh (Eds.), *Biobehavioral measures of dyslexia* (pp. 177–214). Baltimore, MD: York Press.

Vellutino, F. R., & Scanlon, D. M. (1988). Phonological coding: Phonological awareness and reading ability: Evidence from a longitudinal and experimental study (pp. 77–119). In K. Stanovich (Ed.), *Children's reading and the development of phonological awareness.* Detroit, MI: Wayne State University Press.

Vellutino, F. R., Scanlon, D. M., Sipay, E. R., Small, S. G., Pratt, R., Chen, R., & Denckla, M. B. (1996). Cognitive profiles of difficult-to-remediate and readily remediated poor readers: Early intervention as a vehicle for distinguishing between cognitive and experiential deficits as basic causes of specific reading disability. *Journal of Educational Psychology, 88,* 601–638.

Vellutino, F., Scanlon, D. M., & Tanzman, M. S. (1998). The case for early intervention in diagnosing specific reading disability. *Journal of School Psychology, 36,* 367–397.

Venezky, R. L. (1965). *A study of English spelling-to-sound correspondences on historical principles.* Unpublished doctoral dissertation, Stanford University, Stanford, CA.

Vinovskis, M. A. (1996). An analysis of the concept and uses of systemic educational reform. *American Educational Research Journal, 33,* 53–85.

Vreeland, E. (1998). *Handwriting: Not just in hands: A comprehensive resource.* Hanover, NH: Maxanna Learning Systems.

Vygotsky, L. S. (1978). *Mind and society: The development of higher psychological processes.* Cambridge, MA: MIT Press.

Wade, S. E. (1990). Using think-alouds to assess comprehension. *The Reading Teacher, 43,* 442–451.

Walker, B. G. (1992). *Diagnostic teaching of reading: Techniques for instruction and assessment* (2nd ed.). New York: Macmillan.

Walker, S. C., & Poteet, J. A. (1989). Influencing memory performance in learning disabled students through semantic processing. *Learning Disabilities Research, 5,* 25–32.

Walmsley, S. A. (1978–1979). The criterion referenced measurement of an early reading behavior. *Reading Research Quarterly, 14,* 574–604.

Walton, P. D. (1995). Rhyming ability, phoneme identity, letter-sound knowledge, and the use of orthographic analogy by prereaders. *Journal of Educational Psychology, 87,* 587–597.

Wasik, B. A. (1998). Volunteer reading programs in reading: A review. *Reading Research Quarterly, 33,* 266–292.

Watson, A. J. (1984). Cognitive development and units of print in early reading. In J. Downing & R. Valten (Eds.), *Language awareness and learning to read* (pp. 93–118). New York: Springer-Verlag.

Weaver, B. M. (1992). *Defining literacy levels.* Charlotteville, NY: Story House.

Weaver, B. M. (2000). *Leveling books K–6: Matching readers to text.* Newark, DE: International Reading Association.

Weaver, C. (l994a). *Reading process and practice* (2nd ed.). Portsmouth, NH: Heinemann.

Weaver, C. (l994b). Understanding and educating students with attention deficit hyperactivity disorders: Toward a system-theory and whole language perspective. In C. Weaver (Ed.), *Success at last: Helping students with AD(H)D achieve their potential.* Portsmouth, NH: Heinemann.

Wechsler, D. (1974). *Manual for the Wechsler Intelligence Scale for children–Revised.* Cleveland, OH: The Psychological Corporation.

Wechsler, D. (1989). *Manual for the Wechsler Preschool and Primary Scale of Intelligence—Revised.* Cleveland, OH: The Psychological Corporation.

Weinstein, C., & Mayer, R. (1986). The teaching of learning strategies. In M. C. Wittrock (Ed.), *Handbook of research on teaching* (pp. 315–327). New York: Macmillan.

West, J., Denton, K., & Germino-Hausken, E. (2000). *Early childhood longitudinal study: Kindergarten class of 1998–99.* Washington, DC: National Center for Educational Statistics. Available at http://nces.ed .gov/pubsearch/pubsinfo.asp?pubid=200070

West, R. F., Stanovich, K. E., & Mitchell, H. R. (1993). Reading in the real world and its correlates. *Reading Research Quarterly, 28,* 34–50.

Westby, C. (1999). Assessing and facilitating text comprehension problems. In H. W. Catts & A. G. Kamhi (Eds.), *Language and reading disabilities* (pp. 154–223). Boston: Allyn & Bacon.

White, T. G., Sowell, J., & Yanagihara, A. (1989). Teaching elementary students to use word-part clues. *The Reading Teacher, 42,* 302–308.

Wigfield, A., & Asher, S. R. (1984). Social and motivational influences on reading. In P. D. Pearson, R. Barr, M. L. Kamil, & P. Mosenthal (Eds.), *Handbook of reading research* (pp. 423–452). New York: Longman.

Wiig, E. H. (1994). The role of language in learning disabilities. In A. J. Capute, P. J. Accardo, B. K. Shapiro (Eds.), *Learning disabilities spectrum: AD, ADHD, & LD* (pp. 139–154). Baltimore: York Press.

Wilde, S. (1992). *You kan red this! Spelling and punctuation for whole language classrooms.* Portsmouth, NH: Heinemann.

Wilde, S. (1995). *Twenty-five years of inventive spelling: Where are we now?* Paper presented at the Annual Meeting of the International Reading Association, Anaheim, CA.

Wilhelm, J. D. (1995). Reading is seeing. *Journal of Reading Behavior, 27,* 467–503.

Wilkins, A. J. (1995). Helping reading with colour. *Dyslexia Review, 7*(3), 4–7.

Willcutt, E. G., & Pennington, B. F. (2000). Comorbidity of reading disability and attention-deficit hyperactivity disorder: Differences by gender and subtype. *Journal of Learning Disabilities, 33,* 179–191.

Williams, P. L., Reese, C. M., Campbell, J. R., Mazzeo, J., & Phillips, G. W. (1995). *1994 NAEP reading: A first look.* Washington, DC: Office of Educational Research and Improvement, U.S. Department of Education.

Willows, D. M., Kruk, R. S., & Corcos, E. (1993). Are there differences between disabled and normal readers in their processing of visual information? In D. M. Willows, R. S. Kruk, & E. Corcos (Eds.), *Visual processes in reading and reading disabilities* (pp. 265–285). Hillsdale, NJ: Lawrence Erlbaum.

Wilson, M. M. (1979). The processing strategies of average and below average readers answering factual and inferential questions of three equivalent passages. *Journal of Reading Behavior, 11,* 235–245.

Wilson, P. (1992). Among nonreaders: Voluntary reading, reading achievement, and the development of reading habits. In C. Temple & P. Collins (Eds.), *Stories and readers: New perspectives on literature in the elementary classroom* (pp. 157–169). Norwood, MA: Christopher-Gordon.

Winkler, H. (2004, May 3). *Keynote address.* Paper presented at the annual convention of the International Reading Association. Reno: NV.

Winograd, P., Lipson, K. K., & Wixson, M. Y. (1989). *Improving basal reading instruction.* New York: Teachers College Press.

Winograd, P. N. (1984). Strategic difficulties in summarizing text. *Reading Research Quarterly, 19,* 404–425.

Wixson, K. K., & Durto, E. (1998). *Standards for primary-grade reading: An analysis of state frameworks.* (CIERA Report 3-001). Available at http://www .ciera.org/ciera/publications/report-series/

Wolf, M., & Goodglass, H. (1986). Dyslexia, dysnomia, and lexical retrieval. *Brain and Language, 28,* 154–168.

Wolf, M. A. (1991). Naming speed and reading: The contribution of the cognitive neurosciences. *Reading Research Quarterly, 26,* 123–141.

Wolf, S., & Gearhart, M. (1994). Writing what you read: Narrative assessment as a learning event. *Language Arts, 71,* 425–444.

Wood, E., Pressley, M., & Winne, P. H. (1990). Elaborative interrogation effects on children's learning of factual content. *Journal of Educational Psychology, 82,* 41–48.

Wood, F. P. (1994). *Cortical activation patterns in normal reading and dyslexia: PET and ERP.* Paper presented at the New York Branch of the Orton Dyslexic Society Annual Conference, Language and Medical Symposia on Dyslexia, New York.

Wood, K. (1984). Probable passages: A writing strategy. *The Reading Teacher, 37,* 496–499.

Wood, K. D., Lapp, D., & Flood, J. (1992). *Guiding readers through text: A review of study guides.* Newark, DE: International Reading Association.

Woodcock, R., & Mather, N. (2001). *Woodcock–Johnson–III Tests of Achievement Standard and Supplemental Batteries: Examiner's manual.* Chicago: Riverside.

Worthy, M. J., & Invernizzi, M. (1990). Spelling errors of normal and disabled readers. *Annals of Dyslexia, 40,* 138–151.

Wright, J. (2004). *Curriculum-based measurement: A manual for teachers.* Available at http://www.interventioncentral.org/download.shtml

Yaden, D. B., Tam, A., Madrigal, P., Brassell, D., Massa, J., Altamirano, S., & Armendariz, J. (2001). *Early literacy for inner-city children: The effects of reading and writing interventions in English and Spanish during the preschool years.* (CIERA Article #00-04). Available at http://www.ciera.org/ciera/publications/report-series/

Yopp, H. K. (1988). The validity and reliability of phonemic awareness tests. *Reading Research Quarterly, 23,* 159–199.

Yopp, H. K. (1995). A test for assessing phonemic awareness in young children. *The Reading Teacher, 49,* 20–29.

Yuill, N. (1996). A funny thing happened on the way to the classroom: Jokes, riddles, and metalinguistic awareness in understanding and improving poor comprehension in children. In C. Cornoldi & J. Oakhill (Eds.), *Reading comprehension difficulties: Processes and intervention* (pp. 193–220). Mahwah, NJ: Erlbaum.

Yuill, N., & Oakhill, J. (1991). *Children's problems in text comprehension: An experimental investigation* (Cambridge Monographs & Texts in Applied Psycholinguistics). New York: Cambridge University Press.

Zakaluk, B. L., & Samuels, S. J. (1988). Toward a new approach to predicting comprehensibility. In B. L. Zakaluk & S. J. Samuels (Eds.), *Readability: Its past, present, and future* (pp. 121–144). Newark, DE: International Reading Association.

Zakaluk, B. L., Samuels, S. J., & Taylor, B. M. (1986). A simple technique for estimating prior knowledge: Word association. *Journal of Reading, 30,* 56–60.

Zecker, S. G. (1991). The orthographic code: Developmental trends in reading-disabled and normally achieving children. *Annals of Dyslexia, 41,* 178–192.

Zeno, S. M., Ivens, S. H., Millard, R. T., & Duvvuri, R. (1995). *The educator's word frequency guide.* Brewster, NY: Touchstone Applied Science Associates.

Zentall, S. S. (1993). Research on the educational implications of attention deficit hyperactivity disorder. *Exceptional Children, 60,* 143–153.

Zwaan, R. A., Radvansky, G. A., Hilliard, A. E., & Curiel, J. M. (1998). Constructing multidimensional situation models during reading. *Scientific Studies of Reading, 20*(3), 199–220.

CHILDREN'S BOOKS AND SCHOOL TEXTBOOKS

Abbye, S., & Donahue, B. C. (1991). *Our country's geography.* Austin, TX: Steck-Vaughn.

Bains, R. (1993). *Thurgood Marshall: Fight for justice.* Mahwah, NJ: Troll.

Blaine, M. (1986). Giants of the city. In J. Stanchfield and T. Gunning (Eds.), *Wings* (New Directions in Reading) (pp. 162–169). Boston: Houghton Mifflin.

Bledsoe, L. J. (1988). *Biology, The kingdom of life.* Castro Valley, CA: Quercus.

Bledsoe, L. J. (1990). *Fearon's biology.* Paramus, NJ: Globe Fearon.

Bledsoe, L. J. (1994). *Fearon's general science* (2nd ed.). Paramus, NJ: Globe Fearon.

Brown, C. (1989). *Big red barn.* New York: Greenwillow.

Brown, C. (1995). *Tractor.* New York: Greenwillow.

Bulla, R. C. (1987). *The chalk box kid.* New York: Random House.

Byars, B. (1970). *Summer of the swans.* New York: Viking.

Cameron, P. (1990). *Donna: A helping hand.* Hayward, CA: Alemany Press.

Carle, E. (1987). *Have you seen my cat?* New York: Scholastic.

Carroll, L. (1871/1969). *Alice in wonderland and Through the looking glass.* Chicago: Children's Press.

Cole, J. (1986). *Hungry, hungry sharks.* New York: Random House.

Cowley, J. (1980, 1990). *The hungry giant.* Bothell, WA: The Wright Group.

Degen, B. (1983). *Jamberry.* New York: Harper.

Domanska, J. (1969). *The turnip.* New York: Macmillan.

Duncan, L. (1976). *Summer of fear.* New York: Dell.

Eastman, P. D. (1961). *Go, dog, go.* New York: Random House.

Ehlert, L. (1987). *Growing vegetable soup.* Orlando, FL: Harcourt Brace.

Fleischman, P. (1988). *Joyful noise: Poems for two voices.* New York: HarperCollins.

Freeman, D. (1978). *A pocket for Corduroy.* New York: Puffin.

Gág, W. (1928). *Millions of cats.* New York: Coward.

Gantos, J. (1994). *Heads or tails: Stories from the sixth grade.* New York: Farrar, Strauss, & Giroux.

Geisel, T. S. (Dr. Seuss) (1974). *There's a wocket in my pocket.* New York: Beginner.

Gelman, R. G. (1977). *More spaghetti I say.* New York: Scholastic.

Goodall, J. (1992). *Writers' voices: Selected from In the shadow of man.* New York: Literacy Volunteers of New York City.

Gottlieb, J. S. (1991). *The wonders of science: The human body.* Austin, TX: Steck-Vaughn.

Greenfield, E. (1978). *Honey, I love and other poems.* New York: Harper.

Gutelle, A. (1990). *Baseball's best.* New York: Random House.

Hill, E. (1986). *Spot goes to the circus.* New York: Putnam.

Hopkins, L. B. (1984). *Surprises.* New York: Harper.

Hopkins, L. B. (1987). *More surprises.* New York: Harper.

Kimmel, E. A. (1992). *Anansi goes fishing.* New York: Holiday House.

King, W., & Napp, J. (1998). *Our nation's history.* Circle Pines, MN: American Guidance Service.

King, W., & Napp, J. (1998). *United States history.* Circle Pines, MN: American Guidance Service.

Kuskin, K. (1992). *Soap soup and other verses.* New York: HarperCollins.

Leedy, L. (1992). *Blastoff to earth: A look at geography.* New York: Holiday House.

Lefkowitz, W. (1990). *Fearon's United States geography.* Belmont, CA: Globe Fearon.

Lionni, L. (1959). *Little blue and little yellow.* New York: Astor-Honor.

Lowery, L., & Lorbiecki, M. (1993). *Earthwise at home.* Minneapolis, MN: Carolrhoda Books.

Marshall, J. (1990). *Fox be nimble.* New York: Penguin.

Martin, B., Jr. (1983). *Brown bear, brown bear, what do you see?* New York: Holt.

McKissack, P. C. (1983). *Who is who?* Chicago: Children's Press.

McMullen, K. (1989). *Dinosaur hunters.* New York: Random House.

Minarik, E. H. (1958). *Little Bear.* New York: Harper.

Minarik, E. H. (1959). *A kiss for Little Bear.* New York: Harper.

Modesitt, J. (1990). *The story of Z.* New York: Simon & Schuster.

Morris, A. (1992a). *Tools.* New York: Lothrop, Lee & Shepard.

Morris, A. (1992b). *Vegetable soup.* New York: Lothrop, Lee & Shepard.

Morris, R. A. (1975). *Dolphins.* New York: Harper.

Nentl, J. A. (1983). *Big rigs.* New York: Crestwood House.

Parish, P. (1974). *Dinosaur time.* New York: Harper.

Piper, W. (1961). *The little engine that could.* New York: Platt.

Reef, C. (1991). *Ellis Island.* New York: Dillon Press.

Robart, R. (1986). *The cake that Mack ate.* Boston: Little, Brown.

Roe, E. (1990). *All I am.* New York: Bradbury.

Sattler, H. R. (1993). *The earliest Americans.* New York: Clarion Books.

Schade, S. (1992). *Toad on the road.* New York: Random House.

Schade, S. (1994). *Railroad toad.* New York: Random House.

Scott, M. (1993). *A picture book of reptiles and amphibians.* Mahwah, NJ: Troll.

Shaw, N. (1986). *Sheep in a jeep.* Boston: Houghton Mifflin.

Shea, G. (1992). Amazing rescue underground. In G. Shea, *Amazing rescues* (pp. 28–48). New York: Random House.

Steele, P. (1991a). *Pocket facts: Birds.* New York: Crestwood House.

Steele, P. (1991b). *Pocket facts: Insects.* New York: Crestwood House.

Steele, P. (1991c). *Pocket facts: Wild animals.* New York: Crestwood House.

Stott, C. (1991). *Observing the sky.* Mahwah, NJ: Troll.

Strasser, T. (1993). *Help I'm trapped in my teacher's body.* New York: Scholastic.

Torres, L. (1993). *Subway sparrow.* New York: Farrar, Strauss, & Giroux.

Walker, A. (1992). *Writers' voices: Selected from The temple of my familiar.* New York: Literacy Volunteers of New York City.

Wildsmith, B. (1982). *Cat on the mat.* New York: Oxford University Press.

Wiseman, B. (1959). *Morris and Boris.* New York: Harper.

Yep, L. (1989). *The rainbow people.* New York: Harper.

Ziefert, H. (1988). *Dark night, sleepy night.* New York: Penguin.

INDEX